With
Sincere
appreciation

Hillel Found.
Rabbi Saul Kraft

Israel:

A HISTORY OF THE JEWISH PEOPLE

Behold, the bush burned with fire, and the bush was not consumed. EXODUS III, 2

ISRAEL: A HISTORY OF THE JEWISH PEOPLE

BY RUFUS LEARSI

Meridian Books
THE WORLD PUBLISHING COMPANY
CLEVELAND AND NEW YORK

A MERIDIAN BOOK
Published by The World Publishing Company
2231 West 110th Street, Cleveland, Ohio 44102
Published simultaneously in Canada by
Nelson, Foster & Scott Ltd.
First Meridian printing May 1966.

Library of Congress Catalog Card Number: 49-8382
Printed in the United States of America. FD566

TO SUNDEL DONIGER

with affection and esteem

Foreword

Not the achievements of renowned individuals, not even the rise and fall of great communities across the centuries, but the career of a single people should stand before the reader as the dominant theme of this narrative. In this drama, altogether unique in the annals of the nations, the leading actor is the Jewish people.

Moreover, a reading of this odyssey should, in spite of diversions and retreats, engender a sense of direction and goal. A river may twist and wind, but its general course is nonetheless definite. The sense of destiny—a destiny not in terms of "might and power, but of spirit"—is, of course, explicit in the traditions that began with the first Hebrew, but it seems to emerge also from the career of his descendants. The history of man, like man himself, "doth not live by bread only"; not, at any rate, the history of the Jewish people.

This book appears at a time when the nations of the world have, knowingly or unknowingly, aligned themselves with the millennial goal by decreeing the reestablishment of the Jewish state in Palestine, and when the heroic Jewish community in that land has actually transformed itself into the State of Israel. After sustaining a disaster of unparalleled magnitude in the Second World War, the Jewish people may now achieve one of the essential conditions of a dignified and creative life. In the making of that event the tragic present joined hands with the imperative past—the present which all who run may read, and the past which, it is hoped, the following pages will help to reveal.

After years of labor spent on this work, it is pleasant to recall the friends who upheld the author in his task. First among them are Dr. Israel S. Wechsler and Sundel Doniger. Others are Mrs.

Frank Cohen, Maurice J. Waldinger, Dr. Joshua H. Neumann and Dr. Joshua Bloch, of whom the last two read the proof and made many sound suggestions. I am greatly indebted to my son, David Emanuel, for his help in connection with the last chapters of the book and with the preparation of the manuscript for publication. Finally, the generous assistance of the Jewish History Foundation, Inc., and of the Esco Fund Committee, Inc., is gratefully acknowledged.

RUFUS LEARSI

Contents

List of Maps

Part One 2000 B.C.E. TO 586 B.C.E.

The First Commonwealth

Faith, Land, and People

CHAPTER ONE

Abraham, Isaac, Jacob

THE Bible as history has found remarkable support in the testimony of archaeology, and chronicles of the Jewish people may well continue to follow its lead and begin with the three Patriarchs. They, like the rest of the Bible, have of course been exposed to various theories, some of which have even shed doubt on their existence. But as we read their lives in the sacred text the theories fade and vanish: the conviction that they were men, real men, grows on the reader and becomes indelible.

The first of the three, Abraham son of Terah, as the progenitor of the twelve tribes of Israel, is the founder of the Hebrew nation. This nomad shepherd, tradition reports, received the most momentous illumination in the spiritual ascent of man—the recognition of the One God, maker of heaven and earth, holy and righteous, champion of the weak and oppressed. On Abraham was also conferred the Great Covenant with its promise that his descendants would forever possess the land of Canaan. Thus, out of the first Patriarch emerge the three leading strands of this narrative: faith, land, and people.

2

BORN some forty centuries ago in Ur of the Chaldees, not far from the Gulf of Persia, Abraham belonged to a clan of nomads whose remote origins must be sought in Arabia. And from Ur the clan resumed its wanderings, moving north and sojourning a space of time in Haran on the upper reaches of the Euphrates.

Now the world through which the first Hebrew patriarch wandered was already old. A thousand years before him, the country, inhabited by a people called Sumerians, was already dotted with cities where the arts and vices of civilization flourished profusely. Kings waged war with standing armies; merchants traded near and far; scribes wrote skillfully and durably in wedge-shaped letters on clay tablets, and architects built huge temples where many and strange deities were worshipped—gods and demons of earth, air, and water, of sun, moon, and stars. Centuries later, the Sumerian cities were overrun by hordes of bearded Semitic warriors and, about the time of Abraham, the Semites had produced a ruler of genius named Hammurabi (2123-2081 B.C.E.*), who bound the bickering cities to his will, made Babylon, his own city, the capital of the Empire of Babylonia, and established a system of laws which has become famous as the Code of Hammurabi. As Abraham drove his flocks along the Euphrates, it was the civilization of Babylonia that he found everywhere predominant.

But Abraham was not to end his days in Mesopotamia. The Voice of the One God he heard and obeyed ordered him to leave his country and his kindred for "a land that I will show thee." Crossing the Euphrates River, the patriarch, with his flocks and herds, his menservants and maidservants, turned west and then south toward Canaan. It was one of the momentous river crossings in history; thereafter Abraham was to be known as *Ibri*, "the man who crossed over."

To the people of Canaan the newcomers were, of course, just another nomad band. The land was inhabited by a number of nations at different stages of development, from the cave dwellers, who have been traced back to 12,000 B.C.E., to the highly civilized Amorites. The latter were agriculturists, artisans, and traders. They lived in walled cities, possessed skillfully constructed fortresses, and were so dominant that in the earliest inscriptions the country as a whole is called the Land of Amurru. The religion of the Amorites, like all primitive religions, was essentially a nature idolatry, with deities who presided over the different natural forces. The male Baal and the female Asherah were worshipped on the so-called "high-places" with gory and lewd ceremonies, often accompanied by human sacrifice.

In Canaan, moreover, the Hebrew nomads found the civilization of Babylonia challenged by the power and glamour of Egypt. For

* Before the current era.

in the valley of the Nile there flourished a civilization even more splendid than the Babylonian. Egypt's pyramids and temples, her palaces, paintings, and statues, the might and magnificence of her rulers, were the envy and dread of all the lands. And the animal divinities of Egypt clashed and mingled in Canaan with the gods and demons of Babylonia.

The Hebrew nomads pitched their tents at Shechem, moved on to Bethel, and wandered farther south. In a year of drought and famine, they trekked through the Desert of Shur to find sustenance in Egypt. But they returned to Canaan, growing steadily stronger, richer, more numerous.

3

THUS, between two hoary civilizations, moved a little band of nomads charged with a new destiny. Between two idolatries appeared the first sprouts of a new faith, the faith of the spirit. For the journey of the first Hebrew, we learn, was already stamped with the seal that marks the career of his descendants. He was not merely searching for greener pastures: he was carrying out the Covenant between himself and his Deity, the pact in which God had declared: "I will make of thee a great nation, and I will bless thee and make thy name great . . . and in thee shall all the families of the earth be blessed."

So the patriarch walked through the land with the tread of a conqueror. Under stress of necessity, he pitted his clan victoriously against a coalition of four kings. The kings in question, led by Chedor-laomer of Elam, had invaded Canaan to punish certain cities, among them being Sodom and Gomorrah, which had rebelled against his suzerainty. One of the four, Amraphel, King of Shinar, has been identified as none other than the great Hammurabi of Babylon. After overcoming a defensive alliance of five Canaanite kings, the invaders departed, carrying off among their captives Abraham's nephew Lot together with his household. But Abraham pursued and defeated the kings, rescued his kinsman, and recovered the booty.

On his return the local rulers courted his good will and he dealt with them shrewdly and masterfully. The patriarch is not pictured as a flawless saint; in difficult situations he resorts to guile.

But Abraham is magnanimous and compassionate; his justice is tempered with mercy. When an edict of doom goes out against the depraved cities of Sodom and Gomorrah, his heart is moved with pity for their inhabitants and, vain though his plea, he implores God to spare them. He sits at the door of his tent and receives wayfarers with lordly hospitality. He stands before men with assurance and dignity, before God with humility. Nor does he conceive his God as only a family or tribal deity. "Shall not the judge of all the earth do justly?" he cries in his plea for the wicked cities.

In old age, his wife Sarah bears him the son they had long despaired of, and when the infant Isaac is eight days old, the father, in token of the Great Covenant, performs upon him the rite of circumcision. Thus, with Isaac, the line is continued and the Covenant confirmed.

But a strange doom is pronounced upon the boy: to prove his utter devotion to God, Abraham must offer him up as a sacrifice. All the nations of antiquity, Aryan as well as Semitic, worshipped their gods with human sacrifice; Moloch, a deity of the nations among whom Abraham wandered, delighted especially in the charred bodies of first-born sons. The Hebrew Patriarch and his descendants were to learn that their God abhorred such sacrifice, and the lesson was to be so vivid that neither he nor his descendants would ever forget it. At the crucial moment he hears the Voice say: "Lay not thy hand upon the lad, neither do thou anything unto him!" The story of that ordeal, the *Akedah* or the "binding" of Isaac, still makes human hearts shudder and thrill.

Sarah, the first mother of her people, died in Hebron, a city destined to be the scene of great events in the career of her descendants. There were Hittites in the city, and from one of them Abraham acquired his first stake in the soil of the Promised Land: the field "which was in Machpelach . . . and the cave that was therein," and in that cave the first mother of the Hebrews was laid to rest.

4

ISAAC has entered into manhood, but his wife must not be of the daughters of Canaan, for the land reeks with idolatry and pollution. So the patriarch's steward, Eliezer, journeys to Haran and brings back Rebekah, granddaughter of Nahor, his master's brother, to be Isaac's wife. In the regal narrative of the Bible the first meeting of Isaac and Rebekah is thus related:

> And Isaac went out to meditate in the field at the eventide; and he lifted up his eyes, and saw, and, behold, there were camels coming. And Rebekah lifted up her eyes, and when she saw Isaac, she alighted from the camel. And she said unto the servant: "What man is this that walketh in the field to meet us?" And the servant said: "It is my master." And she took her veil and covered herself. And the servant told Isaac all the things that he had done. And Isaac brought her into his mother's tent, and took Rebekah and she became his wife; and he loved her. And Isaac was comforted for his mother.

Other sons besides Isaac had been born to Abraham; one of them, Ishmael, is famous in story and legend. With his mother Hagar, the lad has been thrust into the desert by the jealousy of Sarah, and is near to die of thirst when God's angel intervenes and saves him. Ishmael, whose mother was an Egyptian, could not be the bearer of the Covenant: he became the father of the Arab nomads. To Isaac alone fell the glory and the burden.

5

"IN A GOOD old age, an old man, and full of years," Abraham died and was gathered to his people. Ishmael and Isaac, their feud forgotten, took up their father and laid him beside Sarah in the cave of Machpelah. Now Isaac, the second patriarch, commanded the Hebrews, and God blessed him in all his ways, reaffirming unto him the Great Covenant.

The Hebrew nomads become stronger, and Abimelech, a king of the Philistines, orders them out of his borders and sets his people to destroy their wells. In the end, however, the Philistine monarch is forced to sue for a treaty of peace and alliance with them. Gradually the nomads take up the ways of settled life: they learn to plow and plant and reap. So Isaac, we learn, "waxed great, and grew more and more until he became very great."

In the meantime Rebekah, whom God in His mercy saved from barrenness, bore the patriarch twin sons. The parents named one Esau, "the hairy one," for he was covered with hair from birth, and the other Jacob, for he gripped his brother's heel (Hebrew: *ekeb*), striving with him while still in the womb. Though twins, the brothers were as unlike as two human beings could be. Esau was wild and rude, a hunter and man of the field. Jacob was gentle and wise, "a quiet man dwelling in tents."

A tense drama unfolds, a struggle for supremacy between the brothers. Esau is obviously unfit to be the carrier of the Covenant, for he lacks the gifts by which men apprehend God. Moreover, he marries Hittite women who are "a bitterness of spirit unto Isaac and unto Rebekah." Coming home one day from the hunt and famished for food, Esau sells his birthright to his brother for "bread and pottage of lentils," thus despising the great prerogative.

The long duel reaches its climax when Isaac is old and his eyes are dim. One of the brothers is to receive the patriarch's final blessing. The father chooses Esau, but Rebekah, with the cunning of an Oriental queen-mother, puts Jacob in Esau's place and Isaac speaks the irrevocable words over Jacob. A fury of hatred against the supplanter blazes up in Esau, and Rebekah sends Jacob away to Aram, or Mesopotamia, to find safety with her brother Laban.

6

ON THE way to Aram the fugitive, we read, hears the voice of God reaffirming the Covenant. "The land whereon thou liest, to thee will I give it and to thy seed . . . And in thee and in thy seed shall all the families of the earth be blessed."

And at last Jacob comes to "the land of the children of the east," the land of Aram. At a well surrounded by shepherds and flocks, he meets the comely Rachel, daughter of Laban, coming to water her father's sheep. Unaided, Jacob rolls away from the well's mouth the great stone which always required the united strength of all the shepherds to move.

Seven years Jacob serves Laban for Rachel the beautiful, only to find himself, through Laban's deceit, wedded to her plain sister Leah; but he serves seven more and obtains the cousin he loves. Finally, he labors six more years for flocks of sheep and goats, outwitting the wily Aramaean who tries to defraud him again. And sons are born to Jacob of his wives and concubines: Reuben, Simeon, Levi, Judah, Issachar and Zebulun, whose mother was Leah; Dan and Naphtali, whose mother was Bilhah, Rachel's handmaid; Gad and Asher whom Zilpah, Leah's handmaid, bore. And, finally, there was Joseph, whom Rachel the beloved bore unto Jacob, God having heard her prayers and taken away from her the shame of barrenness.

Twenty years have passed, and the call of Canaan comes strong upon Jacob, but on the way he faces a great peril. Esau has become a warrior chieftain in the land of Edom, and when Jacob's messengers bring him tidings of his brother's approach, Esau hastens to meet him—with four hundred armed men. Jacob's courage and ingenuity are severely tested, but neither fails him. His strategy is remarkable for its shrewd understanding of human nature, particularly the fickle nature of a desert sheik. Esau's designs, if they were hostile, melt in the warmth of his brother's generosity. Both brothers are deeply moved. "And Esau," we read, "ran to meet him and embraced him, and fell on his neck, and kissed him; and they wept." The night before, an angel had come and wrestled with Jacob. Unable to prevail against him, the angel had bestowed on him a new name: *Israel*, "prince of God," expressive of the patriarch's power with God and men.

7

SO ISRAEL returned to Canaan with wives and sons and daughters, with menservants and maidservants, with flocks of sheep and herds of cattle. His advent must have created no little stir in the country. Israel pitched his tents before Shechem, and his sons wreaked terrible vengeance on that city for an insult inflicted on their sister Dinah. He went on to Bethel, and on the way to Bethlehem, Rachel gave birth to another son whom she was just able to name Ben-oni, "son of my agony," later called Benjamin, before giving up the spirit. In Hebron, Jacob found his father Isaac "old and full of days," and when Isaac died, Esau came up from Edom and the brothers laid their father in the cave of Machpelah.

The years pass and a new drama fraught with immense consequences unfolds itself, the drama of Joseph and his brothers. In the Bible narrative it throbs with passion and pathos and glows with the color of the East. Joseph has dreams of domination and as he foolishly boasts of them, hatred grows in the hearts of the brothers against the favorite son whom Israel has singled out for special marks of affection, the most provoking being a gift symbolizing authority, "a coat of many colors." So they seize their brother and cast him into a pit. "And they sat down to eat bread; and they lifted up their eyes and looked, and behold, a caravan of Ishmaelites came from Gilead, with their camels bearing spicery and balm and ladanum, going to carry it down to Egypt."

And while the sons of Jacob deliberate, deciding at last to sell their brother into bondage instead of letting him die in the pit, some Midianite merchants happen along and anticipate them. They draw the youth out of the pit and sell him to the Ishmaelites "for twenty pieces of silver." And when the brothers find him gone, they dip the hated coat of many colors in the blood of a slain goat and lay it before their father as proof that Joseph has been torn by a wild beast. Alas for the old man with the blood-stained coat in his hands! Alas for Israel weeping and refusing to be comforted for the dearest of all his sons!

But down the coastal plain and across the desert, the caravan now bears a new freight, a Hebrew youth given to dreaming dreams, sold to the merchants and going down to be sold again in the fabulous land of Egypt.

Such, in swift review, is the story of the Hebrew Patriarchs, the first "heroes" of the Jewish people. But they are wholly unlike the first heroes in the annals of any other people. They are neither demigods nor men of giant mold, brandishing sword, spear, and club, hacking their way through hosts of enemies, performing incredible deeds of valor. Nor are they perfect knights and saints, *sans peur et sans reproche*, fearless and stainless. On the contrary, they are men, real men, moved by the earthy passions of the human heart, nor are they free from error and sin. But, in all their journeys and tribulations, a strange and unique light beats upon them, an awareness that the Spirit of all flesh has chosen them for a sublime purpose.

CHAPTER TWO

Bondage and Freedom

THE Egypt to which Joseph was brought was altogether a marvelous land. It teemed with cities and villages, it glittered with palaces and temples, with stately mansions and public buildings, with pyramids, obelisks, and statues. The king, or Pharaoh, ruled it in might and splendor and the people worshipped him as a god, toiling and dying for his glory. Led by a numerous priesthood, the Egyptians venerated a great many gods, including birds and beasts, reptiles and insects. They worshipped bulls, cats and ibis, snakes, lizards and beetles. Their religion, moreover, was intensely preoccupied with the dead: their bible, the *Book of the Dead*, consisted of directions and incantations to aid the departed in the nether world. The priests, moreover, were masters of the art of embalming, and the exalted dead were laid away in tombs inside the pyramids which have not been equaled for magnitude and opulence.

By trade and conquest the civilization of Egypt had overflowed its borders. The "sand dwellers" of the North, as the Egyptians called the nomads of Canaan, as well as the walled cities of the Canaanite princes, were frequently brought under the sway of the Pharaoh. Sometimes the armed forces of Egypt—spearmen and bowmen, chariots and horsemen—swept up the coastal plain of Canaan, swung east at the foot of Carmel into the Valley of Jezreel, and there they set their array and locked in battle with the Hittites or Babylonians. With the recession of the armies, the merchant caravans reappeared, going down into Egypt for pottery, glassware, and jewelry, and bearing for exchange the spices of Gilead as well as leather and wool, and, perhaps, a handsome youth who might be picked up on the way to fetch a high price in the slave market of Memphis or Thebes.

2

JOSEPH, we learn, was bought by a wealthy Egyptian named Potiphar, and soon rose to a place of importance in his master's household. But the youth's fortunes were brought down by the rage of his master's wife, whose lustful advances he dared to spurn. Now he was in the prison house awaiting the fate of all the wretched in Egypt who incurred the displeasure of the mighty.

But the young Hebrew was marvelously gifted. He "was of beautiful form and fair to look upon," and to outward charm he added wisdom and intuition. He had above all the gift of action: he knew what to do at moments when others were dismayed or bewildered. "The Lord made all that he did to prosper in his hand."

And suddenly the Hebrew slave finds himself in the presence of the monarch. The Pharaoh has dreamed strange, disquieting dreams: seven lean cows consume seven fat cows; seven ears of corn, "thin and blasted with the wind," swallow up seven ears "full and good." The official magicians and dream interpreters can make nothing of it, but the keen vision of the Hebrew reveals the hidden meaning. Before the startled king and courtiers he raises the famine signal. Let Egypt take heed! Seven years of drought are coming upon the land and grain must be stored up against the famine, or Egypt will die. Let power be entrusted to one man, for the menace is grave. "You are the man," says the Pharaoh to the Hebrew slave.

So Joseph becomes the food dictator of the empire and his power is second only to the monarch's. Seven years of plenty come and go: Joseph fills up the granaries of Egypt. His word is law. Then come the lean years; the Nile is too low to water the fields, the irrigation buckets shrivel in the heat. Famine comes down like a conqueror over all the lands of the East: in Egypt alone there is food.

In Canaan, Joseph's brothers sit and wonder whence food is to be gotten for their hungry children. "Why do you look one upon another?" says their old father. "I have heard that there is corn in Egypt. Get you down thither and buy for us from there: that we may live and not die." So they go down into Egypt and stand before their brother Joseph, who knows them—but they know him not.

Now Benjamin, whose mother was also the mother of Joseph, is not with them, for Israel feared to expose the lad to the hazards of the journey. But Joseph yearns for Benjamin and, charging his brothers with being spies, he holds Simeon as a hostage and sends the rest away with the admonition that they can clear themselves only by bringing Benjamin. "And," we read, "he turned himself about from them, and wept."

The famine continues; the clan of Israel in Canaan cries aloud for bread. Benjamin is forced to take the journey with his brothers and face the harsh man who rules in Egypt. But the man receives and feasts the Hebrews in his own house. "Is your father well," he asks them, "the old man of whom you spoke? Is he yet alive? Is this your youngest brother of whom you spoke to me? God be gracious unto thee, my son." And Joseph retires to his own room to weep.

The sacks are filled and the brothers depart, but they are brought back posthaste. Joseph had ordered his favorite silver goblet placed in Benjamin's sack, for he would hold the lad as a thief. But Judah, who had gone as surety for Benjamin with his father, steps forward and pleads to be held and punished in place of the boy.

Now Joseph can no longer contain himself: the flood breaks every bound. "I am Joseph," he cries, "Doth my father yet live?" The news is brought to Israel. "It is enough," cries the old man, "Joseph my son is yet alive. I will go and see him before I die."

Such is the story of Joseph and his brothers, a tale that still excites the imagination of poets and dramatists, that will never lose its hold on the heart of humanity. But the story is not only drama; it is also history, for it leads to a strange turn in the career of the Hebrews, the long sojourn in Egypt which changed the nomad clan into a people.

3

THE famine shows no abatement, and Joseph sends his father an eager invitation, which the Pharaoh endorses, to come with all his household and settle in Egypt. The Hebrews shall eat "the fat of the land." The fertile region of Goshen in the eastern delta of the Nile is thrown open to the shepherds and their flocks. On the way to Egypt Israel is visited by the God of Abraham and Isaac, who reassures him: in Egypt his seed shall become a nation.

Who was the Pharaoh to whom Joseph owed his elevation and his brothers their rescue from famine? He has not yet been identified, but the internal evidence of the biblical narrative—the names of the persons that figure in it, the customs it reveals, as well as the general atmosphere in which it moves—is so convincing, that there is no reason to doubt its authenticity. The most probable date of Joseph's arrival in Egypt is about 1850 B.C.E. The land was still ruled by a line of Semitic invaders, nomads from the north known as Hyksos, or "shepherd kings," a circumstance that would account for the welcome accorded the kindred Hebrews under Joseph and Jacob, and for the complete reversal of attitude toward them when, many years later, the Hyksos were overthrown and expelled. Remarkable parallels have been found in Egyptian inscriptions to the biblical account of Joseph's elevation and to the measures he took before and during the famine to save the land from starvation.

Thus, under favor of man and God, began the long sojourn of the Hebrews in Egypt. Their abode was not far from the land they regarded as their own. On the fat grasslands of Goshen where the Hebrew shepherds pastured their flocks, they kept alive the memory of their origin, the knowledge of the God of their fathers, and the sense of destiny that ruled their consciousness. The lure of the Egyptian way of life reached them, if at all, with attenuated force: the shepherd clans preserved their spiritual personality. Moreover, as the generations followed one another the danger of absorption dwindled and vanished. For the seed of Jacob was "fruitful and multiplied exceedingly." The seventy who came from Canaan became a nation.

4

THE "shepherd kings" were expelled in 1580 B.C.E. and a new Pharaoh, we read, ascended the throne of Egypt, one who "knew not Joseph." This Pharaoh is believed to have been

Amosis (1580-1557 B.C.E), founder of the Eighteenth Dynasty. He saw the children of Israel grown numerous and strong, and he felt alarmed. The Hebrews, moreover, had been the protégés of the hated Hyksos and what if the land were invaded and they joined the enemy? They might then "get them up out of the land." The Pharaoh wanted them in Egypt, for there were cities to be built near the border, military store-cities, and the children of Israel could be put to labor. Other sections of Egypt's population toiled for the ruler, dug and quarried and dragged huge blocks of stone for pyramids, temples and palaces. Why should the Hebrews be exempted?

So the shepherds were reduced to slavery; but while the Egyptians may have looked on bondage as part of the order of nature, to the Hebrews it was an insufferable wrong. They groaned aloud in their misery and shame. "And God heard their groaning, and God remembered his covenant with Abraham, with Isaac, and with Jacob."

5

THE plight of the Hebrews in Egypt called out the greatest leader of men the human race has known, Moses son of Amram, emancipator and lawgiver, teacher, prophet and saint. No feet that have trod this earth have borne a spirit wiser and humbler and more exalted. No life has been more perfect and beneficent.

His childhood and early manhood were spent in the court of the Pharaoh as the adopted son of the monarch's daughter. A royal princess, we learn, had saved him from the Nile to which his mother herself had consigned him; for the Pharaoh, determined to put an end to the children of Israel, had decreed that all male infants be cast into the river. This princess is believed to have been Hatshepsut, the favorite daughter of Thotmes I (1539-1501 B.C.E.). But the milk that nourished the infant Moses was his own mother's, for the princess engaged her to be the child's nurse; and the people he came to know as his own were the Hebrews.

The sight of an Egyptian taskmaster beating a Hebrew slave is more than the youth Moses can bear. He slays the Egyptian, but his deed becomes known and he is forced to flee. He comes to the

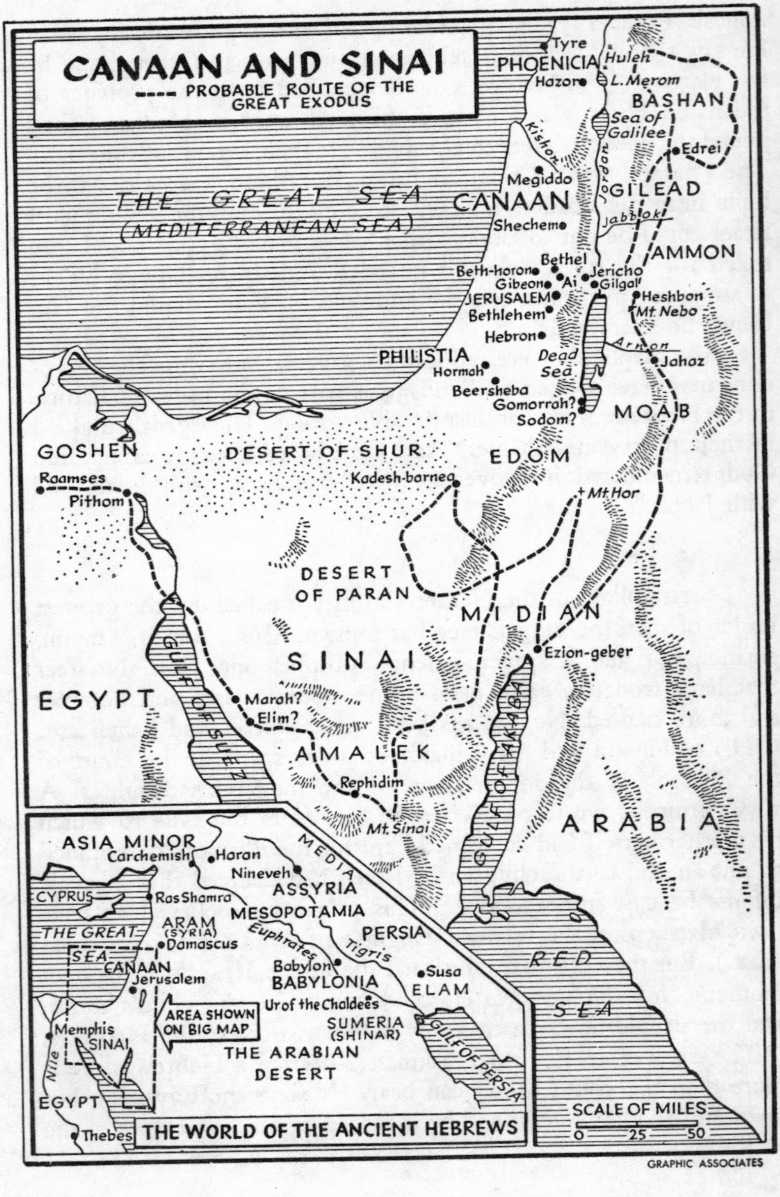
CANAAN AND SINAI
---- PROBABLE ROUTE OF THE GREAT EXODUS
THE GREAT SEA
(MEDITERRANEAN SEA)
Tyre
PHOENICIA
Huleh
Hazor
L. Merom
BASHAN
Sea of Galilee
Kishon
Jordan
Edrei
Megiddo
CANAAN
GILEAD
Shechem
Jabbok
AMMON
Bethel
Beth-horon
Jericho
Gibeon
Ai
Gilgal
JERUSALEM
Heshbon
Bethlehem
Mt. Nebo
Hebron
Arnon
PHILISTIA
Dead Sea
Jahaz
Hormah
Beersheba
Gomorrah?
Sodom?
MOAB
GOSHEN
DESERT OF SHUR
EDOM
Raamses
Kadesh-barnea
Pithom
Mt. Hor
DESERT OF PARAN
MIDIAN
SINAI
Ezion-geber
EGYPT
GULF OF SUEZ
Marah?
Elim?
GULF OF AKABA
AMALEK
Rephidim
Mt. Sinai
ARABIA
RED SEA
SCALE OF MILES
0 25 50
ASIA MINOR
Carchemish
Haran
MEDIA
Nineveh
ASSYRIA
CYPRUS
Ras Shamra
MESOPOTAMIA
ARAM (SYRIA)
THE GREAT SEA
Damascus
Euphrates
PERSIA
CANAAN
Tigris
Jerusalem
Babylon
BABYLONIA
Susa
ELAM
Ur of the Chaldees
AREA SHOWN ON BIG MAP
Memphis
SUMERIA (SHINAR)
SINAI
GULF OF PERSIA
Nile
THE ARABIAN DESERT
EGYPT
Thebes
THE WORLD OF THE ANCIENT HEBREWS

GRAPHIC ASSOCIATES

bleak land of Midian in the Sinai Peninsula, and lives the life of a shepherd pasturing the flocks of one Jethro whose daughter, Zipporah, he takes to wife.

On Mount Horeb, a place sacred to the God of his fathers, he sees a strange sight. It is a bush wrapped in flames; it burns, but the flames are powerless against it: "the bush burned with fire, but the bush was not consumed." And a Voice speaks out of the flames: "I will send thee unto Pharaoh to bring my people the children of Israel out of Egypt." The shepherd is dismayed by the charge, but all his pleading is in vain: he must go. But what shall he say when they ask him the name of Him Who sent him? And the Voice answers: "I AM THAT I AM." The name is like a veil hiding the Mystery yet vouchsafing a faint glimpse of it. And the bush which the flames were unable to consume, and out of which came the voice of God, has become the symbol of Israel through the ages.

Moses goes back to Egypt, where he speaks first to the elders of his people. Accompanied by his brother Aaron as his spokesman —for Moses is no orator—he then appears before the ruler with the bold demand: "Let my people go!" The Pharaoh is angry and adamant. He lays heavier burdens on the slaves who now cry out bitterly against Moses.

In the end, however, the Pharaoh is forced to let the Hebrew slaves go. All the plagues that fester in the air of Egypt fall upon the land, plagues of insects and frogs, of murrain and boils, of hail and thick darkness, climaxed by the smiting of the first born. The king sees the hand of a Higher Power lifted up against him.

6

WHEN Thotmes I died, the princess Hatshepsut became the virtual ruler of Egypt. The Pharaoh on the throne was her brother Thotmes III (1501-1448 B.C.E.) for whom, until her death, she acted as regent. Thotmes III is now believed to have been the Pharaoh of the Oppression. Like his father he was a great conqueror or, at any rate, he saw to it that posterity should so regard him. An inscription found in the temple at Thebes and dated 1479 B.C.E., proudly records a campaign he fought in Canaan which netted him a vast booty, including

> 2,041 mares, 1,949 oxen, 2,000 goats, 296 bulls, 20,500 sheep, 200 suits of armor, 892 chariots, 32 gold-plated chariots, 7 silver-plated tent-poles, 1,784 pounds of golden rings, 966 pounds of silver rings, ivory and ebony ornaments, a golden plough, cedarwood tables inlaid with gold and precious stones, golden sceptres, embroidered robes, 208,000 bushels of corn.

And whether or not the inventory is correct, for several centuries thereafter Canaan, with its kings and kinglets often in revolt, was a province of Egypt.

On his death in 1448 B.C.E., Thotmes III was succeeded by Amenophis II, and a year later the Exodus is believed to have taken place. That date receives remarkable confirmation in the First Book of Kings, 6;1, which states that Solomon began to build the Temple "in the four hundred and eightieth year after the children of Israel were come out of the land of Egypt." Now, the date of the Temple is 967 B.C.E., which also sets the Exodus at 1447 B.C.E.

Archaeology, it is true, has thus far failed to produce specific evidence in support of the biblical narrative but the failure need not occasion surprise, for Egyptian rulers always omitted from their records whatever might detract from their glory. However, archaeology does confirm the general historic background as revealed in the Bible. The death of the oppressor was the signal for revolt in Syria and Palestine, and Moses may well have taken advantage of the difficulties in which the new monarch became involved. On purely psychological grounds, moreover, it is impossible to believe that a story like the sojourn in Egypt or the Exodus could have been invented. Why should a people choose to identify its beginnings with the shame of slavery? Invention, indeed, pursues an opposite course: nations love to surround their origins with circumstances that are heroic and glorious. The Bible, in fact, is the only ancient historic document that shuns the vainglory of embellishment and apotheosis.

7

SO GREAT was the haste of the Hebrews to leave Egypt that the dough they carried had no time to become leavened. They ate the unleavened cakes which, through the ages that follow, serve as a symbol of the Great Exodus. The Hebrews made up a vast assemblage "with their sons and their daughters, with their flocks and their herds." The men alone numbered six hundred thousand, and there was in addition "a mixed multitude," strangers who attached themselves to the Israelites. Thus did Jacob's children multiply in the centuries of their sojourn in Egypt.

From Raamses, one of the cities they had built for the Pharaoh, the Hebrews moved on to Pithom and they encamped on the shore of an inlet of the Red Sea. Suddenly the army of Egypt appeared in the distance: the ruler had repented of his weakness and was pursuing the fugitives. But a wind came up and blew the waters away, the Hebrews passed to the other side in safety, and when the waters returned the pursuing hosts were engulfed. A cry of jubilation arose from the multitude:

Thou didst blow with thy wind,
The sea covered them;
They sank as lead in the mighty waters!

Now the slaves were free. Before them stretched the desert and beyond the desert beckoned the Promised Land.

CHAPTER THREE

Desert and Torah

THE short route from Egypt to Canaan, the path followed by caravans and armies, lay due north through the Wilderness of Shur. But Moses avoided this route, for the warlike Philistines dwelt on it and the newly liberated slaves were not prepared for so strong an adversary. Moses turned south, past Marah of the bitter waters and Elim of the twelve springs and seventy palm trees. Southward also lay the mountain of the burning bush, where a momentous experience lay in store for the Hebrews.

But on the road he chose there also lay in wait a powerful enemy. The Amalekites appeared at Rephidim and challenged the desert invaders. The battle was long and bitter. Israel's warriors, led by the young captain Joshua son of Nun, looked up from the field to an elevation where Moses sat, and when they saw his arms uplifted, they pressed valiantly forward upon the enemy until they defeated him. Such was the inspiration that flowed from the leader. It is clear, moreover, from the account of this battle that the fugitives were no mere rabble. They were, on the contrary, an organized expedition, marching by tribes behind their elders or chieftains, each tribe furnishing its tale of fighting men to meet emergencies as they arose.

Now Jethro, the father-in-law of Moses, who dwelt in near-by Midian, came to bless his son-in-law, and with him came Zipporah and the leader's two sons, Gershon and Eliezer. Jethro was a wise old sheik, and Moses organized the administration of justice in the nomad nation in accordance with his counsel. He appointed "rulers of thousands, rulers of hundreds, rulers of fifties and rulers of tens," who acted as judges in ordinary cases, referring the more important disputes to the leader.

But the Israelites were not a docile people. They were, on the contrary, clamorous and rebellious. Apparently the transition from bondage to freedom had been too sudden. Amid the privations of the desert they pined for the good and abundant food of Egypt, and this nostalgia of the fleshpots became for all time the symbol of their lower nature.

But, we are told, the Hand that took them out of the house of bondage made provision for the journey. It fed their hunger and quenched their thirst. It pointed the way to them with "a pillar of cloud by day and a pillar of fire by night."

2

NOW these wayward children of Israel whom, nevertheless, the Lord loved, are to receive the most precious of His gifts, the Torah. *Torah* is usually translated as "Law," but it embraces a great deal more than law. It includes everything else contained in the Written and Oral Tradition: history and prophecy, proverb and parable, wisdom and homily, song and psalm. A legend relates that God had previously offered the Torah to the other nations, all of whom refused it. Israel alone said: "We will do and obey." The consecration, attended by signs and wonders, occurs at Mount Sinai, the mountain of the burning bush. Now the career of Israel is stamped with the seal of a great teaching: this nomad troop is to become "a kingdom of priests and a holy nation."

The Ten Commandments are the freshets from which flows the river of Torah that has watered the earth. They make up the groundwork of the faith and ethics of humanity. The First and Second of the Ten Commandments proclaim the omnipotence and unity of God, and represent the most revolutionary doctrine in the religious history of mankind. No illumination of the intellect and spirit of man, before it or since, can compare with it in grandeur of conception or vital implications. Ethical monotheism, as this doctrine is designated, is the first and foremost contribution of the Jewish genius to humanity, and the most fruitful seed of progress toward the higher life lying imbedded in the heart of mankind, and still waiting to sprout and flourish.

The doctrine, in all its majestic simplicity, is expressed in a verse (Deuteronomy 6;4) spoken by Moses to his people in later years. That verse, called after its first word, meaning "hear," is the *Shema:* "Hear, O Israel, the Lord is our God, the Lord is One!" The six Hebrew words of the *Shema* are not a cold mathematical formula: they are a confession of faith, a passionate affirmation, a ringing manifesto. They have been the watchword of the Jew through the ages, holding the central place in his daily prayers. They have been his last words on his deathbed and at other supreme moments, especially when face to face with martyrdom. Every dilution of the doctrine, every compromise with it, be it the equal powers of light and darkness of Zoroastrianism, or the Trinitarianism of Christianity, has been implacably rejected.

Monotheism, which proclaims the One God to be creator and ruler of all nature, begins by destroying the foundations of paganism. For the many gods of paganism only reflect the many and often conflicting forces of nature. Monotheism goes on to replace the apparent conflict and chaos of nature with design and harmony;

and, since God controls human destiny also, monotheism replaces the apparent capriciousness of human history with moral purpose and goal. The goal is "to make the world perfect under the kingship of the Almighty," as the *Alenu* prayer expresses it. Monotheism, in other words, proclaims a goal that is ethical, universal, and holy, and demands that human life be dedicated to its achievement by rising to the level of purity and holiness.

Ethical monotheism is a rigorous doctrine, as exacting as it is sublime, nor is it to be expected that the frail children of men who will be led to pay lip-devotion to it will overflow with gratitude toward the people who first proclaimed it.

3

THE Third Commandment prohibits the frivolous invocation of the name of God to which men are so prone. The Fourth establishes the Sabbath as a day of rest in which even the beast of burden must be allowed to share.

If the distinction can be made, the first four commandments are primarily religious in character, while those that follow are ethical or social. The Fifth, "Honor thy father and thy mother," is one of the two safeguards of the family, the basic institution of society; the other is the Seventh, "Thou shalt not commit adultery." The Sixth, "Thou shalt not murder," the Eighth, "Thou shalt not steal," and the Ninth, "Thou shalt not bear false witness against thy neighbor," make up the keystone of the arch that supports all human relationships. The Tenth, "Thou shalt not covet anything that is thy neighbor's," seeks to control the passions leading to antisocial conduct.

4

THE Great Tradition relates that Moses remained forty days on the mount in solitary communion with God, and when he reappeared, he carried two tablets of stone on which the Ten Words were inscribed. It was a common practice in the lands of the East to inscribe laws and other important records on tablets or steles, and the conclusion that Moses possessed the art of writing is abundantly justified by the evidence of archaeology. At a place not far from Mount Sinai, Sir Flinders Petrie. the famous Egyptologist, discovered inscriptions dating a century and a half before the Exodus.

The script that Moses used was most probably an early form of the Hebrew or Phoenician alphabet, in which the symbols represented not syllables and words, as in early cuneiform and hieroglyphic writing, but sounds. This phonetic alphabet represents an enormous advance in the art of writing: twenty-odd letters took the place of the great number of symbols required by the pictographic or syllabic systems. This alphabet, in fact, is believed to have been invented in the Sinai Peninsula, whence it eventually reached the Phoenicians and Aramaeans who carried it to all the known lands.

The language of Moses and the children of Israel was Hebrew, a Semitic tongue of Canaanite origin, which Jacob and his household took with them into Egypt. There, though modified by the influence of Egyptian, the language was preserved throughout the long sojourn.

5

HAVING accepted the Ten Commandments, the children of Israel were soon to demonstrate how difficult it was to observe them. Almost immediately they violated the First. Coming down from the mountain with his tablets, Moses saw the people beneath him dancing around a golden calf. The old idolatry of Egypt had reared its head. "This is thy god, O Israel," they said, pointing to the image, "which brought thee out of the land of Egypt!" Moses shattered the tablets he carried; but in his heart mercy fought with justice and mercy prevailed. "Forgive their sin," he pleaded with God, "and if not, blot me, I pray thee, out of the book which Thou hast written." And God answered, "Go, lead the people to the place of which I have spoken unto thee."

Instructed by Moses, the people set up a portable tabernacle as a visible symbol of their faith and for a center of worship. It foreshadowed the temple which, centuries later, was to rise up in Jerusalem. Around the Tabernacle public worship was elaborately organized after Aaron and his sons, as well as the other men of the tribe of Levi, had been solemnly invested with the priesthood.

But while the craftsmen were building the Tabernacle, Moses labored at the still greater edifice of Torah. His aim, however difficult of attainment, was clear: to fashion a nation physically and morally pure, and practicing justice and righteousness toward their fellow-men. He understood that a nation so ordered must be zealously devoted to the One God. Laws and institutions, priests and judges, penalties and rewards—all these were necessary, but the foundation must be: "And thou shalt love the Lord thy God with all thy heart, and with all thy soul, and with all thy strength." So the teacher never tires of denouncing idolatry and warning the people against its lure. Idolatry was the sin of sins, the foundation of impurity and iniquity. Idolatry meant human sacrifice, sexual depravity, slavery and oppression. Israel was going to a land teeming with idolatry. Israel must beware of contamination.

Higher and higher rose the structure of Torah. To regulate and elevate every aspect of private and public life, in work and worship, at home, in the field, and in the marketplace, on weekdays, Sabbaths and festivals, a stream of commands and prohibitions, warnings and appeals, flowed from the leader to his people. Purity and justice are their touchstone; forbearance and mercy have sat as their interpreters. Thus the injunction "an eye for an eye and a tooth for a tooth," was early explained as meaning monetary compensation: the spirit of the Mosaic Code makes a literal interpretation of this ordinance impossible.

At moments a command appears that taxes our modern viewpoint. In this connection the dietary prohibitions, distinguishing between clean and unclean animals, as well as the prohibition that developed into the "milk and meat" regulations, are often cited. Apart from their obvious disciplinary value, however, there lies behind these so-called taboos a vast experience which no wise people would ignore. They have been shown to be closely related to the health of the body as well as of the soul. The prohibitions, for example, disqualify foods like pork and shellfish which, it is now known, may carry the germs of disease. But the explicit premise on which the regulations are based is: "For I am the Lord your God; sanctify yourselves, therefore, and be ye holy; for I am holy." The dietary laws were to have a share in fashioning and preserving "a holy people."

6

WHENCE came these "statutes and judgments," these warnings and pleas, these signposts for the labyrinth of life? Did they all flow from the inspired genius of the leader? Did he owe nothing to other men, other nations, other eras?

In 1901 a stone slab, or stele, was discovered in Susa, capital of ancient Persia, on which some three hundred laws were found inscribed in cuneiform beneath two figures representing the great Hammurabi and the Babylonian sun-god Shamash. The stele was deciphered, the laws were hailed as the Code of Hammurabi, and striking resemblances were discovered between them and those of Moses. The "eye for an eye and tooth for a tooth" laws were there, as well as many other enactments not unlike those in the Mosaic Code for the regulation of a pastoral and agricultural society. Certain scholars and "higher critics" now believed that at last they were in possession of the source of the Mosaic Code. All that Moses did, they declared, was to copy Hammurabi, and some of them went further, finding Hebrew civilization generally to be a mere imitation of the Babylonian. Of late, moreover, the claim has been advanced that Egyptian influence upon the language, customs, and institutions of the children of Israel has been undervalued in favor of the Babylonian, while with the discovery of the Minaean inscriptions in South Arabia and the Ras Shamra tablets on the Syrian coast an increasing amount of "credit" has been claimed for the influence of Arabia.

But the claims of the Babylonians to originality or priority over the Hebrews are no longer honored.* The laws of both may have had a common source that is lost in the nebulae of prehistoric times, or each code may have grown up independently of the other, developing similarities because of the similar con-

* "A comparison of the Code of Hammurabi as a whole with the Pentateuchal code as a whole, while it reveals certain similarities, convinces the student that the laws of the Old Testament are in no essential way dependent upon the Babylonian laws."—George A. Barton, *Archaeology and the Bible,* p. 367.

ditions under which both arose. The resemblances between the two codes, in fact, are far less remarkable than their differences. The Hebrew Sabbath, for example, may be said to bear the same relation to the Babylonian Nubattum and Shabbattum as the human species bears to the ape. The Nubattum, which also occurred every seventh day, is, as described in the Babylonian Seven Tablets of Creation, "an evil day," a day of gloom and dread when "cooked flesh he shall not eat: he shall not change his coat: he shall not put on clean clothes . . . the physician shall not heal the sick." The Shabbattum, which others believe may have been the origin of the Sabbath, occurred in the middle of the month when the moon was at full and about to wane, and for that reason was also a day of gloom and foreboding. The Jewish Sabbath, on the other hand, is a day of rest and joy and spiritual replenishment. In the Code of Hammurabi the ideal of holiness is conspicuous by its absence, while the Mosaic Code is saturated with it. The harsh customs of the desert, like blood revenge, the Mosaic Code aims to abolish or moderate, and with the hideous practice of human immolation prohibited, sacrifice is exalted into a means of releasing the purest human emotions: gratitude, repentance, and reverence. All that the great teacher ordains is stamped with the seal of spirit: whatever he touches becomes holy.

7

A PROFOUND concern for social justice permeates the Torah. The universal institution of slavery, after being shorn of its cruelties, is discredited by being made contemptible in the sight of men. The weak and the helpless—the poor, the widow, the orphan and the stranger—are the special wards of God. The husbandman reaping his harvest is not to crop the "corners" of the field; he is not to return for the sheaf he has forgotten; he is not to beat his olive tree twice; he is not to glean his vineyard after gathering the grapes: all that is left over shall be "for the stranger, for the fatherless, and for the widow." The poor man who has pledged his garment must have it restored to him in the evening "that he may sleep in his garment, and bless thee." The laborer is to receive his hire the same day, "for he is poor and setteth his heart upon it." The stranger is as much an object of God's care as the widow and orphan. "And if a stranger sojourn in your land with thee," says the Torah, "ye shall not do him wrong. The stranger that sojourneth with you shall be unto you as the homeborn among you, and thou shalt love him as thyself; for ye were strangers in the land of Egypt."

But in none of its provisions does the sacred code reveal such insight into social problems as in those that ordain the Sabbatical and Jubilee years. Every seventh year the fields were to lie fallow and all debts were to be cancelled. It was to be a "sabbath" year for the reparation of the soil and for lifting the burden from the homesteads of the poor. At the end of seven Sabbatical cycles, or every fiftieth year, the Jubilee was ordered to be proclaimed in all the borders of Israel. In that year all land was to be restored to the original owners or their heirs, and all slaves were to be liberated. The Jubilee was for restitution and redemption. Were not the worst of the social evils—slavery and prostitution, excessive wealth and exploitation of the poor—the results of those economic wrongs that stripped the peasant of his holding and enabled the rich, as the prophet Isaiah later expressed it, to "join house to house" and "lay field to field, till there be no room"? Israel must not be a nation of landless serfs in the clutches of a few landed barons. Israel must be a nation of freemen before the Lord, and men who are economically enslaved cannot be free. The Jubilee was to be the season of emancipation, when Israel was to "proclaim liberty throughout the land unto all the inhabitants thereof."

8

"A HOLY nation," the ever-recurring demand of Torah, may sound austere and forbidding, but such is not the spirit of the sacred code. Life is for joy, as well as holiness. "Thou shalt rejoice before the Lord thy God" is an injunction repeated again and again by the prophet and lawgiver. And for increase of joy as well as holiness, the year was adorned with a series of gracious and exalted festivals.

There were, first, the three "pilgrimage" festivals, Passover, Shabuoth, and Sukkoth, when every man of Israel was required to repair to the national center for worship. These festivals bear a double significance. They signalize first some turning point in the agricultural year, and second, they commemorate a decisive experience in the career of the nation. Passover is the time when "the sickle is first put to the standing corn"; it is also for remembrance of the Exodus, "the season of our liberation." Shabuoth, or the Feast of Weeks, when the Story of Ruth, redolent of the earth in its freshness and beauty, is read, marks the season of the ripening harvest; it also commemorates the promulgation of the Ten Commandments at Sinai. Sukkoth, or the Feast of Booths, is the "season of rejoicing" with the final ingathering from field, orchard, and vineyard; it also recalls the years of wandering through the Sinai Desert, when the people dwelt in tents or booths.

To the three "pilgrimage" festivals, each of them a season of joy, were added two solemn occasions, both falling just prior to the Feast of Booths. One is Rosh Hashana, the first of the year; the other, ten days later, is Yom Kippur, the Day of Atonement, the holiest day of all.

Through all the round of the year came, of course, the Sabbath, the vehicle of ascent for the soul of man from the sordid to the sublime. Numerous and momentous are the appeals and warnings touching the Sabbath. Without the Sabbath, no holy nation, no kingdom of priests.

Thus in the web of Torah there entered as warp and woof a marvelous mingling of holiness and joy. With the promulgation of the Written Torah, moreover, began the tradition of Oral Torah, handed down by word of mouth from father to son, from teacher to scholar. Generation after generation the web was extended. The pattern, though it remained always essentially the same, was constantly elaborated. Israel became the Torah-people. Israel and the Torah became inseparable.

Later, the Jewish sages expressed the relationship in a terse and tremendous statement. "The Holy One, blessed be He," said they, "and Israel and the Torah are One."

9

NORTH of the sacred mount, across the wild wastes of the Sinai Peninsula, lies the oasis of Kadesh-barnea. This verdant spot springs out of the dreary desert like a magic apparition. Shepherds from pastures near and far gather there to water their flocks, and not far away winds a pass that leads into the Negeb, or southern section of Canaan.

To this oasis Moses marched the children of Israel. They moved in order, tribe by tribe, guarded by their armed men. Frequently the craven spirit born of slavery came out in loud complaints. Now they demanded water, now meat. Nor was the spirit of rebellion confined to the rabble. Once the leader faced a serious revolt led by Korah of the tribe of Levi with whom other Levites, "princes of the congregation, the elect men of the assembly, men of renown" associated themselves. The revolt, we read, failed ignominiously, for God Himself intervened for His chosen prophet. Korah and his followers were swallowed up in an earthquake.

From Kadesh-barnea the leader's gaze turned to the Promised Land; the hour to strike seemed to have come. First he sent twelve scouts to survey the land, its people, its towns, its defenses. The scouts returned with a tale of wonders and terrors. The land was marvelous, it flowed with milk and honey, but alas, they could not hope to conquer it. The inhabitants were fierce giants, the cities "fortified and very great." Fear gave wings to their imagination. Through the camp ran the rumor: beside the Canaanites the Hebrews were as grasshoppers. The scouts may have seen some of the massive prehistoric monuments that still stand in Palestine: monoliths, dolmens and menhirs, consisting of huge stone slabs arranged in circles or avenues, which they decided only giants could have set up.

Two of the scouts, Caleb of Judah and Joshua of Ephraim, stood forth and denounced the fears of their comrades. "We should go up at once and possess the land," cried Caleb, "for we are well able to overcome it!" But the former slaves were in panic. "Let us make a captain," they cried, "and return to Egypt."

Now Moses became convinced that these former slaves were not fit to enter the Promised Land: they must die in the wilderness and the task would be accomplished by their children. Such, indeed, was the stern decree, and when the people heard it they were dismayed. A strange courage took possession of them, the courage of despair. They marched up into the hills, unmindful of the leader's warnings, and the Amalekites and Canaanites came out and routed them.

The desert generation resumed its wanderings, moving south again toward the Gulf of Akaba. For forty years they marched and halted, and marched again. Young men became old, men in their prime aged and died. And a new generation arose, nurtured by the great leader and his aides, a generation that knew not the fleshpots of Egypt.

10.

AGAIN the nomad nation assembled at Kadesh-barnea, eager to strike for the Promised Land. The tribe of Judah, led by Caleb, had already broken through the Negeb and established itself in the region around Hebron. But Moses decided to take possession first of the regions east of the River Jordan.

The road to the Jordan lay through Edom and Moab, and Moses petitioned Edom to let Israel through. "We will not pass through field or through vineyard," ran the message, "neither shall we drink of the waters of the wells; we will go along the king's highway, we will not turn aside to the right hand nor to the left, until we have passed the border." The answer was a curt refusal, and Israel had to make a hard journey around Edom's borders. Then followed victory on victory. At Hormah the Canaanites of the south were decisively defeated. The wild Midianites, led by five of their kings, suffered disaster and spoliation. At Jahaz, Israel smote the Transjordanian Amorites led by Sihon, King of Heshbon, and conquered the region from the Arnon to the Jabbok. The warriors of Israel swept on. At Edrei they overwhelmed the forces of Og, King of Bashan, and became masters of Transjordania to the foot of Mount Hermon.

Edom, Moab, and Ammon were spared for reasons of kinship, for Edom was descended from Esau, brother of Jacob, and Moab and Ammon from Abraham's nephew Lot. Nevertheless, Balak, King of Moab, was seized with great fear, and hired Balaam, a famous magician, to pronounce a doom on Israel. But every curse in Balaam's mouth, we read, was changed to a blessing. The magician spoke in a trance, he was not his own master. "Behold a people," he cried, "that riseth up as a lioness, and as a lion doth he lift himself up!" King Balak was enraged. "What hast thou done?"

he cried. And Balaam answered: "Must I not speak that which the Lord putteth in my mouth?"

The East Jordan plateau, now held by the Israelites, was excellent grazing land. The tribes of Reuben and Gad, who possessed much cattle, were especially attracted by it. They, together with half the tribes of Manasseh, asked to be allowed to settle there, promising, however, that their armed contingents would cross the Jordan with the rest of Israel and would not return until Canaan had been conquered. "We will build sheepfolds here for our cattle," said they, "and cities for our little ones, but we ourselves will be ready armed to go before the children of Israel." With solemn emphasis on this engagement, the petition of Reuben, Gad, and half of Manasseh was granted.

The people encamped in the plain of Moab near the Jordan opposite Jericho, but their leader was not to go across the river with them. He had already placed his hands on Joshua son of Nun, and ordained him his successor. Now in words of passionate eloquence, he delivered his final charge to the people he had nurtured and led. Then, with a final blessing and farewell, he turned and left them: he went away alone to die. He climbed to the summit of Mount Nebo and looked out upon the Promised Land which his feet were forbidden to tread. Then he gave up his spirit to God, and a legend reports that the Holy One, blessed be He, took up his soul with a kiss.

CHAPTER FOUR

The Land and the Conquest

THE new leader, Joshua son of Nun, was no stranger to his people. Through the forty years of desert wandering he had stood by the side of Moses and led the embattled hosts of Israel against their enemies. He was one of the twelve scouts whom Moses had sent to spy out the land, and one of the two who had returned undismayed. Essentially a soldier, Joshua was nevertheless imbued with the spirit of his great master.

The days of mourning for Moses came to an end and the new leader ordered the nation to march. Headed by the priests bearing the Ark of the Covenant, the children of Israel streamed across the Jordan and stood at last on its western bank.

2

FROM time to time the boundaries of Canaan or Palestine have varied, the only fixed line being its coast on the Western Sea. Its eastern limit has generally embraced Transjordania, while the traditional formula "from Dan to Beersheba," designed to indicate its north and south borders, has proved exceedingly elastic.

Within its area of some 50,000 square miles, the land is remarkable for its topographical contrasts. West of the Transjordanian plateau, the relief map reveals three longitudinal zones of which the Jordan Valley, where the invaders now stood, is one. Starting with the Huleh swamps in the north and embracing the Sea of Galilee, the Jordan River, and the Dead Sea, this valley is a great gash between the mountains of Transjordania and those of western Canaan. The gash becomes broader and deeper as it cuts south; the thick waters of the Dead Sea, which are part of it, lie in the earth's deepest hollow, almost 1300 feet below sea level. The shores of this strange sea are wild and torrid wastes, but its waters have been found to harbor immense wealth: asphalt and vast quantities of other minerals, especially compounds of potassium and magnesium.

The Jordan, or "downcomer," as the name signifies, rises in the glades of Mount Hermon and in a flow of only ten miles through the swampy plain of Huleh and the shallow Lake Merom to Lake Kinnereth, the river drops almost 700 feet. Kinnereth is the beautiful "Lake of the Harp," or Sea of Galilee. The Jordan comes rushing out of it, and, in a serpentine flow of sixty-five miles, it drops an additional 600 feet to the Dead Sea.

Up from the Jordan Valley rises steeply the middle zone, the broad mountainous backbone, extending 150 miles through the length of the land and setting its seal upon the country as a whole.

In the north the slopes of this range are craggy and precipitous. As they roll south, the hills become broken by many vales of which the largest is the Valley of Jezreel. This low, undulating plain is roughly triangular in shape, with its eastern corner at the ridge of Mount Gilboa, its apex at the foot of Mount Tabor, and its western limit at Mount Carmel where the River Kishon falls into the Great Sea.

The Valley of Jezreel opens Palestine to the world north and south of it, and has enormously influenced the destiny of the country. The traders from Egypt, moving north along the coast, turned at the foot of Carmel into this plain to go on to Damascus and beyond, or to veer south into the interior of Canaan. The traders from Mesopotamia, with merchandise for Palestine or Egypt, reversed the same route. And often enough the route was followed not by the peaceful caravans of trade but by the hosts of warring empires. Down from Mesopotamia or up from Egypt, the armies swept into Jezreel and camped there. It was a good camping ground, and it was also a good battleground. Jezreel became famous as a battlefield and the belief arose that the final battle of the nations before the advent of Messiah the Redeemer, the Battle of Armageddon, would be fought on this plain, "Armageddon" being a name derived from the city of Megiddo that stood sentinel above the valley on the south.

Below Jezreel the mountainous backbone resumes its march through the district of Mount Ephraim or Samaria, with Carmel on the west and Gilboa on the east. Near Shechem, where Gerizim and Ebal rise to a height of 3000 feet, the Samarian upland reaches its highest altitude. Intersected here and there by small secluded vales, the hills roll on into Judea where they form the fulcrum of the country. There the hills rise in gentle slopes to broad rounded summits. Today they are for the most part treeless and desolate, their soil washed away by the rains of centuries, their rock-ribbed sides naked in the glare of the sun. In Joshua's time, however, they were covered with forests and orchards and vineyards. At Jerusalem the hills, rising to a height of 2500 feet, represent the most important point in the Judean range. Farther south, in the neighborhood of Hebron, the hills reach their highest elevation. They become low east-and-west ridges as they move down into the Negeb, or southland, merging finally with the rocky wastes of the Sinai Peninsula.

Westward the hills slope gently down toward the Great Sea, and sea and mountains are separated by the third zone, the maritime plain. As it stretches southward, this plain grows wider. At Haifa, Mount Carmel almost obliterates it, leaving a passage only 600 feet wide, but enough to enable the caravans from Egypt to plod on to Phoenicia. The Plain of Sharon which, in the spring, becomes transformed into a vast field of flowers, makes up the northern section of this zone, and the Plain of Philistia, at some points as much as 20 miles wide, is its southern portion. In the winter or rainy season, this maritime plain is watered by numerous torrents that rush across it to the sea; in the summer dry pebbly gullies or wadies reveal the beds of these streams. There are a few rivers that flow all year round of which the most important are the Kishon that empties near Haifa, the Yarkon north of Jaffa, and the Rubin in the Plain of Philistia.

3

THE climate of the country is as varied as its surface: on neighboring plain and mountain, the palm and pine grow within sight of each other. From Jerusalem to Jericho a brief but sharp descent takes the traveler from a temperate climate to a tropical one. In the north there are similar contrasts such as that between temperate Safed and subtropical Tiberias.

The summer is a long succession of hot days followed by cool refreshing nights, and only when the fiery sirocco blows in from the southeast are the days and nights oppressive. The winter is a season of rain, but in the mountains heavy snowfalls are not unknown. In October and November come the "former rains" which prepare the ground for ploughing. In the months that follow, the "latter rains" continue up to the early spring. Egypt and a considerable part of Babylonia depended for their crops on irrigation, but Canaan, we are told, "drinketh water as the rain of heaven cometh down." Even during the dry summer the absence of rain is relieved by the exceptionally heavy dew. Rain and dew are the life of the land; they are the great boons which evoked eager and constant prayer. With the rain and dew coming in season, the land blossomed like the rose and flowed with milk and honey. It was "a good land, a land of brooks of water, of fountains and depths springing forth in valleys and hills; a land of wheat and barley, and vines and fig trees and pomegranates; a land of olive trees and honey."

The vegetation varied, of course, with the topography. The coastal plain, the Valley of Jezreel, and especially the uplands across the Jordan, were covered with fields of wheat and barley. Throughout the land rose the watchmen's lodges amid the vineyards. The twisted grey-leaved olive tree grew everywhere, and along the coastland and in the Jordan Valley the fig tree and palm lifted their graceful foliage. In the higher altitudes rose forests of timber trees: cedar and cypress, sycamore and oak. Southward the hills of Judah became craggy and bare, but even there the herdsman found pasture for his sheep and goats.

And altogether Canaan was a land that enchanted the eye and uplifted the soul. Its varied aspects had each its own mood, but they were all clad in beauty. Sea and sky, mountain and plain, forest and desert spoke in a chorus of symphonic grandeur. What strains of ecstasy this beauty was to evoke from the soul of a gifted people! The heavens will declare the glory of God, the firmament show His handiwork. The mountains will skip like rams, the trees of the field clap their hands. It was a land well fitted to ripen a God-hungry people into prophets and psalmists.

4

THE country lies like a bridge between Asia and Africa. Up and down the coastal plain and the Jordan Valley, the caravans linked the two continents in a continuous stream of commerce. From the south came camel caravans laden with the arts and crafts of Egypt; from Mesopotamia came donkey caravans with bales of wool and leather, and merchants of the Hittites came from the north. In the markets of Palestine they met and traded. In the gates of its cities sat Babylonians poring over their invoices inscribed in cuneiform on clay tablets, and Egyptians were there with their rolls of papyri covered with hieroglyphics. Native merchants and money-changers joined in the babel of many

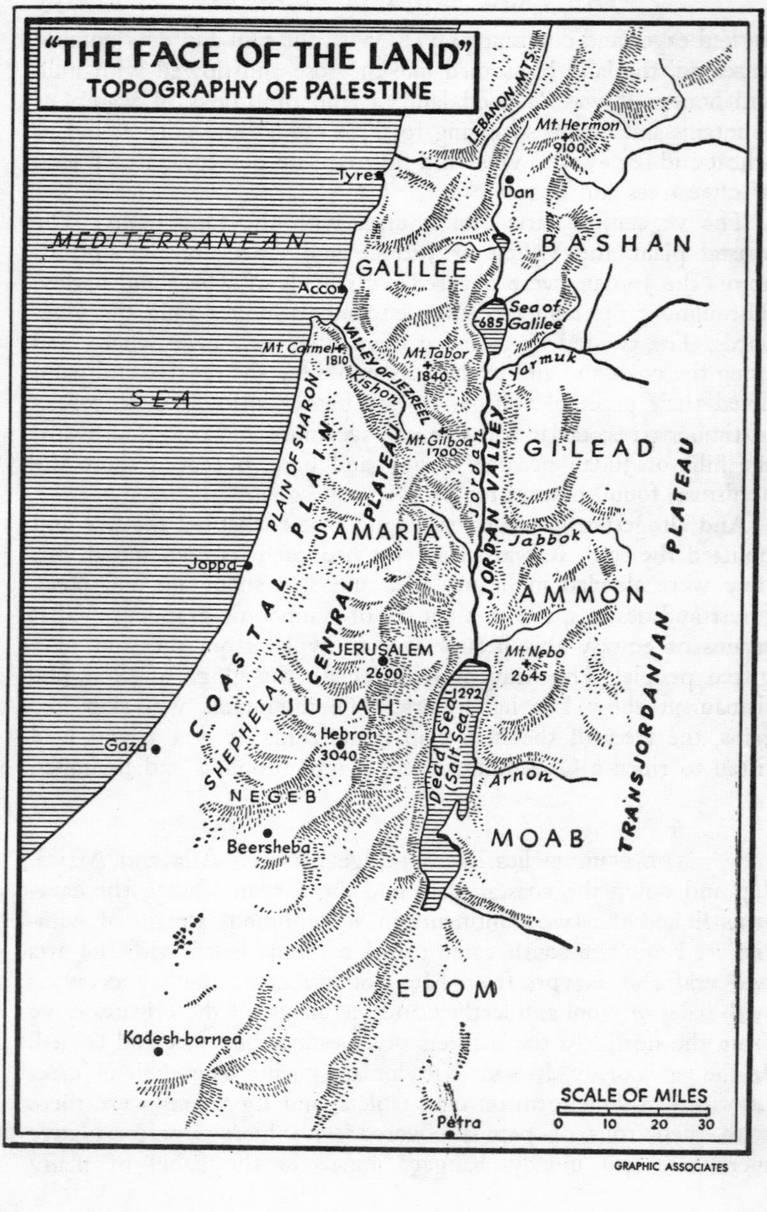
"THE FACE OF THE LAND"
TOPOGRAPHY OF PALESTINE
LEBANON MTS.
Mt. Hermon
9100
Tyre
Dan
MEDITERRANEAN
SEA
BASHAN
GALILEE
Acco
Sea of Galilee
-685
Mt. Carmel
1810
VALLEY OF JEZREEL
Kishon
Mt. Tabor
1840
Yarmuk
Mt. Gilboa
1700
Jordan
JORDAN VALLEY
GILEAD
PLAIN OF SHARON
PLAIN
PLATEAU
SAMARIA
Jabbok
Joppa
COASTAL
CENTRAL
AMMON
JERUSALEM
2600
Mt. Nebo
2645
-1292
Dead Sea
(Salt Sea)
JUDAH
SHEPHELAH
Hebron
3040
Gaza
Arnon
NEGEB
Beersheba
MOAB
TRANSJORDANIAN PLATEAU
EDOM
Kadesh-barnea
SCALE OF MILES
0 10 20 30
Petra
GRAPHIC ASSOCIATES

tongues, while the whir of wheels and the clanging of hammers came from the neighboring workshops of potters, goldsmiths, armorers, and other artisans.

Except for the Philistines, the inhabitants of Canaan belonged to the Semitic race. The two leading stocks, Amorites and Canaanites, had mingled and become practically one. Across the Jordan also, Edomites, Moabites, and Amorites meant political rather than ethnological distinctions. The broken character of the country favored division. Each city was ruled by its own king who fought his neighbors or intrigued with them against the foreign suzerain, Babylonian or Egyptian. Sometimes, when faced by a common enemy, a number of cities united for mutual defense, but such unions fell quickly apart. Only the Philistine cities on the coastal plain—Ekron, Ashdod, Ashkelon, Gath, and Gaza—managed to maintain a more or less stable confederation.

From every point of the compass the land had always been the goal of invading armies. They came from Babylonia on the north, from Egypt on the south, from the isles of the Western Sea and from the desert on the east. Even the incursion of the Hebrews is sometimes represented as just another descent of famished nomads upon the rich cities and fat pastures of Canaan.

5

BUT the invasion of the Hebrews was marked by a difference that makes their story significant and memorable—the difference which lay in the religious gulf between them and the natives. The beliefs and practices of the Canaanites made up a confused nature-cult derived from many sources, principally Babylonian, Hittite, and Egyptian. Every political group had its own special deity, in addition to the gods, goddesses, and demons they all had in common. The principal objects of devotion were the male Baal and the female Baala, or Asherah. Baal was not a single, definite god: every field and spring, every village and city had its own Baal: he was its master and protector. Baala was his consort, and she is frequently identified with the lewd Astarte of the East and the wanton Aphrodite of the West. A leading figure among the demon-gods was Moloch, who delighted in human sacrifices.

The worship of these deities was conducted with gory and lecherous rites. Priests, priestesses, and people abandoned themselves to unrestrained orgies. The wooded places on the hilltops, where this worship took place, the "high places," as they are called in the Bible, were so many plague-spots of physical and moral corruption.

But a new conqueror now stood in the gateway of Canaan, claiming the land in the name of a new God, a God of justice and purity, whose people were to wage eternal war against idolatry and all its vices.

6

FROM the Plain of Gilgal, where the Israelites pitched camp, rose the mountains on whose crags and summits stood the cities of the Canaanites. These strongholds were prepared for irruptions from the desert, but the Hebrews were not the customary nomad raiders. Rumors of their exploits in Transjordania had already come to the ears of the cities, and the hearts of their inhabitants, we are told, "melted, neither was there spirit in them any more."

The city of Jericho stood in the Plain of Gilgal like an outpost guarding the ascent into the mountains. Against that city the strength of the nation, moral and physical, was brought to bear. The Ark of the Covenant, making a circuit about the walls, struck the inhabitants with terror. The walls of Jericho, the chronicle relates, fell suddenly, and the city was captured and destroyed.

7

EXCAVATIONS that have been made on the site of ancient Jericho have furnished amazing confirmation of the biblical account of its downfall. Proof has been found that about the year 1400 B.C.E., the approximate date of the Hebrew invasion, the walls of Jericho collapsed and the city was destroyed by fire. The evidence unearthed at Jericho indicates also that Canaan was then under Egypt's domination. The reigning Pharaoh, Amenhophis III (1411-1375 B.C.E.), claims to have raised his country to an unprecedented height of power and glory, but his inscriptions, like those of all the Pharaohs, must be taken with many grains of salt.

There is, in fact, reason to believe that at the time of the Hebrew invasion his authority in Canaan was already waning.

Toward the end of his reign and during that of his successor Akhenaten (1375-1358 B.C.E.), Egypt was deluged with appeals for help from the vassal kings of Palestine. Some of these appeals, written in Babylonian cuneiform on clay tablets, were discovered in 1887 in Tell el-Amarna, the site of Akhenaten's capital. The kinglets of Canaan implore their suzerain to send them reinforcements against the Hittites who are invading the country from the north, and against the *Habiru* who are breaking in from the south and east. The *Habiru*, it is now generally believed, were the Hebrews. "I am like a bird caught in a trap," writes Rip-Adda of Byblus. Arad-Hiba, King of Jerusalem, writes frantically: "The *Habiru* are now capturing the fortresses of the Pharaoh . . . Lo, if no reinforcements come this year, all the countries of my lord the king will be utterly destroyed . . . What have I done against my lord the king, that thou lovest the *Habiru*, and hatest the governors?" There is evidence also that some of the kings, while appealing for help against the invaders, were actually in collusion with them.

8

THE outpost city having been taken, the ascent began, and the first mountain city to feel the strength of the invaders was Ai. After a first attempt that failed, Joshua drew the defenders away from the city by stratagem, and Ai suffered the same fate as Jericho. Thereupon Joshua held a solemn convocation of his people and re-dedicated them to the law of Moses.

Shortly afterwards some natives appeared in the Israelite camp and laid their submission at the feet of the commander. Their garments were tattered and covered with dust, their shoes worn through. They were from a distant city, they said, and begged the Hebrews to make a treaty of alliance with them. A covenant was duly concluded but the men, it turned out, were from near-by Gibeon. The marks of long travel had been craftily feigned in order to obtain the desired pact. Despite the deception, however, the covenant was honored by the Israelites.

But the other cities were not disposed to follow Gibeon's example. Jerusalem, Hebron, Lachish, Eglon, and Jarmuth formed an alliance and began by attacking Gibeon. The Gibeonites appealed to Joshua to save them, and in a swift movement the Hebrew chieftain struck at the allied forces and overwhelmed them. The survivors, fleeing into the foothills through the pass of Beth-horon, were beaten down by a terrific hailstorm. The victory at Gibeon opened the southern half of the country to the invaders.

In the north, as the Israelites continued to penetrate slowly but steadily, the Canaanite cities finally bestirred themselves. Led by King Jabin of Hazor, they set out to halt the invaders and a decisive battle was fought on a plain near Lake Merom where the Canaanites were routed. The city of Hazor was captured and destroyed.

Thus, bit by bit, the greater part of the land was conquered. Hills and valleys yielded to the steady pressure of the Hebrews. The natives, however, continued to dwell beside the conquerors. There were places, moreover, which the invaders were unable to seize. The southern portion of the coastal plain, for example, continued to be held by the Philistines and certain cities, among them Jerusalem, proved impregnable.

The struggle lasted for a long time, and Joshua, now grown old, pronounced his task completed and sent the warriors of Reuben, Gad, and Manasseh back to their wives and children and flocks across the Jordan. He then allotted to each of the other tribes its "inheritance" in Canaan. South of Jerusalem the largest portion went to Judah. Simeon, lying south of Judah, merged finally with its stronger neighbor. In the north, the leading tribe was Ephraim, and between Judah and Ephraim lay Benjamin and Dan. North of Ephraim were the portions of half-Manasseh, of Issachar, Zebulun, Naphtali, and Asher. The Levites alone received no allotment: as priests they dwelt among the other tribes, even as Moses had commanded.

The Tabernacle containing the Ark of the Covenant was set up in the city of Shiloh. The high priest Eleazar took up his abode in the sanctuary, and the solemn assemblies of the people were held there. Shiloh became the religious center of the tribes. There Joshua accomplished the allocation of the land, the act that marked the completion of his task. He had led his people for twenty-five years and his work was done. After solemn warnings and adjurations to be faithful to the teachings of his master, the rugged old warrior died and was gathered to his fathers.

CHAPTER FIVE

The Judges

For three and a half centuries after Joshua no leader arose in Israel strong enough to command the obedience of all the tribes. It was a period of disunion that threatened to end the career of Abraham's descendants. Enemies swarmed against them within and without their borders, and the tribes showed little inclination to aid each other in time of need. The sense of kinship and common destiny, which the perils of the desert had quickened, went slowly glimmering.

Moreover, the beliefs and customs of the Canaanites began to make inroads on the faith of the Hebrews. The former desert nomads, now settled agriculturists, were surrounded by neighbors whose way of life they found hard to resist. They forsook the God of justice and purity whom their fathers had worshipped in the desert, and joined the Canaanites in the worship of Baal and Asherah on the "high places." "The children of Israel," we read, "dwelt among the Canaanites, the Hittites, and the Amorites, and the Perizzites, and the Hivites and the Jebusites; and they took their daughters to be their wives, and gave their own daughters to their sons, and served their gods." Thus apostasy made common cause with disunion to undermine the Hebrew nation.

Against these disintegrating forces the great memories of their past struggled valiantly. The sense of divine selection, nourished by the Great Teaching that had been placed in their keeping, could not be entirely erased. In every generation there were zealots who kept alive the fires of the old faith in the hearts of the people. From time to time, moreover, men of might and daring rose up who met the enemies of Israel in battle and overthrew them. The grateful people made these heroes their leaders and rulers: they were the *shofetim* or judges.

2

IN THE Book of Judges the exploits of some of these *shofetim* are recorded. Like all the figures that move through the Bible, the judges are men of large mold, but intensely human. The book is a glowing canvas of epic heroes and deeds, and out of it emerges the picture of a people struggling against overwhelming odds to save its body and soul.

There emerges also a picture of the religious and political anarchy that reigned in Israel during this period. Those were the days when "there was no king in Israel, and every man did that which was right in his own eyes." We read, for instance, how men from the tribe of Dan, on their way to a new home in the far north of the land, forced a certain Levite to go with them and serve as priest to the idols they carried. Such was the confusion of creed and practice among those whose fathers had stood at Sinai! We read, further, how the tribe of Benjamin, having committed a heinous moral offense, was nearly annihilated by the other tribes, an incident bearing testimony to the higher ethical perceptions which nonetheless persisted in Israel.

The first judge named in the chronicle is Othniel of Judah who delivered Israel from the oppression of Aram. The second is Ehud of Benjamin, left-handed, but swift with the dagger. The oppressor of his day was Eglon, King of Moab, whom Ehud slew in an exploit of great daring. Ehud then "blew a horn in the hill country of Ephraim," and, at the fords of the Jordan, the Moabites were overwhelmed by the Hebrew warriors who had responded to the summons.

But a new oppressor arose in the north. He was Jabin, King of the Canaanites, whose yoke lay on Israel for twenty years. It remained for a woman to rouse the people to revolt: Deborah, whose proudest title was "a mother in Israel." Barak, the man she chose to command the warriors of Israel, would march only on condition that she accompany him. In a great battle fought at the River Kishon, the Canaanite forces, led by the overconfident Sisera, were routed, and Sisera himself met his fate at the hands of another woman, Jael of the Bedouin Kenites, who were allies of Israel. In a passionate song of triumph Deborah contrasts vividly the disgrace endured by her people at the hands of the oppressor and the glorious victory which she inspired. The battle of the Kishon broke the power of the Canaanites for all time.

But from the eastern desert came Midianite and Amalekite raiders, stealing crops and cattle, burning and slaying. The deliverer this time was Gideon of the tribe of Manasseh, whose first act was to destroy the idols in his father's household. Then, on a dark night and with only 300 followers, he surprised and routed a large Midianite encampment. Many had come to march behind his standard but Gideon had sifted his men until the bravest only were left. The victory won, Gideon proved he had wisdom as well as courage. He knew how to placate the blustering and unruly Ephraimites, and when his grateful people offered him a royal crown he refused it. All his life he was content to be only their "judge." When Gideon died, however, his son Abimelech determined to be king. Abimelech began by murdering his brothers, a measure frequently resorted to by royal aspirants. But the attempt at monarchy failed: the people rose up against the usurper and he met an inglorious death while besieging one of his rebellious cities.

The scene shifts to the other side of the Jordan, where the tribes of Reuben and Gad groaned beneath the oppression of the Ammonites. Then rose up a certain Jephthah of Gilead, "a mighty man of valor," who rallied the Israelites and inflicted a crushing defeat on the children of Ammon. On the eve of the battle Jephthah rashly vowed to sacrifice "whatsoever cometh forth of the doors of my house to meet me." There came to meet him his only daughter. The savage vow may have been kept—the account is not clear. What is clear, however, is that Torah had not yet triumphed in Israel: in the religious confusion of the times, human sacrifice still exercised its hideous lure.

Again the Ephraimites blustered and challenged. Why had Jephthah proceeded against the enemy without them? But Jephthah, unlike Gideon, minced no words with them. He set his warriors upon the men of Ephraim who paid a terrible price for their insolence.

3

WHAT light does archaeology shed upon the Age of the Judges? The Egyptian records upon which we are chiefly dependent are extremely meager and their interpretation is still, in large part, a matter of controversy. But a little light does break through them.

A period of 480 years, says the Great Tradition, runs from the Exodus (1447 B.C.E.) to the building of Solomon's Temple (967 B.C.E.), and the latest archaeological findings, as already noted, confirm the statement with startling exactitude. In this stretch of nearly half a millennium, the three and a half centuries from the death of Joshua (1377 B.C.E.) to the accession of Saul, the first King of Israel (1025 B.C.E.) may be regarded as the period of the Judges.

It appears that during these centuries Canaan continued to owe allegiance to Egypt. It was a debt on which the country was always more or less in arrears; the amount paid depended on the degree of power possessed at different times by the suzerain. Nor did Egyptian domination prove an obstacle to the Israelites. On the contrary, a remarkable correspondence in time has been pointed out between the periods of Egyptian ascendancy and the years when the children of Israel had "rest" from their enemies. Conversely the periods of Egyptian decline correspond with those when Israel bore the yoke of oppressors.

It may be taken for granted that the armies of Egypt, in the Age of the Judges, marched up and down the coastal plain, but they interfered little with the Israelites who occupied the central and southern portions of the land. The Pharaoh Seti I (1314-1292 B.C.E.), for example, has left inscriptions and pictures recording triumphs in Palestine. His successor, Ramses II, called the Great, whose long reign extended from 1292 to 1225 B.C.E., fought an indecisive battle with the Hittites in the far north, followed by a treaty of peace which has been discovered and deciphered.

But the most important discovery bearing on the period is a stone inscription left by Merneptah (1225-1200 B.C.E.), the successor of Ramses the Great. It is known as the Israel Stele, for on it Israel is for the first time found mentioned in a record other than the Bible. The inscription tells of Merneptah's triumphs in Palestine and Syria.

Devastated is Tehennu;
The Hittite land is pacified;
Plundered is Canaan with every evil;
Carried off is Ascalon;
Seized upon is Gezer;
Yendam is made a thing of naught;
Israel is desolated, her seed is not;
Palestine has become a defenseless
widow for Egypt;
Everyone that is turbulent is bound
by King Merneptah,
Giving life like the sun every day.

It goes without saying that Merneptah's victories were not as decisive as he desired posterity to believe. Shortly afterwards, in fact, Egypt was attacked by new enemies from the north and west. They were defeated, but the empire was reduced to a state of exhaustion and Egypt entered upon a long period of decline.

The new enemies were probably the Philistines. They are first found mentioned in the records of Ramses III (1198-1167 B.C.E.), although they must have begun their raids many centuries earlier. They are believed to have fled from their original home in Crete or elsewhere as a result of the pressure of the Greeks whom, in many ways, they resembled.

4

GENERATIONS followed one another with alternations of freedom and oppression. Gradually Israel gained the upper hand over the surrounding nations, over the Canaanites on the north and the desert marauders east and south. On the coast, however, dwelt the Philistines, the most formidable enemy of all, whose united cities the Israelites had not yet been able to breach.

The most humanly appealing of the heroes that stride through the Book of Judges is associated with the struggle against the

Philistines. He is Samson the Danite, the man no enemy can subdue but who is himself unable to subdue his passions.

From birth Samson has been ordained to the service of God; he has taken the vows of a Nazirite which require him to forego the pleasures of the senses. His prowess strikes terror into the Philistines, but the strength against which their men are helpless is brought down by the wiles of a woman. In his death as well as in his life, however, Samson inflicts terrible punishment upon the Philistines. In a supreme effort he brings down their temple on their heads and on his own, his last words being, "Let me die with the Philistines."

But the Philistines recovered and began a career of new conquests. They marched north along the coast, apparently intending to drive a wedge between the tribes of Israel by seizing the Valley of Jezreel. At Aphek the Israelites attacked the invaders and were repulsed. The Hebrew warriors sent to Shiloh for the Ark of the Covenant, to be borne by them against the enemy. It was a desperate measure and it failed; a second time the Israelites were defeated.

The Philistines pressed on; they captured Shiloh and destroyed it. Philistine garrisons were stationed in the towns of Israel, Hebrew blacksmiths were forbidden to make arms, and the proudest tribes, Ephraim, Manasseh, and Benjamin, were forced to pay tribute. The sun appeared to be setting for Israel in Canaan.

5

A YOUTH named Samuel, who had been living with the priest in the sanctuary at Shiloh, returned after the defeat at Aphek to his birthplace, the village of Ramah. Samuel became the greatest of the judges. For fifty years he led his people in the struggle against Philistine domination, and where the strength of Samson failed, the sword of the spirit, which Samuel wielded, brought eventual victory.

From early childhood, Samuel had displayed remarkable spiritual gifts, and on his return to his native village, people flocked to him for counsel and comfort. Samuel believed that Torah alone would save his people. Were they sinking in the mire of idolatry? Torah would lift them out of it. Were the tribes forgetting their common past? Torah would recall them to it. Have they become indifferent to each other's welfare? Torah would remind them of their common destiny.

Such was the faith that determined the career of the great judge and prophet Samuel. And groups of young men came forward to assist him. They led peculiar lives and displayed peculiar powers in the midst of the people. They were the *B'nai Nebiim*, "Sons of the Prophets," or young prophets, who wandered up and down the land, appearing suddenly in the gates of villages and towns, and calling on the people to be faithful to the God of Moses. They punctuated their appeals with singing and dancing, and their zeal and enthusiasm proved infectious.

Of these young men Samuel became the guide and inspiration. He too traveled through the land, holding court, teaching Torah, instilling hope and courage. In Mizpah, in Bethel, in Gilgal, as well as in his native Ramah, the elders frequently came together at his call. Even the tribe of Judah, until then secluded in its own rugged hills, became aware of its kinship with Israel. Adversity proved more effective for restoring the solidarity of the tribes than prosperity and triumph.

In a manner unexpected, the people became aware that subjection to the Philistines was not inevitable. An attack by the oppressor on one of the assemblies at Mizpah was repulsed by Israel's warriors. Though not a decisive victory, it nourished the hope of eventual liberation.

But the leader was growing old and the elders of Israel perceived with sorrow that his sons were not worthy of succeeding him. They came to Samuel with the startling demand that he choose a king to rule over them. Only thus, it appeared to them, could they have union in the face of the enemies who, they pointed out, were all ruled by kings. Must Israel alone be different?

In words that have become classic, Samuel warned the elders against royalty. The king, he told them, would take away from them all that was most precious to them, their sons and daughters, their fields and vineyards, even their lives.

> He will take your men-servants, and your maid-servants, and your goodliest young men, and your asses, and put them to

> his work. He will take the tenth of your flocks; and ye shall be his servants. And ye shall cry out in that day because of your king whom ye shall have chosen you; and the Lord will not answer you in that day.

Thus did Samuel sound a warning against autocracy and tyranny which has re-echoed through the ages.

CHAPTER SIX

Saul and David

But the immediate dangers were too great for the prophet's warnings to be heeded. The elders insisted on a king, and Samuel had to assume the task of finding someone qualified for the exalted and dangerous post.

There came to him one day a youth of heroic aspect, tall and handsome, and the seer, moved by a prophetic impulse, poured oil on his head and kissed him. The young man was Saul son of Kish, of the tribe of Benjamin.

On his way back to his native Gibeah, Saul stopped to sing and dance with a group of the *B'nai Nebiim.* Neighbors who knew the modest youth were surprised: "Is Saul, too, among the prophets?" they asked. And soon afterwards Samuel presented him formally to a large assemblage of elders, who confirmed the choice. "Long live the king!" the people shouted, the first time this cry sounded in Israel. But it became established that a king of Israel was subject to the free choice of the people's representatives.

Not long afterwards the king performed a deed that vindicated Samuel's insight. Across the Jordan the Ammonites were besieging the Israelite stronghold of Jabesh. Prepared to surrender, the men of Jabesh were met by the shameful demand that they give up their right eyes to the victors. So they sent messengers across the Jordan appealing for help. The king was in the field, plowing, when the message reached him. Roused to fury, he slashed the oxen that pulled his plow and sent the pieces to the tribes. The men of the nation understood the summons and warning. They flocked to his standard and he led them across the Jordan and overwhelmed the insolent foe.

It was a great victory, and all the tribes hastened to do homage to the king. Saul set up a government, made Gibeah his capital, and created a standing army with his cousin Abner as commander. No voice of disaffection made itself heard, not even in fractious Ephraim. Nevertheless, Samuel's authority was greater than Saul's, the young king submitting to the guidance of the priest and seer.

The years passed, Saul came to full manhood, and his dependence on Samuel became a burden to him. His chief task, however, the liberation of his people from the yoke of the Philistines, was still to be accomplished. At last the revolt against the oppressor broke out. It was set off by Jonathan, the king's heroic son, who began by wiping out the Philistine garrison in Gibeah, the capital. Thereupon the Philistines marched against Israel in full force, and Saul's case appeared desperate. Samuel himself, offended by the king's growing independence, seemed to have deserted him.

Again Jonathan came forward and saved his people's cause. At Michmash, where the enemy was encamped, the daring youth, followed only by his armor-bearer, climbed a sheer ascent, slew the sentries, and threw the Philistine camp into panic. The enemy sought safety in flight. Saul's summons rang through the hills and even the timid came out and joined in the pursuit. The Philistine flight became a rout.

The king had triumphed against his strongest enemy: the king should have been joyous and happy. Yet Saul was not happy. Samuel's change of attitude had, no doubt, a great deal to do with it, but the final source of the king's unhappiness lay in himself. A mood of profound melancholy settled upon him and under its baleful spell joy turned to bitterness, victory to wormwood.

2

THE Philistines, for the time being, at least, were discomfited; on the east the desert marauders kept a respectful distance. Only on the south the Amalekites, hereditary foe of Israel, needed to be punished. Samuel appeared and ordered Saul to strike the

Amalekites a crushing blow, to give no quarter, not even to take booty. Saul obeyed except for the last injunction: he permitted some of his men to drive off the enemy's cattle. Thereupon the prophet publicly denounced the monarch and rejected him.

Saul became more gloomy and bitter, and he sought relief in battle and victory. He fought the Moabites, the Ammonites, the Edomites, and the kings of the north as far as Damascus. But neither clash of arms nor shouts of victory could soothe his tormented spirit.

His officers, who loved their noble king, thought that music might bring him relief, so they brought him one day a young shepherd and harpist who had come up from Bethlehem in Judah, one David son of Jesse. At once Saul was captivated by the charming youth, and David's playing brought him respite from the melancholy that preyed on his soul.

But David was no mere plucker of harp-strings; he was cast for a far greater role. The shadow of the youth grew longer and soon he had the opportunity to prove the stuff he was made of. The Philistines had again invaded Israel, and the two armies stood facing each other on opposite heights. For a number of days a giant Philistine, one Goliath, had come and taken his stand in the valley between, defying the Hebrews to send down a champion to engage him in combat. At last the champion of Israel stood forth. He was the harpist from Judah, armed only with a sling and "five smooth stones out of the brook." One of them flew swift and true and the giant fell like a blasted cedar. The Philistines abandoned their camp, pursued by the Hebrews, and David was hailed as Israel's savior.

David's star continued to rise, but as yet the king's love was undiminished. No one seemed able to resist the youth's charm. Jonathan became his fast friend; Michal, the king's daughter, loved him; the people idolized him.

Suddenly Saul's mood changed. David returned one day from a triumphant raid against the Philistines, and the women came out to greet him and the king heard them sing:

Saul had slain his thousands,
And David his ten thousands!

Now the king became aware that David was taking precedence over him in the thoughts of the people. He recalled the wrath of Samuel and how the prophet had renounced him, and with the clairvoyance that madmen are said to possess, he saw David as the man for whom the prophet had rejected him. Suspicion, fear, and hate took possession of the king's heart. Saul sought to slay him, and David was compelled to flee. Grief-stricken, he bade farewell to Jonathan, the comrade of his bosom, and to Michal, who had become his wife.

He stopped at a sanctuary in Nob near Jerusalem, and the priests gave him the sword of Goliath which had been entrusted to their keeping. Then he fled south and came to his own Judah. He sent his parents away into Moab for safety, and took refuge in the hills, where before long he became the leader of a company of outcasts like himself. They numbered some 400 desperate men, and the caves near Adullam became their place of refuge.

3

SAUL pursued the fugitive relentlessly. First he massacred the priests of Nob for having befriended David, then he followed him into Judah. The people had welcomed the help of David's outlaws against Philistine raiders, but once the enemy was driven off, they were eager to be rid of their wild and hungry deliverers. So they sent word to Saul informing him of the fugitive's presence among them. David fled deeper into the southland.

He had hairbreadth escapes from Saul. Twice he had the king in his power and could have slain him, but he would not stretch out his hand against "the Lord's anointed." On one of those occasions, as the king lay asleep, David cut off a piece of his garment; on the other, he made off with the king's spear and pitcher. On learning how his foe had spared him, Saul was overcome with remorse, but the ravening monster of suspicion took possession of him again, and the hunt continued.

Finally, David was compelled to take refuge in Philistine territory. Achish, King of Gath, welcomed the conqueror of Goliath, believing that David, embittered by the ingratitude of the Hebrew monarch, would turn his arms against his own people. Achish assigned the stronghold of Ziklag to David and his followers. The Philistine ruler reckoned without David's cunning. With Ziklag as his base, David took his followers on raids, but the victims of his sallies were not his own people; they were Amalekites and other of his people's enemies.

4

AT LENGTH the hunter was forced to leave his quarry, for the Philistines were gathering to strike a decisive blow at Israel. Their plan of campaign was one followed frequently by invaders of Palestine. They marched up the coast, turned at the foot of Carmel and swept into the Plain of Jezreel. It was good ground for them: it allowed them to make full use of their equipment, especially the war chariots of which they had large quantities.

But a new crisis arose for David also. His host and patron, the King of Gath, invited him to march with the Philistines, an invitation too dangerous to decline. At Aphek, however, the other Philistine chiefs demanded to know what David was doing among them. Recalling what they had suffered at his hands in the days when he fought for Saul, they insisted on his discharge. David was saved! Returning to Ziklag, he found the place in ruins: in his absence an Amalekite band had raided it, carrying off the women and children. David pursued the Amalekites, routed them, and rescued the captives.

For David the crisis was over; for Saul it swept on to its tragic climax. Having concentrated his forces on Mount Gilboa, the king looked out on the Philistine encampment at Shunem. Was this to be the end? A fierce desire to know the answer took possession of him. Against the prohibition of Torah, he resorted to the black arts of divination by which all his forebodings were confirmed.

The armies clashed and Israel was overwhelmed. Three of the king's sons were slain in the field, among them Jonathan. As the enemy pressed closer, the king commanded his armor-bearer to slay him. The man, dismayed, held back; whereupon Saul "took his sword and fell upon it."

The soul of the unhappy king found repose at last.

CHAPTER SEVEN

David the King

DAVID was still a fugitive in Ziklag when he heard of Saul's defeat and death, and he was overcome with grief. He mourned aloud for the "Lord's anointed" and for Jonathan, the friend of his bosom. "Thy beauty, O Israel," he cried, "is slain upon thy high places!" And of Jonathan he sang:

Wonderful was thy love to me,
Passing the love of women.
How are the mighty fallen,
And the weapons of war perished!

But soon the urge to action came strong upon him. His nation lay broken and bleeding; the frail ship of state would founder in a sea of anarchy unless a strong and skillful hand seized the helm. That hand was his: he knew it with the self-assurance of genius. He shook the dust of the Philistines from his feet, and with his band of followers, faithful to him unto death, he came to Hebron in Judah. There the elders of his tribe assembled and elected him their king.

David proceeded to make overtures to the northern tribes, but for a long time without success. Saul's general, Abner, had rescued one of his master's sons from the disaster at Gilboa, and this prince, Ishbaal by name, challenged David's right to succeed his father. There was civil war between Ishbaal and David until Abner was won over. But David's general, Joab, slew Abner, who in the course of the previous fighting had slain Joab's brother. This ruthless act of blood revenge was denounced by David: nevertheless the removal of Abner strengthened the position of the new monarch, for between Abner and Joab peace would have been impossible.

Not long afterwards Ishbaal, too, was the victim of assassins, and only a crippled child, a son of Jonathan, remained who might challenge David's right to the throne. The star of Jesse's son continued to rise. Seven years after receiving the crown of Judah, the elders of the north came together at Hebron and proclaimed him king over all Israel. The year was 1006 B.C.E.

2

DAVID thus became the founder of a dynasty whose title to succession has persisted longer than that of any other in recorded history. In the traditions of his people, David is the king par excellence; his descendants alone may rightfully reign over Israel. The double light of temporal greatness and of holiness illumines David's crown, for, in the same tradition, this mighty ruler is also the devout singer of the Lord, the author of the incomparable Psalms. And the belief arose that from him would descend mankind's ultimate Redeemer, "Messiah son of David."

Nevertheless, his greatness and glory have not blinded the generations to his faults: the Great Tradition has neither omitted nor condoned them. Full-blooded and passionate, he was guilty of sins and errors for which he suffered grievous penalties, including shame and remorse. And not the least of his sorrows sprang from his military prowess. For David was denied the supreme joy of building a temple to the Lord: "God said unto me," he declared: "Thou shalt not build a house for My name, because thou art a man of war, and hast shed blood."

But David was a statesman of genius, and as his reign advanced his greatness became more and more manifest. To the diplomatic business of consolidating his authority over Israel was added, in the early years of his reign, the formidable task of freeing his people from the yoke of the Philistines. The war of liberation lasted many years. David's fortunes rose and fell, and there were times when he seemed to be pursuing a forlorn hope. Again David became a fugitive, seeking the protection of the caves in Adullam. With a band of desperate men, his *gibborim*, heroes for whom no exploit was too hazardous, David resorted to guerrilla warfare. His men adored him. When they saw him as ardent in battle as they were themselves, they forced him to guard his life, fearful lest he quench "the lamp of Israel." Then his fortunes rose. In a swift northerly movement he met the Philistines in the plain of Rephaim, near Jerusalem, and defeated them. He went on and even invaded their territory, capturing the city of Gath. The Philistine yoke fell from the neck of Israel.

The early years of David's reign saw still another decisive event: Jerusalem was taken and became the capital of the Hebrew nation. This well-nigh impregnable fortress was still being held by the Jebusites, but its location and natural strength recommended it to David as the ideal center of his kingdom. It was neutrally situated between the mutually jealous tribes of Judah and Ephraim, and east, south, and west of it lay valleys which made it almost unapproachable. The Jebusite chieftains laughed at David when he called on them to surrender the citadel, taunting him that the blind and the lame would suffice to defend it. David's *gibborim* led the attack on the fortress of Mount Zion and captured it. They crawled through a tunnel, clambered up a vertical shaft, made their way through another passage, reached the city, and smote down the unsuspecting garrison. The actual tunnel through which they passed, now called Warren's Shaft, has been discovered and identified.

Shortly after the capture of Jerusalem, the Hebrew monarch built himself a splendid residence on Mount Zion, and he made Jerusalem the religious capital of the nation as well by bringing to Zion the sacred Ark of the Covenant which had formerly rested in Shiloh. The progress of the Ark was a solemn and festive occasion; the king himself danced before it as the Levites bore it to the Mount. There, in the Tabernacle which had been prepared for it, the sacred object was reverently lodged. David felt that it deserved a more impressive accommodation: he longed to build a magnificent temple to his God; but the prophet Nathan, whose voice he had learned to heed, ordered him to leave the building of a temple to his successor.

Thus did David launch Jerusalem on its career as the stronghold of Israel and the Holy City of many nations.

3

HAVING secured his throne against all possible pretenders, subdued the Philistines, and created a national center, David turned his abundant energies to the task of organizing his kingdom and extending its borders. He appointed ministers, commanders, priests. He set up his *gibborim* as a personal bodyguard, but shrewdly placed at his call still another guard composed of Philistine mercenaries, foreigners who would not be likely to take sides with a pretender. Joab and his brother Abishai were put in command of the army; Zadok and Abiathar were appointed chief priests.

On the other side of the Jordan the inveterate enemies of Israel seemed to be anxious to try the mettle of the new king, nor was David loath to accept their challenge. An ambassador whom he sent to Ammon with condolences to the new ruler of the kingdom on the death of his father, was made the victim of an outrageous insult. At once David dispatched an army commanded by Joab to Ammon, and a war followed which lasted several years. The Ammonites drew the Aramaeans into an alliance against Israel, but both allies were eventually defeated. David himself took an army to the north and overthrew the forces of the Aramaean kings of Zobah and Damascus, annexing both kingdoms to his own. Joab overcame the resistance of the Ammonites whose capital, Rabbath Ammon, was seized together with a vast booty. The arrogant king of Ammon was dethroned, and his possessions made tributary to Israel.

Farther south, Moab, Edom, and Amalek were added to David's conquests. Amalek was crushed, Moab and Edom made tributary. The ports on the Gulf of Akaba were drawn into David's borders. Thus, stretching from the Euphrates on the north to the Gulf of Akaba on the south, from the Mediterranean on the west to the desert on the east, David's kingdom became an empire. Among his allies were the Phoenicians, those skillful craftsmen and seagoing traders, whose cities lay on the coast north of Canaan.

Such was the greatness and the glory to which Israel was elevated by David. The monarch's skies were darkened by no menace. His enemies feared him. His allies admired him. His people idolized him.

4

BUT all the wisdom and prowess of the king proved powerless against two demons that have plagued monarchs from time immemorial. The first was the demon of domestic dissension to which the polygamous households of eastern potentates are especially exposed. The second was the fiend of lawless passion which even those who conquer cities are unable to hold in leash.

The blot on David's escutcheon was the work of the second of these demons. The king became sinfully enamored of Bathsheba, wife of Uriah the Hittite, an officer in his army. With Uriah away fighting the Ammonites, the king had Bathsheba conducted into his palace, and sent secret word to Joab to expose Uriah in battle. Uriah was slain. It was a foul crime, but one of those which rulers permitted themselves without exciting a murmur either in their own consciences or on the lips of their people.

In Israel, however, a spirit was at work which brooked no wrong even from monarchs. The prophet Nathan came and stood before David, calm words on his lips, a storm of wrath in his heart. He asked the king to pass judgment on a certain rich man, owner of many flocks and herds, who had nevertheless stolen the "one little ewe lamb," sole possession of a poor neighbor, and killed it for a feast. And when the indignant king pronounced death upon the rich man, the prophet thundered: "Thou art the man!" And David bowed his head. "I have sinned before the Lord," he said.

5

THE years of David's reign became many. Israel's farmers and burghers had peace at last. The frontiers were well-defended. Internal dissension dared not raise its head.

In his palace on Mount Zion the king saw his sons and daughters, born of different wives, grow into manhood and womanhood. Then came conflicts that darkened his days. His eldest son, Amnon, guilty of a shameful deed against his half-sister Tamar, was slain by Tamar's brother Absalom. Absalom escaped into exile, but David loved the brave and handsome youth and permitted him, after several years, to return to his palace and his favor. The young man looked upon himself as his father's successor.

But Absalom was impatient; he would not wait until his father was dead. So he raised the standard of revolt against the king and was joined by enough malcontents to menace his father's throne.

The king, accompanied by his faithful *gibborim*, fled from Jerusalem across the Jordan to Mahanaim.

He was already old, but the keen mind and great spirit held firm. With the precision of genius he took his measures for quelling the rebellion, augmenting his fighting forces and throwing confusion into the councils of Absalom. In a bloody battle fought in the jungles east of the Jordan the revolt was crushed. Absalom, his head caught fast in the branches of an oak as he rode under the tree, was slain by Joab. David's throne was saved, but the victory brought him no joy: bitterly the king wept for Absalom, the faithless son whom he loved.

The elders of Israel were bringing David back to Jerusalem in triumph when a fierce quarrel broke out between Judah and the other tribes. David had to put down another rebellion led by a Benjamite named Sheba. Between north and south jealousy and hate were always festering.

With faltering steps the aged king mounted his throne again. In spite of his sorrows, God's goodness and mercy, he felt, had followed him all the days of his life. His heart overflowed with thankfulness and adoration, and out of his tribulations sprang new psalms to the Lord who "drew me out of many waters."

6

AGAIN David's throne stood secure, his enemies subdued, his people contented. The drift toward idolatry which had, for generations, menaced the integrity of the nation, was now checked. For David was the servant of the God of Moses, and under his mighty scepter Israel strove to achieve the way of life prescribed by Torah.

In extreme old age, the king still found the strength and resolution to put an end to a new rivalry which arose in his household around the succession. The rivals were his sons Adonijah and Solomon. Adonijah was the oldest, but Solomon's mother was the well-loved Bathsheba. Solomon, moreover, had the support of the prophet Nathan.

Adonijah attempted to follow in Absalom's footsteps. On a certain day he solemnly declared himself successor and king. Thereupon Bathsheba, who had been promised by David that her son should reign after him, came and stood before the king, demanding that he proclaim Solomon his successor. The king so ordered, and Solomon's rival fled for safety to a sanctuary.

Thus was the nation saved from another civil war, and David could meet his approaching end with serenity. With a final admonition to Solomon and a warning against Joab, for Joab had slain Absalom and supported the pretender Adonijah, David, after a reign of forty years (1013-973 B.C.E.), died, and was gathered to his fathers.

CHAPTER EIGHT

Solomon

THERE was enough of David's genius in Solomon to insure another long and prosperous reign in Israel. Solomon's splendor even surpassed his father's, for the son inherited a realm so strong and united, its enemies so thoroughly subdued, that his sword could rest in its scabbard and the king could apply his wealth and talents to the embellishment of his kingdom. Later chroniclers looked back upon the forty years of his reign (973-933 B.C.E.) with pride and wistfulness. It was a period when Judah and Israel from Dan to Beersheba dwelt safely, "every man under his vine and under his fig tree, and there was none to make them afraid."

Solomon was a monarch of whom a people might well be proud. In his palace in Jerusalem, splendidly aloof from his subjects, he dwelt in pomp and grandeur. Foreign rulers came to pay him homage and gaze upon his magnificence. His wisdom, moreover, was phenomenal; it "excelled the wisdom of all the children of the east and all the wisdom of Egypt." He had "a wise and understanding heart": it was the one gift he chose when, in a dream, gifts of all sorts, among them wealth and long life, were set

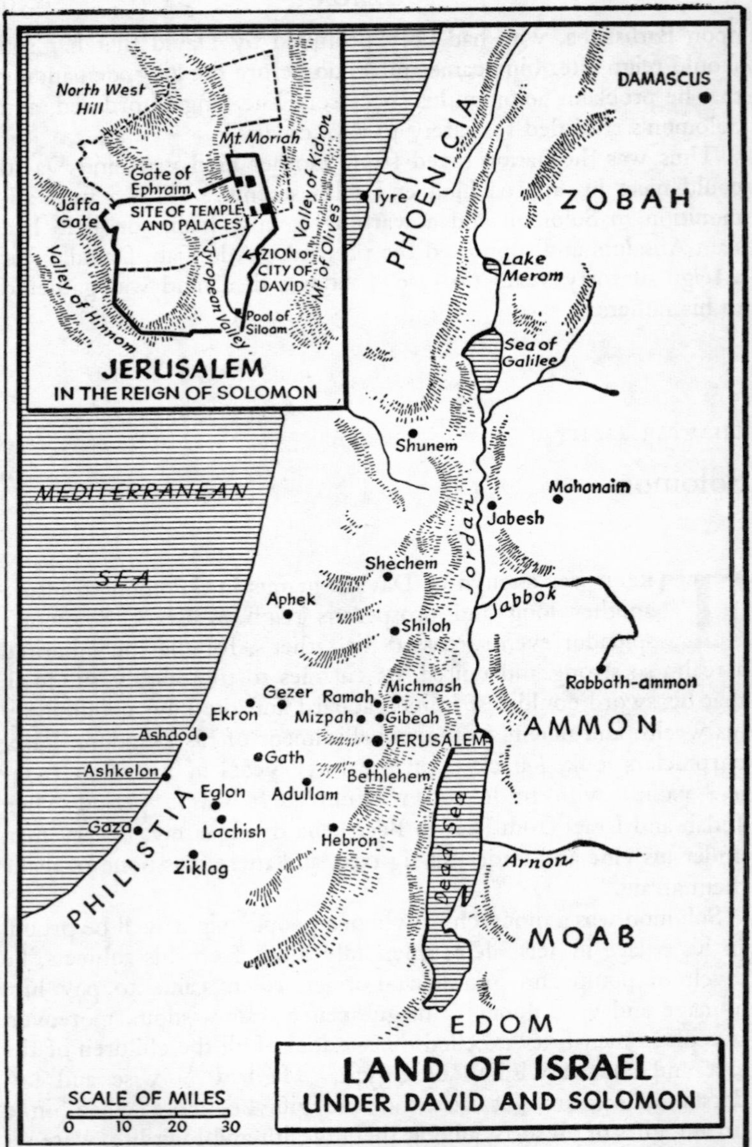

North West Hill
Mt. Moriah
Gate of Ephraim
Jaffa Gate
SITE OF TEMPLE AND PALACES
Valley of Kidron
Mt of Olives
Tyropean Valley
ZION or CITY OF DAVID
Valley of Hinnom
Pool of Siloam
JERUSALEM
IN THE REIGN OF SOLOMON
PHOENICIA
Tyre
DAMASCUS
ZOBAH
Lake Merom
Sea of Galilee
Shunem
MEDITERRANEAN
SEA
Mahanaim
Jabesh
Jordan
Shechem
Aphek
Jabbok
Shiloh
Rabbath-ammon
Michmash
Gezer
Ramah
Ekron
Mizpah
Gibeah
Ashdod
JERUSALEM
AMMON
Gath
Ashkelon
Bethlehem
Eglon
Adullam
Dead Sea
Gaza
Lachish
Hebron
Arnon
Ziklag
PHILISTIA
MOAB
EDOM
SCALE OF MILES
0 10 20 30

LAND OF ISRAEL
UNDER DAVID AND SOLOMON

before him. To Solomon was credited the garnered wisdom of the race, as well as the possession of powers that made him master of the secret forces of life.

He was an Oriental monarch vying with other Oriental monarchs in the parade of pomp and power, and he began his reign in the manner characteristic of Oriental monarchs—by removing every potential rival and rebel. Pretexts were found readily enough, and among those who forfeited their lives were Adonijah and the grizzled old warrior, Joab.

Solomon went on to overhaul and strengthen the administrative establishment he inherited from his father. He made Benaiah, the captain of the guard, commander in chief of the army. He named head priests, a recorder, a palace steward, two scribes, and a collector of the revenue. The latter was Adoniram, a minister of exceptional importance. For Solomon divided the country into twelve districts with twelve officials charged with the duty of securing annually from each a month's supplies for the maintenance of the king's expanding household; and Adoniram was the chief of the twelve. Thus did Solomon in his wisdom organize his administration and revenues.

In addition, wealth came pouring into the land from foreign countries. The "Pax Hebraica" maintained by his father and himself among the surrounding nations kept the caravans moving in a steady stream between Babylonia and Egypt. Solomon, moreover, widened his commerce to include the fabled land of Ophir, which may have been India. With the help of his friends and allies, the seagoing Phoenicians, he sent a fleet to that distant land. Two years later, the fleet returned to Ezion-geber, his port on the Gulf of Akaba, laden with the spices and luxuries of the Far East.

On the site of Ezion-geber recent excavations have uncovered the remains of a great factory town which, the excavators report, Solomon alone in his day "had the ability and the vision and the power to build." In this industrial city the copper and iron ores taken from Solomon's mines in Akaba were smelted, refined, and made into finished products which went out by sea and land "to be exchanged for the spices, ivory, gold, and precious woods of Africa and Arabia and India." At various points in his realm Solomon established depots for controlling the commercial traffic and policing the country. At one of these depots, Megiddo in Jezreel, Solomon's stables, together with a hangar for his chariots, have actually been discovered. There was little in the arts of industry, commerce, and statecraft in which Solomon the wise did not prove himself adept.

2

IT MAY be taken as evidence of Solomon's wisdom that throughout his long reign war was a rare and unimportant occurrence. Military glory had no lure for this king who, unlike his martial father, had spent his youth amid the pleasures and amenities of a royal court, and it was probably this aversion for war that led to a shrinkage in the boundaries of his empire. In the north, the city of Damascus fell away, while in the south Edom revolted and won its freedom. But Damascus was too distant to excite keen regret in Solomon's heart, and as for Edom, he retained, probably by treaty arrangement, the important harbor of Ezion-geber. As for the rest of that forbidding region, Solomon felt, no doubt, that it was not worth the blood of Israel's warriors.

The keystone of Solomon's foreign policy, in fact, was not war but alliance. He made an alliance with Egypt and cemented it by marrying the daughter of the Pharaoh, his royal father-in-law giving him the city of Gezer, lately conquered by Egypt, as dowry. He followed the same policy with his other neighbors, and with every *entente cordiale* a foreign princess was added to his harem. His most lucrative alliance was with the Phoenicians from whom he obtained ships and sailors for his trade with distant lands, and artisans and materials for his buildings.

Jerusalem began to lose its provincial aspect. The high-born ladies whom Solomon married brought their retinues to the capital. They also brought their religious cults into the city, and Solomon, for diplomatic reasons, refrained from interfering with the innovations. Strange forms of worship now appeared in Jerusalem, exercising a lure which the king himself was at times unable to resist.

Moreover, these elegant ladies, the Egyptian princess in particular, had been reared in a splendor beside which Solomon's capital must have seemed barbaric. What were the rude structures of Jerusalem beside the monuments and palaces of Egypt? The king determined to remove the reproach. Jerusalem must not be inferior to the capitals of his neighbors.

3

SOLOMON proceeded to transform his capital. First he strengthened its defenses, encircling the city with a wall that embraced the western hill, the Tyropean Valley, and the hills on the east above the Vale of Kidron. On the northern area of the eastern hill, or Mount Zion, he erected a new city, indulging to the full his taste for splendor and his ambition to figure as a great builder.

He required for these structures armies of laborers and vast stores of material. He required also skilled artisans of many crafts, masons, carvers of wood and stone, workers in metal and ivory. His Phoenician allies supplied the principal craftsmen as well as the timber from the forest of Lebanon; the stones were quarried near Jerusalem. For unskilled labor he had recourse to the method employed by the despots of Egypt: he drafted thousands of his subjects to labor in the forests and quarries.

Gradually there rose up a palace for the king, another for his wives, and still another for the Pharaoh's daughter. A gold and ivory throne was fashioned for the king, and set up in a great Hall of Justice. Below the palaces and Hall of Justice an arsenal was erected—called, because of its cedar columns, the House of the Forest of Lebanon.

North of the palaces rose the most illustrious of all of Solomon's structures, the Temple. Great courts surrounded it, and two enormous pillars of bronze, before which stood the Brazen Altar, flanked the entrance to the sanctuary proper. The latter had two principal chambers. The first was the *hechal*, into which the priests alone could enter; the second was the *debir*, or Holy of Holies, where, beneath the wings of two giant cherubim, rested the Ark of the Covenant. The *debir* could be entered by the High Priest alone, and only on the Day of Atonement. It was this Temple that became the national shrine of the people, their glory in prosperity, their consolation and hope in adversity. And wherever, in the centuries that followed, the tides of history bore them, the memory of the Temple on Mount Zion filled their hearts with pride and sorrow and expectation.

The dedication of the Temple was a memorable event in Israel; Jerusalem was thronged for the occasion with pilgrims from every corner of the land. The king's dedication address rang with eloquence and spiritual exaltation. In deep humility he offered the Temple to the God of Israel. But his conception of God was not merely that of a local or national deity. "Behold!" he cried, "heaven and the heaven of heavens cannot contain Thee: how much less this house that I have builded!" The Temple, moreover, was declared open to all nations, "that all the peoples of the earth may know Thy name."

Having listened to their king and seen his greatness and glory, the pilgrims set their faces homeward. The shepherds returned to their flocks and pastures, the husbandmen to their fields, groves, and vineyards, the craftsmen to their shops, the merchants to their wares. Their hearts were filled with pride and gratitude, for Israel was great among the nations.

Solomon's fame swept across the boundaries of his empire to distant lands, and foreign potentates, impelled by interest and curiosity, came to his capital on visits of state. The most illustrious of these visitors was the Queen of Sheba, a faraway land on the southwestern coast of Arabia. The Queen went away awed by Solomon's splendor and dazzled by his brilliance. "The half was not told me," said she when at last she tore herself away and returned to her country.

4

IT IS pleasant to dwell on Solomon's glory, and later generations have done so in full measure. Nevertheless, all was not well with the nation. Too high a price was demanded for all that magnificence. The people found the taxes too high, particularly the maintenance tax for the king's household, and they resented even more the forced labor the monarch exacted from them for his building operations. Moreover, the King of Tyre had obtained twenty Israelite towns for the help he gave Solomon. Was it right, the people asked, to barter away the patrimony of Israel? In addition Solomon pursued a policy that alienated the religious leaders of the people, especially the prophets. True, the king in the main remembered his father's behest to be loyal to the Great Teaching. At the same time, however, to please his foreign wives, he did permit the introduction of idolatrous cults into Jerusalem.

Finally, it must be set down that Solomon did nothing to allay the old hostility between the north and the south. Ephraim could not forget that the king was a son of Judah, and the king himself helped them to remember it, for in the imposition of the hated maintenance tax, the tribe of Judah, foolishly enough, was exempted.

While the king was alive, however, the discontent, despite the abundant fuel it had to feed on, was not a serious problem. Only one incident is recorded which disturbed the king's serenity. A certain bold fellow, Jeroboam son of Nebat, attempted to launch a rebellion in Ephraim. The attempt was quickly suppressed, but Jeroboam escaped into Egypt, where a new Pharaoh gave him refuge. The rebel, it seems, had been encouraged by the prophets. One of them, Ahijah of Shiloh, having cut his garment into twelve pieces symbolizing the twelve tribes of Israel, had presented ten of them to Jeroboam.

There came a day when the news was brought to Jeroboam in Egypt that Solomon was dead. The great king had died peacefully, without premonition, apparently, of the troublous heritage he was leaving to Rehoboam, his son and successor.

CHAPTER NINE

The Kingdom of Israel

Not a trace of the genius of David or the wisdom of Solomon fell to Rehoboam: he bears the inglorious distinction of having been the immediate cause of the breakup of the kingdom. His conduct, as soon as he ascended the throne, was precisely calculated to make the embers of discontent burst into flame. For when the elders of the northern tribes, gathered to confirm his selection, demanded relief from the oppressive burdens of his father, the arrogant young man, spurred on by a coterie of youthful counselors, told his subjects: "My father made your yoke heavy, but I will add to your yoke; my father chastised you with whips, but I will chastise you with scorpions."

Thereupon, the traditional cry of revolt: "To your tents, O Israel!" rang out in the multitude; the leader was the former rebel Jeroboam who had returned to Israel. The king then made another mistake. He sent an ambassador to the elders to reason with them, choosing for this delicate mission none other than Adoniram, the man who had been in charge of Solomon's tax levies. The people stoned the messenger to death. Rehoboam fled to Jerusalem, and the northern tribes proclaimed Jeroboam their king. The year was 933 B.C.E.

It was the end of the united kingdom: the commonwealth created by David was no more. In its place arose two Hebrew kingdoms, each one pursuing its own destiny. The two were unequal in extent and resources. The northern kingdom, sometimes called Ephraim in deference to its leading tribe, but more often called Israel, had three times the area of the southern kingdom, which came to be known as Judah. The south embraced the tribes of Judah and Benjamin only, the other ten being credited to Israel.* The north was more fertile; its cities were larger and more numerous. Israel was in closer contact with the currents of world commerce and world events.

In spite of its advantages, however, Israel ended its career almost a century and a half sooner than Judah. The northern kingdom encountered more enemies, and it was internally weakened by numerous dynastic revolutions. The people of Judah, on the other hand, were spared the turmoil of dynastic changes by their unshakable loyalty to the House of David. Moreover, the attachment to Torah and the Torah way of life, which augmented the power

* Of the original tribes, Simeon also may be assigned to the kingdom of Judah. Simeon, however, had practically lost its identity in the tribe of Judah, so that only the latter and Benjamin are included in the kingdom of the south. In the north there would be only nine tribes, but the two parts of Manasseh, divided by the Jordan, came to be looked upon as separate tribes. Thus, Israel is frequently called the Kingdom of the Ten Tribes.

of national resistance, was much stronger in the south than in the north.

2

WAR broke out at once between the two kingdoms and continued throughout the reign of Jeroboam, whose defeat was only averted by the intervention of his patron, the Pharaoh of Egypt. The latter invaded Canaan and captured many cities.

The prophets, from whom the northern rebel had received encouragement, were compelled in the end to turn against him, for he set up shrines in his kingdom where the bull, sacred to the Egyptians, was worshipped. These shrines, he hoped, would wean his subjects from the temple in Jerusalem which they continued to visit. At the same time he was paying homage to his protector by worshipping his gods.

Jeroboam's son survived his accession for only two years. A number of bloody palace revolutions followed, out of which there finally emerged a military leader of exceptional prowess—Omri, who seized the throne of Israel about the year 884 B.C.E. Israel's army, which proclaimed Omri king, was at the moment besieging the Philistine stronghold of Gibbethon. Apparently the ancient enemy, after a period of decline, had again become formidable.

During a reign of only twelve years Omri, who possessed the gift of statesmanship, brought Israel to a high place of power and importance. To begin with, he established peace between Israel and Judah. The other enemies, the Philistines on the west and the Moabites across the Jordan, were made to feel the strength of Omri's arms. Finally, Omri built a new capital for Israel. He built it on a hill overlooking a plain, and he rendered it almost impregnable. It was the city of Shomron or Samaria, which became the metropolis of the north and the religious and political rival of Jerusalem.

3

OMRI was followed by his son Ahab, the most notorious of Israel's kings. Ahab attempted to emulate the opulence of Solomon, strengthening his capital and other cities in Israel, and embellishing them with fine edifices, including a sumptuous "ivory palace," remains of which have been discovered by excavators. But it was Ahab's misfortune to reign at a time when the smoldering hostility between the zealots of the ancient faith and the idolaters burst into flame. The conflict had been prepared by Ahab's father. Having formed an alliance with the Phoenician city of Tyre, Omri had thought to cement it by a marriage between the crown prince and the Tyrian princess Jezebel. The princess brought her national idols with her, and Samaria became infested with the cult of Baal, Asherah, and Moloch. Jezebel was determined to foist the Phoenician worship upon her adopted land, and she brought in hundreds of priests of Baal to assist her.

The prophets became aroused. No such insolent defiance of the God of Moses had ever been attempted before. Idolatry, moreover, brought its normal brood of social vices: luxury and licentiousness, oppression of the poor, perversion of justice. The prophets, of course, stood for the ancient purities and simplicities. There were Nazirites among them and Rechabites; the latter were named after Aminadab son of Rechab, and lived, like their remote ancestors, as nomad shepherds. In that life alone, they felt, could the ancient virtues be preserved.

A leader rose up among the prophets, Elijah the Tishbite, a man of irresistible power and passion. His zeal was for the God of justice and righteousness, and he spurned all compromise with idolatry and vice. The nation, he demanded, must stop vacillating between Torah and idolatry.

With incredible boldness Elijah defies king and queen, and challenges the prophets of Baal to a supreme test of faith. The scene of the great contest is Mount Carmel. The priests of Baal offer their sacrifices, but in vain: no fire comes down to consume them. "Louder, shout louder!" Elijah taunts the frantic priests, "Perhaps your god is asleep and needs to be awakened." Then the prophet offers his sacrifice and, we are told, a bolt from heaven comes down and consumes it. Elijah's victory is so spectacular that the people turn on Jezebel's priests and annihilate them.

To escape the fury of Jezebel, Elijah flees to the deserts of the south. There, in a revelation of incomparable beauty, he finds his

God, not in a strong wind that rends the mountains, nor in an earthquake, nor in a fire, but in a "still small voice." The voice commands him to return to Israel and continue the struggle against the faithless house of Omri.

Elijah, his aspect gaunt and terrifying, returns to the north. On the way he meets Elisha son of Shaphat plowing his father's field, and throws his mantle over him in token of selection as his successor.

Again Elijah appears before Ahab, for the king has permitted his wife to commit a heinous crime. She has caused an innocent man, Naboth the Jezreelite, to be put to death in order to rob him of a vineyard which the king coveted. Elijah's return strikes terror into Ahab. "Hast thou found me, Oh mine enemy?" he cries; and Elijah pronounces doom upon him and his house.

The day of Elijah's final departure arrives. "What shall I do for thee before I be taken from thee?" he asks Elisha who is with him. "Let a double portion of thy spirit be upon me," Elisha answers. And the young disciple, we read, sees his master caught up in a fiery chariot and lifted by a whirlwind to heaven.

4

AHAB was killed in battle fighting the Aramaeans, Israel's principal enemy. His father had also suffered from Aram: he had been compelled to set aside a special section in the city of Samaria for the Aramaean merchants. Ahab was, on the whole, more fortunate. He routed the Aramaeans while they were besieging his capital, and later he defeated them again at Aphek in the Valley of Jezreel, compelling the King of Aram to let the merchants of Israel trade in Damascus. The final war against them was fought with the King of Judah as Ahab's ally. They met the Aramaeans at Ramoth-gilead, both Hebrew monarchs fighting in the thick of the fray. Ahab, mortally wounded by an arrow, remained standing in his chariot until the evening, when he died. The day was won by the enemy.

The fate of Israel was left in the hands not of Ahab's sons, but of the queen-mother Jezebel: Ahaziah, who reigned only two years, and Jehoram who followed him, were completely dominated by her. The house of Omri continued to be the fountainhead of idolatry and corruption.

Jehoram's career as a warrior was checked by Moab, whose king, Mesha, was an aggressive ruler. Mesha refused to pay tribute to Omri's grandson, and even raided Israelite territory. Jehoram set out to punish the arrogant Moabite, and the King of Judah accompanied him. The allies were besieging the Moabite capital when Mesha brought out his eldest son upon the city's wall and burnt him as a sacrifice to his god Chemosh. The besiegers were seized with dread and retired.

A remarkable record of Mesha's rebellion was found on the site of ancient Dibon in 1868, confirming the account in the Bible. It is the famous Moabite stone on which Mesha set down in Phoenician script and in the current Hebrew language, his successes against Israel. Mesha omits the sacrifice of his son, but he ascribes all his victories to his god Chemosh, to whom he "devotes," or sacrifices, his booty and his enemies. "I am Mesha, son of Chemosh, King of Moab, the Dibonite," the inscription begins, and then it goes on to tell of the afflictions visited upon Moab by Ahab and of Mesha's defiance and defeat of Israel. "And Israel perished everlastingly," the Moabite magniloquently adds. Mesha fought also against the tribe of Gad who still dwelt in the land. He writes:

And Chemosh said unto me, "Go, seize
Nebo against Israel!"
And I went by night, and fought against
it from dawn unto noon.
And I seized it, and slew all of it . . .
For to Chemosh I had devoted it.

Jehoram then fought against the Aramaeans. He took from them the city of Ramoth-gilead, but, wounded in battle, he returned to his summer palace in the city of Jezreel, leaving the army in command of his general Jehu. The prophets, to whom the house of Omri was anathema, now encouraged this ruthless soldier to put an end to it. Jehu began by obtaining the support of the army, then proceeded to Jezreel and with his own hand slew Jehoram, throwing his body into the vineyard which had belonged to

Naboth. He then rode to the palace where, from a window, the queen-mother Jezebel, painted and bedizened, looked down upon him and defied him. She was seized and thrown down in front of his chariot wheels. Jehu went on, nor did he desist until all the princes of the dynasty, and even some of the royal family of Judah who had fallen into his hands, were slain.

5

JEHU's long reign of twenty-eight years (843-816 B.C.E.) was a turbulent period in the career of the northern kingdom. By his bloody deeds he forfeited the friendship of Judah and Phoenicia, Israel's former allies, while its inveterate enemies, Moab and Aram, became more aggressive than ever.

Meanwhile, north of Aram a new power was reaching out for world dominion. It was Assyria, planted on the upper reaches of the Euphrates, whose shadow was growing ever longer across the neighboring lands. Assyria lived only by and for conquest: its armies were the most efficient instruments of devastation of the age.

The red shadow lengthened, pointing toward Egypt. In 854 B.C.E. the nations that lay between the two great powers, including Israel, had made common cause against the advancing Assyrians, led by their emperor Shalmaneser III (859-825 B.C.E.). At Karkar, where Shalmaneser claims to have won a great victory, the allies had nevertheless succeeded in checking his march.

A record of Shalmaneser's "victory" at Karkar has been found, inscribed on a stone slab known as Shalmaneser's Monolith Inscription. His principal victims, according to this inscription, were Ben-hadad the Syrian, and "Ahab the Israelite," who thus has the distinction of being the first biblical personage definitely found mentioned in a non-biblical source. Says Shalmaneser:

> Karkar, his royal city, I destroyed, I devastated, I burned with fire. 1,200 chariots, 1,200 cavalry, 20,000 soldiers of Hadadezer of Damascus . . . 2,000 chariots, 10,000 soldiers of Ahab the Israelite . . . thousands of soldiers of Baasa son of Ruhubi the Ammonite . . . I defeated. I rained destruction

upon them. I scattered their corpses far and wide . . . the plain was too small to let their bodies fall. With their bodies I spanned the Orontes as with a bridge.

Now Jehu, harassed by Aram, sent tribute to Shalmaneser, hoping that the Assyrian would save him from his foe. On the famous Black Obelisk of Shalmaneser where, in picture and word, the triumphs of this monarch are vividly recorded, the King of Israel, erroneously called "Jehu son of Omri," is shown kneeling before the Assyrian ruler. But Jehu's hope was vain. The Aramaeans overran Transjordania and, in the reign of his son, they even besieged Samaria. It was only in the reign of his grandson, Jehoash, that the longed-for respite came. The Assyrians had captured Damascus, the capital of Aram, and the King of Israel was able to defeat his hereditary enemy.

Jehoash defeated Judah also. The Judean monarch had sent him an arrogant challenge, and Jehoash entered Jerusalem, seized the treasures of the Temple and palace as well as hostages, and returned to Samaria. Nevertheless, victorious Israel did not deal harshly with Judah. Amid all the bitterness between the two kingdoms, the sense of kinship was still alive.

CHAPTER TEN

Prophets in Israel

IN THE two-century career of the northern kingdom, a century and a half had already passed. The sun of Israel was soon to set, but before the final darkness the kingdom was destined to have its day of glory.

The monarch to whom this day was granted was Jeroboam II, son of Jehoash. In a reign of forty years (785-745 B.C.E.), he lifted Israel to its pinnacle of worldly power. Aram had been greatly weakened by the Assyrians and Israel had its opportunity against its principal enemy. Jeroboam brought the Aramaeans under his yoke, capturing Damascus and sweeping on to the Euphrates. He forced the Moabites to pay tribute again. The Phoenicians and the Philistines were kept within their borders, and Israel dwelt in safety.

2

IN THE events that crowd the political history of the kingdom, there is little or nothing that distinguishes Israel from the surrounding nations. Palace revolutions and bloody dynastic changes stain the domestic record of all of them, while in their foreign affairs, war, frequent if not continuous, marks their "normal" relations with their neighbors. Why then have Moab and Aram, Phoenicia and Philistia been forgotten while Israel is remembered?

Nor does Israel reveal any striking divergence from its neighbors in the social and economic spheres. Two of these neighbors, the Phoenicians and Aramaeans, were keen traders, the first by sea, the second by land. The Aramaeans, whose language eventually became the vernacular of the East, were a ubiquitous people, trading in every land. Their principal kingdom lay west of the Euphrates, in the region called Syria; the name resulted from the fact that the Greeks confused the Aramaeans with the Assyrians. The Phoenicians occupied a string of cities along the northern coast, whence they sent their argosies sailing to all the coasts and islands of the Mediterranean, and beyond the Pillars of Hercules as far as Britain. The cities of Aram and Phoenicia grew large and populous, serving as depots and marts as well as centers of industry, and those of Israel developed along the same lines. In the main, of course, the Hebrews were still a nation of farmers, planters, and herders, and the village was still the foundation of their social life. But the cities had grown enormously, with slums that swarmed with artisans and laborers, with warehouses and bazaars for the traffic of the traders, with palatial residences for the merchant princes and bankers.

In these cities, Aramaean and Phoenician as well as Israelite, the gulf between rich and poor made its inevitable appearance. The evils of excessive wealth as well as those of poverty lifted their ugly heads. Idleness and luxury became the fertile breeding-ground of ostentation, vice, and oppression. The poor and the needy were pawns in the hands of the rich, and justice was perverted in favor of the powerful.

Nor was the city alone the dwelling place of greed and exploitation. The small farms that once supported a numerous peasantry gave way to large estates, to absentee landlords and rural proletarians, to all those evils which the Jubilee Year was designed to prevent. But the Jubilee was not observed, the large estates became larger, the position of the landless peasants more precarious.

In all these things Israel was like its neighbors. Nor would its annals deserve the special place they hold in the interest and hopes of mankind were it not for one difference. It was the difference that had its origin in Torah. A light had been kindled in the Sinai Desert which violence and oppression could obscure but not extinguish, and in every generation there were priests and prophets who kept it burning. In Israel, above the tumult of war and revolution, above the clamor of the market place and the orgies of the oversated, rose "the still small voice" of the Lord.

3

IN THE Book of Kings where the reign of Jeroboam II is briefly recorded, no mention is made of a man named Amos, a shepherd from Judah who, in the days of that monarch, came to Bethel in Israel on a strange mission. Apparently his visit was not regarded by the chronicler as an event of importance. Bethel was the religious center of Jeroboam's realm; the place was thronged with priests and worshippers; numerous sacrifices smoked on the altars. Suddenly words of incredible boldness fell on the ears of the people, terrifying words, announcing doom. It was Amos speaking in the name of the Lord:

Hear ye this word which I take up for a
lamentation over you, O house of Israel:
The virgin of Israel is fallen.
She shall no more rise;
She is cast down upon her land,
There is none to raise her up.

Amos turned to the pampered wives of the wealthy and shriveled them with his irony and wrath:

Hear this word, ye kine of Bashan,
That are in the mountain of Samaria,
That oppress the poor, that crush the needy,
That say unto their lords: "Bring,
that we may feast."
The Lord God hath sworn by His Holiness:
Lo, surely the days shall come upon you,
That ye shall be taken away with hooks,
And your residue with fish-hooks.

And lest they or their husbands imagine they can atone for their wrongdoing by bringing sacrifices to the priests, this peasant assures them that the Lord takes no delight in their solemn assemblies, that He will not accept their burnt offerings. Or do they comfort themselves with the doctrine of Israel's selection? The shepherd tells them they were selected not for ease and luxury, but to be a light unto the nations; and in his wrath and anguish he cries out:

You only have I known of all the families of earth!
Therefore I will visit upon you all your sins.

It was the ancient and true doctrine of Israel's selection that he proclaimed, the doctrine which the worldly rich had perverted, accepting its favors and rejecting its obligations. And what finally did Amos demand? The prophet makes no secret of it, he is as outspoken in his demands as in his accusations:

Let justice well up as waters
And righteousness as a mighty stream!

Apparently the words of Amos roused his hearers. There must have been muttering among the poor and protest among the rich. At any rate, Amaziah, the presiding priest of Bethel, became alarmed and urged the king to expel the agitator. "Go into the land of Judah and prophesy there," says the priest to the prophet. He was apparently ignorant of the nature of the prophetic call;

he was unaware that the true prophet has no choice. Amos states it very simply:

The lion hath roared,
Who will not fear?
The Lord God hath spoken,
Who can but prophesy?

4

THE stormy career of the northern kingdom was moving to its close, Jeroboam II being its last great king. Jeroboam died in 745 B.C.E., and only twenty-three years later, after a number of dynastic upheavals, the final curtain fell on the "pride of Ephraim." The prowess and diplomacy of its rulers were futile. Israel lay in the path of the Assyrian juggernaut and its doom was sealed. Egypt, itself menaced by the same peril, gave niggard help and only bedeviled the counsels of the smaller nations. They vacillated continually between submission to Assyria and hope in Egypt.

Of the kings there remains but a meager memory. It is the prophets who make Israel's story vivid and memorable. Of the many "Sons of the Prophets" who must have raised their voices against idolatry and injustice in Israel there is, besides Amos, only one other whose words were written down and saved. He was Hosea son of Beeri, whose sayings are recorded in the book that bears his name.

In their denunciations and demands, there is little difference between Amos and Hosea. Both cried out against the sins of Israel: against the idolatry that polluted the land, against the iniquity and oppression that made a mockery of the ancient covenant. But while the shepherd from Judah heaped scorn and derision upon the evildoers, Hosea's heart is full of pity for the backsliding children, whom God loves despite their faithlessness. The prophet knew the bitterness of infidelity: his own wife, whom he loved, had been unfaithful to him. So, while he accuses he also pleads, and his heart overflows with sorrow.

In his very denunciations there is a tenderness that finds expression in a matchless lyricism; as when he cries:

O Ephraim, what shall I do unto thee?
O Judah, what shall I do unto thee?
For your goodness is as a morning cloud,
And as the dew that early passeth away.
Therefore have I hewed them by the prophets,
I have slain them by the words of my mouth;
And thy judgment goeth forth as the light.
For I desire mercy, and not sacrifice,
And the knowledge of God rather than burnt
offerings.

And when his love for his people sweeps away all other emotions, God speaks through him, saying:

How shall I give thee up, Ephraim?
How shall I surrender thee, Israel?
My heart is turned within Me,
My compassions are kindled together.
I will not execute the fierceness of Mine anger,
I will not return to destroy Ephraim.

So, in the midst of his sorrows, Hosea has the vision of a day when a new betrothal will take place between the Lord and His people.

And I will betroth thee unto Me forever;
Yea, I will betroth thee unto Me in righteousness,
and in justice,
And in lovingkindness, and in compassion.
And I will betroth thee unto Me in faithfulness;
And thou shalt know the Lord.

But for all his compassion Hosea does not mince words when dealing with the iniquity of Israel. The seal of the true prophet is upon him: his mission is to cleanse the human soul. His final utterance, however, is one of hope and healing. He sees a time when his people will no longer put their trust in Assyria or Egypt, but in God. And God, speaking through the prophet, declares that in that day

I will heal their backsliding,
I will love them freely;
For Mine anger is turned away from him.
I will be as the dew unto Israel;
He shall blossom as the lily,
And cast forth his roots as Lebanon.

5

IN 745 B.C.E., the year when Jeroboam II died, Tiglath-pileser III came to the throne of Assyria. The conqueror set his cohorts moving and swept on toward Israel. Israel's ruler, Menahem, held him off with a large tribute. Pekah, who usurped the throne of Israel, allied himself with Rezin, King of Aram, against the Assyrians, and even made war on Judah to compel it to join the coalition. The Assyrians came down and captured Damascus, Rezin's capital. They overran Gilead and Galilee, and drove many of the inhabitants into exile.

Tiglath-pileser has left us a record of his gory triumph over Rezin. Concerning the hapless king of Aram, he writes:

> That one fled alone to save his life and like a mouse he entered the gate of his city. His nobles I captured alive with my own hands and hanged them on stakes and let his land gaze on them. His gardens and plantations without number I cut down, not one escaped . . . Sixteen districts of Syria I destroyed like mounds left by a flood.

What he did to the "Land of Omri," or Israel, he reports as follows:

> The Land of Omri, all its people together with their goods, I carried off to Assyria. Pekah their king they deposed, and I placed Hoshea over them as king.

Hoshea, however, played fast and loose with the Assyrians, relying on Egypt for help. The Assyrians, led by a new emperor, Shalmaneser IV, came down and besieged Samaria. For three years the city held out against the invaders. Finally, in 722 B.C.E., with

Sargon II now emperor of Assyria, the capital of Israel fell to the enemy.

Sargon's own account of his capture of Samaria has been found in an inscription on the walls of the palace at Khorsabad, and it reads as follows:

> In my first year of reign the people of Samaria to the number of 27,290 . . . I carried away. Fifty chariots for my royal equipment I selected. The city I rebuilt. I made it greater than it was before. People of the lands I had conquered I settled therein. My official I placed over them as governor.

Thus were the people led away captive into distant provinces of the empire and became the Lost Ten Tribes. Samaria, as Sargon informs us, was colonized with strangers, and the Kingdom of Israel became a tale that is told.

CHAPTER ELEVEN

Judah and Isaiah

For nearly a century and a half the kingdom of Judah survived its sister and rival on the north. Judah was less vulnerable than Israel; its capital had stronger defenses; its rugged territory was less tempting to the greed of neighbors. Moreover, Judah's loyalty to the House of David saved it from the bloody revolutions that stain the annals of Israel. In fact, with only one short break (843-837 B.C.E.), the Davidic line continued to reign over Judah to the end.

Rehoboam, whose folly was the immediate cause of Israel's defection, fought against Israel, as did his son and grandson. To his grandson Asa is ascribed the merit of attempting to clear the land of the "high places" where heathen rites were still practiced, an attempt which was only partly successful. His aim was to make the Temple the only place of worship for his people. Asa

ISRAEL AND JUDAH
AND THEIR NEIGHBORS
ASSYRIA
ARAM
(SYRIA)
PHOENICIA
LEBANON MTS.
Orontes
Leontes
MEDITERRANEAN
SEA
Sidon
Tyre
DAMASCUS
Mt. Hermon
Dan
Mt. Carmel
Valley of Jezreel
Jezreel
ISRAEL
Samaria
Shechem
Jordan
GILEAD
Gibbethon
Bethel
Ramoth-gilead
AMMON
Ekron
Ashdod
Anathoth
JERUSALEM
Mt. Nebo
Libnah
Tekoa
Dead Sea
Gaza
Hebron
Dibon
PHILISTIA
JUDAH
Beersheba
MOAB
EDOM
SCALE OF MILES
0 10 20 30 40

was a capable and warlike ruler. With the aid of the Aramaeans, whom he bribed lavishly, he humbled the king of Israel and turned back an invasion from Africa.

A policy of peace with Israel was inaugurated by Asa's successor, whose son married Athaliah, daughter of Jezebel, the idolatrous queen of Israel. When Athaliah became queen of Judah, Phoenician idolatry began to flourish in the land, and years later this faithful daughter of Jezebel seized the throne after slaying her own grandchildren. That was the one break in David's line, but one of the royal grandchildren, an infant boy, had been saved, and six years later he was acclaimed by the priests of the Temple and by the army as King of Judah. Athaliah's career was speedily ended and the line of David restored.

The restored king, Jehoash, reigned over Judah from 837 to 798 B.C.E. He labored hard to stamp out the idolatry which still infested the land. He fought his neighbors, but his wars brought him no glory, for he suffered defeat at the hands of the Aramaeans and Edomites. His son retrieved Judah's pride against Edom, but he was worsted in an encounter with Israel whose king he foolishly challenged. Then came Uzziah (780-740 B.C.E.) whose reign was contemporaneous with that of Jeroboam II in Israel. There was peace between the two, and both reigns were long, prosperous, and brilliant. The Philistines, Ammonites, and Edomites were made to feel the power of Judah's king.

A grave situation confronted Uzziah's grandson, Ahaz. Threatened by Assyria, Aram and Israel had formed an alliance which they sought to compel Judah to join. The allies besieged Jerusalem but in the end Ahaz foiled them: he sent a huge tribute to Tiglath-pileser, acknowledged the Assyrian as his suzerain, and prayed for deliverance from Israel and Aram. The Assyrian was only too willing to grant the petition, and the allies were compelled to withdraw from Judah in order to defend their own capitals.

But Ahaz paid a heavy price for his deliverance. He surrendered not only the gold of the Temple and the independence of his country, but also the pure faith of his fathers. The King of Judah brought the idolatry of his Assyrian master into Jerusalem. The heavenly bodies were worshipped in the capital, as well as statues of horses which were set up in the Temple. Nor was the country spared the ultimate abomination: children were sacrificed to Moloch, the king himself offering up his son. What better way for a vassal to flatter and appease his suzerain than to adopt his gods and his rites?

In 722 B.C.E., when Samaria fell, Ahaz still sat on the throne of Judah. The rivalries of former days were now forgotten: the downfall of Israel threw a pall of sorrow and anxiety over Judah and Jerusalem.

2

THERE was at least one man in the capital of Judah who did not mince words in condemnation of the foreign policy of King Ahaz. He was the prophet Isaiah, in many respects the greatest in the long line of the Hebrew seers.

Isaiah had begun his prophetic career in 740 B.C.E., the year when King Uzziah died. In that year the youthful prophet had a vision: a glowing coal from the altar of the Temple was pressed to his lips by an angel, and the voice of the Lord sounded in his ears, saying: "Whom shall I send, who will go for us?" And Isaiah answered and said: "Here am I; send me." And that was the manner in which Isaiah was inducted into his mission.

In the years that follow, the prophet moves against the dark background of the times, robed in light and splendor. His voice thunders above the din of Judah's capital; his utterances are magnificent beyond compare. Nevertheless, he is no mere commentator on the events of the day, for nothing of importance occurs in which Isaiah does not play an important role. He rises immeasurably above his age, but he is also part and parcel of it.

During the reign of Ahaz, the prophet, because of his opposition to the king's policies, could have but little influence at court. But other questions besides those of international politics disturbed Judah and Jerusalem. Isaiah blasted the idolaters with all the force of his irony; he denounced the luxury and the callousness of the rich and their oppression of the poor and humble. Never has the cry of the disinherited and the summons to righteousness been uttered in words more stirring. In the name of God, Isaiah cries to his people:

Wash you, make you clean!
Put away the evil of your doings
From before Mine eyes.
Cease to do evil!
Learn to do well!
Seek justice, relieve the oppressed,
Judge the fatherless, plead for the widow.

First and last Isaiah is the uncompromising moralist. Human problems are conflicts between good and evil, and man comes nearer to God in proportion as he sees what is good and does it. Not by mere sacrifices is God to be worshipped,

But the Lord of Hosts is exalted through justice,
And God the Holy One is sanctified through righteousness.

3

ISAIAH, though the greatest seer of the age, was not the only one. In Judah, as in Israel, there were many prophets who expressed the living conscience of the people. They came from all classes and they were heard in the countryside as well as in the city.

Through the storms of the centuries the words of one of the village prophets have also been saved. He was Micah of Moresheth who, simple peasant though he was, gave the most lofty expression to the ideal life of the spirit. He asks the supreme moral question of the age and of all ages, and answers it:

"Wherewith shall I come before the Lord,
And bow myself before God on high?
Shall I come before him with burnt-offerings,
With calves of a year old?
Will the Lord be pleased with thousands of rams,
With ten thousands of rivers of oil?
Shall I give my first-born for my transgression,
The fruit of my body for the sin of my soul?"

It hath been told thee, O man, what is good,
And what the Lord doth require of thee:
Only to do justly, and to love mercy, and to
walk humbly with thy God.

For the rest, Micah voices the wrath of the simple husbandman upon whom the city has laid its talons.

Woe to them that devise iniquity
And work evil upon their beds!
When the morning is light, they execute it,
Because it is in the power of their hand.
And they covet fields, and seize them;
And houses, and take them away;
Thus they oppress a man and his house,
Even a man and his heritage.

The city is the home of greed and oppression, and both Isaiah and Micah see the "day of the Lord" advancing, the day when the city shall pay the price of its follies and vices.

4

IN 720 B.C.E., Prince Hezekiah became King of Judah and there was great rejoicing among Isaiah's followers. Hezekiah sided with the prophets against the idolaters, and he began his reign with a sweeping religious reform. The "high places" where idolatry and its vices still flourished were demolished, and the Temple in Jerusalem, purified and purged, was proclaimed the only legitimate place of worship in the land. The following Passover, Jerusalem overflowed with the pilgrims who, in obedience to the king's decree, came to sacrifice at the national shrine. They came from every corner of Judah, and among them were many Israelites who had escaped the Assyrian dragnet and whom Hezekiah invited to join in the festivities. Thus the Temple was invested with new authority. It became the chief bond of national union, and, as the only recognized center of worship, the principal means of checking the ever-recurring drift toward idol worship.

To Isaiah the moralist, as to Moses the lawgiver seven centuries earlier, idolatry was the fountainhead of sin and corruption.

Eagerly the prophet now looked forward to the dawn of a new day in Judah. "The people that walked in darkness" he cried, "have seen a great light!"

5

BUT Judah, because of its parlous situation between Assyria and Egypt, was not permitted to work out its religious and social problems in peace. The two giants were measuring each other for mortal combat, and the fate of Judah hung in the balance.

It was inevitable that two parties, one pro-Egyptian, the other pro-Assyrian, should come into existence in Judah. Galled and humiliated by their country's vassalage to Assyria, the pro-Egyptian party clamored for rebellion. Egypt, they were sure, would come to their aid. The party included many of Judah's princes and magnates and was led by one Shabua, who stood at the head of the king's ministerial council. The rival party was led by Isaiah. Having chosen to pay tribute to Assyria, his country, he felt, should abide by its choice: the alternative was fraught with greater evils. Besides, Judah should devote its strength to spiritual regeneration, not to conspiracy and rebellion. As for Egypt, Isaiah had nothing but contempt for it and its promises.

The ambitious intrigues of Shabua and his henchmen filled Isaiah with alarm. He struggled against the minister and finally brought about his downfall. Hezekiah held fast to his prophetic counselor: he rejected the invitations of his neighbors to join a coalition against Assyria. Hanno, King of Gaza, had extended him such an invitation in 720 B.C.E., and Hezekiah had to defeat the Philistine king in order to be clear of his machinations. Ten years later the city of Ashdod rebelled against Sargon, and Judah was nearly drawn into the vortex. Again it was saved by the influence of Isaiah.

Inscriptions have been discovered in which the Assyrian emperor records the attempts of the neighboring rulers to induce Hezekiah to join them in rebellion against him. In one of them, dated 711 B.C.E., Sargon writes:

> Azuri king of Ashdod plotted in his heart to withhold his tribute, and sent messages of hostility to the kings round about

> him. To the kings of Philistia, Judah, Edom, Moab . . . payers of tribute to Assyria, he sent numberless inflammatory messages . . . to set them at enmity with me. To Pharaoh king of Egypt, a prince who could not save them, they sent presents . . . to gain him as an ally.

Sargon records that he dethroned the bold Azuri, captured Ashdod and other rebellious Philistine cities, and colonized them with strangers.

6

FINALLY, about the year 705 B.C.E., Hezekiah could no longer resist the pressure to throw off the Assyrian yoke. The moment seemed auspicious. Sargon, the cruel and invincible, had been murdered, and his son Sennacherib became ruler of an empire in revolt. Assyria's vassals became inflamed with the hope of immediate liberation. Jerusalem became a focal point in the general uprising, which extended from the lower reaches of the Tigris and Euphrates, where the Chaldean Merodach-baladan led the revolt, to Egypt, where the Pharaoh So threw down the gauntlet to Assyria. Padi, King of Ekron, who chose to remain loyal, was dethroned and placed in a dungeon in Jerusalem. Not even the passionate pleas and warnings of Isaiah could prevent Judah from throwing itself into the conflagration. The king stopped paying tribute to Assyria.

Hezekiah took steps to fortify Jerusalem, and one of his accomplishments was to secure the city's water supply by digging a tunnel from a spring outside the city to the Pool of Siloam. This tunnel or conduit has been discovered, as well as an inscription in the ancient Hebrew characters carved upon the rock. The words convey the excitement of the two groups of excavators when they heard each other's pickaxes from opposite sides of the rock, and their joy when they finally met.

For all that Hezekiah could do, however, Judah found itself face to face with disaster. Sennacherib proved a worthy successor of Sargon and Tiglath-pileser. After crushing the rebellion in Babylonia, he turned west and swept down the Mediterranean coast, where in 701 B.C.E., he defeated the combined forces of the rebels: Philistines, Egyptians, and Ethiopians. The cities of Phoenicia and Philistia hastened to pay tribute and beg for mercy.

Hezekiah and his counselors continued to defy the Assyrians and the hosts of Sennacherib began the ascent to Jerusalem. One after another the intervening fortresses were taken and given away to the Philistine cities of Ashdod, Ekron, and Gaza, inveterate enemies of Israel and Judah. "Himself," writes Sennacherib, referring to Hezekiah, "like a bird in a cage in the midst of Jerusalem, his royal city, I shut. The dread of the splendor of my reign overpowered him."

Finally, the King of Judah shook off his illusions. He humbly acknowledged his guilt and offered the conqueror a huge tribute. Sennacherib took the gold and silver, then demanded the surrender of Jerusalem. He was determined that the capital of Judah should suffer the fate of Samaria. Like Israel, Judah was to be led away into distant captivity.

Hezekiah rejected Sennacherib's demand and prepared his capital for defense. The hosts of Assyria came up and the siege of the city began. An Assyrian deputation approached the walls of Jerusalem and called upon the city to surrender. The spokesman, Rab-shakeh, taunted the people and defied their God.

> Hath any of the gods of the nations delivered his land out of the hand of the king of Assyria? And have they delivered Samaria out of my hand? Who are they among all the gods of these countries, that have delivered their country out of my hand, that the Lord should deliver Jerusalem out of my hand?

The people, including the king and his ministers, were struck with dismay. But there was one man who remained unafraid. The prophet Isaiah, roused to wrath and scorn, came forward and defied the blasphemous invader, accepting the challenge flung at the Holy One of Israel. "The Assyrians," he declared with the confidence born of faith, "shall not come into this city."

The Assyrians never did. A strange thing occurred which, the people were convinced, only the intervention of the Most High could have brought to pass. Suddenly Sennacherib withdrew his forces and marched them down into Egypt to meet a new foe hailing from Ethiopia. The Assyrians lay down in their tents one night; the next morning, we are told, they were lifeless corpses: some dreadful pestilence had mowed them down. The survivors, including the emperor, fled in terror to their own borders.

Thus was Jerusalem delivered and the faith of Isaiah vindicated in the sight of his people. The influence of the prophet rose to its zenith and stood there for another decade, until the end of the reign of Hezekiah in 692 B.C.E.

7

FROM the sublime utterances of Isaiah which have come down to us, it does not appear that the power he achieved made him happy. Happiness, alas, is never the lot of the true prophet. The political skies of Judah were still overcast, nor could he be at ease in the moral climate of Jerusalem. For, as with all the Hebrew prophets, Isaiah's dominant passions were love of justice and detestation of wrong. He was an aristocrat, but his heart overflowed with pity for the poor and weak, and he excoriated the oppressors with words that fall like hammer-strokes.

He cries to the nabobs and nobles of Jerusalem:

Hear the words of the Lord, ye rulers of Sodom,
To what purpose is the multitude of your sacrifices unto Me?
Saith the Lord.
Bring no more vain oblations;
It is an offering of abomination unto Me.
And when you spread forth your hands,
I will hide Mine eyes from you;
Yea, when you make many prayers,
I will not hear:
Your hands are full of blood.

It was only in visions of the distant future that the prophet's soul found repose, visions of the perfect king, or Messiah, holding the nations in benign sway; of universal peace, with the specter of war forever banished; of Israel, saved and restored, dwelling securely in its own land, and practicing justice and righteousness.

And it shall come to pass in the end of days,
That the mountain of the Lord's house shall be
established as the top of the mountains,
And shall be exalted above the hills;
And all nations shall flow unto it.
And many peoples shall go and say:
'Come ye, and let us go up to the mountain of the Lord,
To the house of the God of Jacob;
And he will teach us of his ways,
And we will walk in his paths.'
For out of Zion shall go forth the law,
And the word of the Lord from Jerusalem.
And He shall judge between the nations,
And shall decide for many peoples;
And they shall beat their swords into plowshares,
And their spears into pruning-hooks;
Nation shall not lift up sword against nation,
Neither shall they learn war any more.

That was the supreme vision of the great prophet spoken in words which only amplify the promise of the Great Covenant: "In thee shall all the families of the earth be blessed."

CHAPTER TWELVE

Judah and Jeremiah

SOME ten years after the invasion of Sennacherib, the good king Hezekiah died and the voice of Isaiah fell silent. The king's successor was his twelve-year-old son Manasseh, and the court party found their long-awaited opportunity to overthrow the influence of the prophet and restore the idol worship which Hezekiah had suppressed.

They were the princes and magnates of the land, these men who were so lightly lured by the gods of their neighbors. They only sought to resemble these neighbors, rather than tread the hard road enjoined by the command: "Ye shall be unto me a kingdom of priests and a holy nation." That was the road of Isaiah and his followers, who came to be known as *Anavim*, "the humble." The *Anavim* became the objects of relentless persecution. Isaiah himself, according to legend, fell victim to the rage of the reactionaries.

The licentious Astarte, the unspeakable Moloch, the demons of the Babylonians and Assyrians, now ruled the moral and social life of Judah. The "high places" reappeared, and a shrine to Moloch was set up where first-born sons, among them the first-born of the king himself, were sacrificed to the monster. The voice of justice and mercy was stifled. Luxury and oppression flourished, all the vices abhorred by the prophets lifted their heads. Yet, in hidden corners of the land, the *Anavim* continued to feed the flame of Torah and prophecy for the day when it should again illumine the land.

2

IN THE meantime Judah continued in vassalage to Assyria. That vast robber empire held together, notwithstanding Sennacherib's disaster in Egypt, notwithstanding rebellions and upheavals. Whatever hopes in the might of Egypt persisted among the princes of Judah must have been rudely shaken when, in 671 B.C.E., Sennacherib's son, Esar-haddon, invaded Egypt and captured the city of Memphis. Esar-haddon, it seems, held the King of Judah for a time in captivity, suspicious, no doubt, of Manasseh's loyalty.

In 638 B.C.E., after a weary reign of fifty-four years, Manasseh died, and a year later his son and successor Amon was slain by a palace cabal, and Amon's eight-year-old son, Josiah, was crowned king. The assassins, apparently anti-Assyrians, were punished, but idolatry continued unabated. The *Anavim*, though not without friends in high places, still labored in secret.

In 621 B.C.E., came a sudden change, a religious revolution led by the still youthful King Josiah, whom secret prophetic influences had prepared for the event. With the force of revelation, the young king was brought face to face with the Great Teaching. In that year, the High Priest Hilkiah found in the Temple a copy of the Book of Deuteronomy, the last of the Five Books of Moses, and took it to Josiah. The eloquence of the great lawgiver, his solemn warnings against idolatry, his clarion summons to purity and probity, swept like a cleansing storm through the hearts of king and people.

Judah was ripe for a religious revival. The voice of prophecy, long suppressed, had grown bold again. The few prophetic voices of the period which still speak to us across the millennia must have been part of a much more numerous chorus, with the "Sons of the Prophets" in zealot bands again rousing the fires of the ancient faith.

The thunderous voice of Nahum strikes our ears, as well as the somber accents of Zephaniah. Nahum has left us a great cry of jubilation as he sees in his vision wicked Nineveh, capital of Assyria, trampled by its foes. The prophet reports his vision with a vividness that is almost terrifying:

Woe to the bloody city!
It is all full of lies and rapine;
The prey departeth not.
Hark! the whip, and hark! the rattling of wheels;
And prancing horses, and bounding chariots;
The horseman charging,
And the flashing sword, and the glittering spear;
And a multitude of slain, and a heap of carcasses;
And there is no end of the corpses,
And they stumble upon their corpses.

Indeed the doom of Assyria was fast approaching. Early in Josiah's reign a horde of savage horsemen from the Scythian uplands broke through the empire's defenses and swept down the Mediterranean plain toward Egypt. Zephaniah, who may have witnessed this invasion, sees the dread "day of the Lord" advancing against all the nations, his own included, and he calls upon Judah to put away its idols and return to its God.

That day is a day of wrath,
A day of trouble and distress

A day of waste and desolation,
A day of darkness and gloominess,
A day of clouds and thick darkness,
A day of the horn and alarm,
Against the fortified cities, and against the high towers.

A mood of repentance seized upon the people. Throughout the land, and including the former territory of Israel, the "high places" were demolished and the idols destroyed. The Passover festival of the year 621 B.C.E. saw the climax of the great revival. At the summons of the king, the people gathered in Jerusalem, bearing offerings to the purified Temple and rejoicing in their new-found faith. Again the Temple was established as the sole shrine of the nation.

3

AMONG the celebrants of that unforgettable Passover in Jerusalem there must have been a young priest named Jeremiah who, five years earlier, had left his village of Anathoth near Jerusalem, driven to the capital by the same urge which a century before had brought Amos from Judah to Bethel. It was the implacable call of prophecy which the true prophet must obey. Jeremiah belonged to a priestly family of wealth and distinction, but the summons had come to him, and he set out

To root out and to pull down
And to destroy and to overthrow;
To build and to plant.
And if I say I will not make mention of Him,
Nor speak any more in His name,
Then there is in my heart as it were a burning fire
Shut up in my bones,
And I weary myself to hold it in,
But cannot.

Thus began the great and tragic career of the prophet Jeremiah, tragic because the true prophet, a stranger to the smooth ways of the courtier and demagogue, can hope for neither honor nor comfort from men. Jeremiah, moreover, prophesied in a period of world confusion, war, and disaster, a period of supreme crisis for his people. In the forty years of his career (626–586 B.C.E.), he never faltered, speaking and acting always without fear or favor, undeterred by threats of persecution.

What did it matter to Jeremiah that his words cut across the pet beliefs of his people, the belief, for example, in the efficacy of sacrifice? Not sacrifice had the Lord commanded when He brought their fathers out of Egypt, declared the prophet, but this He had commanded them: "Hearken unto My voice, and I will be your God, and ye shall be My people; and walk ye in the ways that I command you, that it may be well with you." And did the people believe the Temple to be impregnable and inviolate, expecting God's house to be their refuge no matter what might befall? It was a foolish and wicked hope, and the prophet minces no words about it:

> Will ye steal, murder and commit adultery, and swear falsely, and offer unto Baal, and walk after other gods whom ye have not known, and come and stand before Me in this house, whereupon My name is called, and say: "We are delivered," that ye may do all these abominations? Is this house, whereupon My name is called, become a den of robbers in your eyes?

He is a great searcher of hearts, this prophet of the searing word. He will not accept a formal devotion to which the heart does not solemnly assent. A new covenant shall come into existence between God and His people, a covenant to which every man's inner self shall be so attuned as to require no formal engagements. "I will put my law in their inward parts, and in their hearts I will write it," says the Lord by His prophet Jeremiah.

Amid a present dark with forebodings of rack and ruin, visions of moral perfection mingle in Jeremiah with tender memories of the idyllic past. Bent with a burden of inescapable woes, this "man of sorrows," as he calls himself, towers above his age like a lone mountain over a plain.

4

IN THE meantime, the game of war and empire among the nations of the Eastern world followed its fateful course. Assyria, a brigand power fit only for war and plunder, was brought down at last. North, south, and east, the nations that groaned beneath its yoke rose up and in 612 B.C.E. they poured into its capital, Nineveh on the Tigris, and left it a heap of ruins. Mighty among the avengers were the Chaldeans, a Semitic people which had possessed itself of Babylonia, now to be known as Chaldea.

What part in this game was played by Egypt, Assyria's arch-rival and the hope of the anti-Assyrian party in Jerusalem? Egypt tried to save Assyria from destruction! Egypt had no desire to see Chaldea take Assyria's place among the powers, a place it was eager to seize for itself. The Pharaoh Necho II led an army north to assert the might of Egypt among Assyria's conquerors. At Megiddo in the Valley of Jezreel, the Pharaoh found his passage barred by King Josiah of Judah. In the encounter that followed Judah was defeated, and in the thick of the battle the good and brave king Josiah was slain.

That was in 609 B.C.E. In the next twelve years Judah was the scene of swift and tragic changes. For four brief years the Pharaoh Necho was arbiter of the nations. He deposed Josiah's son Jehoahaz and put his brother Jehoiakim on Judah's throne, after wringing a huge tribute from him. In 605 B.C.E., however, Jehoiakim had to change masters, for in that year Egypt and Chaldea fought it out in the decisive Battle of Carchemish on the Euphrates, and Egypt was overwhelmed. In Jerusalem the prophet Jeremiah exulted:

The swift cannot flee away
Nor the mighty men escape;
In the north by the River Euphrates
Have they stumbled and fallen.

The Chaldeans, led by Nebuchadnezzar, now laid their yoke upon the nations. Eventually Jehoiakim yielded to the Pharaoh's threats and blandishments, and refused to pay tribute to Chaldea. At once, Judah was invaded and Jerusalem beleaguered. Its inveterate enemies, Aramaeans, Moabites, Ammonites, were unleashed against it. Jehoiakim died and his young son Jehoiachin fell heir to the crisis. There was nothing for him to do but throw himself on Nebuchadnezzar's mercy, and the Chaldean ruler wreaked a terrible revenge. He deposed Jehoiachin and, together with ten thousand of the leading men of the nation, including the armorers and other craftsmen, exiled him to Chaldea. It was the first Babylonian captivity, in the year 597 B.C.E.

5

ON JUDAH'S vacant throne Nebuchadnezzar placed Zedekiah, a remaining son of King Josiah. For a few years Zedekiah paid his tribute submissively to the conqueror. But soon enough Egypt recovered from the blow it suffered at Carchemish, and the pro-Egyptian party in Jerusalem took heart again. The hope of freedom, fed by the lying promises of Egypt, once more threw the small nations into a ferment. Zedekiah, torn between longing and fear, leaped at length into the vortex and the scene was prepared for the final agony of Judah.

Jerusalem became the center of the rebel ferment: from the neighboring nations emissaries gathered in Judah's capital to plan revolt. Jeremiah donned a wooden yoke in dramatic warning to the people to bear the yoke of the Chaldean or suffer disaster, for like the prophets before him, Jeremiah scorned Egypt, putting no trust in its promises. Besides, his nation, engrossed like the others in the sordid business of international intrigue, mistook its destiny. What mattered political subjection, if only it left Judah free to execute God's law of righteousness and holiness? Let the Chaldean have his tribute; Israel had his Torah.

For a number of years Zedekiah continued to vacillate: it was a bitter choice that confronted him. He understood the risks, nor did he fail to be impressed by Jeremiah's warnings, but he lacked the prophet's conviction and strength of spirit. So it came to pass that in 588 B.C.E., the year being the sixth of his reign, Zedekiah stopped paying tribute to his suzerain.

Other dependencies of Nebuchadnezzar were also in revolt, but the emperor sent the major part of his vast armament against Zedekiah. It swept through the lesser cities of Judah, and in the tenth month of the year of revolt, appeared before Jerusalem. The city's supreme trial was now upon her.

King and people had made her ready for the siege, and the Chaldeans, past masters in the art of siege-craft, found her impregnable to assault. So they girdled her about with counter-fortifications, trusting to famine to bring to slow fruition what their arms and engines were unable to achieve. Their plan was aided by the congestion in the city, for throngs of fugitives from other parts of the country had taken refuge in the capital.

Gripped in the vise of famine, the city nevertheless held firm, still hoping for succor from Egypt. Month followed month in growing agony, until, at the turn of the year, the hope in Egypt seemed vindicated! The besiegers abandoned their posts and departed hurriedly to meet an enemy from the south. Jerusalem exulted; and men who, obeying the law of Moses, had in fear and contrition liberated their slaves, now repented of their piety and compelled their slaves to return. Such were the magnates of Jerusalem, their righteousness like the grass on the housetops which the sun dries up. Jeremiah denounced the backsliders and warned the king against overconfidence: the Chaldean, he predicted, would return. The prophet was not without influence upon the king, but the leaders of the war party were in full control, the king a more or less unwilling tool in their hands.

Nor did Jeremiah escape their persecution, to which the aged prophet, were it not for Zedekiah's friendship, would have succumbed. They cast him into a miry pit from which the king rescued him, but not a single word of comfort would the prophet give the king in return.

The Pharaoh Hophra, whose incursion had drawn the besiegers away from Jerusalem, was, like his predecessor Necho II, decisively defeated, and the Chaldeans reappeared before the unhappy city. Now the twin scourges of famine and pestilence made common cause with the enemy. The heroic defenders still manned the walls, but their strength was ebbing. On the seventeenth day of Tammuz the wall was breached. The foe poured into the city, venting his rage and lust upon the survivors.

The king attempted to escape, but near the Jordan he and the greater part of his retinue, including his household, were captured. He was taken north to Riblah where Nebuchadnezzar sat over him in judgment. The Chaldean decreed a dire fate for Judah's last king. Zedekiah was compelled to see his sons slain, and it was the last thing he saw; immediately after, he was blinded.

The conqueror then pronounced doom upon Jerusalem: he ordered his commander Nebuzaradan to destroy the city. On the ninth day of Ab, the day when Jews still mourn for the great disaster, the enemy set fire to the Temple. Jerusalem, the beautiful and holy, was destroyed, its walls, houses, and palaces became a heap of ruins, and the Temple, the nation's pride and glory, was no more. A mere remnant of the people, the very poorest, were permitted to remain in the land. The others, in chains, were driven into Babylonia, to join their fellow-exiles who had preceded them eleven years before.

Among those whom the Chaldeans allowed to remain was Jeremiah. His heart, overflowing with sorrow, poured itself out in lamentation. On the Fast of Tisha b'Ab (Ninth of Ab), in houses of worship the world over, the strains of his mourning are still heard:

How doth the city sit solitary
That was full of people!
How is she become as a widow,
She that was great among the nations!

Part Two 586 B.C.E. TO 70 C.E.

The Second Commonwealth

A Torah People

CHAPTER THIRTEEN

Exile

The singular career of Israel from bondage to liberation, from desert trials to Revelation, from battle and conquest to defeat and disaster—this unique surge of a whole people toward the higher reaches of the spirit, seemed now to have come to a tragic and inglorious conclusion. The citadels of Judah were rubble and ashes, its defenders decimated and the survivors dispersed or led away captive to the land of the enemy. What fate could the exiles expect in Babylonia but absorption and dissolution?

Four generations earlier, the road of the captives had been traveled by their brothers of the northern kingdom. Had the exiles from Judah undergone the fate that befell their predecessors, this story would now be a tale that is told. To the Lost Ten Tribes of Israel would have to be added the two tribes of Judah, and the rest would be silence.

The new exiles, however, carried an elixir of life, an invisible baggage that was beyond the reach of the enemy or the attrition of time. It was the burden bequeathed by their unique past. All that is embraced in the word Torah—doctrine and creed, ritual and law, history and prophecy, memories and aspiration—had laid its indelible stamp upon them. The roots had struck too deep to be torn up by adversity or withered by prosperity. Teaching and experience had produced an integrated and tenacious spiritual personality.

Imbedded in it was a profound nostalgia for the homeland which one of the psalms has preserved with powerful poignancy:

By the rivers of Babylon,
There we sat down, yea, we wept,

When we remembered Zion.
Upon the willows in the midst thereof
We hanged up our harps
For there they that led us captive asked of us
words of song,
And our tormentors asked of us mirth:
"Sing us one of the songs of Zion."
How shall we sing the Lord's song
In a foreign land?
If I forget thee, O Jerusalem,
Let my right hand forget her cunning.
Let my tongue cleave to the roof of
my mouth,
If I remember thee not;
If I set not Jerusalem
Above my chiefest joy.

That sentiment was more than home longing: it was part and parcel of their faith, of the mission of holiness which Torah had laid upon them. For the land had been promised to Abraham's descendants, and only there could His house be built, only there could the Covenant be fulfilled. With the first step across the border was born the hope of restoration, and the name the exiles chose for themselves was "Mourners of Zion."

2

BUT even in the ruined homeland life was not wholly extinct. Shortly after the destruction of Jerusalem, a new center, small but promising, made its appearance in Mizpah, north of the former capital. Gedaliah, a man of wisdom and courage, was appointed by the Chaldeans as governor of those survivors whose unimportance had earned them exemption from exile. They were the old and the destitute, but others came and joined the feeble community, fugitives who slowly gained courage to come out from the caves and jungles. Jeremiah also came to Mizpah, eager to devote his remaining years to the work of reclamation.

But among those who returned were desperate men who had fought the Chaldeans and looked upon Gedaliah as a traitor. They had found refuge in Ammon, across the Jordan, and, it is thought, the king of that country instigated them to commit the bloody deed which extinguished the new promise. They slew the Chaldean garrison stationed at Mizpah as well as the governor, and the entire community, to escape the wrath of Nebuchadnezzar, fled into Egypt. The Fast of Gedaliah, on the day following the New Year festival, is still kept in memory of the governor's assassination.

To the sorrows of Jeremiah was now added the bitterness of exile in the land of his loathing. In Egypt the refugees found many of their countrymen who had gotten there before them: some of the earlier settlers even bore arms for the Pharaoh, and there was a Jewish military colony in the south defending Upper Egypt against incursions from Nubia. But Jeremiah had no happiness among his brethren in Egypt, for they remembered their own faith but dimly and, in spite of the prophet's appeals and warnings, clung to the idolatry of Egypt.

For the next two generations the main current of Jewish life, narrow though it was, flowed neither in Palestine nor in Egypt, but among the exiles in Babylonia.

3

IN BABYLONIA, it appears, the captives were permitted to live in large, well-knit communities, and perhaps they were joined by descendants of the northern exiles. They struck root in the agriculture, industry, and commerce of the land, and in time some among them acquired wealth, power, and influence.

The decades followed each other, the hope of immediate restoration dimmed, but the pious fervor of the Mourners of Zion did not diminish. A new institution, the synagogue, which centuries later became the model for the Christian church and Mohammedan mosque, sprang up among them. The synagogue may have been regarded at first as a temporary substitute for the Temple: prayer certainly became the substitute for sacrifice. But the new institution answered to a vital need; it spread and flourished, developing its own forms of organization and ritual. A new mode of worship came into existence consisting of prayer, devotion, and study. Thus an instrument was created to express the urge for collective communion, which is one of the roots of the religious impulse.

The synagogue, always virile and supple, became, like the tabernacle in the desert, the focus of Jewish life.

4

FOR thirty years after his conquest of little Judah, Nebuchadnezzar, who is remembered among men only because of that conquest, continued to reign over the Chaldean Empire. His death in 555 B.C.E. set off the usual Oriental byplay of intrigue, cabal, and palace revolution. His son Evil-merodach, who was brought down by assassins only two years after his accession, found time to release Jehoiachin from prison and show the former king of Judah special favor. Then came a few more inglorious reigns until there sat on the throne in Babylon a certain Nabonidus, who, having no taste for the court or the camp, left those things to his son Belshazzar.

In the meantime, the eastern world had become a prey to new convulsions. First the Medes, then the Persians threatened to upset its unstable equilibrium. Finally, Cyrus the Persian, a remarkably gifted conqueror and statesman, having brought the Medes under his sway, shattered an alliance which Babylonia, Lydia, and Egypt formed against him, and in 539 B.C.E. his united Medes and Persians laid siege to Babylon.

The Mourners of Zion saw the impending collapse of Chaldea with mingled hopes and fears. Nearly half a century had now elapsed since the fall of Judah, but in their hearts the longing for restoration was as keen as ever. What awaited them at the hands of the new master? Under Nabonidus their lot had grown worse: in place of liberation, which the ill-starred Evil-merodach had appeared to promise, there was suppression and persecution. Might not deliverance come from Cyrus the Persian?

5

THE mysterious force called prophecy, which for so many centuries had denied the seed of Abraham the "right" to be like the other nations, accompanied the captives into Babylonia. Two glorious figures stand out among the heirs of Elijah, Amos, and Isaiah in the Exile, the first being the priest Ezekiel who had been carried away with King Jehoiachin in 597 B.C.E., the other the

Great Unknown, whose utterances are believed to make up the latter part of the Book of Isaiah.

Ezekiel is a perfect blend of the God-intoxicated prophet and the pious priest. Like the other great prophets, Ezekiel denounces and consoles. He denounced the idolatry of which his first fellow-exiles were guilty, as well as their foolish expectations of speedy deliverance. But when the disaster of the year 586 B.C.E. came upon Judah, and the first exiles saw the new contingents who came to join them, Ezekiel, true to his name (God will strengthen), became the great strengthener and consoler. Now he prophesied restoration and the reunion of Israel with his God in holiness of life and purity of worship.

> For I will take you from among the nations, and gather you out of all the countries, and will bring you into your own land. And I will sprinkle clean water upon you, and ye shall be clean; from all your uncleannesses, and from all your idols, will I cleanse you. A new heart also will I give you, and a new spirit will I put within you; and I will take away the stony heart out of your flesh, and I will give you a heart of flesh. And I will put My spirit within you, and cause you to walk in My statutes, and ye shall keep Mine ordinances, and do them. And ye shall dwell in the land that I gave to your fathers; and ye shall be My people, and I will be your God.

And were the exiles skeptical of their future? Were they oppressed by a sense of guilt? Ezekiel proclaims the revolutionary doctrine of individual responsibility, removing from the children the moral taint of their fathers. The Lord will restore His people if only to vindicate His holy name among the nations. In his firm assurance, Ezekiel sees a new Temple rise up on the ruins of the old. He even prepared plans for the new structure with elaborate architectural detail. And to those who continued to doubt and despair, Ezekiel addressed the vision of the Valley of Dry Bones, a vision which has become the supreme symbol of rebirth and restoration. And this is the manner of Ezekiel's vision:

> The hand of the Lord was upon me, and the Lord carried me out in a spirit, and set me down in the midst of the valley,

and it was full of bones; and He caused me to pass by them round about, and, behold, there were very many in the open valley; and, lo, they were very dry. And He said unto me: "Son of man, can these bones live?" And I answered: "O Lord God, Thou knowest." Then He said unto me: "O, prophesy over these bones, and say unto them: 'O ye dry bones, hear the word of the Lord: Thus saith the Lord God unto these bones: Behold I will cause breath to enter into you, and ye shall live. And I will lay sinews upon you, and will bring up flesh upon you, and cover you with skin, and put breath in you, and ye shall live; and ye shall know that I am the Lord.' " So I prophesied as I was commanded; and as I prophesied, there was a noise, and behold a commotion, and the bones came together, bone to its bone. And I beheld, and, lo, there were sinews upon them, and flesh came up, and skin covered them above; but there was no breath in them. Then said He unto me: "Prophesy unto the breath, prophesy, son of man, and say to the breath: 'Thus said the Lord God: Come from the four winds, O breath, and breathe upon these slain, that they may live.' " So I prophesied as He commanded me, and the breath came into them, and they lived, and stood up upon their feet, an exceeding great host. Then He said unto me: "Son of man, these bones are the whole house of Israel; behold, they say: Our bones are dried up, and our hope is lost; we are clean cut off. Therefore prophesy, and say unto them: 'Thus saith the Lord God: Behold, I will open your graves, and cause you to come up out of your graves, O My people; and I will bring you into the land of Israel.' "

6

AS THE Babylonian Exile draws to a close, Israel's destiny is lighted up by the other prophetic luminary of whom nothing is known except the words in the Book of Isaiah that are attributed to him. He has been called the Second Isaiah, and the utterances ascribed to him lift the prophetic line to a summit of dazzling splendor.

The universalist outlook, apparent in prophecy from the beginning, finds in this seer its most brilliant expression. The God of Israel is the God of all the nations; His temple shall be a "house of prayer for all peoples"; Israel redeemed shall bring redemption to all mankind.

Look unto Me, and be ye saved,
All the ends of the earth;
For I am God, and there is none else.
By Myself have I sworn,
The word is gone forth from My mouth
in righteousness,
And shall not come back,
That unto Me every knee shall bow,
Every tongue shall swear.

But the immediate task of the prophet is to comfort and inspire the exiles, and he does it in words that have brought consolation to the exiles of all times:

Comfort ye, comfort ye My people,
Saith your God.
Bid Jerusalem take heart,
And proclaim unto her,
That her time of service is accomplished,
That her guilt is paid off;
That she hath received of the Lord's hand
Double for all her sins.
Hark! one calleth:
"Clear ye in the wilderness the way of the Lord,
Make plain in the desert
A highway for our God.
Every valley shall be lifted up,
And every mountain and hill shall be made low;
And the rugged shall be made level,
And the rough places a plain;
And the glory of the Lord shall be revealed,
And all flesh shall see it together;
For the mouth of the Lord hath spoken it."

Like the other Mourners of Zion, the great prophet looked toward the horizon where the star of Cyrus the Persian was steadily rising.

CHAPTER FOURTEEN

Restoration

In the forty-seventh year of the captivity (539 B.C.E.), proud Babylon fell to the Persians and Medes, and the mighty empire of Nebuchadnezzar went the way of Assyria. The night before the city fell, the prince Belshazzar, we are told, was feasting in the royal palace when a mysterious hand appeared and wrote upon the wall the strange words: *mene mene tekel upharsin.* These words a young Hebrew captive named Daniel interpreted to mean: "Thou art weighed in the balance and art found wanting. Thy kingdom is divided and given to the Medes and Persians."

The people of Babylon, Cyrus relates, welcomed him, and the city was his "without fighting and battle." The rest of the empire was also his, including the little land on the Mediterranean toward which the Mourners of Zion looked with so much longing.

A year later their hope became a reality: the new ruler put an end to their captivity in a proclamation which permitted the exiles to return and rebuild the Temple. This was the great King's Declaration as recorded in the Book of Ezra:

> All the kingdoms of the earth hath the Lord, the God of Heaven given me; and He hath charged me to build Him a house in Jerusalem, which is in Judah. Whosoever there is among you of all His people—his God be with him—let him go up to Jerusalem, which is in Judah, and build the house of the Lord, the God of Israel; He is the God who is in Jerusalem. And whosoever is left, in any place where he sojourneth, let the men of his place help him with silver, and

with gold, and with goods, and with beasts, beside the free-will-offering for the house of God which is in Jerusalem.

Rarely do the favor of kings spring from pure benevolence: Cyrus, no doubt, weighed the advantages of having a grateful and loyal community on the road to Egypt, a road which, sooner or later, he or his successors were bound to follow. The declaration recorded by Ezra, however, is in accord with the general policy of the Persian conqueror. "The gods dwelling within them [the cities of Chaldea]," he writes on his famous Cylinder, discovered in Babylon, "I returned to their homes, and caused eternal shrines to be built. All their people I collected and restored to their homes."

2

FROM all over the Captivity the Mourners of Zion gathered in Babylon for the journey back to the homeland. The first contingent of returning captives, as recorded in the Book of Ezra, numbered 42,360, "besides their menservants and their maidservants." Escorted by a Persian military guard, and bearing with them the sacred vessels of the Temple which Nebuchadnezzar had plundered, the returning remnant retraced the road of exile and at length beheld the ruined site where Jerusalem once stood in her glory. But all sorrow was swept away in a transport of joy. A psalmist sang:

When the Lord brought back those that returned to Zion,
We were like unto them that dream.
Then was our mouth filled with laughter,
And our tongue with singing.

Under the leadership of Sheshbazzar, a son of Jehoiachin, they took possession of Jerusalem and a small area around it, divided the land among the clans, and began the labor of building a new life on the harsh and neglected soil. They also found themselves ringed about with enemies. The ancient foes were all there, astonished and alarmed at the reappearance of the nation which they thought had been destroyed. There were the Moabites and the Ammonites on the east, the Edomites on the south, the Philistines on the west. On the north, moreover, a new and peculiar enemy had come into existence. In Samaria, once the capital of the Kingdom of Israel, which the Assyrians had colonized with strangers, a mingling of race and religion had taken place between the remaining Israelites and the newcomers. The Samaritans, as the product of this mixture became known, felt that they were true heirs of the Hebrew tradition. They welcomed the exiles and desired to share in the rebuilding of the Temple, but the returned captives found them unqualified for partnership and rejected them.

Spurned affection turned into hatred, and the Samaritans became the bitterest enemy of all. For twenty-five years their intrigues with the Persian officials, before whom they charged the Jewish community with aiming at revolt and independence, prevented the rebuilding of the Temple.

In the meantime, Cyrus died and the Persian Empire went through a series of violent convulsions. Usurpation and rebellion threatened to undo all that Cyrus had accomplished. Peace was finally restored by Darius, a member of a younger branch of the royal family. In Jerusalem, as in the rest of the far-flung empire, events were watched with anxiety and hope. Zerubbabel, a grandson of Jehoiachin, now headed the community, with Jeshua, who traced his descent from the last high priest, exercising the priestly functions. Hopes of independence may have stirred in the governor's heart, but they were checked by the priest. The Persian master, suspicious of Zerubbabel's intentions, decreed that the higher authority should be vested in the priest, a decree which fixed the political constitution of the Jewish community for several centuries.

At length, in 515 B.C.E., the Second Temple was rebuilt. A direct appeal to Darius and to the Declaration of Cyrus overcame the machinations of the Samaritans and their allies. Darius proved himself as magnanimous as his predecessor, ordering that the taxes paid by the Jews should be applied to the rebuilding of the sanctuary. The dedication, which occurred on the Passover of that year, was celebrated with solemn and moving rites. Hearts were stirred by old memories and uplifted with new hopes. The symbol of their national life stood again on Mount Zion.

3

LIKE an island in a stormy sea, the new community lay amid the foes that surrounded it, and completion of the Temple became the signal for new hostilities. The embittered Samaritans retaliated by building a temple of their own on Mount Gerizim. Nor did they cease their accusations before the Persian authorities, and the calumnies were not without effect: the Persian officials denied the Jews permission to build a wall around Jerusalem, and the city was almost defenseless against the raids of its enemies.

Nor did the inner life of the community develop in a manner to satisfy the disciples of Ezekiel. In the ritual sphere there was much to be desired, especially with regard to the observance of the Sabbath and the Temple sacrifices. Moreover, the ancient social inequalities reappeared, with the poor receiving scant mercy from the rich, who violated the safeguards which the Mosaic Code prescribed for the protection of the unfortunate and the needy.

Furthermore, as the years passed, a new menace rose up against the community. In the crucible of time old enmities began to dissolve; gradually better relations arose between the Jews and their neighbors, and with religion interposing only feeble opposition, the inevitable consequence was intermarriage. Even Samaritan wives were not rejected by the grandchildren and great-grandchildren of the returned exiles. Naturally, the offspring of such unions spoke the language of the foreign mothers and were taught the worship of foreign gods. Again the little community stood on the brink of dissolution.

4

JUDEA was saved by the indomitable will and resolution of Ezra the Scribe. Ezra came from Babylonia, with authority from the reigning emperor to govern the Jewish community according to the law of Moses. He was apparently a personage of high standing in the court, for the Persian ruler not only showered him with gifts for the Temple, but permitted him to lead back to the homeland a new and large group of exiles.

In 458 B.C.E., eighty years after the arrival of the first contingent under Sheshbazzar, Ezra, with several thousand followers, came to

Jerusalem. His appearance was a great event, but he was dismayed by the prevailing religious indifference. For Ezra's primary interest was to reestablish the ancient faith in Judea.

At a large gathering of the people which he assembled in Jerusalem he branded intermarriage as the worst of the evils that flourished in the community. He proceeded to apply heroic measures, calling upon the men to divorce their foreign wives. "As thou hast said, so it is for us to do," they answered.

The drastic decree, which no doubt saved the struggling community from extinction, was duly enforced by a tribunal headed by the new governor, and the foreign wives were divorced. But this action brought a recrudescence of all the ancient animosities. Again Jerusalem was attacked by the neighboring nations. Bands of Samaritans led by the crafty Sanballat, Ammonites led by Tobiah, and other enemies as well, raided the open city. Thereupon Ezra set out to rebuild the walls of Jerusalem. But the grant of power under which he governed gave him no authority to fortify the city. Again their enemies accused the Jews of planning rebellion, and Ezra was forced to desist. His prestige declined, the old evils raised their heads, and all his labor seemed lost.

5

IN THE apathy and stagnation that followed, there suddenly appeared a new leader who poured a fresh wave of energy into the community. He was Nehemiah son of Hacaliah and cupbearer to the Persian emperor in Shushan, the imperial capital. On being told that the Holy City lay helpless in the face of its enemies, Nehemiah's heart was fired with indignation and resolve. The emperor, whose favor he enjoyed, conferred upon him the powers of governor, with authority to rebuild the city's defenses. Escorted by a military guard and accompanied by numerous followers, Nehemiah, in the summer of 445 B.C.E., presented himself to the startled inhabitants of Jerusalem.

The people flocked to his standard. "Let us rise up and build!" they cried. In an incredibly short time, and in spite of all that Sanballat and Tobiah could do to prevent them, they raised the city's walls, making it secure against sudden attack. In a graphic account of his mission, Nehemiah reports the measures he took to foil the enemy:

> And it came to pass from that time forth, that half of my servants wrought in the work, and half of them held the spears, the shields, and the bows, and the coats of mail; and the rulers were behind all the house of Judah. They that builded the wall and they that bore burdens laded themselves; every one with one of his hands wrought in the work, and with the other held his weapon; and the builders, every one had his sword girded by his side, and so builded. And he that sounded the horn was by me. And I said unto the nobles, and to the rulers and to the rest of the people: "The work is great and large, and we are separated upon the wall, one far from another; in what place soever ye hear the sound of the horn, resort ye thither unto us; our God will fight for us." So we wrought in the work; and the half of them held the spears from the rising of the morning till the stars appeared.

Having fortified the city, Nehemiah turned his attention to the internal affairs of the community. He was particularly incensed at the exploitation of the poor by the rich. Many a destitute husbandman had been compelled to put his possessions and even his children in pawn. Nehemiah called upon the rich to make restitution and they answered: "So we will do, even as thou sayest," a promise which they actually kept. A spirit of solemn exaltation took possession of the restored community. It seemed ripe for full acceptance of the Torah way of life.

Ezra the Scribe now came forward and resumed his labors, he and Nehemiah working in loyal partnership for the preservation of people and faith. In the festival month of Tishri, 445 B.C.E., the leaders convoked a Great Assembly (*Keneset Hagedolah*) where Ezra read and expounded the Torah and a covenant was signed by the heads of families who bound themselves to its observance. In particular, they agreed to ban intermarriage, hold sacred the Sabbath and festivals, maintain the priests and Levites, and observe the sabbatical year. The ancient constitution was thus reaffirmed and amplified into living laws.

CHAPTER FIFTEEN

The Life and the Book

THE foundations of the Second Commonwealth were now laid: at last the community was free from the shame of helpless exposure to hostile neighbors and from the danger of dissolution by intermarriage. It proceeded now to embody its unique tradition of spirit and law in institutions and ways of life that have, down to our own times, withstood the onslaughts of a thousand enemies.

But the victories of Ezra and Nehemiah did not remain unchallenged: like all precious possessions, their retention demanded eternal vigilance. Nehemiah, thinking his mission fulfilled, returned to his duties in the imperial household at Shushan. But reports soon reached him that brought him back to Jerusalem in haste. The ban on intermarriage was being violated. Manasseh, grandson of the high priest himself, was among the guilty: he had married a daughter of the Samaritan chief Sanballat. Nehemiah acted with characteristic sternness: he exiled the delinquents from the city. Manasseh fled to Shechem where he was elevated to the priesthood of the temple which the Samaritans had built on Mount Gerizim to rival the sanctuary that stood on Zion.

2

CONCERNING the following century and more, the meager records from which we glean our knowledge of the Second Commonwealth are altogether silent. Apparently no startling events came to disturb the current of its life. The period, therefore, was well adapted for social and spiritual consolidation.

The records speak again, briefly and in the hazy voice of legend, when a young conqueror from the West swept through Asia Minor and overthrew the Persian Empire. For, until the Battle of

Arbela in 331 B.C.E., when Alexander the Great overcame the hosts of Darius III, the empire established by Cyrus in 539 B.C.E. stood firm.

Another record, moreover, the Book of Esther, reveals that, besides the community in Palestine, the Jews already formed a Diaspora that extended through the length and breadth of the empire. Some twenty-three centuries have passed since the days of Esther and Mordecai, but the tale of peril and deliverance, of malicious intrigue and steadfast courage, has a strangely familiar ring. Haman has become a stock character in dramas that were still to be enacted, and the Feast of Purim* which celebrates his downfall has provided a measure of comfort in the face of his numerous descendants. Ahasuerus, the bibulous and amorous monarch whom Haman sought to manipulate, was probably Artaxerxes II who reigned between 404 and 358 B.C.E.

In the vast empire, little Judea lived its own self-contained life. The suzerainty of Persia did not weigh heavily upon it. The Persian governor collected the taxes for his master and kept a watchful eye for rebellious intrigue that might emanate from Egypt or other quarters. The internal life of the community was free to follow its own course.

It was a rich and intense life, cast into forms to which the people became passionately attached. Nor was it a static life which the Jews developed, for notwithstanding its fixed devotion to certain fundamentals, like the Oneness of God and the ideal of holiness, it was essentially flexible and progressive. The Torah was like a living tree, its roots sunk deep in the soil of basic faith, but always striking out new branches. The weaving of the fabric of Oral Law and legend had been long in progress, its beginnings going back to the First Commonwealth, back even to the very promulgation of the written code; and this tradition was always at work, interpreting and adapting, illuminating and molding, building a "fence around the Torah," a fortress of the spirit against the days of trial that were to follow.

* The name is derived from the Persian *pur* meaning "lot." The fourteenth day of Adar, the day fixed for the destruction of the Jews, was determined by Haman by casting lots.

3

THE political headship of the community continued to be vested in the high priest, and this union in one person of the secular and sacerdotal powers prevented the tension and conflict which their separation nearly always engendered. The high priest, however, notwithstanding the solemn and divine sanctions under which he exercised his functions, was far from possessing unlimited authority. His powers were circumscribed by the Sanhedrin, a body of seventy-one notables and sages, with the high priest, as a rule, the presiding officer.

The Sanhedrin had its origin in the Great Assembly (*Keneset Hagedolah*) convoked in 445 B.C.E. by Ezra and Nehemiah; some trace its beginnings further back to the "seventy men of the Elders of Israel," whom Moses was commanded to choose "to bear the burden of the people with him." It was at once a legislative and judicial body. From it emanated decisions that established laws and precedents. The general temper of this tribunal is illustrated by the treatment it meted out to defendants charged with capital crimes. So manifold were the safeguards with which the accused was surrounded that a Sanhedrin which, in the course of its life, imposed the death penalty on more than one person, achieved the unenvied appellation of "the bloody court."

For purposes of local government, small councils or courts came into existence, consisting as a rule of seven men, "the seven worthies of the town" as they came to be called; while in the larger towns "little Sanhedrins" of twenty-three members arose, modeled upon the national Sanhedrin in Jerusalem.

It was a simple and wholesome life which the Sanhedrins, national and local, were called upon to govern. Agriculture continued to be its economic basis. In field and fruit grove, in pasture and vineyard, God's power was seen in the periodic renewal of life, and the people testified to this vision in daily prayers to Him "Who in His mercy giveth light unto the earth and unto them that dwell thereon, and in His goodness reneweth every day continually the deeds of creation." Again the hard soil of Judea blossomed like the rose. The hills became terraced with vineyards and groves of fig trees and olives, the fields gave bountiful harvests of grain, the pastures nourished flocks of sheep and cattle. Every seventh year, the pious farmers observed "the sabbath of the soil" when the fields lay fallow.

In the cities and towns, where life was more complex, many crafts were plied by artisans, and commerce too had its place in the economy of the land. For Palestine was still the highway between the people of the Nile and those of the Two Rivers, and it is the way of men that when they do not fight they trade.

Thus the economy of the new Commonwealth was essentially like that of the neighboring lands or those beyond the sea. In one important respect, however, it was different. In other lands, notably in Greece and Rome, slavery was an essential part of the economic system. To the philosophers of those lands slavery was indispensable for the ideal human society: in their Utopias, human labor is the labor of slaves. In the Jewish Commonwealth, that evil institution, pernicious alike to master and slave, gradually disappeared, primarily because in the law of Moses it found not sanction but reprobation. The Commonwealth became a society of free men, equal before God, equal before the law by which they lived. Labor became not a token of degradation, but a patent of nobility.

In order to live and flourish, this society of free men had to know the Torah and be deeply attached to it. Reason united with instinct to make learning and popular education the cornerstone of the Commonwealth. Learning was the principal qualification for honor and public preferment. Every place of worship became also a school for the young; the teachers were the *soferim* or scribes, who taught and transcribed the Book, making it accessible to the people.

In the synagogues, successive portions of the Five Books of Moses, called Sidrahs, were read on the Sabbath, and smaller portions on Mondays and Thursdays, when the farmers came to town with their produce. On the Sabbath, portions of the Prophets known as Haftorot or "conclusions," were added. By the process known as Midrash, or interpretation, the sacred text was elaborated and illumined; and since the Aramaic tongue had displaced the

Hebrew as the general language of intercourse, the reading of the portions on the Sabbath was supplemented by an Aramaic translation called Targum.

That remarkable institution, the synagogue, was alike the religious, the educational, and the communal center of each locality. It was the *Bet Tefillah*, or House of Prayer, the *Bet Hamidrash* (House of Study), and the *Bet Hakeneset* (House of Assembly). Three times daily, corresponding to the services of song and sacrifice in the Temple, the synagogue was the scene of public worship by prayer. The order of prayer became fixed, affording sustenance to the deepest human emotions: love and hope, veneration and ecstasy.

No picture of the life of the Second Commonwealth, however cursory, can omit the Sabbaths and festivals. The Sabbath rested men from toil and replenished their souls. The festivals, especially the three pilgrimage festivals, brought days filled with glamour and rejoicing. The boundaries of the Commonwealth were narrow enough to permit the farmers who lived within them, and many who lived without, to repair to Jerusalem on Passover, Shabuoth, and Sukkoth, bearing the fruit of their toil for the Temple and its ministers. The roads were thronged with pilgrims; the city resounded with jubilation; the courts of the Temple echoed with praise and thanksgiving.

4

UNDERLYING and shaping this unique life was the Book in which the nation had stored its experiences, its thoughts, and its longings. So dominant a role has this Book played in the career of the Jews and in that of a great portion of mankind in general, that the people who created it are often called the People of the Book, and the leading nations of the world have found in it guidance, inspiration, and delight. It moves men profoundly by the surge of passion and lofty aspiration that throb in its pages; the Book has been the most potent influence in the art of the medieval and modern world: in architecture, sculpture, and painting; in music, poetry, and the drama. In it men find the ideals of justice, love, and peace exalted not only as individual virtues, but as the essentials of social order.*

It was during the Second Commonwealth that this Book, which is really a collection of books, took definite form. Every mode of literary expression is represented in it: history and law, homily and philosophy, prophecy and psalms, prose and poetry. The books of the Hebrew Scriptures, twenty-four in number, are divided into three groups of which the first is called the Torah. Now the word "Torah" is applied also to the Book as a whole and to the vast system of law and lore which resulted from its interpretation. But the Pentateuch, or Five Books of Moses, are *the* Torah, for their authorship is ascribed to Moses, who was not only the great emancipator and the first among the prophets, but also the inspired lawgiver.

After Torah comes the division called Nebiim, or Prophets. Nebiim contains eight books of which the first four, Joshua, Judges, Samuel, and Kings are narratives, telling the story of the Hebrew nation from the death of Moses to the downfall of the First Commonwealth. The remaining four books record the actual words and some of the deeds of fifteen prophets. Three of them, Isaiah, Jeremiah, and Ezekiel, because of the volume of their recorded utterances, are called the Major Prophets, and the remaining twelve, among whom are the great poets and moralists Hosea, Amos, Jonah, Micah, and Nahum, only because of the meagerness of the record, are known as the Minor Prophets.

In the third division of the Hebrew Scriptures, called Ketubim, or Writings, there are twelve books. As set down in the Hebrew canon,† they are: Psalms, Proverbs, Job, Song of Songs, Ruth, Lamentations, Ecclesiastes, Esther, Daniel, Ezra, Nehemiah, and Chronicles. Ketubim, as these titles indicate, is extremely diversified. It includes history and prophecy, poetry, philosophy, and even

* "The Bible has been the Magna Charta of the poor and the oppressed; down to modern times no state has had a constitution in which the interests of the people are so largely taken into account, in which the duties so much more than the privileges of the rulers are insisted upon, as that drawn up for Israel in Deuteronomy and in Leviticus." Thomas H. Huxley (1825-1895).

† "Canon" means order or arrangement. The Christian canon differs in a number of ways from the Jewish.

drama, the Book of Job having been found to follow in the main the dramatic form. The Song of Songs, Ruth, Lamentations, Ecclesiastes, and Esther are the Five Megillot, or Scrolls. The Song of Songs, comprising the most exquisite love songs in any literature, and interpreted by the Orthodox as an allegory of the love between God and Israel, is read in synagogues on Passover. Ruth, that enchanting idyll of field and harvest, is read on Shabuoth. Lamentations is a dirge for the destruction of the Temple and is chanted on the Fast of the Ninth of Ab. Ecclesiastes, consisting of the broodings of a pessimistic moralist, is read on Tabernacles, perhaps to temper the high joy of the festival. Esther, which relates the story of Purim, is of course read on that feast. Esther is the "Megillah" *par excellence.* Unless another of the five is indicated, "Megillah" is taken to mean the Book of Esther.

The compilation of the canon, not to speak of the actual composition of the books, was the work not of years but of centuries. The art of writing, as we have seen, was known even to the generation of the Exodus, and events were probably recorded when, or shortly after, they occurred. Nor are the books that make up the canon the only ones that sought admittance into the sacred fraternity. Others applied but were not admitted. Some of those rejected make up a compilation of their own under the name of Apocrypha, derived from a Greek word meaning "hidden," since those books were believed to contain secret meanings.

Who were the authors of the books that make up the Hebrew Scriptures? Tradition answers the question about each of them and answers it with assurance. The author of the Pentateuch, for example, was Moses. Most, though not all of the books whose titles are the names of persons such as Joshua, Samuel, Jeremiah, and Isaiah, were written by those persons. Psalms is the work of David; Proverbs, the Song of Songs, and Ecclesiastes that of Solomon. Other books, among them Esther and Daniel, are ascribed to the "men of the *Keneset Hagedolah,*" or Great Assembly.

In recent times, however, certain scholars, the so-called "higher critics," have rejected the answers given by tradition. Having subjected the text of the Bible to microscopic analysis, they have declared it to be a blending of a number of literary streams which, before being channeled into writing, flowed by word of mouth down the generations among the people. With the recent discovery, however, that the art of writing must have existed among the Hebrews even in Egypt, that hypothesis has lost one of its chief supports. An even more important prop for that theory was found in the different names of God which occur in the Pentateuch, the use of different names being ascribed to different authors. But that hypothesis, too, was badly shaken when it was shown to be based on a misapprehension of the passage—Exodus VI, 3—which served as its starting point. The "higher critics" have been eagerly preoccupied with precise dates, exact authorship, and linguistic problems, but of much greater importance to men are the beauty, the holiness and the inspiration which they find in the Sacred Scriptures.

CHAPTER SIXTEEN

Greek Dominion

JUDEA was a mere mite in the vast realms which Alexander the Macedonian gathered beneath his scepter. For to Greece, Macedonia, and Thrace in Europe; to Asia Minor, Syria and Palestine in Asia; and to Egypt in Africa, he added Mesopotamia and the unbounded regions stretching east along the Caspian Sea and the Indian Ocean as far as the River Indus. Never before in recorded history had an empire so immense been assembled. And only little more than a decade elapsed between the day when the twenty-three-year-old Alexander crossed the Hellespont and the day in June, 323 B.C.E., when he died.

But rapid as the conquest had been, the dissolution of Alexander's empire, which began immediately after his death, was still more rapid. His leading generals seized different portions of it and fought over them like wolves. The provinces of the former Persian Empire became the prey of three of the generals until a battle fought at Ipsus in Asia Minor in 301 B.C.E. reduced the number of rivals to two. Four years earlier, one of the two, whose principal domain was Egypt, had proclaimed himself ruler of that land with the title of Ptolemy I. The other, who claimed sovereignty over the rest of the former Persian Empire, was Seleucus. Ptolemy's capital was Alexandria, a city which the great conqueror had built at one of the mouths of the Nile. The capital of Seleucus was Antioch, a city on the River Orontes in Syria, which Seleucus had built and named in honor of his father Antiochus.

There were Jewish communities in both capitals; the one in Alexandria was particularly large and influential. It was not long before Alexandria became the chief center of commerce and culture on the Mediterranean, with the Jews playing a leading part in both spheres. Antioch strove hard to rival Alexandria and, by granting the Jews equal rights, Seleucus induced thousands of them to settle there.

The Jewish Diaspora, or Dispersion, had in fact begun long before and was steadily expanding. In Egypt, for example, there existed a Jewish military colony at Elephantine or Yeb as far back as the Persian period. It may have begun even before the fall of Jerusalem in 586 B.C.E. Letters have been discovered which members of this colony, bearing such names as Jonathan, Azariah, and Hosea, addressed to each other, as well as the copy of a letter of complaint against certain Egyptians, which the high priest of the Jewish Temple in "Yeb the fortress" addressed to Bogoas the Persian governor of Judea in 407 B.C.E. In this letter mention is made of "Jehohanan the high priest of Jerusalem" and of "Sanballat, governor of Samaria." To Egypt and Syria should be added Babylonia, where Jewish communities had their origins in the deportations of Sargon and Nebuchadnezzar.

2

THE hostility between the Seleucids, as the Syrian rulers came to be called, and the Egyptian Ptolemies went further than the rivalry between their capitals. The two heirs of Alexander and their successors found it impossible to divide the inheritance peacefully. And between them lay Judea, intent on its own life, indifferent as to which of them was the suzerain, but condemned to bear the brunt of their collisions.

As early as 318 B.C.E., only five years after the death of Alexander, Ptolemy stormed Jerusalem and took many of the people captive into Egypt. He assaulted the holy city on a Sabbath and met with no resistance: the use of weapons on the sacred day was forbidden to the Jews.

Through the greater part of the century that followed the Battle of Ipsus, Palestine was held by the Ptolemies. But, by war or diplomacy, every Seleucid ruler attempted to add the little land to his dominions. It changed hands several times until in 198 B.C.E., at the Battle of Panion, the Seleucid ruler Antiochus III, called the Great, overwhelmed the forces of Egypt, and the destiny of the Jewish nation became linked with the rulers of the north.

3

EGYPT and Syria had many scores to settle, but in the vital matter of culture and way of life, they were essentially at one. For Alexander the Great had conquered not only the cities and fortresses of the nations, but their spirit as well. They succumbed to the culture of the conqueror even more promptly and much more permanently than to his arms.

It was the civilization of the Greeks, known as Hellenism, which thus became the prevailing mode and fashion of the eastern world. It was a brilliant civilization which, over a period of a thousand years, the city-states of Hellas or Greece, with Athens in the lead, had brought to perfection. This culture was a complete expression of the spirit of paganism, the spirit that revels in the joy of life and the exercise of power, that sees the entire universe of nature and man as a blind interplay of ruthless forces, that knows no higher law than the struggle for existence and the survival of the fittest.

It was destined that this spirit should find as its leading exponents a remarkably gifted people. For the Greeks, or Hellenes, as they preferred to call themselves, contrary to other pagans, ancient and modern, knew how to embody this outlook on life into institutions and works of such power and fascination that their attraction is still potent in the world of today. Indeed, according to many of its pundits, the legacy of Greece is the most important element in modern civilization.

In the ancient world, at any rate, Hellenism had no difficulty in establishing its empire over nations and men. It came to them clad in all the graces of the plastic arts, of sculpture and architecture, of painting and craftsmanship. It spoke to them in the subtle music of abstract sound and in the lofty or intimate strains of passionate verse. It lured them with bold excursions of the intellect into new worlds of speculation and science. It summoned them to cultivate all their faculties of mind and body in libraries and museums, in theatres and athletic contests. It gave sanction and license to the clamorous urge of the instincts for self-assertion and self-indulgence.

Moreover, hand in hand with these lures and gifts went a religion which the nations found no difficulty in assimilating to their own. Like their own, it was a profuse polytheism that deified the phenomena and forces of nature. Sky, earth, and sea; sun and stars; fields, forests, and fountains—all had their tutelary deities; and there were divinities who presided over the forces that move in nature and man, over storm and thunder, fate and death, the arts of war and peace, with emphasis always on the forces of procreation.

In this assemblage of Greek gods and goddesses, demigods and demons, there existed a measure of organization, for they all acknowledged the supremacy of Zeus the Thunderer. But Zeus is a genial and indulgent master, himself rather lax and irresponsible, occupied with numerous amours in which beautiful mortals and goddesses figure promiscuously; and his subordinates exhibit the same proclivities, imposing their capricious will upon men with little regard for considerations of right and wrong.

The nations of the East accepted these divinities, admitted them into their own pantheons, and recognized in most of them familiar spirits. To the worshippers of Baal the transition to Jove presented no serious obstacle. They entered with enthusiasm into the bacchanalian mysteries of Dionysus, the dissolute god of wine whose wanton feasts were celebrated with drunkenness and debauchery. And as for Aphrodite, the goddess of love, she had been worshipped under the name of Astarte from time immemorial, and the lewd rites of her priests and priestesses were prevalent throughout the East.

4

THERE was one people, however, and only one, which resisted resolutely the refinements and depravities with which Hellenism beguiled the nations. Every instinct of the Jews, every tradition, belief, and institution rebelled against it. How could the sublime conception of the One God who transcends and rules the universe of nature make peace with a multitude of divinities who were themselves the slaves of nature? In a world controlled by those gods, purity and justice, the stern law of the God of the Hebrews, was impossible. Holiness, or the elevation of man to the plane of spirit, was a thing undreamed-of. Man's eternal soul was unrecognized, his individual worth and dignity denied, cruelty and torture flourished, and slavery was the basic institution of society.

Nor could the graces and seductions of Hellenism be harmonized with the teachings of Torah. The beauty that appeals only, or primarily, to the senses was met with profound distrust. The statues of the Greeks were incitations to idolatry: they vindicated the ban which the Decalogue pronounced against graven images. The Greek enthusiasm for bodily prowess was childish and frivolous and, moreover, it went hand in hand with shameless immodesty. The Greek theatre was a nest of lewdness, or a forum for doctrines that denied the justice of God. And even the wisdom of Hellenism, its philosophy, poetry, and science, was regarded with suspicion. For what did this poetry celebrate but the exploits and crimes of the Greek gods and heroes? To a people steeped in the passionate pity of the prophets and the God-hunger of the psalmists, the blood-lusty chants of Homer were nothing but blasphemy. In the name of Greek science, human beings—condemned criminals, but still human beings—were undergoing vivisection. And as for Greek philosophy, it was, as the later Jewish sages expressed it, a plant that "bears flowers but no fruit."

What was to happen when the two antagonists, Judaism and Hellenism, would come to grips?

5

FOR a period of four or five generations the antagonists lived side by side, measuring each other, as it were, without coming to grips. Neither the Ptolemies nor the Seleucids attempted during that period to impose the religion and culture of Hellenism upon the Jews. Changes of suzerainty meant little to this people whose rich and peculiar life continued to flourish under one political domination or another.

It was natural, of course, that in the Jewish communities outside Palestine, living as they did in close relations with Greeks and Hellenized Egyptians or Syrians, the opportunity as well as the practical necessity of adopting the Greek language and customs should arise much sooner than in the homeland. Among the Jews of Alexandria, for example, the Greek language had, as early as the reign of Ptolemy II (285-247 B.C.E.), replaced the sacred Hebrew and the Aramaic vernacular to such an extent that the leaders of the community felt the need for a Greek translation of the Torah. Accordingly, the famous translation known as the Septuagint came into existence.

The circumstances surrounding the production of the Septuagint, its name derived from a Greek word meaning seventy, are shrouded in legend, and according to one account the Egyptian ruler invited Eleazar, the Jewish high priest, to send seventy or seventy-two scholars to Alexandria to perform the task. The scholars worked separately, but when their translations were compared they were found to be miraculously identical! The early history, laws, and concepts of the Hebrews were now open to the Greek mind and, no doubt, a desire on the part of the Jews in Alexandria to reveal the excellencies of their faith and laws to their neighbors figured in the enterprise.

6

AGAINST Judea itself, guarded by the watchful zeal of the High Priest and Sanhedrin, the waves of Hellenism beat in vain. The records of those generations continue to be vague and meager; the only eminent personality disclosed is that of the high priest Simon the Just who held office about the year 300 B.C.E. Simon may have been the high priest who, at the head of a solemn retinue, met Alexander the Great outside the walls of Jerusalem. The records reveal that Simon was a man of courage as well as wisdom and gentleness. He repaired the Temple, strengthened the defenses of the city, and improved its water supply. To him is attributed the following saying: "The world is upheld by three things: Torah, worship, and good deeds."

Simon was succeeded in the office of high priest by his son Onias II. But a nephew of Onias, the bold and crafty Joseph, found an opportunity to discredit his uncle and ingratiate himself with the Egyptian sovereign Ptolemy III (247-221 B.C.E.). Onias was not blameless: he had joined a pro-Seleucid party in Jerusalem which aimed to repudiate the suzerainty of Egypt. Joseph denounced Onias, and Ptolemy rewarded the informer with the lucrative post of taxgatherer for his northern province, which included Judea.

When Joseph died, his place and prestige fell to his youngest son Hyrcanus, whose brothers before long found an opportunity to satisfy their natural resentment. About 200 B.C.E., when the insatiable Antiochus III appeared before Jerusalem, they opened the gates of the city to the Syrians. Shortly afterwards, the Egyptians succeeded in recovering the city, but in 198 B.C.E. came the Battle of Panion and the final victory of the Seleucid. Hyrcanus, however, was not abandoned by his Egyptian patron: he was made taxgatherer of a region in Transjordania which continued under Egyptian sovereignty.

7

THE close relations which Joseph and his son were compelled to maintain with the court of the Ptolemies, as well as their natural zeal to please their sovereigns, led them to embrace the fashions and customs of their masters. With the weakening of moral fiber that often accompanies great wealth, they, as well as their agents, yielded to the lure of the Greek way, and Judea itself began to be inundated by the ever-advancing tide of Hellenism. Nor were they and their satellites the only carriers of the germs in Judea. The government officials in Jerusalem, the merchants who traded with Syria, Egypt, and other lands, as well as the Jews who were domiciled in foreign parts and made pilgrimages to the Holy City, became the conscious or unconscious agents of Hellenism.

There was, of course, no suggestion of religious apostasy in their attitude, but the Hellenists, as the Jewish admirers of the foreign culture may be called, saw no good reason for rejecting the art and wisdom, as well as the adornments and amenities, of Greek life. Gradually they brought into their homes the Greek banquet, with its music and dancing. They Hellenized their Hebrew names: Joshua became Jason, or Jesus, Choni became Menelaus, and Jakim was changed to Alcimus. They taught their children the Greek language and Greek sports. The cynosure that drew their gaze was no longer Sinai but the Acropolis of Athens. They wanted nothing better than to disappear in the huge Hellenistic melting-pot which the entire East had become.

Numerically, however, the Hellenists were a minor portion of the nation. The great majority clung to Torah and *mitzvot*. The laborers and craftsmen of the cities, the peasants of the countryside, the humble priests and Levites, the *soferim* or scribes—all looked upon Hellenism with profound misgivings. They formed a party in opposition to it, and called themselves Chassidim or pietists. The Chassidim despised the postures and pretensions of the Hellenists and suspected their loyalty to the faith of Israel. Beneath the elegant veneer of art and poetry and philosophy, the Chassidim discerned the same greeds and lusts, the same cruelties and superstitions against which the prophets had thundered and which the laws of Moses were designed to eradicate. A synthesis of Judaism, which affirmed the existence of absolute moral law, and of Hellenism which denied it, seemed to them impossible.

In the great outer world of intrigue and conflict by which Judea was surrounded, as well as within the little Commonwealth itself, the lines were being drawn for one of the decisive struggles in the history of humanity.

8

AT THE Battle of Magnesia in Asia Minor, fought in 190 B.C.E., only eight years after his victory at Panion, the triumphant career of Antiochus the Great was brought to a disastrous close by Rome, the great western power that was now reaching out its tentacles to the East. The victors compelled Antiochus to send his young son, who bore his father's name, as a hostage to Rome. Three years later Antiochus the Great died, and for eleven years another son held his throne as Seleucus IV. Then Seleucus was murdered by his treasurer Heliodorus, who is better known for an unsuccessful attempt he made to rob the Temple at Jerusalem.

Now came the turn of young Antiochus. He had been replaced as hostage to Rome by his nephew Demetrius to whom, on the death of Seleucus IV, the throne rightfully belonged. Antiochus, however, was not disposed to allow a scruple like that to stand in his way. He came to Antioch and mounted the throne of the Seleucid Empire as Antiochus IV.

To this imperial title Antiochus added the Greek word *Epiphanes*—the divine—but posterity has accorded him the sobriquet *Epimanes*—the madman.

CHAPTER SEVENTEEN

The Maccabaean Revolt

EVEN before the accession of Antiochus IV, the tension in Jerusalem between the Hellenists and their opponents had grown acute. Partisan bitterness reared its ugly head in the leading families of the nation, including that of the high priest; and, as in all party strife, unscrupulous men utilized the conflict for the promotion of personal ambitions.

The high priest in the reign of Seleucus IV was Onias III, whose own brother, Jason, espoused the Hellenist cause as a means of usurping the office. Harassed by Jason and his minions, Onias proceeded to Antioch to lay his case before the royal court. He was still there when Antiochus ascended the throne, and the new ruler, immersed in plans of conquest for which he required huge sums of money, accepted an offer from Jason of a large payment and a bigger annual tribute in return for the coveted office. To ingratiate himself with his suzerain, Jason built a Greek gymnasium in Jerusalem; on one occasion when games were held in the city of Tyre in honor of Hercules, he sent costly gifts to be offered to the hero-god. At the last moment, however, the high priest, afraid of his people's wrath, offered the gifts to the Emperor's navy instead.

But after four years of insecure tenure, the usurper was removed by Antiochus to make way for a higher bidder, one Menelaus, who, to pay the price, rifled the Temple of its treasures. The animosity between Hellenists and Chassidim became more bitter and sanguinary. The deposed high priest Onias was murdered at the instigation of Menelaus, while the latter's brother fell victim to the wrath of his opponents. Menelaus who, besides other disqualifications, was not even a member of the high priestly family, brazenly urged his sovereign to stamp out the religion over which he presided.

2

THE plans of conquest with which Antiochus fed his vainglory began with Egypt, and were calculated to end with Rome. In 170 B.C.E. he invaded his southern neighbor, but found himself checked at Alexandria. On his way back he entered Jerusalem and, escorted by Menelaus, he defiled the Temple by entering the Holy of Holies.

Two years later he again invaded Egypt. This time he was more successful against the Egyptians, but the Roman envoy ordered him out of the country. When Antiochus hesitated, he drew a circle around him demanding his yea or nay before stepping out of it. Antiochus, who remembered only too well the might of Rome, abandoned Egypt, his dreams shattered and his glory turned to shame and dishonor.

Again Antiochus stopped at Jerusalem, and there he found what he sought: an outlet for his rage. False rumors of his death produced intense excitement among the Jews, and Jason, the deposed high priest, had returned to Jerusalem and forced Menelaus to take refuge in the Acra or citadel. Antiochus avenged himself to the hilt. On a Sabbath day, when he knew the pious inhabitants would offer no resistance, his mercenaries broke into the city, butchered the men, plundered the homes, and carried off women and children to be sold into slavery. The defenses of the city were razed, and a garrison was quartered in the Acra for the protection of Menelaus and his fellow traitors.

Antiochus followed up his "victory" with a decree commanding "that all should be one people, and every one should leave his laws," an edict aimed at the Jews alone, since the others had no scruples about accepting the culture of the Greeks or worshipping their gods. On the fifteenth day of the month of Kislev, 168 B.C.E., a statue of Zeus was erected in the sanctuary, and the king ordered a swine, an animal held in special abhorrence by the Jews, to be sacrificed on the altar. In towns and villages throughout the land, shrines were set up for the same loathsome rite. The people were compelled to join in the shameful processions in honor of Dionysus, and the glory of the nation, the Temple of the God of Israel, was profaned by the revelries and debaucheries of pagan worship.

To enforce the edict "that all should be one people," Antiochus decreed the penalty of death for loyalty to the Jewish faith. Circumcision, the observance of the Sabbath and dietary laws, and the possession of Torah scrolls became capital crimes. The land swarmed with spies and the victims were numerous. Tradition has preserved in particular the memory of Eleazar, who died under torture for spurning the flesh of the swine, and of Hannah and her seven sons, all of whom perished for their faith, refusing to bow down to the heathen idols.

Jerusalem became a desolate city inhabited by strangers. The Chassidim fled to the hills and sought refuge in the caves. One Sabbath day a thousand of them were surprised in their retreats by soldiers of the king, and all the thousand perished. In the court of the Temple, beside the altar, stood "the abomination of desolation," the statue of Zeus, symbol of the triumph of Hellenism and the subjugation of the Hebrew spirit and nation.

3

A TROOP of Syrian soldiers, charged with enforcing the imperial edicts against the Jews, came one day to the village of Modin in the Judean foothills. Following their customary procedure, they summoned the villagers to the market place, erected an altar, and prepared to sacrifice a swine in honor of Zeus. The leader of the troop ordered an old man who stood among the people to come forward and perform the sacrifice.

The man was Mattathias of the family of Hasmonaeus. He had been a priest in the Temple, and when the sanctuary was desecrated by Antiochus, he had fled with his five sons to Modin. Now Mattathias stood in the market place with his sons, and saw the sacrilege follow him to his place of refuge. The old priest defied the order, and when another Jew, a renegade, prepared to perform the foul deed, Mattathias rushed forward and slew the man by the altar. Behind him came his sons, who fell upon and routed the Syrians. The soldiers fled, leaving their captain among the slain.

A village brawl—but it was the signal for the revolt that saved the Jewish faith and people. The old man and his sons fled into the mountains. News of their exploit spread through the countryside and from far and near men flocked to join them. They spent a year in guerilla warfare, cutting down patrols of the king's soldiers and swooping down on towns and villages to demolish pagan altars and bring hope to the faithful and terror to the renegades.

In these forays the man who stood out for skill and daring was Judas, the third of the old priest's sons. Men called him the "Maccabee," which means "the hammerer," and Judas Maccabaeus is the name by which he is known to posterity. His brothers were Johanan, Simon, Eleazar, and Jonathan.

Two more important deeds were accomplished by their father before he died: he declared it lawful to use weapons on the Sabbath against the enemy, and he commanded his followers to make Simon their counselor and Judas their leader in battle.

4

THE long and desperate struggle that followed is one of the most unequal contests recorded in history: for the first time a people rose up in arms to defend its religious freedom. It was, no doubt, the victories of Judas, won by his intrepid courage and brilliant generalship, that proved the decisive factor. In Judas the revolt found a superb leader, one who combined military genius with a stainless character. He was the fearless and faultless knight, a soldier of God, true-hearted and with no taint of personal ambition. "In his acts," records the chronicler in the First Book of the

Maccabees, "he was like a lion, and like a lion's whelp roaring for his prey."

In his first open battle Judas defeated a large force of Syrian troops and slew their leader Apollonius. Shortly afterwards came a larger force, led by a general named Seron, whom Judas ambushed and routed in the pass of Beth-horon.

News of these defeats reached Antiochus and he swore to exterminate the Jewish people. Confronted, however, with uprisings in Parthia and Armenia, he led half his forces away to subdue the rebels in the east, and gave the other half to Lysias, a prince of the royal family, appointing him guardian of his young heir and governor of his western provinces, and charging him with the task of dealing with the Jews.

Lysias assembled a force of nearly 50,000 footmen and horsemen, and placed them under the command of three veteran generals. They moved down the coast and, turning east from the Plain of Philistia, encamped at Emmaus midway between Jerusalem and the sea. The outcome of the campaign appeared to be a foregone conclusion: a large contingent of slave merchants, with ample bags of gold, marched with the Syrian forces.

The Jewish warriors who, though greatly outnumbered, were now well-armed and disciplined, went first to Mizpah where they heard the reading of the Torah and prayed and fasted. Judas then led them to Emmaus where, by a combination of ruse and daring, he won an amazing victory. On a dark night, under pretense of having abandoned the field, he lured a portion of the enemy into the hills and, in the gray of dawn, surprised and overwhelmed the remainder. When, after their fruitless search, the first contingent returned and saw their encampment in smoke and flames, they fled in every direction. There was great rejoicing throughout Judea. Judas gathered an immense booty, including the silver and gold of the slave merchants and the weapons which the Syrians discarded in their flight.

The following spring—it was the year 165 B.C.E.—Judas won another great victory. This time Lysias had resolved to strike from the south, and with a still greater force. At Beth-zur, just north of Hebron, the Jewish patriots, who now numbered 10,000 seasoned warriors, fell upon the Syrian mercenaries and routed them.

Secure against further immediate attacks, Judas, in the late fall of the same year, entered Jerusalem and cleansed the Temple of its pagan pollutions. He removed the idols and replaced the sullied altar and its vessels. On the twenty-fifth day of Kislev and for the seven days that followed, the dedication, or *hanukkah*, of the purified sanctuary was solemnized with praise and sacrifice, with music of voice and instrument, and the relighting of the Menorah. It was a festival of thanksgiving for the victory of "the weak over the strong, of the few over the many."

5

THE festival of Hanukkah, which is known also as the Feast of Lights, was ordained as a perpetual observance and the city once again became the habitation of the faithful. But Judas and his brothers were well aware that the final victory was not yet won. The city itself, in fact, was not yet clear of the enemy. Above the Temple loomed the citadel of the Acra which sheltered a Syrian garrison together with a band of extreme Hellenists, whom the patriots were unable to dislodge.

Moreover, the ancient enemies of the Jews, Idumaeans and Ammonites, Philistines and Phoenicians, alarmed by the victories of the Judean warriors and egged on by Lysias, made common cause with the Syrians. They raided Jewish territory, gave asylum to Syrian troops and Hellenist traitors, and persecuted the Jews who lived in their midst. The Battle of Beth-zur was followed by a lull that lasted for two years, and Judas and his brothers used the opportunity to punish these hostile neighbors and rescue their Jewish victims by removing them to Judea. The Maccabaean brothers captured and burned the Idumaean strongholds, defeated a large force of Ammonites, drove the Phoenicians back into their cities on the coast, and punished the Philistines by destroying the city of Ashdod and raiding the port of Jaffa, where they burned the ships in the harbor.

The lull in major operations which enabled Judas and his brothers to settle old scores with their neighbors was occasioned by a change of heart in Lysias. Unlike his master, the viceroy was not a rabid Hellenizer. He saw no good reason for draining the resources of the empire in order to compel an obstinate people to renounce their faith. Accordingly, he issued a decree restoring freedom of worship to the Jews. And shortly afterwards came the news that Antiochus, the arch-enemy of the Jews, was dead in distant Persia.

But Lysias was unwilling to remove Menelaus and his henchmen, and the Maccabaean brothers declined the olive branch which he extended. They were fighting not alone against the foreign oppressor, but against the Hellenist traitors who stood in his service. When, therefore, Lysias learned that Judas was preparing to attack the Acra, he repented of his offer and made another and even more formidable attempt to crush the Jewish patriots.

Again a huge Syrian army moved up toward Jerusalem from the south, and Judas moved down to meet it. This time the enemy was furnished with a new terror in the shape of fighting elephants, and a rumor spread that the regent and his boy-king would themselves ride into battle on one of the beasts. At Beth-zacharias, not far from the field of Beth-zur, Judas clashed with the mighty host of Syria and suffered his first defeat. Also, he lost one of his devoted brothers. Eleazar, believing that one of the elephants he saw plunging into the melee was bearing the Syrian king, broke through the enemy ranks, drove his spear into the beast, and died under its huge bulk as it fell. Judas took his shattered forces back to Jerusalem and found himself besieged behind the walls of the Temple.

6

THE Jewish cause seemed lost, when a series of events began, born of the sordid rivalry and intrigue in the court of Antioch, which time and again brought providential respite and new hope to the hard-pressed Jews. The events moved with confusing swiftness. The regent was forced to make peace with the Jews, even going so far as to put Menelaus to death, in order to deal with a rival regent whom Antiochus had appointed before his death. Lysias defeated his rival, but his triumph was brief; suddenly Demetrius, the victim of Antiochus' usurpation, appeared on the scene supported by Rome, and Lysias and his boy-king went down to disgrace and death. But the new ruler appointed another Hellenist, one named Alcimus, as high priest in Jerusalem, and the struggle between Hellenists and patriots flared up again. Alcimus had the support of the emperor, and the Chassidim fell on evil days again. Sixty of them were put to death by order of Bacchides, the governor of the province.

Again Judas took to the hills where he gathered fresh strength for the struggle. He won two brilliant victories against the Syrian general Nicanor; in the second victory, the Battle of Adasa in 161 B.C.E., the Syrian was slain. The anniversary of this battle, the 13th day of Adar, was observed for many years as the Day of Nicanor. But Judas and his brothers had no illusions about the chances of ultimate victory. Accordingly, they sought and obtained a treaty of alliance with Rome, in which the mightiest of the empires recognized the independence of the Jewish nation.

But before his ambassadors returned from Italy, Judas fought his last fight. At Elasa in 160 B.C.E., he faced a huge Syrian force led by Bacchides. The patriot army, hopelessly outnumbered, melted away just before the battle to a band of eight hundred men, with whom Judas and his brothers performed mighty deeds of valor. All day long, and with dwindling numbers, they held the Syrian hosts at bay, but when night fell Judas lay dead on the field.

The survivors, under cover of darkness, fled into the hills, and Jonathan, Simon, and Johanan took their brother and bore him to the village of Modin where they buried him beside their father, the valiant priest Mattathias.

7

FROM the hills of Judea the survivors of Elasa fled to the jungles on the banks of the Jordan. Their case was desperate indeed, and they lost another of the Maccabaean brothers when Johanan, while guarding the baggage of the fugitives, was attacked and slain by Arab plunderers.

The command now fell to Jonathan, who proved himself a worthy successor of the great Judas. He avenged the death of Johanan and for several years conducted relentless guerilla warfare against the Hellenists and their Syrian protectors.

In the capital, Alcimus and his followers, supported by Bacchides, obtained a free hand against the Chassidim, many of whom were slain. Egged on by the Hellenists, Bacchides pierced the Jordan jungles and attacked Jonathan in force. Again the incredible happened: the Syrians were defeated. The governor turned his rage on his Hellenist counselors. He was willing to protect them, but not at so high a cost; and he had as little enthusiasm for Hellenism as a policy as his predecessor Lysias. Bacchides came to terms with Jonathan, who returned to Judea, established himself at Michmash and, for a number of years, was looked upon as the unofficial head of the nation.

In 152 B.C.E., eight years after the death of Judas, another series of court revolutions began in Antioch which carried the patriotic cause still further. A pretender arose who claimed to be a son of Antiochus IV and challenged the emperor Demetrius. Both sides made generous bids for Jonathan's support, and he was enabled to enter and fortify Jerusalem and assume the office of high priest. Jonathan finally threw in his lot with the pretender and the choice proved fortunate. Judea had six years of peace. Jonathan was a strong and resourceful ruler and added some of the Philistine cities to his dominions. Then a new pretender arose who overthrew the first; but, in spite of war and confusion, Jonathan was able to add further strength and territory to the Jewish Commonwealth. He improved the fortifications of the capital, built up a large army, and renewed the treaty of friendship with Rome.

In the court of Antioch, the turbid current of intrigue and treachery ran on. Finally Jonathan's skill and wariness failed him. A Syrian general named Tryphon who, after espousing the cause of a third pretender, murdered his protégé and took his place, lured Jonathan into the city of Ptolemais, massacred his bodyguard, and held him prisoner. Tryphon moved on Jerusalem with a large army but had to fall back; the roads had become impassable because of a heavy snowfall, a rare occurrence in Palestine. In his rage, Tryphon ordered Jonathan, still his prisoner, to be slain.

Simon, the last of the lion's brood, had already assumed the headship of the nation. The oldest of the five brothers, Simon was already advanced in years, but he was nothing behind them in heroic zeal. Besides, he commanded a strong army, a devoted people, and a country with enlarged borders and a well-fortified capital where the only remaining symbol of subjection was the Acra.

Simon laid siege to this fortress. At the same time, he threw in his lot with Demetrius II, the reigning Seleucid monarch, against the bloody Tryphon, and in return Judea was freed from all taxes and tribute. The year was 142 B.C.E.

A solemn assembly was convoked of priests and elders who conferred on Simon the title of "high priest, commander of the army, and prince of the nation." He was king in everything but name, and the name was withheld because of the belief that it should only be borne by a descendant of David. Judea was now independent and recognized as such by Rome, the leading world power. Simon struck his own coins and the year 142 became Year One of a new era.

The same year the Acra was taken. The last symbol of servitude was overthrown; the twenty-five year struggle was over and the victory complete.

CHAPTER EIGHTEEN

The Hasmonaean Dynasty

SIMON, records the chronicler, "made peace in the land, and Israel rejoiced with great joy: for every man sat under his vine and under his fig-tree, and there was none to make them afraid." This picture, perhaps too idyllic, reflects the pride of the nation in the new era of unity and independence, achieved after twenty-five years of intense struggle and suffering. But the independence of Judea under the rule of Simon and his descendants lasted only little more than two generations (142 B.C.E. to 63 B.C.E.), and its existence in the rapacious world that surrounded it was always precarious. As for unity, while the victory of the Hasmonaeans did away with the Hellenist party, a new division arose before long to plague the nation; and, what proved equally mischievous, the harmony that had reigned among the five sons of Mattathias gave place among their successors to the feuds and rivalries which, with few exceptions, stain the annals of every dynasty.

In the seven brief years that he ruled as "high priest, commander of the army, and prince of the nation," Simon was compelled to renew the struggle for the freedom of his people, and he ended his career as the first victim of the discord that undermined the dynasty he founded. The new Seleucid ruler, Antiochus VII, as soon as he felt strong enough to hold his scepter without the support of his Jewish ally, ordered Simon to surrender the coastal cities and when Simon refused, Antiochus invaded Judea. At Jabneh, on the coastal plain, the Syrians were met by the Jewish forces commanded by Simon's two sons, John and Judah, and were decisively defeated.

The freedom of his nation was saved, but shortly afterwards the aged Simon was slain in a conspiracy hatched by his own son-in-law at the instigation of the Seleucid monarch. Thus died the last of the Maccabaean brothers, giving his life, as did the other four, in his people's service. Simon's son John, or John Hyrcanus, as he now called himself,* was also marked for death, but he was warned in time and escaped.

John Hyrcanus made his way to Jerusalem and the people hailed him as their ruler. He avenged the death of his father, but Antiochus VII came down with an immense array and besieged Jerusalem. In spite of famine the city held out: the Syrians, suffering heavy losses, were unable to storm it. But in the end Hyrcanus was compelled to accept a peace under which, after losing the coastal cities, he became a vassal of Syria.

But shortly afterwards Syria was again thrown into a welter of confusion by contending rivals for the Seleucid throne, and Hyrcanus lost no time in shaking off his vassalage. He took back the cities on the coast, renewed the treaty with Rome, and, with the help of hired troops, made war on his enemy neighbors. He crossed the Jordan and took the city of Medeba; and after capturing Shechem, he demolished the Samaritan temple on Mount

* Cendebeus, the Syrian general whom John defeated, hailed from Hyrcania, a country near Parthia, and in accordance with a prevailing custom, John, after his victory, called himself Hyrcanus.

Gerizim. He seized and destroyed the Idumaean fortresses on the south compelling the Idumaeans, on pain of exile, to embrace the Jewish faith. Thus for the first time, and contrary to its spirit and traditions, Judaism was endowed with the dubious gift of forced converts.

Toward the end of his long reign of thirty-one years (135-104 B.C.E.) the son of Simon captured and destroyed the city of Samaria, and pushing farther north, took Scythopolis as the former Beth-shean was now called. Since the days of Solomon, the borders of the Jewish Commonwealth had not been so wide. On his coins Hyrcanus stamped his title as "High Priest and Chief of the Commonwealth of the Jews."

2

THE title of king was first assumed by Hyrcanus' son Aristobulus, whose reign of only one year was marred by the bitter and sordid family discord which in the end was to bring a new servitude upon the nation. He imprisoned his mother and three brothers, while another brother, Antigonus, who had been his favorite, the two having fought their country's enemies side by side, was put to death by his orders. And all because their father, out of deference to the teachings of a new party that had sprung up in the nation, had provided by will that the functions of ruler and high priest should be separated, with his wife to be queen and Aristobulus high priest.

Aristobulus extended his borders farther north to the foot of Mount Hermon, continuing his father's mistaken policy of forced conversion. When he died—from grief and remorse for his crimes, it is said—his brother Alexander Jannaeus was released from prison and promptly became both high priest and king.

3

THE new party that John Hyrcanus had been so eager to placate was new in name only. Its members called themselves Pharisees but, in spirit and doctrine, they were the direct heirs of the Chassidim. Against them stood the Sadducees who, although they rejected the aims and affectations of the Hellenists, may nevertheless be identified with their general disposition and outlook. For, in the career of the nation, two tendencies have been at work, sometimes running side by side, more often crossing and clashing: one of them resolved to preserve the Jews as a "peculiar" people, the other striving to make them "like all the nations." The Pharisees, like the Chassidim, represented the first tendency; the Sadducees, like the Hellenists, the second.

The Sadducees, in Hebrew *Zadukim*, derived their name from Zadok, the progenitor of the family from which the high priest, before the office was conferred on Simon and his successors, used to be selected. The party included most of the leading priests, the army officers, the state officials, the notables and merchants, and in general, the men of wealth and station. The Sadducees were staunch patriots, proud of their country's new power and eager to augment it. At the same time they were "men of the world," in contact with other nations and attracted by some of the foreign customs they met with. In the Sanhedrin the Sadducees were in the majority, and at court they naturally wielded considerable influence.

In the reign of John Hyrcanus, a minority of the Sanhedrin, finding themselves in disagreement with the majority, "separated themselves" and formed what may be called an opposition. They came to be known as Separatists, in Hebrew *Perushim*, whence arose the name Pharisees. But there are other theories to account for the name, one of them connecting the "separateness" of the Pharisees with their scrupulous observance of the laws of ritual purity, and another with their insistence that Israel must be a nation separate and distinct from all others. The Pharisees looked upon themselves as keepers of the Great Covenant that ordained their people "a kingdom of priests and a holy nation."

Although the Sanhedrin, the palace, and the Temple were controlled by the Sadducees, the bulk of the nation stood behind the Pharisees. The latter ruled the synagogue, the center of the religious and social life of each community. The Pharisees were the local communal leaders, the teachers of young and old, the custodians of the noble tradition of learning. They were not the dry religious formalists which a long-standing prejudice charges them to have been, nor were their teachings and practices marked by a joyless austerity. They sought, on the contrary, to make religious observance a source of joy, while in the administration of justice they were, as against the Sadducees, noted for leniency rather than rigor. The Sadducees acknowledged the validity of the Written Law only; the Pharisees recognized the Oral Tradition also, thus admitting the necessity of continually interpreting and adapting the ordinances of Torah. As in the days of the Maccabees, the nation at large, while deploring the excesses of the partisan spirit, was inclined to entrust its destiny to those who exalted the historic faith and clung to the ancient customs.

4

IN THE long and hectic reign of Alexander Jannaeus (103-76 B.C.E.) the smoldering antagonism between the two parties broke into civil war. The monarch was a man of violent temper; he sided openly with the Sadducees, and, out of recklessness or incomprehension, flouted the sensibilities of their opponents.

Alexander began his reign auspiciously. He made conquests on both sides of the Jordan, and although he was once threatened with disaster by an invasion from Cyprus, he was rescued by an Egyptian army commanded by Hananiah and Hilkiah, sons of the high priest of the Jewish community in Egypt. The Queen of Egypt was preparing to annex Palestine when she was warned by her Jewish commanders and desisted.

In the beginning, also, Alexander endeavored to keep the scales even between the Pharisees and Sadducees. He even appointed Simon ben Shetach, the queen's brother and a leader of the Pharisees, to the Sanhedrin, of which Simon subsequently became president. But the Pharisees, for two reasons they deemed sufficient, refused to be reconciled with Alexander. The title of king, they held, could be borne by a descendant of David only; and one who wields the sword should not officiate as high priest. Had not David himself been told by God: "Thou shalt not build a house for My name, because thou art a man of war, and hast shed blood?"

The people had still another grievance against their ruler: his army contained too many mercenaries. The justice of this complaint received terrible confirmation during a celebration of the Feast of Tabernacles in Jerusalem, when Alexander, flushed with military successes, deemed the moment opportune for defying the

Pharisees. He was officiating as high priest, and at the ceremony of "pouring water," instead of pouring on the altar, as the ritual prescribed, he deliberately poured it on the ground. There was a violent outburst of resentment, and some of the people hurled at the king their citrons and palm branches, objects which enter into the ceremonial of the day. Thereupon Alexander unleashed his mercenaries who slew six thousand of the worshippers in the court of the Temple.

Alexander's turbulent spirit craved for war and violence, and he crossed the Jordan for fresh conquests. But this time he was ambushed and routed, barely escaping with his life. When he returned to the capital he found his people in open revolt. For six years the civil war raged and many more thousands fell victim to the king's hirelings. The Pharisees were driven to desperation. They persuaded the Seleucid ruler to come to their aid; Alexander's mercenaries were defeated, and he became a fugitive. His plight induced a change of heart in many of his opponents; and when the Syrians withdrew, Alexander rallied and overcame the remainder. He crucified eight hundred of his captives in an orgy of degenerate cruelty, and thousands of Pharisees fled the country. Alexander continued fighting to the day of his death, adding the habit of excessive drinking to his other vices. He died while besieging a city across the Jordan.

Alexander's widow, Salome Alexandra, now mounted the throne, and her reign of nine years (76 to 67 B.C.E.) was a period of peace and recovery. She reversed her husband's policy, favoring the Pharisees against the Sadducees. She made her brother, Simon ben Shetach, her chief counselor and Judah ben Tabbai, another Pharisee leader, became president of the Sanhedrin. She appointed her son Hyrcanus high priest, and his brother, Aristobulus commander of the army. It was the intention of the aged queen that on her death the secular and sacerdotal functions should thus be divided between them.

But while she lay dying, Aristobulus, with the aid of the Sadducees who regarded him as their protector, revolted, and there was civil war again. After a year of fighting in which the older and weaker Hyrcanus was worsted, the brothers met and made peace on terms that accorded with their mother's wishes. But the peace lasted only three years: Hyrcanus gave ear to the promptings of one Antipater, a crafty Idumaean who, having wormed himself into the high priest's favor, made it his business to feed his grudge against his more successful brother. The result was a renewal of the conflict. This time Aristobulus was defeated and driven for refuge behind the walls of the Temple. Hyrcanus was aided by a large force of Nabataeans, a people to the south of Idumaea whose ruler, Aretas, had been persuaded by Antipater to inject himself into the bitter feud of the Hasmonaean brothers.

5

AT THIS critical juncture in the affairs of the Commonwealth, a new power, beside whom King Aretas was less than a pygmy, appeared on the scene in Judea. The year was 63 B.C.E. The Roman conqueror Pompey the Great, having subdued Mithridates, King of Pontus, obtained the submission of Armenia, put an end to the inglorious Seleucid line, and made Syria a Roman province. Now he scanned the horizons to see what other laurels he could gather before returning to Rome for the prodigious triumph that awaited him. He determined to "settle" the bloody quarrel that raged in Jerusalem and sent down an emissary whose decision favored Aristobulus. The Nabataeans, ordered by the Romans to return to their own country, were overtaken by Aristobulus and defeated. To make doubly sure of Pompey's favor, the lucky brother sent the Roman a magnificent golden vine. Suddenly, however, the conqueror ordered both brothers to appear before him. A third party appeared also, a deputation that spoke in the name of the nation, pleading that both be removed and Judea be permitted to become a republic.

But Pompey, influenced by the wily Antipater, decided that the interests of Rome would be served best by elevating the weaker of the two brothers. Aristobulus, after surrendering a fortress in which he had taken refuge, fled to Jerusalem, with the Roman legions in pursuit. His supporters shut the gates against them, but the followers of Hyrcanus opened them. For three months a large body entrenched behind the walls of the Temple defied the Romans. But the enemy broke through the walls, fell upon the helpless people, and massacred twelve thousand of them, sparing not even the priests who refused to abandon the sacred rites. Like the Greek Antiochus before him, Pompey defiled the Holy of Holies by entering within its precincts. But the Roman, according to one account, was so greatly awed when he saw neither statue nor other object of worship in the chamber, that he refrained from robbing the Temple treasures.

The Roman reduced the boundaries of Judea and abolished the crown, leaving a mere shadow of authority to Hyrcanus, with Antipater in possession of the real power. And among the captives he took with him to Rome to be led in his public triumph were Aristobulus and his two sons and two daughters.

CHAPTER NINETEEN

Roman Dominion

AMID the bewildering changes in the quarter century (63 to 37 B.C.E.) that separates the rape of Jerusalem by Pompey from the elevation of Herod, son of Antipater, to the throne of Palestine, the two basic factors that stand out clearly are the strangle hold of Rome upon the body and soul of the nation, and the desperate efforts of the Jews to break it.

In Rome a greater man than Pompey, Julius Caesar, appeared on the scene and, together with one Crassus, set up the First Triumvirate for possession of the Roman world. Crassus, who came to gather military laurels in the East, stopped in Jerusalem, robbed the Temple of an immense treasure, but met defeat and death at the hands of the Parthians. Led by Pitholaus, the patriots in Palestine rose up in arms. They were put down and thirty thousand of them, together with their leader, were executed.

For a number of years Caesar and Pompey managed to share the Roman world between them. They finally broke, and in 48 B.C.E., at the Battle of Pharsalia in Greece, the clever Pompey was outmaneuvered by Caesar and overthrown. But only four years later, on the fateful Ides of March, 44 B.C.E., a band of

LAND OF ISRAEL
IN THE SECOND COMMONWEALTH

assassins led by the high-minded Brutus and the "lean and hungry" Cassius, stabbed Caesar to death, and Rome fell into the hands of his adopted son, Octavian, and his friend Mark Antony. Two years later, at the Battle of Philippi in Macedonia, the new masters of Rome extinguished the hope, by which Brutus and Cassius had been beguiled, of preserving Rome as a republic. Those events are well-remembered: the poets and dramatists have not permitted the world to forget them, for closely associated with them is the Egyptian Queen Cleopatra, whose charms overcame both Caesar and Antony.

In Palestine the little nation of Jews lay clamped in the vise of Roman dominion, with Antipater a puppet in the hands of the Roman governor and Hyrcanus a puppet in the hands of Antipater. One after another the luckless Aristobulus and his two sons, Alexander and Antigonus, escaped from Rome, and, with the Jewish patriots rallying round them, Palestine became the scene of one revolt after another. But they were all suppressed; Aristobulus and Alexander forfeited their lives and Antipater tightened his hold on the land.

It was not long, moreover, before the crafty Antipater was able to win the good will of Caesar by bringing him timely help in putting down an outbreak in Egypt. Caesar was grateful, and he requited the service by conferring rights and privileges upon the Jews in Palestine and elsewhere. He permitted the restoration of Jerusalem's defenses, augmented the power of the high priest and Sanhedrin, and restored the possessions of which the country had been deprived by Pompey.

2

THE favors of Caesar, however, granted as they were through a foreign usurper and sycophant, failed to placate the Jewish patriots. The hotbed of insurgency was Galilee, and Antipater decided to appoint his son Herod governor of that district. Thus began a career of crime and power for which a posterity none too discriminating has conferred upon Herod the title of "the Great." It was a career wherein amazing good fortune seemed to play as large a role as Herod's exceptional qualities and vices.

From his father he inherited a boundless ambition and indomitable will, and at their service stood a fund of energy, cruelty, and cunning that seemed inexhaustible.

Herod began by seizing Ezekias, a leader of the Galilean patriots, and, without the formality of a trial, he put him to death together with a number of his followers. The people were shocked. The clamor was so great that Hyrcanus was forced to order Herod to stand trial before the Sanhedrin. Herod, sure of Roman support, treated the august body with insolent contempt, appearing before it in royal purple and surrounded by a bodyguard. Hyrcanus found it expedient to allow the young man to escape from Jerusalem. But Herod soon returned in command of an army, determined to put his enemies to death, a pleasure which, on the advice of his crafty father, he decided to postpone.

Mark Antony having become the man of destiny, and Antipater having been poisoned, Herod labored alone—and successfully—to win the favor of the new master of Rome. The son of the Idumaean took his father's place as virtual ruler of Judea. Then came the Parthians, whom the Roman legions had never conquered, and invaded Palestine. With their help Antigonus, the last son of Aristobulus, became king and high priest of the Jews. Herod fled for his life and Hyrcanus was carried off, a captive, to Parthia.

But Herod was not dismayed. For a time he found refuge in the fortress of Masada; then he set out to repair his fortunes. He got to Rome where he had no difficulty persuading Antony and Octavian that he and not Antigonus would best serve the interests of the empire. The Roman Senate declared him king of the Jews and in 39 B.C.E. he landed in Acco. Finding the Roman authorities in Syria lukewarm to his cause, he raised an army of mercenaries and gradually conquered the country. He defeated Antigonus and laid siege to Jerusalem. For five months the city held out, and when it was finally taken by assault, the mercenaries and their Roman allies indulged in an orgy of pillage and massacre which Herod himself, to save the city from destruction, could only bring to a halt with costly bribes. Antigonus was captured and beheaded. The Idumaean adventurer, under the protecting wings of the Roman eagle, became the unchallenged master of the nation.

3

HE WAS not unaware of the importance of winning the good will of the people he conquered, and while the siege of Jerusalem was still in progress, he celebrated his nuptials with Mariamne, a grand-daughter of the exiled Hyrcanus, hoping through this alliance with the royal Hasmonaean family to ingratiate himself with his subjects. He even proclaimed himself a descendant of an exile who had returned with Ezra from Babylon, and he made a special bid for the allegiance of the Pharisees by declining to assume the office of high priest. But all his efforts were futile. They were nullified by his servility to the hated Romans, and even more by his morbid suspicions and sadistic cruelty. Throughout his long reign of thirty-three years (37 to 4 B.C.E.) Herod won nothing from the people he ruled but hatred and contempt.

He began by ordering the execution of the leading supporters of Antigonus and seizing their property. Among them were the members of the Sanhedrin, of whom only Shemaya, the president, and Abtalion, the vice-president, were spared. He instigated the murder of Mariamne's young and popular brother Aristobulus, and after enticing Hyrcanus to come and live under his patronage in Jerusalem, he brought about the old man's death on a false accusation. Thus he rid himself of the two male survivors of the Hasmonaean line, but his fears and suspicions were never at rest. He even came to suspect his wife and children, and his reign became tarnished with foul and unnatural crimes.

The gloomy record is only slightly relieved by a passion for building which, in the intervals between war and intrigue, he fully indulged. He built cities and fortresses, temples and palaces. He rebuilt the city of Samaria, renaming it Sebaste, which is Greek for Augustus, in honor of the Roman emperor. He erected a splendid city on the coast, calling it Caesarea, also in honor of the emperor. Two new fortresses he named Herodium, and in his capital he set up an amphitheater for gladiatorial shows which outraged his God-fearing people. His thirst for fame carried his building operations to foreign lands, to Asia Minor, to Greece, to the islands.

The edifice on which his fame principally rests is the Temple in Jerusalem, which he rebuilt. It was a structure of immense strength and surpassing beauty, this temple of Herod. A resplendent mass of white marble and gold, it rose on the summit of Zion, surrounded by three walled-off courts, the whole enclosed in a lofty and impregnable rampart. But the evil genius that possessed him brought his best intentions to ruin. He adorned the principal gate of the Temple with a golden Roman eagle, defying the law against graven images and violating the deepest religious instincts of his people.

Early in his reign he fought a successful war against the Nabataeans, in which he displayed great personal courage and military skill. The war had been fomented by Cleopatra, as crafty as she was seductive, in the hope of weakening both contestants, and with the consent of her lord and slave Mark Antony, she possessed herself of Herod's kingdom. But with all her advantages, Herod proved more than a match for her in the strategy of diplomacy as well as of war.

It was not long, moreover, before Cleopatra and Egypt ceased to be a menace to him altogether. For in 32 B.C.E. the inevitable conflict between Octavian and Antony broke out, and the following year, at the naval Battle of Actium off the western coast of Greece, Antony and Cleopatra were decisively defeated. Antony, who proved to be a greater lover than warrior, on being informed that his mistress was dead, took his own life; and Cleopatra, who was not dead, but found Octavian immune to her charms, ended her life symbolically and magnificently by laying a poisonous viper to her bosom. Thus perished Cleopatra and with her the Ptolemaic line which for nearly three centuries had reigned over Egypt.

But, strangely enough, where Cleopatra failed, Herod succeeded. He had been a loyal henchman to Antony and now, he felt, he was in great peril. At once he brought into play all his energy, cunning, and audacity. He sent his children, his mother, and his sister Salome to the stronghold of Masada; and Mariamne with her mother Alexandra he confined in another fortress with orders to execute the two women if his worst fears for himself should prove true. Then he met the new master and first emperor of Rome on the Island of Rhodes and employed his wiles with such consummate skill that the Roman not only confirmed him in his possessions but, before long, even added to them, making the boundaries of his kingdom as wide as they had been in the days of David.

Notwithstanding the end of Herod's fears, the fate of Mariamne and her mother Alexandra was sealed. His love for Mariamne was genuine, but he listened with morbid avidity to false accusations which the venomous Salome whispered in his ear, and finally ordered his wife's execution. To the end of his life that crime gave him no rest and exacerbated a nature already a prey to the most violent passions. Alexandra attempted a feeble rebellion against her son-in-law which ended in her death.

The detestation of his subjects became more intense, but Herod had the favor of Rome and he needed nothing more. The emperor and his heir were his friends, for he earned their gratitude by aiding them in their wars and accompanying them on their campaigns. The campaigns were successful, the civil wars to which Rome had been a prey for a century came to an end, and the accession of Octavian, renamed Augustus, as first emperor of Rome ushered in a long period of peace and prosperity in which Palestine shared in full measure. Its old harbors were improved and new ones built, commerce expanded and flourished, and considerable wealth, of which a great deal made its way into the king's coffers, flowed into the country.

4

A STORM upon the sea lashes the surface into huge waves, but the depths below may be calm and tranquil. Beneath the tumult of war, revolution and crime, ran the steady stream of the nation's life, pursuing the course marked out for it by its traditions and destiny.

The economic structure of this life, although affected by the turmoils of political change, continued to rest on its agricultural base, with a steady increase in the number and size of the cities where, of course, industry and commerce made their home. The merchants exported corn, wine and oil, wool, purple and linen, while the imports included textiles, implements, ornaments, and other wares. There were flourishing cities on the coast and on both sides of the Jordan. East of the river, the cities, which included Gadara, Gerasa, Pella, Philadelphia,* and others, made up a province called the Decapolis, or ten-city district. In some of the cities dwelt heathens, but the Jewish population of the country as a whole is estimated to have numbered some 3,000,000, a number that testifies to the skill with which the soil was cultivated.

The labor in field and workshop was arduous, but it was a labor of devotion and love. For the teachers of the nation never wearied of extolling the virtues of the toilsome life, demanding that the sage shall not use the Torah "as a spade to dig with," but should "combine Torah with a worldly occupation"; and the psalmist too exalted the beauty and dignity of labor.

When thou eatest the labor of thy hands,
Happy shalt thou be and it shall be well with thee.
Thy wife shall be as a fruitful vine, in the
innermost part of thy house;
Thy children like olive plants, round about thy table.

It was, of course, the Torah, and the observance of its precepts, especially the observance of the Sabbaths and festivals, that invested even the lowliest lives with dignity. Only by a steady perception of this truth is it possible to realize the profound attachment of the people to their way of life, and to understand the tragic and heroic events to which this passionate devotion gave rise. Education, based as it was on Torah, became a national necessity; every synagogue was also a school for young and old. Towards the end of the Second Commonwealth, a decree of the high priest Joshua ben Gamala made it obligatory upon every community of ten families or more to provide a school for the male children, the first instance of compulsory education that history records.

The Temple to which, on the pilgrimage festivals of Passover, Shabuoth and Sukkoth, the men of the nation flocked, filled the worshippers with reverent pride. The New Year, when the ram's

* The name is the Greek version of "Rabbath-ammon." It is the modern Amman, capital of Trans-Jordan.

horn was sounded, the solemn Day of Atonement, the Feast of Lights, or Hanukkah, and the Feast of Purim, brought additional joy and exaltation. An aura of holiness clung to all of them, but each possessed its own savor, bringing into the lives of the people a rich variety of inspiration and joy.

5

NOR was the spirit that produced the Sacred Scriptures exhausted. On the contrary, in days of wrath and menace, as if impelled by an instinctive awareness that the spirit alone provided a safe refuge, the Jewish mind gave itself over to intense activity. With the Scriptures as a springboard, it struck out into new realms, not only in the disciplined pursuit of legal elaboration, but in the free play of poetic fancy. The age of the *tannaim* (singular, *tanna*), as the teachers of the period are called, had begun. Herod was building imposing structures which the fury of foes or the ravages of time were destined to obliterate. The *tannaim* were building up the edifice of Torah which neither time nor enemies could demolish.

The greatest of these builders in the reign of Herod was Hillel, who left the deepest impress on the generations that followed. Driven by a thirst for knowledge, he left Babylonia, where he was born, to study in the schools of Shemaya and Abtalion. He rose to be president of the Sanhedrin, but, what is more important, he was the founder of an academy, the *Bet Hillel* (House of Hillel) and of a system of interpretation which rose to the rank of highest authority.

His system was the natural outgrowth of his character, and both are best understood by contrasting them with the character and teachings of Shammai, his contemporary and rival. Shammai too was a great *tanna*, a leader of the Pharisees and founder of a school known as *Bet Shammai*. But Shammai was stern, while Hillel was gentle; Shammai was inflexible, while Hillel was liberal. The character of the two men is illustrated by the story of the insolent heathen who came to Shammai and demanded to be taught the whole Torah in the time he could stand on one foot. The irascible Shammai drove the man away, but when the scoffer came to Hillel, the gentle teacher told him: "Do not unto others what you do not wish them to do unto you. This is the whole Torah: all else is commentary."

Hillel, as tradition portrays him, was a man of singular force and charm, while Shammai stands out as a tower of strength in his zeal for Torah. The two schools locked horns on many questions, and their disputations continued for a long time after the death of the founders. In the end, it was *Bet Hillel* that triumphed, and in the evolution of Oral Torah it was the liberal method of Hillel that prevailed. Nevertheless, Shammai too had his place in this evolution; and a legend relates that when a certain student, unable to reconcile the opinions of the two schools, cried out in his perplexity, a voice from heaven answered him in the cryptic pronouncement: "Both are the words of the living God!"

6

AS HIS life drew to a close, the morbid suspicions that tortured King Herod became darker and deeper, and the crimes with which he sought to allay them became more hideous. His sister Salome went on with her role of incendiary, and among his victims were three of his sons, two of whom had been borne him by Mariamne, the beloved wife whose death preyed on him continually. News of these crimes reached the imperial capital. "Better to be Herod's swine than Herod's son," was the comment of Emperor Augustus.

The people were eager for Herod's death. Once a rumor that he was dead spread through the capital, and a band of youthful zealots gave vent to their joy by tearing down the Roman eagle from the gate of the Temple. But the rumor was false, and Herod, though his end was approaching, sent forty-two of the offenders to the stake. In the torments of a malignant disease, he conjured up the most fantastic crime of all. Knowing that his end would be hailed with joy, he determined that the day should be one of mourning and left orders that the same day the leading men of the nation should be executed.

But Herod's final command was not obeyed, and the day of his death was a day of general rejoicing.

CHAPTER TWENTY

Messiah Longing

ROME ruled over many nations, and, sullen or resigned, they accepted her dominion and obeyed her laws, bending to the yoke of her brutal legions and rapacious governors. The Jews alone, with a unique passion for freedom, remained irreconcilable. It was more than Rome could understand, more than Rome could tolerate. She continued to tighten her grip, but with every turn of the vise the wrath and bitterness of the Jews became only more intense.

Helpless against the might of the tyrant, the exasperated yearning for freedom turned upon itself, feeding on expectations of immediate divine intervention, and producing strange aberrations. Men found refuge in desperate deeds or in dreams and hallucinations. And, naturally, what moved the people most powerfully was the belief that the time was ripe for the advent of the Great Deliverer, scion of David, the King and Messiah.

2

IT ADDED greatly to the misfortunes of the Jews that not only the Romans but their own immediate rulers, notably Herod, were strangers to their blood and spirit. As if his kingdom belonged to him in fee simple, Herod, before he died, divided it among three of his sons, leaving to Herod Archelaus, whose character was most like his own, the southern half of the realm together with the royal title. The paternal character declared itself without delay. The people demanded the punishment of the men they held guilty in the execution of the Pharisees who had torn down the Roman eagle. They demanded also the removal of the Sadducee high priest, Joezer, who was a servile tool in the hands of the rulers. Archelaus, seeing his people on the verge of rebellion, set the garrison upon them and again the courts of the Temple were stained with blood.

But soon Archelaus found it necessary to travel to Rome, for his two brothers, who had their grievances against him, had taken them to the imperial capital. Palestine was left to the tender mercies of Varus, the Roman governor of Syria. Varus quartered a Roman legion on Jerusalem, and under its protection, but not without a bloody affray, the Romans plundered the treasures of the Temple. Galilee rose up and Palestine seethed with revolt. Varus overran the country with his legions and nailed two thousand of the patriots to the cross.

In the imperial capital a deputation of the people pleaded in vain that Palestine be ruled by a high priest alone. Rome confirmed Herod's will, placating the brothers of Archelaus by depriving him of the royal title. From 4 B.C.E. to 6 C.E. Archelaus, under the title of ethnarch, was the hated ruler of Judea until, having incurred the suspicions of Rome, he was removed and exiled to Gaul.

3

THERE followed a line of Roman governors appointed by the emperor with the title of procurator. The procurators were charged with the maintenance of public order and the collection of taxes. They were given power to appoint the high priest and to intervene in the judicial functions of the Sanhedrin, particularly in capital cases. In practice, the procurators abused their power, selling their favors to the highest bidders. They aimed at one thing: to make their tenure of office as lucrative as possible for the emperor and, even more, for themselves. As in the days of Antiochus, men bribed their way into the exalted office of high priest, while the august Sanhedrin was left with only a shadow of its authority.

The first procurator was Coponius, who nearly plunged the country into a general revolt. He ordered a census to be taken of the people, a procedure to which they had a traditional aversion and which, they well knew, portended higher taxes and new restrictions. In Galilee the patriots, led by Judas, whose father Ezekias had been murdered by Herod, prepared to resist. In the end, however, they yielded to the pleas and warnings of the high priest and submitted.

There were now two new parties in the nation, who, though poles apart, represented a natural reaction to the fever and anguish through which it was passing. The first consisted of men who called themselves Zealots, reckless and fearless men who swore undying hatred against the Romans. Be the prospect victory or defeat, they were always ready to throw themselves upon the enemy, and to avoid capture, did not hesitate to slay their wives and children and put an end to themselves.

At the other extreme were the Essenes,* who bore the closest resemblance to a monastic order ever developed in Judaism. The Essenes turned their backs on the labors and sorrows of the world and went off to live in communities of their own, most of them located in the desert regions near the Dead Sea. They surrendered their property to the community and spent their days in deeds of piety, observing the laws of their faith with exceeding scrupulousness and practicing every form of self-denial, including celibacy. They renounced all hope of happiness in the brutal world that surrounded them and looked forward to the bliss of the World to Come.

4

FOUR procurators came and went in the twenty years that elapsed from the removal of Archelaus to the year 26 C.E., the year when the emperor Tiberius appointed Pontius Pilate, the best-remembered procurator of all. Pilate is remembered best because it was during his administration that a young preacher named Joshua, but better known as Jesus, the son of a carpenter of Nazareth in the province of Galilee, was convicted of blasphemy and sedition and put to death by the Roman method of crucifixion.

No great stir was produced either in the capital or in the country at large by the execution of the Galilean preacher. Josephus, the most important historian of the period, who was born only seven

* The origin of the word is uncertain. One explanation derives it from a word meaning "to bathe" and refers to the scrupulousness with which the Essenes observed the laws of ritual purity.

or eight years after the crucifixion, makes no mention of Jesus.* The capital was witnessing too many executions to be startled by any one of them, for Pilate was as brutal a tyrant as Rome ever inflicted upon the Jews. He made free with the treasures of the Temple and executed many Zealots without trial. He violated the dearest sentiments of the people by displaying the hated regimental images in the capital, answered complaints by giving his soldiery a free hand against the complainants, and in the end was ordered back to Rome to answer charges against him. Pilate was anything but the compassionate and amiable official which certain Christian traditions, bent on laying the odium of the crucifixion on the Jews alone, make him out to have been.

For the rest, preachers like the Galilean aroused the fears and suspicions, above all, of the Roman authorities. The air was rife with rebellion, and any concourse of people, assembled for no matter what purpose, might take a seditious trend. Wandering preachers and their followers were particularly suspect, and the most dangerous orators were those who enflamed their hearers with extravagant hopes and messianic notions. A year or so before the conviction of the Galilean, a certain Johanan, better known as John the Baptist, also a preacher and bringer of messianic tidings, had been beheaded as a public menace. John, we are informed, had taken his stand beside the Jordan, calling upon all men to confess their sins and be baptised in the river, for, he declared, the Great Redeemer was at hand; and among those who had heeded his call was the young preacher from Nazareth. John, it may be assumed, belonged to the Essenes; his manner of dress, the food he ate, and the importance he attached to ritual ablution, or baptism, all point to that conclusion.

People flocked to hear the preacher of Nazareth, and not a few followed him wherever he went. He spoke of a better world which he called the kingdom of God, a place apparently not of this earth. The world of sorrows through which he moved, the world that writhed in the merciless grip of Rome, was a matter of small concern to him. "Render unto Caesar the things that are Caesar's," he told his hearers, "and unto God the things that are God's." He

* The passage on Jesus in Josephus' *Antiquities of the Jews* (XVIII; 3) is undoubtedly a pious interpolation by a later hand.

exhorted men to be compassionate to one another, to love one another, to love even their enemies. "If any man will sue thee at law, and take away thy coat, let him have thy cloak also," he commanded. And he taught the doctrine of non-resistance, saying: "Resist not evil, but whosoever shall smite thee on the right cheek, turn to him the other also."

Whence came the teachings and exhortations of this itinerant preacher, his pity for the poor and the oppressed, his burning indignation against evil-doers, his withering scorn for hypocrites and sycophants? They came from Amos and Hosea, from Isaiah and Jeremiah, from Nahum and Micah. They harked further back to the Decalogue and the laws of Moses, nor do we have to strain our hearing to discover echoes in them of the later sages, of Ezra, and Simon the Just, and Hillel. In fact, Jesus himself acknowledged his debt to his predecessors by proclaiming it to be his mission not to nullify their teachings but to fulfill them. "Think not," said he, "that I am come to destroy the law or the prophets: I am not come to destroy but to fulfill. For verily I say unto you, till heaven and earth pass, one jot or one tittle shall in no wise pass from the law, till all be fulfilled."

Notwithstanding this pronouncement, however, the Galilean took liberties with certain of the laws, treating them in a manner that could not but shock the pious. In particular, he made light of the laws governing the observance of the Sabbath. "The Son of man is Lord also of the Sabbath," said he in answer to those who protested against his violations.

Perhaps the best known of his revisions was the one that resulted in the so-called Golden Rule. Jesus took the famous dictum of Hillel, "Do not unto others what you do not wish them to do unto you," and revised it to say, "Whatsoever ye would that men should do unto you, even so do ye also unto them." Was the change a happy one? It has been so acclaimed, and the positive version of Jesus rather than the negative version of Hillel is offered as the basic rule to guide men to the good life. Nevertheless there are those who doubt the wisdom of that choice. The most obvious fact in nature, including human nature, say the doubters, is its infinite diversity. The things I would have done to me are not always a proper guide as to what I should do to my neighbor. The positive version of the golden rule, they point out, has provided well-intentioned meddlers and bigots with a sanction for interfering with the lives of others. As a guide to the good life, Hillel's version, though it enjoins restraint rather than zeal, is wiser and safer; and, as for positive deeds of charity, certainly the traditional teaching, both written and oral, did anything but underrate them. "Torah, worship and good deeds," declared Simon the Just, are the three pillars of the universe.

5

"AND there followed him great multitudes of people from Galilee, and from Decapolis, and from Jerusalem, and from Judea, and from beyond the Jordan." Apparently the Galilean preacher was causing great excitement throughout the land. He attracted the poor especially; and many who came to him were diseased or crippled, for the word had spread that Jesus performed miracles, that he could heal the halt and the blind, eject evil spirits, and even raise up the dead.

Soon the belief arose among his followers that the man from Galilee was the Messiah himself, the anointed savior for whom the people yearned so passionately. And by his words and manner the Galilean encouraged the belief, for now he began to lapse into strange silences or speak in riddles, using common expressions with a new and startling purport. The words "son of man," which Ezekiel and Daniel had used before him, thus acquired a vague messianic connotation, while the expression "son of God," which to the Jews meant simply that all men were the children of their Father in heaven, took on a special and fantastic significance.

The only testimony on the arrest, the trial, and the execution of Jesus is to be found in the four gospels of the New Testament, and not only do the witnesses contradict each other, but it is extremely doubtful if they are unprejudiced. The record was set down at a time when feeling ran high between the devotees of the new faith and the guardians of the old, and the witnesses are bitter against the Pharisee leaders and teachers of the people and, in particular, against the Sanhedrin. They lay the onus of the execution upon the Jews, and find amazing extenuations for the Roman master. But, with a knowledge of the background against which the tragedy was enacted, a glimpse of the truth may be obtained from this record, confusing and biased though it is.

It was Passover of the year 30 C.E. and Jerusalem was thronged with pilgrims. The Galilean preacher was also there, and with him came a band of disciples and followers. He preached in the courts of the Temple and large crowds gathered to hear him. In his utterances the messianic note had become more pronounced. A peculiar exaltation took possession of him and his disciples. There were money-changers in the courts of the Temple and men who sold doves for sacrifice: the wrath of the preacher and his disciples turned on these men. Who were these money-changers? Twenty centuries of odium lies heaped upon them and it is almost impossible to dig them out of it. But they were not scamps and malefactors; they performed a useful function: they exchanged the coins of pilgrims from foreign lands for the currency of the realm. The preacher and his followers overturned the tables of the money-changers and drove them, as well as the dove-sellers, out of the courts. Undoubtedly the incident must have had all the earmarks of a riot. Jesus was arrested, tried before a court of the Sanhedrin, and convicted of blasphemy. The evidence against him was his claim to be, in a special sense, the "son of God."

From now on the records begin to strain ordinary credulity to the breaking point. Jesus is sentenced to death, but the sentence must be confirmed by the procurator, and the bloody Pilate is represented as a genial and merciful judge! He, who had more reason to fear the Galilean agitator than anyone else, pleads for his release! But the first question, which, according to the same records, the procurator addressed to Jesus, reveals the mind of the Roman quite clearly. The question was: "Art thou the king of the Jews?" that being the seditious title by which his followers had acclaimed him. Jesus replied: "Thou sayest it." And upon the cross to which the Roman executioners nailed him, they placed the derisive inscription: "Jesus of Nazareth king of the Jews." The question and the inscription leave no doubt as to the crime for which Jesus suffered.

Seldom does it happen that one who has become the focus and lodestar of men's hopes loses his power with his death. Too bitter was the thought that the Redeemer had died on the cross like any other victim of Roman "justice," and the belief soon spread among his followers that he had risen from his grave and been assumed to heaven. They believed also that he would, before long, return and accomplish his mission; and this belief in his second coming has been held by countless millions of his devotees in the centuries that followed.

About thirty years later, Saul, or Paul, of the city of Tarsus in Asia Minor, carried the evangel of the Galilean preacher to many lands and nations. But among the great body of the Jewish people the new religion failed to take root. The reasons are not hard to find. To begin with, in order to win converts among the heathens, the new creed abrogated the immemorial laws and practices of Judaism; the missionaries of the new faith embraced a policy which the Jews always regarded with deep distrust, the policy of easy conversion. The new faith, moreover, clashed too violently with the basic credo of Judaism, the Unity of God. For out of this credo flows the sublime conception of a universe controlled by design and moral purpose and, to vindicate it, numberless Jewish martyrs have died with the words of the *Shema* on their lips: "Hear, O Israel, the Lord is our God, the Lord is One!"

CHAPTER TWENTY-ONE

Mounting Crisis

THE Roman emperor Tiberius, in whose reign the events just related occurred, died in 37 C.E. His successor was Caligula, whose mentality and character are sufficiently illustrated by the fact that he seriously proposed to have his favorite horse elected consul of Rome. But this madman befriended the Jewish prince Agrippa, whose father was one of the unfortunate sons of Mariamne and Herod. With his own hands Caligula, as soon as he ascended the throne, released Agrippa from the prison in which Tiberius had incarcerated him, and made him king of the northern provinces of Palestine, the regions formerly governed by Herod's son Philip. Two years later Caligula removed Philip's brother, Herod Antipas, who still ruled over Galilee and the lands across the Jordan, and added those provinces to Agrippa's possessions. Agrippa's good fortune continued: in 41 C.E., Caligula's successor Claudius bestowed on him the remainder of Palestine, Samaria and Idumaea. Thus it came about that Agrippa reigned over a kingdom of even greater extent than his grandfather's.

He reigned wisely and well, but all too briefly. Only three years after the country had become united under his scepter, he died suddenly and under circumstances that lent color to the suspicion that he was the victim of Roman treachery. He was too solicitous of his people's welfare, too energetic in strengthening his country's defenses, and too popular to suit the policy of Rome. With this policy, as well as with the depravity of Rome's ruling class, Agrippa was only too familiar, for he had spent most of his life in the imperial capital. No doubt he saw the impending struggle and endeavored to prepare for it, but although he enjoyed the favor of the emperor, his efforts were thwarted by Marsus, the governor of Syria. Marsus prevented Agrippa from building a third wall around Jerusalem, and once, when the Jewish king was meeting with five neighboring rulers in the city of Tiberias, the Roman suddenly appeared on the scene and ordered each of them to return to his own country.

Agrippa owed his popularity primarily to a delicate regard for his people's sensibilities. He celebrated the festivals with them and read aloud from the sacred books in the court of the Temple. Once, it is recorded, when he came to the passage, "One from among thy brethren shalt thou set king over thee; thou mayest not put a foreigner over thee, who is not thy brother," Agrippa, remembering his grandfather Herod, burst into tears. But his people chose to remember instead his Hasmonaean grandmother Mariamne, and their answer was: "Thou art our brother! Thou art our brother!"

His people remembered still other things for which they were grateful to Agrippa. Earlier in his reign, when the maniac Caligula was still on the throne, an imperial edict had gone out ordering the emperor's statue to be set up and worshipped in all the shrines and temples of the empire. The edict threw the Jews into consternation. Previous emperors had also required their subjects to worship them as gods, but in Palestine the Roman officials, aware of the danger of trying to enforce this command upon the Jews, connived at its nonobservance. Now Caligula, with the obstinacy of madness, refused to grant the Jews exemption from an edict which all his other subjects accepted without demur, and ordered his statue to be erected in the Temple of Jerusalem. Petronius, the governor of Syria, sent word to Caligula that enforcement would entail an enormous amount of bloodshed, but the message made the madman only more determined. As a result of Agrippa's efforts and influence, however, the imperial edict was repealed.

2

IN THE city of Alexandria, where a numerous and wealthy Jewish community flourished, the edict of Caligula did not have so fortunate an outcome. The other inhabitants of the city, who envied the Jews their privileges and prosperity, found in the edict a welcome pretext for giving vent to their resentment.

It was 38 C.E., and Agrippa, on the way to take over his possessions in Palestine, had stopped in Alexandria, where the Jews welcomed him with high honors and the Greeks made public mockery of him. Flaccus, the Roman prefect of the city, sided with the Greeks, and to curry favor with Caligula he sought to compel the Jews to worship the emperor's statue. But the Jews refused to set up the image in their houses of prayer, and the prefect, after depriving them of their civil rights, left them to the mercy of the Greek mob.

The result was a bloody pogrom. The synagogues were desecrated and destroyed and the Jewish quarters looted. Many Jews were slain and their leaders scourged in public. Agrippa intervened and effected the removal of the prefect, but the situation in the city continued dangerous, with venomous anti-Jewish propaganda conducted by Apion, a Greek writer of unsavory character and reputation.

The quarrel was carried to Rome. In 40 C.E. the Jews of Alexandria sent an embassy to the emperor headed by their foremost citizen, the sage and philosopher Philo, and the Greeks sent a deputation headed by Apion. Philo, who holds an important place in Greek philosophy, was an ardent admirer of Greek culture, especially of the system of Plato, but at the same time he was deeply attached to his faith, convinced that the truths of Greek philosophy lay imbedded in the Sacred Scriptures. He sought to bring these truths to light by the allegorical interpretation of the Bible, a method which looks for hidden meanings beneath the surface of the text. Philo was an elegant and facile writer, and his *Embassy to Caligula* reveals the Rome of his day, the strange vagaries of the ruler, the intrigues of his corrupt courtiers. Philo's mission was a failure: Caligula's final verdict on the Jews was: "These men do not appear to me to be wicked so much, as unfortunate and foolish in not believing that I have been endowed with the nature of God."

3

IN HIS *Embassy to Caligula*, Philo quotes a letter of appeal which King Agrippa addressed to the emperor. Agrippa writes:

> Concerning the holy city I must now say what is necessary. It, as I have already stated, is my native country, and the metropolis not only of the one country of Judea, but also of many, by reason of the colonies which it has sent out from time to time into the bordering districts of Egypt, Phoenicia, Syria in general, and especially that part of it which is called Coele-Syria,* and also those more distant regions of Pamphylia, Cilicia, the greater part of Asia Minor as far as Bithynia, and the furthermost corners of Pontus. And in the same manner into Europe, into Thessaly, and Boeotia, and Macedonia, and Aetolia, and Attica, and Argos, and Corinth, and all the most fertile and wealthiest districts of Peloponnesus. And not only are the continents full of Jewish colonies, but also all the most celebrated islands are so too; such as Euboea, and Cyprus and Crete.
>
> I say nothing of the countries beyond the Euphrates, for all of them except a very small portion, and Babylon, and all the satrapies around, which have any advantage whatever of soil or climate, have Jews settled in them. So that if my native

* Coele-Syria means "Hollow Syria." It is the valley north of Palestine between the Lebanon and Anti-Lebanon mountains.

> land is, as it reasonably may be, looked upon as entitled to a share in your favor, it is not one city only that would be benefited by you, but ten thousand of them in every region of the habitable world, in Europe, in Asia, and in Africa, on the continent, in the islands, on the coasts and in the inland parts.

Thus the king vividly portrays the great Jewish world that had grown up around Palestine, a world that reached out into all the known lands, with communities, large or little, linked to the motherland by the silver cords of a common tradition and a common faith. The Jewish population beyond the borders of Palestine may have even exceeded the 3,000,000 who dwelt within them.

The largest of these communities was domiciled in Mesopotamia, and it possessed the advantage of lying outside the boundaries of the Roman Empire. In the fertile plain between the Tigris and Euphrates, the descendants of the captives whom Sargon and Nebuchadnezzar had driven from Israel and Judah, now numbered a million souls. They were destined for an important role in their people's career. Firmly rooted in the soil of the land they inhabited and deeply attached to their faith, they enjoyed a large measure of autonomy under a governor of their own whom they called Exilarch, or "chief of the exile."

The prophet Jeremiah had sent the early captives the advice: "Build ye houses, and dwell in them, and plant gardens, and eat the fruit of them; take ye wives, and beget sons and daughters . . . And seek the peace of the city whither I have caused you to be carried away captive, and pray unto the Lord for it; for in the peace thereof shall ye have peace." This counsel the Jews of Babylonia observed in letter and in spirit; and untouched by the glamour and vices of Hellenism, the Babylonian community was preparing for the role that lay in store for it.

The second largest concentration in the Diaspora was the community in Alexandria which, geographically as well as by fortune and misfortune, was closely linked with the motherland. There, too, Jeremiah's advice was followed and the Jews prospered greatly. They lived in quarters of their own, for security as well as common worship. They had large and splendid synagogues, and at Leontopolis, not far from the land of Goshen which a Pharaoh once allotted to the sons of Jacob, a temple had been erected by a son of the hapless high priest Onias III. This son, also named Onias, had fled to Egypt where, after a brilliant military career, he was named Ethnarch, or ruler of the Jews, and permitted to build the temple.

In Alexandria, the influence of Hellenism was powerful and corrosive. Not all the Jews of the city were, like the illustrious Philo, able to combine an enthusiasm for Hellenic culture with unswerving loyalty to Torah. Many of them became lukewarm to Judaism and some fell away from it altogether; among the renegades was a nephew of Philo himself, the notorious Tiberius Alexander, who was to add to the miseries of the people he renounced.

On the River Tigris, north of Mesopotamia, lay a country called Adiabene, whose queen, Helen, and her son Izates who reigned after her, became converts to Judaism. The royal family continued Jewish for several generations and some of its members took part in the struggle against Rome. There were proselytes in other places also. In Damascus most of the women were at one time reported to have embraced the Jewish faith. There were converts in Alexandria and in Rome itself where the Jews, though not numerous, had grown to great influence. The most distinguished of the Roman proselytes was Fulvia, the wife of a senator. Her conversion incited the enemies of the Jews, and in 19 C.E. Sejanus, minister of the emperor Tiberius, expelled them from the city. The ban continued until the removal of the minister twelve years later.

Judaism was no longer a sealed book. In addition to the Septuagint and the writings of Philo, other works had appeared in Greek explaining the laws of the faith and defending them against the attacks of enemies like Apion.

Many were the ways by which the settlements of the Diaspora had come into existence. Some of them, especially those on the coasts and the islands, owed their origin to Jewish traders and sailors. Others were begun or augmented by captives whom their fellow-Jews ransomed from heathen masters. Colonies of Jewish soldiers defended the borders of Egypt against the Ethiopians, and in Babylonia also Jews were selected by the government as frontier guardsmen. Even the Romans sent a contingent of 4,000 Jews against the brigands in Sardinia. Wherever they settled, the Jews were quick to adapt themselves, learning the language of the land for their secular needs, and entering into every economic field, agricultural, industrial, commercial, and professional. Nor were they absent from the civic and political affairs of their communities, including service in the military and naval forces.

But when they prayed, the Jews of the Diaspora turned their faces to the motherland. For all the scattered communities the religious authority of the Sanhedrin was supreme. Jerusalem was their pride and the Temple their glory. From Media and Babylonia, from Asia Minor, Syria, and Egypt, from Greece and Italy, from the islands of the seas and from the coasts of Africa the annual poll tax of half a shekel, decreed in the reign of Salome Alexandra (76-67 B.C.E.), flowed into the treasury of the Temple; and on Passover, Shabuoth and Sukkoth, pilgrims from all the lands streamed to Jerusalem to feast their eyes and souls on its beauty and holiness.

4

AGRIPPA S son, who bore his father's name, was only sixteen years old when the king died, and again Rome sent a procurator to rule over Palestine. His name was Fadus and his successors, until the fateful year 66 C.E. when the revolt against Rome broke out, were Tiberius Alexander, the renegade nephew of Philo, Cumanus, Felix, Festus, Albinus, and Florus. But the names matter little. They were all alike in their brutal callousness to the sensibilities of the people they governed, and in their rapacity which reduced the Jews to poverty and despair.

The procurators were faithful mirrors of the Rome they represented: the imperial city had become a hot-bed of corruption, with the successive wives of the emperor Claudius setting the fashion in depravity and vice. It was in this atmosphere that young Agrippa grew to manhood, and the fact that he became a favorite with the court and its monarch was a portent of the ignoble part he was to play in the tragedy of his nation.

The messianic yearning continued to agitate the people. The first of the new procurators was faced with a messianic aspirant in the person of a certain Theudas who attracted large throngs with fantastic predictions and promises of miracles. The procurator dealt with him in Roman fashion: he crucified the would-be messiah together with a large number of his followers. The tragic tale repeats itself again and again, particularly in the time of the procurator Festus (60-62 C.E.). The country was like a tinderbox, and the Romans stamped out every spark that might produce the conflagration.

But with a policy of plunder and brutal suppression the Romans could not hope to subdue the Jews. Tiberius Alexander, whom the Jews hated as an apostate, captured and crucified the two Zealot leaders, Jacob and Simon, but the Zealots grew in number and audacity, and from their midst sprang a band of men who became notorious as the Sicarii, or dagger-men. They were the terror of Romans and friends of Rome alike. Many husbandmen whom Roman rapacity had ruined joined the Zealots and Sicarii, and the struggle against Rome was complicated by a struggle of the poor against the rich, who, in the main, were not disposed to challenge the might of the master.

Nor were those the only conflicts that afflicted the land. The ancient antagonism between Jews and Samaritans persisted, and in the procuratorship of Cumanus (48-52 C.E.) it broke into violence. Cumanus had already earned the hatred of the Jews: earlier in his administration, when the people had demanded the punishment of a Roman soldier for insulting their Passover service in the Temple, Cumanus had set his legionaries upon them and three thousand of them had been crushed to death in the panic that followed. Now, when some Galilean Jews on the way to Jerusalem were murdered by Samaritans and the procurator failed to act, the Zealots took the matter into their own hands. The governor of Syria intervened; the issue was carried to Rome; and, with the help of young Agrippa, Cumanus was removed and exiled.

Agrippa had come of age, and Claudius conferred upon him the northeastern provinces and the power to appoint the high priest. But Judea was given a new procurator, a former slave named Felix who, as is customary with former slaves, proved an abominable master. After eight years of misrule, during which he hunted down and crucified many of the Zealots, he was removed by the new emperor Nero. The Sicarii became more active. In their choice of victims they eschewed fine distinctions, and one of the men they struck down was the high priest Jonathan, who appears to have deserved a better fate.

But Agrippa made poor use of his power to name the high priest. Jerusalem became the scene of violent brawls between rival high-priestly families. Agrippa's appointees, moreover, robbed the lower priestly orders and maintained large bodies of retainers with whom they terrorized the people.

The procurators resided not in Jerusalem but in Caesarea, the city on the coast built by Herod and inhabited by mutually hostile Jewish and heathen communities. In other cities also there was friction between the religious groups, a condition that added to the maze of conflicts that enveloped the country. But the bloodiest affray took place in Caesarea. First, as had been the case in Alexandria, the Jews were deprived of their civil rights, and when a riot broke out in the city, the legionaries who were called in to suppress it attacked the Jews of whom great numbers were slain. It was apparent that the soldiers acted with the connivance of the procurator Florus (64-66 C.E.).

He was the last of these officials, this Florus, and a concentrate of all their vices. His passion was plunder, and the recklessness with which he indulged it drove many who had stood for patience and moderation into the camp of the Zealots. He looted the treasures of the Temple, took bribes from the enemies of the Jews, and even shared in the spoils of the professional assassins who had attached themselves to the Sicarii.

5

JUST before the final break, a series of events took place in Jerusalem that have the unreality and terror of a nightmare. Florus demanded a huge sum from the treasury of the Temple. In rage and derision the people passed the basket to collect alms for "poor Florus." The procurator unleashed his legions who, in an orgy of slaughter, slew thousands of men, women, and children. Even the wiles of the beautiful and profligate Berenice, sister of Agrippa, failed to soften the heart of the Roman governor.

Nevertheless the peace leaders prevailed on the people to go out and extend the customary greetings to a new contingent of

Romans who, shortly afterwards, came to Jerusalem from Caesarea. But the soldiers, under orders from Florus, provoked the people to new rage by failing to return the gesture. The Jews were driven into the city: they were first to reach the Temple and defied the Romans, whereupon the latter took possession of the opposite fort of Antonia.

Agrippa, friend of Rome and leader of the peace party, came to Jerusalem with 3,000 horsemen. The Zealots, led by Eleazar ben Hananiah, drove them off, burned down the house of the high priest, another leader of the peace party, and the palace of Agrippa. They captured the fort of Antonia and slew the Roman soldiers to a man.

Now the city belonged to the Zealots. The usual sacrifice for the welfare of the emperor was suspended, as well as the payment of taxes. The tiny nation threw down the gauntlet to Rome, mistress of the lands, the seas, and the nations.

CHAPTER TWENTY-TWO

The Great Revolt

THE war that followed and lasted four years (66-70 C.E.) was one of the most desperate and amazing struggles in the annals of mankind. To many, of course, it appeared from the very beginning a forlorn hope: how could little Palestine pit itself successfully against the mistress of the world? Nevertheless, the courage and tenacity of the Jews were so great that were it not for the perfidy of traitors and the dissensions among the patriots, it is not impossible to believe that the outcome might have been different. Were not the early prospects of the Maccabaean revolt just as hopeless?

The situation in Jerusalem, which Florus seems to have deliberately provoked, was now too much for him, and Agrippa prevailed on Cestius Gallus, the governor of Syria, to intervene, offering to assist him with a force of 3,000 footmen and 1,000 horsemen. Gallus assembled an army of 30,000 men, overran Galilee and the coast, and in short order stood before Jerusalem. But the siege was scarcely under way when the Roman, to the great chagrin of the traitors, ordered a retreat. Undoubtedly, the strength of the Zealots who nearly routed him on his first appearance before Jerusalem had convinced him that with the forces at his command, he could not hope to take the city.

The retreat was a terrible ordeal for the Romans. The Zealots poured out of the city and attacked their rear and flanks, cutting them down in large numbers. In the pass of Beth-horon, where invaders had come to grief in the past, Gallus managed to extricate himself by a ruse, but he lost his war material and 6,000 of his men. The patriots were jubilant, the peace party was submerged, and coins were struck with the inscription "The deliverance of Jerusalem."

2

BUT the Zealots had no illusions: the struggle had only begun. They prepared for it with feverish energy, forging weapons, strengthening the defenses of the city, drilling and training the young men. But they failed to achieve what was most important of all: unity of policy and command. It was not they who controlled the capital but the Sanhedrin, a body of rich notables whose insurgent ardor was not above suspicion. Eleazar ben Hananiah, probably the ablest Zealot leader, was sent by them to Idumaea; Joseph ben Gorion and a former high priest named Hanan were put in charge of the capital; while the defense of Galilee, the key post in the struggle, was entrusted to Joseph ben Mattathiah, who is better known as Josephus the historian.

The fame of Josephus as an historian rests principally on his account of this war, an account devoted in large measure to apologies for his own conduct. Josephus had a great deal to explain and apologize for: it is clear from his own record that he was never a single-minded patriot and ended by turning traitor.

Galilee was the nursery of Zealotism and the first line of defense. The men of Galilee were renowned for their bravery, and the province bristled with strongholds. Josephus made a great display of patriotic fervor, but there promptly sprang up a feud between him and John of Giscala, a fiery Zealot leader who ruled over a fortress in the far north. John suspected and despised the young aristocrat whom Jerusalem had sent up to take over his beloved Galilee, nor was it long before his suspicions became certainties. But Josephus, bold and adroit, defeated his attempts to expose him. Finally John sent a deputation to the capital with charges against Josephus, and a military force was dispatched to remove him. But Josephus stayed. He sent his own emissaries to Jerusalem to defend him, and when the Sanhedrin's commissioners appeared before him, he had the audacity to order them back in chains.

Galilee was in a state of virtual civil war: the first line of defense became weaker instead of stronger. In the meantime Vespasian, the best general the empire possessed, was named commander in chief of the Roman forces in Palestine. His son Titus having brought up two additional legions from Egypt, Vespasian commanded a host of 60,000 men—footmen and horsemen, archers and slingers, hardened legionaries, equipped with all the engines of war and siegecraft.

In the spring of 67 C.E. Vespasian reached Ptolemais. The stronghold of Sepphoris surrendered without a blow. The Romans advanced and the army of Josephus melted before them. Josephus himself took refuge in Tiberias.

The next citadel to fall was Gabara, whose defenders the Romans put to the sword. Then they laid siege to Jotapota, the most redoubtable fortress of them all. The cliff on which Jotapota stood was surrounded by rugged hills, and on its northern side, which alone was open to assault, the defenders had raised a high wall. On the fifth day of the siege, Josephus appeared in Jotapota and took over its defense. The Romans raised their breastworks and brought into play their battering rams and other siege-engines. The defenders made almost daily sorties, destroying the works and engines of the Romans, penetrating into their camp, and on one occasion wounding the commander in chief himself. The stronghold, Vespasian decided, could only be taken by starving the garrison into surrender. After forty-seven days of siege, with the water supply cut off, the heroic garrison, starved and exhausted, was overcome and massacred and the women and children carried off to be sold into slavery.

The capture of Jotapota brought an end to the career of Josephus as a leader of the revolt. He managed to escape the massacre of the garrison and, according to his own account, by a combination of luck and duplicity, he managed also to circumvent a suicide pact with a group of forty other survivors who had taken refuge with him in a cave. Josephus gave himself up to the Romans, was received by them with cordiality, and thereafter served as adviser of the Roman command in the war against his people.

The Romans swept on through Galilee, taking Tabor and Tiberias and, after a month's siege, capturing Gamala which was defended with true Zealot heroism. Finally, Giscala, where the fearless and high-spirited John commanded a little army of Zealots, was forced to open its gates, but not until John himself escaped with some of his men, going south to continue the struggle in the capital.

Galilee, the first bulwark of the nation, was lost. All hope and resolution were now concentrated on Jerusalem, and from every corner of the land streams of refugees and warriors flowed steadily to the capital.

3

JERUSALEM's defenses appeared impregnable, and the vast multitude of a million souls that, for refuge or combat, had gathered within its walls, felt little alarm at the approach of the enemy. Protected on the west, south, and east by the encircling valleys of Hinnom and Kidron, the city on the hills could be effectively attacked on the north only. And there a series of walls and other defenses, of which the Temple itself was the most formidable, seemed capable of defying every assault. With such fortifications and, more important still, with the indomitable spirit that animated its defenders, the city looked out unafraid upon the supreme trial that awaited her.

Besides, the enemy seemed to be in no hurry to attack Jerusalem.

Having conquered Galilee, Transjordania, Idumaea, and the lower regions of Judea, Vespasian spent the greater part of the years 68 and 69 in apparent inactivity. The general, in fact, had a greater preoccupation than the revolt of the Jews. Nero had died a suicide, and the legions were making and unmaking emperors. Vespasian, the ablest soldier of the empire, was the idol of the legions of the east, and the great prize which a number of hands weaker than his had been forced to relinquish, fell, in the middle of the year 69, into his own. The legions of Syria, Palestine, and Egypt proclaimed him emperor, and Vespasian set out for Rome, leaving his son Titus to finish the war against the Jews.

But there was still another reason for the Roman's apparent idleness. In Jerusalem the Jews were fighting his battle, and Vespasian knew it. The factional strife among them was steadily increasing and took on the proportions of a civil war. The Zealots were profoundly dissatisfied with the men who were in control of the city: that was but natural, for they were the men who were responsible for Josephus, and others among them were suspected of collusion with Agrippa and the peace party. The Zealot leaders, however, were incapable of agreeing among themselves, making unity of command impossible and insanely thwarting each other's efforts to prepare the city for effective resistance.

After a bitter and bloody struggle the Zealot leaders John of Giscala and Eleazar ben Simon settled their scores with the Sanhedrin and the peace party. The high priest Joshua ben Gamala was removed, and a humble priest put in his place. With the help of a body of Idumaean Jews, to whom they opened the gates of the city, the Zealots put down an uprising of their foes and executed the leaders. John then began to prepare the city for the siege.

But, the traitors having been suppressed, a fierce rivalry sprang up between the two Zealot leaders, and they turned their weapons on each other. The remnant of the peace party, finding the bloody strife suited to their purpose, added to it by opening the gates of the city to Simon bar Giora, a famous firebrand, intrepid leader of a band of desperate Zealots and Sicarii in the neighborhood of the fortress of Masada, near the Dead Sea. John, Eleazar, and Simon, holding different sections of the city, spent their strength in internecine conflict, instead of saving it for the common enemy. They even went to the insane extent of setting fire to each other's stores of grain.

4

IN THE early spring of the year 70, just before Passover, Titus came up with a host of 80,000 men and the siege began. He pitched his camp on Mount Scopus, the northern extension of the Mount of Olives, and brought his engines around north opposite the outer or third wall. He began with a call on the city to surrender. But the Zealots spurned his ambassador, who was none other than the subtle and ubiquitous Josephus, now the protégé and adviser of Titus; and shortly afterward, in sorties from the city, the Zealots wrought havoc in the camp of the Romans and almost slew the commander himself.

But soon enough the battering rams were crashing at the outer wall, and what reason and sanity had been powerless to accomplish, the enemy engines brought to pass: the Zealot leaders, of whom one, Eleazar ben Simon, had been eliminated, put an end to their suicidal strife. They rushed out of the city and destroyed the embankments and engines, but the enemy set up new ones. To terrorize the defenders, Titus ordered his prisoners crucified within sight of the city.

Fifteen days of continuous battering breached the outer wall; five days later the rams broke through the second wall, and the Romans were facing Fort Antonia. Here the struggle was stupendous. John of Giscala, leonine in might and daring, burned down the first works set up by the enemy against the fortress, and when the wall of Antonia came down, the Romans stood before a new wall which the Zealots had quickly erected. But new legionaries came to replace the slain, new embankments and engines were set up, and Titus used all the arts of martial eloquence to bolster the waning morale of his soldiers. Antonia fell and the Jews were driven to their last citadel—the Temple.

And now there came two grisly allies, famine and pestilence, and joined forces with the Romans. The people in the crowded city died by the thousands. Titus, who knew that the strength and valor of his legions would not suffice to take Jerusalem, had completely encircled the city with a stone wall, permitting no food to be brought in and none of the starving to escape. On the seventeenth day of the month of Tammuz the most important rite, the daily sacrifice in the Temple, came to an end. No more animals were obtainable.

In the battle for the Temple the epic struggle soon reached its climax. The Jews inflicted enormous losses on the Romans, demolishing their earthworks and defeating their attempts to scale the walls by ladder. Even the battering rams proved futile, and on the ninth day of the month of Ab Titus ordered the huge gates that opened on the courts to be set on fire. They burned for a night and a day, and the legionaries charged through. The starved and exhausted defenders, though they hurled themselves again and again on the shields and swords of the Romans, were unable to throw them back.

A burning brand, flung by a legionary, fell into one of the surrounding chambers of the sanctuary, and before it could be extinguished the Temple itself was in flames. The courts were thronged with a great concourse of people, men, women, and children, whom the legionaries, crazed with all they had suffered at the hands of the Jews, slaughtered indiscriminately. Not even Titus who, according to Josephus, was anxious to save the Temple, could restrain the fury of his men.*

The Zealots died fighting to the last. Some threw themselves bare-handed on the foe, others leaped into the flames, unwilling to survive the destruction of the Temple. The din of clashing arms and tumbling walls, of roaring flames and shrieking men, was heard for miles around, and when it died down, the glory of Judea was a heap of smoking ruins.

5

BELOW the Old Wall and the hill on which the Temple stood lay the sections of Jerusalem known as the Upper City and the Lower City. To the latter the torch was quickly applied, but

* Josephus, *The Jewish War,* VI; 4. This book is our principal source on the uprising against Rome. It should be read with caution. It was written at the command of Titus, and its bias in favor of Rome is evident throughout. There is reason to doubt that Titus was really anxious to save the Temple.

the Upper City, protected by the Old Wall, held out. The Romans raised their siege-works, the battering rams went into action, and the starved and exhausted remnants of the Zealots were overwhelmed. The garrison which Titus now lodged in the towers of Herod's palace stood guard over a dead city.

Outside the devastated capital, the enemy sought out and destroyed several thousand Zealots who had escaped and were hiding in the Jordan forests. The fortress of Herodium in Judea held out for a time, and it took a long siege to reduce Machaerus on the eastern shore of the Dead Sea. The climax of heroic resistance was reached by Masada. This almost impregnable natural fortress was held by a thousand Zealots under command of Eleazar ben Jair, who traced his descent to the founder of the party. When, after breaking down two walls, the Romans finally came through, they found only the bodies of the defenders. The Zealots, after slaying their wives and children, had turned their weapons upon themselves.

Palestine was proclaimed a Roman province, and a great part of the land became the personal property of the emperor. But the country was in ruins, its once flourishing towns and villages almost without inhabitants, dogs and jackals prowling through the devastated streets and houses. In Jerusalem, a million people are reported to have perished, with a hundred thousand taken captive to glut the slave markets of the empire. The tall and handsome youths were held for the arena, to die fighting, or to be torn by wild beasts for the entertainment of Egyptian, Syrian, and Roman spectators.

Some bands of Zealots escaped into Arabia where the long arm of Rome was unable to reach them; they settled in the neighborhood of Medina where their descendants dwelt for many centuries. Those who found themselves within the empire were not so fortunate. In the Jewish communities where they sought refuge their mere presence enflamed the smoldering hatred of the Jews against Rome. Revolts, which were put down with great cruelty, were attempted in northern Africa including Alexandria.

Sorrow and despair came down like a pall upon all the communities of the Diaspora. All that they loved and gloried in was extinguished: Jerusalem the holy and beautiful, the Sanhedrin and the Temple. With refined cruelty, Rome continued to collect the Temple-tax from the Jews but applied it to a temple of Jupiter in Rome.

6

THE magnitude and splendor of the public triumph with which Rome hailed the conqueror of Judea is a measure of the fierceness of the struggle and the losses which the embattled Jews inflicted upon her. It is doubtful if Rome ever saw a more imposing spectacle. Among the trophies that were carried in the procession were the seven-branched candlestick, the table of shew-bread and other objects taken from the Temple; and among the prisoners who were dragged in chains before the Roman populace were Simon bar Giora and John of Giscala. When the triumph was over the first was put to death, while John suffered the worse fate of lifelong incarceration.

But Rome signalized her victory in more durable symbols as well. Special coins were struck to commemorate the event, and a magnificent arch in honor of Titus who, in 79, succeeded his father as emperor, was erected in the Forum of the city. On a sculptured panel inside this arch, the spoils of the Temple borne in triumph can still be seen, and one can almost hear the shouts of the Roman multitude witnessing the procession.

Still stands the arch of Titus, its proud inscriptions dimmed, its marble crumbling slowly into ruins. But it stands rather as a monument to "the grandeur that was Rome," than as a symbol of the conquest of the Jews. For ancient Rome is only a memory, and the "conquered" Jews, in spite of that disaster and others which were to follow, are still unconquered.*

* On November 30, 1947, almost nineteen centuries after the fall of the Jewish State, the Arch of Titus was the scene of a remarkable demonstration. Thousands of Italian Jews and Jewish "Displaced Persons" in Italy marched beneath the Arch in a symbolic and jubilant procession. The day before, the General Assembly of the United Nations, meeting at Flushing Meadows, New York, had voted to re-establish in Palestine what the Romans had destroyed—the Jewish State.

Part Three 70 C.E. TO 1492

Dispersion

The Spirit Lives On

CHAPTER TWENTY-THREE

New Life

UNTIL the year 70, when the legions of Rome completed their work of devastation in Palestine, the Jews possessed the conditions that are deemed essential for national life. In its outward aspects, at least, their career was like that of other nations that have their day, brief or long, on the stage of history and vanish. They had, to begin with, a geographical center, a land of their own. They had, in addition, a polity and civilization of their own, owing allegiance to the same government, obeying the same laws, adhering to the same customs, speaking the same language, and cherishing common memories, all of these possessions being part and parcel of a common faith. Can a people, it may well be asked, pursue a distinctive career without at least a land and polity of its own?

The year 70, however, may be taken to mark the Great Divide when the career of the Jewish people became wholly unique. Broken and scattered, stripped of all the possessions that appear to be indispensable for national survival, they nevertheless preserved their integrity and remained a distinct people. And the story that records their career also becomes unique, for now it lacks a focus in space: it must wander with them over the face of the earth. It is a pageant, moreover, from which the customary sights and sounds are absent. There is no parade of pomp and power, no glitter of kings and conquerors. There is no tramp of marching armies, no thunder of battle or shouts of victory. The heroes of the story lack the glamour that captivates the eye and excites the facile imagination: they are sages and scholars, singers and dreamers, martyrs, mystics, and saints. It is a story like no other in the annals of the nations.

2

THE story, however, is not without a focus, dwelling not in space but in spirit, and beyond the reach, therefore, of fire and sword. It dwells in all that is embraced in the word Torah—faith and practice, law and doctrine, prophecy and aspiration. The loss of land and freedom only added to the power of this supreme possession, only led to a fiercer concentration around the spiritual standard. The Jewish people, conquered and dispersed, withdrew into its fortress of faith and law and lived on.

The Roman engines were still crashing against the walls of Jerusalem when out of the stricken city issued the man who was to set up anew the ancient standard. He was a *tanna*, a teacher and interpreter of Torah, and his name was Johanan ben Zaccai. Convinced of the futility of resistance, Johanan had advocated peace with Rome. Who the political master might be was a matter of indifference to him: all he desired was that he and his people should be undisturbed in the study and observance of Torah.

Johanan determined to quit the beleaguered city and set up a center of Torah in another place. It was no small task to escape the watchfulness of the Zealots, and legend has embellished ben Zaccai's enterprise with the glamour of adventure. The *tanna*, we are told, was carried out of the city in a coffin by two of his disciples, and taken before the Roman commander who granted him permission to transfer his school to the little town of Jabneh near Jaffa.

A troop of disciples quickly gathered about the teacher. Some of them expected to resume their studies before long in Jerusalem, and when they learned that the city was taken and destroyed, the Temple burnt down, and the Sanhedrin slain or scattered, they gave way to despair. Their leader, however, stood firm. True, the daily Temple sacrifice, considered an essential of the national cult, was no longer possible; but Johanan, with the prophets for authority, declared that good deeds and the study of Torah were more pleasing to God than sacrifice. Had not the prophet Hosea proclaimed:

I desire mercy and not sacrifice,
And the knowledge of God rather than burnt offerings.

Before long Johanan was compelled to take another important step. The religious life of the people, not only in Palestine but in the numerous communities of the Diaspora, required direction and regulation. These functions had formerly been exercised by the Sanhedrin, and Johanan proceeded to establish a new Sanhedrin at Jabneh. It could not, of course, compare with its august predecessor, but in time the Romans granted it a measure of recognition. It came to be known as the *Bet-Din*, or Court of Justice, and its authority as the supreme Jewish tribunal was established when it assumed the right of fixing the dates for the observance of new moons and festivals.

Thus Judaism acquired a new national center under a wise and firm leader. His influence derived solely from intellectual and moral preeminence, and his wisdom sprang from an insight into the character and destiny of his people. He saved his people at a time when an overwhelming national disaster and the advent of a new faith and new doctrines combined to threaten the Jews with extinction. These doctrines, soon to eventuate in the new religion of Christianity, sprang from passionate Messianic yearnings, from despair of the world and the renunciation of life. Already Paul of Tarsus, having accepted Jesus of Nazareth as the Christ or Messiah, had proclaimed the abrogation of the laws of Torah, and called on men to despise the things of this world and prepare for the second coming of Jesus. Johanan and his disciples rejected the new teaching: like other generations who had lived in times of crisis, they faced their problems not in a spirit of surrender, but of affirmation and renewed faith.

The source whence the fresh streams of living waters issued was the old fountain, the Torah. The master and his disciples continued to weave the fabric of Oral Torah, which not only sheltered them against the harsh winds that blew around them, but brought them relief and delight. For Oral Torah consisted not only of Halachah, or law in the strict sense of the word, but also of Haggadah, or poetry and legend; and even the study of

Halachah had a fascination of its own. The school at Jabneh was open to all who were willing and able to follow the discourses of the master and the intricate discussions of his disciples. They were not a body of professional teachers and students: it had now become a fixed tradition that Torah must not be used as "a spade to dig with." Every scholar, no matter how distinguished, was expected to obtain his livelihood from some other occupation, preferably of a manual character. Teachers and students usually met for study and discussion after the day's work in field or workshop.

3

JOHANAN died in the arms of his disciples. His piety and shrewd wisdom are manifest in his final admonition to them: "May the fear of God influence your actions as much as the fear of man."

Johanan's successor, known as Gamaliel II, had a stormy career. Gamaliel was a man of distinguished lineage, a descendant of the great Hillel and of several generations of heads of the Sanhedrin in Jerusalem. With the consent of the Roman governor, Gamaliel assumed the title of *Nasi*, the meaning of which is "prince" or "patriarch." He thus became the founder of the Patriarchate, which became hereditary and continued as the highest office of the community in Palestine for more than three centuries.

Gamaliel succeeded in putting an end to the controversy that broke out afresh between the followers of Shammai and those of Hillel. There was danger of a serious division in the doctrines and practices of Judaism, which the *Nasi* averted by decreeing the interpretations of Hillel and his school to be valid in practice, granting at the same time that those of Shammai also possessed divine origin. "Both are the words of the living God," was the formula by which the acrimony of the strife was allayed. Gamaliel himself, however, became involved in serious differences with his colleagues at Jabneh, in particular with the learned and gentle Joshua ben Hananiah and the equally learned but ungentle Eliezer ben Hyrcanus, the *Nasi's* brother-in-law. The *Nasi*, who was not distinguished for tactfulness, used his power of excommunication too freely. He was removed from his position for a time, but in recognition of his merits and after a reconciliation with Joshua, he was reinstated.

Thus the annals of the decades after the year 70, though meager, disclose an intense intellectual activity, with the Sanhedrin at Jabneh gaining steadily in respect and authority. A new national center had come into existence, holding together the remnants of the people. Vacancies in the Sanhedrin were filled with scholars who, through the ceremony of "laying on of hands,"* or ordination, were declared to be qualified for the honor and responsibility. Nor were legal matters alone dealt with by the Sanhedrin. In Gamaliel's day an important and hotly debated question was whether the Song of Songs and Ecclesiastes should be received into the Bible canon. The two books were subsequently admitted but others, like the Proverbs of ben Sira, were excluded and became part of the Apocrypha.

4

SOME fifty years after the fall of Jerusalem, when Gamaliel II was at the zenith of his career, the fields and vineyards of Palestine were again being cultivated. A new generation of Jews now lived in the land, repairing its ruins and rebuilding the national life. In towns and villages communities arose with law courts of their own and elected councils that managed communal affairs, including education, philanthropy, and public safety. The synagogue took the place of the Temple, prayer and the study of Torah the place of sacrifice.

The principal prayer was the *Amidah*,† called also *Shemoneh-esreh*, or "Eighteen Benedictions." Before the *Amidah* came the *Shema*, which proclaims the basic doctrine of the faith: "Hear O Israel, the Lord is our God, the Lord is One." The Torah was read in the synagogues on Sabbaths and festivals. It was also read on Mondays and Thursdays, when the farmers, many of whom had no synagogues where they lived, came to town to sell their produce. The Torah is still read in synagogues on those days.

Education, which was compulsory for boys, was one of the

* Hebrew, *semichah,* a word still employed to mean the act of certifying a rabbi.
† Derived from the word meaning "to stand," the prayer being recited standing.

chief cares of every community. To every house of worship was attached an elementary as well as a higher school. In the first, the principal study was the Bible; in the second, it was Oral Torah as handed down by the *tannaim.* Children of the poor and orphans were educated at the expense of the community.

Jewish life in Palestine appeared to be on the road to recovery. The ancient faith found new props, it evolved new safeguards for the preservation of the people. But the fires of hope and hate which the new generation had inherited continued to smolder, and before long burst into new and devastating conflagrations.

CHAPTER TWENTY-FOUR

Rebels and Sages

THE hate was directed against Rome, the tyrant who had laid waste their land, given its fairest fields to strangers, and was still diverting the tax they paid for the Temple at Jerusalem to a temple of Jupiter in Rome. The hope that stirred the new generation was that their Temple would be speedily rebuilt and its glories restored. "Let our eyes behold Thy return in mercy to Zion," they prayed three times a day, a prayer the Patriarch Gamaliel had inserted into the "Eighteen Benedictions."

Forty-five years after the fall of Jerusalem, the old flame of Zealotry burst with a strange and savage violence. Exactly what happened the annals do not make clear, but throughout the Mediterranean world, it appears, the Jews were roused to fury by an attempt of Emperor Trajan to extend the boundaries of Rome eastward into Mesopotamia and Parthia. This attempt, if successful, would have put the yoke of Rome upon the large and flourishing Jewish community of Babylonia. Trajan was a brilliant soldier. Early in his reign he added regions that are now part of Rumania and Hungary to the empire. About the year 105 he carved out a new province east of Syria and Palestine including the Sinai Peninsula, enabling Rome to control the trade routes from Arabia.

Ten years later he subdued Armenia and Mesopotamia and prepared to invade Parthia.

The following year, however, the conquered provinces, with the Jews of Mesopotamia in the lead, revolted. At the same moment, apparently in accordance with a preconcerted plan, the Jews of Cyprus, North Africa, Egypt, and Palestine rose up in arms, and with incredible ferocity fell upon their heathen rulers and neighbors. The victims of their fury are reported by the Roman chroniclers to have numbered hundreds of thousands. In the meantime, Trajan had suffered a humiliating defeat in Parthia which, owing in large part to the Jewish uprisings, he was never able to retrieve.

That the motherland was a formidable factor in this second challenge of the Jewish people to the might of Rome may be inferred from the fact that Lucius Quietus, the general who quelled the uprising in Mesopotamia, was made governor of Palestine. The leaders of the revolt in Palestine seem to have been two brothers, Pappus and Julianus, who were afterwards joined by the leader of the revolt in North Africa. The uprising came to an end when Quietus, after a relentless siege, captured and destroyed the city of Lydda where the Jewish forces were gathered. In Egypt and Cyprus the rebellions were put down by Marcius Turbo after bitter fighting and wholesale slaughter.

2

MESOPOTAMIA was abandoned by Trajan's successor, Aelius Hadrian, and the Babylonian Jewish community was saved from Roman domination. Under Hadrian, however, the Jews again threw down the gauntlet to Rome, and this time the motherland was the principal theater of revolt. The new emperor had inherited the task of bringing the second Jewish uprising to an end and seems afterwards to have adopted a policy of conciliation. He recalled the brutal Quietus and had him executed. He even promised to permit the Jews to rebuild the Temple.

The promise was not fulfilled: the Samaritans, it appears, again opposed the project as their ancestors had done in the beginning of the Second Commonwealth. The Jews were bitterly disappointed. In the year 130, moreover, Hadrian ordered Jerusalem to be rebuilt, not as the capital of the Jews, but as a Roman city to be named Aelia Capitolina, with a temple to Jupiter on the site of the Jewish sanctuary. The disappointment of the Jews changed to fury.

The old sage Joshua ben Hananiah, who had probably succeeded Gamaliel as Patriarch, managed for a brief interval to curb his people's wrath. It is recorded that he told them the fable of the lion and the crane. The lion was feasting with too much relish and a bone stuck in his throat. Thereupon he promised the crane a handsome reward if she would insert her long neck between his jaws and pull the bone out. When, however, after performing the service, the crane claimed her reward, the lion answered: "Is it not enough that your head is safe after having been in the jaws of a lion?" The crane insisted no further. Should the Jews, asked Joshua, insist that the Roman lion fulfill his promises?

Not long afterwards, however, Hadrian issued another edict which made revolt inevitable. It was not, it is said, directed against the Jews in particular—it was an old Roman law against mutilation which Hadrian saw fit to revive—but under it the Jews were forbidden to practice the rite of circumcision. The records of the period are confused, and it may well be that the rebuilding of Jerusalem as Aelia Capitolina as well as the ban against circumcision were consequences rather than causes of the third uprising of the Jews against Rome. What is certain is that the deeper causes of the revolt must be sought in the thwarted hopes of the Jewish patriots who had fought against Trajan, and beyond that in the implacable hostility of the Jews against Rome. The fact is that in the interval of fifteen years after the suppression of the second outbreak, the Jewish patriots had made extensive preparations for the next attempt. They fortified the caves in which the country abounded, connected them with subterranean passages, and stored arms in secret places.

3

THE uprising that followed found two brilliant leaders who, against a less formidable adversary than Rome, might have won the freedom of their people. They were the scholar Akiba ben Joseph and the warrior Simon bar Kochba. Akiba is a figure of fabulous splendor. He was the leading *tanna* of his generation, perhaps even of his century, and to his luster as a sage he added the crown of a patriot and martyr. His epic career has been embellished with legend and romance. It is told of Akiba ben Joseph that in his youth and early manhood he was only a shepherd. Rachel, his master's daughter, fell in love with him and, defying her father's commands, became his wife. Notwithstanding her love, however, she sent him away with the admonition not to return until he had become a great scholar. Years later the former shepherd came back followed by a great retinue of students who addressed him reverently as "Rabbi" or master.

Akiba belonged to the circle of Gamaliel II, and about the year 95 he accompanied the Patriarch on a journey to Rome, undertaken, it appears, for the purpose of petitioning the emperor Domitian to allay his persecutions against the Jews. Later Akiba made many other journeys. He visited Parthia, Asia Minor, and perhaps Africa and Europe, in all likelihood seeking the support of the Jewish communities of the Diaspora in preparation for the struggle against Rome.

Akiba was inspired with the conviction that the advent of the Messiah was at hand, and he saw the deliverer in the warrior Simon bar Kochba. Not much that is certain is known of bar Kochba: he looms against the period more than half hidden in the mists of legend. His name, it is thought, was originally bar Kozba, and in token of his messianic mission it was changed, perhaps by Akiba himself, to bar Kochba, meaning "son of a star." Bar Kochba, we are told, was gifted with incredible strength and prowess: among other feats, he could stop with his knees the stones the Romans hurled from their ballistae. He was undoubtedly a soldier of heroic mold, worthy of taking his stand beside the Zealot leaders of the year 70.

4

IN 131, Emperor Hadrian was visiting Egypt, Palestine, and Syria; the Jewish patriots waited for his departure, and the following year the revolt broke out. From every corner of Palestine and from other countries too, the Jews flocked to bar Kochba's standard. Even Samaritans made common cause with them: only the Nazarenes, as the new sect of Christians was called, held aloof, an attitude which bar Kochba regarded as treason and for which he made them pay dearly. The forces of bar Kochba are reported to have numbered hundreds of thousands, and although the report is no doubt an exaggeration, bar Kochba must have commanded a formidable array. The power of recovery displayed by the Jews is nothing short of amazing: it was the third major war in less than two generations fought by a little nation against the mightiest empire on earth.

The war lasted three years and exacted the best that Rome possessed in generalship and arms. The Roman governor of Palestine, the depraved Tinnius Rufus, suffered one defeat after another, and the same fate befell the legate of Syria, Publius Marcellus, who went to the governor's assistance. Fifty fortified places and numerous other towns and villages were seized by the victorious rebels. Finally, Jerusalem itself was captured by bar Kochba, who thereupon proclaimed the restoration of the Jewish state, striking coins to signalize the event and stamping them with the words: "For the freedom of Israel."

Hadrian himself hurried back to Palestine and shortly afterwards he summoned Julius Severus, his ablest general, to leave England, where he was putting down a rebellion of the Britons, and quell the uprising of the Jews. Slowly but relentlessly the huge war machine that was Julius Severus' to command swept down from the north, recapturing one stronghold after another and forcing the Jewish patriots to their retreats in the mountains. The Romans fought over fifty battles before they were again masters of the country; and so great were their losses that when the emperor reported his final victory to the Senate he omitted the customary formula, "I and the army are well."

After holding the capital for two years bar Kochba was compelled to abandon it and in Bethar, a fortified place southwest of the city, he made his last stand against the enemy. For a long time Bethar defied the Roman legions and their siege engines. Famine decimated the defenders, but the survivors fought on. Once the Romans were on the point of giving up the siege, but Bethar finally fell, as a result, according to one report, of Samaritan treachery; and among the many who were slain defending the citadel to the last was bar Kochba himself.

Over half a million, it is estimated, fell in the war fighting the Roman legions, besides those who succumbed to famine and pestilence. The victorious Romans avenged themselves on the Jews with more than their customary ferocity: they massacred great numbers and seized many others to be sold in the slave markets, which became glutted with Jewish captives. Palestine, and particularly Judea, again became a desolate waste. Jerusalem alone stood up among the ruins, but it was a pagan city, with its temple to Jupiter and other heathen gods. Hadrian colonized it with Roman, Phoenician and Syrian legionaries. Jews were forbidden on pain of death to approach it.

Bethar, according to tradition, fell on the ninth day of Ab, a portentous day in the annals of the Jews. But Jewish resistance was not over: the Romans had to put down a formidable Jewish force near Tiberias. They enticed some of the fugitives out of their retreats by false promises, and established a cordon of garrisons to capture those who sought safety in flight to other lands. There were many, however, who made their way to Arabia where they were safe from the avenging arm of Rome.

CHAPTER TWENTY-FIVE

The Mishnah

BUT Hadrian was not satisfied with crushing the rebellion and transforming Jerusalem into a pagan city: he determined to destroy Judaism altogether. Like Antiochus IV in his day, Hadrian issued a series of edicts making it a capital crime to follow the basic practices of Judaism, such as circumcision and the observance of the Sabbath. The Roman, however, went even further than his predecessor. Advised in all likelihood by traitors or by members of the new sect of Nazarenes, the emperor included among the capital crimes the teaching of Torah and the ceremony of ordination. Hadrian was well advised, for Torah, as well as the practice of ordination which perpetuated its teaching, was the very breath of the faith he was determined to stamp out.

A reign of terror was instituted against all those who remained loyal to the faith, the Roman officials being particularly zealous in hunting down the sages and their pupils. The leaders of the bleeding remnants of the people thereupon held a secret meeting and voted to distinguish between laws of primary and laws of secondary importance, condoning a breach of the latter which might be committed in order to escape death and torture. The laws of primary importance were declared to be those that prohibited murder, adultery, and idolatry, and were declared inviolable. The teachers, however, decided that they themselves must be denied any immunity: as leaders of the people they must bear the full burden of the faith. They were especially resolved to continue the teaching of Torah and many of them suffered martyrdom. The martyrs included men of the highest eminence; among them was Akiba ben Joseph, who died under torture with the *Shema* on his lips, rejoicing that he was privileged to sanctify God's name with his death.

Another of the illustrious martyrs was Judah ben Baba, whom the Romans surprised in the act of ordaining seven of Akiba's disciples. Judah performed the rite in a valley in Galilee near Usha, for the school at Jabneh had come to an end and the students and teachers sought refuge in the north. Judah was seized by the Romans, but the young scholars he ordained escaped to Babylonia.

2

BEFORE long, however, these scholars returned to their native land, where a change for the better had taken place. In 138 Hadrian died, and his successor, the humane and wise Antoninus Pius, ended most of the persecutions against the Jews, including the prohibitions against the observance of the faith. The school and Sanhedrin could again be set up, and a gathering of scholars took place in the town of Usha, which before long replaced Jabneh as the center of the community. However, the edict that barred the Jews on pain of death from Jerusalem or

Aelia Capitolina, as the city was now called, remained in force, and they were forbidden to make proselytes, a restriction that testifies to the attraction which Judaism still exerted upon other faiths.

A son of Gamaliel II, known as Simon II, was recognized as Patriarch. Simon had escaped from the massacre at Bethar and spent a number of years in Babylonia, where he was impressed by the power and dignity of the Exilarch (chief of the Exile), as the head of the Babylonian Jewish community was called. As Patriarch, Simon was eager to enjoy the same status but he lacked the preeminent scholarship which alone could sanction his claim. Like his father before him, Simon found himself in difficulties with some of his colleagues. His leading opponents were Meir, the most brilliant scholar of his generation, and Nathan of Babylonia, a son of the Exilarch. The dissensions, however, did not impede the paramount task of the period—the elaboration of the Oral Tradition.

This elaboration was, of course, accomplished by the collective labor of generations of *tannaim*. Each of the generations was illumined by stars of the first magnitude: Hillel, Johanan ben Zaccai, Akiba ben Joseph, Meir, and others. The culmination of the process was the great code known as the Mishnah, the most important step toward its completion having been taken by Akiba. It was he who brought the whole process back to its origin, the Torah, by discovering new and hidden meanings in every word and letter of the sacred text. What is even more important, he arranged the vast body of Halachah and Haggadah into an orderly system, without, however, writing it down.

Meir, who had been a pupil of Akiba, continued in the path laid out by his master. Meir was also a man of broad sympathies and varied interests. He numbered Samaritans and learned pagans among his friends, and even kept up relations with the famous renegade Elisha ben Abuyah, better known as Acher.* The spirit that lived in these sages is illustrated by the story of Meir and his wife Beruriah, the modest and learned daughter of Chanina ben Teradion. Meir and Beruriah had two young sons and one Sabbath

* The name means "another," signifying that Elisha's apostasy had completely transformed him.

afternoon both of them died. When Meir came home from the synagogue, his wife said nothing until the close of the Sabbath, when she told him that someone had entrusted some jewels to her and had now come to claim them. Was it right, she asked, to give them up? "But how can you ask such a question?" her husband replied. She led him to the room where their sons lay dead. "Behold," said she, "Here are the jewels! The Lord gave and the Lord has taken away."

3

THERE were other bright stars whose light pierced the gloom in which the Jews of Palestine were still shrouded. There was Judah ben Ilai who delighted as much in deeds of kindness as in learning. There was Jose ben Halaftha, sage and historian, who supported himself as a worker in leather. There were numerous others, but the most picturesque figure among them is undoubtedly Simon ben Yochai. Condemned to death by the Romans, Simon escaped and hid in a cave where he lived with his son Eleazer for thirteen years. Many marvelous stories grew up about Simon: he was credited with power to work miracles, and centuries later he came to be regarded as the founder of the mystic lore of Cabala.

The terrible wounds which bar Kochba's revolt left on the Jewish community of Palestine began to heal, but the longing for deliverance never died. The year 161 saw this longing in fresh ferment. That year two emperors in joint partnership, Verus Commodus and Marcus Aurelius, came to the throne of Rome, and her inveterate foe, the Parthians, declared war and invaded Syria. Many of the Jews saw deliverance on their borders and rose up against the oppressor. But the revolt, it seems, was a mere flare which was quickly extinguished by the governor of Syria. The Parthians, after some initial victories, were compelled to retire, and still another dream of freedom lay shattered.

The Romans imposed new restrictions on the Jews. They deprived them of their courts of justice, and kept a special watch on the Sanhedrin at Usha. But after Verus died and the Empire was ruled by the wise and just Marcus Aurelius, the special laws were repealed. According to one report it was Simon ben Johai who traveled to Rome and secured their abrogation.

4

ABOUT the year 170, the patriarch Simon II was succeeded by his son Judah Ha-Nasi. Judah was first in learning as he was first in authority. Moreover, he possessed great wealth which he employed wisely and unselfishly. He was respected by the Roman officials, and tradition records that he was on intimate terms with the emperor. Throughout his patriarchate, which lasted nearly half a century, no one presumed to challenge his authority. So great was the esteem in which his colleagues and disciples held him, that they referred to him simply as "Rabbi," implying that he was the rabbi or teacher *par excellence*, and by that name he became best known to posterity. He died in 217, having spent the last years of his life in the Galilean town of Sepphoris, where his school and the Sanhedrin also established their domicile.

The generation of Judah Ha-Nasi was the last of the line of *tannaim:* it saw the completion of the Mishnah toward which the labors of all of them converged. Under the direction of the Patriarch, this compilation of the Oral Tradition received its definitive form, and about the year 200 it was reduced to writing.

This great compendium of law and lore names one hundred and forty-eight *tannaim*, but many others contributed to the work who are anonymous. Its language is Hebrew, although the vernacular of the Jews at the time was probably Aramaic, and its foundation, of course, is the Bible; more particularly, the Five Books of Moses. The Mishnah is divided into six parts or "Orders," which are in turn divided into *messichtot* or tractates. The Order of "Seeds" deals with agriculture; "Seasons" with festivals and fast days; "Women" with marriage and divorce; "Damages" with crimes and compensation. Appended to "Damages" is the famous collection of ethical maxims known as *Pirke Aboth* or "Sayings of the Fathers." The fifth Order is called "Holy Things" and contains the laws governing religious observances; and the sixth and last is "Purities," and deals with the laws of ritual purity and impurity.

Thus, notwithstanding persecution, war, and terror, the mind and spirit of the remnant in Palestine continued to labor and bear fruit. The Mishnah, as we shall see, served as the foundation for the Talmud, just as the Bible was the foundation for the Mishnah, and all three made up the citadel of the Jewish people in the dark ages that followed.

CHAPTER TWENTY-SIX

The Patriarchate

THE disaster of the year 70, which put an end to the ascendancy of the Jews in Palestine, lifted none of the other national groups to the place the Jews relinquished. The land became the home of a motley population with no common memories, interests, or aspirations to weld them together. In this human potpourri, moreover, we miss nearly all of the nations that march through the pages of the Bible. In the west, we now look in vain for the redoubtable Philistines who gave their name to the entire land, the terror of Israel in the days before King David. Gath, Ashdod, and Ekron of their proud "Five City District" have become mere memories; while Gaza and Ashkelon still remain, the people that dwelt in them are gone. The same is true of the Phoenician cities in the north: centuries of subjection to Seleucid and Roman rulers had thoroughly Hellenized them and made the descendants of the ancient sea rangers indistinguishable from the immigrants who hailed from Greece and Macedonia. In the markets and workshops of those cities the language spoken was not the ancient Phoenician which was so much like the Hebrew, nor even the Aramaic which had once held dominion throughout the east, but Greek. The Ammonites and Moabites were no more, as well as the Midianites and the other ancient prowlers of the desert; and even the Edomites, or Idumaeans as they were later called, became absorbed by the Nabataean Arabs who occupied the Transjordanian regions and whose capital Petra, a rocky fortress of fantastic beauty and immense natural strength, became an important commercial center.

In fact, of the many nations other than the Jews who have a place in the Bible narrative we now encounter only the Samaritans who still regarded themselves, as indeed their handful of descendants still regard themselves today, as the custodians of the genuine Jewish faith. After the Great Revolt, when the Samaritans made common cause with the Jews, the relations between the two communities fluctuated from friendliness to hostility until, about the year 300, the Sanhedrin issued a decree enjoining complete separation between them.

In the cities once held by Moabites and Ammonites, by Philistines and Phoenicians, as well as in many others formerly inhabited by Jews, now swarmed "a mixed multitude" whom it would be difficult to designate by any ethnographic term. They are sometimes called Greco-Romans, and there were no doubt Greeks and Romans among them. But there were also Syrians, Egyptians, and newcomers from the other lands of the vast Roman Empire. They made up the bulk of the population of Aelia Capitolina, the former Jerusalem; they dwelt in large numbers in the cities of the coast and of Transjordania; they occupied many of the choice agricultural regions, particularly in Samaria. And they had, of course, brought with them the gods of the lands from which they hailed, so that Palestine became the home of nearly every variety of heathen cult and strange worship.

2

BUT a new religion had now made its appearance in Palestine, which was destined to spread over the greater part of the earth and make the place of its birth a holy land to the leading nations of mankind. By every token the Roman world, with its wretched and brutalized masses, was ripe for a new faith. The pagan cults were moribund, they failed to satisfy the yearnings of the human spirit; the Greek gods were too hard and aloof for men whose daily lot was oppression and sorrow. Even in Greece and Italy, the classic pagan lands, the cult of the more intimate and "human" gods of the East, of Mithras and Serapis and other Oriental deities, had won numerous proselytes; and the elements of the old faiths were combined into new and fantastic beliefs, into the mystic doctrines of the Gnostics, early Christians, and other sects who sought an answer to the eternal problem of human suffering.

That problem, in the cruel world to which the great masses of humanity were doomed, had become acute. Life was terribly hard. The lot of the numerous slaves on the estates of the wealthy few was literally worse than that of cattle, while the small farmers and craftsmen found themselves crushed beneath the constantly growing burden of taxation. Emperor Caracalla, in the year 212, granted the rights of Roman citizenship to all the inhabitants of the Empire. The aim of this apparently liberal measure, however, was to increase the public revenues so that the ruling classes, from the emperor down to the petty officials, could live in opulence and debauchery, while the millions of slaves, husbandmen, and artisans were sunk in hopeless toil and misery. Small wonder that these millions were eager to embrace the promise of something better, even if its fulfillment should be postponed beyond the grave.

In the general search for a nobler faith, Judaism, although it pursued no aggressive missionary policy, had won many adherents among the pagans. There were numerous converts to Judaism in the west as well as in the east. The synagogues in Rome were attended by Romans, and Jewish rites made their appearance in Roman homes. In the year 95 Emperor Domitian, brother and successor of Titus, sentenced to death his own nephew, Flavius Clemens, for having embraced Judaism. There were even proselytes in Alexandria, despite the hostile relations between the Jews and pagans of that city. But the most illustrious convert was Aquila, a native of Pontus on the Black Sea and a relative of Emperor Hadrian. Aquila, who had at first joined the Christians, became a disciple of Akiba ben Joseph under whose guidance he made a new translation of the Hebrew Scriptures into Greek.

But Judaism was not only a faith and a body of doctrine; it was also a stern discipline and its progress among the pagans was bound to be slow. The Jewish teachers were not anxious to make their faith an "easy" one. On the contrary, they continued to build higher "the fence around the Law," multiplying rites and duties which, while congenial to their own people, looked forbidding to others.

The new religion of Christianity, on the other hand, adopted a wholly different policy It began, it is true, as an apparently unimportant departure from Judaism, its first followers being all Jews who only differed from their fellows in the belief that the Messiah had already come in the person of Jesus of Nazareth. In their mode of life the Nazarenes, as these first Christians were called, were very much like the Essenes, living in separate communities, renouncing marriage, and holding their property in common. A radical change of policy, however, was launched by Paul of Tarsus. He traveled through the heathen world as far west as Rome, and he knew how to address himself to the pagans of his day. Paul gave the new religion its greatest impetus by declaring the Jewish laws no longer binding. Now it was easy to become a Christian, and the new faith spread rapidly: the missionary policy initiated by Paul carried it to every part of the Roman Empire.

In Palestine the Jewish Nazarenes refused to accept Paul's abrogation of the law and continued as a separate sect under the name of *Ebionites* (Poor Men), but the apostle's teachings found many converts among the other inhabitants of the land, who looked upon the *Ebionites* as heretics. Now the breach between Judaism and Christianity became too wide to be healed and the missionaries and bishops of Palestine, whose church came to be regarded as the mother church of the new faith, conceived a special hatred against Judaism, the only one of the old faiths that refused to give way to the new.

3

BUT as long as Christianity was itself a persecuted sect, its hostility did not seriously affect the Jews of Palestine. For somewhat more than two centuries after the death of Judah Ha-Nasi, the Jewish community continued to be governed by the patriarchs. There were occasional flurries of revolt, like the one in 193 when Septimus Severus was fighting for the imperial crown against Pescennius Niger, the governor of Syria. It was this Niger who once told a Jewish deputation which came to complain of the unbearable burden of taxation that he was sorry he could not tax the very air they breathed. But the Roman emperors were frequently at war with Parthia or Neo-Persia and they sometimes thought it wise, in view of the powerful Jewish community in

Babylonia, not to be too harsh with their Jewish subjects in Palestine. There were times, therefore, when the relations between Jews and Romans were almost friendly.

Judah I was followed in 217 by his son Gamaliel III, who after holding office for eight years, was succeeded by Judah II. The latter, unlike his illustrious grandfather, was not the greatest scholar of his age: he was eclipsed in learning by Johanan bar Nappacha who, as his name testifies, was the son of a blacksmith; by Eleazar ben Pedath, who came from Babylonia; and by Simon ben Lakish, who in his youth was a gladiator but, under the guidance of the blacksmith's son, became a formidable dialectitian.

But though others might surpass the patriarch in scholarly attainments, the office invested its holder with authority that extended to the Jewish communities of other lands, including Babylonia. It was an authority that was recognized by the Roman master: the emperors Antoninus and Alexander Severus, we gather, were on terms of friendship with the patriarchs Judah I and Judah II respectively. Severus, who reigned from 222 to 235, was particularly friendly to the Jews and sympathetic to their faith.

The era of the *tannaim* was now over, the completion of the Mishnah having signalized the end of their labors. The new era in the growth of Torah is known as that of the *amoraim*, a word meaning "speakers" or interpreters. The new generation of scholars expounded the terse sayings of the Mishnah, and applied them to new needs as they arose. The most important school in Palestine was now located in Tiberias, but there were other centers of learning like the one in Lydda, which was headed by the illustrious Joshua ben Levi. He, we are told, once visited Rome. He saw many things in the imperial capital that excited his wonder and admiration; but he saw also a statue covered with a fine cloth to protect it from the rain and, lying at its base, a half-naked beggar shivering in the cold.

4

JUDAH II died in 255, and was followed by his son Gamaliel IV, who held office for twenty years. For some twelve years of the patriarchate of Gamaliel IV, Palestine was subject to Palmyra, a city located on an oasis in the Syrian desert, known also by its

Hebrew name of Tadmor and believed to have been founded by King Solomon. In 260 Odenathus, prince of Palmyra, defeated the Persians and the Romans allowed him to take possession of Palestine. But twelve years later his widow, the celebrated Queen Zenobia, incurred their wrath. She was defeated and dethroned, and Palestine returned to the dominion of Rome.

Gamaliel IV was succeeded by his son Judah III, who was patriarch from 275 to 320. It was in his time that the Roman imperial throne was seized by a general named Constantine, who was destined to have a profound influence on the course of history in general and on the fate of Palestine and the Jews in particular.

CHAPTER TWENTY-SEVEN

Christian Palestine

THE Christian communities throughout the empire, with their clergy and laity, had, despite the persecutions visited upon them by previous emperors and to a large degree even because of those persecutions, become a power, and Constantine, fighting for the imperial throne against formidable rivals, took the shrewd course of enlisting those communities on his side.

After defeating one of his rivals in a great battle fought in 312 at Milvian Bridge near Rome, a victory which made him master of the western part of the empire, Constantine issued an edict from the city of Milan proclaiming equal toleration for all religions. Thirteen years later, having in the meantime also defeated Licinius, the ruler of the east, Constantine, seated on a throne of gold, presided over a Christian Council at Nicaea in Asia Minor. The leading clergy of the empire, numbering nearly 300, had gathered to deal with certain dissensions which had risen up among them and threatened to undermine the new faith upon which Constantine relied to check the disintegration of his vast empire. The most alarming issue concerned the question of the divinity of Jesus: the followers of Athanasius of Alexandria insisted that the Nazarene was another "person" of the same godhead; the followers of Arius, also of Alexandria, were equally adamant in their contention that he was on a plane lower than God. The bishops wrangled and even came to blows but in the end Athanasius triumphed. The Council adopted the Nicene Creed requiring all Christians to believe that Jesus was "of the same substance as God," and a later ecumenical or world council, held at Constantinople in 381, completed the Trinity by declaring still another "person," the Holy Ghost, as being "of the same substance." Constantine himself was not baptized until shortly before his death in 357, but the year 325, the year of the Council of Nicaea, may be taken as the date when Christianity became the official religion of Rome.

It was only natural that Palestine should be an object of special interest and veneration to Christians. The church at Jerusalem became known as the mother church of Christendom; and soon pilgrims began to stream toward Palestine from all parts of the empire. Numerous spots that were associated, correctly or mistakenly, with the life and death of the Nazarene were proclaimed holy places. The most famous of the early pilgrims was Helena, the mother of Constantine, who claimed to have discovered the very cross to which Jesus was nailed and the tomb or sepulcher in which he was laid. On the site of the sepulcher the emperor ordered the immediate erection of magnificent churches. The number of pilgrims continued to multiply as well as the holy places, many of which were destined to become a source of violent contention among different sects and to play an important role in history.

2

THE edicts of Constantine extended toleration to Judaism also, but the victory of Christianity added enormously to the power of the clergy in Palestine and they lost no time in imposing upon the Jews the same repressions of which they themselves had been the victims. The Jews were forbidden to make converts and the old law of Hadrian, which barred them from Jerusalem, was revived. The persecutions became especially severe in the reign of Constantine's son and successor, Constantius II.

In 351 the Jews of Palestine were goaded to rebellion, and a new "Messiah," who called himself Natrona, and whom the Romans called Patricius, arose in Galilee and defied the Roman legate Ursicinus and his legions. The Romans, it appears, were preparing to march against Neo-Persia and were no doubt imposing new tax burdens on the Jews. Natrona and his followers were crushed. The three principal centers of Jewish learning, Tiberias, Lydda and Sepphoris, were destroyed. The Patriarchate fell into decline: Hillel II, who succeeded Judah III in 320 and held office until 365, was the last of the patriarchs to exercise real authority.

Toward the end of Hillel's incumbency, between 361 and 363, the Jews of Palestine enjoyed a breathing spell under the liberal and brilliant emperor Julian, whom historians have stigmatized as Julian the Apostate. He restored the ancient Roman religion as the religion of the state and treated the Jews with singular liberality, even promising to let them rebuild Jerusalem and the Temple. The promise, which Julian knew would rally the Jews to his support, was announced on the eve of a campaign against the Neo-Persian monarch Shapur II. At the emperor's expense, material and workmen were assembled at Jerusalem, but fires, which the Christian chroniclers ascribe to divine intervention, broke out in the ruins and the work was suspended. Julian met his death in the campaign against Neo-Persia. He was slain by an arrow, shot, it is said, by one of his own archers, a Christian.

The principle of religious toleration, which the Roman emperors who followed Julian adopted as their policy, was of little benefit to the Jews of Palestine, who found themselves more and more at the mercy of the clergy. Palestine, in fact, became a Christian country. Many of the pilgrims came to stay and churches, chapels, and monasteries rose up everywhere, especially on the "holy places," whose number continued to grow. The restrictions against the Jews multiplied: they were barred from public office; they were prohibited from owning Christian slaves; they were forbidden to build new synagogues. Liberal emperors like Theodosius the Great (379-395), endeavored to protect their Jewish subjects, but the local officials found it more profitable to cultivate the good will of the clergy. The latter were determined to convert the Jews, while the Christian merchants, for more practical reasons, favored the suppression of their Jewish competitors.

3

THE Patriarchate continued for sixty years after Hillel II, but while the office still possessed a certain prestige, its real power was gone. Three patriarchs, all in the direct line of descent, came after Hillel II: Gamaliel V (365-385), Judah IV (385-400), and Gamaliel VI (400-425). The latter died without an heir, and Emperor Theodosius II (408-450), whose reign was marked by repressive laws against the Jews, abolished the patriarchate altogether. Thus came to an end the exalted office which, since the year of disaster 70 C.E., served as a unifying and directing force for the Jews of Palestine and every other land.

4

THE Roman Empire had, in the meantime, undergone far-reaching changes. The vast structure had begun to disintegrate. From north and east, hordes of barbarians were beating against its frontiers and breaking through them, and a deep fissure appeared along a line between Italy and Greece, between the western provinces that spoke Latin and the eastern that spoke Greek. Constantine the Great had moved his capital from Italy to a new one in the east, on the site of the old Greek town of Byzantium, which he renamed Constantinople. Theodosius the Great, reigning in Constantinople, had been the last emperor to hold sway over east and west: on his death in 395, the west went to his son Honorious and the east to his son Arcadius. The split became permanent, and the Jews of Palestine, as well as those of Asia Minor, Syria, and Egypt, became subjects of the Byzantine emperors.

In the western empire the real rulers were now the barbarians from the north who, after breaking through the frontiers, had compelled the emperors to let them remain. In 410, only fifteen years after the death of Theodosius the Great, one of the barbarian leaders, Alaric the Goth, captured and sacked the city of Rome. Fifteen years later, the Vandals seized the south of Spain; they pushed across into North Africa whence they made incursions into Sicily and the Italian mainland. In 455 they, too, captured and plundered the capital of the west and, included in the loot they carried off, were the golden candlesticks and other spoils of the Temple which, after the conquest of Judea, had been borne in triumph through the streets of Rome. In 476, the last emperor of the west whose name, as if in mockery, was Augustulus, "little Augustus," was murdered by the barbarians and one of their own leaders mounted the throne of Rome.

The eastern empire, with many changes of fortune and boundaries, lasted nearly a thousand years longer: it was not until 1453 that its capital fell to the conquering Turks. After 425, when Theodosius II extinguished the Patriarchate, Palestine, however, continued under Byzantine sway for only two centuries: in 636, as we shall see, the land was seized by a new power that burst upon the arena of history out of the deserts of Arabia.

We know little of what befell the Jews of Palestine during those two centuries. All that is certain is that their imperial masters were dominated by the church and lent themselves, willingly or unwillingly, to the policy of the clergy, aimed at the conversion or suppression of non-Christians throughout the empire.

The wrath of the clergy burned more fiercely against the Jews than against other nonconformists: it was intolerable to them that the founder's own people should reject the new faith. The persecutions extended, of course, to Jewish communities outside of Palestine—to Antioch, Alexandria, and other cities. In 415 the Jews of Alexandria were plundered and driven out of the city after bloody riots instigated against them by the bishop Cyril.

In Palestine, the victims of this policy were the Samaritans as well as the Jews. Several times the Samaritans rebelled against their oppressors, wreaking bloody vengeance on the Christians, and for a time defying the emperors' legions. But the uprising brought almost total annihilation upon them. Justinian (527-565) was especially merciless. He slew large numbers of them and reduced the survivors to the condition of pariahs.

Justinian distinguished himself by his hostility against the Jews also. The oppressive laws of Theodosius II were enforced and extended. The Jews were barred from all positions of honor except one, the magisterial post of decurion which, however, imposed heavy burdens on its holders. The testimony of Jews as witnesses against Christians was declared invalid, and no Jew could set foot in Jerusalem. Spurred on by the bishops and abbots, who were now the real rulers of Palestine, Justinian invaded also the religious practices of the Jews, with which the previous emperors had not interfered. He denied them the right to celebrate their Passover before the Christians celebrated Easter, and even went so far as to require Jewish congregations to listen to a Greek translation of the Bible abounding in Christian interpretations. The reading of Isaiah, the great consoler and herald of better days, was altogether forbidden.

The bitterness of the Jews against their Christian oppressors was so great that in 556 a violent clash occurred in the city of Caesarea. It was at the time of the chariot races, often the occasion of racial and religious conflicts in that and other cities. Justinian's governor Stephanus, together with many other Christians, fell victim to the fury of the oppressed. The outbreak was put down and cruel penalties were imposed on the rebels, but Justinian found it necessary to increase his garrison in Palestine.

5

THE immediate successors of Justinian left the Jews of Palestine more or less at peace, and there is reason to believe that the half-century that followed saw a substantial increase in their numbers and strength. For the year 614 saw them involved in a remarkable movement aiming at nothing less than the liberation of the land from Christian rule and the restoration of the Jewish Commonwealth. Again war had broken out between the Byzantine Empire and Neo-Persia, and in 614 the Persians invaded Palestine. Led by Benjamin of Tiberias, the Jews rallied to the standard of the Persian ruler Chosru II, from whom, it appears, they obtained assurances for the restoration of their national life. The meager reports that are available suggest a movement of considerable magnitude. Jewish contingents came flocking from Tiberias, Nazareth, and other cities of Galilee and, later, from the cities of the south also. One of the incidents of the movement was an attempt by a force of 20,000 Jews to seize the city of Tyre.

In the summer of 614 the Jews and Persians stormed Jerusalem and 90,000 Christians are reported to have been massacred by the victors. The patriarch of the Christians, together with the "true cross," was carried off by the Persians to Ctesiphon, their capital. Churches and monasteries throughout the country went up in flames. The pent-up wrath of centuries of oppression and humiliation broke loose, and Christian rule in Palestine seemed to be definitely ended.

In the fourteen years during which the Persians were masters of the country, however, the Jews had full opportunity to become disillusioned with them. The Persians not only failed to carry out their promises but imposed heavy burdens upon them. In the meantime, Heraclius, the Byzantine emperor, took vigorous measures to expel the invaders from his realms. In turn, he entered into an agreement with the Jews, promising them amnesty for renewed loyalty and assistance.

After a long struggle Heraclius was successful. In 627 he defeated the Persians near Nineveh and was marching to Ctesiphon when the Persian monarch was murdered by his own son, who hastened to make peace with the Romans. In 628 the Persians evacuated Palestine, and the following year Heraclius carried the "true cross" on his own shoulders back into Jerusalem.

Palestine again belonged to the Christians, who in their turn betrayed the Jews. The monks and priests demanded their total extermination; when Heraclius displayed qualms of conscience, the ecclesiastics, headed by the Patriarch Sophronius, quieted the scruples of the pious emperor by taking full responsibility for the breach of faith. Moreover, they declared a week of fasting as an anticipatory atonement. Thereupon Heraclius proceeded to carry out their wishes. The Jews were hunted down and massacred. The survivors were those who found refuge in the caves of the mountains or escaped into Babylonia, Egypt, and Arabia.

But the resumption of Christian rule over Palestine was destined to be brief. For a new power came sweeping up from Arabia, bringing a new era in the history of Palestine and of the Jewish people in that land and in many other lands.

CHAPTER TWENTY-EIGHT

The Talmud

WHILE the remnant in the homeland was thus spending itself in the unequal struggle against Roman oppressors and Christian persecutors, a Jewish community grew big and strong in the Tigris-Euphrates valley where, some twenty-five centuries earlier, the Jewish people was born. From the loins of the exiles who had stayed on in Babylonia sprang a proud center of creative life. It flourished for fifteen hundred years and, except for the motherland itself, left the deepest mark on the generations that followed. And again it was a Book, this time the Talmud, whence came the power and the glory.

During the six centuries of the Second Commonwealth and the generations of spiritual ingathering that produced the Mishnah, the Babylonian community was content to be a mere satellite of Palestine. It is only in the third century C.E., when the Parthian monarchs known as the Arsacids still reigned over the lands east of the Euphrates, that we become aware of a vigorous, self-contained, and populous Jewish society, resting on strong economic foundations, enjoying a large measure of political autonomy, and bearing rich fruit of mind and spirit. In the year 226 the Hellenistic Arsacids were overthrown by the Sassanids, better known as the Neo-Persians, zealous fire-worshippers and fanatically devoted to the faith of Zoroaster. Although the Jews, like the Christians and other nonconformists, suffered persecution at their hands, the community continued to flourish—so deeply was it rooted in the soil of the country and in its own institutions.

The region inhabited by the Jews of Babylonia, a region so definitely dominated by them that it came to be called the "Land of Israel," lay in the central portion of the great plain between the two rivers. The principal cities of the district were Nehardea, Pumbeditha, and Sura along the Euphrates, and Mahoza, not far from Ctesiphon, the capital on the Tigris. These were practically Jewish cities, inhabited by Jewish merchants and industrialists, craftsmen and laborers. Outside the cities, on a soil crisscrossed by canals and irrigation ditches, dwelt Jewish cattlemen and farmers whose toil and skill transformed the rainless plain into a fruitful garden. This region, with a population believed to have numbered in the millions, was practically self-governing. Its recognized political head bore the title of *Resh-Galutha* or Exilarch, meaning "Prince of the Captivity." The Prince, who inherited his office and claimed descent from the royal line of David, was invested by the sovereigns with executive, judicial, and fiscal powers. He appointed judges, police officials, inspectors of canals, controllers of weights and measure, and other officers. He maintained a body of retainers and cultivated the pomp of a court and palace. His power was great and he sometimes abused it.

2

FOR centuries the wealth, freedom, and learning of the Babylonian community made it more important than Palestine, but the love of the exiles—for such they deemed themselves—for the motherland never wavered. As long as the Temple stood in Zion, the flow of their gifts for the national shrine continued: from Nehardea, their leading city, the treasure was taken by armed caravan to Jerusalem. The inner life of the community was governed by Torah and Mishnah; its local institutions for worship, education, and charity were modeled after those in Palestine. The prayers and scriptural readings in the synagogues were much the same as in the homeland; the judges sat in the gates of the city; and the voices of teachers and pupils resounded in the houses of study.

The hardships and foibles that go with human life were, of course, not absent: in the pages of the Talmud they are clearly reflected. Farming by irrigation, with canals and ditches often overflowing, was arduous toil. The small traders and peddlers, the porters, blacksmiths, tanners, and other artisans worked hard for a bare living and envied the industrial and commercial magnates who were served by slaves and lived in luxury. But pride of lineage was common to all of them, and all were proud of the Exilarch,

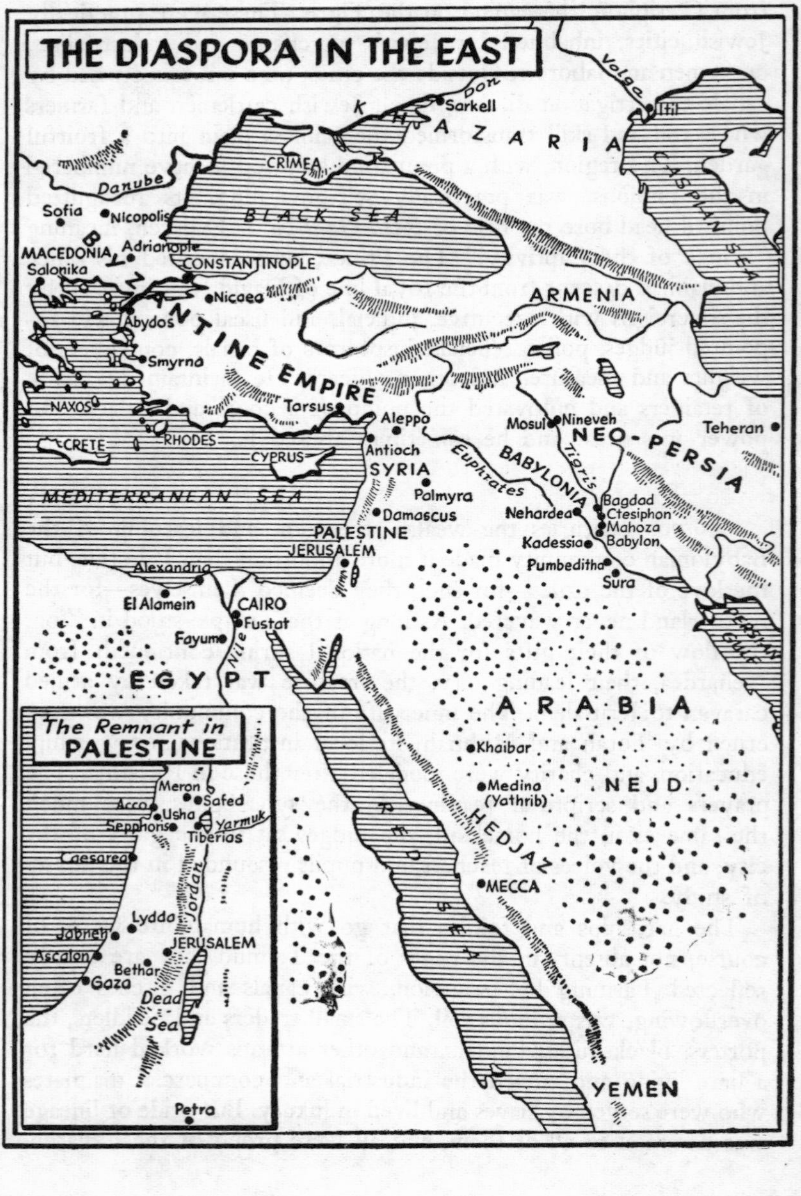
THE DIASPORA IN THE EAST
Volga
Don
Sarkell
Itil
KHAZARIA
CASPIAN SEA
CRIMEA
Danube
BLACK SEA
Sofia
Nicopolis
MACEDONIA
Adrianople
Salonika
CONSTANTINOPLE
BYZANTINE EMPIRE
Nicaea
Abydos
Smyrna
ARMENIA
NAXOS
Tarsus
Aleppo
Mosul
Nineveh
Teheran
CRETE
RHODES
CYPRUS
Antioch
SYRIA
NEO-PERSIA
Euphrates
BABYLONIA
Tigris
MEDITERRANEAN SEA
Palmyra
Damascus
Nehardea
Bagdad
Ctesiphon
Mahoza
PALESTINE
JERUSALEM
Kadessia
Babylon
Pumbeditha
Sura
Alexandria
El Alamein
CAIRO
Fustat
Fayum
Nile
EGYPT
PERSIAN GULF
ARABIA
The Remnant in PALESTINE
Meron
Safed
Acco
Usha
Yarmuk
Sepphoris
Tiberias
Caesarea
Jordan
Lydda
Jabneh
JERUSALEM
Ascalon
Bethar
Gaza
Dead Sea
Petra
Khaibar
Medina (Yathrib)
NEJD.
HEDJAZ
RED SEA
MECCA
YEMEN

who bore himself like a monarch. There were other compensations, and on the whole life was pleasant. There were the Sabbaths and the festivals; weddings were celebrated with lighted processions and music; the women adorned themselves with finery and cosmetics. Monogamy was the rule and the wife was mistress of the home.

Such were the external aspects of life in the Babylonian community. Its inner life is reflected first and foremost in the crowning achievement of Babylonian Jewry, the Talmud. It is also reflected in certain prayers that had their origin in Babylonia and that are still part of the liturgy in synagogues throughout the world.

Among these prayers, the *Kaddish* and *Alenu* are the most important. The first is now chanted in memory of the dead; in content however, the *Kaddish* is a hymn of glorification and a prayer for the advent of the messianic era. The *Alenu*, which has suffered calumny and persecution, is an expression of hope for the redemption of mankind, couched in language of incomparable grandeur. Composed originally for the services of the New Year, it is now recited by the Orthodox thrice daily, at the conclusion of the morning, afternoon, and evening prayers. The second paragraph of the *Alenu* may be set down as one of the great spiritual achievements of Babylonian Jewry:

> Therefore do we hope in thee, O Lord our God, that we may speedily behold the glory of Thy strength, when Thou wilt remove abominations from the earth, and the idols will be utterly destroyed; when the world will be made perfect under the kingdom of the Almighty, and all children of flesh will call upon Thy name, and all the wicked of the earth will be turned unto Thee. Then will all the inhabitants of the world acknowledge and perceive that unto Thee must bend every knee and swear every tongue. Before Thee, O Lord our God, will they bow and prostrate themselves, and give honor to Thy glorious name; and they will all accept the yoke of Thy kingdom, and Thou wilt reign over them speedily and forever. For Thine is the kingdom, and in all eternity Thou wilt reign in glory, as is written in Thy Torah: "The Lord shall reign forever and ever." And it is also said: "And the Lord shall be

King over all the earth; on that day the Lord shall be One and His name be One."

But the most characteristic and revealing of the prayers is the *Yekum Purkan* ("May salvation come") which is still chanted on Sabbath immediately after the scriptural reading. The prayer is in the stately Aramaic vernacular and it glows with the local color of the remote life in which it originated. *Yekum Purkan* is a prayer for "the teachers and the rabbis, a holy company, whether in the Land of Israel or in Babylonia," for the "heads of the student assemblies, the Exilarchs, and the masters of the academies, and the judges in the gates, and all the disciples and the disciples of their disciples, and all who engage in the study of Torah." For them, the congregations pray not only for "grace and loving kindness" and the material things of life, but also for the "higher enlightenment."

3

FOR Torah and piety were the only attainments that could vie with the power of the Exilarch. Great academies of learning rose up in Babylonia where the lore of the *tannaim* was taught and refined and ripened by thousands of teachers and students, and the masters of these schools became the spiritual heads of the community. Beginning with the Exilarch Mar-Huna, a contemporary of the compiler of the Mishnah, the line of the Exilarchs proceeds without a break for nearly a thousand years; but more important than these secular dignitaries were the heads of the academies where, on the foundations of the Mishnah, rose up the imposing edifice of the Talmud.

Only the master builders of the Talmud can be admitted into this brief narrative. Two of the early ones who left a lasting mark on the life and lore of their people and whose names have been like magic in the ears of the generations that followed, were friends and fellow-students in the school of Judah I in Galilee. They were Abba and Samuel. The first was nicknamed "Arika" (the tall). "I can see further than most men," he jested about his height; but to his colleagues and students the saying was no jest. For Abba is better known by the name of Rab, the word meaning master or teacher and the name signifying that Abba was *the* teacher. Some years after his return from Palestine, Rab was asked to become head of the academy at Nehardea, then the leading city of the "Land of Israel." But he felt that Samuel was more entitled to the post and declined in his favor. His modesty, however, did not prevent Rab from being regarded by his contemporaries as the leading scholar of his age and by later generations as the founder of Babylonian learning.

This learning was no diversion from the stream of tradition, although the special conditions of the land and the times are reflected in it. In the broad stream the two currents, Halachah and Haggadah, law and legend, continue to flow together. The age of the *tannaim*, makers of the Mishnah, was over. Now came the generations of *amoraim* who interpreted and expanded the Mishnah.

The Exilarch appointed Abba Arika inspector of markets, and as the sage traveled through the land he noted with sorrow the ignorance that prevailed among his people as well as the laxity in religious observance. Nehardea in the north had its academy but there was none in the south, and Abba proceeded to supply the lack: he founded a school at Sura and became its head. Before long thousands of students, including farmers, artisans, and merchants who gathered for instruction in the early morning or late at night, came to listen to the teachers. For just as in Palestine, learning was an obligation or privilege that belonged alike to the rich and the poor, the great and the lowly. For nearly thirty years Rab was the master of Sura, and the school he founded flourished for eight centuries. When Rab died in 247, he was so deeply mourned by his people that for a whole year the myrtle and palm branches were not displayed at weddings.

During all these years Samuel was the great *amora* of Nehardea, and when the master of Sura died the mantle of spiritual leadership fell upon his shoulders. Samuel was a man of balanced intellect and broad learning which he knew how to put to practical use. His knowledge of astronomy enabled him to devise a fixed calendar; an eye salve of his invention made him famous as a physician; he served with distinction as a jurist; and he displayed skill and tact in handling men. To guide his people in their relations with the sovereign, Samuel reduced to a legal formula the exhortation "to seek the peace of the city whither I have caused you to be carried away captive and pray unto the Lord for it," which the prophet Jeremiah had addressed to the exiles in Babylonia seven centuries earlier. Samuel's formula, *dina de-malchuta dina* (the law of the government is binding law), applied to all laws that did no violence to religious convictions, and the rule has been honored and observed by Jews in all the lands of their dispersion.

4

IN THE meantime the liberal Parthian monarch Artaban IV, last in a line that had reigned for nearly four centuries, was overthrown by the bigoted Neo-Persian Ardashir I (226-241). Spurred by the fire-worshipping Magi, or priests of Zoroaster, the new emperor moved to suppress all the other faiths in his realms. The Jews were deprived of important civil rights; synagogues were burnt down; restrictions were imposed on the ritual slaughter of animals for food and the use of fire and light. One of the strangest beliefs of the Magi concerned the disposal of the dead: the corpse, they believed, would desecrate the soil, so they left their dead to be devoured by beasts and birds of prey. The Jews were forbidden to bury their dead and Jewish corpses were even dug up to be disposed of after the manner of the Magi.

But as time went on the fanatical zeal of the Neo-Persians abated: Samuel even succeeded in winning the friendship of Ardashir's son and successor, Shapur I (241-272). As a result of minor concessions made by the Jews and the financial and military help they gave the monarchs in their wars, the persecutions were relaxed. Yet from time to time, during the four centuries of Neo-Persian domination, new persecutors arose, some of them even more ruthless than Ardashir I.

The wars the Neo-Persians fought were chiefly against Rome. Shapur conquered Syria and in 260 defeated the Roman emperor Valerian, whom he took prisoner. Shortly afterwards, however, the desert freebooter Odenathus, whose native city was Palmyra or Tadmor, defeated the Persians and, as we have already noted, set up a short-lived kingdom which included Palestine, and on which his wife, the famous queen Zenobia who reigned after him, shed a legendary luster. Odenathus, whom the Jews of Babylonia fiercely resisted, destroyed the city of Nehardea with its famous seat of learning. Samuel was spared the sorrow of this tragedy: he died in 254, five years before it occurred. Eventually the academy of Nehardea was transferred to Mahoza, but thereafter the principal centers of learning were the school founded by Rab in Sura and another that arose in the city of Pumbeditha.

5

TO THE galaxy of the *amoraim* whose labors produced the Talmud, all three schools contributed stars of the first magnitude of whom only the most brilliant can here be noted. In Pumbeditha, early in the fourth century, there was the amazing "mover of mountains," Rabbah son of Nahmani (died 330), who attracted so many students that the government ended his career to prevent a slump in production and taxes. Then came Rabbah's nephew Abaye, whose name is among those most often repeated wherever the wistful chant of the Talmud is heard. A simple and kindly soul, Abaye heeded the wholesome advice of the *tannaim*, farming his own little plot for a living, and spending his devotion on his many disciples.

Among the sages of Mahoza, the most illustrious was Raba (died 352). When in 338 Abaye died, his students flocked to Mahoza to sit at Raba's feet. Raba was no recluse in the ivory tower of Halachah and Haggadah, although he was master of both. He was also a mystic and moralist and he brought the wisdom of law and legend down to the people, striving to improve their manners and morals and lead them to the study of Torah. He had great influence in the court of Shapur II (310-379); the king's mother was his friend, and he served his people well by mitigating the persecutions of her bigoted son. Raba's influence, in fact, was greater than that of the Exilarch.

The next figure of splendor in the line of *amoraim* was Ashi, who for more than fifty years (375-427) was master of the academy at Sura. Ashi's learning, wealth, and renown made Sura the center of the "Land of Israel" in Babylonia, a position it continued to hold for several centuries.

In the meantime the law and lore accumulated by the *amoraim*, to which was given the general name of Talmud or Gemara,* had grown to vast proportions, and it was still stored in the incredible memories of the sages. But even they were finding it difficult to retain: mnemonic devices were not sufficient. Ashi had recourse to the more effective method of organization. He did for Talmud what Akiba and Meir had done for Mishnah: he arranged the vast body of argument, opinion, and decision, as well as the tales and homilies of the Haggadah, into a definite system without writing it down: only the sacred scriptures, it was felt, should be in writing. Legend has it that the work, in which Ashi was assisted by many disciples, took thirty years, and thirty years more were spent in going over and confirming it.

Ashi died in 427. His son Mar bar Ashi continued the work of compilation, adding his father's contributions to the system of Talmud. About this time, however, the Babylonian community fell on evil days. First the Emperor Jazdejerd II (438-457), then his son Firuz (457-484) bore down hard upon their Jewish subjects. The first forbade them to observe the Sabbath and festivals; the second, who earned the title of "Firuz the Wicked," had many of them slain, took their children away to be brought up by the Magians, and imposed harsh restrictions on the academies. Among the victims of his executioners was the Exilarch Huna-Mari. It was during these persecutions that a group of Jews fled from Persia and settled in India.

What lay in store for the proud Babylonian community in the near or more distant future? The sages had many forebodings: the schools might be closed and the line of *amoraim* extinguished. Rabina (474-499), the master of Sura, and Jose, the head of the academy at Pumbeditha, took the only measure open to them to guard against such calamities: they completed the compilation of Ashi and put it into writing. Thus the Talmud of Babylonia, which had been growing for several centuries and was nurtured by a thousand sages, the book that gave content to the life of the Jewish people in the centuries that followed, received its final form.†

* The word means "completion"—the completion, that is, of the Mishnah.

† There are, in fact, two Talmuds. Besides the Babylonian, there is the Palestinian or Jerusalem Talmud, which was completed half a century earlier, but failed to achieve the authority of the first.

6

OF THE books that have influenced the course of humanity, the most important is no doubt the Bible: it has swayed the mind and spirit of a larger portion of mankind than any other work. Since the same Book is the ultimate source from which the Talmud derives its authority, the Bible has remained supreme, but the day-to-day life of the Jewish people in the scattered communities of the Diaspora has been dominated by the Talmud.

Structurally, as we have seen, the Talmud is an extension of the Mishnah. Passage after passage of the Mishnah is quoted and followed by questions, answers, and rejoinders, opinions, obiter dicta, and decisions. The language of the Gemara, or Talmud proper as distinguished from Mishnah, is principally Aramaic, the style is compact and terse, the transitions sudden and swift. In the midst of a legal argument that calls for the keenest concentration, a flash of poetic fancy breaks through the intricate web, a glow of pious fervor, a homily or proverb, a quaint tale or parable. Not every question is answered, not every doubt resolved. The sages joust and wrestle through the pages, their polemics ring like the swords of fencers. The student is captivated and charmed; the conclusion of every argument, the solution of every problem, is an arrival and a triumph.

Thus the Talmud is a unique and altogether remarkable book; a true understanding of it is almost inaccessible to minds operating with the usual conceptions concerning books. The familiar connotations that go with the word "literature" are foreign to it. To its devotees the study of the Talmud is an act of worship: the ruling quality of the Book is holiness, and from this quality stems the authority it has exercised in all spheres of life. Primarily a code of laws to govern man's relations to God and to his fellows, the Talmud at the same time ministers to his intellectual and emotional needs. Its dialectics have produced keen and athletic minds; its exuberant flights into wisdom and fancy provide a feast for the imagination. From the sorrows and perils that surrounded them, men could retire to it as to an ideal and enchanted world.

The Talmud has had a checkered career: enemies of the Jews have distorted and slandered it, on occasion made bonfires of it.

Others have judged it by the criteria of another age and another intellectual climate. Among its own people, as we shall see, it provoked before long a schismatic revolt, while in modern times it has been subjected to harsh judgment by those who rejected its authority in the name of reform and "enlightenment." For the Talmud is not a mere book; it is a distinct world and a unique way of life and was bound to have its critics and insurgents, its foes and rivals. But it commanded the fervent devotion of scores of generations and still commands it today.

CHAPTER TWENTY-NINE

The Rise of Islam

For nearly a century and a half longer, and through varying fortunes, the Jews of Babylonia lived on under Neo-Persian monarchs. There were periods of persecution when the academies, where the heart of the community was located, remained closed. But the Talmud, towards which the labor of the schools had converged, was completed; the sages who followed, known as *saboraim*, or explicators, were content to review and clarify the opinions of their revered predecessors. In the tribulations that were only too often inflicted upon them, the people rallied to the Talmud for resolution and solace.

The reign of Kovad I (488-531) was particularly grievous for the Jews of Babylonia. The monarch came under the influence of a fanatical reformer who persuaded his master that the triumph of light over darkness was being thwarted by the two dominant human passions: greed for possessions and sexual lust. Thereupon Kovad issued a decree ordering that property and women should, throughout his realm, be held in common. At least half of the startling innovation struck at a basic tenet of the Jewish faith: the sanctity of the marriage tie. Led by their youthful Exilarch, Mar-Zutrah, the Jews rose up in revolt. For nearly seven years the Exilarch maintained the independence of Jewish Babylonia, with

Mahoza as its capital. In the end Mar-Zutrah's diminutive army was overcome, he himself executed, and an amazing episode in the history of Babylonian Jewry came to an end.

Kovad's successor, Chosru I (531-579) abolished the fantastic reforms that were to have ushered in the millennium. Chosru was a vigorous and enlightened monarch: he extended his empire to the east and as far south as Yemen in Arabia. He was nearly always at war with Justinian, the Christian Byzantine emperor, and gave refuge to the Greek philosophers whom Justinian persecuted. Chosru put an end to the persecutions against the Jews, and the Talmudic academies reopened. Then came the weak and dissolute Ormuz IV (579-590) who permitted the Magian priests to vent their animosity on Christians and Jews alike. The academies were closed again and the teachers had to flee. It was a turbulent period in the history of Neo-Persia. The king's brilliant general Bahram overthrew his degenerate master and seized the throne. But Bahram suffered defeat at the hands of the Byzantine emperor, and the respite the Jews enjoyed came to a swift and tragic end: the Romans seized Mahoza and slew most of its Jewish inhabitants.

It was during the reign of the next monarch, Chosru II (590-628), that the Persians invaded Palestine and, as we have seen, brought the persecuted Jews of the homeland a brief hope of deliverance and freedom. In Babylonia the persecutions again subsided and the academies reopened and flourished. It was about this time that the heads of the academies assumed the title *Gaon* or "Excellency."

Chosru II was murdered by his own son, and in the decade that followed ten monarchs succeeded each other on the tottering throne of Neo-Persia. The wars between the Neo-Persian and Byzantine empires, which had been going on for nearly two centuries, had sapped the strength of both contestants. The wretched masses of both empires felt no loyalty to their rulers, no attachment to the state. Both were now ripe for the sword of a new conqueror who burst upon them out of the wastes and oases of Arabia, imposing a new sovereignty upon the lands of western Asia, shattering the power of Magian priest and Christian prelate alike, and bringing new turns of fortune to the scattered communities of the Jewish people.

2.

IT WAS, to begin with, a passionate resolve to convert mankind to a new faith that set the Arabs on their spectacular career of conquest. But added to missionary zeal was the immemorial drive of the desert which again sent its lean and hungry children swarming across the frontiers of more favored lands. And both impulses were strangely commingled in the enigmatic personality of Mohammed, founder of the new faith and first leader of the Arabs in the battle for Allah and for the green lands beyond the deserts.

It was about 610, when he was already forty years old and a prosperous citizen of his native Mecca, that Mohammed, who belonged to the distinguished Koreish family, began to preach the new faith. The ideas that had come to a ferment in his mind, giving rise to that hectic book called the Koran and the simple and austere faith called Islam, were undoubtedly of Jewish origin. Earlier in his life, when he was a camel driver in the caravans that plodded from Yemen to Medina and up farther into Syria, he had come into contact with Jews whose communities lay along the route. "There is no God save Allah!" is only a paraphrase of the Hebrew *Shema:* "Hear, O Israel, the Lord is our God, the Lord is One!" Nor when he added "and Mohammed is his prophet," did it mean that he rejected the teachers and prophets of Israel. On the contrary, Mohammed insisted on his descent through Ishmael from Abraham, whom he also regarded as a prophet of Allah, and he acknowledged the other prophets of Israel, among whom he included Jesus of Nazareth. Early in his apostolic career he even adopted some of the practices of Judaism: he appointed the Day of Atonement as a fast day and directed his adherents to turn their faces toward Jerusalem when they prayed. Of all the prophets, Mohammed was, of course, the crown and culmination. To him Allah, through the angel Gabriel, had vouchsafed His final revelation.

That revelation, both as theology and ethics, was an enormous advance over the primitive idol worship that flourished in Arabia. Of this coarse worship Mecca had become the center and shrine. Thither from near and far came pilgrims to worship in an ancient temple that housed the tribal deities, some three hundred in number, and to kiss the Kaaba, a sacred meteorite stone and the only object of veneration the tribes had in common. The town, lying on the principal caravan route, developed also into a great trading center, and from the pilgrims and traders Mecca derived its prosperity. Naturally, the worthies of the place frowned upon Mohammed and his doctrine of a single deity which threatened to undermine the prestige of their temple and its revenues.

For ten years the prophet's progress was desperately slow, his converts forming but a small circle, nearly all of them his own relatives. Mohammed decided to quit Mecca and go north to the rival city of Yathrib, later called Medina, the city of the prophet, where the prospects for the new faith appeared much brighter and where most of his converts had already established themselves. Mohammed's journey became a flight: the Meccans had become aware of his plans and early one morning a group representing the leading families broke into his home with the object of slaying him, notwithstanding the prohibition against the shedding of blood within the bounds of the sacred city. But the "committee" found his adopted son Ali in the prophet's bed. He himself, with his faithful friend Abu Bekr, was already on his way by circuitous trails to Medina where, after eluding a determined pursuit, he finally arrived and was warmly welcomed. It was the year 622, the year of the Hegira or flight, which became Year One of the Mohammedan calendar.

3

THE welcome Mohammed found in Medina can only be explained by the large number of Jews who inhabited that city and by the influence of Judaism in predisposing its Arab residents to accept the basic doctrine of the new faith. Medina, in fact, is believed to have been founded by Jews, who in the course of centuries had established themselves also in many other parts of the western fringe of the peninsula from Hedjaz in the north to Yemen in the south. They trickled down from the motherland as traders, soldiers of fortune, and fugitives, and there must have been a particularly large influx of refugees after the Roman conquest in 70 C.E., five hundred years before Mohammed was born. Similarity of race and language simplified the process of adjustment, and although the religious difference brought occasional conflict and persecution, Jewish religious ideas made important penetrations among the Arabs. There is even a recorded instance of a mass conversion of Arabs to Judaism. It took place about the year 500 in the kingdom of Yemen, the region known as Arabia Felix, "Arabia the Happy," at the southwestern tip of the peninsula opposite Abyssinia. Dhu Nawas Masrug, King of Yemen, embraced the Jewish faith, changed his name to Joseph, and his subjects followed him into the new fold. Not long afterwards, however, the Jewish kingdom was invaded and conquered by the Christian rulers of Abyssinia, aided by the Byzantine emperor.

The most important Jewish settlements, however, were located in the Hedjaz around Medina and farther north in the region of Khaibar. Although in language, dress, and general mode of life they were indistinguishable from their neighbors, the Jews were proudly attached to their faith. In Medina they maintained a school for the study of the Bible, and the degree of literacy among them must have been comparatively high, for the Arabs, among whom they won many converts, called them "the People of the Book." The Jews of the Hedjaz were farmers, fruit-growers and traders, and many of them were artisans renowned for their skill as jewelers and armorers. Like the Arabs, the Jews became divided into tribes of which the Banu* Kainuka, the Banu Nadhir and the Banu Kuraiza were the most prominent; the last two claimed descent from the priestly tribe of Levi. The tribes erected strongholds in their settlements for defense against marauding Bedouins, nor did they differ from the Arabs in their contentiousness and zest for combat. Sometimes, in alliance with Arab tribes, they even fought each other. But when a Jewish prisoner was in danger of being sold into slavery, even his Jewish enemies came forward to ransom him. Every other consideration was put aside in face of the duty of *pidyon shevuyim*, the redemption of the captives of their faith, which that faith laid upon them.

4

THE fugitive prophet, who had so narrowly escaped to Medina with his life, based the hope of repairing his fortunes in

* Equivalent of the Hebrew *B'nai*, "Sons of."

that city largely upon the Jews. They, he was sure, would be among the first to acknowledge his mission and accept the new faith, which he called Islam or "submission to God." Did he not come to them in the name of the One God, the God of Abraham and Moses and Isaiah? Did he not pray with his face turned toward Jerusalem the Holy? And were they not waiting and hoping for the advent of the last great prophet, the Messiah? "O children of Israel," he pleads in the second Sura, or chapter, of the Koran, "Remember my favor wherewith I have favored you; and perform your covenant with me, and I will perform my covenant with you; and revere me: and believe in the revelation which I have set down, confirming that which is with you."

It was not long, however, before Mohammed realized that the Jews would not follow him. A few there were who did embrace the new faith of Islam, but the majority, including the leading men of the Jewish tribes, looked askance at the prophet and his pretensions. Some of them even treated his claims with levity. The unity of God was a doctrine they did not need to be taught by him; rather it was he who had learned it from them; and as for his claims to messianic ordination, they found his manner of life, particularly his eagerness to add to his worldly possessions and to his harem, incompatible with their conception of the redeemer.

The prophet soon realized that the Jews would impede rather than promote his progress. He resolved to destroy them and in the seven years of his sojourn in Medina, Mohammed waged implacable war on them. During the same period the Meccans waged war on him, sending one expedition after another against the prophet who menaced their prestige and prosperity. "War is enjoined you against the infidels," Mohammed commanded his followers. He defeated the Meccans in 624 and followed up his victory by besieging the stronghold of the Banu Kainuka after they defied his summons to embrace the new faith. The Jewish tribesmen, unaided by their Arab neighbors with whom they had a treaty of alliance, were compelled to capitulate. They were exiled and migrated to Palestine, settling east of the Jordan.

A year later came the turn of the Banu Nadhir. Mohammed, who had now suffered a reverse at the hands of the Meccans, was informed by the angel Gabriel that the Jews had plotted to slay him.

He invested their fortress and, in violation of the desert code of warfare, he cut down their date palms, a shocking procedure for which he required and obtained a special revelation. "What palm trees ye cut down or left standing on their roots," he tells his faithful, in the Sura called "The Emigration," "we so cut down or left by the will of God; and that he might disgrace the wicked doers." The plight of the Banu Nadhir, deprived of their principal source of food, became desperate; in vain they pleaded with their Arab allies and the Banu Kuraiza to bring them help. They were conquered and exiled. They proceeded north to the Jewish communities in Khaibar, and like the Banu Kainuka, eventually found new homes east of the Jordan.

In 627 the Meccans, in confederation with other foes of Mohammed, failed ignominiously in an effort to capture Medina and crush the prophet and his new faith, an effort instigated by tribesmen of the Banu Nadhir. Flushed with victory, Mohammed turned on the Banu Kuraiza, accusing them of having aided his enemies. After a valiant defense, the Jewish tribe was starved into surrender and seven hundred of the men were massacred. The women and children were sold into slavery, but not before the prophet had selected one of the widows for his harem.

The proud Jewish community in and around Medina was now practically obliterated, and the following year Mohammed attacked the northern settlements in the district of Khaibar. Here the Moslems met with even more formidable resistance and Mohammed was compelled to call into the field his three ablest generals, Abu Bekr, Omar, and Ali, all three of whom later became caliphs or successors to the prophet. The Jewish fortresses were stormed or compelled to surrender, and though allowed to remain in the land, the Jews were plundered and reduced to a condition of semi-servitude. It was in the course of this campaign that another Jewess—Safiyya, wife of Kinana—was selected by the prophet for his harem, after her husband had been tortured and slain by his orders.

Arabia and the Arabs now lay in the palm of the prophet's hand. The Jews were either massacred, exiled, or reduced to bondage, and his Arab opponents defeated and demoralized. His followers were no longer a tattered mob: victory and the spoils of victory had transformed them into a well-equipped and confident fighting force. "God hath caused you to inherit their land, and their houses, and their wealth, and a land on which ye have not trodden," he told his true believers of the Jews they had conquered. No wonder that in 628 Mohammed had the superb audacity to address a letter to the rulers of the earth, including Heraclius in Byzantium and Kovad II in Ctesiphon, calling upon them to acknowledge Allah and his prophet or take the consequences. He had already severed his former ties with Judaism: no longer were the faithful to pray with their faces toward Jerusalem but toward Mecca; instead of fasting on the Day of Atonement they were to fast every day from dawn to sunset during the month of Ramadan. He even permitted them to make pilgrimages to Mecca and to kiss the Kaaba! Like Paul of Tarsus and other religious innovators, Mohammed knew the art of making terms with the old beliefs and practices for the greater glory of the new.

The proud and bellicose Jewish tribes who defied Mohammed sank into oblivion, but in succeeding centuries, and right down to the present, travelers have continued to bring reports of Jewish tribes in Nejd and other remote regions of Arabia, tribes of nomads, raiders, and desert warriors.

5

IN 629, seven years after the great flight, Mohammed returned to Mecca in triumph. He was now ruler of the city and the temple, ruler of Arabia. In 632 he died, and the stern and faithful Abu Bekr, who became the first caliph, proceeded to carry into effect his master's resolve to subdue the earth to the new faith.

In a magnificent rush of conquest, the Arabs in less than a decade wrested from both the Byzantine and Neo-Persian empires all those provinces, including the motherland, where the principal Jewish communities were established. The battle of the river Yarmuk in 634 was the climax of the campaign against Heraclius: the river became the grave of the motley Byzantine host that endeavored to stem the pious fury of the Moslems. In 637, at Kadessia on the Euphrates, not far from Sura and Pumheditha, the power of Neo-Persia was overthrown, never to rise again. With the help of the Jews, and many Christians also, the conquerors drove on and captured Ctesiphon the capital, and three years later the Moslem arc of the Near East was completed with the conquest of Egypt.

The Moslems, of course, did not stop there: they pushed on to the east and west for another hundred years, and it was under their rule that, in addition to lesser Jewish communities, the great center in Babylonia flourished for another four centuries and, as we shall see, the equally great center in Spain grew up and reached its zenith.

CHAPTER THIRTY

Decline of the East

The Jews in the lands of the East had suffered too long and too cruelly at the hands of Christian prelates and Magian priests not to welcome the conqueror. The Moslems, who divided mankind into believers and unbelievers, imposed on the latter a special poll and ground tax, as well as certain civil and religious disabilities, but they proved, on the whole, more humane and tolerant masters than their predecessors. Omar, the rough and pious warrior who in 634 followed Abu Bekr as caliph, obeying Mohammed's admonition that "there cannot be two religions in Arabia," ordered the Jewish remnants expelled from the Hedjaz; but apparently the order was not thoroughly enforced, for in later times Jewish communities were still there. In 638 when Sophronius, the bishop of Jerusalem, after a four month siege, surrendered his city to Omar, he stipulated that no Jews were to be allowed to dwell there; nevertheless, despite that condition, which Omar apparently accepted, a Jewish community shortly afterwards rose up in the Holy City.

On the site of the ancient Temple Omar laid the foundation of a mosque which he, austere pietist, built of wood, but which under a successor was transformed into the magnificent structure it is today. With Mecca and Medina, Jerusalem became one of the three holy cities of Islam, a place of pilgrimage for the faithful. The year of Jerusalem's surrender saw also the capture of Caesarea, which completed the Moslem conquest of Palestine. The fall of Caesarea, it is related, was hastened by the help the invaders received from the Jews.

The Moslems, in fact, came to look upon the Jews, whom they delivered from the Byzantine yoke, as their allies. It took a surprisingly short time for the stern puritanism with which the new faith began, and of which the first two caliphs were the most distinguished exemplars, to wear off; and while, as unbelievers, the Jews were bound to occupy a station of civil and social inferiority, the restrictions were less galling in practice than in theory. The new rulers even permitted the schools in Tiberias to reopen.

2

THE unity and concord which the prophet enjoined upon the true believers came to grief even sooner than their austere pietism. A bitter rivalry sprang up almost immediately between the faithful of Medina, whose zeal and loyalty had brought Mohammed in triumph through the critical years after the Hegira, and the aristocratic families of Mecca who, after that triumph, found it advantageous to embrace the new faith and were shown special favor by the prophet. He was particularly partial to the Omayyad family, distinguished for its able men of affairs, but in deadly rivalry with other Meccan families among whom the Abassids were most prominent.

The first Omayyad caliph was Othman: in 644 he succeeded Omar who had died at the hands of an assassin. Twelve years later Othman too was murdered and he was followed by Ali, the prophet's son-in-law, husband of his daughter Fatima. The Omayyads rose in revolt. In 661 Ali was dispatched like his two predecessors, and until 749 the caliphs were Omayyads, imposing, from their capital in Damascus, their autocratic will on the Islamic world. For another half century and more Islam continued to expand eastward toward China and westward to the Pillars of Hercules. Asia Minor and Byzantium, however, remained unconquered until many centuries later when a new and more vigorous nation, the Mohammedan Turks, appeared on the scene.

In the meantime, Islam had become rent by a religious division which went hand in hand with the political rivalries and exists to this day. On the one hand were the Sunnites and on the other the Shiites. The latter cling to the conviction, which they have elevated to a religious dogma, that the Omayyads were usurpers and that the caliphate belonged rightfully to the descendants of the prophet through his daughter Fatima and her husband Ali. The Abassids, ancient rivals of the Omayyads, espoused the Shiite cause, or appeared to do so. In 749 they seized the caliphate and secured it by a wholesale massacre of their opponents. According to one account they invited some eighty Omayyads to a banquet in Damascus, and after murdering them all, spread a carpet over the victims and continued the feast, using the heap of corpses as a board. They then sought out and slew the descendants of Ali. The Abassids moved their seat of government east: near Ctesiphon, the ancient capital of Neo-Persia, they built the new and splendid metropolis of Bagdad.

The Abassid line continued for some two and a half centuries until, about the year 1000, it was swept out by the conquering Turks. The zenith of its glory is identified with the caliph Harun-al-Rashid (786-809), the glamorous monarch of the *Arabian Nights;* but notwithstanding the political upheavals and rebellions that followed, Bagdad remained the center of a vast and opulent imperial system and of a brilliant literary and scientific culture.

3

IN THIS Moslem empire of western Asia, as well as in the Moslem states that stretched across northern Africa and into Spain, old communities of the scattered Jewish people carried on and new ones arose, each one having its cycle of prosperity and affliction, of vigor and decline. By different courses and with different degrees of success they sought to adapt themselves to the political, social, and intellectual pressures that bore down upon them from outside and, at the same time, to keep alive the ancient tradition of which they were the heirs and trustees.

The Moslem world, unlike the Christian world in which for many centuries later they languished and suffered, did not rebuff or segregate them. In short order the Jews of Babylonia abandoned the Aramaic as their vernacular, and spoke and wrote in Arabic.

The caliphs, especially the Abassids, as well as the provincial governors, admitted them into the administrative functions of the state, and many of them rose to high station and power. They shared in the expanding industry and commerce of the empire and made brilliant contributions to its literature, science, and art. Arabs and Jews seemed to constitute an ideal partnership for the advancement of civilization at a time when the western Christian world was in a state of mental torpor and civic barbarism.

The community in Babylonia, with the Exilarch as its secular head and the masters or *Gaonim* (Excellencies) of the academies in Sura and Pumbeditha as the religious authority, continued for several more centuries to retain the hegemony of the scattered nation. The records of the period are scanty, but there is enough to testify to the existence of a large and well-knit community with an intense inner life, drawing its principal nourishment from the Talmud. Nor was Babylonian Jewry immune to the doctrinal divisions and the personal and party dissensions that are the lot of all human societies, and that sometimes make for growth and sometimes for decay.

4

WITH respect to the community in the motherland the records are even scantier. Like Judea in the Empire of Cyrus and his successors more than a thousand years earlier, Palestine was but a tiny spot in the dominions of the Omayyads and Abassids. There is sufficient evidence, however, of a rich and organized intellectual and religious life headed by a Sanhedrin, with its probable center in Tiberias, and with Jerusalem, of course, as its lodestar. In Tiberias also, the masters bore the title of *Gaon*, and in its schools the Sacred Scriptures became an object of intense study, particularly after the Karaite schism which for a time had its headquarters in Palestine. The scholars in Tiberias developed the system of vocalizing the Bible text (the *Masorah*), which won general acceptance, and there, also, liturgical poetry (*piyyut*) is believed to have had its first strong impulse. Like the rest of the population, the Jews of the motherland suffered from the chronic wars between the Moslems and Byzantine Christians, particularly in the tenth century when the Byzantines more than once invaded Palestine, bringing ruin and devastation.

The larger and more important community in Babylonia continued to look upon the teachers in Palestine as their masters, particularly in Biblical scholarship and in the matter of fixing the calendar, the latter a highly important function since the feast days and fast days depended upon it. In time, however, Palestine lost its authority in those fields also.

5

THE Moslems, who swept the Neo-Persians out of Babylonia in 637, recognized the Exilarch Bustani and even conferred special privileges upon him. The Jews had no doubt been helpful to them and so, for that matter, had been the Nestorian Christians, who had also suffered persecutions at the hands of the fire-worshippers. Bustani was permitted to have a signet ring—a highly coveted distinction—and the symbol he chose for it was the image of a fly. As he stood once in the presence of his sovereign, the Exilarch, it is reported, was stung by a savage fly but refrained from brushing it away out of respect for his master; hence the choice of the symbol. This and other legends have clustered about the first Prince of the Captivity under the Moslems.

In addition to the Exilarch, the conquerors recognized the heads, or *Gaonim*, of the academies in Sura and Pumbeditha. Needless to say, this triangular arrangement was not conducive to community concord, and the rivalries of wives and half-brothers, in which polygamous households are generally embroiled, sometimes involved the succession to the dignity of Exilarch in bitter dissension. But the four centuries during which Babylonian Jewry continued to hold the hegemony of the Diaspora is known as the Age of the *Gaonim:* in accord with the Jewish genius it was they, rather than the secular princes, who imposed their impress upon the period.

The *Gaonim* exercised a unifying influence over the entire Diaspora, which spread through the lands of the Inland Sea from Asia Minor to Spain. Wherever Jews lived they looked to the masters in the land where the Talmud had been created as their teachers and guides. Questions on law, ritual, and other matters flowed to the *Gaonim*, especially to the *Gaon* of Sura, from near and far, and their answers, or *responsa*, were accepted as having final authority. Those *responsa*, moreover, were more than individual opinions, for learning was not the exclusive possession of the *Gaon* and a few intellectual aristocrats: learning was largely democratized. The tradition of the Pharisees lived on. In the months of March and September the *Kallah*,* or gathering of students and teachers from all over the land, took place in Sura and Pumbeditha where the Talmud was zealously studied and *responsa* were prepared for the questions that had come in.

In the ninth century the distant community of Spain still leaned heavily on the *Gaonim*. Amram of Sura, who was *Gaon* from 856 to 874, arranged the order of prayers for them. Paltoi, who was *Gaon* of Pumbeditha from 842 to 858, sent them the Talmud together with aids for its study.

6

IT WAS inevitable that movements of dissent and rebellion against the authority of the Talmud should, from time to time, make their appearance among the Jews of Babylonia. The intellectual climate that surrounded them, the climate created by Zoroastrian superstition, Moslem dissension, and Christian mysticism, was bound to seep in among them. In particular, the mystic impulse which nourishes the roots of all religion, but which, if uncontrolled, produces crops of fantastic and idle vagaries, beguiled a great many minds. It lingered with special fondness about the longing for the advent of the final redeemer, giving rise to Messianic pretenders who renounced the Talmud and provoked tragic social upheavals.

Early in the eighth century came a self-proclaimed Messiah named Serenus, who flouted the Talmud and promised a miracle which would restore Palestine to the Jews. He attracted numerous followers, some of them in far-away Spain. Before the caliph Yazid II (720-724) Serenus quailed and recanted, but another Messianic movement arose not long afterwards under the leadership of Abu Isa of Persia. Abu Isa was a man of sterner stuff than

* The origin of the word is in dispute. It is probably derived from the Hebrew word meaning "all" or "everybody,"

Serenus. He was content to proclaim himself only the forerunner of the Messiah. Nor did Abu intend to rely on miracles only: he gathered a force of 10,000 armed men to liberate Palestine from Moslem rule. His plan was not altogether fantastic. The Omayyad dynasty was about to fall and the Moslem empire was rent with civil strife. Abu Isa, however, was compelled to flee from the wrath of Mansur (754-775), the second Abassid caliph, and died a hero's death in battle against the Moslems. For generations afterwards there were Jews in Persia who still believed in Abu Isa. They rejected many ordinances of the Talmud and were, to all intents and purposes, a separate sect.

7

BUT the most important secession from the Talmud, the rebellion that gave rise to a sect which has persisted to our own day, was not inspired by the Messianic impulse although it must have been very much influenced by it. The movement known as Karaism was largely a revolt against the Oral Tradition and the numerous interpretations and laws of which the Talmud was the compendium. The authority which the movement invoked against the Talmud was, of course, the Written Tradition or the Bible—hence the name by which its followers became known, "Karaite" being derived from the word which means "reading" or "Scripture." Their opponents the Karaites called Rabbanites, or followers of the rabbis.

The man who started the revolt was probably animated as much by personal pique as by animosity against the Rabbanites. He was Anan ben David, who in 760 stood next in line for the office of Exilarch, but whose choice was thwarted in favor of a younger brother by the *Gaonim*, who already doubted his loyalty. Thereafter the events in Anan's life are veiled in legend. His followers, it is related, refused to abide by the choice of the *Gaonim*. For a time the caliph kept Anan in prison as a rebel, then permitted him to settle in Jerusalem, where he built his own synagogue and devoted his zeal and knowledge to relentless war against the Rabbanites.

Anan ben David enjoined strict adherence to the laws and statutes of the Bible, but instead of making religious observance less rigorous, he made it more so. He reduced the number of feast days and increased the number of fast days. He made drastic reductions in the kinds of food that might be eaten. The Sabbath ceased to be a day of joy. No warm food was to be eaten on the Sabbath, Friday must be spent indoors, and Friday night must be spent in darkness. Anan arrived at all these hard regulations because he happened to be an ascetic. He failed to realize that the Talmud was not an arbitrary dictate, but a slow and laborious growth, and that often—perhaps most often—its conclusions were not in the direction of severity but moderation. Was it not the liberal house of Hillel rather than the rigorous house of Shammai that generally prevailed in its decisions?

Anan ben David, however, found many followers. He found them among those who for one reason or another rejected the Talmud, and among those who were unfamiliar with it. The second included the Jews from Arabia who had lived in a Jewish backwater and had taken no part in the creation of the Talmud. He found followers also among those who preferred more to less religious observance, for a religious reform, to be successful, need not necessarily offer the easier way.

The Karaite teachers who followed Anan did not always adhere to the conclusions of the master: dissent had become a virtue. Such was the attitude of Benjamin Nehawend who flourished early in the tenth century. Daniel al-Kumisi, a later Karaite teacher, finally went so far as to reject the founder, deriving his own laws from the Scriptures. Benjamin's method was haggadic and allegorical; Daniel's was severely literal.

Communities of Karaites sprang up in Babylonia, Syria, and Egypt. The rebellion made its way into the Byzantine Empire and across northern Africa into Spain. Eventually Karaites migrated into southern Russia where there were some 10,000 members of the sect before the First World War; and Karaite remnants are still to be found in Jerusalem.

8

IN SPITE of rivalries and defections, in spite of the infiltration of alien superstitions and mystic absurdities, in spite of the increasing jars and cracks in the empire of the Abassid caliphs, to whose fortunes it was inevitably bound, the Babylonian community continued to be the center of Jewish life in the Diaspora. Its sun had long passed the meridian, but before its final setting it was destined to flare up in a new burst of glory. In the line of *Gaonim* appeared Saadia ben Joseph and Babylonia was stirred to new creative life.

Since men often owe their progress to their rivals, a large portion of the credit for the new surge of energy should not be denied to the Karaites. As the latter grew in numbers and boldness, the Rabbanites, or traditionalists, were spurred to self-defense and attack, to establish anew the foundations of Oral Torah and, in particular, to meet the opponents on their own ground—that of the Written Word.

But the effective force that stemmed the spread of Karaism did not flow from the *Gaonim* of Sura and Pumbeditha who consumed too much of their strength in mutual rivalry. The Exilarch had lost his prestige with the caliph and each of the *Gaonim* was anxious to inherit his power. Of the two colleges, Pumbeditha, because it lay nearer to Bagdad, had the advantage; when in 928 Sura found itself without a head, Cohen-Zedek, the *Gaon* of Pumbeditha, proposed to the Exilarch that the rival school should be closed altogether. The Exilarch, David ben Zaccai, thought otherwise: he refused to close the school that had been founded by the great Rab, the school where the Talmud had been compiled. Moreover, it was obviously more in his interest to have two rival *Gaonim* than to have one who would concentrate all his fire on him. After a long and bitter quarrel, the Exilarch secured the selection as *Gaon* of Sura of a man who was not a Babylonian, but whose fame as a brilliant upholder of the traditional faith had already spread throughout the communities of the East.

Saadia ben Joseph (882-942) was a native of Egypt where another dynasty of caliphs—the Fatimites, who claimed descent from Fatima and Ali, dear to the heart of the Shiites—were now reigning. There were prosperous Jewish settlements and schools in Egypt, and when Saadia had learned what those schools could teach him, he moved on to Palestine. Early in his career he entered the lists against the Karaites, and he fought them relentlessly all his life. He met them on their own ground, the Bible, which he translated into Arabic, and he wrote the first grammar of the Hebrew language as an aid to a correct understanding of the sacred text. Saadia's translation is still used by the Jews of Yemen.

The new *Gaon* of Sura was a man of regal intellect and unbending principles. He loved to fight the good fight. He defeated an attempt made by Aaron ben Meir, head of the schools in Palestine, to assert the former authority of the motherland: Saadia rejected a new calendar proposed by Ben Meir and wrote the *Book of the Seasons* to disprove his claims. It was not long, however, before he became involved in a bitter feud with the man to whom he owed his high office. David ben Zaccai called on him to approve a verdict in a lawsuit of which the Exilarch would be the beneficiary. Saadia, finding the verdict unjust, refused to comply. In the course of the feud that followed the Exilarch removed the *Gaon* and had him excommunicated. Saadia retaliated by declaring the Exilarchate vacant and appointing a brother of David to the office. Both sides sought the support of the caliph, his ministers, and his courtiers. The Babylonian community was divided into two warring camps.

At last, after seven years of strife, the leading men got together and managed to heal the breach. In 937, on the day before Purim, the *Gaon* and Exilarch were brought together and peace and friendship restored. For the rest of his life Saadia remained scrupulously loyal to his former enemy. When, three years later, the Exilarch died, the *Gaon* saw to it that David's son should be chosen in his place, and when the son died shortly afterwards, Saadia adopted David's grandson and educated him to be worthy of the high office.

During the period of his rupture with the Exilarch, Saadia lived in retirement and produced his greatest works. He compiled a systematic code of Talmudic law, made his own arrangement of the traditional prayers, and wrote new ones. He continued to wage war on his opponents including those who, like the Exilarch, wielded despotic power, and the arsenal he stored up against the Karaites provided weapons against them for generations.

He ventured also to seek a solution for the conflict between science and religion, a problem that bids fair to challenge the human mind to the end of time. Saadia offered his solution in his greatest and most enduring work, his *Emunoth Ve-Deoth*, which may be freely translated "Faith and Reason." The book constitutes a system of what we would today call religious philosophy. Saadia may be described as a rationalist in the sense that he does not reject reason but, on the contrary, invokes it to vindicate his faith. He answered the eternal question for his own age and more cannot be expected from any man.

That Saadia Gaon and his works still command admiration and homage is attested by the fact that in 1942, amid the anguish and toils of the Second World War, the Jews of the world reverently observed the one thousandth anniversary of the death of the great master of Sura.

9

WITH Saadia's death began the sunset and twilight of the Babylonian centers of learning and of the Babylonian community. It was, however, a sunset of lingering splendor, for up to the eve of the final closing of the schools, which occurred about the middle of the eleventh century, they still produced luminous spirits who shed their luster on other lands and later generations.

The decline of the Babylonian community was undoubtedly hastened, if it was not principally caused, by the ravages and disasters that befell the empire of the Abassids. A new people, the warlike Turks, swarmed down from central Asia, adopted the faith of Islam, filled the ranks of the empire's armies, and did pretty much as they pleased. The old line of lusty caliphs degenerated into a succession of impotent rulers whose power was usurped by their viziers or by brigand chiefs. Outlying provinces defied the mandates of Bagdad and became practically independent under dynasties of their own. And all the time the process of religious cleavage continued, producing numerous sects and schisms in the two original camps of Shiites and Sunnites, and adding to the confusion and conflicts in Islam.

Before it faded from history Pumbeditha produced two great teachers, father and son, men of splendid intellect and saintly life. Sherira, who died in 998, traced the growth of Mishnah and Talmud as the original tradition was passed on from one *tanna* and *amora* to the next. His son Hai, who died in 1038, codified the civil law of the Talmud and brilliantly maintained the prestige and authority of his school at home and abroad.

A hundred years after the death of Saadia, the glory of Babylonia was a thing of the past. The last important *Gaon* of the school in Sura, the great nursery of the Talmud, was Samuel ben Hophni who died in 1034. The last *Gaon* of Pumbeditha was Hezekiah, a descendant of David ben Zaccai, who also held the office of Exilarch. Hezekiah had powerful enemies at court; he was imprisoned and executed, and with his death both offices were extinguished.

CHAPTER THIRTY-ONE

Westward to Spain

WE TURN now to the West, and not until the resurgence of the ancient homeland in our own generation will the East recapture its central place in this narrative. The present goal of our journey is the land at the other end of the Mediterranean, but on the way we stop to take brief note of the Jewish communities in the intervening lands on both sides of the Inland Sea.

In Asia Minor, Greece, Macedonia, and other provinces of the Byzantine Empire, the lot of the Jews under the monarchs who reigned in Constantinople was not a happy one. The general policy was to force them into baptism by making life as hard for them as possible. They were forbidden to build new synagogues, and crimes committed against them were allowed to go unpunished. In the larger cities they were often at the mercy of the mob. In Antioch, for example, during the chariot races in the year 507, the synagogue was attacked and burned down, and many Jews were murdered. The illustrious Justinian (527-565), as we have seen, even undertook to tell them how to conduct their religious services. A later emperor, Leo III, tried to solve the problem more simply: he issued a decree in 722 ordering his Jews to become Christians.

Many of them fled north to the Crimea and the Caucasus, and some of them came where the Volga empties into the Caspian Sea to a land inhabited by the Khazars of whom we shall hear more anon.

2

IN ITALY, the next stage in our journey westward, there were Jewish communities all over the land from Milan in the north to Calabria in the south, as well as in Sicily across the Straits of Messina.

The origin of the first community in Rome is lost in conjecture: in Caesar's day it was already well established, its members enjoying religious and civil rights, taxing themselves for the support of the Temple in Jerusalem and, without indulging in active proselytism, attracting numerous Romans, many of high rank, to observe Jewish rites and even become full converts to Judaism. Their numbers were augmented by the revolts against Rome in the first and second centuries: Jewish captives were brought to Italy whom the Italian Jews, as their faith enjoined, ransomed from bondage. Although they suffered the cruel humiliation of seeing the tax they raised for their sanctuary in Jerusalem diverted for a temple of Jupiter, they were later allowed to raise funds for the support of the Patriarch in Palestine.

In the large cities of Italy and Sicily they belonged to every trade and profession. There were Jewish weavers and dyers, tailors, metal workers, and artisans of every other sort. There were even Jewish painters, sculptors, and actors, and a considerable number embraced soldiering as a career. Like their neighbors, the Jews owned fields, orchards, and vineyards, and engaged in agriculture on a large or small scale. Some began as small peddlers and became merchant princes, shipowners, and bankers. The community or congregation was headed by a *parnes*, and the scribe who wrote the Torah scrolls was held in almost equal regard. The education of the young was not neglected, and eventually there were schools of higher learning also, especially in the cities of the south, Bari, Otranto, Oria, and others. For guidance and inspiration every community, of course, looked to the motherland and later to Babylonia.

When Rome turned Christian, the Jews became the victims of official persecution and mob violence. They did not therefore look upon the incursion of the barbarians, who put an end to the western Roman empire, with the same dread as the rest of the population. When in 489 Theodoric, chief of the Ostrogoths, became king of Italy, their lot actually improved: he protected them against the pious venom of the bishops and the greed of the mobs. Theodoric and his barbarians were also Christians but they, like other barbarian nations, rejected the orthodox Nicene Creed, professing instead the doctrines of Arius, which denied the divinity of Jesus; and Arianism was curiously lacking in zeal for persecution. But half a century later, Ostrogothic Italy was conquered by Belisarius, the brilliant general of Justinian, emperor of the east, and the Jews, who fought bravely against the invaders, again became the victims of persecution under the famous Code of Justinian.

In the meantime the bishops of Rome were growing in the power and prestige that before long made them supreme in the Christian world of the west, a supremacy that meant so much for the weal or woe of the Jewish communities scattered in that part of the world. Italy itself was breaking up. In 566 came another barbarian nation, the Lombards, who ousted the Byzantine rulers from a great part of the peninsula and ruled its northern reaches for more than two centuries. The Lombards, originally Arian, became orthodox, and the shadow of the bishop of Rome, now designated as Pope or "father," continued to grow. In 774 he was powerful enough to bring about the downfall of the Lombards by the sword of his ally, the great Charlemagne.

The papal attitude toward the Jews across the centuries was not uniform, but the popes were, in the main, more liberal than their subordinates. Gregory I (590-604), called the Great, set the general pattern of papal policy. He was anxious to convert the Jews, but by persuasion rather than by force: forcible conversion, he realized, was futile. He was not in favor of molesting them but he denied them the right to employ Christian servants or possess Christian slaves, not because he disapproved of slavery, an institution to which only the Jewish religious conscience had shown itself hostile, but because it was wrong that an infidel should be the master of a true believer.

In the south the Byzantines continued to hold sway until in 827 Sicily and parts of the mainland were conquered by the Moslems, who held on for more than two centuries. The Jewish communities grew and prospered, maintaining contact with Palestine, Babylonia, and Spain, and even with communities north of the Alps. Wherever the doors were not shut against them, they served the state and rose to high station, like the famous family whose achievements over two centuries have been found quaintly and piously recorded in 1054 in the memoirs of a descendant, Ahimaaz, son of Paltiel of Padua.

Everywhere they studied their own tradition, adding to the Talmud the absorbing and sometimes disturbing mysteries of the Cabala. Many Talmudic academies rose up and flourished, the most famous in Rome, and many scholars labored to enrich the lore of the past. Among them we can only mention the anonymous author of the *Joseppon* (Little Josephus), an historic compendium that achieved wide and enduring popularity; and Nathan ben Jechiel of Rome, famous for his dictionary of the Talmud which he finished in 1100 and called *Aruch* (Arrangement).

3

IN NORTHERN Africa, old Jewish centers revived and new ones came to life in the wake of the conquering Moslems. In Egypt the principal communities were in Alexandria, where Jewish life persisted in defiance of all the bishops could do to uproot it; in Fostat near Cairo, where the great Maimonides was to find refuge; and at Fayum, birthplace of Saadia Gaon. In all these places, Rabbanites and Karaites dwelt in separate communities and in uneasy propinquity, each with its own head and its own institutions.

Westward along the African coast new centers arose, of which the most important was Kairwan, located near the site of ancient Carthage in Tunisia. The pulse of Jewish life beat high in this new Moslem stronghold and shrine, capital of the state of Ifrikia, whose rulers were only nominally subject to the caliphs. The secular head of the community bore the title of Nagid, and many of its religious leaders rose to distinction as teachers and scholars.

There was a continuous intellectual flow between Kairwan and the other communities of the Diaspora. Hushiel ben Elhanan, on his way from Rome to Egypt, remained in Kairwan and established a school for higher learning. Both he and his son Hananel won wide recognition in the Jewish world of the eleventh century. Another international figure was Nissim ben Jacob, who was in touch with some of the greatest figures among the Jews of Spain. Isaac Israeli, teacher and friend of Saadia Gaon, came to Kairwan from Egypt and served as court physician to a succession of rulers.

A curious and glamorous personage, who stands out in this exotic and colorful world of the Mediterranean Diaspora and is identified chiefly with the community of Kairwan, is Eldad the Danite. He is a figure out of a Jewish Arabian Nights who, about the year 870, came down as on a magic carpet to Kairwan and told wonderful tales about descendants of four or five of the ancient tribes of Israel, redoubtable warriors who were living in a Shangri-la beyond Ethiopia, where the waterless river Sambation flowed with a torrent of sand and stones all week, and rested on the Sabbath. And he brought a ritual written in Hebrew which, he reported, was in use among those castaway Jews, and which impressed many of the scholars! There is enough in Eldad's marvelous stories to suggest the existence of Jewish settlements in faraway lands; his reports, at any rate, found wide acceptance and stirred vague messianic hopes: were not God's people scattered through all the known and unknown lands while the motherland lay desolate waiting for their return?

4

THERE were Jewish settlements in other cities of North Africa, notably in Fez, but we hasten westward to the Strait and across into Spain.

It was natural that Jews, on the bitter road of exile, should prefer Spain to almost any other land; they became passionately attached to it, for in many ways Spain resembled Palestine. Its climate is largely subtropical, with hot rainless summers and mild winters. It is a land of steep hills and sunny plains, of olive groves and vineyards, grainfields and pastures.

Jews must have come to Spain very early in their history: there were Jewish families in Spain who proudly claimed descent from King David and whose ancestors, they averred, had come to the land right after the destruction of the First Temple (586 B.C.E.). It is certain, however, that by the year 305 C.E. they were already important in number and influence, for in that year the Christian clergy of Spain met in the small city of Elvira near Granada and adopted measures against them. The prelates forbade all Christians to trade with them, to intermarry with them, and to let them bless their fields. Apparently the relations between the Jews and their neighbors were altogether friendly.

But the people, it seems, paid little heed to the dictates of the priests and, besides, the rural inhabitants were still pagan. The Jews followed the same occupations as their neighbors. They owned fields, vineyards, and olive groves. In the cities they were artisans and merchants and their ships sailed to all the ports of the Mediterranean. For a hundred years after the Council of Elvira they flourished under the Roman governors in spite of the bishops.

In 409 the barbarians broke into Spain. First came the Vandals, who passed on into Africa whence they crossed over into Italy and sacked the city of Rome. Then came the Visigoths who, like the kindred Ostrogoths, belonged to the Arian creed. They treated the Jews well; better, in fact, than they treated the Catholics, whom they looked upon as Romans and enemies. The Visigoth rulers elevated many Jews to important government posts and Jewish military contingents defended the Pyrenees passes against the incursions of the Franks. The Jews were even permitted to convert their slaves to their faith. It was during this period of nearly two centuries of Visigoth-Arian rule that the Jews established themselves so firmly in Spain that not even the persecutions that followed were able to uproot them.

The change came in 589 when King Reccared I renounced the Arian creed and became Catholic. His conversion stemmed from political rather than religious motives: he found it expedient to have the support of the Catholic clergy against the nobility who elected the monarch and frequently defied him. At once the Jews were forbidden to hold public office or own slaves. Intermarriage was banned and all children born of such marriages were to be baptized by force. But the nobles found the Jews too useful to persecute and, to a large extent, the laws remained a dead letter. Then came King Sisebut, who was more determined and more drastic. He issued a decree ordering all Jews to choose between baptism and exile. There were many who chose baptism but continued to practice their faith in secret, while thousands fled from the country and sought refuge in France or Africa.

The story of the Jews in Spain during the century preceding the descent of the Moslems is one of remorseless oppression, interspersed with brief and rare periods of relaxation. The wrath of the clergy burned even more fiercely against the converts who practiced their faith in secret than against those who refused to be baptized. After ten years of respite from persecution under Sisebut's successor Swintilla, the baptized Jews caught practicing their former faith were ordered enslaved and their children torn from them and brought up in convents. The highest pitch of cruelty came under Euric and Egica. The first placed the secret Jews wholly at the mercy of the clergy, and declared forfeit the property of all others who clung to their faith. The second decreed all Jews to be slaves forever, stripped them of land and houses, and tore all children of seven and over from their parents to be brought up as Christians.

The proud and tortured Jews of Spain whose spirit, despite all cruelties, remained unbroken, grasped at every opportunity that offered relief from their pitiless oppressors. Once they supported a rebel noble who claimed the throne of Spain and promised to abolish the laws against them. The rebel was defeated and the Jews were in worse plight than ever. More and more they looked toward Africa where the Moslem hosts were advancing and coming nearer.

By the turn of the century the Visigoth kingdom was ripe for destruction. The court was seething with conspiracy, the nobles were unruly and defiant, the clergy corrupt and insolent. King Egica, the last and worst of the oppressors, died in 701. The reign of his son, who was probably murdered, ended in general disorder, and when Roderic, the last Visigoth king, came to the throne, Tarik the Moslem already stood at the tip of Africa opposite the great rock which bears his name.*

* *Jebel Tarik,* Mount Tarik, has become "Gibraltar."

5

IN JULY of the year 711, Tarik took his 12,000 Berbers and Arabs across the straits, and in a three-day battle at Jerez overthrew the last Visigoth ruler of Spain. He was, of course, hailed by the Jews as their deliverer, but he was welcomed and assisted by Christians also: Spaniards who looked upon Roderic as a usurper provided Tarik with ships and many of them fought at his side. The Moslems, moreover, were not persecutors. Christians and Jews, as unbelievers, were of course compelled to pay the poll tax, but they could worship as they pleased. Many a Christian became a willing convert to the religion of the conqueror.

The fire and fervor as well as the austere simplicity that marked the faith of Abu Bekr and Omar were now gone. The invaders were worldly men who sought to reap as much wealth and power from their conquests as they could, and they made excellent progress. In less than three years, they overran the entire country to the Pyrenees Mountains. Cordova became their capital, and they made it a city of grace and splendor, rivaling the magnificence of Bagdad, the metropolis at the other end of the Moslem world. The centers of Christendom were like rude encampments compared to the elegant cities of the Moslems with their public buildings, mosques and palaces—cities where, under the patronage of the rulers, artists and scientists, philosophers and poets, forgathered and pursued their labors.

It was natural that in the affairs of the new regime, as well as in the cultural efflorescence that came in its wake, the Jews of Spain should play a leading part. Not only was there an affinity of race and language between Jew and Arab which promoted understanding and in short order enabled the Jews to make the Arabic tongue their vernacular; the Moslems also found in the Jews a convenient link between themselves and the Christians, and entrusted to them the administration of many of the centers they occupied. A broad path of freedom and opportunity opened for the Jews of Spain, and as they grew more numerous, more wealthy, more influential, they spread their wings and mounted to dazzling heights of cultural achievement. While the great center of the East was sinking into twilight and dusk, Spain became the Babylonia of the West, and for five hundred years held the hegemony of the Dispersion.

The primacy did not descend suddenly upon the Jews of Spain: the Moslem conquest was two centuries old before the remarkable talents of Chasdai ibn Shaprut raised Spanish Jewry to pre-eminence. It was first necessary that Moslem power in Spain should itself be consolidated, a process long retarded by internal dissension and strife which enabled the Christians to reconquer the northern and western parts of the peninsula and establish kingdoms with which the Moslems had to be constantly at war. In 758 Abdurrahman, one of the few Omayyads who escaped massacre at the hands of the Abassids, became the first independent and effective ruler of Moslem Spain, but for a century and a half under his weak successors the country fared badly. It was not until 912, when Abdurrahman III, the first to assume the royal title of caliph, came to the throne that a long period of power and splendor was ushered in for Moslem Spain.

6

ABDURRAHMAN III reigned for fifty years, and it was under him and under his son Hakam II (961-976) that Chasdai ibn Shaprut displayed his versatile and brilliant attainments. Chasdai, to begin with, was a physician and watched over the health of the rulers. Being a master of Latin, he served as interpreter to the caliph and ambassador to Christian monarchs. He was, in fact, a remarkably adroit diplomat: he won his greatest triumph when he persuaded a Christian king as well as a queen-regent and her ward to come to Cordova and sign a treaty of peace with the caliph. In addition Chasdai was an able financier and man of affairs: he served the caliph also as minister of finance and commerce.

With all that, however, Chasdai was not accorded the title of vizier or any other official rank: such a distinction and token of equality could not be conferred upon an unbeliever. And Chasdai was first and last a Jew whose deepest concern was the honor and welfare of his people. He was particularly zealous for the exaltation and diffusion of Torah. For students, he secured copies of the Talmud from the college of Sura, and men of learning and talent, like the poets and grammarians Menaḥem ben Saruk and Dunash ben Labrat, could always count on his assistance. Nor was he insensible to the fallen estate of his scattered people, to the glory that was no more, or to the jibes of Moslems and Christians who would have it that since "the scepter had departed from Judah," it could only mean that God had cast them aside, that they were no longer His people.

7

CHASDAI and his people in Spain were deeply stirred one day to learn that in a faraway land to the east the scepter had not departed from Judah. Rumors about a Jewish kingdom in the nebulous regions north of the Byzantine Empire had long been current among them, and people connected them with the fantastic tales of Eldad the Danite. This time, however, Chasdai's information was definite: it came to him from the Byzantine and other foreign ambassadors who arrived in Cordova. On the western shore of the Caspian Sea, between the Volga and the Don, they told him, there dwelt the Khazars, a powerful nation, and they were ruled by a Jewish king named Joseph.

Chasdai determined to establish contact with King Joseph. He tried first to correspond with him through Constantinople and failed, but finally a letter was delivered to the king by a Jew from Germany named Isaac ben Eliezer. The letter was long; it was written with the assistance of the poet and grammarian Menahem ben Saruk. Some years later Chasdai received King Joseph's reply. The Khazars, he learned, were not, as many people supposed, descended from the lost tribes of Israel; they were not, in fact, of Jewish origin. The Khazars were a people of uncertain stock and must have come originally from Asia. Centuries ago they had established a kingdom near the mouth of the Volga and conquered the tribes around them, forcing them to pay tribute. They were formidable warriors, these Khazars, and struck terror into the hearts of the Persian and Byzantine rulers.

King Joseph went on to answer the question that was uppermost in Chasdai's mind: How did it come about that the Khazar kingdom became Jewish? In the beginning, the ancestors of the king were worshippers of idols, but in 740 or thereabout the reigning monarch, King Bulan, became converted to Judaism. How that happened Joseph did not know exactly. Already, it seems, there were many foreign merchants in Itil, the Khazar capital, and many Jews must have found refuge there from Byzantine persecution. One record had it that King Bulan, seeking a new religion for himself and his people, had summoned learned Christians, Moslems, and Jews to debate before him the merits of their respective creeds, and when he learned that the first two were the offspring of Judaism, he and his nobles and some of the people decided to embrace the mother faith. Later a law was enacted that only a Jewish king could sit on the throne of the Khazars, and a successor of Bulan, named Obadiah, had established schools for the study of the Bible and Talmud, the Khazars in the meantime having made contact with the schools in Babylonia. The fact must be noted that there was no persecution in the Khazar kingdom: the members of all faiths were on a footing of equality.

"You state that you long to see me," King Joseph writes to Chasdai ibn Shaprut. "I too long to know you and your wisdom. Could I but speak to you face to face, you should be my father and I your son, and I would place the government of my land into your hands." How marvelous the king's words must have sounded in Chasdai's ears! But, alas, the Jewish kingdom was already on the verge of downfall. In 965 the Russian prince of Kiev captured Sarkell, the chief Khazar stronghold; four years later Itil, the capital, was taken, and in time the Jewish kingdom of the Khazars became only a tale and a memory.

CHAPTER THIRTY-TWO

High Noon

IN THE west, the sun of Spanish Jewry was mounting to a brilliant noon, and the chronicle glows with the names of statesmen and warriors, scholars, scientists, and philosophers, poets, mystics, and moralists. But the dazzling light they shed should not blind us to the community which they crown. It was a community of noble men and women in whom the Arabic culture that had come to a fine fruition in Spain appeared to be perfectly blended with their own millennial tradition.

Outwardly their life was stamped with the grace and dignity that wealth bestows upon those who deserve to possess it. They lived in beautiful houses, wore handsome attire, gathered at rich banquets, and walked abroad with poise and assurance. They mingled freely with their Moslem neighbors, nor was their devotion to their own faith or their pride in the great past of their people weakened by this intercourse. Their basic culture was still Jewish, grounded in the Bible and Talmud; nor was the structure they built on it less Jewish for being cast in the graceful mold of a rich and colorful age.

The Jews of Spain, moreover, considered themselves a single people with common interests and aims, and they were recognized by Christians as well as Moslems as distinct communities or *aljamas*. In the tenth century, when they lived under one caliph; in the eleventh, when Moslem Spain broke up into rival states; as well as in the twelfth and later centuries, when the Christians made heavy inroads upon the Moslems, the Jews were normally free to manage their own communal institutions, and they possessed a large measure of autonomy in judicial and fiscal matters as well. They recognized a common leadership, secular as well as religious, and delegates from different communities met from time to time in assemblies to consider their common interests.

Five centuries is a long span even in Jewish history, and the career of Spanish Jewry is not free from suffering and disaster, but it still casts the richest glow across the two millennia of the Jewish Dispersion.

2

THE lore of the Talmud was brought from Babylonia to Spain by a scholar named Moses ben Enoch after an odyssey of high adventure. Moses was one of four emissaries from Sura who were charged with the mission of obtaining support for the ancient academy from communities in other lands. They were sailing west on the Mediterranean near Italy when their ship was seized by Ibn Rumahis, admiral of the Spanish caliph Abdurrahman III, then at war with the caliph of the east. Moses ben Enoch's wife threw herself into the sea to escape dishonor, and he and his young son were taken to Cordova where they were duly ransomed by the Jewish community. The fate of his three companions is veiled in legend: one account has it that they were taken to different lands where each became the head of a Talmudic academy.

Such, however, was certainly the dignity achieved by Moses ben Enoch. His superior learning was quickly recognized, and under his guidance and with the support of Chasdai ibn Shaprut, Cordova became an important Talmudic center which attracted students from all parts of Spain and North Africa. The caliph looked with favor upon the event: he was glad to see the Jews of his realm no longer dependent on the schools in the land of his rival and enemy. Moses ben Enoch died in 965 and, after one of those bitter contests that too often disturbed the harmony of the community, his son was chosen to take his place. Chasdai, still the secular head of the community, survived Moses for five years; his successor, appointed in the reign of Hisham II (976-1013), was the wealthy Jacob ibn Jau, who became the Nagid or secular head of the Jews in all the realms of the caliph, in Africa as well as Spain.

But the caliphate that was centered in the gorgeous city of Cordova was approaching evil days. Hisham reigned but he did not rule: the real power was his chief minister Almanzur, and when this strong and crafty man died a period of fierce civil strife and chaos ensued. The armies which were composed of slaves and mercenaries turned on their masters, and in 1013 the Berbers seized the capital and looted it. The Omayyad princes fought among themselves like wolves, and the Caliphate of Cordova fell to pieces.

3

PEOPLE fled from Cordova to other cities in Spain and many Jews found refuge in Granada, the beautiful city of the famous Alhambra, where a thriving Jewish community had existed for centuries. The Arabs, in fact, sometimes called Granada *Karratta-al-Yahud*, the "City of the Jews." Before long Granada became the capital of a new kingdom which included the port of Malaga, and in 1013 a remarkable young man named Samuel ibn Nagrela left Cordova and came to live in Malaga.

Samuel's story reads like a tale from the *Arabian Nights,* but his career may nevertheless be considered symbolic of his people in Spain. His education was typical of the cultured Spanish Jew: mathematics and philosophy went hand in hand with the Talmud and Hebrew, and Samuel knew six other languages besides. Young Samuel derived his living from a little spice shop, but people came to him to write letters and petitions for them addressed to the vizier of King Habbus in Granada. Impressed by Samuel's epistles, the vizier sought out the young spice merchant and persuaded him to come to Granada and be his secretary. Samuel became also his friend and adviser, and when the vizier died the king, to the amazement and chagrin of all pious Moslems, put Samuel in his place, conferring upon the Jew not only the powers but the title as well. But Samuel knew how to win over his enemies, and there seemed to be no limit to his talents. He was the king's war minister and often led his troops in battle. He conducted the foreign affairs of the kingdom, raising it to a high position among the states into which Moslem Spain had become divided. In 1038 King Habbus died, and Granada became the scene of a bitter contest for the crown between his two sons. Samuel won the succession for Badis, the elder of the two, and his position in the kingdom became even stronger.

Samuel was, of course, the official leader of the Jews of Granada: he is best known as Shmuel Ha-Nagid, or Samuel the Prince. His influence and good deeds extended to the whole of Spain and into the other lands of the Mediterranean Diaspora. He corresponded with its leading men, among others with Hai and Hezekiah of Pumbeditha and Nissim ben Jacob of Kairwan. He found time, moreover, to conduct his own Talmudic academy, decide questions on law and religion, and write philosophic and scholarly works as well as poetry, the latter an exercise that attracted most cultured men of the age. He even found time to engage in a literary feud with the great Joseph ibn Janah of Saragossa, the foremost grammarian and biblical scholar of the period. Such feuds were not infrequent and furnished entertainment as well as enlightenment to wide circles especially when, as in the war between the two grammarians Dunash ben Labrat and Menahem ben Saruk, the controversy descended to personalities.

Shmuel Ha-Nagid, said the poets after his death, wore the quadruple crown of priestly descent, exalted station, Torah, and good deeds; and the last, they added, was the brightest of all.

4

WITH all the wealth and elegance that adorns the Jewish communities in Spain, and with all the prestige to which so many of their leaders rose, their position as a racial and religious minority was always more or less insecure. A terrible demonstration of this truth came to the Jews of Granada shortly after Samuel's death, which occurred about 1056. His son Joseph, who possessed much of his father's brilliance but lacked his tact and wisdom, succeeded to his dignities. Joseph was arrogant and indiscreet. He incurred the bitter hatred of the Arabs and Berbers of the city, long resentful of the power exercised by his father. In December 1066, after spreading rumors that Joseph was in treasonous correspondence with a neighboring ruler, they overran his palace and crucified him at the gate of the city. The mob then turned on the Jews of Granada and in a single day, December 30, massacred four thousand of the community.

5

THREE years later, there died in the city of Valencia the poet and philosopher Solomon ibn Gabirol, a star of the first magnitude in the galaxy of Spanish Jewry. He had spent his brief and restless life in many cities of Spain, including Malaga, Granada and Saragossa. In Saragossa he was befriended by Yekutiel ibn Hasan, who held high office with the ruler of the land, and in Granada Shmuel Ha-Nagid was his friend and protector. Ibn Gabirol, like the prophet Jeremiah, was a man of sorrows: he was the victim of envy and malice. His patron Yekutiel was put to death by a usurper, and he saw the calamity that befell the Jews of Granada. Like Jeremiah also, Ibn Gabirol sought refuge in an unshakable faith in divine justice, and gave expression to it in songs of towering grandeur. Many of Ibn Gabirol's poems are still included in the synagogue ritual. His majestic *Royal Crown* glows with the whole gamut of emotions experienced by the devout soul before the impenetrable mystery of the universe. But as a philosopher Ibn Gabirol's merit has only recently obtained recognition. When still a young man he wrote in Arabic a book called *The Fountain of Life*, and a century later, in a Latin translation, it became a textbook in philosophy widely adopted by the universities of Europe. In the translation and copying, however, the name of the author was garbled into Avencebrol and Avicebron, and only in the nineteenth century was the author's identity discovered.

A legend has come down concerning the death of Ibn Gabirol which reflects the love and admiration in which he was held. It reports that an Arab poet in a jealous rage slew Gabirol and buried his body under a fig tree. At once the tree burst into bloom and bore fruit!

"The Lord anointed him his nation's king of song," was the verdict pronounced over Ibn Gabirol by Al-Harizi, himself a distinguished poet who lived a century later. Both belonged to the monarchs of the spirit who, in the annals of the Jewish people, now took the place of the more common variety of kings. They were well described by Abraham ibn Daud, also a member of the royal company, as the men "who strengthened the hands of Israel with songs and with words of comfort."

6

THE generation of Ibn Gabirol and Shmuel Ha-Nagid is rich with many other luminaries, among whom the moralist and mystic Bachya ibn Pakuda deserves special mention. He is the author of *The Duties of the Heart*, a book that is still a source of pious inspiration to thousands of his people. Bachya is not satisfied with mere observance, which he calls "the duties of the limbs"; he demands the inward piety that leads to the soul's ascent and absorption with the infinite and he teaches how it may be achieved. He was called *Chassid*, or saint, and many centuries later, at the other end of the European continent, his teachings had no small share in giving impulse to a powerful religious movement whose followers also called themselves *Chassidim.*

The position of the Jews in the other Moslem kingdoms of Spain does not seem to have deteriorated as a result of the catastrophe that overtook the Jews of Granada in 1066. From Saragossa in the north to Seville in the south, learning continued to flourish, and

Jews rose to high station in the service of the rulers. Isaac ibn Albulia, for example, who had escaped from the massacre in Granada, was raised to the distinguished post of astrologer in the court of Seville, and being a Talmudic scholar as well as an astronomer, he was made head of the Jewish community. By the middle of the eleventh century, Spain had in fact become the center of Talmudic learning, and the laurels of Sura fell to the city of Lucena, situated not far from Seville. There the school of Isaac Alfasi, a lion among the savants of the age and the author of a great commentary on the Talmud, became the nursery of many of the choice spirits of Spanish Jewry.

7

IN THE meantime, the power of the Moslems in Spain continued to wane: the Christians, taking advantage of their feuds and divisions, kept pressing down upon them. Moreover, after a long period of wrangling, in the course of which one Christian king sometimes called in the Moslems to help him against another, the Christians began to unite. Thus in 1065 Alphonso VI, who reigned till 1109, found himself the ruler of the three kingdoms of Galicia, León, and Castile, and with little opposition extended his suzerainty over the petty Moslem rulers south to Andalusia. In 1085 the important city of Toledo surrendered to him and became the capital of Christian Spain.

Now for the first time the Moslems found the will to act together, but the course they took was a counsel of despair. They invited Yussuf ibn Tashufin, who ruled over a wide Berber empire in Africa, to come to their aid. They knew the invitation was dangerous to its senders, for Yussuf might come and choose to stay; but, said the king of Seville, he would rather drive camels in Africa than tend pigs in Castile. Yussuf came over with his fierce Berbers, who are known as the Almoravides, defeated the Christians—and stayed. Moslem Spain became a province of his African empire.

As the Christians moved down, absorbing one community after another, their treatment of the Jews was surprisingly fair. The Jews were declared equal before the law, and so many of them held important positions in the government of Alphonso that the Pope, Gregory VII, chided him for allowing them to hold sway over Christians. The Almoravides, however, who were a savage lot and had only recently become converted to Islam, began by bearing down hard upon all unbelievers. Yussuf summoned the Jews to redeem a pledge which, he informed them, their ancestors had made: that they would all turn Moslem if, five hundred years after the Hegira, the Messiah had not yet appeared. Yussuf's missionary ardor, however, was cooled with a handsome bribe, and before long the Almoravides became less fanatical. Yussuf's successor Ali (1106-1143) received the Jews into his service and Spanish Jewry, under Moslem rule or Christian, went forward to new heights of achievement.

8

THE twelfth is the century of high noon in the career of Spanish Jewry. It is the century of Yehudah Halevi, of Moses ibn Ezra, Abraham ibn Ezra, Abraham ibn Daud, Benjamin of Tudela, and of other giants, too numerous to be contained in this chronicle. It is, above all, the century of Moses Maimonides, the giant among the giants.

The life of Yehudah Halevi, ardent champion of his people and the most inspired singer since the days of the psalmists, is a miniature of the saga of Spanish Jewry as a whole. It was a noble life, filled with high aspiration and achievement, and it ended in tragedy. Born in Toledo in 1086, a year after that city was wrested from the Moslems by Alphonso VI, Halevi went for his education to Lucena. There he studied in the school of the renowned Alfasi and met the most learned and gifted men of the day.

Among them was Moses ibn Ezra, scion of an illustrious family which produced a constellation of bright luminaries. From Granada an unhappy love affair had sent Moses wandering through Spain, pouring out his sorrows in song. But no Jewish poet of that day could sing only of "love and the sorrows of love." Moses wrote songs of pious devotion, many of which have entered into the synagogue ritual. In Yehudah Halevi, however, he recognized his master.

Halevi absorbed all that Lucena could teach him of Hebrew and Talmud as well as the secular subjects, including Arabic, mathematics, philosophy, and science, and returned to his native city to practice medicine. But he was not happy in that profession or in the city itself. "I busy myself with the vanities of medical science, although I am unable to heal," he wrote to a friend; "I physic Babel, but it continues infirm." Toledo was a Babel to him, so he went to Cordova, a center of Arab-Jewish culture for centuries. There he practiced his true vocation of inspired philosopher and poet, singing in words that fall on the ears like music, of love and friendship and joy in the beauty and majesty of God's creation. But the full passion of his love he lavished on Zion, the abode of his people's former glory. On the Ninth of Ab, the day of mourning for the destruction of Jerusalem and the Temple, his *Ode to Zion* is still chanted in synagogues the world over. It is the chant that begins with the famous lines:

Zion, wilt thou not greet thy captive sons,
The remnant of thy flock, who bid thee Peace?
From west and east and north and south they cry
Their Peace, from near and far and every side.
And Peace from this poor prisoner of hope
Who yearns to shed his tears upon Thy hills!

His love of Zion grew until it became the ruling passion of his life, and his songs rose to an ecstasy of rapture and longing. Of Jerusalem he sang:

Could I but fly on eagle's wings to thee
And mingle with thy sacred sod my tears!
How tenderly thy stones and dust I'd kiss,
Their taste than honey sweeter to my lips.

Cost what it might, he determined at last to satisfy his longing. He took ship and after a stormy voyage came to Egypt where his fame had preceded him and where the leaders of his people, including the Nagid, Samuel ibn Mansur, tried to detain him. Ibn Mansur lived in Fostat near Cairo; he held high office in the court of the Fatimite caliph who ruled over the country, and was probably the recognized head of the community. Halevi tore himself from his admirers and came at last to Palestine, where he becomes lost to view suddenly and completely. He visited Tyre and Damascus, but legend places his death near the mount of the Temple, where, as he lay prostrate in prayer, he was trampled and slain by an Arab horseman.

The year was 1141, the country was again in Christian hands, and Halevi must have found more sorrow than joy in the land of his longing. But he had the never-failing refuge of song; he visioned the redemption of his people and sang:

When in dreams I see thy captive throngs,
Then straight am I a harp unto thy songs!

But Halevi the poet must not be allowed to eclipse Halevi the philosopher and defender of the faith. From within and without, the faith he loved was under attack. From within, it was directly attacked by Karaism, which had made its way into Spain, and by Jewish disciples of the ancient Greek philosopher Aristotle, some of whose teachings, like his doctrine of the eternity of the universe, conflicted with the tenets of Judaism. From without, it was of course under constant attack by Christian and Moslem theologians.

Halevi embodied his momentous defense of Judaism in his book *Kitab al Khazari* (Letter of the Khazars), an inspired work which may still be read for pleasure as well as instruction. As a frame for his ideas Halevi used the debate that was reported to have taken place before King Bulan of the Khazars when he sought a new faith for himself and his people. "Israel among the nations," declares Halevi through the mouth of the Jewish champion in this debate, "is like the heart amid the organs of the body"; God is glorified in Israel, and Palestine is the "inheritance of the Lord and His footstool."

9

IN NORTH AFRICA a new Moslem ferment had sprung up and boiled over into Spain. Combining religious frenzy with a lust for conquest, it started again among the African Berbers who, in the name of the true faith, smote the Almoravides who had grown lax and tolerant. The leader, a certain Ibn Tumart, proclaimed himself the Mahdi, or appointed prophet, and his followers took the name of Almohades. By 1149 the whole of Moslem Spain was in their hands.

To the Jews they offered the choice of Islam or exile. There were some who rejected both and died the death of martyrs. Others renounced their faith in the open but continued to practice it in secret. The majority chose exile and sought refuge in the Christian kingdoms of the north. The Talmudic schools of Seville and Lucena were closed, the beautiful synagogues of Cordova were laid in ruins. Toledo, where Alphonso VII (1126-1157) reigned as King of Castile and León, became the most important city of refuge. Judah ibn Ezra, a nephew of the poet Moses, was in high favor with the king and held important posts in the government. He was appointed *Nasi* of the Jews in the kingdom, and helped the victims of the Almohades to find asylum in Toledo and elsewhere in Christian Spain. In Portugal in the west, in Aragon in the east, and in Navarre in the far north, Jewish communities gathered new strength and flourished. Saragossa and Barcelona in Aragon and Toledo in Castile became leading centers. Meir ibn Megas, pupil and successor of the great Alfasi, became the head of a Talmudic academy in Toledo, the city where Yehudah Halevi had been so ill at ease. Jews rose to high station in the service of the Christian monarchs and they fought with distinction in the wars, both foreign and civil, to which there was never an end.

Many names were added also to the roster of the illuminati. There was Abraham ibn Daud, philosopher, scientist, historian, and moralist who, to the confusion of the Karaites, traced the origin and continuous progress of Oral Torah. There was Judah al-Harizi, poet, critic, and traveler. There was Benjamin of Tudela, a small city which was a perennial bone of contention between Navarre and Aragon, and where the Jews fought from their own citadel. Benjamin, whose fame rests on his travels, epitomizes the bold spirit that stamped the Jews of Spain. He visited many lands in Europe, Asia, and Africa, and wrote a fascinating account of what he saw of the life of his own and other people.

An even more striking example of boldness and versatility is Abraham ibn Ezra, whose fame has been embellished by Robert Browning in the well-known poem *Rabbi Ben Ezra*. Abraham, who died in 1167, was the most picturesque member of the illustrious family to which belonged the poet Moses and the *Nasi* Judah. He became familiar with all the learning as well as with the world of his day, traveling as far east as Babylonia and as far west as London, sojourning in many lands and writing books wherever he stopped. His stay in Italy profoundly influenced the cultural life of his people in that country. He wrote extensively on the Bible, on mathematics, astronomy, and astrology; he wrote poetry and philosophy also. He was a man of restless spirit, a sparkling wit and a good deal of a paradox. He lived to a ripe old age with unimpaired intellectual vigor, but he was always poor in worldly goods. "If I should deal in shrouds," he once declared, "men would stop dying; and if I should take to selling candles, the sun would never set."

10

THE labors and journeys of Yehudah Halevi, Al-Harizi, Benjamin of Tudela, and the amazing Ibn Ezra, highlight the existence of a Jewish world not confined to Spain alone. It lay scattered in large and small concentrations throughout the Mediterranean lands; it overflowed north into the realms of the Franks, the Germans, and the Anglo-Saxons; it carried on in good and evil days, thriving and suffering under Christian and Moslem dominion alike. But the man whose life is the clearest reflection of the cosmopolitan range of the Jewish community, and who is regarded as the peak which the Jewish mind attained in the twelfth century, is Moses ben Maimon, better known to the world at large as Maimonides and among his own people as the Rambam.* His influence on succeeding Jewish generations was incalculable and is still, after a lapse of eight centuries, unexhausted; it is reflected in the terse saying that compares him to his greater namesake: "From Moses unto Moses there has been none like Moses."

In 1148, at the age of thirteen, his family became refugees from the fury of the Almohades. That year the stately city of Cordova, where the sage was born, was seized and ravaged by the Berber savages and the family of Maimon, after years of wandering in Spain, made their way to North Africa and sought asylum in Fez.

* *Rambam* is derived by combining the first letters of "Rabbi Moses ben Maimon," a device followed in the case of many other Jewish sages, ancient and modern, e.g.: *Rashbag* for Rabbi Shimon ben Gamaliel, *Rashi* for Rabbi Shlomo Itzhaki, *Besht* for Baal Shem Tov, *Shadal* for Shmuel David Luzzatto, etc.

But that was only the beginning of their exile. Fez was ruled by the Almohades, Jews had to pretend they were Moslems, and the family fled and resumed their travels. They set sail for Palestine, having decided to seek a haven in the land of their fathers. After landing in Acco they proceeded to Jerusalem, but the land was still in the hands of the Christians and their people were few and poor and persecuted. Like Jacob's clan in the days of Pharaoh, they migrated to Egypt and settled in Fostat, near Cairo, where the sage lived for the rest of his life. The education of this youthful wanderer, however, had not been neglected. His father, who had been a student of Alfasi, taught him the Bible and Talmud, and from Arab teachers he learned physics and medicine. Nor did his travels prevent him from beginning some of those works which were to make him the ranking authority of his own and later generations.

In Egypt things went hard for Moses in the beginning. Soon after his arrival his father died; then his brother David, who supported the family by trading in precious stones, went down in the Indian Ocean together with his fortune. Moses took to the practice of medicine and became so famous as a healer that he was appointed physician to the court of Saladin, the ruler of Egypt. This was the gallant and knightly Saladin, the first and greatest of the Ayyubite dynasty, who in 1169 became Sultan of Egypt and in 1187 drove the Crusaders out of Jerusalem and the greater part of Palestine. His opponent was the equally famous and chivalrous English monarch Richard the Lion-Hearted, who is reported to have tried, without success, to induce Moses ben Maimon to desert his rival and accept the post of physician to himself. Moses had every reason to remain in the service of the Egyptian sultan. Since Saladin was always in the field, the real ruler of the land was his vizier Alfadhel, a friend and admirer of the sage, whom he elevated to the leadership of the Jewish community with the title of Nagid. Maimonides made good use of his influence to improve the lot of his people in Egypt and other lands. They were again permitted to dwell in Jerusalem, from which the Christians had banished them, and he was successful also in alleviating the hard lot of the Jews of Yemen.

Immersed in professional, communal, and literary labors, the Rambam's life was a continuous round of toil. "When night falls I am so exhausted I can scarcely speak," he writes to a friend. The fame of his wisdom and erudition spread far and wide, and from every land his people sought counsel from him in matters small and great, just as in former days they sought it from the academies in Babylonia. The light he shed in dark and grievous moments is illustrated by the famous reply he sent the Jews of Yemen who had turned to him for help in evil days on which they had fallen. Their troubles were laid before him in a letter from Jacob al Fayumi, one of the Yemenite scholars. Not only, wrote Al Fayumi, were they tormented by their rulers, who were forcing them to embrace Mohammedanism, but they were bedeviled by two self-proclaimed prophets, one of whom had turned renegade, contending that Islam was the true faith, while the other admonished them to divide their wealth among the poor and prepare for the speedy coming of the Messiah.

In his "Letter to Yemen" (*Iggeret Teman*), remarkable both for courage and elevation, the Rambam exhorted them to be steadfast in their own faith, compared to which, he told them, the others were but as dead likenesses to the living original. "The nations hate us," he declared, "on account of the divinity that lives in our midst." But, he warned them, they must not be tempted to calculate the advent of the Messiah, who would come in God's own time. The Rambam's words were like a tonic to the Jews of Yemen, who were so grateful that they included him in the *Kaddish* prayer. "May God's kingdom," they revised the *Kaddish* to read, "be established in your lifetime, and in the lifetime of our teacher Moses ben Maimon, and in the lifetime of all the house of Israel."

The same zeal for the ancient faith produced his thirteen credos, which Jews the world over still recite in their daily prayers. These Articles of Faith the great teacher embodied in one of his monumental works, a commentary on the Mishnah which he called the *Luminary*, and on which he labored during his years of wandering. The Articles are so framed as to refute not only the claims of the rival religions, but the philosophical heresies as well, including atheism and the denial of free will. The second and third Articles, for example, proclaim the unity of God in such a manner as to render impossible a belief in polytheism or the Christian Trinity.

The second great work of the Rambam, a complete code of Biblical and Talmudic law, contributed even more than the *Luminary* to establish his authority with his people. This colossal work, known as *Mishneh Torah* (Torah Repeated) and also as the *Yad Ha-Chazakah* (The Mighty Hand) is an ordered classification of the vast jurisprudence of the Talmud, together with illuminating explanations which the sage drew from his rich store of philosophic and scientific knowledge. The *Mishneh Torah* was acclaimed throughout the Jewish world and exalted the Rambam to a plane unattained by a Jewish leader since Saadia Gaon, two and a half centuries earlier.

But the work had its opponents also. There were those who frowned upon its rationalistic outlook; others were afraid it would supplant the Talmud; and still others were envious of the prestige it conferred upon its author. Among the latter was Samuel ben Ali, master of a Talmudic college in Bagdad with the title of *Gaon;* for the *Gaonate* had, it seems, been restored in Babylonia, shedding a false glow and striving to recapture its ancient authority. In the sharp controversy that ensued the sage of Fostat stood aloof: unlike Saadia he found no zest in combat, but his cause was valiantly upheld by his favorite pupil, Joseph ibn Aknin.

II

THE Rambam's lucid mind produced another work which provoked even more controversy. He called it *Guide to the Perplexed,* and wrote it for those whose minds were lured by the philosophy and science of the age and found their faith incompatible with reason. "The object of this treatise," he writes, "is to enlighten a religious man who has been trained to believe in the truth of our holy Torah . . . and at the same time has been successful in his philosophical studies. Human reason has attracted him to abide within its sphere, and he finds it difficult to accept as correct the teaching based on the literal interpretation of Torah . . . hence he is lost in perplexity and anxiety." In the realm of philosophy and "human reason" Aristotle was still the reigning monarch.

One way by which the Rambam seeks to enlighten the perplexed is to interpret passages of the Bible not literally but figuratively. Another is to reconcile the teachings of philosophy and science with those of Torah. He is not, however, a thick-and-thin follower of Aristotle. On the contrary, he clashes with him on a number of fundamental questions. Is the universe, or matter, without beginning or end, and without aim, or is it the product of God's creative will and purpose? Is man a creature held fast in the shackles of predestination, an irresponsible slave of necessity, or is he endowed with free will, and responsible, therefore, for what he does or fails to do? With brilliant dialectic, Maimonides, taking issue with Aristotle, upholds the doctrines of creation and design, of free will and responsibility, doctrines which are basic not only to Judaism, but to all theistic religion.

The Rambam, moreover, is well aware of the limitations of the human intellect, nor does he invoke the judgment of reason in all questions. "Do not imagine," he writes, "that these most difficult problems can be thoroughly understood by any one of us. This is not the case. At times the truth shines so brilliantly that we perceive it as clear as day. Our nature and habit then draw a veil over our perception, and we return to a darkness almost as dense as before. We are like those who, though beholding frequent flashes of lightning, still find ourselves in the thickest darkness of the night."

From the Arabic in which Maimonides wrote it, the *Guide* was translated into Hebrew and Latin, and the work has given its author an honored place in the history of philosophy. But among his own people the conflict that began with the *Mishneh Torah* grew more bitter with the appearance of the *Guide*, and although such controversies may be a tribute to the intellectual vigor of an age, it did not add to the strength and serenity of the Jewish communities in exile.

The sage himself continued his round of arduous labor until his death, which occurred on December 13, 1204. His remains were taken to Palestine for burial, and the entire Diaspora went into mourning for the great light that had gone out in Israel.

CHAPTER THIRTY-THREE

France, Germany, and the Crusades

BEFORE pursuing the tale of Spanish Jewry to its tragic finale, we raise the curtain on the communities in what are today France, Germany, and England, the classic lands of European civilization. For the Spain we have so far dealt with was Moslem and Oriental rather than Christian and European; and, although the current of Jewish history has flowed through many civilizations, it is Christian Europe which, by reason of the faith it adopted, that the Jewish spirit has influenced most profoundly; and it is Christian Europe which, for better or worse, has left the deepest mark on the Jews themselves.

2

THERE came a time, toward the end of the fifth century, when the Roman legions holding the Rhine frontier of the empire broke before the pressure of the barbarians swarming in from the forests of Germany. Clovis the Frank set up a great kingdom which took in what is now France and most of Germany. He and his warriors embraced the Catholic faith, but it was a conversion that was only an immersion, without relation to the ethical teachings of the founder. It left the lusts and savagery of the converts unaffected, but it had an important influence on the fate of the Jews who were scattered among them.

There were Jews in those lands centuries before the invasion of the Franks; they came as early as the first century with the Roman armies that pressed up into northern Gaul; and there were little Jewish communities along the Rhine frontier, the largest of them in the fortified outpost of Cologne. They were farmers, traders, artisans, and physicians, and they lived at peace with their neighbors: Romans, Gauls, or Franks.

Their troubles began when Christianity became the state religion and the bishops sought to put an end to all intercourse between them and their neighbors. For a long time the prelates were only moderately successful: the special laws forbidding them to own slaves, to employ Christians or intermarry with them, and to be employed in government service had to be enacted over and over again, for the people generally, including the lower clergy, bore them no ill will. A great deal, of course, depended on the ruler: a strong man like Clovis dominated the bishops and checked their zeal for persecution. But Clovis was followed by a succession of weaklings known in history as "the do-nothing kings," and the bishops raised their heads. Life became hard for the Jews in the Frankish realms. Although the official papal policy did not favor forced conversion, that method was often attempted. In 596 the synagogue of Clermont was destroyed by a mob, and the Jews who rejected baptism were driven from the city. When the Spanish Jews fled from the cruelties of King Sisebut they found the gates of France closed to them. Finally in 629, the Frankish king forced all his Jews to accept baptism or leave the country, and for 150 years thereafter their story is a blank. Many of them must have made their way to the region around Narbonne, which was ruled by the Visigoths, and farther south into Spain.

After conquering Spain the Moslems swept on into France, and for a time it looked as if the Jews of that country would share in the new era of freedom and culture which had been ushered in for their brothers in Spain. But this was not to be. The Moslems were approaching the river Loire when in 732 they were met near Tours and defeated by a mighty host assembled and led by the great Carolus or Charles Martel. The son of Charles dethroned the last do-nothing king and established the Carolingian dynasty, of which the greatest ruler was Charlemagne (768-814), under whom we again pick up the thread of the Jewish story in the land of the Franks.

3

CHARLEMAGNE was a relentless converter: with fire and sword he brought the faith to the heathens on his borders, but he seems to have let the Jews alone. He even appointed special officers with the title of "Master of the Jews" to protect them. No doubt Charlemagne found them very useful. They were the leading merchants of the land; through connections with their coreligionists in other lands, they carried on a large international commerce, and a tithe of their profits went into the king's coffers. Charlemagne employed them also in the service of his government: a certain Isaac was a member of an embassy he sent to the caliph Harun al-Rashid in Bagdad. Charlemagne is best remembered as the man whom, in 800, Pope Leo III crowned Emperor of Rome, thus restoring a title that was now empty, but which for many centuries haunted Europe like a ghost.

The son of Charlemagne, Louis the Pious, also resisted the efforts of the bishops, of whom the most determined was Agobard, Bishop of Lyons, to persecute his Jews. Agobard and his colleagues had abundant cause for complaint against them. They often converted their heathen slaves to Judaism, their Christian servants rested on Saturdays and worked on Sundays, and every now and then prominent personages embraced the Jewish faith.

After Louis, the empire his great father had built up fell apart. Now for the first time we see France and Germany emerge and go their separate ways, for the western Franks had become Latinized, speaking a Roman language which is the French of today; while the eastern Franks, too far removed from Roman influence, clung to their German dialects, as well as their barbarous ways.

In neither country, however, were the monarchs strong enough to control their dukes and counts, and the fortunes of the Jews varied with the interests or whims of the local lords. But the general state of confusion and division was not without its compensations. Banished from one city, as they were from Sens in 875, from Limoges in 1010, and from Mayence in 1012, they could find refuge in another in the same country.

Gradually the chaos gave way to the feudal system, but while feudalism helped to make life tolerable in those dark and bloody centuries, it provided no room for the Jew. Under that system all men except the king were protégés or vassals of some protector or suzerain to whom they swore fealty and service. The religion of the Jew, however, prevented him from taking the feudal oath. Nor was it possible for him to join in the feasting, fighting, and gaming that made up the life of the knights and nobles who left all useful labor to be performed by their serfs. Moreover, as the system tightened, it became practically impossible for those outside of it to own land, for every landowner had to become the vassal of some larger and more powerful owner or find himself landless. In France, particularly in the south, Jews continued to own landed property, but their possession was precarious. In 900 the Jews of Narbonne, for example, were despoiled of their vineyards and other real property, which the king handed over to the church.

In Germany the only occupation freely open to the Jews was commerce, and communities sprang up on the banks of the principal rivers. Along the Rhine the most important were in Cologne, Mayence, Worms, Speyer, and Strasbourg. On the Danube and its tributaries there were communities in Ulm, Augsburg, Munich, Regensburg, and other towns, and there were still others on the Elbe and its tributaries, the most important in Magdeburg, Merseburg, and Prague.

In 962 a German king, Otto I, was crowned Emperor of Rome, a title which brought his successors a heritage of troubles: wars in Italy and bitter feuds with the popes. In one of his battles in Sicily, his successor Otto II was saved by an Italian Jew named Calonymus who then, it appears, migrated to Germany and settled in Mayence, where his family achieved great distinction for learning and good deeds.

4

IT WAS a hard and harassed life that the Jews of France and Germany lived amid the coarseness and violence of the Dark Ages, but by the practice of their faith and the pursuit of learning it acquired grace and elevation. From Provence, the region adjacent to Spain, the study of the Talmud spread northward to the Rhine. Legend has it that it was brought to Narbonne by Nathan ben Isaac, one of the four emissaries from Sura; and Judah ben Meir, better known as Leontin, the first important teacher of the academy in Narbonne of whom we have definite knowledge, may have been one of Nathan's pupils.

But it is certain that Gershom ben Judah, a pupil of Leontin, born in France in 960, left his native land and established a school in Mayence on the Rhine, which became the most important center of Jewish learning north of the Pyrenees. The learning of the north lacked the breadth and elegance of Spain, where it was embellished with the poetry, the philosophy, and the science that surrounded it. But it was deeper and more thorough. The Talmud was like a fortress to which its devotees fled for refuge, and with every nook and cranny of which they became familiar.

Gershom became "the Light of the Exile." Pupils flocked to his school from France, Germany, and Italy, bringing the learning they acquired from the master back to their own communities. His authority surpassed that of Hai, the last *Gaon* who was then striving to uphold the prestige of Pumbeditha. Questions on law and ritual poured in on him from communities all over the continent, and he issued decrees that were accepted without question. The one on which his fame is most securely founded was a decree formally abolishing polygamy, and another required a husband to have the consent of his wife before he could divorce her.

The master's teachings may have been too persuasive, for it happened that a Christian priest became converted to Judaism and evil days fell on the Jews of Mayence and other cities in the Rhineland. They were ordered to accept baptism or be expelled. Before the persecutions were checked by the wealthy and learned Simon ben Isaac, Gershom sustained the sorrow of seeing his own son embrace Christianity. When the Jews were finally able to return to their own homes and faith, Gershom issued a decree forbidding any slur to be cast on the former converts. Their sufferings, he declared, had already been great enough.

5

AFTER his death the school of Gershom ben Judah declined, but before it disappeared it gave instruction to one who was destined to surpass its founder in learning and prestige. The new light of Israel was Rabbi Shlomo ben Isaac, better known as Rashi. He was born in 1040, and when still a youth left his native city of Troyes in France and set out, poor and friendless, to quench an insatiable thirst for knowledge. He studied in Mayence and Speyer and found teachers also in Worms, where the chapel in which he studied has been reverently preserved. At twenty-five he returned to his native city and lived there for the remaining forty years of his life, teaching the young men who flocked to him for instruction; but, like the sages of old, he earned his livelihood by the labor of his hands. From near and far, his answers were sought to questions on Talmudic law, and so highly regarded was his school at Troyes that its students were in demand as rabbis and teachers even by the communities of Spain.

Rashi is the great illuminator of the Bible and Talmud. His commentaries, which are still an essential part of the traditional education of the Jew, are remarkable for their incisiveness and clarity. A single word or short phrase, often with the French and German equivalent, lights up the meaning of a difficult passage, and when something escapes his understanding he very frankly states: "This I do not understand."

His personal life was a model of saintliness, and his children and grandchildren proved worthy of him. His work on the Talmud was completed after his death by his son-in-law and grandsons, who also made additions (*tossafot*) to the commentaries of the master. His mantle of authority fell on the shoulders of his grandson Jacob Tam,* who became recognized as the master Talmudist of his generation. He too was the recipient of interpellations from near and far, and in order to give his answers greater validity he referred them to a congress of rabbis which, from time to time, assembled at his call in the city of Troyes.

6

IN 1095 Rashi and his disciples were peacefully pursuing their studies in Troyes, and the Jewish communities on the Rhine and Danube felt safe under the protection of the "Roman Emperor" and the lesser German rulers. But the same year an assembly of bishops and princes, meeting in the French city of Clermont, was roused to a frenzy by Pope Urban II, who called on all true Christians to march on Jerusalem with cross and sword and deliver the Holy City from the Turks. The infidels, he thundered, were torturing and murdering the pilgrims who came to kneel at the Holy Sepulcher. That assembly marked the beginning of those

* *Tam* in Hebrew means "perfect."

fantastic mass movements of the Middle Ages known as the Crusades which, before marching to their objective, swept like a devastating storm over the Jewish communities of Western Europe.

The Turks had come from the plateaus of central Asia, a region boiling over with barbarians who descended on the provinces of the Abassid caliphs and the Byzantine emperors. By 1073 they were in possession of Jerusalem and were holding Nicaea, not far from Constantinople. The Byzantine emperor Alexius appealed for help, and the shrewd Pope Urban saw in the situation an opportunity to become head of the Christians of the east as he was already the head of those of the west.

A monk named Peter the Hermit took up the cry sounded by the Pope. He travelled through France and along the Rhine, and in response to his flaming speeches, people left their fields, hovels, and castles and assembled in motley throngs to march on to Palestine, two thousand miles away. Something like a fever took hold of Christian Europe. Here was an adventure that broke with bright promise on the drab and bitter life of the masses. In addition to those who were fired by simple religious enthusiasm, the movement swept in vagabonds, criminals, camp followers, and those who loved excitement regardless of what it was all about. Needy knights and bankrupt nobles were lured by the fabled riches of the East. They dreamed of acquiring little kingdoms or principalities, nor did it matter very much to them whether they wrested them from the infidel Turks or the Christian Greeks.

7

EARLY in 1096 the strange aggregations in northern France and along the Rhine were ready to move. The Jews, especially in France, watched the growing excitement of their neighbors with fear and foreboding. The pious crusaders were asking why, before dealing with the unbelievers in Palestine, they should not deal with those in their own midst. Would it be less pleasing to God to kill a Jew than to kill a Mohammedan? Godfrey de Bouillon, one of the foremost leaders of the Crusade, declared that the blood of Christ must be avenged with the blood of the Jews. And cupidity joined hands with fanaticism: for the Jews, it was rumored, possessed great stores of gold and silver.

To their brothers on the Rhine the Jews of France sent word of their peril, imploring them to fast and pray for them. It turned out, however, that with the exception of Rouen, the Jewish communities in France suffered but little, while those in Germany, who felt secure in the rights which emperors, bishops, and nobles had granted them, bore the brunt of the crusaders' fury.

In the spring of 1096, a horde of crusaders turned up in the region of Metz and Treves. The procession was headed by a goose and some goats, who were to lead the way to Jerusalem. In Metz they slew twenty-two Jews; in Treves they offered the Jews the choice of baptism or death. After appealing in vain to the bishop of the city for protection, most of the Jews accepted baptism, hoping that as soon as the Emperor Henry IV, who was away in Italy, came back to Germany they could return to their faith.

Early in May a horde of crusaders broke into Speyer. There the Jews were enjoying special rights and occupying a section of their own protected by a wall. After repelling an attack on the synagogue, many of them found refuge in the palace of the bishop who even seized some of the mob and executed them. A week later, however, the crusaders, joined by peasants and burghers, surrounded the palace and demanded the surrender of the Jews. The bishop told his wards he was unable to hold out and advised them to accept baptism. They asked for time to consider it, and when he returned there lay before him a heap of corpses. The Jews of Speyer had taken their own lives.

Equally grim and sublime was the fate which, in May of the same year, overtook the communities at Worms and Cologne. The great majority of them preferred death to baptism, and many died by their own hands, fathers and mothers first slaying their children. In Cologne the bishop, as well as the Christian burghers, did their best to protect the Jews, but the crusaders tracked them down in their places of refuge. In Mayence over a thousand Jews perished, many of them suicides. A descendant of the famous Calonymus slew his own son before he died. A desperate act of vengeance by a Jewish youth of Worms is recorded. He was Simcha Cohen, who had seen his father and seven brothers murdered. He agreed to be baptised and, in the midst of the ceremony, plunged his dagger into the heart of the bishop's nephew.

By July of 1096, more than 10,000 Jews had perished in the cities of the Rhine alone. As the crusaders moved eastward still other Jewish communities lay in their path, and wherever they came—in Regensburg, Prague, and other places—they gathered a rich harvest of plunder, forced converts, and corpses. In Hungary, however, they met with terrible retribution. Alarmed by the incursion of the rabble horde, the Hungarians met them and slew scores of thousands of them. Those that escaped and went on were later massacred by the Turks.

Such were the exploits and such the climax of the so-called people's part of the First Crusade. There was another part which consisted of mustered armies led by princes and dukes. These potentates distrusted and hated each other, and all of them despised the Byzantine emperor whom, ostensibly, they had come to succor. Some went so far as to ally themselves with the Mohammedans and Turks against their brother crusaders.

A portion got to Palestine, and in 1099 they captured Jerusalem and massacred its inhabitants, the Jews of the city perishing in the flames of the synagogue into which the crusaders herded them before setting it on fire. The "Franks," as the Moslems called the crusaders, met fierce resistance from Jews and Mohammedans alike, but managed to establish themselves also along the coast of Syria and Palestine. They were still there in 1141 when Yehudah Halevi set foot in Palestine and in 1165 when the Rambam passed through the land on his way to Egypt.

On his return from Italy, Emperor Henry IV, outraged by the crimes, did what he could for the survivors. He ordered their property to be restored and, against the protests of the Pope, he permitted the forced converts to return to their faith. From his study in Troyes the great Rashi raised his voice, admonishing those who had remained steadfast not to reject their repentant brothers, but to welcome them back into the fold. On the surface, life resumed its former course, but the soldiers of the cross had inflicted wounds on the Jewish communities of the Germanies that never quite healed.

CHAPTER THIRTY-FOUR

Martyrdom and Exile

FOR another century and a half crusades flared up and flickered out, providing an outlet for the miseries and passions of the multitude, as well as a channel for the ambitions of princes and potentates. The Crusades became more and more sordid and futile as they continued. The Second Crusade, which came in 1147 after the Turks had wrested the Syrian county of Edessa from the "Franks," was led by the king of France and the German emperor; they hated each other and were distrusted by those whom they came to succor.

The adventure was a failure, but it "succeeded" against the Jews of France and Germany, whom the crusaders attacked and forced into baptism or suicide. Jacob Tam, grandson of Rashi and leading rabbi of the age, suffered grievous wounds at their hands and barely escaped with his life. During this crusade, however, there were Jews who met their foes arms in hand. A pitched battle took place at Carentan in France, where the small Jewish community was overcome only after slaying a large number of the assailants.

Forty years later when Saladin, the Sultan of Egypt, had retaken Jerusalem, came the Third Crusade, copiously besung by bards and troubadours. Its leaders, who wasted no love on each other, were the French king, Philip Augustus, the German emperor, Frederick Redbeard, and the English king, Richard the Lion-Hearted. The only bright spot in that affair was the mutual respect and admiration that developed between Richard and Saladin. In Germany the emperor took the Jews under his personal protection, and they were saved from massacre. Philip Augustus, on the other hand, was a ferocious persecutor who murdered and exiled many of his Jewish subjects until, on his return from the crusade, he discovered that by making them his property and affording them a measure of protection, he could extort a handsome revenue from them. His barons adopted the same policy. In 1182 Philip had banished his Jews; in 1198 he recalled them and encouraged them to engage in moneylending in order to plunder them.

The Crusades continued. Some of them, like the Fourth Crusade in 1202, which was really a war not against the infidels, but against the Byzantine Empire, and the crusades against heretics and monarchs who incurred the wrath of the Pope, were directed against Christians rather than infidel Moslems. In 1212, there was even a Children's Crusade in which thousands of French and German boys perished or were captured and sold into slavery. The innocent children, it was urged, would succeed where the wicked elders had failed. In 1229 Emperor Frederick II, the *enfant terrible* of the century and a liberal skeptic who preferred Jewish and Moslem companions to orthodox Christians, after having been himself the target of a crusade, made off to Palestine and conducted an *opera bouffe* crusade of his own.

The ferment abated, the glamour became tarnished, and the movement ebbed away. It was seven centuries later, in 1918, that an army of a Christian power wrested Palestine from Moslem rule, and that army, as we shall see, contained battalions of Jews, descendants of those who survived the crusaders' fury, who fought for the restoration of their people in its ancient land.

2

BUT the Crusades inflicted upon the Jews of Germany and France even worse ravages than snuffed-out lives and forced conversions. Changes were brought about in their economic, legal, and social position, from which they found it more difficult to recover and which fixed their status for centuries to come.

The feudal system had already made it practically impossible for Jews to own and till the soil. As for the handicrafts, they were barred from the guilds of artisans in the towns, and so were unable to ply the manual trades except within the narrow confines of their own communities. Commerce, however, was open to them, and they had occupied an important and often dominant place in it, particularly in international trade. But the Crusades brought large numbers of Christians into contact with foreign lands and foreign commodities. Christian tradesmen now appeared on the scene who, finding themselves hampered by their Jewish competitors, secured the enactment of laws that cut the ground from under the feet of the Jewish merchants. Only the meanest forms of trading, such as pack-peddling and dealing in second-hand merchandise, remained open to them.

Another occupation which was still permitted the Jews was that of moneylending. Its practice was forbidden to Christians; the church took the position that all interest was usury and therefore sinful, a position, it may be noted, that it no longer holds, the leading bankers or moneylenders of today being not Jews but Christians. It was not inclination but necessity that impelled the Jews of the Middle Ages to resort to moneylending, for the occupation was fraught with hazards and perils. It roused against them the resentment and greed of the very people it served, and in the popular fancy it gave rise to the fantastic and dangerous legend that every Jew was possessed of fabulous wealth.

It was greed that was chiefly responsible also for a change in the legal position of the Jews. Kings and emperors, princes, dukes and bishops, having discovered they could derive a lucrative income from the Jews inhabiting their realms, made them their personal property and sold them protection for a price. Always in need of money for their wars or pleasures, they contrived all sorts of devices for extorting it from "their" Jews, and when the latter sought to escape ruin by emigration, they prevented them from leaving their borders. In the reign of Philip Augustus, for example, the dukes and barons agreed that each of them would keep out of his territory Jews belonging to the others. It was these "protectors" who benefited from the usury; it was they who were the real usurers.

Still another change was imposed upon the Jews, a change in their social status even more catastrophic than the economic and legal changes already noted. In 1215 the Fourth Lateran Council in Rome, convened by the illustrious Pope Innocent III, re-enacted the old laws that aimed to prevent all intercourse between Jews and Christians, and added new ones. Among the latter was one requiring all Jews to wear a special mark that would distinguish them from their neighbors. The yellow patch, which they were now forced to wear on their outer garments, reduced them to the status of social outcasts. The patch was an invitation to every scoundrel and ruffian to insult and attack them. The yellow patch was responsible for untold physical suffering and moral anguish.

To the Christian masses of the Middle Ages, the Jews became not only an object of aversion and derision; they became also a mystery and a dread. In the popular mind, always beguiled by the bizarre and the lurid, fantastic ideas took root concerning the Jews, including the insane belief that they use the blood of Christians in preparing their Passover bread, a belief that brought death and ruin to thousands of innocents. Nor is it amiss to point out that this belief and others like them still persist in our own day for the ready use of charlatans, bigots, and demagogues.

3

UNTIL 1189, when Richard the Lion-Hearted became king, the Jews of England were on the whole more fortunate than their brothers on the continent. Jewish traders must have come to England from France and Germany before the Norman conquest in 1066; they may, in fact, have come with the Roman legions that descended on Britain in the first century. It is certain, however, that William the Conqueror was accompanied by a group of them from Rouen, his capital in Normandy, and his son Henry I granted them a charter of rights and privileges as traders.

Their legal and economic status, to be sure, was not secure, for they were the wards and virtually the property of the rulers, and subject to his whims and greed. By levying special taxes on them and naming themselves their heirs, the kings took care that their Jews should not become too wealthy. When, for example, the rich banker, Aaron of Lincoln, died, Henry II made himself his heir. The kings found the Jews useful also in improving their relations with their proud and unruly vassals. Every now and then the monarchs permitted the barons to liquidate the debts they owed the Jews on terms favorable to them and to the royal treasury, but not, of course, to the creditors.

Nevertheless, in spite of oppression and chicanery, the Jews of England increased and prospered. Communities sprang up in the principal towns, the largest of them in London. There, in 1158, the famous traveler and philosopher Abraham ibn Ezra came to visit them. Jacob of Orleans, a pupil of Jacob Tam, came to live there and they made him their rabbi. A few of them even managed to become rich and lived in fine palaces: they might have chosen to live in hovels could they have foreseen what the future held in store for them. Already in 1144, the ghastly blood accusation had been laid against the Jews of Norwich, and many of them had been murdered by the mob.

But the First and Second Crusades left the Jews of England unscathed: to belong in fee simple to the monarch had its advantages. Henry II, who reigned from 1154 to 1189, resorted to all the royal devices for fleecing them and when, toward the end of his long reign, he made ready to take part in the Third Crusade, he extorted a huge sum from them for his expenses. But the Jews of England were grateful that they were not faced with the crusaders' choice of baptism or death. Henry, moreover, reigned also over many of the provinces of France, having acquired them by inheritance or marriage, and the Jews of those regions also enjoyed his protection.

Henry II did not set out on the Crusade. He died of a broken heart, his sons having rebelled against him and made war on him in open or secret alliance with Philip Augustus of France; it was his son Richard who was destined to gather laurels in Palestine as a soldier of the cross. On September 3, 1189, Richard was crowned king, and the same day a series of bloody outbreaks against the Jews of England began which made their lot one with their brothers in France and Germany.

4

THE king himself, it appears, was not to blame. A Jewish deputation headed by Benedict of York and bearing gifts for the monarch, had come to the coronation, and the Archbishop of Canterbury prevailed on Richard not to admit them into his presence. The multitude outside the palace saw the Jewish notables not only dismissed, but insulted and beaten. At once the rumor spread among them that their pious king wanted them to do with the Jews as they pleased. The good people of London, like the good people of other places and times before and since, became a bloodthirsty mob. They set fire to Jewish homes, hunted the victims to their places of refuge, and gave them the choice of baptism or death. The Jews chose death and many of them, including their rabbi, Jacob of Orleans, died by their own hands. The king tried to stop the butchery; he even had two of the mob executed. He issued an edict proclaiming the Jews to be under his protection, but the passions that were roused were out of control and he himself, moreover, had to leave for Palestine.

From London the violence spread to other towns. The barons, who were generally in debt to the Jews, made little or no effort to check it, and some of them even aided and abetted it. Before embarking on the Crusade, the soldiers of the cross gave full vent to their religious zeal at home. They wiped out a little congregation of twenty English families who had embraced Judaism, and Jews were slain or driven to self-immolation in Lynn, Norwich, Stamford, York, Bury St. Edmunds, and other places.

The most somber and heroic tragedy was enacted in the city of York. Benedict of York had died from the wounds he received in the London outbreak, and the mob attacked and looted his home. The Jews took refuge in the town citadel to which the mob, led by a baron who was heavily in debt to the Jews, laid siege. The besieged beat off every attack, the ardor of the rabble began to wane, and they were about to abandon the enterprise when a monk dressed in a white robe appeared among them and roused them to fresh enthusiasm. The enthusiasm changed to frenzy when a stone from the tower killed the monk in his pious exercises. But the frenzy was of no avail; the Jews continued to hold out.

Before long, however, they saw themselves faced with starvation and capture, and one morning—it was the morning of the Great Sabbath: March 17, 1190—the besiegers, noting the absence of the usual signs of resistance, broke into the citadel. When they reached the tower they stood facing five hundred corpses. The defenders had performed the supreme act of martyrdom. The men, after slaying their wives and children, had slain each other. Joseph, the lay leader of the community, sought and obtained the honor of being slain by the rabbi, Yom Tob of Joigny.

5

A CENTURY later, in July 1290, Edward I issued an edict ordering all Jews, on pain of death, to be gone from the soil of England by November 1 of that year. It had been a century of mounting misery for the victims. Legally they belonged to the king and Henry III, whose long reign lasted from 1216 to 1272, once leased them for a year to his brother Richard! But the kings "protected" them only in order to rob them, the bishops and abbots insisted on their right to persecute the unbelievers, and behind kings and bishops lowered the coarse and bestial mob, easily incited and always ready to vent its wretchedness on the helpless.

In 1222, an assembly of the clergy had met in Oxford and passed laws forbidding the Jews to build new synagogues or employ Christian servants, and ordering them to wear the shameful patch on their clothing. The king, on the other hand, professed to be interested in their welfare. In 1241 Henry III had assembled a "Jewish Parliament" to which every community in England sent representatives; but all it did was to raise a huge sum of money for the royal treasury. The principal function of the chief rabbi, whom the king chose, was to collect the special taxes levied upon them.

The credulous mob was particularly fascinated by the blood accusation. Torture was used to obtain confessions from the innocent, and in 1255 eighteen Jews of Lincoln were put to death when the body of a boy named Hugh was discovered, and the Jews were accused of having murdered him. During a disturbance in 1264 the Jews of London and other places were plundered and many of them slain.

Early in his reign Henry III had been petitioned by his Jews for permission to emigrate. By 1211 many of their rabbis had left and gone to Palestine with another group of rabbis from France. But the king refused permission and took measures to prevent them from leaving the country. In time, however, the usefulness of the Jews to the crown declined. The extortions had almost wrung them dry; in 1275 they were forbidden by Edward I in his Statute of Judaism to engage in moneylending. About the same time, moreover, they began to be supplanted by Italian bankers—

the Lombards, as they came to be known in England. Economically the Jews were left dangling in the air, and morally the persecutions instigated by the clergy became more and more galling. Finally came the Edict of Expulsion, and some 16,000 Jews left English soil. The royal policy was enforced to the hilt, the real property of the exiles as well as the debts which Englishmen owed them were taken over by the king.

It was not until 1656, more than three and a half centuries later, that Jews were readmitted into England, but although they themselves were absent, the weird legends about them persisted. The trail of those legends moves in the literature of those centuries: in ballads about little Hugh of Lincoln, including a famous one by Chaucer; in Christopher Marlowe's *The Jew of Malta*, in Shakespeare's *The Merchant of Venice*, the latter still a fertile breeding ground of prejudice against a people whom the author could only have known through legend and rumor.

6

MOST of the exiles from England found refuge in France, but not for long did they remain unmolested. Here too they were exposed to the greed of kings and nobles, the bigotry of bishops and friars, and the ferocity of the mob. France, in fact, was even more dominated by the clergy than England; in 1242, during the reign of the pious Louis IX, known as Saint Louis, Paris had been the scene of the first public burning of the Talmud. An apostate named Nicholas Donin, one of those twisted souls whose bitterness and hate added greatly to the woes of the people they renounced, had charged that the Talmud contained insults to the Christian faith, and the king's officers had seized twenty-four wagon loads of the sacred and precious books and burned them. Saint Louis loved converts. He often honored the ceremony of baptism by his presence; and once he manifested his generosity to his people by cancelling a third of the debts they owed the Jews.

In 1306 the refugees from England, together with a much larger number of native Jews whose ancestors had lived in France for a thousand years, were ordered by Philip IV to leave the country. It was a simple device for replenishing the royal coffers: the king left to the exiles only the clothes they wore and enough money for a day's maintenance. Nine years later, however, Louis X recalled them for a period of twelve years: the people, it appears, preferred the Jews to the moneylenders who had taken their place. But their lot in France until the final expulsion in 1394 was hard and bitter. In 1320 they were the victims of a crusade of shepherds and peasants who destroyed more than a hundred Jewish communities, some in northern Spain, most of them in southern France. The "shepherds" were suppressed only after, in their warped fanaticism, they had begun to attack the clergy also. A year later, thousands of French Jews lost their lives following a charge made by lepers that the Jews had hired them to poison the wells. This accusation was not to be the last of its kind: the wretched populace believed it avidly, the clergy countenanced it, and the kings profited from the victims' possessions which they confiscated.

There was another expulsion, followed after nearly forty years by another invitation to return, which many of the exiles pathetically accepted. What happened was that in the Battle of Poitiers in 1356, John the Good had been taken prisoner by the English, and France was unable to raise the ransom for its king. So the Jews were asked to come back; but the mob and the clergy were not appeased. Finally in 1394, when it was found that a French Jew who had accepted baptism had had the audacity to return to his faith, the clamor became greater than the king could withstand. On the Day of Atonement of that year, Charles VI signed the order of expulsion. It went into effect on November 3 and for the next four centuries, until the Great Revolution swept out the old regime, the history of the Jews in France is a blank page.

7

IN THE political crazy quilt of Germany, only nominally ruled by the head of the Holy Roman Empire, the same social conditions prevailed that made Jewish life precarious all over Europe. Emperors, princes, and bishops granted Jewish communities charters of rights and privileges to protect them in their life, property, and worship; charters which were, of course, well paid for. Frederick II, who reigned from 1215 to 1250, even allowed them to settle their disputes in their own courts. The rulers of the neighboring lands, Austria, Bohemia, Moravia, Hungary, Silesia, and Poland, conferred similar grants upon their Jews. But those parchments were no talisman against the primitive passions that surged around them. Not even Frederick II could save them from outbreaks that took place at Erfurt, at Frankfort on the Main, at Meiningen, in Baden, in Wuerttemberg, in Bavaria. Thirty-two Jews perished in Fulda as the result of a blood accusation. The emperor denounced the legend, pointing out that the Bible and Talmud prohibited the Jews from using even the blood of animals; Innocent IV and Gregory X issued papal bulls proclaiming the accusations to be false; but nothing could dislodge the insane belief from the mind of the mob.

Under the emperor Rudolph of Hapsburg (1273-1291), the plight of the Jews grew worse; many of them secretly left Germany, and some of them decided to migrate to Palestine. Their leader was Rabbi Meir of Rothenburg, the outstanding Jewish personality of the century. As a scholar, Rabbi Meir belonged to the *Tossafists;* that is, to those who wrote additions to Rashi's commentary on the Talmud. Meir was educated in the *Tossafist* schools in France; as a young man he had seen the public burning of the Talmud in Paris and written a lament which is still read on the Ninth of Ab. In Rothenburg he conducted a school of his own, and his disciples carried his teachings to foreign lands, including Spain and Austria. Questions on law and religion came to him from distant communities in many parts of the world.

The project of migrating to Palestine was not new; it dovetailed, of course, with the hope of eventual restoration which is part and parcel of the ancient faith. The urge to live and die on the holy soil had impelled others besides Yehudah Halevi to brave the hazards of the journey. About 1211, for example, some 300 rabbis of France and England, led by another famous *Tossafist*, Samson ben Abraham of Sens, had made their way to Palestine and settled there. Meir of Rothenburg, however, was not destined to be so fortunate. He was stopping in Italy, waiting to be joined by his community, when he was recognized, taken back to Germany, and imprisoned in a fortress near Colmar. It was a crime to deprive the emperor of "his" Jews. But the large sum that was raised for Meir's ransom never reached the emperor's coffers. Meir of Rothenburg refused to be ransomed; he refused to show the wicked a new way of oppressing his unhappy people. In 1293, after an incarceration of six years, the noble and courageous teacher died in his prison.

8

THE centuries that follow provide little comfort for those who are eager to discover in history a progressive refinement of the human mind and character. Perhaps the basic cause was the appalling misery and squalor that prevailed in Europe, and the blind rage of those who suffer and hunt for a scapegoat. But the capacity of the human intellect to believe the weird and incredible, and of the human character to descend to the level of the beast of prey, is no less appalling. And woe to the helpless who find themselves caught between the millstones of credulity and greed!

In 1298, five years after the great-hearted Meir of Rothenburg died in prison, a new chimera of the human imagination, more ghastly even than the blood libel, was born in Germany. The Jews were accused of "bleeding the host." It should be recalled that the sacrament of the Eucharist is based on the belief that by the recital of the mass, a piece of bread, or "host,"* is changed by the priest into the body of Christ. The Jews of Roettingen in Franconia were accused of stealing the host and beating it until it bled! The duty of avenging the sacrilege was assumed by a nobleman named Rindfleisch, and his task was rendered easier by a civil war in which the empire was embroiled. Beginning with Roettingen, Rindfleisch and his horde swept on through Bavaria and Austria. About 140 Jewish communities that lay in his path are believed to have been destroyed. Forty years later came another orgy of destruction, led by two noblemen with leather arm-bands who called themselves *Armleder*. The pope, Benedict XII, denounced the new libel, but his words had little or no effect on the popular mind. The advantages of destroying the Jews were too obvious.

But the terror of those years, and even that of the First Crusade two and a half centuries earlier, appears small when compared to the desolation that descended on the Jews of Europe in 1348 and 1349. In those years the nations were in the grip of a great horror.

* From the Latin word *hostia,* meaning "sacrifice."

By way of Africa and through Spain the Black Death had spread through the continent. A third of the population is believed to have been carried off by it, and in some parts as many as two-thirds and three-quarters perished. Soon, rumors began to circulate that the pestilence was the result of a plot, an "international conspiracy" hatched by the Jews to destroy the Christians. The Jews did it by poisoning the wells and rivers, the poison being compounded of spiders, frogs, lizards, hearts of Christians, and the host! Haggard bands of Flagellants, religious maniacs who scourged themselves and each other with whips, moved from town to town, performed their penance in public, and called on the people to kill the Jews.

The fact that the plague was rife in France and England where there were no Jews, and that Jews also perished from it, meant nothing to the inventors of the rumors or their dupes. Or it may be true that the Jews, by reason of the hygienic mode of life which their religion enjoined upon them, did not so readily succumb to the pestilence as did their neighbors. Confessions were wrung from the innocent by torture, and whole communities in Spain, Switzerland, and Germany were wiped out. Some of the victims set fire to their quarters and perished in the flames which, in many instances, spread and destroyed the rest of the towns. More than two hundred communities, it is estimated, were annihilated.

Some of the city councils, as well as the pope and, half-heartedly, the emperor also, tried to check the fury of the rabble, but without success. The intervention of the councils, dominated as they were by the nobility, only added fuel to the flames. For the guilds of the towns were in revolt against the privileged nobility, and they regarded the Jews as the allies of the oppressors: the pattern of European society was undergoing a change and the principal victims were the Jews. Where the guilds succeeded in seizing the councils they set about liquidating the Jewish communities "legally" and methodically. But the wealth they acquired by pillaging their victims proved illusory. The cancellation of debts only strengthened the nobles who were the principal debtors, and the liquidation of the Jews brought a decline not only in the revenues of emperors, dukes, princes and bishops, but in the general prosperity of the towns themselves. For the Jews played an immensely important role in the economy of the Middle Ages, and their disappearance was apt to be followed by stagnation and decay.

Before long the fever of insurrection and violence in the Germanies subsided, and those who had managed to escape the holocaust through flight were invited to return. The special quarters to which they were consigned were now closed off, the gates locked every night. The ghetto became a separate world, in the physical as well as the spiritual sense. The emperor, nobles, bishops, and town councils composed their differences as to who should own and despoil the Jews, and for about thirty years the ghettos were not assaulted.

New disturbances broke out in 1384. This time the Jews were prevented from leaving: they remained between the hammer and anvil of the contending classes, the matter in dispute being who should benefit from the spoliation of the victims. In 1389 a frightful massacre occurred in Prague when the host, which was being carried in a religious procession through the ghetto, was accidentally sprinkled with sand by Jewish children playing in the street. In 1400, eighty Jews of Prague perished when a Jewish renegade charged that the *Alenu* prayer insulted the founder of Christianity.

9

THROUGH the fifteenth century, the dreary tale of extortion, libel, violence, and exile continues. The fate of the Jewish communities in the numerous political units into which the empire was divided and over which the authority of the emperor often failed, hung on the interests, the whims, and the passions of rulers, clergy, and mobs. In the wars against the religious rebel and reformer, John Huss, which lasted from 1419 to 1436, the Jews were accused of helping the heretics. The friars called upon the faithful to treat Jews and Hussites alike, and Jews suffered as they did centuries earlier at the hands of the crusaders. In 1421, after a series of bloody persecutions, all Jews were expelled from Austria. The same fate befell those of Cologne, Augsburg, and other towns.

In the middle of the century the center of the stage was held by the Franciscan monk John Capistrano, styled "the Scourge of the Jews." His eloquence led to their expulsion from Bavaria and Franconia, and to the hideous accusation of bleeding the host against the Jews of Breslau in Silesia. Israel Isserlein, the leading rabbi of Germany, challenged Capistrano to go with him to the stake and let God decide between them, but the monk declined the offer.

A colleague of Capistrano named Bernardinus won even greater glory in the Tyrolean city of Trent. In 1475 he accused the Jews of that city, who had been living in friendship with their neighbors, of having murdered a Christian child for Passover, and all of them, with the exception of four who accepted baptism, were buried alive. The child became an object of worship. Not even a later investigation, clearing the accused, not even a bull issued by Pope Sixtus IV, could shake the belief of the populace in the guilt of the Jews and the miraculous virtues of the child's grave. The affair of Trent had wide repercussions: it led to large-scale persecutions in other places, particularly in Regensburg.

Such was the social and moral atmosphere in which this "peculiar people" struggled to exist and preserve its soul.

CHAPTER THIRTY-FIVE

Inner Life

NEVERTHELESS, it would throw the picture of Jewish life during those somber centuries out of focus if we dwelt solely on the woes and disasters that crowd the annals of the European Diaspora. Endowed with an inner strength that bordered on the mysterious, Jewish life displayed an incredible capacity for recovery and renewal. The communities stood always in the shadow of a smoldering volcano, but in the intervals between eruptions their wounds healed and they resumed their own inner life, the exuberance and elevation of which were a sealed book to their neighbors.

2

THIS life became completely inaccessible to their neighbors when, after the Black Death, the Jews were compelled to live in walled ghettos, and intercourse with Christians was drastically curtailed. Of course the ghetto was decreed with the object of preventing such intercourse; at the same time, however, it afforded its residents a measure of protection and was therefore not wholly unwelcome to them. Even before the ghetto was established by law in Germany and other lands, the Jews dwelt together in sections of their own, for apart from the desire of human beings to live with their own kind, it was only natural for them to group themselves around the synagogue where the heart of the community pulsated.

The ghetto was usually the dingiest street of the dingy medieval towns, and so narrow that a vehicle was unable to turn around in it. The gables and dormers on both sides of the street nearly met, shutting out the light almost completely. At one end of the street was the gate, kept locked from sundown to sunrise and all day on the Sabbath; at the other end lay the burial ground. The ghettos were usually overcrowded; only rarely were they allowed additional space for increased population, and congestion, as is well known, is an effective check on the graces and adornments of life. Such were now the gloomy and squalid habitations of a people whose ancestors had once lived in a green and sunny land of their own, cultivating fields, groves, and vineyards, or shepherding their flocks on its hillsides and valleys. Those days when "every man sat under his vine and fig tree and there was none to make them afraid," were now only a memory, but a memory that never ceased to glow and beckon.

3

THE denizens of the ghetto were surrounded also by a wall of economic restrictions, but they clung to every jut and crevice they could find in it. They took to the soil wherever the legal barriers were not yet raised against them, and they labored at every handicraft wherever the guilds did not block them. As artisans they were unexcelled. They were known in northern Italy, Prague, and other places in central Europe as the best goldsmiths; in southern Italy as the best dyers and silk weavers; in Sicily where, according to a contemporary report "nearly all the artisans of the realm are Jews," as the best craftsmen in iron and other metals, making "horseshoes, agricultural implements and equipments for ships, galleys, and other conveyances."* They were among the best craftsmen in the art of printing, and in all countries tailoring became one of their principal trades.

In the professions they were distinguished in the art of healing. The church tried hard to prevent Christians from employing Jewish physicians, for doctors often acquire influence over their patients. But the sick paid no attention to the prohibitions; not only kings and princes, but even bishops and popes entrusted their health to Jews. In Spain, as we have seen, there were many Jews in the public service, and before the thirteenth century they even served in the papal household! There were Jewish soldiers and sailors as well as navigators, geographers, and cartographers. They contributed not a little to the success of the epoch-making voyages of Christopher Columbus who, it is believed by many, was himself of Jewish origin.

It was in commerce and banking, however, that the Jews of the Middle Ages were most prominent. They brought life and vigor into the local markets and fairs, and before the Crusades gave rise to a class of Christian traders who suppressed their Jewish competitors, they were the leading international merchants of Europe. Such cities as Montpelier and Marseille in southern France became great commercial depots where Jewish merchants exchanged the grain, wine, and manufactures of France for the spices, perfumes, carpets, and other luxuries of the East. In Germany, a similar role was played by the cities of Regensburg, Augsburg, and Nuremberg.

In popular fancy, of course, the medieval Jew figured principally as a moneylender, and literature and legend have combined to keep the illusion alive to our own day. Forgotten are the Jewish blacksmiths, glass blowers, weavers, and printers of the Middle Ages. The Jewish merchant princes, physicians, statesmen, and

* La Lumia, *Gli Ebrei Siciliani,* Palermo, 1870; quoted in Israel Abrahams' *Jewish Life in the Middle Ages.*

THE DIASPORA IN THE WEST

public servants are only dimly remembered. It was of course in his role as moneylender that the Jew, after the Crusades, came into most frequent contact with Christians. It was a role which by its very nature was bound to engender hostility against its practitioners—Jews, Lombards, or whoever they might be. Nevertheless too much needless apologizing has been done for the Jewish moneylender: today the banker, who is primarily a moneylender, is looked upon as a useful member of society, and commands general deference. Nor should it be forgotten that the stigma of usury had nothing to do with the rate of interest, for all interest was branded as usury. No doubt there were Jewish moneylenders—and Christian also—who charged exorbitant rates of interest, most of which, in the case of the Jews, found its way into the coffers of kings, nobles, and town councils. But their willingness to follow the hated and dangerous calling should be taken rather as a measure of the extent to which they were barred from other sources of livelihood.

4

NEEDLESS to say, it was not their material but their spiritual resources that gave the Jewish communities of the Middle Ages the power to suffer and endure. The economic roots of their existence hung in the air, but their spiritual roots were sunk deep in the soil of a vital faith and creative tradition. Out of this faith and tradition had been evolved the pattern of a self-contained and integrated life, equipped with forms and institutions which had stood the test of a millennial experience, and which nourished the mind and spirit of a gifted people. The survival of the Jewish communities of the Middle Ages offers perhaps the most convincing proof that "man doth not live by bread only, but by everything that proceedeth out of the mouth of the Lord doth man live."

The central institution of the community was the synagogue, which continued to perform the three functions it acquired from its origin: as a house of prayer, a house of assembly, and a house of study. The ritual of prayer for weekdays, Sabbaths, and festivals, including the readings from the Scriptures, followed in the main the order and content that had been fixed toward the end of the Second Commonwealth, although minor variations arose as between the Sephardic or Spanish ritual and the Ashkenazic or German. The highest religious authority was of course the rabbi, and the principal functionary during the worship was the *chazzan* or cantor, but the services, unlike those in the church, did not depend on the ministrations of a priest. The Jewish community, in fact, had no religious or clerical caste: all worshippers were eligible to perform any of the functions.

Nor was there any formal distinction between the religious and secular affairs of the community, so that the synagogue was also the place where communal business, such as the election of officials or the allocation of taxes, was transacted, and where the people met to share their joys and sorrows. It was the place where the bridegroom came to be congratulated and the mourner to be consoled. It was the place where any man who had a grievance could publicly proclaim it and demand redress, and where the dread sentence of excommunication was pronounced upon members of the community who were deemed dangerous to its welfare. The roaming preacher or *maggid* held forth in the synagogue, and the people who in all ages, benighted or "enlightened," cherish an assortment of superstitions, flocked to hear his grim and picturesque warnings against sin.

The officers whom the people chose to conduct the affairs of the community were the *parnes* or president, the *gabbai* or treasurer, and a council that varied in size, often consisting of seven men known as the *tobei ha-ir*, the "good men" or notables of "the city." Two *dayyanim* (judges) handed down decisions in disputes or passed sentence on offenders in matters that fell within their jurisdiction.

In Spain the routine administration of the affairs of the community or *aljama* was in many instances entrusted to a smaller executive body of *mukdamim* who had a wide range of duties and powers, from assigning seats in the synagogue to proclaiming edicts of excommunication, and even passing the death sentence if the right was included in the *aljama's* charter. In most of the communities, however, the administration of justice, civil as well as criminal, was entrusted to a special court or *bet din*. And from time to time representatives of communities in a region met to deliberate on their common interests.

A highly respected official in every community was the *shochet* or ritual slaughterer, who had to possess considerable learning as well as skill. The *shamash*, or sexton, performed many functions in addition to those connected with the synagogue, from executing judicial sentences on offenders to delivering invitations to weddings.

5

THE synagogue was also the center of a network of philanthropic societies, each one devoted to a special charity. There was a society that furnished dowries for orphans and daughters of the poor, another that provided Passover food to the needy, still another that ransomed Jewish captives. And there were societies to raise money for the relief of the needy in Palestine, to visit the sick, to bury the dead. In addition to these voluntary philanthropic associations, there was a communal charity fund raised and administered by designated officials, with power to levy assessments based on the ability of each donor. The well-to-do were expected to give a tenth of their income, and the observance of this tithe was fairly common. It was even found necessary to check some who were inclined to give too much: the Talmud itself fixes a maximum of 20 per cent to prevent the overcharitable from impoverishing themselves!

Begging in the open or from door to door was discouraged by distributing food to the poor, and when, after the ravages of the Crusades, troops of roaming beggars began to descend upon the ghettos, they were provided for by special societies, and communities built inns to accommodate them. Entertaining an *oreach* or stranger over the Sabbath was a highly coveted privilege: it added greatly to the sanctity of the day. All deeds of charity were, of course, looked upon as religious duties, and in their performance, the greatest care had to be taken to safeguard the self-respect of the recipient. The Talmud not only enjoins charity as a supreme virtue, but it multiplies warnings and pleas not to offend the sensibilities of the poor. The true dispenser of charity was he who gave anonymously or in secret. To the Jew of the Middle Ages the practice of charity was a natural corollary of the spirit of loving-kindness which permeated his faith and which, in turn, permeated every aspect of his life. Charity was justice: the same Hebrew word, *zedakah*, stands for both.

6

ANOTHER religious duty, which ranked even higher than charity, was education and study. The Biblical injunction, "And thou shalt teach them [the commandments] diligently unto thy children," repeated three times every day, was the foundation for a system of compulsory education that has kept the Jews the most literate people in the world. In the Middle Ages, when kings and nobles never learned to read and write, every Jewish boy began going to school at the age of five. He stayed there under a regime of rigorous instruction until he was at least thirteen, and there were schools where many acquired higher learning, whether it consisted only of the Talmud and the commentaries as in France and Germany, or included philosophy, poetry, mathematics, and science as in Spain and Italy. Education required no legal enforcement to be compulsory. Its cost, except for orphans and the children of the very poor, was met by the parents of the pupils, but fathers and mothers would no more think of depriving their sons of education than of depriving them of food. Girls, on the other hand, were exempted from formal schooling; the knowledge they required for the conduct of a household was imparted to them in the home. Exemption, however, did not mean prohibition: women could read the prayer book and some, like the daughters of Rashi, were even distinguished for learning.

From the first day when the five-year-old was carried by a learned man of the community to the synagogue and school in a quaint but solemn initiation ceremony, the boy's schooling became an arduous occupation. He left his home early in the morning—in winter, when it was still dark—and returned after sunset. By the time he was ten years old, he had mastered the Pentateuch, the Prophets and the other books of the Bible together with the *targum* or Aramaic translation, and was ready to begin the Mishnah; his elementary education even included portions of the Talmud.

He translated the original into the language of the land, which the Jews used as their everyday speech. Many Hebrew words gradually entered into this speech and special Jewish vernaculars arose, the most important of them being the Germanic, out of which modern Yiddish developed. Hebrew, of course, continued to be the literary language and, in large part, the language of official and even commercial transactions. The Jews of the Middle Ages spoke French or German, Arabic, Spanish, or Italian, but in all the lands of their dispersion, the Hebrew language was one of the bonds that united them.

Education and study, however, were not limited to particular periods of life or particular institutions such as elementary schools and academies. For study was not only an alluring exercise; it was also a supreme religious duty. Study was worship. There was no period, therefore, in a man's life when study could be discontinued, and among the societies that clustered around the synagogue must be included the many groups that met for the study of the Bible, Mishnah, or Talmud. Each of the societies had its own membership and ritual, and the completion of a course was the occasion for a solemn celebration. They were an integral part of the educational system of the Jews of the Middle Ages.

7

IF THE synagogue was the common sanctuary of the ghetto, the refuge of the individual Jew was his home. In the street and market place oppression and derision might bend his back and subdue his glance; in the serenity of his home he regained his dignity and became aware of his superiority over his oppressor. For in spite of insecurity and poverty, the typical ghetto home was the abode of affection, sobriety, and sanctity.

Of this home the presiding genius was the wife and mother. Polygamy had by force of custom become virtually nonexistent centuries before the decree of Gershom ben Judah made it illegal, although exceptions to the rule of monogamy existed in lands where Mohammedanism held sway. Polygamy, in fact, had practically become a thing of the past as early as the Second Commonwealth: the domestic code of the Mishnah and Talmud takes monogamy for granted. True enough, from the standpoint of the modern feminist the legal position of the woman left much to be desired, but the tenderness, respect, and devotion the Talmud demands from the husband on behalf of his wife more than made amends for the legal inequality. And from all that can be gathered it appears that compliance with these demands was the rule and not the exception. On Friday night, when the husband returned from the synagogue to a home pervaded by the sanctity of the Sabbath, he chanted the glowing song to "the woman of valor" from the Book of Proverbs, exalting the busy and God-fearing housewife who "reacheth forth her hands to the needy" and "the law of kindness is on her tongue."

Her children rise up and call her blessed;
Her husband also, and he praiseth her:
"Many daughters have done valiantly,
But thou excellest them all."

The fifth command of the Decalogue, "Honor thy father and thy mother," controlled the relations between parents and children. The family gathered at the table not merely to eat and drink; the meals were sanctified by the precepts that called for washing of the hands, benedictions, and grace, and on Sabbaths and festivals the spirit was heightened by special table hymns. Excessive eating and drinking were frowned upon; moderation and sobriety were the rule and the only occasions when a certain latitude was allowed were the Purim Feast and Simhath Torah (Joy-in-Torah) which concludes the autumn festival season.

Frivolous conversation at the table was also discouraged for, says the Mishnah, "If three have eaten at a table and have spoken no words of Torah, it is as if they had eaten of sacrifices to dead idols," i.e., as if they were guilty of idol worship. Torah furnished the themes for conversation at the typical table. This was particularly true at the special repasts, the so-called "commandment" or devotional meals which were served at marriages, betrothals, circumcisions, and other festive occasions. At these banquets, it may be noted, luxury and ostentation were not uncommon, and many communities imposed special taxes as a curb on extravagance.

The Jewish home of the Middle Ages was governed by a spirit of moderation and order, as well as a peculiar delicacy in the relations among its members that extended to servants, Christian as well as Jewish. No doubt the clergy had reason to oppose the employment of Christian domestics by Jews: the servants became too strongly attached to their masters and might even embrace their religion. For in all those qualities that transform a house into a home, Jewish life stood on a much higher level than the life that surrounded it.

The same is true in the matter of cleanliness which, in a quite literal sense, stood next to Godliness, for cleanliness was commanded and regulated by religious ordinance. No community was without the *mikvah,* or ritual bath for women, and in nearly all of them a bathhouse for men was one of the public institutions. The hygienic value of those observances in the intimate relations between husband and wife, of which the ritual bath is a part, has been generally acknowledged; among the Jews of the Middle Ages they were universal, and contributed greatly to the elevation of the moral atmosphere of the home.

8

THE color and vitality that characterized the inner life of the Jew flowed largely from the Sabbaths and festivals. These were like brilliant splashes of light against the drabness that surrounded him, and the special observances in the synagogue had their counterparts in the home. On every seventh day the home was transformed into a shrine; with the lighting of the candles on Friday night the "Sabbath Queen" reigned in the home, and the "oversoul" of the Jew emerged and held sway until the "going out" of the Sabbath on the following night.

Except for Purim and the Feast of Lights, the festivals were those his ancestors had celebrated in Biblical times. They were "the appointed times for gladness, festivals and seasons for joy." In the squalid ghetto, the fragrance of field and vineyard exhaled by the ritual aroused a profound nostalgia, which only added to its charm. The festivals were a round of varied delights that feasted the body and uplifted the spirit. There was the exaltation and awe of Rosh Hashana and Yom Kippur, the gladness of Sukkoth, the joy of Simhath Torah, the cheer of Hanukkah, the hilarity of Purim. In the early spring came Passover, the "season of our freedom," with the stately *seder* in the home bringing a sense of liberation and new life; and in the early summer came the festival of Shabuoth, a hymn of Torah and a song of corn waving in golden sunlight. And even the Fast of Tisha b'Ab, when he sat on the floor of the synagogue mourning for the glory of the past, brought the shrinking denizen of the ghetto a species of consolation. For he never doubted that the past would live again, that in God's own time, and perhaps soon, the bitter exile would come to an end, and the prayer "Let our eyes behold Thy return in mercy to Zion" which he repeated three times daily, would be granted at last.

CHAPTER THIRTY-SIX

Christian Spain

FOR two centuries after Maimonides, Spain was still a shining contrast to the other lands of western Europe. Moslem power on the peninsula was on the wane; in 1212, only eight years after the Rambam's death, the Almohades, whose fierce bigotry had driven him into exile, were overthrown by the Christian kingdoms of the north. By 1265 all that was left to the Mohammedans was Granada and some ports near Cadiz; but until the black year of 1391 the Jews did not, on the whole, fare worse under Christian than under Moslem rule. The monarchs of the four Christian kingdoms—Castile, the largest, in the center; Portugal on the west; Aragon on the east; and tiny Navarre, tucked in between Castile and Aragon—were not very keen about enforcing the edicts of the church councils, particularly the law of the patch. In fact, every now and then the popes found it necessary to censure the kings for their laxness, or for favors bestowed on their Jewish subjects. The kings, however, found these subjects too useful to persecute: they were the best artisans, merchants, and physicians in Spain, and when the state coffers became empty they could be relied upon to replenish them. Under royal charters, moreover, the Jewish communities enjoyed a large measure of internal autonomy, each one being governed by its own council and paying its taxes as a body. At times, they formed regional unions to promote their common welfare.

2

TOLEDO in Castile and Gerona in Aragon harbored the most important Jewish communities of Christian Spain. Gerona was the mother of great scholars and rabbis, and the greatest of them was Moses ben Nachman, better known as Nachmani. He was rabbi of his native city during the greater part of his life, but his authority extended throughout the land and into other countries also. He is best known, however, as the leading opponent of Maimonides' philosophic doctrines in the bitter and far-flung controversy which for several generations after the Rambam's death disturbed the peace of Jewish communities.

Maimonides found his stoutest defenders in Italy and in the communities of southern France, in the district known as Provence which, in language and climate, resembled Spain. Narbonne, Montpelier, Lunel, Marseille, and other cities of Provence had become flourishing centers of Jewish life and learning. For a long time the local potentates paid little attention to the anti-Jewish edicts that emanated from Paris. The Jews enjoyed a large measure of self-government and, in Narbonne especially, they owned and cultivated land and vineyards. The communities of Provence, where the science and philosophy of Spain mingled with the Talmudic and *Tossafist* learning of France and Germany, served as a bridge between the south and the north, and it was only natural that the most famous translators of the age, the Ibn Tibbon family, should hail from that region.

One of the Ibn Tibbons translated the Rambam's *Guide to the Perplexed* from its original Arabic into Hebrew, and together with David Kimchi of Narbonne, they became the leading champions of the renowned philosopher. Kimchi even left his native city and went to Spain in an effort to win over the Spanish rabbis. But the controversy, which had its roots in the ancient and perhaps irreconcilable conflict between faith and reason, between the mystic *élan* of the heart and the cold logic of the head, became more bitter and violent. Some of the opponents of the Rambam resorted to a dangerous expedient: led by Solomon of Montpelier, they brought accusations against his teachings before the Dominican friars, who thereupon seized as many copies of his writings as they could ferret out and in 1234 destroyed them at public burnings in Narbonne and Paris. Those were the same Dominicans who instigated the crusade against the Albigensian heretics, a crusade that became a civil war between the north and south of France and wiped out the fine civilization of Provence. It ended by bringing the region under the domination of the French kings who, together with the friars and bishops, saw to it that the Jews of Provence were shorn of their wealth and freedom.

Moses ben Nachman who, by temperament and education, was an opponent of the Rambam, nevertheless exerted himself to allay the bitterness of the conflict. He was not a stranger to the philosophy and science of his day; like the Rambam, he derived his living from the practice of medicine, refusing to make the rabbinate a source of income. But he considered Torah the most important object of study, and he found every "beauty of wisdom sealed in her treasures." Nachmani indeed was not only a profound student of the Talmud, but essentially a poet and mystic. He saw life as a procession of miracles, most of them beyond the reach of the senses, by which man is in constant communion with the Divine, and he saw all of it alike—body and soul, joy and sorrow—the work of God and equally good and beautiful. When toward the end of his life Nachmani, as an exile, saw the ruins of Jerusalem, he could say: "I wept bitterly, but I found joy in my tears."

Notwithstanding the gulf that lay between Nachmani the mystic and the analytical author of the *Guide*, he was not blind to the Rambam's greatness. He was shocked when the friars burned the master's writings, and he addressed letters to the communities of France and Spain imploring both sides to end or at least to moderate the bitter feud. His pleadings, however, had little effect: the differences were too fundamental, the passions they stirred too profound.

3

IN THE meantime the Dominican friars, who had shown themselves so efficient with the Albigensians in France, were entrusted by the pope with the task of stamping out heresy in Castile and Aragon also, and the means provided them for the purpose was the Inquisition. This instrument, consisting of an elaborate system of investigation, trial, and punishment, was designed for Christians only; its primary aim was to induce suspects to confess to the crime of heresy, that is, of holding beliefs that were contrary to the teachings of the church, confessions which were often wrung out of them by torture. Technically, Jews were not heretics; their conversion, the church hoped, would come about in due course, especially if the process were stimulated by segregating them from their neighbors and degrading them socially. However, once a Jew, voluntarily or under compulsion, had submitted to baptism, he too was answerable to the Inquisition for heresy, especially if he relapsed to the practices of his former faith.

Now, there was one Dominican who found the process of conversion too slow, and he hit upon a device for expediting it. He was Pablo Christiani, himself a converted Jew, and he persuaded King James of Aragon to order Moses ben Nachman to meet him in public debate where he, Pablo, would prove that Jesus of Nazareth was the true Messiah, and the Jews would all be converted en masse! The debate, which went by the solemn name of Disputation, took place at Barcelona in July 1263, and it was not to be the last of these tragi-comedies so fraught with peril for the Jews whether they won or lost. Pablo, of course, was no match for Nachmani. Before an august audience that included the king, the court, and the highest clergy, the Jewish champion with dignity and skill demolished the claims and arguments of the renegade.

Fortunately the Jews of Aragon escaped the consequences they feared from the victory, but Nachmani himself fell under the king's displeasure through a report of the event which he wrote for the Archbishop of Gerona. Egged on by the friars, the king condemned him to a two-year exile, and in 1267 the sage, already advanced in years, arrived in Palestine where, with superb courage, he continued his labors until his death three years later.

Nachmani found Palestine in ruins. Twice in a period of twenty years the land had been overrun and devastated by savage hordes from central Asia: in 1240 by the Mongolians and in 1260 by the Tartars. In Jerusalem he found only a handful of Jews, most of them pilgrims and beggars. But his brief sojourn brought new life into the scattered remnants. He established a school for the study of Talmud and spent his remaining days completing a commentary on the Pentateuch. In words that echo the passionate love of Yehudah Halevi, who sang his songs of Zion more than a century earlier, Nachmani writes from Jerusalem:

> I am a man who has seen affliction . . . I forsook my family and home . . . and with the dear children whom I brought up on my knees I left also my soul . . . But the loss of all this, and of every other glory my eyes beheld, is repaid by the joy of being a day in thy courts, O Jerusalem, visiting the ruins of the Temple and wailing over the desolate sanctuary where I am permitted to caress thy stones, to fondle thy dust, and to weep over thy ruins.

4

FOR more than a century after Nachmani's death the Jewish communities in the Christian kingdoms of Spain continued to prosper, despite the ill will of the clergy, the hostility of the nobles, and the zeal of the friars to bring about their conversion. There were more than a hundred communities in Castile alone, the largest of them in Toledo, Burgos, and Carrion. They were proud communities, strong in numbers, wealth, and influence, and it was not safe to insult or to attack them. In 1348-49, the years of the Black Death when the populace of Europe was transformed into raging mobs and thousands of Jews in Germany perished at their hands, the Jews of Spain repelled the rabble, arms in hand.

They owed their safety in large measure to the kings to whom they rendered outstanding service as physicians, collectors of taxes, financiers, and men of affairs. It was the kings who reduced to a dead letter the special laws passed against them, like the law the Castilian parliament adopted in 1293 forbidding them to own land or houses.

Not that dependence on the monarchs was a uniform blessing, for there were times when it was a dangerous honor to be employed by them. In 1280, for example, Alphonso X of Castile put to death his treasurer, Isaac de Malea, who had been compelled to deliver a large sum to the king's rebellious son. Alphonso XI (1312-1350) had many Jews in his service including Joseph ibn Benveniste, scion of an illustrious family, who was his treasurer, and Samuel ibn Wakar, who was the royal physician. As it happened, the two were bitter rivals, but they both incurred the hostility of the king's general, Gonzalo Martinez, a typical Haman, who coveted their wealth and plotted successfully against them, his machinations being aided by a venomous anti-Jewish agitation conducted by the renegade Abner of Burgos. Samuel was tortured to death and Joseph died in prison.

But the most famous object lesson in the perils of the court is furnished by the career of Samuel Abulafia, the treasurer and favorite minister of King Peter of Castile, who reigned from 1350 to 1369. Peter's reign was disturbed and finally overthrown by the rebellion of his step-brother Henry, and the Jews of the kingdom, who supported Peter, paid a huge price in blood and treasure for their loyalty. In 1355 Henry's mercenaries were driven back by the Jews of Toledo when they attacked their inner quarter, but in the final siege of the city, more than ten thousand of them perished by sword and famine. Samuel Abulafia, who led his people in loyal support of the king, met his doom at the hands of Peter himself. The Jewish minister whose enemies poisoned the king's mind against him was stripped of his possessions and tortured on the rack until he died.

The part the Jews of Castile played in the civil war between Peter and Henry is a measure of the important position they held in the kingdom, but Henry's victory in 1369 marks the beginning of their decline. They could no longer count on the king to protect them against the clergy and nobility.

5

THE three centuries of Jewish life in Spain after the death of Maimonides failed to produce a line of philosophers and poets who could vie with those of the previous generations. Perhaps it was the somber and repressive atmosphere of Christian dominion that affected the spirit of the Jews; perhaps it was a pervasive sense of insecurity and foreboding: but the leading minds of those centuries concentrated on the traditional lore of their people and, in the hunger of the heart and fancy, they turned to the exciting mysteries and speculations of Cabala. North of the Pyrenees, in the freer atmosphere of Provence, the tradition of Maimonides lasted longer, reaching its highest expression in the philosopher and scientist Levi ben Gershon, better known as Gersonides (1288-1344), who was also, of course, a thorough Talmudist and profound commentator of the Bible. In Spain, however, the Talmud and the Zohar became the two books which nourished the inner life of the Jews.

The word Cabala means "tradition," and the mystic knowledge was so called because for many generations, so it was believed, it was handed down by word of mouth only. This fantastic medley of exalted doctrine, numerological mysteries, and compelling formulas, this revelation of the hidden forces of heaven and earth, was meant only for the elect, and the cabalist, in his search for the divine essence and the destiny of man, was eager above all things to know the signs presaging the advent of the Messiah and the redemption of his suffering people. At various times, this strange lore stimulated messianic movements that gave rise to wild hopes and desperate efforts, but its cultivation was not confined to the restless and fanciful. It attracted many of the great minds of the age, even those who, like Nachmani, were well grounded in the sober spirit of Halachah, although they, unlike others, did not allow its mysteries to possess them and disturb the even tenor of their lives.

Among those who allowed themselves to be enthralled by it, the man who figures most prominently is Abraham Abulafia (1240-1292), scion of a clan that produced great scholars and statesmen. It would be difficult to say which was more fantastic, his life or the beliefs to which he clung. Obeying the command of a mystic voice, Abulafia proceeded to Rome to convert the pope to Judaism! He was arrested and imprisoned but his judges, impressed by his strange talk, set him free and he wandered down to Sicily where he made a great stir, especially in the flourishing communities of Messina and Palermo, by proclaiming himself the Messiah. There were some who made ready to follow him to Palestine but the Jewish leaders, alarmed by the agitation, obtained a letter from the most distinguished rabbi of Spain denouncing Abulafia as a dangerous person. His followers fell away and the movement expired, but like all messiahs, Abulafia left behind him a trail of longing and loyalty which long survived him.

But the most important master of Cabala was Moses de Leon (1250-1305), the compiler of the book called Zohar (Brightness). In it Moses assembled the mystic knowledge that had been handed down through the generations, the authorship of which he ascribed to the famous *tanna* Simon ben Yochai who, to escape persecution, had, it was said, lived for thirteen years in a cave in Palestine where the secrets of heaven and earth were unlocked to him. These secrets the Zohar undertakes to derive from the Bible, every word and letter of which is believed to abound with hidden meaning. Life is conceived as a struggle between good and evil, both of which, however, serve the divine purpose; and every right deed, every fervent prayer, produces spiritual influences that bring nearer the triumph of good over evil, a triumph that will appear in all its fullness and glory with the coming of the Messiah.

The Zohar itself is a triumph of the fervid and unfettered imagination. It appealed powerfully to all in whom the longing for redemption was intense, nor is it surprising that with all its crudenesses, it attracted students of the Talmud who looked for something that gave freer rein to the fancy than the labyrinthian discussions of the Babylonian *amoraim*.

6

THE distinguished scholar to whom the leaders of the communities in Sicily appealed against Abraham Abulafia was Solomon ibn Adret (1235-1310), rabbi of Barcelona in the kingdom of Aragon. Solomon's fame and influence covered the whole of Spain and reached out into other lands. Like Nachmani, he subordinated the philosophy and science of the day, of which he had considerable knowledge, to the Bible and Talmud, and he took his stand against the Rambam when the old controversy flared up anew. In addition, Ibn Adret defended his faith valiantly against the Dominicans, one of whom, Raymund Martin, made a study of the Bible and Talmud in order to vilify Judaism.

It was Ibn Adret who persuaded the Jews of Toledo to receive the German refugee Asher ben Yechiel (1250-1328) and appoint him their rabbi. Asher's prestige rose even higher than Ibn Adret's. His learning was only equalled by his piety and good deeds, and his school attracted students from many lands. He too frowned on the pretensions of philosophy and science, although he encouraged the study of astronomy as a useful aid in determining the holy seasons and festivals. His son Judah succeeded him as rabbi of Toledo, and proved worthy of his illustrious father. Another son, Jacob, whose learning entitled him to be rabbi of the foremost community, desired no place of honor or profit but spent his life in pious study and works of charity. The three Asheris, as they are known, all fugitives from the fury of the German rabble, symbolized the plight of their exiled people, as well as the qualities of their mind and spirit.

CHAPTER THIRTY-SEVEN

Twilight in Spain

IN 1371 the clergy and nobility of the proud kingdom of Castile scored a great triumph: Henry II, who had overthrown King Peter and seized his throne, issued a decree ordering the Jews of his kingdom to wear the shameful yellow patch on their clothing. Now began the twilight of Spanish Jewry which was to end with the total blackout of 1492.

The clergy, who found it intolerable that those who rejected "the true faith" should be the equals of those who professed it, felt triumphant because the yellow patch degraded its wearers and created a gulf between them and their neighbors. The nobility triumphed because the Jews would now find it harder to hold positions of honor and profit which, they felt, belonged by right to themselves. Before long, in fact, a law was passed by the Cortes, or parliament, that made it impossible for the king to appoint a Jewish treasurer, and in 1385 the clergy gained another victory when Jews were forbidden to live among Christians or to employ them as servants.

The yellow badge of shame inflicted untold suffering on the proud Castilian Jews, and the relations between them and their neighbors continued to deteriorate. But even more serious was a decline in the moral fiber of the Jews themselves, for while persecution may at times have a bracing effect on its victims, it may also lacerate the spirit and enfeeble it. The old-time reverence for piety and learning was no more. Luxury and ostentation, which inflamed the envy and hostility of the populace, increased. In the allocation of communal taxes the rich threw the greater burden on the poor. Vanity and oppression raised their heads, and there was no Amos or Isaiah to cry out against the evildoers.

That vile creature, the informer, who together with the slanderous apostate was the bane of the Jews in the Middle Ages, made his appearance among the Jews of Spain, poisoning the minds of their neighbors for profit and advantage. Joseph Pichon, chief tax collector of Henry II, became the victim of informers together with Nissim ben Reuben, illustrious scholar and rabbi of Barcelona, and other prominent men of that community. The case of Pichon, in particular, illustrates the low level to which the community in Castile had sunk. After being cleared of the charges, Pichon informed against those who had informed against him, whereupon a Jewish court condemned him to death, and the sentence was carried out by order of the king under conditions that cast suspicion on the court's integrity.

2

A STORM was brewing in the sultry atmosphere that surrounded the Jews of Spain, and it broke in 1391 with incredible fury. It started in Seville, the ancient and beautiful city on the Guadalquivir, famous for its splendid synagogues and illustrious scholars. For years the archdeacon Ferrand Martinez had conducted a vicious campaign of incitement, and in June 1391 the populace stormed the ghetto from all sides, looted and burned the houses, and slew more than four thousand of the inhabitants. Most of the survivors saved their lives by accepting baptism.

From Seville the storm swept north and overwhelmed one community after another. In Cordova, the Jewish quarters went up in flames, thousands perished in Toledo, and in small communities like Ecija and Carmona not a Jew was left alive. The storm crossed the border into the kingdom of Aragon and broke over Valencia, Barcelona, Gerona and other cities. Even the sea was unable to stop it: the community in Palma on the island of Minorca was practically wiped out. By the time the fury spent itself, some seventy communities in Castile alone were devastated and the number of forced converts rose to scores of thousands. Only in Portugal and in Granada, the latter still held by the Moslems, were the Jews safe.

The destruction of property and the disruption of industry and commerce, from which the whole of Spain suffered, could before long be remedied, but the moral havoc was another matter. The gulf between the Jews and their neighbors became wider, and the spirit of Spanish Jewry was humbled and nearly broken. Their enemies, flushed with victory, became more insolent, and thought to make an end of Judaism in Spain altogether.

But the most serious menace to the future of Spanish Jewry lay in those who, to save their lives, had accepted baptism. They were called New Christians, but they held in horror the religion that had been thrust on them with the torch and the sword. They continued to love the faith that had been theirs and their fathers', and they loved it the more passionately from a sense of guilt, having proven too weak to die for it. Many of them sought the first opportunity to return to it by escaping into North Africa, Granada, Portugal, and other lands, and those unable to escape wore the mask of Christianity in public and practiced their own religion in secret. Their devotion to Judaism was all the stronger because the practice of it was not only a joy but a penance and a peril.

The secret, of course, could not be indefinitely kept, and the wrath of the clergy burned even fiercer against the New Christians than against the Jews. They called them Marranos or "the damned," a name which is still borne by many of their descendants, but which has become a badge not of scorn, but of tragedy and pride.

3

THE Jews of Spain became like a city besieged. All the power of the church and all its learning and skill were brought into play to undermine their faith and break their spirit, and there were apostates and traitors who joined the hue and cry against their people. The most effective and violent of the renegades was Paul of Burgos. He was one of the converts of 1391, and rose fast and high not only in the government of Castile but in the church itself. In 1412 he induced the Cortes to pass a law which outdid all previous ones for insult and injury. It became a crime for Jews to trim their hair and shave their beards. Their clothes had to be of inferior material and ugly cut. They were forbidden to carry arms. They were forbidden to engage in handicrafts and professions, or deal in wine, flour, meat, or bread. The aim was clear: the Jews of Castile were to be brought down to the level of pariahs and paupers. All debts which Christians owed to Jews had already been declared null and void.

But Paul's zeal and ingenuity were not exhausted. There was a Dominican friar named Vincent Ferrer, a redoubtable preacher, and Paul invited him to exercise his talents on his former people. Accompanied by a gang of ruffians, Vincent traveled through Castile and Aragon, and the Jews were forced to listen to his threats and ravings in their own synagogues. Vincent, of course, claimed many converts.

In Aragon, however, there was a man at the time who was sure he could convert the Jews faster than was being done by Vincent and Paul. He was none other than the pope, or rather the anti-pope, Benedict XIII, for since 1378 there had been two rival popes, one in Rome, the other in the French city of Avignon. Benedict had encouraged both Paul of Burgos and Vincent Ferrer. Then he lost the anti-papal throne and sought to retrieve his fortunes by bringing about a mass conversion of the Spanish Jews.

The method he chose was that of the public disputation which Pablo Christiani had first tried a century and a half earlier. Pablo had failed but he, Benedict, proposed to stage it on a grand and crushing scale. Accordingly, in answer to his summons, twenty-two Jewish representatives, headed by Vidal Benveniste and Joseph Albo, were confronted by the most learned and adroit Christian theologians, including a number of Jewish renegades. From February 1413 to November 1414, the two sides debated the merits of their respective faiths. This, the most famous of the disputations, took place at Tortosa in the kingdom of Aragon.

But Benedict took care that his appeal should be directed not only to reason, but above all to fear. The Jews saw facing them not only the Christian advocates, but an imposing array of knights and bishops. Vincent Ferrer, who was operating in Tortosa at the time, paraded his converts before the disputants. The keynote was sounded by one of the renegades. "If ye be willing and obedient," he quoted from Isaiah, "ye shall eat the good of the land; but if ye refuse and rebel, ye shall be devoured with the sword." He could not have expressed himself more plainly.

The Jewish spokesmen, however, held their ground with courage and dignity. Their opponents began by seeking support in the Talmud; they ended by denouncing it and demanding that its study be banned. The grand disputation was a failure, and seeing he could not convert the Jews en masse, Benedict prevailed on the government to lay upon the Jews of Aragon the same crushing burden of social, economic, and moral indignities as had already been enacted against their brothers in Castile. They were deprived of their internal autonomy, forbidden to study their sacred books, compelled to put on the disgraceful patch, and three times a year they had to listen to Christian sermons in their own synagogues. All that, of course, was in addition to the ruinous economic restrictions that had the double aim of pauperizing those who remained steadfast and seducing those who vacillated.

4

THE Jews of Castile and Aragon suffered but remained, on the whole, steadfast; and even those who, in face of the uplifted sword, abjured their faith, continued for the most part loyal to it in secret. Nor was the age deficient in men of light and learning, although the stress of the times drove them into narrower channels, contracting the free flow of reason and imagination which distinguished the poets and philosophers of former generations. Isaac ben Sheshet Barfat (1326-1408), rabbi of Saragossa and later of Valencia, stood like a rock against every attempt to compromise with Talmudic law in deference to the science and philosophy of Aristotle. His contemporary and friend, Hasdai Crescas (1340-1410), also frowned upon philosophy, but he was a fine thinker and able to challenge it on its own ground. Both men wielded authority not only in the communities of Spain but in those of France, Germany, and other lands. The deplorable character of the times they lived in is illustrated by the fact that they and other Jewish notables of Aragon, including the aged and renowned Nissim of Gerona, who had been the teacher of both men, were kept in prison for a long time as the result of a denunciation lodged against them by an informer.

The man whose work influenced not only his own but later generations was Joseph Albo, who had been among the foremost Jewish spokesmen in the disputation of Tortosa. He was a persuasive writer and his book *Ikkarim* (Fundamentals) plunges boldly into the deep waters of religious philosophy. He even dared to cross swords with the Rambam, asserting that the belief in a Messiah is not a fundamental of the Jewish faith. Albo's aim is not far to seek. He, like the other Jewish scholars of his day, desired to strengthen his people against the pressure of Christianity in which the Messianic belief is the central dogma.

5

IN 1432, twelve years before Joseph Albo died, action of a more direct sort was taken by the communities of Castile to strengthen their religious and communal life and eradicate abuses that had crept in among them. Politically, their situation had improved. John II (1406-1454) was king, and Alvaro de Luna, his favorite minister, needed the help of Jewish money and brains in the perennial conflict between the throne and the nobility. Abraham Benveniste, one of Alvaro's closest friends and advisers, was named chief rabbi of Castile; the internal autonomy of Castilian Jewry was restored; and Benveniste convened a congress of representatives to remedy the sad state into which the communities of the kingdom had fallen. The deliberations of this congress, which met in the city of Valladolid, hold up a mirror to the internal problems that beset the Jews of Spain. The Congress denounced extravagance and ostentation as a danger to the community; it dealt with the plague of apostates and informers; it sought means for the restoration and maintenance of communal institutions; and it labored, above all, to promote learning and the education of the young.

Nor did the Jews of Castile fare badly under John's successor Henry IV (1454-1474), whose personal physician, Jacob ibn Nunez, was chief rabbi of the kingdom. In Aragon also the monarch's physician was a Jew, and in both kingdoms, notwithstanding the protests of nobles and bishops, Jews were again received into the employ of the state. Their lot, in fact, might have continued to improve and the tragedy of 1492 perhaps been averted or at least deferred, if their situation had not been bedeviled by the New Christians and Marranos.

6

IT WAS against the New Christians, in fact, that the general wrath burned hottest and kept steadily mounting. It was not simply that they were suspected of clandestine loyalty to the faith they had renounced, although in the eyes of the clergy no crime could be more heinous than such heresy. The New Christians aroused bitter resentment even more because they were too successful. Too many of them, now that religion no longer barred their way, became rich and powerful. They held high positions in the government, the army, the universities—in the church itself! They went even further. Their sons and daughters married into the nobility, and to such an extent that before long there was hardly a noble family in Spain without an admixture of Jewish blood, and even royalty itself was not immune to this "invasion."

Altogether the New Christians, even more than the Jews, furnished excellent fuel for zealous bigots, frustrated mediocrities, and ambitious demagogues. When the sovereigns, whose coffers were always being drained by endless wars, increased the burden of taxation, the fury of the populace was shunted to the tax collectors, many of whom were New Christians. In all of them, even in those who wore the habits of the church, the priests and friars saw heretics, and they inflamed the passions of the people against them to the point of violence. In 1440 and again in 1467 the mob broke loose in Toledo, and many New Christians were slain and their homes sent up in flames. Six years later bloody riots against them occurred in Cordova, Saen, and Segovia.

Thus, by a strange irony, those who thought they could escape the wrath by renouncing their faith, found themselves in deadlier peril than those who remained loyal to it. It was clear, however, that the comparative safety of the latter would not long endure. The two groups were too closely identified: the Jews, in fact, were suspected of aiding and abetting the Marranos in their secret heresies.

In the New Christians the bishops and friars found proof of the futility of conversion as a solution for the Jewish problem in Spain. They looked for a new solution and they found it.

CHAPTER THIRTY-EIGHT

Exile

THE year 1479 is an important landmark in the history of Christian Spain. On the throne of Castile sat the pious but hardheaded Isabella, and that year her husband Ferdinand fell heir to the throne of Aragon. Thus were united the two kingdoms which comprised by far the greater part of the peninsula. Both rulers, whom the pope designated as "the Catholic Sovereigns," were competent, aggressive, and unscrupulous, the queen leaning toward bigotry and the king toward greed. The policy which the monarchs adopted called for absolutism at home and expansion abroad and, in pursuit of the first objective, the nobles were to be stripped of their ancient prerogatives and heresy stamped out as treason to the state.

A most important instrument for promoting this objective was the Inquisition, but the Catholic Sovereigns were not willing that their Inquisition should be under papal jurisdiction, and in 1480 they established a national and royal Inquisition of their own. It began operations in the south, and a year later its first auto-da-fé was staged in Seville where twelve Marranos, six men and six women, were burned at the stake with all the solemnity and festivity that befitted the occasion. Thousands of Marranos who fled to Cadiz were brought back and thrown into dungeons. Thousands of Jews who were accused of aiding them were banished to other parts of the kingdom. All Christians were ordered, on pain of excommunication, to become spies and informers. They received careful instructions. They were told, for example, to note if New Christians bought meat from the Jewish butcher or wore clean linen on Saturdays.

The flames of the autos-da-fé continued to blaze, and in the dungeons the torturers were busy. Even corpses were not allowed to lie in peace. Charges of having practiced Judaism were brought against many of the dead, and their bones were disinterred and burned at the stake. The property of the victims, which swelled the royal coffers, provided the sovereigns with the means to finance other undertakings.

The proud Marranos did not take the Inquisition submissively. They appealed to the pope, they exploited their powerful connections, they plotted against the leading inquisitors. Some of them succeeded in escaping its clutches, and in 1485 one of the two chief inquisitors of Aragon was assassinated. But these efforts were of little avail. The great majority of Spaniards approved of the Inquisition, convinced that its work was holy and patriotic.

2

IN 1483 the Inquisition gained immensely in reach and power when the Dominican monk Thomas de Torquemada, already inquisitor-general of Castile, was elevated to the same rank for Aragon. The holy office was now centralized, its jurisdiction was gradually extended to every nook and corner of the united kingdoms, and in Torquemada it had a servant of ferocious zeal and rare ingenuity. The business of detecting, torturing, and punishing was organized into a perfect system, with the penalties, based on the principle of panic, graded in proportion to the promptness of confession. Besides, Torquemada was confessor to their "Catholic Majesties," and he had little difficulty in impressing the king and queen with the spiritual and material advantages of liquidating the heretics.

Thousands of Marranos confessed "voluntarily," and if they did so after the period of grace, they were stripped of their possessions and imprisoned for life. At the solemn and imposing autos-da-fé, the more fortunate, principally minors, were only compelled to wear the grotesque penitential robe called the sanbenito. The others, including even friars and priests of the church, after being tortured into confession, were consigned to the holy flames.

Torquemada was indefatigable, but the work of purification, he felt, should include the Jews also, and since they were not eligible for the ministrations of the Inquisition, the only alternative, he concluded, was expulsion. He took his measures toward this end with thorough care, and he made particularly good use of a blood accusation which brought death at the stake to six Marranos and five Jews in the city of Avila near Madrid. The victims had been charged with slaying a Christian child that never existed.

3

IN 1492 the reign of Ferdinand and Isabella attained its zenith. In January of that year, the monarchs made a triumphal entry into the city of Granada, the last stronghold of the Moslems in Spain. Nearly eight hundred years earlier, the land had been overrun by them, and for centuries they ruled in it in power and splendor. For the Jews, those centuries were a bright memory, and it was a bitter irony that a special tax was levied upon them to finance the final war against the Moslems. The reigning princes of Granada, it may be added, deserved no better fate. They were torn by rivalries and betrayed each other to the Christians without scruple.

The year 1492, moreover, witnessed two other great events in Spain: the departure of Christopher Columbus on his momentous voyage across the Atlantic and the fall of the final curtain on the tragedy of Spanish Jewry. In view of the important part played by Jews and Marranos in making the voyage of Columbus possible, and in view, further, of what the discovery of the New World has meant for the future of the Jewish people, the concurrence of those two events has exerted a peculiar, almost mystical, fascination on many minds, a fascination which the recent discovery of evidence supporting the theory that Columbus was himself of Jewish descent, has naturally intensified. Whatever the merits of that theory may be, there is no doubt that Jewish money and brains contributed greatly to the success of the daring enterprise. Jewish scientists had prepared the ground for it, including Abraham Zacuto, astronomer-royal of Portugal, whose perpetual almanac and astronomical tables guided the voyager; Zacuto's pupil, Joseph Vecinho; Yehuda Cresques, the map-maker of Majorca; and other Jewish mariners, navigators, and scholars. The funds for the voyage came from Marranos and Jews: from Luis de Santangel, controller-general of Aragon, from Gabriel Sanchez, chief treasurer of the kingdom, from Abraham Senior, chief rabbi and principal tax collector of Castile, from Isaac Abarbanel, and others. And there were even Jewish sailors who accompanied Columbus, among them Rodrigo Sanchez, a relative of Gabriel; Maestro Bernal, the ship's physician; and Luis de Torres, the interpreter, who is believed to have been the first man of the expedition to set foot on the soil of the New World.

Whether it was because the expulsion of the Jews from Spain was the news sensation of the day, or because Columbus' consciousness of his origin overcame his customary vigilance on this occasion, as indeed it seems to have done on others also, he himself couples the two events in his diary. "In the same month in which their Majesties issued the edict that all Jews should be driven out of the kingdom and its territories," the diary begins, "in the same month they gave me the order to undertake with sufficient men my expedition of discovery to the Indies."

4

THE edict of expulsion was issued on March 30, 1492, from the Alhambra in newly conquered Granada, and it provided that by the end of July, any Jew found in the realms of Ferdinand and Isabella would escape death only by baptism. The exiles were forbidden to take their gold or silver with them, and although they might sell their land and houses, the market became so glutted with their possessions that a house was sold for a cart and a vineyard for a donkey. They made desperate last-minute efforts to ward off the blow. It is related that Abraham Senior and Isaac Abarbanel appeared before the monarchs and offered their own immense fortunes for the annulment of the edict, and as the king began to waver, Torquemada came rushing in and, extending a crucifix to the rulers, he cried: "Here! Take him and sell him!"

The edict was not recalled and the exiles made ready to depart. To the very end Torquemada and his minions continued their efforts to force them into baptism, inventing a variety of new devices for the purpose. But the great majority held firm. They wept at the graves of their fathers, said farewell to the land they still loved, and with the cry, "Let us go in the name of the Lord," they set out, some 300,000 of them, for lands across the waters and for the neighboring kingdom of Portugal.

Terrible beyond description were the hardships and cruelties suffered by the exiles on the ships at sea and on the shores of Europe, Africa, and Asia where they sought refuge. Many were lost in wreck and storm, others died from pestilence or at the hands of brigands, still others were sold into slavery by the masters of the ships on which they sailed or by pirates who overtook and captured them. Only in the lands of Bayazid II, Sultan of Turkey, who understood how valuable the exiles would prove for the prosperity of his empire, did they find welcome.

5

BUT most of the exiles got across the border into Portugal where they bought permission to remain for a period of eight months. When the term expired and there were not enough ships for them, many of those who were left behind were sold into slavery and their children torn from them to be baptized. Four years later, the King of Portugal ordered those who still remained to leave the country, but they were too valuable for him and he did not really intend to let them go. Instead he proceeded to baptize them by force. A few escaped, and many parents, after slaying their children, put an end to their own lives.

A large body of Marranos thus came into existence in Portugal and their misfortunes were the same as those of the Marranos in Spain. In 1506 two thousand of them perished at the hands of a mob, and in 1531 the Inquisition, with its trials and tortures and autos-da-fé, came to nest in Portugal. For a long time Marranos continued to escape from that country and seek asylum in other lands of the Old World as well as the New, but to this day there are thousands of descendants of the forced converts in Portugal who still remember their proud and tragic lineage.

And thus the glory and tragedy of Spanish Jewry also becomes a tale that is told.

Part Four 1492 TO 1789

In Medieval Europe

A People Besieged

CHAPTER THIRTY-NINE

Light and Shadow in Italy

"ALL things," says the Talmud, "are in the hands of God, except the fear of God." The winds of destiny had swept the Jewish people westward through the lands washed by the Mediterranean, with remnants still in the east, and tributaries from the main stream branching north and south. From England the current was turned back in 1290; from France in 1394. In the foul ghettos of the Germanies it lay stagnating. Now from the fallen grandeur of Spain it was set moving back toward the east. Back and forth like driftwood, this people seemed buffeted on the tides of history. Nevertheless, one thing, which is well described as "the fear of God," lay within the power of their own hands and souls. For wherever they went, they still carried the ancient lamp with them, they still chose to cling to the fire that had been kindled for them at their birth as a people in the Sinai desert.

Not since the year 70, when the Romans extinguished their corporate life and devastated their land, had the Jewish people sustained a disaster so shattering as the expulsion from Spain. Spain had been the largest, proudest, and most brilliant center of the Diaspora; for half a millennium it had held the primacy in the life of the scattered nation; and now, at a single stroke, it was no more. How great the anguish, how bitter the shame! The invincible Romans had at least felt the edge of the Jewish sword on their necks; the struggle had dowered the generations that followed with a glorious memory. In Spain, the victims were like sheep led to the slaughter; and, as the exiles dragged their sorrow from one land to another, the full meaning of the catastrophe came home to every other community, and wherever Jews lived—in Europe, Africa, Asia—lamentation rose up as if for a third time their Temple had been defiled and destroyed.

2

TO the communities in Italy, particularly in the so-called Kingdom of the Two Sicilies, which embraced the island of Sicily and the southern half of the peninsula, the fugitives from Spain brought a sharp awareness of the sword that hung suspended above their own heads. In that segment of the Italian political chaos, and north of it in the republics and duchies that jostled each other to the foot of the Alps, numerous Jewish communities persisted under varying fortunes through the centuries. The political disunion was not without certain advantages: when life became impossible for them in one state they found refuge in another. Italy, indeed, was a land of many contrasts. It was the land of the sublime poet Dante Alighieri (1265-1321) whose *Divine Comedy* is a mirror of the medieval mind at its loftiest and purest. It was also the land of Niccolò Machiavelli (1469-1527), who lifted the infamy and cruelty that marked the political life of the Italian states to the dignity of a philosophy and a guide to the art of statecraft. The Jewish poet Immanuel of Rome is said to have been a friend of Dante, and commentators on the Italian poet have expressed wonder that in the region of hell which he reserved for usurers, he found only Christians and noblemen! Moreover, the edicts of the church, which were designed to keep Jews segregated from their neighbors, were less effective in Italy than in other lands. Many famous and fruitful friendships are on record. Pico della Mirandola, one of the luminous spirits of the Renaissance, was a friend and disciple of the grammarian and cabalist Elijah del Medigo (1460-1497). Elijah Levita (1469-1549) who, in the course of his long life was buffeted about between Germany and Italy, had among his friends and pupils a number of distinguished churchmen, including Cardinal Egidio di Viterbo. In both countries, in fact, the Renaissance awakened in Christian scholars a lively interest in the Hebrew language and in the books of the Jewish people, an interest which led not only to friendships between men of learning of both faiths, but, as we shall see, added greatly to those deeper stirrings which eventually gave rise to the Protestant Reformation.

3

THE steady flow of refugees from Germany to the relative safety of Italy and Turkey, and the sudden flood of exiles from Spain bear testimony to the basic unity of destiny and character that stamped the Jewish people throughout the Dispersion. In their internal tensions also, they were all very much alike. The clamor that rose up around the teachings of the Rambam echoed loudly in Italy where, in addition to the Talmud and Cabala, philosophy and poetry were held in high esteem. It was an esteem, however, which the scholars and rabbis from Germany frowned upon, and there was fierce dissension in Padua, Mantua, and elsewhere. But when the Spanish exiles arrived, many of them in the condition of captive slaves, the communities knew their duty and united to discharge it. They hastened to obey the ancient command to ransom their captive brothers and make them welcome.

The exiles, however, were no mere pensioners on the bounty of their hosts. They still possessed the qualities that made them great in Spain: they brought with them not only energy and practical skill, but also learning and prestige. Of these qualities, as well as of the changing fortunes that hounded the refugees from Spain, and, for that matter, the Jews of Italy also, Isaac Abarbanel (1437-1509) and his sons provide a striking illustration. They were a noble and remarkably gifted family, claiming direct descent from King David. After his vain attempt to ward off the fatal decree, Isaac found asylum in Naples, where the king took him into his service. It was not long, however, before the kingdom was conquered by Spain, and Isaac resumed his wanderings, until finally he joined his son Joseph in Venice. There too Isaac played an important role in state affairs, but his chief interest was scholarship. He was a philosopher and Biblical commentator. His *Herald of Salvation* is a cabalistic work which he wrote in order to sustain the spirit of his people with the promise of a speedy fulfillment of the Messianic hope.

Joseph Abarbanel was a physician; his older brother Judah Leo, after a distinguished career with Gonzalo de Cordova, the conqueror of Naples for Ferdinand of Spain, joined his father and brother in Venice, for the Spanish conquest had, of course, brought the Inquisition with it. Nor should Isaac's youngest son Samuel (1473-1550) be omitted from the roster. Samuel inherited his father's financial skill, which he too placed at the service of the government of Naples. Himself a fine Talmudic scholar, Samuel was also a patron of learning and his people's protector. But the Spanish monarch was determined to extend the expulsion decree to his Italian possessions, and after one edict had been suppressed by the efforts of Samuel and his brilliant and noble wife Benvenida, the expulsion finally took place. In 1540 the Jews of the Kingdom of Naples took up the wanderer's staff. They sought asylum across the Adriatic in the realms of the Sultan and in other Italian states, principally in Ancona and Ferrara. Samuel and Benvenida, although they were exempted from the edict, chose to share their people's exile and spent the remainder of their lives in Ferrara.

4

THE states and cities of Italy were nearly always in the throes of civil turmoil, war, and political change, and the fortunes of the Jewish communities fluctuated continually. Nevertheless their records contain many bright and noble pages, to which Sephardic and Ashkenazic refugees, as well as natives, contributed. Ferrara, for example, was developed by the exiles into an important commercial center and for a hundred years the community flourished, although each of the three groups maintained its own communal institutions and only rarely united for common action. Ferrara produced a brilliant scholar in Azariah dei Rossi, and among its distinguished leaders we come upon a grandson and namesake of Isaac Abarbanel. In 1597, however, the duchy was annexed to the Papal States, half the community migrated, and the rest were confined in a ghetto and forced to listen to conversionist sermons delivered by zealous monks.

Perhaps the best example of tenacious life is furnished by the community of Venice, the largest in the Venetian republic and the second largest in the peninsula, the first being in Rome. In 1566, earlier than in any other Italian city, a ghetto was established in Venice, and from time to time decrees of expulsion were issued and revoked. But the community, with its various groupings, persisted and even flourished, playing an important part in the far-flung commerce of the republic and yielding a substantial revenue to its coffers. There were schools for secular as well as religious learning, and the duty of purchasing the freedom of captives was not neglected. The Venice community had its distinguished personalities, among them two poetesses, Deborah Ascarelli and Sarah Sullam. Nor did the frivolities and foibles of the age leave it unaffected, a condition which Rabbi Simeone Luzzatto, in his *Status of the Jews,* frankly exposes and condemns, lamenting in particular a lack of interest in the public weal and a tendency on the part of many of his people to be too obsequious toward their neighbors. Strangely enough, it was a colleague of Luzzatto's, the brilliant and erratic Judah Leon Modena (1571-1648), who exhibited not a few of those deplorable traits, including a passion for card-playing and a general lack of intellectual stability. Modena, however, possessed considerable learning and was capable of lofty poetic and devotional flights. His contradictions are perhaps explained as the result of a conflict between his Hebraic heritage and the Hellenistic influences of the Italian Renaissance that surrounded him.

5

THERE was hardly a sizable place in northern Italy that did not have its Jewish community, clinging, in fair political weather or foul, to all that made life possible. Their story in Milan, Cremona, Pavia, and other cities is shadowed with persecutions and expulsions, but it contains bright pages also. In Leghorn, or Livorno, for example, Duke Ferdinand was anxious to expand the city's commerce. He invited some Marranos and Jews to settle there, and in 1597 granted them a charter of rights by which they enjoyed complete autonomy and acquired a leading place in the cultural life of their people. They were prominent in industry as well as commerce, particularly in the manufacture of soap and textiles. Leghorn, which was sometimes called the Jerusalem of Italy, became also an important center of the art of Hebrew printing, of which, it may be noted, there were many other centers on the peninsula, the most famous in Soncino, Mantua, and Bologna.

In the Papal States, which cut across the peninsula north of the Kingdom of Naples, the Jewish communities in the first half of the sixteenth century had little to complain of. Clement VII, who headed the church from 1523 to 1534, even permitted Marranos from Portugal in his city of Ancona to return openly to their former faith, and to the community in Rome he extended a large measure of internal autonomy. In both cities, to be sure, the Jews were an important economic factor, but there can be no doubt that both Clement VII and his successor Paul III (1534-1549) had no zeal for persecution and sought to allay the bitter lot of the Marranos.

6

BOTH Clement VII and Paul III tried hard, also, to keep the Inquisition out of Portugal, or at least to mitigate its horrors. But all their efforts, stimulated in large measure by the influence and largess of the Marranos, had little success. In 1531 the dread tribunal was authorized in Portugal and promptly began its fiendish work, with escape for the victims made practically impossible. A year later it was suppressed, then re-established and extended to the Portuguese possessions in the New World. Too many interests and passions were concentrated against the Marranos in Portugal: the bigotry and hatred of the clergy and populace; the dread of heresy, augmented now by the rising tide of Protestantism in the north; the avarice of the king, who of course fell heir to the fortunes of the condemned; and the machinations of the wily and unscrupulous Emperor Charles V who sought to make the papacy subservient to himself by depriving it of independent action.

7

THE liberal and humane policies of Clement VII and Paul III were completely reversed when Paul IV (1555-1559) ascended the papal throne, and the change lasted for three centuries. The old church laws were now invoked, and even the traditional papal policy against forced conversion was violated. The Jews were herded into miserable ghettos with the gates kept locked from dark to dawn. They could own neither land nor houses; were barred from most occupations, including the professions; and a system of cruel humiliations was imposed upon them, with the yellow hat for men and the yellow veil for women. They had to listen to conversionist sermons by priests, monks, and renegades, and from time to time there were public burnings of the Talmud. The Marranos were ordered back to Christianity, and in Ancona twenty-four of them who defied the command suffered martyrdom at the stake. In 1569 and again in 1593 all the Jews of the Papal States, except those in Rome and Ancona, were ordered into exile. In those two cities the Jews could not be spared: in spite of their impoverishment and degradation they still furnished too large a share of the state revenues.

8

AGAINST this shifting background of light and shadow in sixteenth century Italy, we come upon a strange drama springing from the intense longing of a homeless and harassed people. In 1524, in the reign of the liberal Clement VII, a curious stranger appeared in Rome with a tale about a brother of his, a Jewish king somewhere in the nebulous east, who had sent him as ambassador to the Christian rulers of the west. The inhabitants of his brother's kingdom, he stated, were a brave and warlike people, descended from the tribe of Reuben, and they were eager to make war on the Turks and reconquer Palestine. But, he reported, they lacked arms which he, David Reubeni, as he called himself, had come to obtain from the rulers of Europe.

Many, including the pope himself, believed the mysterious ambassador. He was an odd personage, of pigmy size, dark-skinned and alert, pious and solemn, and he stirred vague messianic longings. The pope gave him letters to King John III of Portugal, Italian Jews supplied him with funds, and Reubeni sailed on a ship flying a Jewish flag and arrived in Portugal, where the king received him in grand style and promised to grant his petition. But the Marranos in Portugal were too deeply moved; they saw in Reubeni the harbinger of the Messiah, they saw their deliverance at hand, and some of them rose up in arms. Reubeni was compelled to leave the country and eventually returned to Italy.

Before he departed, however, he had come to know a youthful Marrano who was destined to become the central figure of this fantastic drama. This brilliant mystic whose mind, already excited by the study of Cabala, became enflamed by the appearance of the ambassador from the East, began to have marvelous dreams and visions. He threw off the mask of Christianity and came out openly as a Jew, under the name of Solomon Molcho. On Reubeni's advice Molcho fled from Portugal and went to live in Salonika, Safed, and other cities of the East, where he became still more certain of his messianic mission and roused similar convictions in others.

Now the scene shifts back to Italy where the things that happen surpass the imaginings of the most fertile romancer. The trail of Solomon Molcho takes us to Ancona, Pesaro, Rome, and Venice. Multitudes flock to see him and hear him. Among his own people a few come out against him, fearing the evil that may result from the ferment. More than once his life is in danger. In the presence of the pope, to whom he gains admittance disguised as a beggar, he predicts an inundation of Rome and an earthquake in Portugal, together with the appearance of a comet; and his predictions actually come true! The Inquisition, aided by an informer, steps in and condemns him to death, but with the connivance of the pope, Molcho escapes and someone else, who resembles him, is delivered to the flames.

In Venice and Milan, Molcho and Reubeni meet again, and in 1532 they proceed together on the last stage of their journey. They go to Regensburg and stand before Emperor Charles V, offering the help of the Jewish people in a war against the Turks. Above them flutters a banner embroidered with the initials of the Hebrew words meaning "Who is like unto Thee among the mighty, O Lord!"

But this time their magnificent faith or folly proved unavailing. Charles put them in chains. Molcho was again delivered to the Inquisition in Italy, and with superb courage sanctified the Divine Name at the stake. Some ten years later Reubeni is believed to have suffered a like fate in Spain. It is related that with the fagots piled around him, a messenger from the emperor came posthaste to Molcho, offering him life and pardon if he would return to the church. Molcho spurned the offer. His most ardent desire—the longing for *kiddush hashem*—was at last fulfilled.

CHAPTER FORTY

Turkey—Haven of Refuge

IN THE political patchwork of Italy the lot of the Jews, native and refugee, was spotty and precarious, but eastward now stretched a new Moslem world, where the victims of exile and persecution could find asylum. The Ottoman Empire had been steadily enlarging its borders. In Asia, it now included Anatolia, Syria, Palestine, Mesopotamia, and the regions east almost to the Caspian Sea. In Africa the sultan ruled over Egypt, and many of the Berber states recognized him as their suzerain, while in Europe his domains embraced the Balkan peninsula, as well as Crimea and Hungary to the borders of Austria and Poland. The Aegean Islands fell under his sway, and the Turkish fleet was mistress of the Mediterranean and its inlets.

Millions of Jews, it is estimated, lived in the sixteenth century under the scepter of the sultan, and Constantinople and Salonika harbored the largest Jewish communities in the world. At times, they suffered from the malevolence and greed of a pasha or local governor but, compared to other lands, there was little religious oppression in the Turkish Empire—non-Moslems were only required to pay a special poll tax. In 1532 a blood accusation was fabricated by Greek Catholics against the Jews in a small town in Asia Minor and it claimed a number of victims, but the conspirators were exposed and executed, and a decree was issued making it mandatory for such accusations to be tried in the sultan's courts. The imperial community was headed by a chief rabbi appointed by the sultan, and Jews rose to high station in the service of the state. Joseph Hamon was physician to Bayazid II who opened wide the gates of his empire to the fugitives from Spain, and Joseph's son Moses was physician to the brilliant conqueror and lawgiver Suleiman the Magnificent (1530-1566), and stood high in his favor.

Joseph and his son were both fugitives from Spain, and their career is typical of the progress the exiles achieved in their new homes. In Constantinople and Salonika as well as in Adrianople, Nicopolis, and elsewhere, they rose to commanding positions. Refugees from each of the various provinces and cities of Spain formed congregations of their own, very much like the *landsmannschaft* societies and synagogues that still flourish in America today, each congregation collecting from its members the state poll tax as well as an impost for its own institutions. In time, the exiles imposed the language they spoke upon the communities where they settled, and it became the dialect known today as "Spaniolish" or Ladino. They brought their learning with them also; Salonika, where the Jewish population became a majority, and Safed in Palestine became leading centers of Talmudic and Cabalistic study.

Thus, in the "Vale of Tears," as Joseph Cohen, an historian of the period, calls the Dispersion, Turkey was a veritable city of refuge. In the capital especially, the Jews made up a numerous, wealthy, and powerful community, and because of the empire's importance in the affairs of Europe and the influence the Jews exerted in shaping its policies, they were able to mitigate the hard lot of their brothers in other lands.

2

THE far-flung and variegated Jewish world of the sixteenth century is brought into sharp relief by the epic story of Gracia Mendes, a remarkable exemplar of the Biblical "woman of valor," and her brilliant nephew Joseph Nassi, who rose to power and splendor with Suleiman the Magnificent and his successor. They belonged to a distinguished Portuguese Marrano family of bankers, whose transactions embraced many lands, and among whose debtors were Emperor Charles V and the kings of France. But they sought a land where they could return openly to their own faith, and their odyssey takes us from Portugal to Flanders and across the Mediterranean world to Constantinople and Palestine.

On the death of her husband, Gracia Mendes left Portugal and went to Antwerp, then the leading port of Europe, where a branch of her husband's business was located. But Flanders, a Spanish possession, was a bad place for Marranos and so, after conquering many difficulties and dangers, Gracia reached Venice only to be betrayed, imprisoned, and despoiled. At this point Turkey steps into the picture. Gracia's nephew Joseph Nassi, who with other members of the family accompanied her on her travels, received the aid of Moses Hamon, Suleiman's physician; the sultan's government, alive to the benefits the wealthy family could bestow on Turkey, compelled the Venetian republic to set her free and restore her property. Before proceeding to Turkey, she stayed a number of years in Ferrara and there, as in all places where she dwelt, her nobility and munificence brought her the love and gratitude of the community. She was a generous patron of learning, and always eager to help Marranos who were menaced by the Inquisition.

In Constantinople, where in 1553 Gracia and her nephew arrived with a large retinue, both were at last able to return openly to the faith of their fathers, and it was not long before Joseph won the favor of the sultan. Joseph possessed an intimate knowledge of the European diplomatic labyrinth, and Suleiman, as well as his successor Selim II, found in him a valuable adviser. Like Mordecai in the palace of Ahasuerus, Joseph Nassi "waxed greater and greater . . . seeking the good of his people and speaking peace to all his seed."

The grateful Suleiman gave Joseph the city of Tiberias in Palestine and the district around it to be developed as a refuge for his persecuted people, and Selim made him Duke of Naxos and a group of neighboring islands in the Aegean which the Turks had conquered in 1566. On Joseph's advice, Selim made war on Venice and conquered the island of Cyprus, then a Venetian possession. Ambassadors of the European powers, including those of Emperor Maximilian II himself, came seeking favors from the Jewish duke. The Netherlands, in revolt against their sovereign, the gloomy fanatic Philip II of Spain, besought Joseph to prevail on the sultan to make war on their oppressor.

For Tiberias, Joseph conceived the plan of a large Jewish settlement to which he hoped the sultan would grant self-government. Joseph, in fact, had all his life nourished the dream of creating a Jewish state. He issued a call to his persecuted people to return to their ancient homeland, and provided ships to transport them.

Hundreds of them in the Papal States, suffering brutal persecutions at the hand of Pius V, heeded the call, but some of them were overtaken at sea by pirates and sold into slavery. Joseph went forward with his plans. He rebuilt the ancient city which had fallen in ruins, and tried to establish silk and cloth industries in it. But the experiment did not prove successful; the failure was no doubt due in some measure to Joseph's loss of favor at court.

3

EVEN before the death of Selim II in 1574, the star of Joseph Nassi had begun to wane, owing chiefly to the hostility of the grand vizier, Mohammed Sokolli. But the man who supplanted Joseph in influence at the court was his coreligionist, Solomon Ashkenazi, whose career was almost as remarkable as his rival's. Ashkenazi had served as physician to King Sigismund Augustus of Poland, and one of his achievements was to secure the election as Polish king of Henry of Anjou, later Henry III of France. It was Ashkenazi also who negotiated the peace that concluded the war between Turkey and Venice, and it was his prestige that brought about the revocation by Venice of an edict of expulsion which had been issued against his people in that city.

4

THE capital, with its magnates, courtiers, and diplomats, its palace and harem intrigue, and its international jockeying, presents a striking contrast to other communities in the empire, particularly in the ancient homeland, where men devoted themselves to the study and observance of Talmud and Cabala. By 1521, a sizable community had grown up in Jerusalem, and Safed, the city perched in the hills of Upper Galilee, with its eighteen Talmudic academies and numerous synagogues, became the most important center of Jewish learning in the world.

To Safed in 1538, after a life of exile and wandering, came the wealthy and scholarly Jacob Berab, who dreamed of restoring the ancient Sanhedrin in the motherland as the supreme religious authority for all the communities of the world. He attempted further to revive the practice of ordination or *semicha*, whereby through "the laying of the hands," the right to serve as a rabbi and judge was in olden times conferred upon the scholars of one generation by those of the preceding one. But jealousy arose between the rabbis of Jerusalem headed by Levi ibn Habib, and those of Safed, and Berab's efforts came to naught. Jerusalem, teeming with glorious memories, would not be eclipsed by her northern rival.

But if Berab's attempt to integrate Jewish life by reviving the ancient institutions of Sanhedrin and *semicha* failed, the same end was accomplished in large measure by another man and another method. He was Joseph Karo, poet and scholar, and the instrument he fashioned was a book, the *Shulchan Aruch* (Ready-set Table), which has guided generations of his people in every act of their daily lives. Born in Spain in 1488, Joseph Karo was, shortly after the expulsion, taken by his father to Turkey. He spent thirty-two years of his long life on a vast commentary on the *Four Rows* of Jacob ben Asher, and the *Shulchan Aruch* is really a summary of this commentary. But Karo was a cabalist as well as a legal scholar. He knew Solomon Molcho and was deeply impressed by him, and in Safed, where he believed he was to accomplish a great mission, one of his friends and colleagues was Solomon Alkabez, the author of the strangely beautiful hymn *Lecha Dodi,** the Friday night welcome to the Sabbath Bride which is still part of the synagogue liturgy. Thus a peculiar poetic strain runs through the *Shulchan Aruch*, that legal compendium dealing with prayer and festivals, food and dress, marriage and divorce, business and charity, and all things that concern the life of man from cradle to grave. "Be strong as a leopard, light as an eagle, fleet as a hart, and mighty as a lion, to do the will of thy Father who is in heaven." These words, quoted from an ancient *tanna*, form the opening theme of the *Shulchan Aruch*.

5

JOSEPH KARO, who represents a blending of Talmud and Cabala, died in 1575, surviving by three years the man who made Cabala alone the guide and inspiration for himself and for a little community that gathered around him in Safed. This man was

* *Lecha Dodi* are the first words of the refrain of this hymn: "Come, my friend, to meet the Bride. let us welcome the Sabbath."

Isaac Luria who, born of parents who had come from Germany, was called Ashkenazi Rabbi Isaac. The first letters of the name were, according to custom, combined to make the word *ari*, meaning "lion," and "the Ari" is the name by which Isaac Luria is best known. As a youth he was taken to Egypt, where for several years he lived the life of a hermit near the Nile, developed a mystic system based on the Zohar, and came to look upon himself as the forerunner of the Messiah. He and his followers in Safed, who made up a separate commune, lived with the things "that eye hath not seen nor ear ever heard." Together, in ecstasy, they paid periodic visits to the grave of Simon ben Yochai in nearby Meron.

On Luria's death in 1572 at the age of thirty-eight, the leadership of his mystic community was taken over by Chaim Vital, whose father hailed from Italy. The teachings of the Ari were disseminated before long to all the lands of the Diaspora by men who called themselves "the lion's whelps." One of the outstanding "whelps" was the renowned Talmudic scholar Isaiah Hurwitz of Poland (1570-1628), who in his old age migrated to Palestine where he settled in the Holy City, but had to seek refuge in Safed to escape the persecutions of the local pasha. Another "whelp" was Abraham de Herrera, a prominent member of the important community which had come into being in Amsterdam.

The Cabala of "the lion" and his "whelps," it should be stressed, was not merely an object of study or a system of thought: the creative genius of the Ari transformed it into a collective way of life. Out of its basic conceptions with regard to the emanation or diffusion of the Divine in creation, Luria and his disciples elaborated an applied or "practical" Cabala, the aim of which was to achieve the re-ascent of the individual soul to the Godhead. The system laid special emphasis on ecstasy in prayer and the fervent observance of the Sabbath. Cabala, moreover, was more than nutriment for the individual heart and imagination. Of greater historic significance was its appeal to the longing for national redemption. For the purification of the soul, which was the goal of "practical" Cabala, was intended to prepare it for the coming of the Messiah, every thought and deed being directed to hasten his arrival.

CHAPTER FORTY-ONE

In Germany and Holland

IN THE meantime, a German monk named Martin Luther had launched the first successful challenge to the authority of the Catholic Church, but the religious and social revolutions which followed did little or nothing to improve the lot of the Jewish communities of the north. The nobles and burghers, the artisans and peasants, who rallied to Luther's teachings could not be liquidated as were the Albigensians, the Hussites, and the Marranos; but against the Jews the new sectaries displayed the same old zeal for persecution, and centuries were to elapse before it dawned on men that they could be united in citizenship though divided in religion.

It goes without saying that the segregated denizens of the ghettos had no direct part in the revolt against Rome; indirectly, however, and unwittingly, they played an important and perhaps decisive role. For it was the Bible that served as the chief arsenal of the reformers in their attacks on the pretensions and abuses of the Catholic clergy. Christian scholars mastered the Hebrew language in order to know the Bible in the original. Luther himself spent two years translating the Bible into German, and before long translations appeared in the other European languages also. For the first time, this product of the Jewish genius was brought home to the masses of Europe, and it became the most powerful instrument for the propagation of religious reform.

But, more indirectly perhaps, the Talmud and other Jewish books also played an important part in producing the ferment that resulted in the great schism. In fact, for a number of years before Luther posted his epoch-making ninety-five *theses* on the door of the church in Wittenberg, a bitter controversy had been raging among Christian scholars and clerics over the Jews and their books.

The conflict was set off by Johann Pfefferkorn, a depraved renegade who urged that with the exception of the Bible, all the books of the Jews should be confiscated and burned.

In 1509 this rabid apostate, with the help of the powerful Dominicans, obtained an order from Emperor Maximilian giving him a free hand with the Jewish books, but the following year a new figure appeared on the arena who became the center of the fray. He was Johann Reuchlin, the foremost German scholar of the day. Reuchlin was an enthusiastic student and teacher of the language and books of the Jews and from the brilliant Italian humanist Pico della Mirandola he imbibed a profound veneration for Cabala. Called upon by the emperor to say whether the books should be destroyed, Reuchlin defended them and denounced their detractors. A venomous attack against Reuchlin by Pfefferkorn, printed in the German vernacular under the title of *Handspiegel*, made its appearance, and Reuchlin countered with his famous *Augenspiegel*, also in German, excoriating Pfefferkorn and his abettors and defending the Talmud. Thereafter the *Augenspiegel* and its author were the objects of a relentless pursuit by the Dominicans and their allies, and western Europe became divided into Reuchlinites and anti-Reuchlinites in much the same way as, four centuries later, France was divided into Dreyfusites and anti-Dreyfusites.

For ten years the war, fought chiefly with pamphlets, lawsuits, and investigations, continued. On the side of Pfefferkorn and the Dominicans, with Jacob van Hoogstraten, the Inquisitor and General of the Order in Cologne, at the head, were ranged the forces of bigotry and persecution. On the side of Reuchlin were the men of learning, the so-called humanists, including the gallant and brilliant Ulrich von Hutten, the great Dutch scholar Erasmus, Martin Luther himself, and others whose thoughts were directed to religious reform. The controversy served to open men's eyes to the follies and corruptions of the clergy. A devastating satire appeared entitled *Letters of Obscure Men*, written, some believe, by von Hutten, exposing and ridiculing without mercy the ignorance and vices of priests, monks, and friars. It was a short step from the *Letters of Obscure Men* to the ninety-five *theses* of Martin

Luther. The conflict that raged around the Jewish books now menaced the very foundations of the church.

The War of the Jewish Books was fought not only in Germany but in France and Italy also, and Reuchlin had to stand trial in Rome, as well as in Mayence and Speyer. Inevitably, other interests and passions entered the lists. Thus the Franciscan friars, rivals of the Dominicans, took sides with Reuchlin. Emperor Maximilian II and the worldly Pope Leo X followed a policy of vacillation. They favored Reuchlin, but they dared not show their sympathies openly for fear of the powerful Dominicans. On the other hand, the king of France, who wasted no love on the emperor, and the future king of Spain and emperor, Charles V, took sides against Reuchlin. The University of Paris issued a judgment charging the champion of the Talmud with heresy and ordering him to recant.

The Jewish communities along the Rhine and throughout Germany trembled over the outcome of the conflict. Expulsion and other dangers lowered over them, and they dared not celebrate Reuchlin's victories or lament his defeats too openly. In 1510, while the controversy was at its height, the insane charge of stabbing the host was brought against them in Brandenburg and claimed thirty martyrs.

The matter came finally before the papal court in Rome where it dragged on for six years, with one decision in favor of Reuchlin and a second against him. The second and final verdict was issued in 1520, and it was dictated not by justice but by fear of Luther's revolt, which was making alarming progress and to which Reuchlin and his adherents were lending powerful support.

2

THE progress of the Reformation was bound to produce a messianic effervescence in the ghettos of Germany, for the longing was always quickened by world-shaking events, and Luther's revolt seemed to presage the end of the millennial dominion of Rome. Two Jews, Luther relates, came to him and tried to convert him to their faith, and his attitude toward the people who gave the Christians their Bible and savior began by being deeply sympathetic. *Jesus Was Born a Jew*, is the challenging title of one of his pamphlets, and in it he declares:

> Our fools, the popes, bishops, sophists and monks, these coarse blockheads, dealt with the Jews in such a manner that any Christian would have preferred to be a Jew. Indeed, had I been a Jew and had I seen such idiots and dunderheads expound Christianity, I should rather have become a hog than a Christian.

And Luther concludes with the following advice to his fellow-Christians:

> I would advise and beg everybody to deal kindly with the Jews and to instruct them in the Scriptures: in such a case we could expect them to come over to us.

Luther's aim is clear enough. His purified doctrine, he expected, drawing its inspiration directly from the Bible, would bring the Jews en masse into his fold. It was the old missionary zeal pursuing the old objective, not, however, with cruelty, but with kindness. But it met with the same resistance, and the kindness, as is usually the case, turned sour. In his last years, embittered by other disappointments, Luther's attitude towards the Jews underwent a complete transformation. Now he wrote about "the Jews and their lies," gloated over their expulsion from Spain and more recently from Bohemia, and advised his followers to burn their synagogues, confiscate their books, and tear down their houses. He outdid himself in exercising against them an unusual talent for coarse invective. There was alarm in the ghettos of Germany and Joseph Rosheim, leader of the Jews in Alsace, besought the Strasbourg council for permission, which was denied, to publish a refutation. In general, it was the advice of the later, not the earlier, Luther that the rulers and populace of Protestant Germany followed.

If in the logic of the Reformation there lay the seeds of religious tolerance, it was centuries before they germinated, for logic, alas, is of little avail against habit and self-interest. In 1555, after a generation of religious strife, including a peasant uprising which on Luther's own advice was put down with ruthless cruelty, the princes of Germany adopted the Peace of Augsburg. It permitted each of them to choose between the old and the new faiths, but their subjects were required to follow the faith of their princes, or emigrate. And the Protestant princes, needless to say, were impelled more by political than religious motives; they were tempted not only by the prospect of freedom from the domination of Rome, but by the possessions of the Catholic Church in their domains, which they proceeded to confiscate. The Peace of Augsburg, however, was only a long truce.

The Reformation, moreover, did not follow a single course. Ulrich Zwingli in Zurich, John Calvin in Geneva, John Knox in Scotland, and many others also preached and practiced secession from Rome, but their paths diverged from Martin Luther's and from each other's. Nor would they, any more than Luther, concede religious freedom to those who differed with them. To the Jews it soon became apparent that the Reformation, whatever its ultimate implications might be, meant additional perils, caught as they were between the warring factions of the different faiths.

3

THE Low Countries, today embracing Belgium and The Netherlands, were then part of the scattered domains of the arch-bigot Philip II of Spain, and in 1567 the progress of the Reformation, particularly in the northern provinces, forced the Dutch people into open revolt against their ruler. For heroism and endurance, as well as objective, this revolt may well be compared with the Maccabean struggle against the mad Antiochus and his successors. It was not until the end of the century, and after Philip's power had been dealt a crippling blow by the English seamen who in 1588 destroyed his "Invincible Armada," that the Dutch burghers drove out of their country the armies of the gloomy fanatic, together with the Inquisition and its horrors. And it was this victory of "the weak against the strong, the few against the many" that made it possible for Jews and Marranos to find refuge in those lands.

4

ON THE Day of Atonement of the year 1596, the city magistrates of Amsterdam, amazed and indignant, sent armed men to arrest a group of worshippers whom they took for Catholics. Jacob Tirado, one of the worshippers, explained that they were Marrano fugitives from the Inquisition in Portugal. Although he could only converse with them in Latin, he was able, it appears, to convince the magistrates that the city would benefit from their wealth and commercial connections. Not long afterwards, the little community was allowed to build a synagogue which, in honor of Jacob Tirado, was named the "House of Jacob."

More Marranos fled from Portugal and found asylum in Amsterdam. Somewhat later came refugees from the ghettos of Germany seeking escape from persecution and the terrors of the Thirty Years' War (1618-1648), and still later their number was augmented by fugitives from Poland fleeing from the fury that assailed them with the uprising in 1648 of the Cossacks against the Poles. The land that under the leadership of the great-hearted William of Orange had thrown off the hideous yoke of Spain, became a haven of refuge for the persecuted, at a time when the gates of England and France were still shut against them, and when in Italy, especially in the Papal States, they had fallen on evil days with persecutions of many sorts, crude and refined, practiced upon them. Nor did the Dutch have reason to regret their hospitality, for Jewish wealth and skill contributed in no small measure toward making Holland the leading maritime and trading power of the century. So great indeed were the benefits Holland derived from them that other countries, including Denmark, were anxious to receive them, and they made their way also into the free city of Hamburg.

By 1618 the community in Amsterdam had three synagogues, and twenty years later an academy of learning called "Talmud Torah" was established. It took some time before the three groups, Sephardic, German, and Polish, overcame their mutual aloofness and began to mingle, and it may not be amiss to note that in the same order, these groups later migrated to the New World also, and that there too, for a considerable time, the same aloofness prevailed.

5

ENGLAND was not destined to remain shut against the Jews much longer, and it was Menasseh ben Israel of Amsterdam who opened it. The career of this scholar and statesman, cabalist and man of affairs, is a mirror of his age, Christian as well as Jewish. His friendships embraced the leading lights of the day, including the painter Rembrandt and Hugo Grotius, the savant who laid the foundations of international law. Among those with whom he corresponded was the learned Queen Christina of Sweden. He was rabbi, preacher, and teacher, writer in many languages and printer, and his mind was a strange amalgam of the practical and the mystical.

His cabalistic speculations were, of course, messianic, and his belief in the speedy restoration of Israel was strengthened by a traveler who convinced him that the American Indians were descended from the Lost Ten Tribes. In 1650 he published his faith in his *Hope of Israel*, and from the "Fifth Monarchy Men" of England came a responsive chord. These "Men" believed in the imminent second coming of Jesus, who would establish the fifth and final kingdom on earth, the other four having been the Assyrian, the Persian, the Greek, and the Roman.

It was one of Menasseh ben Israel's convictions, however, that the great fulfillment could not take place until his people were scattered through every land, and England still refused to admit them. But great and startling events had occurred in England, events that could only be messianic in their import. In 1649, the tyrant king Charles I had been led to the execution block; a republic had been established, and at its head stood Oliver Cromwell, a plain God-fearing man, but a soldier and statesman of genius. His followers, the Puritans, drew their inspiration from the heroes of the Bible, Moses and Joshua, Gideon and Saul, and they went into battle singing the psalms of the shepherd-king David. Was it not reasonable to expect that Cromwell and his ministers would remove the ban that forbade the descendants of those heroes and lawgivers to set foot on the soil of England?

The ban, moreover, had to an extent been weakened by the presence in London of a group of wealthy Marranos of whom Antonio Fernandez Carvajal and Simon de Caceres were the most influential. They were both merchants with far-flung connections, which gave them opportunities to serve England not only with their commerce, but with valuable information they were able to gather for the government. Carvajal, who had settled in London about 1635 and some twenty years later returned openly to Judaism, was the owner of ships that sailed to the East Indies and Asia as well as the West Indies and South America. He had agents in every important commercial center in Europe; the merchants in the City of London held him in high esteem and he enjoyed the special protection of the government. De Caceres was the author of a plan for the conquest of Chile which he submitted to Cromwell, offering to organize and command the expedition himself.

6

AS SPOKESMAN for his people before Cromwell and his ministers, Menasseh the mystic and cabalist was powerfully aided by Menasseh the practical man of affairs. He began by translating his *Hope of Israel* from Spanish into Latin and dedicating it to the British Parliament, and in 1652 he was invited to come to London. But it happened that just then the commercial rivalry between England and Holland broke into war, and it was not until three years later that Menasseh laid before the Lord Protector his famous "Humble Address" in which he buttressed his messianic arguments for the readmission of the Jews by pointing out the benefits their wealth and commercial abilities would confer on England. Cromwell was impressed by both arguments: he too was a combination of the mystic and realist.

Menasseh's path in London, however, was not strewn with roses. The lawyers, it is true, found no legal obstacle to the readmission of the Jews, but there were clergymen who raised theological objections and, above all, the London merchants viewed with alarm an influx of competitors. Menasseh ben Israel wrote a spirited reply to the enemies of his people, but shortly afterwards he returned to Holland where he died a sad and broken man. As events proved, however, his mission was not a failure. The gates of England were not formally opened as Menasseh hoped they would be, but his efforts had overcome prejudice and prepared the country if not to welcome, then at least to tolerate, the return of the Jews. Marranos from Spain and Portugal continued to come in, and both Cromwell and his successors permitted them, as fugitives from the hated Inquisition, to remain and openly profess their faith. Quietly and almost unnoticed, other Jews came to England and were allowed to stay. By 1664 there were enough of them in London to establish community life, and Jacob Sasportas, who had traveled to England with Menasseh, became their first rabbi.

7

IN THE summer of 1656, when Menasseh ben Israel was still in London laboring to obtain another asylum for his people, the solemn ban of excommunication was published against a former pupil of his in Amsterdam named Baruch or Benedict Spinoza. The elders of the synagogue found the twenty-four-year-old Baruch guilty of spreading doctrines subversive of their faith and of all religion, and they read him out of their community not only to protect the things they and their fathers had preserved at the risk of their lives, but also in order to disassociate themselves openly from one whose conduct imperiled their standing with their Christian neighbors. In the annals of the Jewish people, that event is not of overshadowing importance, but it looms large in the memory of men because Benedict Spinoza became one of the giants in the history of metaphysical thought.

Some twenty years earlier, in fact, a similar event had occurred in Amsterdam which created a much deeper stir in the community. It was the pronouncement of the ban—and for the second time—upon Uriel Acosta, a former Marrano who in 1617, when he was about thirty years old, escaped from Portugal to Amsterdam and was received into the Jewish fold. Soon afterwards, however, the somber and restless Acosta became intensely dissatisfied. He openly rejected the Talmud, which he found incompatible with the teaching of Scriptures, and laid his views before the community in Venice which, on his refusal to recant, excommunicated him. For fifteen years Acosta lived in Amsterdam as an outcast until, unable to bear it any longer, he agreed to recant. But he was moved not by conviction but despair, and he became even more embittered. He branded the community leaders as Pharisees, using the word, like the Christian theologians, as a stigma and reproach, and denied the immortality of the soul and other Jewish teachings. He dreamed of a religion consisting of faith unencumbered by ritual and observance, and came gradually to deny the authority of the Scriptures also. In 1633 Acosta was put under the ban a second time, and after suffering the shame and hardships of an outcast for another seven years, he again agreed to recant. But the public humiliations that were inflicted upon him during the ceremony of recantation were more than he could bear. Acosta returned to his lodgings, hastily finished a brief autobiography entitled *Specimen of a Human Life,* and shot himself.

Such was the somber tragedy of Uriel Acosta, the memory of which, no doubt, was still fresh in the community when in 1656 the ban of excommunication was pronounced against Baruch Spinoza. In Spinoza's case, however, it led to no tragic consequences. Spinoza had, in fact, withdrawn from the community even before he was excommunicated. He had retired to a village near Amsterdam, and in later years resided in The Hague. He lived serenely, earning his livelihood as a polisher of lenses. All his friends and admirers were Christians. Among those who paid him an extended visit was the illustrious German philosopher Gottfried Leibnitz, who derived some of his basic ideas from Spinoza but later repaid his master with open rejection and derision.

8

THAT the leaders of the Amsterdam community had good reason to disassociate themselves from Spinoza, is indicated by the reception his views met on publication. His *Tractatus Theologico-Politicus,* published anonymously in 1670, was banned by the clergy and suppressed by the States-General of the provinces of Holland, Zealand, and West Friesland. In that work, Spinoza rejects the belief that Moses was the author of the Pentateuch, and contends that with the fall of the Jewish state, the rites and institutions of Judaism had lost their validity—a conclusion defying the group instinct of his people which had led them, after the fall of the Jewish state, to cling to those rites with even greater tenacity.

In this conclusion, as in his basic metaphysical assumptions, Spinoza cannot be reconciled with the teachings of Judaism, notwithstanding the valiant attempts that have been made to do so. Spinoza sees the universe of nature and thought as two of the infinite attributes of the Ultimate Substance, or God, but his universe and his God are fettered in Law and Necessity. It is a static and frozen universe, and the hungry heart beats in it as in a vacuum. Judaism sees the universe as the product of God's creative will, and it sees man endowed with freedom to rise and grow in spiritual stature. Nor is it surprising that the philosopher, immersed in his vast and frigid speculations, should be repelled by religious rites and observance. In relation to their people, both he and Acosta lacked a sense of continuity and progression—the sense of history; and they failed to realize that, by linking every human act with the Divine, the rites of Judaism aimed to regulate the passions that tend to debase human life, and to serve as vehicles for elevating it to higher spiritual levels.

CHAPTER FORTY-TWO

The Great Center in Poland

FROM Spain and Portugal, exiled Jews and fugitive Marranos found asylum, as we have seen, in Italy, in Turkey, in The Netherlands, and later in England; and wherever they came they planted new communities or infused fresh vigor into the old ones. In those countries, however, no concentration arose which, for magnitude and achievement, could be compared with the Spanish community, which was now no more, or with the Babylonian which preceded it. The hegemony of the Diaspora, which belonged first to Babylonia, then to Spain, now fell to a center which arose in eastern Europe.

Where the great rivers that water the steppes of the Ukraine end their courses, Jews had planted their first settlements in what is now the Soviet Union. Centuries before the shadowy career of the Jewish kingdom of the Khazars, whose capital Itil lay at the mouth of the Volga, began, there were Jews in the Crimea who, as early as the first century of the current era, already lived in organized communities. Their language was Greek, and they must have drifted in from Asia and Egypt during the period when the motherland was subject to Rome and perhaps even earlier. The persecutions of the Byzantine emperors drove more of them to the northern coasts of the Black Sea; and Khazars found refuge there when the Russians overthrew their kingdom, as did Karaites from Asia, whose descendants have lived in those regions as a separate Jewish sect to our day.

The warriors who conquered the Khazars hailed from the reaches of the middle Dnieper, and were ruled by the Prince of Kiev, a city to which Jewish traders had made their way at a time when the Russians were still pagans. These traders, it appears, attempted to convert the Russians to the faith that had been adopted by the Khazars. But the prince was assisted in his war against the Khazars by the Byzantine emperor, so he chose instead the Greek Orthodoxy of his ally, which rejected the authority of the pope in Rome. For there had always been rivalry between the bishops of Constantinople and those of Rome, and in 1054 the break between the two churches became final. Toward the end of the tenth century, the Poles were also converted, but they became Roman Catholics, a fact of far-reaching importance for the relations between the two leading Slav nations, as well as for the Jewish communities lying between them.

Moscow and the other principalities into which Russia was divided also became Greek Catholic, and the new church lost no time in persecuting the Jews whose early missionary efforts, it appears, were not wholly fruitless, leaving the Russian clergy with a dread of the "Judaisers" which clung to them for centuries. In Kiev and towns near it, nevertheless, fugitives from Germany, who fled from the fury of the crusaders, were permitted to stay, but the princes of Moscow admitted no foreigners or infidels to their "holy" soil.

For two and a half centuries, Russia was subject to the Tartars, those wild horsemen from central Asia who in 1241 swept westward as far as Germany, and in 1260 overran Palestine. Their domination was brought to an end in 1480 when Ivan III (1462-1505), Duke of Moscow and leading Russian potentate, refused to pay them tribute. His grandson was Ivan IV, called the Terrible (1547-1584), who proclaimed himself the heir of the Byzantine Empire by assuming the title of Caesar, or Czar. In the two centuries that followed, his successors, as we shall see, expanded their domains westward, and toward the end of the eighteenth century swept in beneath their harsh and autocratic scepter the greater portion of a large and vigorous Jewish community which had grown up in Poland.

2

IN POSEN, Kalisz, Cracow, and other cities near the border between Germany and Poland, small groups of Jews must have established themselves in very early times, but it was as refugees from the pogroms of the crusaders that they arrived in Poland in large numbers. They came into a primitive society consisting of nobles and peasant serfs, and they filled the gap between the two classes as craftsmen and traders. The landed gentry, or *shlakhta*, was a numerous and proud caste, but most of its members had little land and revenue. The saying was that a poor nobleman's dog who sat in the middle of his owner's estate rested the tip of his tail on the land of his master's neighbor. But rich or poor, the nobleman could not stain his escutcheon by engaging in useful work. As craftsmen and merchants, therefore, the only rivals the Jews faced were immigrant Germans who, of course, found it profitable to incite the Poles to persecute their Jewish competitors, and found willing allies in the clergy.

The Jews who found refuge in Poland would have fared badly if the kings and the more powerful nobles had not come to their rescue. Not only did the monarchs derive a considerable personal revenue from them, but they could not fail to realize their importance for the prosperity of the country as a whole. The kings like Boleslav the Pious and Casimir the Great (1333-1373) found it useful, therefore, to confirm the rights and immunities of their Jewish subjects by charter, and to facilitate their commercial operations. But not always were the royal charters potent enough to ward off persecution. The Rindfleisch massacres in 1348 sent more and more Jews fleeing into Poland and, particularly in the cities near the German border, the lurid libels against them raised their heads and claimed their victims. Thus, in 1399 the rabbi of Posen and thirteen community notables perished at the stake on the charge of "bleeding the host." In Cracow, a priest in 1407 charged the Jews with slaying a Christian child, and many of them were murdered by the mob which attacked the Jewish quarter. In 1454, the rabid inquisitor John Capistrano, who gloried in the title of the "scourge of the Jews," and whom the Archbishop of Cracow invited to come to Poland, helped the *shlakhta* to pare the powers of King Casimir IV (1447-1492) and terminate the charter of Jewish rights. In Cracow and Posen Jews were again the victims of mob violence.

Nor could the Jews of Poland always count on the protection of the monarchs. There were times when, as in the case of Casimir IV, kings had to make concessions to zealous bishops and arrogant squires, and there were times when they themselves were not inclined to be friendly. Such was the case with Casimir's sons. One of them, John I, on the pretext of shielding them against attack, herded the Jews of Cracow into a ghetto; the other, Alexander, who began by being Grand Duke of Lithuania, plundered and expelled them from his grand duchy. When, however, in 1501 he succeeded his brother to the throne of Poland, and Lithuania became part of the kingdom, he was compelled to let them return, and even incorporated the Jewish charter of Casimir the Great into the constitution. In Lithuania the Jewish settlements, of which the largest were in Grodno, Brest, and Vladimir, were still weak; in Poland, however, the Jews were not to be trifled with, not even by a king: the country's welfare depended too much upon them.

3

FOR a century and a half before 1648, the year of disaster for Polish Jewry, the community increased and prospered. In numbers it grew from 50,000 to 500,000; it developed a rich inner life; it enjoyed wealth and power, as well as a larger measure of internal autonomy than a community of the Diaspora had ever exercised.

The period, of course, had its darker aspects also. In the more populous places, the churchmen, as well as the burghers with whom the Jews competed, made no secret of their hostility. In the villages they were dependent on the whims of idle and brutal squires, and even the peasants were not always friendly, for they were oppressed by the gentry who utilized the Jews as instruments of exploitation.

During the reign of Sigismund I (1506-1548) the Protestant Reformation began to make inroads into Poland, and the clergy, more watchful than ever, accused the Jews also of seeking to make converts. This, and the charge that they were plotting treason with the Turks were proven false; nevertheless they served their purpose. The Diet enacted laws barring Jews from many occupations, restricting their trade, and even ordering them to wear a special headgear of yellow cloth, although the last provision could not be enforced. The king refused to protect those Jews who were living on the estates of the nobles: since he derived no income from them, he was not, he declared, "obliged to secure justice for them."

The same attitude was taken by Sigismund Augustus (1548-1572), although he extended the autonomy of the Jewish communities or *kahals*, permitting lawsuits in which both parties were Jews to be judged in accordance with Jewish law by rabbis or elders of the *kahal*. He also ordered disputes between Jews and Christians to be tried in the royal courts instead of the local tribunals whose judges were not, as a rule, impartial. For the rest, in the campaign to check the progress of the Reformation, the old libels against the Jews were found useful for inflaming the religious fervor of the populace. The blood accusation cropped up again and again, in spite of royal edicts against it. In the towns, the councils devised a variety of restrictions against the Jewish merchants, and at times the mob broke into the ghetto and there was looting and bloodshed. Such was the case in Posen in 1577 and 1618, in Vilna in 1592, in Cracow in 1637.

The attack on the Jewish quarter of Posen in 1618 was led by the teachers and students of the local Jesuit academy. With suppression of the Protestant Reformation as their primary objective, the Polish Jesuits, in the reign of Stephen Batory (1572-1586), acquired control of the schools, and Stephen's successor, Sigismund III (1586-1632), surrounded himself with Jesuit advisers. The Jesuits taught their pupils to hate Jews and Protestants, and their pious hostility extended to members of the Greek Orthodox Church, many of whom lived under Polish rule, for as far back as

1320 the Russian principality of Kiev had been conquered by Lithuania, which later became part of Poland. The Jews suffered at the hands of the Jesuits directly; and indirectly, as we shall see, the persecution of the Greek Orthodox Russians was largely responsible for the catastrophe which swept down upon them in 1648.

4

IN SPITE of the shocks which disturbed it and the dangers lurking around it, the current of Jewish life in Poland ran deep and strong, and no better mirror of this life existed than the annual fairs which took place in the city of Lublin. To these fairs, which were held between Purim and Passover, came Jewish merchants from every province in Poland and its outlying possessions. They came from Great Poland, from Little Poland, and from Galicia or Red Russia, of which the principal city was Lemberg, now called Lwow. They came also from Lithuania, Volhynia, Little Russia, Podolia, and the distant settlements beyond the Dnieper in the Ukraine. They came in sheepskin coats and cloth caps, as well as in silk caftans and great hats of fur. The stalls were crammed with the goods they manufactured: cloth of wool and silk, articles of wood and metal, clothing and shoes, necessities and luxuries. There was considerable traffic also in religious articles: phylacteries and prayer shawls, silver breastplates and crowns for Torah scrolls, great leather-bound folios of the Talmud printed in Lublin itself, and Bibles printed in Cracow and Italy. The fairs swarmed with Poles, Lithuanians and Russians, and there were German merchants also who scowled in the direction of their Jewish competitors.

The economic life of Polish Jewry stood mirrored at the fair, and how richer and more varied it was than that of their brothers in Germany! For in spite of legal restrictions, the Polish Jews followed practically every calling. They were merchants and manufacturers, artisans and farmers. They cut the forests for timber, and opened up the salt mines. Many of them, especially in the outlying districts, lived as *arendars* or renters on the estates of the gentry, operating flour mills and taverns and looking after the interests of the indolent nobles in their relations with the peasants, a function that brought more peril than profit.

But it was not only to buy and sell that they came to the Lublin fairs. Committees representing the widely scattered *kahals* came to engage rabbis for their communities, or to invite a famous *maggid* (preacher) to visit them. Fathers brought their promising sons to be enrolled in the renowned Yeshivah of Lublin, a Talmudic academy authorized in 1567 by King Sigismund Augustus himself; or they sought out the most brilliant students to be their sons-in-law, for learning and piety were more highly esteemed than wealth or lineage.

5

THE most important event, however, which took place at the Lublin fairs, was the meeting of the "Council of the Four Lands," the *Vaad Arba Arazoth*, as it was called in Hebrew. The four "lands" which this body represented were Great Poland, Little Poland, Galicia and Volhynia, the communities of Lithuania having in 1620 set up a council of their own. Under the *Vaad*, which acted, of course, under royal authority, the Jews of Poland achieved a broader and more effective autonomy than had the Babylonian community under the Exilarchs or the Spanish community under the *aljamas*. The *Vaad* has been compared to the ancient Sanhedrin of the motherland, but it was more directly representative. Its thirty-odd members, some of them rabbis, most of them laymen, came from the principal *kahals* of the "four lands." Each "land" had its provincial council, which elected members to the national *Vaad*. Like the Sanhedrin, the *Vaad* was vested with judicial as well as legislative powers: the most important disputes came to it for adjudication.

The ordinances, or *takkanoth*, which the Council enacted aimed to strengthen the internal life of the community and to promote good relations between them and their Christian neighbors. It appointed *shtadlanim*, or agents, to protect their common interests with the king and his ministers: to save them, if possible, from being burdened with special taxes, to be on guard lest their rights and privileges be revoked or impaired. An important duty of the *Vaad* was to allocate among the provinces the taxes which the government levied upon the community as a whole. It did the same with other funds which had to be raised for the general interest, and in turn, each provincial council allocated its share among the local *kahals*.

But the Council of the Four Lands was even more zealous and successful in regulating the inner life of Polish Jewry. It labored to enforce fair practices in commercial transactions with Jews and Christians alike. It prescribed modesty and restraint in dress and demeanor so as not to arouse envy and ill will. It enjoined the strict performance of religious duties, and one of its most important concerns was the education of the young.

6

IN POLAND, as in the other lands of the Dispersion, it was almost impossible to find an illiterate Jew in an age when, among their neighbors, only members of the clergy and the higher nobility were taught to read and write. The Jewish girl was required to know only her prayers, which she was taught at home, but every boy began his schooling when he was four or five, and continued it for at least seven or eight years.

The elementary school, or *cheder*,* kept the boy eight to ten hours a day. The *cheder* was maintained by the tuition fees of the parents, and for orphans and destitute children the *kahal* provided a free school, called *Talmud Torah*. Reading was followed by the Scriptures, which the boy learned to translate into his Yiddish vernacular; then came the commentary of Rashi, the Mishnah, and even the Talmud. The more able and studious went to the Yeshivoth, or Talmudic academies, where they continued with the Talmud and the commentaries of the great rabbis. Drawn by the fame of some illustrious scholar, youths left the shelter of their homes and flocked to the Yeshivoth in Lublin, Ostrog, Cracow, Lemberg, and other cities, where they spent their days, and often also their nights, in intense study, living on the bounty of strangers, who considered it a pious deed to entertain poor students at their boards. Some secular subjects, like science and philosophy, were frowned upon as a menace to faith, but it is doubtful if there has ever existed a community, Jewish or non-Jewish, where the accepted learning was as widespread as it was among the Jews of Poland. There was no learned caste among them; the study of

* The word means "room."

Torah resounded in every home; and every community, large and small, had numerous accomplished scholars, men who earned their bread by the sweat of their brow and found their delight in study. For the rest, the Talmud was not merely an academic subject for them: under the autonomy they enjoyed, their life was regulated by it. Criminal as well as civil cases which came before the rabbis and *dayyanim* (judges) were decided in accordance with Talmudic law.

7

ABOVE this high intellectual plateau rose numerous towering peaks, men of commanding authority, who left their impress on their own and succeeding generations. In 1541 King Sigismund I appointed Sholom Shakhna, who was rabbi of Lublin, as chief rabbi of Little Poland. Shakhna is credited with introducing the method known as *pilpul* in the study of the Talmud, a method that delights in keen and minute analysis, finding differences in things apparently alike and agreements in things apparently different. *Pilpul* has been praised and condemned, but it gained vogue and became the accepted method of study in Poland. A pupil of Shakhna was Moses Isserles (1520-1572), for many years head of the Yeshivah in Cracow, who leaned towards philosophy and was attracted by the Rambam's *Guide to the Perplexed*. With certain additions which Isserles made to the *Shulchan Aruch* of Joseph Karo, that compendium of Talmudic law became the manual and guide of Polish Jewry.

Solomon Luria, who made the Yeshivah of Ostrog in Volhynia a renowned center of learning, was both a friend and opponent of Isserles. Luria was a bold and independent spirit who disapproved of *pilpul* and was attracted by Cabala; each accused the other of incomplete loyalty to the Talmud. There were other scholars in Poland who delved into the mysteries of the Zohar and were attracted by the system of applied Cabala of Isaac Luria and Chaim Vital. Among the people generally, moreover, cabalistic notions were rife, and the advent of the Messiah, who would redeem them from exile and restore their ancient glory, was not relegated to "the end of days," but, on the contrary, was expected to occur "speedily, in our day."

There were also among the great scholars of Poland not a few who combined learning with statesmanship. Mordecai Jaffe (1530-1612), who compiled a Talmudic code of his own and, besides, was at home in astronomy and mathematics, served a number of times as president of the Council of the Four Lands, as did Joshua Falk, rabbi of Lublin. Other illustrious names of the first half of the seventeenth century are those of Meir of Lublin, Samuel Edels, Joseph Serkes, and Yom Tob Lipman Heller, a profound scholar and a man of great courage, who, though born in Germany, lived the last twenty-two years of his life in Poland and, at his death in 1654, was rabbi of Cracow. His stormy career illustrates some of the inner tensions which at times disturbed the peace of Jewish life amid the anomalies surrounding it. As chief rabbi of Prague, Heller antagonized powerful members of the community, who charged him with laying upon them an unjust share of the taxes which the emperor levied upon the community as a whole. In their feud against him, they resorted to a method which the history of their people, as well as every healthy instinct, should have taught them to shun: they accused him before the Imperial Government in Vienna of having insulted the Christian faith in his writings. Heller was removed from office, imprisoned, and compelled to pay a large fine. On his release, he migrated to Poland, where he resumed his distinguished career; he occupied a number of rabbinical posts, playing an important part also in the Council of the Four Lands.

CHAPTER FORTY-THREE

The Disaster of 1648

The long reign of Sigismund III, which witnessed a marked growth of Jesuit influence in Poland and a corresponding rise in hostility against the Jews, ended in 1632, and the *shlakhta* elected his son Vladislav (1632-1648) to succeed him. The right of electing the monarch had, since 1572, been exercised by the nobles, whose power to paralyze the government of Poland was assured by the preposterous *liberum veto*, a constitutional provision which enabled a single member of the Diet, by pronouncing the formula "I do not permit," to make legislation impossible. A grave crisis was impending for Poland, but the "intelligence quotient" of her statesmanship was never lower. In 1643, for example, the Diet fixed the legal profit of Christian merchants at seven per cent, and of Jewish merchants at three. It did not, apparently, occur to the noble legislators that the law made it mandatory for Jewish merchants to undersell and thus drive out of business the very people whom they were so eager to protect.

The new monarch nourished designs for extending the boundaries of Poland at the expense of the Tartars and the Turks, designs for which he counted on the loyalty of the Cossacks, his warlike subjects east of the Dnieper River. But he died in 1648 without obtaining the approval of the *shlakhta*, and the same year the Cossacks launched a revolt against their Polish rulers and oppressors, setting off a train of events which convulsed the kingdom for more than a decade, and brought death and devastation to hundreds of Jewish communities.

2

THE Cossacks, whose name stems from a Tartar word meaning "freebooters," lived on both sides of the Dnieper and owed allegiance to the kings of Poland, who found them useful as a barrier against the Tartars and Turks. Many of them were still nomads, their principal occupation and passion being to make plundering forays on their neighbors; but in many places settled communities of peasant Cossacks had sprung up whose land, however, belonged to Polish nobles. The Polish kings permitted the Cossacks a large measure of autonomy, with the right of choosing their own chief, or hetman, but their real masters were their landlords who kept them in virtual bondage. A fierce hatred against their oppressors sprang up among the wild and primitive Cossacks, and it became greatly intensified when the Jesuits added religious persecution to the economic oppression of the gentry. For the Cossacks were Greek Orthodox, and the Jesuits applied against them, as they did against the Jews, the general policy of making it as hard as possible for anyone in Poland to be a non-Catholic. Already in 1635 and 1636, the Cossacks had risen up in arms, but they were cruelly put down and their ancient rights declared forfeit.

In the fierce hostility between Cossacks and Poles, the Jews were caught as between the upper and nether millstones, for both landlords and Jesuits used them as instruments of oppression. The nobles, who preferred the pleasures of the big cities and rarely lived on their estates, employed them as stewards, with orders to wring the largest possible revenue out of their Cossack serfs. Nor did the Jewish *arendars* to whom the gentry sold the liquor and other concessions, add to the good will of the primitive peasants. But an even greater danger lurked in a device contrived by the Jesuits and designed to humiliate the Cossacks: they placed the keys to the Greek Orthodox churches in the custody of stewards or innkeepers, thus compelling the Cossacks to apply to Jews for the use of their churches.

3

AWARE of their peril, the Jews relied on the Polish lords to protect them, but the year 1648 proved how utterly vain was that reliance. Early that year, the Cossack hetman Bogdan Chmelnitzki raised the standard of revolt, made an alliance with the Tartars of Crimea, and in May, his combined forces inflicted a decisive defeat on the Polish army. Now the Greek Orthodox peasants on both sides of the Dnieper left their plows and joined the uprising to avenge themselves upon the Catholic landlords and their minions. The Cossacks were transformed into bands of ravening beasts, and one after another the little Jewish communities east of the Dnieper were wiped out. They butchered Jews and Poles alike, but reserved their most hideous tortures for the Jews.

East of the River Bug, the fortified city of Nemirov in Little Russia drew thousands of fugitives from the villages and towns which lay in the path of the rebels. The Cossacks besieged the city, but the Jewish refugees defended it with skill and courage. One day, the defenders were overjoyed to see an army with Polish banners approach the city. They opened the gates, but it was a Cossack horde in Polish uniforms whom they admitted. Together with the Russian inhabitants of the city, the Cossacks fell upon the Jews and massacred six thousand of them; among the victims were the rabbi of Nemirov, Yechiel Michel ben Eliezer, and his aged mother.

Across the River Bug, southwest of Nemirov, lay the town of Tulchin where some fifteen hundred Jews, including a number who succeeded in escaping from Nemirov, took refuge. The Jews baffled every attempt of the Cossacks to take the town, and they were assisted by several hundred Poles who had solemnly sworn to stand together with them to the last. The besiegers sent word to the Poles, promising to spare them if they would betray the Jews, and the Polish gentry accepted the proposal. When the Jews discovered the treachery, they prepared to wipe out their faithless allies, but their rabbi, Aaron ben Meir, arose and warned them that by punishing their betrayers, they would draw down upon their people the wrath of the Poles throughout the kingdom. "Let us rather perish," he cried, "and not endanger the lives of our brethren in all the places of their Dispersion!" So the Jews spared their betrayers, and when the Cossacks entered the town they were herded into an enclosure and given the choice of baptism or death. Without exception, they chose death, sanctifying the Name with the *Shema* on their lips.

4

THE bloody tide rose higher, sweeping northward along the Dnieper and westward into Volhynia and Galicia, and engulfing the Jewish communities which lay in its path. The toll of martyrs grew to scores of thousands. Some saved their lives by fleeing to the Tartars, who took them as captive slaves to Turkey, where they were ransomed by their coreligionists. There were women who were spared by the Cossacks only to be forced into baptism and marriage with their captors. The story is told of one girl who assured her enamored captor that she possessed magic powers. "Shoot at me," she commanded him, "and you will see that no bullets can harm me." The simple peasant obeyed, and the girl found the death she longed for.

The Polish nobility and their demoralized retainers failed to rise to the occasion, the only exception being the gallant Count Jeremiah Vishnevitzki who, though commanding but a small force, routed many Cossack bands and took Jewish communities under his protection. But he was unable to stem the raging flood. In September, Chmelnitzki overwhelmed a picked army of 40,000 Poles, and Poland lay open to him in every direction. He laid siege to Lemberg and was bought off by a large sum, most of which came from the Jews of the city. His march towards Lublin and Warsaw was blocked by the stronghold of Zamosc, but he found compensation in wiping out numerous Jewish communities round about.

In the meantime Vladislav IV died, and the country was further paralyzed by the confusion and intrigue which always attended the election of a new monarch. In the spring of 1649, the Cossacks, after a vain attempt by the new king John Casimir (1648-1669) to come to terms with the hetman, were again on the warpath, and more Jewish communities were obliterated. Finally in August of that year, the Poles, after suffering further defeats, accepted Chmelnitzki's terms, which contained a provision that Jews were to be excluded from the regions inhabited by the Cossacks. The peace proved only an eighteen-month truce, but in the interval the Council of the Four Lands labored heroically to salvage and heal, uniting broken families and bringing forced converts back to the faith.

When, early in 1651, the war blazed up again, the hetman found himself facing a new Polish army. John Casimir had determined to rely no longer on the nobility and their retainers. He created a people's militia, which included a regiment consisting entirely of Jews. In July, Chmelnitzki suffered an ignominious defeat. He was forced to accept a new treaty which restored the right of the Jews to live in the Cossack territories.

5

BUT the wily Cossack chieftain was not at the end of his resources. Three years later he transferred his allegiance from the King of Poland to the Czar of Russia, and the same year the armies of the Czar, with strong contingents of Cossacks, marched into Poland. The war that followed was one of the most ruthless in history, but those who suffered most were the Jews. Now the proud communities of Moghilev, Smolensk, Vitebsk, Polotsk,

Minsk, Kovno, Vilna, and many others were added to the black roster.

A year later, the communities in the west were drawn into the maelstrom. This time the enemy came from the north. He was Charles X of Sweden, who quickly overran Great Poland and Little Poland; but the woes the Jews suffered in those provinces were inflicted not so much by the Swedes as by the Poles. The Swedes, who were Protestants, were welcomed by their Polish coreligionists, and when the Catholic Poles turned on the invaders and forced them out, they charged all non-Catholics, including the Jews, with treason. With regard to the Jews, they had, it seemed to them, sufficient proof: the Swedes, although they plundered and burned many of the Jewish communities of the west, had failed to visit upon them the same horrors as the Muscovites and Cossacks were inflicting upon those of the north and east. The Poles lost no time in making up for the omission. The Protestant Poles were granted pardon, but, as the Swedes retreated, the Jewish inhabitants were tortured and massacred, the Poles differing from the Cossacks only in that they gave their victims the choice of embracing Catholicism instead of Greek Orthodoxy. Nearly all the communities in the districts of Posen, Kalisz, Piotrokov, and Cracow were annihilated. The synagogues of Posen and Cracow were confiscated and bestowed upon the Dominican friars.

6

IT WAS not until 1660 that the storm which blew upon Poland from every point of the compass and claimed, according to some estimates, half a million Jewish victims and some seven hundred Jewish communities, began to abate. Many who succeeded in escaping the terror, as well as those who were ransomed from slavery, brought the tragedy of Polish Jewry vividly home to the communities of western Europe and the Turkish Empire. But among them were eminent scholars who established new centers of Talmudic learning in their places of refuge.

In Poland the Jews, despite all their heroic exertions, never quite regained their former prosperity and power. The material devastation they suffered, as well as the primitive passions which the storm unleashed against them, would have made recovery difficult enough. But in addition, the labor of reconstruction had to be carried on in a country greatly reduced in territory, and afflicted to an even higher degree by its traditional weaknesses and inner tensions.

CHAPTER FORTY-FOUR

False Messiahs

But the storms of persecution and terror, however great the havoc they wrought, were unable to quench the hope of restoration in the heart of the exiles. It was, in fact, in times of direst woe that hope shone brightest, and from time to time across the centuries, as we have seen, it converged upon messianic pretenders who rose up like mirages in a desert and beckoned the wanderers. Whether they called themselves Messiahs or precursors of the Messiah, their rise was sure to create a ferment, and their fall leave behind them a trail not only of disillusion and shame, but of tenacious, desperate loyalty.

Even while the great community of Poland was being subjected to its ordeal by fire and sword, a messianic movement was going forward in the Turkish Empire which, in the range and depth of its repercussions as well as in the persistence of its aftermath, far surpassed any similar event in the annals of the Diaspora. It was in 1648, the year of disaster for Polish Jewry, that, in the city of Smyrna, Sabbatai Zevi, a youth of twenty-two, solemnly performed in the presence of a small group of followers the forbidden act of uttering aloud the Ineffable Name of God. The Name, it was held, could only be spoken after the coming of the Messiah, and Sabbatai pronounced it in order to proclaim that the longed-for Redeemer, who was none other than himself, had at last arrived. Thus began a messianic career filled with strange events and fantastic figures, rousing people all over the far-flung Dispersion to frenzied enthusiasm and reckless deeds, and leaving in its wake a devotion which has lingered on to this day.

2

YOUNG Sabbatai believed in himself no less ardently than did his followers. Talmudic studies had scant attraction for him: he was lured instead by the Zohar, and especially by the system of applied Cabala as elaborated by Isaac Luria. Sabbatai fasted a great deal and performed many ablutions. He gave himself up to solitude and mystic rites, and knew the ecstasies of self-mortification. He knew also that in 1648 cabalists expected the reign of the Messiah to begin, and he was informed of the belief held by Christian mystics, particularly the Fifth Monarchy Men of England, that the restoration of the Jews and the beginning of the millennium would occur in 1666. His father, who was the agent in Smyrna for an English trading company, had ample occasion to learn what people in England were thinking.

For nearly twenty years Sabbatai Zevi kept his mission within bounds, for he found not only adherents but also opponents. The rabbis of his native city excommunicated him, forcing him to go into exile. In his journeys, which took him to Constantinople, Salonika, Cairo, Jerusalem, and other cities, most of the rabbis repudiated him. But wherever he went he found people who were fascinated by him. He was tall and handsome, his manner was grave and stately, he seemed always wrapt in mystery and exaltation, and when he spoke or sang he thrilled his listeners with his beautiful voice.

His circle of devotees continued to grow, a motley aggregation of simple and pious folk, hysterical mystics and practical men of affairs, with a sprinkling of impostors. In Constantinople a preacher named Abraham Yakini displayed a book in which Sabbatai Zevi was designated as the Messiah. In Cairo the master of the mint, Raphael Joseph Chelebi, a man of wealth and station but also a fervent mystic, became an ardent follower of Sabbatai. He enabled him to win enormous popularity by providing him with a large sum to relieve the destitute community in Jerusalem, for the disaster in Poland had stopped the flow of charity from that country, and, in addition, the community in Jerusalem suffered from the extortions of Turkish officials. In Gaza, Sabbatai found a powerful supporter in Nathan Benjamin Levi, a youth of twenty who proclaimed himself to be the prophet Elijah reincarnated and the forerunner of the Messiah. Nathan, who became one of Sabbatai's principal lieutenants, promised a series of miraculous events, including the bloodless conquest of the Turkish Empire and the rest of the world, which would speedily elevate Sabbatai Zevi to the kingdom and the power and the glory ordained for the Messiah.

As if to make sure the drama would be complete, a romance entered into it as fantastic as any of its other ingredients. Sabbatai Zevi was sojourning in Cairo in the home of the wealthy Chelebi when it came to his ears that a beautiful maiden named Sarah was looking for the Messiah whose wife, she declared, she was destined to become. Sarah was a native of Poland where both her parents had perished in the Cossack uprising. She had escaped from a nunnery where she was being brought up, and when she was found one morning wandering in the Jewish cemetery, she affirmed it was the spirit of her father that had taken her there. Sarah was enabled to join a brother in Amsterdam where she returned to her father's faith, and before long went journeying through Germany and Italy to fulfill her destiny. The fact that the lady's reputation for chastity was not of the highest mattered nothing to Sabbatai and his followers: the prophet Hosea, it was pointed out, was also married to a loose woman. In the career of a Messiah, in fact, not only persecution but even blemishes could be interpreted as confirming his mission. Sabbatai Zevi had her conducted from Leghorn to Cairo where she captivated him and his followers, and the marriage was duly solemnized.

3

SHORTLY afterwards the Messiah and his mate, with a retinue of devout enthusiasts, set out for his native city, and the journey was a triumphal procession. It was now the fall of 1665: the mystic and momentous year 1666 was at hand. The Messiah was preceded by heralds who prophesied his coming. In Jerusalem, the rabbis were hostile, but in Aleppo, and above all in his native Smyrna, he received a royal reception. In the synagogue of Smyrna the horn of annunciation was sounded, and the joyous multitude shouted "Long live our king, our Redeemer!"

The news spread rapidly. Envoys of the Messiah, chief among them Samuel Primo of Jerusalem and Nathan of Gaza, carried it to Salonika, Venice, Amsterdam, Hamburg, and London. A wave of delirious joy swept through the ghettos of the world. Deliverance was at hand, deliverance and restoration for the exiles and outcasts of the earth! Men fasted and prayed to make themselves worthy of the boon, and they neglected their occupations or wound up their affairs in preparation for the return to Palestine. In the spring of 1666 the entire community of Avignon, for example, was ready to depart.

Nor was it the naive masses alone who were infected by the strange fever. Many of the leaders—rabbis, Talmudists, scholars, and philosophers—succumbed to the frenzy. In Smyrna the rabbi, Chaim Benveniste, was a devotee of the Messiah. In Venice he had the support of the rabbinate and of the distinguished cabalist, Moses Zacuto. In Hamburg there was public jubilation, and hard-headed merchants liquidated their affairs to be ready for the great call. The influential community of Amsterdam went almost entirely Sabbatian. There the enthusiasts included the rabbis Isaac Aboab and Moses Raphael d'Aguilar; the president of the community, Abraham Pereira; and the philosopher Benjamin Mussafia. Even the imperturbable Spinoza responded to it, though in a manner vague and pale: his Christian friend and admirer, the eminent savant Heinrich Oldenberg, wrote him from London that the return of the Israelites "may bring about a revolution in all things"; and many other Christians were also stirred by the sensational news. There were congregations where special prayers were recited for the new redeemer, and in some communities it became dangerous to deny his Messiahship. The zealots and envoys of the pretender who, as is always the case with disciples, went beyond the claims of their master, propagated the most fantastic notions about their idol—notions that bore a close resemblance to the Christian doctrine of the Trinity.

Nevertheless, the extent of the aberration should not be exaggerated. Although, as in every social ferment, the center of the stage was held by the fanatics, the great majority of the people are believed to have held aloof from the frenzy. The *kofrim*, or unbelievers, as the Sabbatians styled their opponents, became more numerous and determined, when in the name of the new Messiah his followers attempted to abolish some of the basic practices of Judaism, ordering, for example, that the Fast of the Ninth of Ab, as well as other fasts, should be changed to days of rejoicing, "for ye shall weep no more . . . because I have appeared." The change, it is true, was in accord with cabalistic doctrine touching the messianic era, but it shocked and alarmed the great number of doubters, to say nothing of those who had definitely rejected the claims of the pretender. Among the latter, one of the most energetic and uncompromising was Jacob Sasportas, rabbi of the new community in London who, to escape the plague that was raging in that city, was now living in Hamburg.

4

THE year 1666, ordained for momentous events, had now begun; and Sabbatai Zevi, accompanied by a retinue of followers, left Smyrna, where he was wielding absolute power, and set sail for Constantinople where he was to achieve his messianic mission. There followed a series of grotesque events which are easy to narrate in a spirit of farce, if not for the suffering and hope out of which they grew and the anguished frustration they produced. Nor is it possible to dismiss the leading actor of this incredible drama as a mere impostor, despite the pitiful and unheroic act with which he climaxed his career. The solution of the riddle must be sought in the contradictions of an abnormal psychology, operating in an atmosphere charged with intense longing and apocalyptic dreams.

The ship that bore him and his "prophets" was compelled by a storm to land on the coast of the Dardanelles. There he was met by Turkish officers who arrested him and brought him in chains to Constantinople, for the grand vizier, Ahmed Coprili, was aware of the strange ferment that was agitating the Jews of the empire and many non-Jews also. Ahmed considered the agitation dangerous, but he felt it would be even more dangerous to exasperate the followers of Sabbatai by extreme measures. For two months he kept the pretender under lock in Constantinople, then, being compelled to leave the capital on an urgent matter of state, the grand vizier thought it best to transfer him to the fortress of Abydos on the Dardanelles. Strangely enough, both imprisonments only added to Sabbatai's power and glory. In the capital he was the sensation of the day, and Turks as well as Jews flocked to see him and were deeply impressed by him. In Abydos his followers had free access to him; it became a place of pilgrimage for devotees from near and far, and in his prison Sabbatai held court like a monarch. Indeed, his imprisonment was looked upon as an essential part of his messianic career. Sabbatai's lieutenants spread the news of his "elevation" far and wide, and excitement in Jewish communities on the three continents continued to mount. Many more prepared for the great migration, but there was also considerable opposition, and sometimes the dissensions assumed violent forms.

5

IT HAPPENED that among the pilgrims to *Migdal Oz,* the "Tower of Strength," as Sabbatai's adherents called his prison at Abydos, there were two who came from Poland, and they informed the august prisoner that in their country a certain Nehemiah Cohen, who pretended to be a prophet, while proclaiming the Messianic kingdom to be at hand, failed to name Sabbatai Zevi as the Messiah. Sabbatai summoned Nehemiah to appear before him, but the prophet from Poland, who in due course arrived, would not recognize him. Abydos became a dangerous place for Nehemiah so he fled to Adrianople where he turned Moslem and informed the governor that the Sabbatian movement was a plot to put an end to the rule of the sultan.

The "plot" was conveyed to Sultan Mohammed IV, Sabbatai was removed to Adrianople, and the sultan and his ministers met to decide what to do with him. The sultan himself, it is reported, was inclined to drastic action, not excluding the extermination of all the Messiah's followers in his empire. Various proposals were considered and rejected, and finally the sultan's physician, another Jew who had turned Moslem, was sent off to persuade Sabbatai to do likewise. The physician succeeded beyond all expectations! On a day in September 1666, Sabbatai, conducted into the sultan's presence, performed the gesture which he had obviously rehearsed in advance: he removed his Jewish headgear and put on a Turkish turban. The Messiah became Mehemet Effendi and a pensioner of the sultan.

Various explanations have been offered for the sudden act of betrayal, of which the most generous assumes that in that way alone could Sabbatai have saved his adherents in the Turkish Empire from destruction. He did not, of course, save them or his followers in other lands from bitter shame and confusion. Nevertheless the movement he started did not come to an end: even his conversion, it was believed, was a necessary part of his messianic calling! He himself encouraged the belief by asserting that "God has made me an Ishmaelite," and by leading a double life as a sort of Marrano Mohammedan. Unrepentant enthusiasts, old and new, men like Samuel Primo, Nathan of Gaza, the physician and cabalist Abraham Michael Cardoso, the preacher Mordecai of Eisenstadt, and others, journeyed far and wide throughout the Jewish world, offering weird theories to explain the Messiah's apostasy, and exhorting the faithful to remain steadfast. Sabbatai was unable to maintain his double role of teaching Cabala to Moslems and preaching Islam to Jews. He was finally banished to the town of Dulcigno in Albania where, in 1676, he died.

6

FOR another half century and more the ground swell of Sabbatianism continued to disturb Jewish communities in different parts of the world. In Salonika it gave rise to the Mohammedan sect known as the Donmeh, or Dissenters, which may have its votaries to this day. Originally, the Donmeh were a group of Jews who were led to believe that a lad named Jacob Querido was the son and reincarnation of Sabbatai. When they found themselves menaced by the hostility of the Jewish and Turkish authorities they became Mohammedans. Secretly, however, they clung to their Sabbatian beliefs and, by banning intermarriage with other Moslems, they have been able to preserve their identity. In Poland, the Sabbatian heresy is associated with the names of Judah the Saint of Dubno and Chaim Malak. The first was a simple and devout soul who, when he found himself an object of suspicion, set out for Palestine with a large troop of followers, some of whom managed to reach Jerusalem where they could not, however, maintain themselves. The second was a dubious character who, after migrating with Judah to Palestine, followed a restless career which took him to Salonika and Constantinople, then back to Poland, always preaching faith in the lost Redeemer.

But the most amazing and unscrupulous of the Sabbatian apostles and adventurers was Nehemiah Chiya Chayun whose trail takes us into nearly every land where Jews dwelt. In Smyrna and Jerusalem, in Venice and Prague, in Berlin and Amsterdam—wherever he appeared he created a sensation by his personal glamour and his cabalistic extravaganzas, which included a new trinitarian doctrine. He kept shooting like a baleful meteor through the communities of Asia and Europe, bringing confusion and strife wherever he came. Excommunicated by the rabbis in Palestine, he retrieved his fortunes in Prague with the aid of the rabbi of that city, the wealthy and scholarly David Oppenheim. In Amsterdam, he gave rise to a serious feud between the Sephardic and Ashkenazic communities of that city, finding favor with the Portuguese rabbi Solomon Ayllon, himself suspected of being tarred with the Sabbatian brush, and bitterly opposed by Chacham Zevi, the Ashkenazic rabbi, perhaps the most distinguished scholar of his generation. Victory already lay within Chayun's grasp when a flood of excommunications against him poured into Amsterdam from other lands, and he was forced to resume his travels, winning fresh victories in Turkey but compelled finally to end his adventures and impostures as an exile in North Africa.

7

THE Sabbatian virus lingered on, and as late as 1750 it was still potent enough to produce a disturbance which rocked the Jewish world. The commotion had its center in "the three communities" of Hamburg, Altona, and Wandsbeck, which really constituted one, and which that year chose as rabbi the eminent Jonathan Eybeschuetz instead of Jacob Emden, Chacham Zevi's son who, like his father, was a relentless enemy of the Sabbatian heresy. Shortly afterwards, Emden, together with some German rabbis, accused Eybeschuetz of being the author of secret formulas which recognized Sabbatai Zevi as the Messiah. Eybeschuetz denied the charge, and a bitter controversy ensued which divided Jewish communities throughout Europe. In Poland, nearly all the rabbis supported Eybeschuetz. Each side issued edicts of excommunication against the other, there were threats of violence, and the matter came before the senate of the free city of Hamburg and, since Altona belonged to Denmark, before the Danish courts and the Danish king himself. First Emden was the victor and the rabbi was removed from his post. But Eybeschuetz was a resourceful man and a hard fighter. He won fresh supporters, Christian as well as Jewish, and in 1756, after the controversy had dragged on for six years, Eybeschuetz was reinstated and "the three communities" held a public celebration of his triumph. That bitter and inglorious conflict was the last important flare-up of the fires left smoldering by the false Messiah of Smyrna.

8

IT IS a relief to turn from the miasmas and impostures of the Sabbatian aftermath to recount the career of Moses Chaim Luzzatto, an exalted spirit, who was not only a cabalist and a dreamer of messianic dreams, but a poet and moralist in direct spiritual descent from Yehudah Halevi and Solomon Gabirol. Luzzatto's intense and stormy life ended in 1747 when he was only forty years old. He was born in the city of Padua, and early in life the Zohar became one of his studies: it influenced him so deeply that he wrote a book in imitation of it which he called the Second Zohar. He became familiar also with the mystic system of Isaac Luria, and the things that are sealed from human sense became real to him. Just as all phenomena are by some modern scientists reduced to waves of energy, Luzzatto saw the whole of creation in terms of spiritual waves all having their origin in God but set in motion also, for good or ill, by men through their deeds. It was a challenging metaphysical system which left every individual man, no matter how humble, the freedom to bring nearer "the perfection of the world under the kingship of the Almighty." The reality of his supersensual world continued to grow on him. He felt that a special guardian angel was guiding him, and he came to look upon himself as God's chosen instrument for the redemption of his suffering people and all mankind.

He confided his faith to a few intimate friends whom he influenced not only by his daring speculations, but also by his poetic achievements; for Luzzatto had already produced a collection of psalms in the style of the Bible psalter, as well as an allegorical drama glorifying virtue. One of his disciples, a young man who abandoned the study of medicine, for which he had come to Padua, to devote himself to Luzzatto's "mission," revealed the secret in letters which he wrote home, and before long it came to the ears of Moses Hagiz, rabbi of Altona, who had fought valiantly against the Sabbatian impostor Nehemiah Chayun. Hagiz became alarmed. Was the Jewish world to be thrown into another turmoil by a false messiah? He appealed to the rabbis of Venice, he admonished and warned Luzzatto, and secured a ban of excommunication against anyone who should presume to write in the language of the Zohar. Luzzatto was persuaded to surrender his manuscripts and undertook to discontinue his cabalistic studies.

But he returned to them, and the rabbis of Venice pronounced the ban upon him. In the meantime, poverty had also come to afflict him, and Luzzatto left his native country and went to Germany where he was taken back into the fold after pledging himself to resume his cabalistic studies only after reaching the age of forty and only in Palestine. Those conditions were accepted by rabbis in Poland, Germany, Holland, and Denmark: the Luzzatto affair had clearly made a big stir in the Jewish world.

Moses Chaim Luzzatto finally found a home and a livelihood in Amsterdam, where he spent ten comparatively peaceful years and produced his two greatest works. The first, which is still widely read and studied, he called *The Path of the Upright*, a fervent moralistic treatise in the tradition of Ibn Pakudah's *Duties of the Heart*. The second was his poetic drama *Glory to the Upright*, a moral allegory of great stylistic beauty. In the exile from Italy Yehudah Halevi had at last found a true heir. And like his great forebear, Luzzatto migrated to Palestine and died there shortly after his arrival. The end came as he was approaching his fortieth year and returning to his visionary world where alone, he was certain, the truth lay hidden.

CHAPTER FORTY-FIVE

Eighteenth-Century Europe

As we follow the dreary trail of the Sabbatian aftermath east or west in the first half of the eighteenth century, we find little in the scattered patches of Jewish life that is splendid or cheering. We look in vain for a single center with power to dominate the Diaspora and exert a cohesive influence: for in the west the communities are politically divided and insecure; in Turkey they have become impoverished and depressed; and in Poland, where such a center had flourished for at least two centuries, the Bloody Decade and its rank aftergrowth had left the survivors despoiled and exhausted. Nor did the period produce men of towering importance—it is only in the second half of the century that movements and personalities came up above the drab level to exert deep and lasting influence.

The walls of the western ghettos stood firm, the people cloistered behind them still living their life apart, still an object of scorn as well as a mystery and a dread to their neighbors. Personal relations between members of the two faiths, though not infrequent in Italy and Holland, were in the Germanies almost nonexistent. From many of the several hundred little states into which that land was broken, Jews were altogether excluded, while in the others they were a people without natural rights, the immunities they received and paid for in each state ending at its borders. Outside these borders, and even at the gates of another city within them, a special body tax was imposed upon a Jew who applied for temporary admission or passage. By an elaborate network of restrictions which taxed marriages and births and prohibited more than one son to remain with his family, governments exercised their ingenuity and fed their cupidity to check the population of the ghetto; but the single squalid street to which the quarter was usually limited was nearly always overcrowded.

Life in its outward aspects was hard and unlovely. The Jew was still kept from the two basic occupations: from agriculture by being barred from the ownership of land; from the handicrafts by being barred from the guilds. As carpenter, shoemaker, or other artisan, he could ply his craft in and for the ghetto only. His commerce was in like manner restricted or, if permitted to emerge from the ghetto walls, it was confined to the pettiest forms of trading. Economic competition between Jew and non-Jew was out of the question: the latter would not permit it. The Jew found his competitor in the ghetto itself, and life within its stuffy confines might have been insufferably harsh and discordant but for the solidarity which sprang from a common faith and the sense of a common destiny, and which the sense of a common peril cemented.

The ethical standards which the ancient faith enjoined had to struggle hard, and did so on the whole successfully, against the corrosive influences of congestion and extreme poverty. In Holland, Hamburg, and London there were still a few wealthy Jews, and there were also a few in Berlin. Isaac Suasso of The Hague, for example, advanced the Prince of Orange, later William III of England, two million guldens without interest to enable him to accomplish the "glorious revolution" of 1689. The Pintos of Amsterdam were among the leading financiers of the city and distinguished for their lavish philanthropy, which embraced all creeds. In Berlin, Israel Aaron held the post of military purveyor to the Great Elector Frederick William (1640-1688), and Jost Liebmann was his mint master and court jeweler. These and a few more like them only served to perpetuate the myth, which still persists, that Jews are fabulously rich, while in reality the eighteenth century ghettos of Germany, Italy, Turkey, and especially Poland, harbored a people that lived in grinding poverty.

Nor could the graces of life, including the cultivation of polite learning, flourish under such conditions, although the traditional learning, as an integral part of the faith, was of course zealously cherished. Talmud and Cabala complemented and often rivaled each other, and it was inevitable that absorption in the mystic knowledge should engender a brood of superstitions which, it may be noted, no age, no matter how "enlightened," has been able to banish from human hopes and fears.

But if the outer aspects of life in the ghetto were ungracious, its people never lost the sound ethical ballast which the ancient faith provided. The ghetto, to be sure, was not without its black sheep —renegades, informers, and overreachers—but the basic virtues of sobriety, continence, and sympathy for the suffering continued to flourish in it, and that in an age when drunkenness, debauchery, and brutality were generally rampant.

2

IT IS one of the bitterest ironies of history that when in the course of time, the prisoners of the ghettos, not only of western but also of eastern Europe, first singly then in large numbers, stepped into the wide world beyond, the culture to which most of them were drawn was that of Germany, the country which is guilty of the most stupendous crime ever perpetrated against them or any other people. The growth, therefore, of the community in Berlin, where the lure started and whence it spread abroad, becomes a matter of special interest. When in 1670, Emperor Leopold I, instigated by the Jesuits, expelled the Jews from the archduchy of Austria, Frederick William, the Elector of Brandenburg, permitted some of the exiles to settle in Berlin. Thus the community had its start. Berlin became enormously important when through the military skill and cynical diplomacy of Frederick the Great (1740-1786), Prussia, of which it was the capital, became a great power. But as early as 1712, in the reign of his grandfather Frederick I, the Jews of Berlin built their first synagogue and, in spite of severe restrictions, their numbers continued to grow. A complicated system of laws came into existence to regulate their status. It provided for two general categories, "protected" Jews and "tolerated" Jews. The first group had three subdivisions, ranging from families all of whose members possessed full rights of trade and residence, to others whose rights were limited in extent and in the number of offspring who could inherit them. The lowest subdivision included physicians and members of other professions, as well as artists! Children who were barred from inheriting "protection" were only "tolerated," and members of one group were prohibited from intermarrying with those of another.

The grandfather of Frederick the Great prided himself on treating the Jews with fairness. It was rumored that he was not indifferent to the charms of the wife of his court jeweler, the wealthy Jost Liebmann; it is certain that he was not indifferent to the substantial revenue he derived from the Jews of his realms. He cleared the Jews of a malicious charge brought against them by two renegades that the *Alenu* prayer contained aspersions on the founder of Christianity, but he failed them when he permitted the publication of a violently anti-Jewish work entitled *Judaism Unmasked*, by a university professor named Johann Andreas Eisenmenger.

This book, "written for the Honest Information of all Christians," omits none of the weird myths that have plagued the Jews in their wanderings, including the libels against the Talmud and the blood accusation. On its first appearance in 1700, Emperor Leopold I, at the solicitation of the banker Samuel Oppenheim, forbade its circulation, and Eisenmenger offered to destroy all the copies for 90,000 marks. The sum was not forthcoming and the author, it is related, died of chagrin, but eleven years later his heirs obtained permission from Frederick I to publish it in Koenigsberg, where the ban of the emperor was unable to reach it. The king's arguments in support of his action were piously hypocritical: similar exposures in the past, he claimed, had done the Jews no hurt and besides, the book only aimed to dissuade good Christians from embracing Judaism. But Eisenmenger's screed, as events proved, furnished the enemies of the Jews with ammunition for many decades.

There were other German professors who devoted their learning and zeal to promote and vindicate persecution, and it is almost surprising to find that one or two of them exhibit a degree of humanity and a little concern for the truth in the process. Thus, Johann Wuelfer of Nuremberg and Johann Christopher Wagenseil of Altdorf, both of whom never tired of fulminating against the *Alenu* prayer and exhorting the princes of Germany to suppress the "blasphemies" of the Jews, nevertheless admitted that Christians were guilty of cruelty against them. They even rejected the testimony of renegades, and denounced the blood accusation which still cropped up from time to time. Wagenseil, though advocating measures for the conversion of the Jews to Protestantism, deplored the baptism of children without the consent of the parents, and when he scolds his countrymen he holds up a mirror to the cruelties and indignities which the Jews of Germany were made to endure. It is wrong, he declares, to throw stones at them or compel them to say "Christ is risen." Nor, he contends, should they be burned, despoiled, or exiled!

In Amsterdam the genius of Rembrandt, in his portraits of rabbis, merchants, and even beggars, reveals the innate dignity and nobility of the Jew; but in the Germanies, the image, refracted by the mists of scorn and by the morbid resentment which the persecutor always generates in his own heart against his victim, is distorted into something sinister or ludicrous. In word or picture, the representations of the eighteenth century German Jew which have come down to us are only caricatures, and in the absence of a Rembrandt, we shall do well to turn to the testimony of a great poet. William Wordsworth, traveling in Germany some forty years after the death of Frederick the Great came upon a Jewish family, "exceedingly poor, and in rags," of which he has left us a memorable description. The poet was almost startled by the grace and the beauty he saw shining through the rags. "The Jews," he states in a prefatory note, ". . . greatly surpass the German peasantry in the beauty of their features and the intelligence of their countenances," and his glowing picture ends with the following stanza:

Mysterious safeguard, that, in spite
Of poverty and wrong,
Doth here preserve a living light
From Hebrew fountains sprung;
That gives this ragged group to cast
Around the dell a gleam
Of Palestine, of glory past,
And proud Jerusalem!

3

IN POLAND, in the meantime, the valiant efforts of the once proud and prosperous community to recover from the havoc of the Bloody Decade, were all but thwarted by the irresponsible greed of the nobility and the zealous bigotry of the clergy, the only two estates that had a voice in the Polish Diet. The principal preoccupation of the *shlakhta* was that the taxes should be paid by someone else. "Who imposes and who pays the taxes?" is a question that occurs in a serious political catechism of the period; and the answer is: "The taxes are imposed by the nobility, and are paid by the peasant, the burgher, and the Jew." Useful labor, of course, was held by the nobility in horror. The same catechism contains also the following questions and answers: "Who is it in this vast country that engages in commerce, in handicrafts, in keeping inns and taverns?" "The Jews." "What may be the reason for it?" "Because all commerce and handicrafts are forbidden to the nobility on account of the importance of this estate, just as sins are prohibited by the commandments of God and by the law of nature." And the *liberum veto*, that incredible contrivance which permitted a single nobleman to block legislation in the Diet and even compel its adjournment, continued in force.

As for the clergy, its primary objective was to suppress the non-Catholic religions in Poland or, at least, to hold them in subjection. In 1720 a synod of the clergy demanded that the Jews be forbidden to build new synagogues or repair old ones. By their degradation and misery the Jews must bear witness to the "tortures of Christ," and to their "unbelief and stubbornness": such was the solemn pronouncement of another synod held in 1733. The clergy, moreover, gave willing support to the Catholic merchants in their crusade to destroy their Jewish competitors; the sordid purpose was dressed up in the vestments of religion, and it became popular with the Polish masses. And not only the merchants, but the artisans also could always count on the support of the priests, as well as the city councils and courts, in their warfare against Jewish competitors.

The kings, now that the real power lay in the hands of the Diets who elected them, could not, as in the past, serve as the bulwark of the Jews of Poland. King John Casimir, it is true, lightened their burden of taxes and in other ways helped them to emerge from the ravages of the Cossack uprising and the wars that followed. King Michael, a son of the gallant Jeremiah Vishnevitzki, who succeeded John Casimir, was also friendly to his Jewish subjects, but in his reign the Diet revived the old church laws against them, including the law which forbade them to employ Christian servants. The next king, John Sobieski (1674-1696), was a warm friend of the Jews and the Diets often complained about it. John was the most brilliant military leader in the history of Poland: it was he who in 1683 finally checked the Turks in their career of conquest across Europe by defeating them outside the walls of Vienna, which they were besieging.

4

POLAND, with its arrogant nobility and narrow-hearted clergy, appeared to be stricken with a mortal malady and in the general decline, the Jews not only suffered with the rest of the population, but were the victims of special misfortunes. Augustus II and his son Augustus III, who reigned between 1697 and 1763, were also the rulers of Saxony, and neither of them had any real concern for the welfare of Poland or the protection of their Jewish subjects. The lawlessness of the nobles and the boldness of the clergy increased by leaps and bounds. In the reign of the first, Poland was invaded by that military meteor, Charles XII of Sweden, and although the Jews suffered greatly, the Diet of 1717 voted a large increase in their poll tax. In 1740 the nobles tried to reduce the Jews on their estates to the legal status of serfs in order that the taxes might be paid them instead of the king; and if Augustus III thwarted the attempt, it was not to save the Jews from serfdom but to protect his revenue. The same monarch permitted Poland to fall completely under the influence of Russia, and thereafter the fate of the country lay in the hands of its eastern neighbor.

The general decline of the Polish commonwealth, the hostility of the merchant and artisan guilds, and the growing burden of taxes imposed upon the Jews, reduced the once prosperous community to a state of poverty bordering on destitution. In the towns, the local councils or *kahals* were always in desperate straits to meet debts and imposts, as well as their share of the head tax for which the community as a whole was held accountable. The *kahals* were forced to enact sumptuary ordinances, limiting private expenditures and even the number of weddings. In many a large city, like Posen and Cracow, the community found itself obliged to pay a species of blackmail, in the form of an annual levy, to the local Jesuit college as the price of safety from attack by the students. In 1644 such an attack by students in Lemberg, assisted by the rabble, led to the loss of a hundred Jewish lives. In 1687 the Jews of Posen fought a three-day battle against a student mob, and there were similar disorders in Cracow, Vilna, and Brest.

In the rural sections, where Jews continued to live as *arendars*, they were wholly at the mercy of the coarse and lawless landowners, and were generally the first victims of their chronic feuds. Moreover, a vile custom arose, peculiar, apparently, to the Polish gentry, which added bitter humiliation to the hard lot of their Jewish dependents. For their own entertainment and that of their noble friends, the landowners invented a variety of cruel and degrading sports with Jews as the butt. And woe to the *arendar* who fell into arrears with his landlord! The arbitrary power of the nobleman extended to his victim's children, whom he could seize and force into baptism.

5

THE pauperized Jews of Poland were further afflicted by an orgy of blood accusations which claimed many victims and kept the community in a state of terror. In the seventeenth century the libel had also cropped up occasionally. In 1657, for example, two rabbis of the little community of Ruzhany, in the province of Grodno, died the death of martyrs as the result of a ritual murder charge. Accused of blaspheming Christianity, Mattathiah Calahora, an immigrant from Italy living in Cracow, was in 1663 done to death with hideous cruelty. Between 1700 and 1760, however, the period when Poland was rapidly decaying, there were no less than twenty blood accusations which brought torture and death to numerous innocent victims. In Sandomir the trial of a *parnes*, accused of ritual murder, dragged on from 1698 to 1710 until, with the aid of the clergy and a Jewish renegade, the innocent man was convicted and the entire community exiled. In 1736, in the city of Posen, the preacher Arye-Leib Calahora, a descendant of the martyr of 1663, and the *parnes* Jacob Pinkasevitch died under torture even before their trial. A particularly revolting case oc-

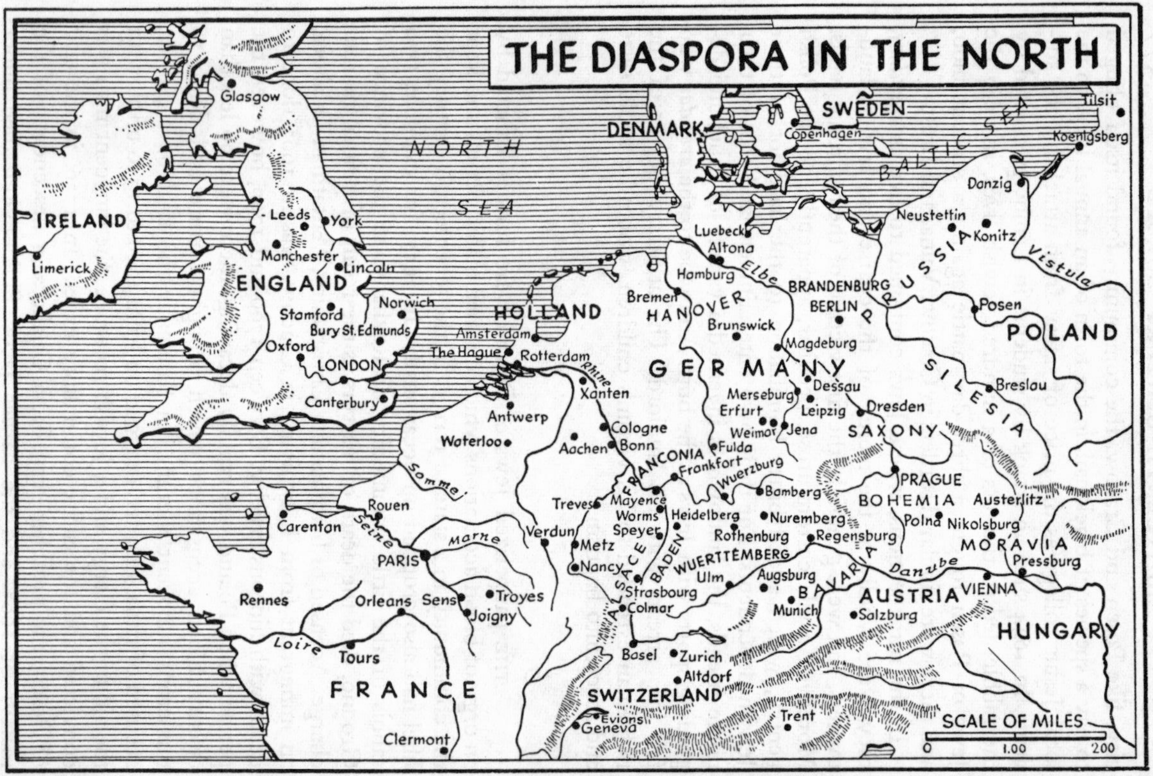
THE DIASPORA IN THE NORTH
NORTH SEA
BALTIC SEA
IRELAND
Limerick
Glasgow
Leeds
York
Manchester
Lincoln
ENGLAND
Norwich
Stamford
Bury St. Edmunds
Oxford
LONDON
Canterbury
HOLLAND
Amsterdam
The Hague
Rotterdam
Rhine
Xanten
Antwerp
Waterloo
Aachen
Cologne
Bonn
DENMARK
SWEDEN
Copenhagen
Tilsit
Koenigsberg
Danzig
Neustettin
Konitz
Vistula
PRUSSIA
Luebeck
Altona
Hamburg
Elbe
BRANDENBURG
BERLIN
Posen
POLAND
Bremen
HANOVER
Brunswick
Magdeburg
GERMANY
Dessau
Merseburg
Erfurt
Leipzig
Weimar
Jena
Dresden
SAXONY
SILESIA
Breslau
Fulda
FRANCONIA
Frankfort
Wuerzburg
Bamberg
PRAGUE
BOHEMIA
Austerlitz
Polna
Nikolsburg
MORAVIA
Pressburg
Treves
Mayence
Worms
Speyer
Heidelberg
Nuremberg
Rothenburg
Regensburg
Verdun
Metz
Nancy
ALSACE
BADEN
WUERTTEMBERG
Danube
Ulm
Augsburg
BAVARIA
Strasbourg
Colmar
Munich
Salzburg
AUSTRIA
VIENNA
HUNGARY
Rouen
Carentan
Seine
Somme
Marne
PARIS
Rennes
Orleans
Sens
Troyes
Joigny
Loire
Tours
FRANCE
Clermont
Basel
Zurich
Altdorf
SWITZERLAND
Evians
Geneva
Trent
SCALE OF MILES
0
1.00
200

curred in Zaslav in 1747; it added five martyrs to the ever-growing list and the case of Zhitomir in 1753 added eleven more.

Something like a nightmare descended on the Jews of Poland. The discovery anywhere of a dead body was sure to bring down upon them an accusation of ritual murder. Finally they sent an emissary to Rome to solicit the help of Pope Benedict XIV, who commissioned Cardinal Ganganelli to make a thorough investigation. The cardinal's report, which recalled that in 1247 Pope Innocent IV had issued a bull condemning the blood accusation, found "no evidence whatsoever to substantiate that prejudice." In 1763, the government of Augustus III was duly informed of the findings, and the king promised to protect his Jewish subjects against the libel. But the virus persisted; not only the ignorant, but the so-called educated also, were infected with it: the lie was too big and had been too often repeated to be eradicated.

6

POLAND, in the meantime, was staggering to its doom. Torn by class hatreds and religious persecution, and ruled by a demoralized nobility and a blindly fanatical clergy, the country was unable to thwart the rapacity of its powerful neighbors. Stanislav II, who mounted the Polish throne in 1764, owed his elevation to the favor of the Russian empress Catherine II. Four years later his Greek Orthodox subjects, relying on the support of Russia, rose again in rebellion and the events of 1648, though not on so large a scale, were repeated. Again the steppes of the Ukraine emitted hordes of savages who unleashed their brutal instincts on the Jewish communities in their path. The bloodiest incident of the uprising was the massacre of Uman, a fortified city in the province of Podolia, where thousands of Jews and Poles had taken refuge. For a time they fought shoulder to shoulder against the rebel Gonta in defense of the city; then the Poles betrayed the Jews to the Cossacks even as their forebears had done in Tulchin in 1648. And, as had happened in Tulchin, the Cossacks, after massacring the Jews, dealt in the same manner with the Poles.

The rebellion, with the help of Russia, was put down, but only a few years later, in 1772, the first of the three acts of international brigandage which resulted in the dismemberment of Poland was carried out by Russia, Prussia, and Austria, each of these neighbors helping itself to the provinces nearest its borders. The chronic state of anarchy in Poland, they asserted with pious hypocrisy though not without a semblance of reason, left them no other course to follow. The second partition was perpetrated in 1793, the third in 1796. Eleven years later, Napoleon, with his grand duchy of Warsaw, gave the Poles a brief illusion of restoration; then the Polish nation for more than a hundred years remained fettered and broken, with the bulk of its Jewish population swept in under the scepter of the czars.

In 1794 the Poles, led by their great soldier and patriot Thaddeus Kosciusko, were up in arms, and Warsaw was under siege by the Russians. The Polish Jews forgot their wrongs and remembered only their unfortunate country. Together with the Poles they manned the trenches outside the city, and a regiment of light cavalry consisting entirely of Jews made up part of the Polish forces. The regiment was almost annihilated in a fierce battle fought at Praga, the eastern suburb of the capital. It had been raised and was commanded by Berek Yoselovitch, a man of bold and adventurous spirit, an ardent patriot and a proud Jew, who summoned his people to fight for the freedom of Poland. Their sacrifices, so he promised them and himself, would be recognized and rewarded.

CHAPTER FORTY-SIX

Chassidism and "Enlightenment"

WITH the terror, destitution, and the encircling anarchy, a depression and gloom which threatened to undermine their spirit had descended on the Jews of Poland, when, toward the middle of the eighteenth century, a fresh spring of living water broke from the ancient fountain, bringing joy to the heavy-hearted and new strength to the weary. Chassidism, as this movement came to be called, also had many roots in Cabala, but unlike the neurotic messianic ferments, it remained loyal to the ancient faith and accomplished a vital historic mission.

Not that the Jews of Poland remained unaffected by the lure of the false messiahs. In their helplessness they became fertile ground for a large assortment of mystic beliefs and superstitions, and when in 1666, with the ravages of the Bloody Decade still fresh, the news came to them of Sabbatai Zevi's messiahship, many of them accepted him eagerly. Swiftly the news traveled from the southern provinces to Lithuania, and everywhere men prepared for deliverance. And even after the disgrace and death of the pretender, many in Poland, as in other lands, continued to hope and believe, and in 1700, as we saw, a large group of them, led by Judah Chassid and Chaim Malak, migrated to Palestine and waited there for his reappearance. Nor did the failure of that pilgrimage put an end to the Sabbatian heresy, for in 1725 the rabbis found it necessary to issue a ban against its followers.

Some thirty years later, moreover, the lingering faith of the Sabbatian die-hards merged with an even more dangerous messianic aberration launched by an impostor known as Jacob Frank. This cunning adventurer, whose real name was Jacob Leibovich, was a native of Podolia. After sojourning in Turkey, where he studied the beliefs and practices of the Donmeh and the other Sabbatians of the east, he returned in 1755 to Poland, and announced himself as the reincarnation of Sabbatai Zevi. He taught a doctrine that bore a striking resemblance to the Christian dogma of the Trinity, rejected the authority of the Talmud, and introduced strange and indecent practices among his followers. In 1756 the rabbis excommunicated them, whereupon they appeared before the bishop of Podolia, spoke vaguely about their belief in a trinity, and lodged false accusations against the Talmud. The accusations led to the seizure and burning of thousands of copies of the book, and the bishop dreamed of leading the Frankists to the baptismal font. Shortly afterwards, in fact, the new messiah and his followers adopted Catholicism, the king himself attending the baptism of the leader as his godfather. Had not Sabbatai also embraced another faith? But Frank was made of viler stuff: he ridiculed and slandered the Talmud, and at a time when blood accusations were rife in Poland, he and his followers did not hesitate to declare the libel to be true.

It was not long, however, before the Polish bishops discovered that the Frankist trinity was not at all like their own; its redeemer was none other than Frank himself. He was arrested and convicted by a church tribunal of heresy and fraud, and kept in prison for thirteen years, but his imprisonment, as might have been expected, only added to his prestige with his followers. In 1772 the Russians released him and he went to Austria and Germany where, for another twenty years, he continued to practice his frauds. Gradually the rank growth withered and died, the descendants of his baptized followers mingling with the Poles and losing their identity as a separate sect.

2

THE sinister aberration spawned by Jacob Frank may be taken as one reaction to the gloom that oppressed the Jews of Poland; it was not, however, the characteristic reaction. The masses of the people recoiled from it, and the Frankist mania went the way of the other excrescences which from time to time arose to afflict the Jewish people and to which, for that matter, no human society is immune. It was rather the movement which sprang from the fervent spirit of the simple man known as the *Besht*, a lime digger of the Carpathian Mountains, that won the masses of Polish Jewry, bringing them wholesome solace and new life.

His real name was Israel son of Eliezer, but they called him the *Baal-shem-tov*, meaning "the good master of the Name." A *baal-shem* was a man believed to possess exceptional spiritual power who, operating with the holy Name, was able to help and heal and save. But Israel was no ordinary *baal-shem*, so he was distinguished by the word *tov*, and the initials when combined made up the word *Besht*, the name by which he is known. He was born about 1700 of poor parents in a little town near the border of Moldavia, and many days of his boyhood he spent not in *cheder* but alone in the neighboring woods. He made no great progress in the study of Talmud, and at twelve he became a teacher's "helper," taking the youngest pupils to and from school and finding peculiar delight in teaching them their prayers. He loved the little ones and they loved him, just as throughout his life his heart overflowed with love for all beings, including those whom others looked upon with contempt or scorn. Later he found other occupations, all of them humble, and although he married into a well-to-do family, the couple went to live in a village in the Carpathians where, for a livelihood, he dug lime which she carted away and sold in the city. In this manner, and always in close touch with nature, he spent many happy years, his spirit undergoing further growth in the solitude of the mountains, in the mysteries of Cabala, to which he devoted many hours of his nights, and in the ecstasy of prayer.

At the age of forty the *Besht* went to live in the little town of Medzhibozh in Podolia where before long disciples gathered around him, and whence his fame as a teacher began to spread. He taught with sayings and parables, by word of mouth only, and everything he said was treasured by his disciples. Legends and wonders grew up and clustered around him. It was no new religion that he taught, nor did he come in the guise of a revolutionary. Far from it. He taught his ever-growing circle that the way of union with God is through the heart rather than the head; did not the supreme lawgiver himself declare that "thou shalt love the Lord thy God with all thy heart and with all thy soul and with all thy might"? He taught his followers to pray not in dejection and with self-torment, but in joy and in ecstasy; does not the psalmist call on men to "serve the Lord with gladness" and "come before his presence with singing"? And in the olden days, before there were kings in Israel, the "sons of the prophets" went about the land worshipping the Lord with singing and dancing. He taught them also that life is good, and that too was in accord with the optimism which underlies the ancient faith.

But the emphasis which the *Besht* put on these teachings did have a revolutionary effect on the lives of his disciples. They were lifted as on a wave of holy joy out of the prevailing gloom and despair. Nor did the teacher, like the Karaites, reject the Talmud. But while study was important, fervent prayer, he taught, was more important; and all men, great or lowly, learned or ignorant, could in simple-hearted piety achieve that union with the Divine which is man's supreme goal, and his greatest good, and deepest joy.

So the followers of the *Besht* called themselves "pious men," or Chassidim. With great rapidity the movement spread through Galicia, Podolia, and Volhynia, the southern provinces of Poland, where persecution and poverty had wrought their greatest havoc, and where Talmudic learning, it should also be noted, had come to a low ebb.

3

IT WAS not long, however, before Chassidism began to move north, where Talmudic learning still flourished and was held in highest esteem. The *Besht* died in 1760, and his successor, Dov-Baer, known as the *maggid*, or preacher, of Mezerich, was a Talmudic scholar also, and the movement began to attract the learned. A definite union of Chassidism and learning was achieved by Shneur Zalman of Liady, who became the leader of a group that called itself *Chabad*, a name derived from the first letters of the words *Chachmah*, *Binah*, and *Deah*, meaning Wisdom, Understanding, and Knowledge.

Before long the Rebbe or *Tzaddik*—the "righteous man"—became the central figure in the Chassidic communities of the south. Special powers of the spirit were ascribed to him, he was revered by his followers, and he often maintained a large establishment, a kind of court, to which they repaired for inspiration, advice, and spiritual comfort. The authority of the Rebbe usually descended to his son, and Chassidic "dynasties" came into existence which have flourished for generations and to this day. The blind veneration in which the *Tzaddik* was held went frequently to excess. It assumed the character of a superstitious devotion which, naturally, was subject to abuse, and was looked at askance by the more sober-minded, particularly in the northern provinces. For their prayers, moreover, the Chassidim adopted the Sephardic ritual of Isaac Luria, and the innovation widened the breach between them and those who were repelled by their demonstrative pietism and lack of enthusiasm for learning.

It happened, therefore, that Chassidism, which made a clean sweep of the southern provinces, only divided the communities of the north, bringing dissension and conflict which at times became acrid and violent. Shortly after the death of Israel *Baal-shem-tov*, his antagonists, who called themselves *Misnagdim*, or "opponents," found a valiant leader in Elijah ben Solomon (1720-1797) who is better known as the Vilna *Gaon*. Vilna, called the "Jerusalem of Lithuania," was the leading center of learning in Poland, and the *Gaon* was the pinnacle of its greatness and glory. He was a man of amazing intellectual prowess; at the age of ten he is said to have held his own in Talmudic discussions with the rabbis. Nor was he a stranger to the science of his day—astronomy, physics, and mathematics. The *Gaon* was revered also for his piety and saintliness; important communal questions were submitted to him but he was not the official head of the community. The cares of communal leadership, he feared, might prove an impediment to the paramount aim of his life: the study of Torah.

In the meantime, Chassidism had gained converts in the north: in Minsk, in Vilna, and other communities large and small; and the rabbis, with the *Gaon* at the head, moved to suppress it. In 1772 the first ban was pronounced against the Chassidim in Vilna, and other communities followed suit. The conflict grew more intense. In 1781, when the teachings of the *Besht* were first published, the assembled rabbis of Lithuania issued a general ban against his followers. The struggle reached its climax toward the end of the century, when Shneur Zalman of Liady came out with a work setting forth the principles of *Chabad*. The author was denounced before the Russian government, now in possession of Lithuania, as a dangerous radical and thrice imprisoned. He was eventually freed, Chassidism was recognized as a legal sect, and, though the strife continued, it became gradually less bitter as the movement continued to spread and the Misnagdim realized that their weapons against it were useless. On many of them, moreover, the realization dawned that the new road and their own led to the same goal, that "both are the words of the living God," to apply the verdict pronounced eighteen centuries earlier on the dissensions between the house of Shammai and the house of Hillel. And in recent decades, Chassidism has been the object of deep and reverent study by scholars and so-called rationalists who have found in it a wealth of truth and beauty.

4

WHILE in eastern Europe Chassidim and Misnagdim, both belonging to a people proscribed and shackled, fought their needless battles, the rumblings of the French Revolution, which was to deal the first effective blow at those shackles, could be heard in the West. The Revolution struck at the ghetto walls from without, but for several decades before it, the walls were being battered from within, and the champion who delivered the lustiest blows was the frail, bent-backed Moses Mendelssohn of Berlin.

In former periods the blending of cultures, which Mendelssohn represented, was not a rare phenomenon. As early as the first century of the Christian era Philo of Alexandria, writing in elegant Greek, made a brilliant attempt to produce a synthesis of the teachings of his faith and the doctrines of Plato; and particularly in the golden period of the Spanish community, we came upon a procession of luminous spirits, pillars of the faith and learning of their people—Ibn Gabirol, the Ibn Ezras, Yehudah Halevi, Maimonides, Gersonides, and numerous others—who were thoroughly at home also in the science, the philosophy, the poetry, as well as the language of the Arab world in which they lived. In the Germany of the eighteenth century, however, Moses Mendelssohn, son of a suppressed and despised community, is a strange phenomenon. He became one of the glories of German philosophy and literature, hailed and befriended by the leading spirits of the age, and sought after by the great and the exalted. Of the Christian world, he demanded civic equality for the Jews, and his own people in Germany he summoned to acquire the language and culture of the country which barely tolerated them. In the changing fashions of philosophy and literature, Mendelssohn's popularity was bound to wane, but as an advocate of German culture and general "enlightenment" to his people, his influence was great and enduring.

Moses was the son of Menahem Mendel, a Torah scribe of

Dessau where, in addition to the Bible and Talmud, the boy received instruction in the philosophy of Maimonides from David Frankel, rabbi of the community. Moses broke down from overstudy, and emerged from his illness with his spine incurably bent. At fourteen he followed his teacher to Berlin, where he struggled hard to earn a living and even harder to increase his knowledge. He learned Latin, French, and English, as well as mathematics, and after seven years of privation he had the good fortune to be engaged as tutor to the children of a rich manufacturer, eventually becoming the manager of his business.

Not long afterwards, he made the acquaintance of Gotthold Ephraim Lessing, the leading German poet, dramatist, and critic of the day, and a remarkable friendship developed between them, one of those friendships which were not uncommon in Spain and Italy but were practically unknown in Germany. Lessing was a rare spirit, ardent, generous, and unprejudiced. The friendship is enshrined in Lessing's play *Nathan the Wise*, in which he took Mendelssohn as his model for the noble Jew who is the leading character of the drama. And other intellectual leaders of the day sought Mendelssohn's friendship, among them the poet Johann Gottfried von Herder, and the philosopher Immanuel Kant. In 1763 Mendelssohn won the prize in a philosophical essay contest in which Kant was one of the competitors, an achievement for which Frederick II of Prussia deemed him worthy of being elevated to the category of "protected Jew." Four years later, Mendelssohn became an even greater celebrity through the publication of his *Phaedon*, a book on the immortality of the soul written in a German that was hailed as a model of purity and beauty. The book was translated into nearly every European language and became the "best seller" of the day. Naturally his coreligionists in Prussia were not among the last to do him honor, and he gave effective help to those in other lands, as in Saxony and Switzerland, who were menaced with persecution and expulsion.

For many years, however, Mendelssohn's chief concern was not with his own people: he seemed content to be part of the rational "enlightenment" in Germany, that pale counterpart of the daring Encyclopedists of France. In 1770, however, Mendelssohn received a rude shock. One of his admirers, the Swiss theologian Johann Kaspar Lavater; who described "the Jew Moses" as the "man with the Socratic soul," had the bad taste to call on him publicly either to refute the "truths" of Christianity or consent to be baptized. Mendelssohn, who shrank from controversy, could not ignore the challenge, and he replied with a vigorous affirmation of loyalty to his faith. Thereafter the defense and welfare of his people became his chief interest, and he saw the improvement of their lot to lie in two directions: the adoption of German culture and the acquisition of equal rights.

The first objective appeared simple enough: he himself was an impressive demonstration of its feasibility and advantages. But first his people must give up their dialect, a mixture of German and Hebrew, and learn to speak the pure German for which he was so justly admired. To help them do so, Mendelssohn translated into German those books of the Bible, the Pentateuch and the Psalms, which with the prayers made up their daily spiritual fare. In some of the communities of Germany, Holland, France, and of England, there were many who hailed the translation with enthusiasm, and Napthali Herz Wessely, a collaborator of Mendelssohn's, wrote a poem in honor of the translator. Nevertheless, the innovation was not as easy to accomplish as first appeared; soon enough it met with determined opposition. Like the Rambam's *Guide to the Perplexed* six hundred years earlier, Mendelssohn's translation of the Pentateuch and the commentaries that went with it became a battlefield, and for much the same reasons. Its general approach was rationalistic; the Bible was held up as great literature, to be relished as a work of art. No, said Ezekiel Landau, chief rabbi of Prague and leading scholar of his generation, and many others: that way lies unbelief and apostasy. The Bible is to be studied not as literature but as divine revelation, to be cherished not for its beauty but its holiness. In Prague, Hamburg, Posen, and other communities the translation was denounced and put under the ban.

But its influence could not be suppressed. In the East, as well as the West, Mendelssohn's translation served not a few of his people as the gateway to European, especially German, culture. The isolation of the ghetto became more intolerable, the longing for the "free enlightened world" more intense. In the view of Mendelssohn's opponents, the moth was rushing for the flame.

5

THE acquisition of equal rights, the second great objective of which Mendelssohn dreamed, was seen of course as more difficult of attainment, depending as it did not on the prisoners but on the jailers. Mendelssohn and his friends could only argue and plead: Lessing's *Nathan the Wise* was, in fact, a powerful though indirect plea for emancipation. A direct appeal to the governments to emancipate the Jews was made in a pamphlet by another friend of the sage, Christian Wilhelm Dohm, a Prussian official, who wrote it at Mendelssohn's request and with his assistance. In 1781 Cerf Berr, leader of the Jews of Alsace, had asked Mendelssohn to draw up a petition for equal rights to be presented to the French Council of State, and the pamphlet of Dohm, which created a considerable stir, was the result. The faults of the Jews, Dohm argued, had their origin in Christian persecution and would be cured by emancipation to their own happiness and the happiness of the state.

It was the age of the "enlightened despots," monarchs who professed an interest in the happiness of their subjects and in the advanced ideas of the age, among whom historians include the cynical Frederick II of Prussia and even the rapacious and dissolute Catherine II of Russia. One of them, however, Emperor Joseph II of Austria, though dismally ineffective, was undoubtedly sincere, nor did he omit his Jewish subjects from his reforming zeal. Influenced to an extent by Dohm's appeal, he abolished in 1782 some of the medieval restrictions against the Jews in his realms, opening to them, at the same time, the public schools and universities. The reforms were hailed by Wessely and other disciples of Mendelssohn who were eager to see a complete revolution in the education of the Jewish child. The previous year a Jewish school had already been opened in Berlin where secular as well as religious subjects were taught, and Wessely and his friends urged all other communities to follow suit. In the Italian regions of Joseph's empire, their advice was followed; in Bohemia and Galicia, however, it was rejected. The rabbis and Chassidim saw the new education as paving the way to the baptismal font.

6

WITH respect to Mendelssohn himself those apprehensions were certainly baseless. By practice as well as profession, he remained loyal to the faith of his fathers, and in his *Jerusalem*, a book which may be considered his final testament on religion in general and Judaism in particular, he declared that his people would not accept emancipation if the price demanded for it should be surrender of their faith. His last days, in fact, were deeply disturbed by a report that Lessing, shortly before his death, had espoused the philosophy of Spinoza which, rejecting as it did a personal God and the immortality of the soul, Mendelssohn regarded as subversive of his own and all religion.

There is, however, quite another story to tell about Mendelssohn's disciples, and the most impressive confirmation of those fears and alarms was furnished by his children and grandchildren. Four of his six children accepted baptism: his eldest daughter Dorothea, who married the celebrated romantic poet, Friedrich von Schlegel; his youngest daughter Henrietta; and his sons Abraham and Nathan. The former led to the baptismal font his little son Felix, who was to become one of the leading European composers. The only son of the sage who remained in the Jewish fold was Joseph; and when in 1871 Joseph's son Alexander died, the line of Moses Mendelssohn the Jew became extinguished.

Three years after Mendelssohn's death the first thunder peal of the French Revolution reverberated through Europe. Now the ghetto walls of western Europe would begin to come down in earnest; Mendelssohn's dreams of emancipation and "Europeanization," it would seem, stood on the threshold of fulfillment. But was the exodus from the ghetto to be a stampede and a dissolution? Was that to be the end of the story that began with Abraham the Patriarch and had gone on through four millennia of unparalleled struggle and suffering and achievement? Such was the supreme question which faced the Jewish people as the so-called modern period of its history began.

Part Five 1789 TO 1914

Emancipation

New Horizons and New Perils

CHAPTER FORTY-SEVEN

A Brave New World

IN AUGUST 1789, after a cataclysmic summer which brought down the pillars of the Old Regime in France, the National Constituent Assembly of France in revolution adopted its momentous "Declaration of the Rights of Man and of the Citizen," with its basic credos that "men are born and remain free and equal in rights," and that "no one shall be molested on account of his opinions, including his religious views." Small wonder that Jews in France and other European lands, for seventeen centuries the pariahs and scapegoats of history, thought they heard the horn of the true Messiah sounding at last. There were men among them who compared the Declaration to the Decalogue, who flocked to worship in the "Temple of Reason," who accepted the Revolutionary calendar which did away with the immemorial Sabbath. It would have been strange if, in the intoxication that seized upon all the disinherited, the Jew had been the least intoxicated.

And yet the French Declaration was modeled on one which had been proclaimed thirteen years earlier on the other side of the world, its first credo being only a paraphrase, more realistically conceived, of the sweeping generalization in the American Declaration of Independence that "all men are created equal." In 1787, moreover, delegates of the independent thirteen colonies of North America had drawn up a constitution which, in Article Six, declared that "no religious test shall ever be required as a qualification to any office or public trust under the United States." Four years later an amendment was added, stipulating that "Congress shall make no law respecting an establishment of religion or prohibiting the free exercise thereof." Thus the process of civil emancipation, which stamps the modern period in the history of the

Jewish people, had its beginnings not in the Old World but in the New.

2

LUIS DE TORRES the interpreter, Bernal the ship's doctor, and the other Marranos who sailed with Columbus on his first voyage dreamed, perhaps, of finding a refuge across the ocean from the bloody reach of the Inquisition. It is certain, however, that this hope promptly drew large numbers of New Christians and Jews from Spain and Portugal to the New World: to Mexico and the West Indies, to Peru, the Guianas, and Brazil. Early in the sixteenth century, Spain and Portugal prohibited them from migrating to their possessions in the Americas, the only "legal" immigrants, many of them children torn from their parents, being those who, together with lunatics and criminals, were deported to hideous penal settlements that were established in the New World. The prohibition, however, proved futile: Marranos continued to arrive.

But soon enough, the Inquisition also arrived in America. In 1570 it was formally established in New Spain, or Mexico, where, fifty years earlier, "Jewish heretics" had already been burnt at the stake. The Inquisition in Mexico was not abolished until 1802.

Of special interest are the fortunes of those who settled in Brazil, for it was they who supplied the first contingent to establish itself in what became the United States. As early as 1548, with Brazil in possession of Portugal, the sugar industry was brought to the colony by Jewish planters from Madeira, but life under the probing eyes of the Inquisition was precarious and the period of prosperity for the Jews of Brazil did not begin until 1630 when Pernambuco, its principal city, was conquered by the Dutch. Shortly afterwards, several hundred newcomers arrived from Amsterdam, among them Isaac Aboab de Fonseca, who was chosen rabbi of the congregation. But the period did not last long. In 1654 the city and the colony, after a valiant defense in which the Jews fought bravely by the side of the Dutch, were reconquered by the Portuguese, and the Jewish community sailed away in sixteen ships and became scattered to the four winds. Many of them returned to Holland, some of them got to London, others found asylum in more proximate regions ruled by the Dutch or English: in Surinam, British Guiana, and the West Indies. But the spotlight of destiny comes to rest on a little group of some twenty-odd fugitives who, after many vicissitudes, arrived on a day in September 1654 in New Amsterdam.

3

THEY stand out as an epitome of the plight which pursued their people through the ages, these anonymous fugitives from the Old World and the New. After being plundered by Caribbean pirates, they reached their destination, only to find the gates guarded by a surly Cerberus in the shape of the wooden-legged governor Peter Stuyvesant, who wanted no "Jewish problem" in New Holland. After a year of growling and barking, however, he was forced to yield to his masters, the directors of the Dutch West India Company, who informed him from Amsterdam that he was "unreasonable and unfair, especially because of the considerable loss sustained by the Jews in the taking of Brazil, and also because of the large amount of capital which they have invested in the shares of the Company." He was to admit them, "provided the poor among them shall not become a burden to the Company or community, but be supported by their own nation." But the governor and his council imposed additional and more serious restrictions. They denied the newcomers the right to build a synagogue, to hold public office, to trade freely, or to serve in the armed guard, though it must be noted that other dissenters from the Dutch Reformed Church, Lutherans, Baptists, and especially Quakers, fared no better in New Holland. Among the Jews, there were at least two, Jacob Barsimson and the indomitable Asser Levy, who fought stubbornly against the disabilities. Asser Levy won the right to bear arms in defense of the colony, then he petitioned "to be admitted a Burgher." The governor and his council thought it best to yield: the shadow of those directors in Amsterdam lay heavy upon them.

4

TEN years after the arrival of those storm-tossed refugees from Brazil, the Dutch colony was conquered by the English and

New Amsterdam became New York. Slowly the little community increased, but it was not till 1730 that the congregation, which called itself Shearith Israel (Remnant of Israel), was free to erect its first synagogue; and for many years Jews were denied citizenship because they were unable to take the prescribed oath "upon the true faith of a Christian."

In the meantime, little groups established themselves in other colonies also: in Pennsylvania, where the congregation Mikveh Israel (Hope of Israel), was founded in Philadelphia in 1740; in Georgia, where they settled in 1733, the year when the colony was founded; and in South Carolina where they arrived eight years later. In 1737 John Wesley, the founder of Methodism, while on a mission in Georgia recorded in his diary that he was learning Spanish in order to converse with the Jews, "some of whom seem nearer the mind that was in Christ than many of those who call Him Lord." In Maryland they were not welcome: in 1658 the physician Jacob Lumbrozo of Baltimore was sentenced to prison for denying the divinity of Jesus. Nor were the Puritans of Massachusetts more friendly to Jews than they were to Quakers and other dissenters.

But the colony to which the cause of religious freedom in America owes its greatest debt was Rhode Island. Roger Williams, who founded it in 1636 as a "shelter for persons distressed for conscience," had been banished from Massachusetts for insisting, among other things, that government had no right to control religious beliefs; and when, twenty-two years later, fifteen Jewish families arrived in Newport, they were at once received as equals. They were followed by others, and it was chiefly owing to their energy and enterprise that Newport came to rival New York as the busiest commercial center on the Atlantic seaboard. That rivalry is now a thing of the past, and of the thriving Jewish community in Newport what remains to stir the memory is the cemetery, which evoked a famous poetic reverie from Henry Wadsworth Longfellow. "Gone are the living, but the dead remain," Longfellow sang a century later, but shortly before the Revolution, Newport had become the seat of the largest Jewish community in the New World, numbering a thousand souls. Its leading merchant, Aaron Lopez, with his argosy of thirty ships bearing cargoes to and from Europe, the Guianas, and the West Indies, was, it is reported by Ezra Stiles, President of Yale College, "a Merchant of First Eminence: for Honor & Extent of Commerce probably surpassed by no Merchant in America." Its rabbi, Isaac Touro, was an immigrant from Jamaica; and the renown and wealth of the community attracted scholars and preachers from the Old World, of whom Hayim Isaac Karigal, who came from Palestine, made the deepest impression.

In New York, Philadelphia, and Savannah also, Jews figured prominently in industrial, commercial, and financial affairs, as well as in philanthropy and public service. They were not yet in possession of complete equality, but compared to the lot of their brothers in Europe, theirs was happy indeed. Equality, they believed, was sure to come, and for two reasons. The first was the fact that their fellow-colonists, from the Puritans in Massachusetts to the Catholics in Maryland, were themselves refugees from religious oppression, and the logic of their position would, they were sure, compel them sooner or later to grant to others what they insisted upon for themselves. The second was perhaps even more important. This New World was free from the poisons with which centuries of calumny had impregnated the air of Europe. Here humanity was making a fresh start, unhampered by the hates and prejudices which the Old World seemed unable to shake off.

5

THE crisis with which the Revolution confronted the colonies found the great majority of the Jewish inhabitants on the side of independence, but there were supporters of the Crown among them also. A few of the latter, notably David Frank of Philadelphia and his vivacious daughter Rebecca, achieved prominence; and at least one of them, the wealthy merchant Isaac Hart of Newport, was mobbed to death for his Tory sympathies. The war dealt harshly with most of the little congregations. The capture and sack of Newport by the British dispersed the community of that town, dealing it a blow from which it never recovered. The occupation of New York drove Gershom Mendes Seixas, rabbi of Shearith Israel, with many of his flock to Philadelphia, and refugees from the South also came to that city which, during the Revolution, remained the most important Jewish center.

Many of the Jews fought for independence, and not a few died for it. The proportion of officers among them, some of whom were promoted from the ranks for gallantry in action, was strikingly high. There was a company of militia in South Carolina two-thirds of which consisted of Jews from Charleston, and Major Benjamin Nones, who came from France in 1777, commanded another unit with a high proportion of his coreligionists. Among those whose names and deeds are preserved in the military annals of the Revolution are Francis Salvador and Major Lewis Bush, who were killed in action, and Colonel Isaac Frank and Lieutenant Colonel Solomon Bush, who were wounded. Other distinguished soldiers were Colonel David Franks, Captain Jacob de Leon, Captain Jacob de la Motta, Captain Isaac Israel, Captain Jacob Cohen of Virginia, the brothers Solomon, William, and Abraham Pinto of Connecticut, Mordecai Davis of Pennsylvania, and Mordecai Sheftall of Georgia.

Nor were Jews absent in the financial crises that plagued the Revolution, and for modest but princely generosity as well as courage, the name of Haym Salomon, an immigrant from Poland living in Philadelphia, became posthumously famous. Of Salomon, a committee of the United States Senate reported in 1850 that he "gave great assistance to the government by loans of money and by advancing liberally of his means to sustain the men engaged in the struggle for independence at a time when the sinews of war were essential to success." Among the leaders who found in Haym Salomon a friend in need were Jefferson, Madison, Randolph, and Morris, the Superintendent of Finance.

6

BUT the Jewish contribution to the revolutionary cause is not to be measured by the men and money furnished by a group which in a total population of three million did not exceed three thousand. A far greater contribution was made by the remote biblical ancestors of those three thousand. It was, in fact, the Bible, that provided the revolutionary ideology and leaven. Concerning the Puritans, who created the intellectual climate of New England, the historian James Truslow Adams asserts that "in spirit they may be considered as Jews and not Christians. Their God was the God of the Old Testament, their laws were the laws of the Old Testament, their guides to conduct were the characters of the Old Testament." In the intellectual ferment which preceded the Revolution, writers like James Harrington, Algernon Sidney, and Tom Paine operated with biblical concepts and ideals. The words inscribed on the Liberty Bell: "Proclaim liberty throughout the land unto all the inhabitants thereof," were found in the Book of Leviticus. From the pulpits of the land—in those days the most effective molders of public opinion—the leading preachers of the time drew on biblical history and prophecy for those concepts and passions that became crystallized in the slogan "Rebellion to tyrants is obedience to God." That was the motto which Franklin, Adams, and Jefferson proposed for the seal of the United States: it was to be inscribed around an engraving representing Israel crossing the Red Sea.

Nor was the influence of the Hebrew Scriptures less potent in the genesis of the basic political institutions of the new republic. The preachers, of whom the brilliant Jonathan Mayhew is an example, inferred from the warning of the prophet Samuel against royalty, that Israel was given a king in order to punish him. Samuel Langdon, president of Harvard, found that "the Jewish government was a perfect republic," and his confrere, Ezra Stiles of Yale, saw the American government as the fulfillment of biblical prophecy. Oscar S. Straus, statesman and scholar, has summed it up in his conclusion that "in the spirit and essence of our Constitution, the influence of the Hebrew Commonwealth was paramount." Those little groups scattered along the Atlantic seaboard bore a burden and a boon out of their past greater and more potent than many of them surmised.

7

THEIR solemn joy in the equality which the Constitution conferred upon them is reflected in a number of formal addresses which Jewish communities presented to the first president of the Republic. The congregation in Newport, in an address dated August 17, 1790, wrote:

> Deprived as we hitherto have been of the invaluable rights of free citizens, we now (with a deep sense of gratitude to the Almighty disposer of all events) behold a Government, erected by the Majesty of the People, a Government which to bigotry gives no sanction, to persecution no assistance, but generously affording to All liberty of conscience and immunities of citizenship . . . For all the Blessings of civil and religious liberty, which we enjoy under an equal and benign administration, we desire to send up our thanks to the Ancient of Days.

In his reply to this address, Washington repeated the terse and statesmanlike assertion that the Government of the United States "gives to bigotry no sanction, to persecution no assistance," and he spoke of toleration in terms that will bear emphasis at a time like the present when the virtue of mere "tolerance" is so highly extolled. "It is now no more," Washington wrote, "that toleration is spoken of, as if it was by the indulgence of one class of people, that another enjoyed the exercise of their inherent natural rights," a statement that echoes the lofty libertarianism of Roger Williams, Thomas Jefferson, and the other great spirits who left their impress on the new republic.

Nevertheless, in some of the states, the ground swell of intolerance and sectarian habits of thought persisted. In Virginia an attempt was made in 1784 to make Christianity the state religion. It was defeated largely through the labors of James Madison. That victory for democracy, wrote Thomas Jefferson, then minister to France, "has been received with infinite approbation in Europe." In Maryland civil and political disabilities against the Jews and Quakers were not abolished until 1825. The Constitution of North Carolina contained provisions, which were not removed until 1868, designed to exclude Jews and Catholics from holding office; and as late as 1876 certain offices were still banned to Jews and Catholics in New Hampshire. Those survivals, however, only served to bring home more vividly the amazing transformation, the new status of dignity and freedom, which had been achieved in the New World by the outcasts of the Old.

CHAPTER FORTY-EIGHT

Europe in Revolution and Reaction

It was only after a long and hard struggle that the equality which the French Assembly proclaimed in its Declaration of the Rights of Man, was extended to the Jews also. The opposition came from Alsace and Lorraine, the so-called German provinces, which Louis XIV had wrested from Austria more than a century earlier, and where lived the majority of the 50,000 Jewish subjects of Louis XVI. The expulsion edict of 1394 had not been applied against the Jews of Alsace and Lorraine, although Strasbourg remained a forbidden city to them; and they were exposed to other restrictions and impositions, of which the poll tax was the most humiliating, for the old religious hostility was now reinforced by economic rivalries. Nor was the edict enforced against the prosperous Sephardim, descendants of Spanish and Portuguese Marranos, who made up sizable communities in the ports of Bordeaux and Bayonne; and some hundreds of Jews managed also to maintain themselves in Paris, where they had no legal right of residence and were often the target of police raids. In all three of these centers, they fought strenuously for their emancipation, but for two years their efforts were balked by the hostility of the Alsatian deputies.

Not that the Jews of France were without friends and champions. Even before the outbreak of the Revolution, a commission headed by Louis' honest but ill-fated minister Malesherbes, and assisted by Abraham Furtado of Bordeaux, Cerf Berr of Alsace, Berr Isaac Berr of Lorraine, and other Jewish notables, had labored, though without results, to introduce reforms. Among the revolutionary leaders, their champions included the Abbé Grégoire and Count Mirabeau, the colossus of the National Assembly. Mirabeau knew and admired the aims and attainments of Moses Mendelssohn, and in 1787 had written a powerful plea for the emancipation of the Jews in which he ridiculed and excoriated their enemies. "There is only one thing to be lamented," he wrote, "that a nation so highly gifted should so long have been kept in a state wherein it was impossible for its power to develop." But the eloquent pleas of these and other advocates, including Clermont-Tonnerre, Robespierre, and Rabaut-Saint-Etienne, were parried by vehement protests and threats from the Alsatian deputies. The threats were underscored by the peasants of Alsace, who, when they rose up against the aristocrats as did the peasants throughout the land after the storming of the Bastille, attacked and plundered the Jews also, forcing many of them to seek refuge in Switzerland.

When the Assembly, staggering under its load of problems, seemed to be in no hurry to grasp the nettle of Jewish emancipation, the Sephardim of the south adopted the dubious course of divorcing their plea from that of their Ashkenazic brothers on the ground that they were "superior" and more deserving. In February 1790 they were granted civil equality, whereupon the communities of the north redoubled their efforts. Led by Salkind Hurwitz, an immigrant from Poland, and a group of young Parisian Jews who had joined the National Guard, they won the support of the Paris Commune, the power that swayed the decisions of the Assembly itself. Early in 1790, a deputation of the municipal commune petitioned the Assembly to extend full civil rights to the Jews of Paris, but again the question was postponed, and it was not until September 28, 1791, two days before it was to adjourn *sine die*, that the National Assembly acted. The deputy Duport demanded that "the motion for postponement be withdrawn, and a decree passed that the Jews in France enjoy the rights of full citizens."

A deputy from Alsace rose to object and was called to order. "Any one who spoke against this motion," said the presiding officer, "would be speaking against the Constitution itself." The motion was adopted, and the Jews of France became free men. Their jubilation knew no bounds. "God chose the noble French nation," wrote Berr Isaac Berr of Nancy, "to restore our rights, just as in former days He chose Antiochus and Pompey to degrade and oppress us."

2

LASHED to a fury by its enemies within and without, the Revolution rolled on with increasing violence. The monarch, after a vain attempt to join his country's enemies, was deposed and guillotined; France stood at war with the most powerful rulers of Europe; and the French Jews hurried to defend the infant republic with their possessions and their lives. The strange innovations of the extremists, like the Republican calendar and the "Worship of Reason," which plowed under the roots of their faith, were received by some of them with enthusiasm, while the others, with the patience and wisdom of age-old suffering, bowed their heads for the storm to pass. Even the unleavened bread for the feast of Passover became suspect. "But these cakes," a housewife in Metz told the commissars, "are a symbol of freedom," and the watchdogs of the Revolution relented. There were even a few Jewish victims of the busy guillotine during the Reign of Terror, but neither the moderate reaction that followed the overthrow of Robespierre in July 1794, nor the Constitution of the Directory which was adopted in the fall of the following year, impaired their hard-won rights.

The Revolution, in fact, now carried the boon of equality to the disinherited of the neighboring lands, for the armies of the Republic, which swept across its frontiers, marched not only as conquerors but as liberators. In Holland, which in 1795 was transformed into the French-controlled Batavian Republic, not all the Jews agreed that equality was a boon and a blessing. Some feared it would undermine the way of life based on the ancient faith, and deprive the community of its privileges as a self-governing body. Others pointed out that privileges went hand in hand with disabilities, and demanded equal rights and duties. There was debate and dissension, but the issue was resolved by the French envoy Noel, on whose insistence the Dutch National Assembly, in September 1796, decreed full rights of citizenship for the 50,000 Jews of the Republic. A few years later two of them were elected deputies to the Assembly, and the following year Isaac de Costa Atias was chosen to preside over it.

3

THERE was no such disagreement, however, among the Jews of Italy, certainly not among the 7,000 prisoners of the foul ghetto in Rome, whom Pius VI was persecuting with all the refinements of medieval barbarism. When, early in 1798, the French entered Rome and the pope became a prisoner of war, the Jews broke down the gates of the ghetto and tore the yellow badge from their garments. They became free citizens, joined the militia, and one of them was even elevated to the Roman Senate. The following year, however, the French had to withdraw, the Jews were driven back to the ghetto, the Inquisition was restored, and the new pope, Pius VII, even compelled them to listen to conversionist sermons. In the Italian cities of the north, events followed the same cycle. In July 1797, for example, the gates of the Venetian ghetto went up in a jubilant bonfire, but later the same year the Treaty of Campoformio, the first of the shrewd international bargains executed by Napoleon Bonaparte, gave the Venetian Republic to Austria, and the dream of freedom was over. At the Congress of Rastadt, called the same year to make peace between France and the German states, the Dutch Jews brought pressure, but without success, to compel the German rulers to relax their discriminations against their Jewish subjects, and in particular to abolish the degrading poll tax which they were compelled to pay at every border. But what the German princes failed to concede to humanity and justice they later yielded to French bayonets.

In November 1799, Napoleon overthrew the unwieldy French government known as the Directory, became master of France, and began his amazing career of conquest in Europe. Earlier that year, in the course of a daring but fruitless campaign to conquer Egypt and the Near East and cut the life line of England to India, he had taken an army to Palestine and summoned the Jews of Asia and Africa to help him wrest the Holy Land from the Turks, promising to restore it to the Jewish nation—a call to which the Jews of Palestine turned a deaf ear. In the Germanic states, the events that brought the dawn of freedom for the Jews were the Battle of Austerlitz where, on December 2, 1805, Napoleon routed a combined Austrian and Russian army, and the Battle of Jena on October 14, 1806, where he broke the power of Prussia. The first erased the still lingering shadow of the Holy Roman Empire and forced the lesser German states into a Confederation of the Rhine headed by Napoleon himself as "Protector." The second deprived Prussia of her Polish provinces, which became the Grand Duchy of Warsaw, and of a portion of her western territory, which became the Kingdom of Westphalia with Napoleon's brother Jerome as king.

Wherever the French exercised direct control, the Jews were emancipated as a matter of course. In Westphalia, a royal decree granting them equal rights was issued in 1808. In the Hanseatic cities of Luebeck and Bremen, which were annexed to France, they also obtained equal rights. In the states comprising the Confederation of the Rhine, on the other hand, where they were still at the mercy of the reigning princes, emancipation dragged slowly and painfully. Frankfort, the capital of the Confederation, drove a particularly hard bargain: in 1811 the Jews paid for equality with a huge sum equal to twenty times the annual "protection" tax. In some of the other states, like Baden and Mecklenburg, some progress was made. But the grants fell short of equality or were subject to a variety of restrictions, like those limiting the right to marry which, like the famous decree of the Pharaohs, were of course designed to check the growth of the Jewish population. In the Grand Duchy of Warsaw, many of the restrictions which had been retained or introduced by Prussia, continued in force, and equality was out of the question.

4

IN PRUSSIA itself, or what was left of it, the disaster of Jena aroused a new conscience in the rulers and led to far-reaching social reforms, of which the emancipation of the peasant serfs was the most important. The Jews also benefited from the new mood. In fact, Frederick William II, who succeeded Frederick the Great, had abolished the poll tax as early as 1787, and even set up a commission to propose further ameliorations which, however, the Jewish communities rejected as offering too little for too much. His successor, Frederick William III, also evinced a benevolent interest in his Jewish subjects, but the attempts at reform were thwarted by his ministers who could not forgive them for being different, a "state within a state" as they put it. But the wave of liberal reform, which Baron von Stein and Chancellor Hardenburg set in motion in Prussia after the defeat at Jena and the humiliating Treaty of Tilsit which followed, finally reached the Jews also. In March 1812, with the country in a state of secret and feverish preparation for the war of liberation, all the disabilities from which they suffered, except the one that banned them from positions in the state service, were removed.

In Austria, on the other hand, the liberal policies of the "benevolent despot" Joseph II were reversed. Francis I, since 1806 no longer head of the Holy Roman Empire but simply Emperor of Austria, subjected the Jews in his realms to a bewildering variety of restrictions, which, however, did not prevent some of the richest among them from being ennobled. In Vienna, a limited number of "tolerated" families were accorded the right of residence, for which they paid a special toleration tax. A larger number of families were allowed to reside there, under restrictions as to occupation and possessions, as their "dependents." Officials who issued residence permits found it a highly lucrative function.

In Moravia and Bohemia also the number of Jewish families was strictly limited. In Hungary they were confined to certain sections and were deprived of elementary civil rights. In Galicia, formerly part of Poland, there were 250,000 Jews, most of them Chassidim, who had no hankering for equal rights, which they looked upon as a bait to lure their children away from the ancient faith. But they were in effect barred from the villages, and were required to pass academic examinations before being allowed to marry! The examination was no doubt calculated to keep down the number of marriages, but it was also part of a larger effort to impose European culture on the Jews of Galicia, an effort which busied itself principally with reforming the education of the children with or without the consent of the parents.

5

AS WE have moved eastward, away from the leaven of the Great Revolution, we found the spirit of the Middle Ages more and more firmly entrenched. But even in France itself the Jews were not permitted to enjoy their equality undisturbed. The spectacle of a people of different blood and religion, for centuries the pariahs of Europe, now suddenly thrown into the national life stream, excited misgivings in the hearts of the rulers. The enemies of the Jews, moreover, were not idle, particularly in Alsace where they charged their Jewish competitors with usury and evasion of conscription. The charges came to the attention of Napoleon himself, and he determined to apply to French Judaism, with appropriate variations, the general policy he pursued with regard to French Catholicism and Protestantism. That policy aimed to subordinate religious loyalties to loyalty to the French state and to himself as its head. In a catechism prepared for the children, they were taught that Christians owed their emperor, Napoleon I, "love, respect, obedience, fidelity, military service, and taxes," besides "fervent prayers for his safety and for the spiritual and temporal prosperity of the state." The Jews must be taught to do likewise. They must abandon whatever national hopes they still cherished and become thoroughgoing Frenchmen.

The emperor, therefore, prepared a catechism for Jews also, but he presented it to them in an altogether novel fashion. Napoleon, who did all things with a glance over his shoulder at the muse of history, first convoked an assembly of Jewish notables, and then proceeded to resurrect the ancient Grand Sanhedrin to pass legislation which all Jews would recognize as binding. The assembly of notables, consisting of 111 deputies under the presidency of Abraham Furtado of Bordeaux, held sessions in Paris from July 1806 to February 1807, and was called upon to furnish answers to the twelve questions that made up the catechism. The Grand Sanhedrin, which convened immediately after the adjournment of the Assembly, consisted as of yore of seventy-one members, forty-six of them rabbis. Its president was David Sinzheim, the rabbi of Strasbourg.

Ostensibly, the notables were free to answer the questions as they deemed proper. Actually, however, Napoleon's commissioners to the Assembly intimated clearly enough what sort of answers the emperor expected. Their attitude was suspicious and unfriendly and some of the questions, the deputies felt, were an affront to their loyalty and integrity. Nevertheless these spokesmen of a long-suffering people had to play their part in the pompous gesture of an histrionic ruler. They answered the questions to his complete satisfaction, and most of them without difficulty. They had no difficulty, for example, in declaring France alone to be their country, which they were prepared to defend "even unto death." They acknowledged all Frenchmen as their brothers, and the laws of France, including the performance of military service, as binding upon their people. They recalled the honored place which Jewish tradition accorded to agriculture and the handicrafts, and condemned usury as a violation of Jewish law, whether practiced against Jews or non-Jews. The only question, in fact, which placed the deputies in a quandary was the one on intermarriage between Jews and Christians. The answer they gave to that question can only be regarded as an ingenious evasion, unavoidable under the circumstances. The ban on intermarriage, the Assembly declared, was not valid against Christians, the Bible having intended it against idolaters only. Since, however, the traditional religious ceremony could not be performed in such marriages, it was not permissible for rabbis to preside over them any more than Catholic priests could officiate under analogous conditions. Mixed marriages, in other words, could receive the sanction of civil law only.

The Grand Sanhedrin duly ratified the answers of the notables, giving them the force of legal enactments to govern all Jews. Its authority, however, failed to reach the lands that lay beyond the French imperial system. Nor were the bright hopes aroused among the Jews of France by the Assembly and Sanhedrin fulfilled. The proclamation concerning the Sanhedrin, which the notables issued to the Jews of the world, promised that it would inaugurate for the Jewish people "a period of deliverance and prosperity," but, as it turned out, the progeny of the two solemn convocations was the harsh and humiliating imperial edict of March 17, 1808, which became known as the "infamous decree." It established a central Jewish consistory, or governing body, in Paris, and lower consistories, embracing rabbis and laymen, for local communities throughout the empire. The principal function of these bodies, however, was to promote conscription, and Jewish conscripts, unlike Christian, were debarred from offering a substitute. Nor were rabbis, like Catholic priests and Protestant ministers, paid by the state. Moreover, for a term of ten years the decree imposed a variety of galling restrictions with respect to residence, trade, and other occupations, depriving thousands of Jews of their livelihood: such was the method the emperor provided for "uplifting" them. Before the term expired, however, most parts of the empire, but not Alsace and Lorraine, were freed from the provisions of the *décret infâme*, nor was it, at the end of the ten year period, renewed.

6

THE Revolution proper which, like the prophet Jeremiah, was ordained "to root out and pull down, and to destroy and to overthrow; to build and to plant," covered the decade between 1789 and 1799. It was followed by the Napoleonic period which, drawing upon the idealistic surge of the Revolution, harnessed it to the chariot of a conqueror who exploited it to trample lands and nations. The first period saw the sweeping emancipation of the Jews of France; the second brought emancipation, in whole or in part, to those of other lands. But in 1812 the star of Napoleon began to pale: that was the year of his shattering debacle in Russia, where he came with an army of half a million of whom only twenty thousand escaped with their lives. Then came the German "War of Liberation," and in October 1813, Napoleon was defeated near Leipzig in the tremendous Battle of the Nations. There for the first time, perhaps, in Europe, Jews fought against each other—French and Italian Jews in the armies of Napoleon against German, Austrian, and Russian Jews. In that battle, as well as at Waterloo in June 1815, many Jews in the German army were killed and wounded; not a few were decorated for gallantry; some were even promoted to officer's rank.

And while the armies were closing for the final decision, the ambassadors of the nations, assembled to "restore" Europe, were already in session in Vienna. What, the Jews asked themselves anxiously, would the exalted apostles of "restoration" do with the hard-won rights which the Revolution and its conquests had brought them?

7

THAT there was ample ground for anxiety, not only for the Jews, but for all men upon whom the Revolution had conferred greater dignity and freedom, was soon apparent enough to all observers. For it was clear that the statesmen who were assembled in Vienna hated the Revolution and all its works. They had, of course, more pressing problems to deal with than the status of the Jews. They had, first, to redraw the boundaries of the European countries—a task which brought the former allies perilously close to war. Second, they had to contrive an effective system for the suppression of every libertarian impulse among the nations, for they were resolved that there must be no more revolutions.

The territorial changes that meant most for the Jews of Europe were, first, the cession of the greater part of the Grand Duchy of Warsaw, with its large Jewish population, to Russia; and, second, the establishment of the German Confederation, with thirty-eight states instead of the several hundred before the Revolution. The Confederation, a loose union which lasted from 1815 to 1866, now confronted the Jews of Germany with so many fewer governments to inspire them with hopes and fears. The Kingdom of Westphalia, where emancipation had fallen to them like manna from heaven, was now, of course, no more, and as the French armies evacuated Napoleon's Confederation of the Rhine, the old abuses against them reappeared. In France, on the other hand, where the embers of liberalism still glowed, not even the restoration of the Bourbon Louis XVIII meant the abrogation of their rights.

While the Congress of Vienna was in session the Jews of Germany were not idle. In an effort to pluck as many brands as possible from the burning, communities sent agents, or *shtadlonim*, to plead with the diplomats, and some of the outstanding ambassadors, like Wellington the conqueror of Napoleon, Talleyrand the leading French diplomat, and the Prussian statesman Hardenburg, were entertained in the brilliant salons of wealthy Vienna Jews. Perhaps the blandishments of elegant Jewish hostesses were not without effect, for after considerable discussion a resolution was presented to the Congress which seemed to provide ample protection for the rights the Jews of Germany had won under the hegemony of the French. "The Congress of the Allies," the resolution stated, "will consider how the civil improvement of those professing the Jewish faith in Germany is to be effected in the most harmonious manner, and how in particular the enjoyment of civil rights and participation in civil duties may be secured to them. The rights already conceded to them in the several federated states will be continued." Of the two sentences the significant one was, of course, the second, of which the key word was the preposition "in."

The diplomats of "the several federated states" became alarmed. Those representing Saxony, Frankfort, and others protested, and the Bremen representative offered an amendment. He proposed a "slight" change in the wording of the second sentence: the preposition "by" instead of "in." With cynical complacency, the Congress accepted the change, and the Jews were despoiled of the rights which had been conceded to them *in* those states but not *by* them.

8

THE Congress of Vienna committed Europe to the velvet grip of the Austrian arch-reactionary Metternich, and the liberal spirit from which alone the Jews could expect help in their struggle for emancipation, was fettered and gagged. From Austria Metternich's system of tyranny extended to Germany, Italy, and other lands, and, particularly in Germany, it seemed to the Jews that the Middle Ages had returned. In Hamburg, Saxony, Bavaria, and other states, they were hedged about with ruinous and humiliating restrictions, both economic and social. From Luebeck and Bremen they were altogether expelled. In Frankfort, where they had paid a huge sum for a grant of equality, they were deprived of all political rights, nor could they reside and trade in the city on equal terms with Christians.

Even in Prussia the arrogant Junkers, who were now again in the saddle, made a mockery of the emancipation which had been enacted in 1812. The new territories which the Congress of Vienna ceded to Prussia were excluded from the grant, and elsewhere a variety of economic and social disabilities were imposed upon the

Jews, among them debarment from positions in the universities and the civil service.

9

TO OMIT nothing from this resurgence of medievalism, German cities in 1819 became the scene of violent anti-Jewish outbreaks, resulting in bloodshed and murder. The old-time bigotry and economic rivalry, which still flourished, were now reinforced by a new passion, a morbid chauvinism which proclaimed the German nation superior to all others, and stigmatized the Jews as an alien element which prevented Germany from achieving its "destiny." Poets, philosophers, and historians united in preaching the new gospel, and university students took the lead in the new crusade against the Jews.

The first pogrom occurred in August 1819 in the Bavarian city of Wuerzburg, where, for the first time, the strange cry of "Hep! Hep!" was heard as students and clerks broke into Jewish shops and homes and attacked their owners. The origin of the word is a mystery: as usually explained, it consists of the initials of the Latin *Hierosolyma est perdita*, "Jerusalem is destroyed." The cry, so ran the legend, was first used by the rabble crusaders of the eleventh century; now it was gleefully echoed by their cultured descendants of the nineteenth. They too would have massacred the Jews, if not in the name of their savior, then in the name of "German destiny," if their victims had not defended themselves until they were rescued by the militia. But the authorities of Wuerzburg yielded to the demand of the citizens that the Jews be expelled, and the fury spread to other cities, among them Karlsruhe, Hamburg, Frankfort, Mannheim, Bamberg, and Heidelberg. Among the houses attacked in Frankfort, the capital of the German Confederation, was that of the famous bankers, the Rothschilds. Most ominous, perhaps, was the fact that while Goethe, the greatest German poet of the period, Fichte, its leading philosopher, and Schleiermacher, the eminent theologian, made no secret of their hostility against the Jews, not a single influential voice was raised in Germany in defense of the victims and in condemnation of the mob.

Exactly thirty years had now passed since the outbreak of the

French Revolution. In the ears of the Jews in Germany and the rest of Europe, the cry of "Hep! Hep!" was like a savage and derisive commentary on all the dreams and hopes which that event had inspired.

CHAPTER FORTY-NINE

The Primrose Path

A FEW months after the "Hep! Hep!" resounded in the streets of German cities, a group of idealistic young men, of whom some were destined to achieve enduring fame, met in Berlin and organized themselves into a "Society for Jewish Culture and Science." Their aims were vague but ambitious. The society was to establish institutions of learning, encourage handicrafts and agriculture among the Jews, teach them the social graces, and above all check the prevailing trend toward baptism. Eduard Gans, a gifted young jurist and historian, was chosen president, and among the members were David Friedlaender and Israel Jacobson, both older men and ardent disciples of Moses Mendelssohn; Leopold Zunz, founder of the new learning called the Science of Judaism; and the poet Heinrich Heine, then in his early twenties.

It was a strange moral and social atmosphere, altogether novel in the experience of their people, on which these men sought to make an impression. On the one hand the new culture, which Mendelssohn and his disciples advocated, was weakening the hold of the ancient faith on those who espoused it; and on the other, emancipation and the rumors of emancipation had whetted the eagerness of these young "moderns" to achieve positions in the world to which they felt their talents entitled them. Among the founders and members of the society itself there were men who stood poised in unstable equilibrium, groping souls who sought support for their vacillating loyalties in a common effort.

The society came to an inglorious end. In 1825 Eduard Gans accepted baptism in return for a university position, and Heinrich

Heine and others did the same for similar reasons. The older men among them, like Friedlaender and Jacobson, lacked the power to guide and restrain. Twenty years earlier, in fact, when he was already fifty, Friedlaender had made a formal offer for himself and others to join the Protestant community, provided they were not required to acknowledge the divinity of Jesus! The offer was of course rejected, and Friedlaender remained in the Jewish fold; but it was a shallow and uneasy affiliation, having little relation to the basic values of Judaism, but preoccupied with forms and practices, particularly in the synagogue ritual, which the gentile might find bizarre or unaesthetic. Jacobson shared the same general outlook. In the short-lived kingdom of Westphalia, he had served the monarchs as financial agent, and utilized his wealth and station to establish schools where, for the first time, Jewish children received instruction from Christian teachers. He also imposed reforms in the synagogue ritual which the Orthodox strongly resented and against which they complained, but to no avail. The changes, which included the public confirmation of girls and the singing of hymns in German, appeared to them a mere aping of Lutheranism.

2

TO HEINE and many others of his generation, the ship of Judaism, which had weathered so many storms across the centuries, appeared to be sinking. In the generation after Mendelssohn, no less than half the members of the community in Berlin had, it has been estimated, left the Jewish fold. In Koenigsberg, Breslau, and other cities, baptism among the cultured and wealthy was a common occurrence, and although the converts did not generally receive the warm welcome they expected, and the Prussian government even passed a law to make baptism harder, devout Christians looked for the speedy conversion of all Jews and in Berlin they established a society to accelerate the process. The flight from Judaism was, of course, advance payment for the boon of emancipation. It held out a world of equality and opportunity in exchange for something which the "spirit of the age" had, so it was believed, already invalidated. When all theologies are equally discredited, why not adopt the least inconvenient? Why continue to stagger under the burden of Judaism which, in Heine's bitter words, was "not a religion, but a misfortune"?

But even where, as in France and Holland, such advance payment was not demanded, and even with those whom honor or conscience forbade the final act of desertion, the ancestral way of life no longer wielded its former authority. For centuries the mind and heart of the Jewish people had been nourished by the Bible, the Mishnah, the Talmud, and Cabala. These constituted a self-contained and self-sufficient culture, by no means closed or static, but deriving its principle of growth out of itself. In Babylonia, in Spain, in Poland, it met the challenge of rival cultures and emerged unimpaired, and in the Germanies the ghetto walls had kept it intact. But now these walls, physical and spiritual, were coming down, the culture of the gentiles beckoned, and emancipation, or the struggle for emancipation, multiplied the motives as well as the opportunities for acquiring it.

Together with emancipation, therefore, and usually anticipating it, has proceeded in the period since the French Revolution the movement called assimilation. The first can be defined with precision as the attainment of civil and political equality. The second is not so definite: it may range from adopting the language and garb of the gentiles to baptism, intermarriage, and total absorption. In its minor manifestations, assimilation had in fact been the rule in every land and period of the Dispersion. Jews spoke Greek in Alexandria, Arabic in Cordova, Spanish in Toledo, German along the Rhine; and, unless prevented, they generally dressed like the people among whom they lived. It was their faith, and the way of life it enjoined, which preserved them as a people. Now, however, what with the eager desire to share in the life of their neighbors—their art and literature, their science and politics—and what with the havoc which the growing spirit of rationalism was working on all faiths, the Jews of western Europe stood before the prospect of total absorption or extinction. Assimilation, therefore, was bound to become a battleground in the internal life of the Jewish people; and the clashes it provoked were not only between those who stood for total preservation and those who aimed at total dissolution, but also among those who differed on the extent and character of the concessions to which "the spirit of the age" was entitled.

3

THE labors of Mendelssohn, coinciding as they did with the dawn of emancipation and the general progress of "Enlightenment," acted like an enzyme on the Jewish youth of Germany and other lands, producing a variety of phenomena all of which moved in the direction of assimilation. His summons and example, of course, created a desire primarily for the German language and literature, but it also stimulated a group of enthusiasts to attempt a renaissance of Hebrew and Hebrew literature. But the language of the Holy Scriptures and the Mishnah, revived and refurbished, was now to serve a secular purpose, to induct the heirs of Isaiah and Akiba into the culture of the new age, to quicken their aesthetic perceptions, to inspire them with a desire for "progress and reform." To promote this program, the young men launched a Hebrew periodical in 1784 which they named *Ha-meassef*, "The Gatherer." The poet Naphtali Herz Wessely and Mendelssohn himself contributed to it, and it found enough material support in Prussia, France, Holland, and Italy to stay alive for a dozen years. But the attitude of the "gatherers" to the faith and culture of their own people was not sympathetic and constructive, and although they wrote in correct and even elegant Hebrew, they contributed little except criticism and satire.

Among the "gatherers" were a few who hailed from Poland, for echoes of the new culture had reached that country also and brought pilgrims to its mecca in Berlin. But their cultural transformation and change of habitat failed to strengthen their moral stamina or promote their mental serenity. The most distinguished of these pilgrims was Solomon Maimon, who hailed from Lithuania. Deeply enamored of the *Guide to the Perplexed*, Solomon had adopted the name of its author and in 1777, when still in his early twenties, turned his back on his native land as well as his wife and children, and made his way to Prussia, where his keen and original mind won the admiration of the intellectual leaders of the day, including Kant, Goethe, and Schiller. But Maimon, who divorced himself from his people, found no lasting happiness in the praise of the stranger. His bitterness overflowed in an autobiography, in which, after the manner of Rousseau's *Confessions,* he revels in his own and other men's foibles and depravities.

Maimon was a zealous apostle and interpreter of the teachings of Immanuel Kant, which seemed to have a particular attraction for those who, having lost the ancient faith, were groping for something to fill the void. Another was Lazarus Ben-David, mathematician and philosopher, who dreamed of a "pure" religion, stripped of ceremonial and dogma. A third was Marcus Herz (1747-1803), physician and metaphysician, who while still a student in Koenigsberg was a favorite of the illustrious Kant. Later, when practicing medicine in Berlin, he delivered lectures on philosophy and science which were attended by the most distinguished personalities in the Prussian capital, including members of the royal family. Herz inherited and extended the influence of Mendelssohn, to whose circle he belonged.

4

THE home of Marcus Herz became the gathering place of Berlin's celebrities, but the magic that attracted them was not so much the erudition of the doctor, as the charms of his beautiful and clever wife Henrietta. Her salon, to which the leading poets, scientists, and artists thought it an honor to be invited, became the social mecca of the capital. One of the frequent and intimate visitors was the great-hearted Count Mirabeau, who was in Berlin in 1786 on a secret diplomatic mission. Among the others were Schleiermacher, the subtly anti-Semitic preacher and theologian; the Prussian statesman Wilhelm von Humboldt and his even more famous brother, the scientist Alexander; Friedrich von Schlegel, the romantic poet, who was first the lover, then the husband of Mendelssohn's daughter Dorothea; the writer and diplomat Varnhagen von Ense, and others. What a leap from the ghetto to the most brilliant salon in the capital!

There were those, however, who thought the change represented a descent rather than a rise, for Henrietta's salon gave the tongue of scandal a great deal to wag about. Apparently the transition had been too swift, and the maudlin romanticism, which had become the literary fashion, contributed its share to the breakdown of the ancient virtues. Eventually Henrietta, like Dorothea, became baptized. She was preceded by her friend and intimate, Rahel Levin, who married von Ense and whose home also became a resort for the brilliant, the influential, and the fashionable. Rahel had a keen intellect but she was greatly distressed by her Jewish birth, and it was only when death stood before her that she declared: "What all my life I considered my greatest disgrace, I would not give up for any price."

In Vienna also, there were brilliant salons presided over by Jewish *grandes dames* and frequented by the celebrities of the day, including the leading diplomats of England, Prussia, and Austria when they attended the Congress of Vienna. The most famous was the salon of Baroness Fanny von Arnstein, daughter of the Berlin banker Daniel Itzig, and wife of the ennobled Nathan Adam von Arnstein of Vienna. The baroness devoted herself zealously to "enlightenment" and general philanthropy, but manifested little concern for the plight of her coreligionists.

5

THE attainments of men like Maimon, Gans, and Herz, and the amazing influence wielded by the Jewish salon queens in Berlin and Vienna, an influence comparable to that of the renowned Madame Récamier in Paris, testified to the ease with which the former residents of the ghetto could adjust themselves to the intellectual and social climate of the gentile world. It was an ease that should have disquieted the impatient apostles of "enlightenment" and assimilation. The echoes of Mendelssohn's summons had not yet died away, and already it appeared that his people was capable of producing a quota of gifted and eager young men and women larger than the nations might be willing to absorb. There could be no doubt that the dogged opposition to emancipation which persisted in the German states, and the savage outburst of their "gilded youth" in the summer of 1819, were rooted not in contempt for Jewish inferiority but rather in fear of Jewish superiority. What lay in store for these gifted men in the immediate and more remote future? Their people's destiny, from which they generally divorced themselves, lay with those in whom the millennial tradition remained a living force, but their own fate is also part of this story.

Among these men, whom the new conditions brought to the surface, were the publicist Ludwig Boerne and the poet Heinrich Heine. Both of them, like many others who followed them, belong more to the history of Europe than that of their own people. They certainly cannot be classed with the giants of the Spanish period who, in the words of one of them, Abraham ibn Daud, "strengthened the hands of Israel with songs and with words of comfort." But their story sheds light on the new and strange path that had opened for their people.

In 1786, the year Mendelssohn died, Ludwig Boerne began life in Frankfort as Loeb Baruch. His father, the wealthy and prominent Jacob Baruch, was one of the deputies whom the Jews of Frankfort sent to the Congress of Vienna to protect their hard-won and dearly-purchased rights. When the reaction demolished those rights, Ludwig was dismissed from the government position he held, and shortly afterwards had himself baptized in order, as he hoped, to serve more effectively the cause of liberty, his dominant passion. "Liberty shall be the soul of my pen, until it becomes blunted, or my hand is lamed," he wrote. Uncompromising in his idealism and gifted with a vein of trenchant satire, he became one of the standard-bearers of the movement known as "Young Germany," which defied and eventually overthrew the tyrannical system of Metternich. He fought the traducers of his people, but he had neither pride in his origin nor understanding of what his people's genius had contributed to the spirit of man and, for that matter, to his own. When the revolution of 1830 swept out the reactionary regime of Charles X in France, Boerne made his home in Paris where, seven years later, he died.

About the same time, and for the same reason, Heinrich Heine (1799-1856), the pet victim of the busy censors in his native land, also exiled himself to Paris, the city where free men could breathe freely, and lived there for the rest of his life. Heine was not like Boerne, a social philosopher or a political leader. He was first and last a poet, generally regarded as one of the three greatest poets who have sung in the German language, the other two being

Goethe and Schiller. The motives that led him to the baptismal font were exceedingly mixed. To a friend he wrote: "I assure you if the law permitted the stealing of silver spoons, I should not have become baptized." Nor would he forgive Gans, the president of the Society for Jewish Culture and Science, for committing the same act of desertion. "The captain," said Heine, "should be the last to leave the sinking ship. Gans, however, was the first to save himself."

Heine's was a temperament teeming with contradictions, a perpetual battleground between the austere imperatives of Judaism and the allurements of Hellenism. But there was one vision within him that always burned bright and never faltered: the vision of liberty and justice enthroned among men in place of the tyranny and oppression which reigned in his fatherland and against which he directed the sharpest arrows of his brilliant and merciless satire. In his last years, when sickness chained him to his "mattress grave," Heine's insight into the world significance of Judaism deepened and his reverence for it, previously stifled and denied, found clear expression. The following passage is from his *Confessions*, which he wrote in the winter of 1853-54:

> Time was when I had no great love for Moses, no doubt because I was dominated by the Greek spirit and could not forgive the Jewish lawgiver his hatred of images, of the plastic arts. I failed to see that Moses, despite his antagonism to art, was, nevertheless, a great artist himself, endowed with the genuine artistic spirit. With him, as with his Egyptian countrymen, the artistic spirit aimed at the colossal and indestructible. But, unlike the Egyptians, he fashioned his works of art not out of bricks and granite; he built pyramids of humanity, he carved human obelisks, he took a poor race of shepherds and created a nation which should also defy the centuries, a great, eternal, holy nation, a people of God, to serve as an example to all other nations, as a pattern, indeed, to all humanity. He created Israel!
>
> As of the artist, so also of his creation, the Jews, I have never spoken with sufficient reverence, and again, no doubt, because of my Hellenic temperament, which was repelled by

Jewish asceticism. My predilection for Greece has since then waned. I see now that the Greeks were only handsome youths, that the Jews, on the other hand, were always men, strong, inflexible men, not only in those days, but also in the present, in spite of eighteen centuries of persecution and sorrow. I have since learned to appreciate them better; and were it not that champions of revolution and democracy must look upon pride of birth as a foolish contradiction, the writer of these pages might be proud that his forebears belonged to the noble house of Israel, that he is a descendant of the martyrs who gave the world a God and a moral law, who fought and suffered on every battlefield of the spirit.

CHAPTER FIFTY

Reform and Neo-Orthodoxy

BAPTISM, as the baptized soon enough discovered, was not the potent charm they had hoped for: that "passport to European civilization," as Heine mockingly called it, failed to sterilize the ingrown antipathies which surrounded them, and it only aggravated their *Judenschmerz,* those inner qualms and tensions to which their sturdy ancestors were at least immune. The way of secession, however, was not the road the great majority chose to meet the new problems and new horizons. Although there were moments, especially in the generation after Mendelssohn, when the exodus from Judaism had the appearance of a stampede, the ancient faith, both as doctrine and way of life, was too firmly rooted in the habits and emotions of the masses, not alone in the East but also in the West, to yield to the new promises and temptations. The apostates belonged to the camp of those to whom all religion had become a matter of indifference.

It was inevitable, however, that many who rejected the way of secession should nevertheless be led to re-examine doctrines and practices which former generations had taken for granted. The impulse to question and challenge flowed from numerous sources. German philosophy, particularly the system of Hegel, another system to which many Jews were attracted, saw religion, like all human institutions, subject to a process of development and change from which Judaism could not, of course, be exempted. Then came the "Science of Judaism," which is essentially an inquiry into the historic origins of doctrine and ritual, and seemed to confirm that view, especially with regard to the Oral Law or Talmud; and the "higher critics" of the Bible, German scholars, many of them not without an anti-Jewish bias, subjected the Written Law also to the same process of adaptation and change. But those ideological motives were powerfully reinforced, and perhaps preceded, by practical considerations, of which the most important was the desire to remove or re-interpret doctrines and rites which seemed to be incompatible with the obligations that flowed from emancipation. And of those doctrines, the one which declared the Jews in dispersion to be in a state of exile from which they were ultimately to be redeemed by restoration to their own land, was considered the most incompatible.

Whether the movement known as Reform Judaism which thus arose in western Europe would have come to life without emancipation or the struggle for it, may or may not be a subject of fruitful speculation. It might be pointed out that Karaism, which, like Reform Judaism, was also a challenge to the authority of the Talmud, arose in a wholly different social and intellectual climate. But the fact remains that the first step in the direction of Reform was intimately bound up with the issue of emancipation: it was taken in Amsterdam in 1796, when those who welcomed the offer of emancipation established a separate synagogue where they introduced changes in the ritual.

2

THAT was but a feeble beginning, and it was not until 1810 that the first thoroughly Reform temple, with an organ and mixed choir, with hymns, prayers, and sermons in German, was established. It was the work of Israel Jacobson, the leader of the Jewish community in the Kingdom of Westphalia, and his chief purpose was to invest the services with more dignity and beauty, to give them greater decorum. That word "decorum" came to play a big role in the controversies the new movement provoked. The traditional services were found to suffer from a lack of aesthetic appeal, to violate the rules of "decorum." The advocates of Reform compared them with the hushed and solemn services in the Catholic and Lutheran churches, weighed them in the aesthetic balance, and found them wanting. Of course the synagogue had for centuries been much more than the scene of a weekly religious service; within its walls men worshipped together three times every day of the week; they came there to study and they met there to deliberate on community affairs. Its informal atmosphere, however, might strike a stranger as unseemly for a place of worship—as lacking "decorum."

In 1815 Jacobson transferred his activities to Berlin, where he conducted a private Reform synagogue and secured the active support of the banker Jacob Herz Beer, father of the famous operatic composer, Giacomo Meyerbeer. But the rabbis of the city were strenuously opposed to every innovation. They were supported by the reactionary Prussian government, which refused to countenance any changes anywhere at all, and Reform in the Prussian capital came to a halt.

3

THE first successful effort at Reform is represented by the Hamburg Temple, dedicated in 1818, of which Eduard Kley, principal of the Jewish Free School of that city, became the preacher. The innovations were the same as those which had been introduced by Jacobson, and when the three rabbis of the city denounced them as a menace to the faith and as a way station on the road to baptism, the reformers solicited and obtained rabbinical opinions justifying the changes on Talmudic grounds. The struggle between the two factions became more and more embittered: the opponents of Reform had no difficulty, of course, in enlisting on their side a much larger number of rabbis, including Akiba Eger of Posen, Moses Sofer of Pressburg, and Mordecai Benet of Nikolsburg. This controversy, however, did not yet define the issues with precision. The Hamburg reformers hesitated to accept the full logic of their position, or they lacked the courage of their convictions: they sought Talmudic support instead of openly rejecting the Talmud, as the reformers did later. They amended the prayers for the coming of the Messiah and national restoration, instead of omitting them as they eventually did.

In the meantime the Temple expanded, and in 1820 it opened a branch in Leipzig, the city where the great fairs brought Jewish merchants from many lands and cities. During the fairs, Reform services were conducted for them, they heard Reform principles expounded, and they brought Reform ideas home to their communities. The movement spread and made its way into Austria, Denmark, and other countries. In some of the German states, including Hanover and Baden, synagogue reforms were even ordered to be introduced by the governments.

4

A YEAR after the Hamburg Temple embarked upon its program of expansion, the Orthodox congregation of that city chose as its chief rabbi, or *chacham*, as he preferred to be called, Isaac Bernays—the first champion of the traditional faith to enter the lists who was equipped with the weapons of the reformers. Bernays combined Talmudic learning with a university education, and he preached eloquent sermons in unimpeachable German. He was not a foe of general culture; on the contrary, he even introduced the secular subjects into the community school, but his conception of Judaism and its world significance made emancipation and European culture, the twin lodestars of Mendelssohn's disciples, relatively unimportant: it made Reform look like the surrender of a noble birthright.

For two decades the temple and synagogue in Hamburg pursued their separate ways in a state of smoldering antagonism; then, in 1841, a bitter conflict flared up between them. The occasion was the adoption by the Temple of a new prayer book, bearing the general title of *Prayer Book for Israelites*, in which, among other changes, the prayers for national restoration were expunged. Isaac Bernays denounced the new compendium and placed it under the ban. The Temple replied with a counterblast, and the discord spread as each side sought support in other communities. The younger rabbis, many of whom preferred to call themselves pastors, hastened to uphold the new prayer book: in the two decades Reform had apparently made large gains and grown bolder.

5

IN FRANKFORT, about the same time, a Reform Society came into existence which displayed even greater boldness. It proclaimed the Mosaic religion subject to unrestricted development, rejected the authority of the Talmud, renounced the hope of national restoration, questioned the validity of the dietary laws, and even denied that the rite of circumcision was binding. The last denial aroused too much opposition, and was dropped from the society's program. But circumcision remained a hotly debated issue, although nearly all the religious leaders, in Italy and Austria as well as in Germany, insisted on its binding character.

The most distinguished dissenter was Abraham Geiger (1810-1874), a native of Frankfort who, after a brilliant career as student, scholar, and author, was serving as assistant rabbi in Breslau. There he and Solomon Tiktin, the first and elder rabbi, were in continuous conflict over Geiger's religious doctrines and reforms, a conflict which only ended with the creation, after Tiktin's death, of two separate congregations. Geiger's general outlook was historical, evolutionary, and "scientific." Although he held that Reform must be patient and reckon with the deep-rooted sentiments that stood in its way, his ultimate objectives were no less radical than those of the Frankfort Reform Society. He had little sympathy with middle-of-the-road men like Zechariah Frankel and Leopold Zunz, whose "Science of Judaism," however, he, like the other Reform rabbis, ardently espoused.

Geiger, however, was not the most extreme reformer of his day. The palm for radicalism belongs rather to a Reform Fellowship, which made its appearance in Berlin, and to Samuel Holdheim (1806-1860) who became its leader. Holdheim stood for the abolition of all those prescriptions, like the marriage and divorce laws, which stemmed from the national character of Judaism. The separateness of the Jewish people, he argued, had been enjoined in order to safeguard their monotheism, but it became unnecessary as soon as the unity of God was acknowledged by the nations among whom they lived. Holdheim had from childhood been a brilliant student of the Talmud, and all the dialectic skill he acquired in its study he now employed in attacking it. As rabbi of the Reform Fellowship, he introduced religious services on Sundays and officiated at marriages between Jews and Christians. Needless to say, his reforms were vehemently denounced by the Orthodox. They branded him as a second Paul of Tarsus, hacking away at the roots of Judaism in order to curry favor with the gentiles.

6

LIKE Karaism a thousand years earlier, the demand for change threatened to produce a schism in Judaism: some of the reformers, notably the Reform Fellowship in Berlin, were prepared to welcome it in the form of a "German Jewish Church." But Reform itself was moving at different rates of speed and in different directions. Was it not possible to resolve the differences? In 1844 Ludwig Philippson, founder and editor of the *Allgemeine Zeitung des Judentums*, a weekly journal which lasted till 1922, published a call for a rabbinical conference, which met the same year in Brunswick "to consider ways and means for the preservation of Judaism and the awakening of the religious spirit."

The conference, which brought together twenty-four rabbis, nearly all advocates of reform, was dominated by Holdheim and Geiger. It accomplished little and evoked a vigorous denunciation from a much larger number of Orthodox rabbis in Germany and Hungary. The following year, another and larger conference was held in Frankfort, and although agreement was reached to eliminate the prayers for national restoration and make other liturgic changes, the incident that made the biggest stir was the withdrawal of the eminent scholar Zechariah Frankel in protest against the decision of the conference to subordinate Hebrew to the vernacular in the ritual. A third rabbinical conference took place in 1846 in Breslau. It dealt with such matters as Sabbath observance, circumcision, and mourning customs, but in general it failed to impress its authority on the congregations. If anything, the war of sermons and pamphlets to which the rabbinical conferences gave rise, only intensified the religious strife that divided the communities in Germany.

7

IN HIS break with the Frankfort conference, Zechariah Frankel made it clear that he occupied a middle position which he described as "positive-historical." In other words, the antiquity of a religious institution and the depth of sentiment that clung to it, invested it with a sanctity which must not be violated. Frankel was a university graduate and a scholar of rare attainments. In 1854, after a rabbinical career in Bohemia, he was chosen to head a newly established theological seminary in Breslau, which came into existence through the efforts of Abraham Geiger. The latter was deeply hurt when the choice fell on some one else: for all the esteem in which the lay leaders held him, they apparently still preferred a moderate like Frankel to be the teacher and mentor of the future religious leaders of their people. Frankel held the post until his death in 1875, holding firm against the extremes of the reformers.

But the acknowledged head of the historical school was Leopold Zunz (1794-1886), creator of the "Science of Judaism," who mastered the vast range of Jewish literature through the ages and drew light from it for the questions of the day, particularly in his monumental work *Die Gottesdienstliche Vortraege der Juden*, which some consider the most important Jewish book of the nineteenth century. The purpose of the work was to demonstrate that the sermon in the vernacular had always had a place in the synagogue; but it was also in effect a powerful plea for Jewish emancipation and a demand for the admission of Jewish science into the universities. That book appeared in 1832, and in 1855 Zunz published his *Synagogue Poetry of the Middle Ages*, another work of vast scholarship. His prodigious labors of research and authorship, moreover, did not prevent Zunz from taking an active part in public affairs, especially after the Revolution of 1848.

Zunz began as an advocate of Reform, but in the course of his long life he saw many things which brought him back to the sacred moorings of the past. He saw the fiasco of the "Society for Jewish Culture and Science," of which he was a founder; he saw the stampede to the baptismal font; he observed the illusions and disillusions of emancipation, and the excesses of Reform. He preferred teaching to preaching, and from 1840 to 1850 held the post of principal of the Jewish Teacher's College in Berlin.

In 1845 Zunz received a letter from Geiger expressing amazement and sorrow over the master's continued adherence to certain practices which had their support only in "habit and fear," like the use of phylacteries in prayer and the dietary laws. "Will you," Geiger demands, "find in the past not merely the history of the spirit, but also the norm for our spiritual life?" To this letter Zunz wrote an ironic reply in which he declared: "We must reform ourselves, not our religion." Abuses must be attacked, he adds, but not a "sacred heritage." As for the Talmud, wrote Zunz, the outcry against it "has ever been the way of the renegade."

8

BUT Germany was not the only land where the Jewish past became an object of study and speculation. In Galicia there was Nachman Krochmal (1785-1840) whose *Guide to the Perplexed of Our Times*, edited after the author's death by Leopold Zunz, aimed to do for Krochmal's generation what Maimonides in his *Guide to the Perplexed* had endeavored to do for his. Maimonides relied to a large extent on the philosophic system of Aristotle; Krochmal on the developmental philosophy of his day. In his *Guide* Krochmal aimed chiefly to clarify the course of Jewish history, which he found to be unique. For while other historic groups were subject to the three stages of birth, efflorescence, and decay, he saw the Jewish people rescued from the third by the power of the "Absolute Spirit," or Divine Providence. Another eminent scholar, who, like others, was greatly influenced by Krochmal, was Solomon Judah Loeb Rappaport (1790-1867) also a native of Galicia. For the last twenty-seven years of his life, he was rabbi of Prague. Rappaport defended Zechariah Frankel against Geiger and the other reformers, but devoted most of his energies to a study of the Jewish past, shedding light on Saadia Gaon and other great figures of the post-Talmudic period.

Rappaport, like Krochmal, wrote in Hebrew and corresponded in that language with Samuel David Luzzatto (1800-1865), the outstanding Jewish scholar of the period in Italy. In 1829 Luzzatto was appointed professor at the rabbinical college of Padua, an institution which owed its existence largely to the efforts of Isaac Samuel Reggio (1784-1855), another Italian savant who was also a distinguished mathematician and painter and who has been called the Italian Mendelssohn. But while Reggio was by temperament a rationalist, Luzzatto was a poet and mystic. In spirit as well as by lineage he was related to Moses Chayim Luzzatto, the poet and mystic of the previous century. His was a mind of exceptional originality and independence. Unlike other devotees of the "Science of Judaism," he refused to bow low to the philosophers, deploring the Rambam's dependence on Aristotle and pouring wrath and ridicule on Spinoza for his Olympian contempt of the quality of compassion, which Luzzatto regarded as the fundamental teaching of Torah. Luzzatto's "science," unlike Zunz's, became a tower of strength to the defenders of the ancient faith.

9

THIS "Jewish science," a child of the rationalist "enlightenment," received nourishment from a variety of sources, not least among them the desire to compel the past to sanction reform in the present. The principle of evolution, now sitting enthroned over every science, must be extended to the beliefs and rites of Judaism, including even the doctrine of revelation which, as interpreted by Geiger and his disciples, was a continuous, never-ending process. But the new learning was a double-edged sword: it could also be employed to confound or, at least, throw doubt on, the conclusions of the innovators; and in the hands of men like Frankel, Rappaport, and especially Luzzatto, it became a weapon against the reformers.

In one respect, at least, the enthusiasts of the new science were certainly destined to be disappointed: it never took the place which the old learning held in the love and devotion of the people. Zunz's

Gottesdienstliche Vortraege and Krochmal's *Guide* were read and relished by scholars and specialists, but how could they substitute for the Mishnah and Talmud, for Rashi and the *Shulchan Aruch?* The books of the new learning might have everything that was claimed for them—erudition, and logic, and style—but one thing they could not claim: the quality of holiness, which clung to the books of the past and gave them their unique hold on the Jewish people.

10

IN GERMANY, the struggle between Reform and Orthodoxy continued unabated until the Revolution of 1848, which diverted general interest from religious to political issues, above all to the prospect of imminent and complete emancipation. In the meantime, champions of Orthodoxy like Isaac Bernays of Hamburg, and opponents of radical Reform like Zechariah Frankel of Breslau, came to the fore in other communities also. In 1845, Michael Sachs, a magnificent preacher and a man of great charm who held a doctorate from the University of Berlin, was chosen rabbi of that community, and fought valiantly against the innovations of the Reform Fellowship, as well as against Reform tendencies in his own congregation. In Vienna, the sweep toward radical Reform was checked by Isaac Noah Mannheimer, whose brilliant sermons, as well as the liturgic music of his cantor, Solomon Sulzer, proved that the reformers had no monopoly on aesthetics.

But the champion of Orthodoxy in those days of storm and strife who left the deepest impression, was Samson Raphael Hirsch (1808-1888). He was born in Hamburg and had sat at the feet of Isaac Bernays, studied in the University of Bonn, and served as rabbi in Hanover, Moravia, and Silesia before 1851, when he accepted the call to head the Orthodox community in Frankfort. There he ministered for the rest of his life, and his labors made Frankfort the citadel of Orthodoxy in Germany. As early as 1836, Hirsch had already published his *Nineteen Letters of Ben Uziel,* an elucidation and panegyric of the time-hallowed institutions and rites of Judaism. The book became the bugle call of the movement known as neo-orthodoxy. Here indeed was something new: a militant defense, in faultless German, of the ancient faith, finding no antagonism between the complete observance of all its prescriptions and the demands of modern culture. The mission of Israel "to perfect the world under the kingship of the Almighty," which the pious affirmed three times daily in the *Alenu* prayer, and which the reformers also proclaimed as a central doctrine, did not, Hirsch contended, require the Jews to surrender their hope of national restoration or to water down their faith for the sake of a *rapprochement* with their Christian fellow-citizens. On the contrary, the very ideal of human brotherhood under God obligated them to maintain their religious separateness, as well as the hope of restoration. Emancipation, which Hirsch welcomed, might render some of the rites more difficult to observe, but the new conditions called for more, not less, devotion from those who would be loyal to the commands of *noblesse oblige*. Men with a mission, Hirsch argued, do not order their lives on the principle of ease and convenience.

Among those who were influenced by the *Nineteen Letters* was a young student named Heinrich Graetz, who was to become the foremost historian of the Jews. The letters of *Ben Uziel*, he wrote the author in 1836, were like "bright sunlight," revealing the abyss which threatened to engulf him. "Already I hovered over the infernal brink . . . when your Letters appeared, every line a rescuing angel, melting the ice of the rigid and frightful skepticism which lay in my heart, rendering my feelings and ideas pure and genuinely Jewish."

The future historian wrote with the enthusiasm of youth, but he was essentially a rationalist and, after a number of years as a disciple of Hirsch, he went his separate way—the way of Frankel and Zunz. Hirsch, on the other hand, was essentially a mystic; he saw the vindication of his faith in something deeper than logic, deeper than what the rationalist scholars called the historical sanction. He stood in direct spiritual descent from those who saw the justification for Jewish survival in the revelation of Sinai, and his distinction rests on his valiant defense of the divine sanction and his denial of the claim that the "spirit of the age" had abolished it.

CHAPTER FIFTY-ONE

Heights and Depths

THE rising tide of religious unrest and reform in western and central Europe may be taken as a measure of the eagerness with which the Jews advanced to welcome the gift or promise of civil equality, or emancipation. Now the current of emancipation, though it wound and twisted with heartbreaking sluggishness, at times even turning back on itself, was nevertheless moving generally in their direction. It received impulse not only from social convulsions like the French Revolution; it was assisted also by the abatement of religious bigotry which resulted from the progress of natural science and skeptical philosophy, and it was aided by the less spectacular but surer forces of the Industrial Revolution.

One need not subscribe to the doubtful conclusions of the economist Werner Sombart, who credits the Jews with a preponderant role in the rise and growth of modern capitalism, to recognize that the same conditions which gave them a large share in the commerce and banking of the Middle Ages would force them into the expanding industry, commerce, and finance of the new age. Their concentration in the large urban centers, which the rise of the factory system multiplied and enlarged, provided the opportunities; their exclusion from other fields which might have employed their energies and talents made them only too ready to seize upon them. Economically, more and more of them in western Europe became part of the up-and-coming bourgeoisie, the class that emerged as the chief beneficiary of the Revolution of 1789 and of the revolutions that followed. By and large, that class was liberal and skeptical, and therefore more favorable to the emancipation of the Jews than the nobility and clergy whose power it curbed. Unlike the feudal system which it replaced, the capitalist system did have a legal place for the Jews.

In every land of central and western Europe, moreover, in the Germanies and in Italy, in France and in England, there emerged Jewish families and individuals so conspicuous for achievement in the economic sphere that they became, like the Rothschilds, almost a legend. They promoted and financed vast undertakings and, in war and peace, governments leaned heavily on their resources and skills. Nor did they limit their interest to the accumulation of wealth. They gave liberally to philanthropic causes, they supported the arts and sciences, they attained influence in society and politics and used it on occasion to obtain justice for their people, in their own and other lands. In performing this function they continued the long-standing tradition of the *shtadlanim*, or court agents, of the Middle Ages and of the highly privileged "Court Jews" of the eighteenth century: men like the wealthy and persuasive Joseph or Joselman of Rosheim in Alsace who, in the first half of the sixteenth century, was a font of salvation to his persecuted people in Germany and Bohemia; like the mint master Jacob Bassevi von Treuenburg of Prague (1570-1634), the first Jew to be ennobled in Austria; like the banker Samuel Oppenheim of Vienna (1635-1703) and his friend and successor, the learned Samson Wertheimer (1658-1724), both of whom used their wealth and influence to suppress Eisenmenger's vicious screed *Judaism Unmasked;* like the ill-starred Joseph Suess Oppenheimer of Wuerttemberg who, after a brilliant but dubious career, ended his life on the gallows in 1738.

But the Oppenheimers and Rothschilds have their place on the debit side of the Jewish ledger also, for no matter how appalling the poverty of the Jewish masses might be, that handful of nabobs was enough to keep alive the myth of "the rich Jew"; and in popular fancy their wealth and power were grotesquely exaggerated, enabling demagogues and hate-mongers to create another myth, that of the "international Jewish bankers," banded together in a world conspiracy to rule or destroy the Christian nations!

2

THE founder of the most fabulous of these clans was Meyer Anselm Rothschild of Frankfort who, in 1760, established a banking house to which both German and foreign princes had recourse in their need. His five sons built up a financial empire that embraced the continent. Two of them, Anselm Meyer and Carl, both of whom died in 1855, conducted operations in Germany and Italy. Solomon established himself in Vienna, where he built the first Austrian railroad and became a baron. James, who founded the French line of Rothschilds, rose to be the trusted adviser of King Louis Philippe, and was also ennobled. These four brothers, however, were outdistanced by Nathan Meyer, who became the outstanding member of the Exchange in London, advanced huge sums in 1814 to England and its allies, and, after the defeat of Napoleon, was the acknowledged ruler of world finance. Nathan's eldest son Lionel, who succeeded him as head of the English Rothschilds, rose to prominence in social and political circles also. He was Disraeli's trusted friend, and provided the funds with which the British government acquired a controlling interest in the Suez Canal. And, as we shall see, it was Lionel who in 1858, after a prolonged and hard struggle, became the first unbaptized Jew to be seated in the House of Commons. The romance of the Rothschilds was crowned in 1885 when Lionel's son Nathan Meyer, the great-grandson of Meyer Anselm of the Frankfort ghetto, was raised to the peerage and, as Lord Rothschild, became the first Jewish member of the House of Lords. A large share of the spectacular good fortune that attended the Rothschilds has been credited to the solidarity which the founder of the house enjoined upon his descendants and which, besides other obligations, required them to look for husbands and wives among their own cousins.

There were other distinguished and wealthy Jews in England and on the continent who, like the English Rothschilds, threw their influence into the scales in the struggle for emancipation. In England, an important place in the story of that struggle belongs to the Goldsmids and the Salomons. Aaron Goldsmid, founder of the famous family of bankers, merchants, and public servants, came to London from Amsterdam in 1765; in 1841, his grandson Isaac Lyon Goldsmid, was knighted, and in 1860 Isaac's son, Sir Francis Goldsmid, after many years of valiant labor for Jewish emancipation, was elected to the House of Commons, where he sat until his death in 1878. Of the Salomons the most distinguished member and the most colorful figure in the battle for emancipation was Sir

David who, in 1855, became the first Jewish Lord Mayor of London.

In England there were also the remarkable Montefiores, who produced not only outstanding financiers, merchants, and men of affairs, but scholars and soldiers as well. The most illustrious Montefiore was Sir Moses, whose journeys and deeds on behalf of his suffering people on three continents have shed the luster of a legend over a life that spanned more than a century (1784-1885).

3

IN FRANCE, the brothers Emile and Isaac Pereire represented an unusual commingling of large-scale, creative business ability and social idealism. Both were ardent followers of Saint-Simon, the founder of French socialism. They published and edited a number of papers to promote his theories, nor did they lose sight of them in their financial creations, which aimed to extend participation and profits to the masses of the French nation. This was particularly true of the *Crédit foncier*, founded by them in 1852, and of the *Crédit mobilier*, which became the most important financial institution of the Second Empire. The Pereires built the first railroads in France and Spain, and were prominently associated with many other industries and public utilities.

Another family of outstanding achievement in finance was the Bischoffsheims, who were noted, in addition, for their contributions to philanthropy and to the advancement of science. The brothers Jonathan and Louis Bischoffsheim founded banks and built railroads in Holland, Belgium, and France. In Germany, the banker Gerson Bleichroeder (1822-1893) was Bismarck's leading financial adviser and the immediate cause of a savage anti-Semitic campaign which did not prevent him, however, from using his influence with the German statesman on behalf of the Balkan Jews when their fate lay in the balance at the Berlin Congress of 1878.

4

BETWEEN the financial and industrial magnates of the West and the oppressed masses of the East the gulf could not, it would seem, be wider. Nevertheless in 1840, the ancient city of Damascus, capital of Syria, became the scene of a blood libel which brought home to the Jews scattered throughout the world, the high as well as the low, that they were all one people, at the mercy of the same foe. For the first time, moreover, the monstrous accusation roused not only the Jews of the world; it outraged also the civilized nations, so that the Damascus Affair, as this series of events came to be known, added considerable momentum to the process of emancipation.

To be fully understood, the affair must be seen against the background of the current international scene. The obscure victims of the medieval legend found themselves caught between the exalted players of a far-flung diplomatic game; and the villain of the piece, strange to relate, was France, the cradle of "liberty, equality, and fraternity" ruled at the time by the "liberal" Louis Philippe with Adolphe Thiers, renowned statesman and historian, as his principal minister. The Turkish, or eastern, question had reached an acute stage and was threatening the peace of Europe: the pasha of Egypt, Mehemet Ali, had rebelled against his master, the Turkish sultan, and possessed himself of Palestine and Syria. Thiers threw France on the side of the rebel, while all the other European powers supported the sultan. Thiers was eager to extend French influence in the Near East and, under French protection, the Catholic institutions in Syria were considerably strengthened.

On February 5, 1840, Father Thomas, head of a Franciscan monastery in Damascus, disappeared, and the monks raised the cry that the Jews of the city had murdered him for ritual purposes. To Ratti Menton, the French consul, it appeared that the interests of France required that the accusation should be sustained. He took charge of the case, and Sherif Pasha, Mehemet's governor in Damascus, felt it his duty to assist the representative of the only friendly power. Several Jews were arrested and one of them "confessed" under torture and named eight others as the "criminals." The eight were then arrested, but though one of them, Joseph Laniado, an old man of eighty, succumbed to the tortures, no confession could be extorted from them. The patriotic Menton, however, was not discouraged. He rounded up sixty Jewish children, locked them in a prison, and starved them in order to wring confessions from the frantic parents. When that device also failed, he arrested three rabbis, together with other prominent men of the community, and, under torture, some of them, eager for speedy death, took the crime upon themselves. The governor of Damascus obtained the permission of Mehemet Ali to execute them, but the prisoners repudiated their confessions and insisted on their innocence.

The zealous M. Menton applied himself also to spread the blood libel among the Moslems and not without success. An Arab mob broke into a synagogue in the city and mutilated the scrolls. Jews were attacked in different parts of Turkey as far as Smyrna, and a blood accusation was trumped up against them on the island of Rhodes which, however, failed in its purpose, the innocence of the accused being plainly proved. In France, the reactionary and clerical newspapers naturally supported the consul.

5

BUT now it became clear to the Jews of western Europe and America, to the emancipated and unemancipated, the influential and the lowly, that they too, and not only those who were being tortured in Damascus, were among the accused. The man who came forward as the leading Jewish champion was the brilliant lawyer and orator, Adolphe Crémieux (1796–1880), who had already delivered some telling blows against the few anti-Jewish discriminations still remaining in France. Five years earlier, when the city of Basel prohibited a French Jew from settling there, Crémieux had intervened and brought about a rupture in consular relations between France and the Swiss city. This time, however, he found his government deaf to his pleas. French political stakes in the Near East were more important than the claims of justice and decency.

Fortunately for the victims, the other governments of Europe were willing to help them; they were, in fact, eager to do so, if only to check the ambitions of France. In June, Lord Palmerston, then British foreign minister, notified Mehemet Ali that the persecutions in Damascus were producing a painful impression in Europe. Metternich, in response, it is believed, to representations from the Rothschilds, took similar action for Austria. Both instructed their consuls-general in Alexandria to intervene with Mehemet Ali, who thereupon ordered his governor in Damascus to put a stop to the tortures and offered to lay the case before a special court to consist of the consuls-general of England, Austria, Prussia, and Russia. But the French consul interfered and thwarted the plan.

All this time the echoes of the Damascus Affair throughout the world grew louder. In the European press, the campaign of slander against the Jews, stimulated by the clerical parties in France, Italy, and Belgium, increased in violence, and for the first time in the somber history of their Dispersion, the Jews of the world invoked the decent opinion of mankind in their behalf. At the call of the Lord Mayor of London, an impressive public meeting took place on July 3, 1840, in the famous Mansion House, where men of distinction voiced their indignation. Some of the speakers went beyond the immediate question and demanded the emancipation of the Jews. In the United States there were meetings of protest in New York and Philadelphia, and President Martin Van Buren, through his diplomatic representatives in Alexandria and Constantinople, informed Mehemet Ali and the sultan that the bare recital of the events in Damascus "has caused a shudder throughout the civilized world." The leaders of French and British Jewry now took an even bolder step: they sent a deputation to the Near East, headed by Crémieux and Sir Moses Montefiore, and accompanied by the renowned Orientalist Solomon Munk.

Early in August, Sir Moses was received by Mehemet Ali in Cairo, and requested letters of safe conduct that would enable the deputation to conduct a thorough investigation on the spot. Under pressure from the French consul, the wily old governor hesitated. When, however, the nine other consuls, representing as many European governments, prepared to send him a collective note in support of the deputation, Mehemet Ali hastened to issue an order for the release of the prisoners. The fact was that the general policy of France in the Near East had already been reversed, Louis Philippe having no stomach to defy the other powers, and French influence with Mehemet Ali was on the wane. The order of release spoke of "pardon," but on the insistence of the deputation that word was changed to "acquittal." On September 6 the prisoners were liberated—there were only nine alive of the thirteen who had been incarcerated—and Mehemet Ali's governor in Damascus paid for his crimes with his life.

6

NOT long afterwards, Syria and Palestine were restored to Turkey, whereupon the Jewish emissaries from the West proceeded to Constantinople and prevailed on the sultan to issue a firman, in which the blood accusation was denounced as a libel. There was great rejoicing among the Jews throughout the world, and all men who loved justice and hated oppression rejoiced with them.

This Damascus Affair, however, seemed to point a number of lessons. It made all Jews, high and low, free or fettered, realize their kinship: with all their differences they were still a world community, if not of common goals, then of common suffering and perils. For the first time, moreover, they became aware of their moral strength, the strength that derives from courageous action and from the support of the decent opinion of the world. And many of them, finally, were sobered by the spectacle of a government representing the most liberal and civilized nation and tradition in Europe, ready, in order to promote a national policy, to resort to the vilest barbarities against the weak and the helpless.

CHAPTER FIFTY-TWO

Emancipation

BUT the removal of the disabilities still cramping the Jews of Europe required more than the sympathy which a Damascus Affair might evoke, nor did the social and political influence of the rich and exalted suffice to bring it about. It called for increasing exertion to awaken the normally sluggish sense of justice in men and nations, and, above all, it depended on social upheavals, which produce a drastic revision in social relations, giving long-standing wrongs a chance of being righted. Indeed, the complete legal emancipation of the Jews of Europe waited a century and a quarter from 1791, when the National Assembly of France in revolution voted the Jews of France free and equal citizens, to the Revolution of 1917 in Russia, which accomplished the same result for those in that country. And the Nazi nightmare, from which the world emerged in 1945, proved with hideous clarity how fragile the growth still was.

The insurrection of July 1830, when the armed workers of Paris forced King Charles X to flee to England, was but a curtain raiser to the revolutionary fever that seized upon Europe eighteen years later. Nevertheless, the Paris uprising had its repercussions in the Low Countries, in Italy, in Poland, and in some of the smaller German states. It led to the extension in 1831 of state support to synagogues and rabbis in France, thus placing Judaism on an equal footing with the other faiths. But it was not until 1846 that the French Supreme Court abolished that degrading vestige of the Middle Ages, the special form of oath required of Jewish witnesses in legal proceedings; and it may be added that in Prussia this humiliation, the oath *more Judaico*, was not abolished till 1869.

Prussia and Austria remained untouched by the ground swell of the July revolution; in Poland, an uprising in 1831 against the Russian master, Czar Nicholas I, was crushed; and in Italy Austrian bayonets restored those rulers, including Pope Gregory XVI, who had been ousted by popular uprisings. The tyrannical system of Metternich, though badly shaken, still held firm in Austria, Italy, and the Germanies, but another and greater surge was gathering to overthrow it.

2

IT CAME in February 1848, and again the first eruption occurred in Paris when the government of the sham liberal Louis Philippe, and his cynical minister François Guizot, who had managed to antagonize all classes of the nation, was overthrown to be followed by a short-lived republic. With "democracy and nationalism" as its watchword, the ferment spread rapidly to Germany, Austria, and Italy. For Germany and Italy, nationalism, of course, meant unification; but for Austria, with its hodgepodge of nationalities, it implied exactly the reverse. The Jews, however, were primarily interested in "democracy," which meant everywhere the same: constitutional government with all citizens equal before the law. Jewish nationalism was not to become an issue until half a century later.

In March 1848, revolutionary riots broke out in Vienna and Count Metternich, his vise on Europe broken at last, fled for his life to England. The same month, there were street battles in Milan and Venice with the soldiers of Austria. In Germany, the rulers of the lesser states granted constitutions and other reforms; and on March 18, 1848, there was a bloody clash between populace and troops in Berlin, in which over two hundred lost their lives. The King of Prussia promised a constitution and appointed a liberal ministry.

The Jews of Prussia and the rest of Germany were thrilled with new hope. Twenty-one of the dead in the Berlin outbreak were Jews, and they shared the common grave in which all the victims were laid. Michael Sachs pronounced a prayer over the grave, and Leopold Zunz saw the rise of "the Dominion of Freedom," with the "recognition of Man unclouded by distinctions of sect or class." And, as if to fulfill this vision, a Constitutional Convention, representing the entire German Confederation, assembled in Frankfort on the Main, and in May 1848 entered upon the Herculean task of unifying Germany on a democratic basis.

The Frankfort Assembly, which remained in session for nearly a year, proved to be one of the most heartbreaking failures in history. The constitution which it drafted for a unified Germany was democratic enough; it recognized the equality of all citizens, irrespective of religion; but the King of Prussia, Frederick William IV, to whom the Assembly offered the imperial crown, refused to accept it from a revolutionary body. Besides, he had no stomach for a war with Austria and the other large German states, who were opposed to a unified Germany under the leadership of Prussia. It was one of the fateful decrees of history, and fraught with disaster for mankind in general and the Jewish people in particular, that a united Germany was to be born, not in the liberal spirit of the Frankfort Assembly, but in the "blood and iron" of Otto von Bismarck.

There were four Jews among the deputies in the Frankfort

Assembly, of whom Gabriel Riesser (1806-1863) was chosen as one of the vice-presidents. He had the doubtful honor, also, of being a member of the deputation which received the "great refusal" from the Prussian monarch. Riesser, the acknowledged leader of the Jews in Germany in the struggle for emancipation, stood firmly on the principle that the grant of equality was an act of justice, in return for which no surrender of any portion of the Jewish faith or practice should be demanded or offered. In 1832, he founded and edited a magazine which he boldly called *Der Jude*, wherein he scrutinized without fear or favor certain half-measures which were brought forward for improving the civil status of the Jews in Baden, Wuerttemberg, Bavaria, Prussia, and other German states, always demanding "unconditional emancipation." Riesser was a persuasive writer, a brilliant orator, and a fearless champion of his people against their traducers. In the Frankfort Assembly he was successful in defeating a constitutional proposal which, in spite of the reforms it provided, would still have given the Jews an exceptional status; he saw clearly, and he made others see, the intimate connection between the denial of full rights to the Jews and the general ascendancy of reaction and tyranny. For Germany, he advocated a constitutional monarchy, and the speech in which he called for unification under the hegemony of Prussia was one of the great moments of the Assembly.

The Frankfort Assembly, which had stirred so many high but vain hopes, was dispersed, and in the summer of 1849 there were new uprisings led, this time, by the republicans. They were all put down, and many of these "forty-niners," among them a good sprinkling of Jews, managed to escape and find refuge in America.

3

IN THE meantime, the revolutionary movements in Austria, bedeviled by conflicts among the numerous nationalities, suffered the same fate. The outbreak in Vienna in March 1848 had wrested a liberal constitution from the emperor, in which religious inequalities were banned; but in June, a Pan-Slavic rebellion in Prague was easily quelled. In the summer of 1849, the Republic of Hungary, which Louis Kossuth had proclaimed earlier that year, was wiped out by the forces of the new emperor, the youthful

Francis Joseph, aided by a large Russian army; and Kossuth became a fugitive. A fine of 2,300,000 gulden was imposed upon the Jews of Hungary for the part they had played in the revolution: they were only about three per cent of the population, but in the revolutionary forces there were 20,000 of them in a total of 180,000. They fought valiantly for Hungarian independence, despite the fact that on the outbreak of the revolution there were mob attacks against them in a number of cities, including Pressburg and Pest. Emperor Francis Joseph, it should be added, reduced the fine to 1,000,000 gulden, with the provision that its income should be used for Jewish educational and philanthropic purposes.

Nor did the revolutions in Italy fare any better. In the spring of 1848, the *Risorgimento* or "Resurrection," as the patriots called the movement for the liberation and unification of Italy, stood on the threshold of victory; in the summer it was snuffed out by a new Austrian army and the Hapsburg princes came back to their thrones. In the interval, the Jews of Piedmont, Venice, Tuscany, Modena, and other Italian states had a taste of emancipation. Early in 1849, an outbreak in Rome, led by Giuseppe Mazzini, transformed the Papal States into a republic; several months later Pius IX, who had been forced to flee, was restored, and similar movements in the south were also suppressed. In the interval, the gates of the Roman ghetto, amid the jubilation of Jews and Christians, were torn down, and the revolutionary assembly decreed civic equality for the Roman Jews. In all these struggles, Jewish volunteers bore arms against the tyrants, they sat in the revolutionary legislative bodies, and they served as ministers in the newly created governments.

4

IN SPITE of the luckless star that dogged the revolutionary movements of 1848-49, they can still be credited with a marked advance in the emancipation of the Jews, just as they were instrumental also in sweeping out the tyranny of the Metternich system and extending the boundaries of liberalism in western and central Europe. In Hungary the sacrifices the Jews laid on the altar of independence did not remain entirely unrewarded, although complete emancipation became a fact only after the *Ausgleich*, or

Compromise of 1867, had established the Dual Monarchy of Austria-Hungary. The same year a law was adopted by the Hungarian Parliament declaring the Jews of Hungary "equal with the Christian inhabitants in the exercise of all civil and political rights."

In Austria, where the Jews were also active supporters of the libertarian movements of 1848-49, the progress toward emancipation was especially marked. The constitution of 1849 made free men of them, its first article providing that "the enjoyment of civil and political rights does not depend on religious profession." Now they could live openly in Vienna or anywhere else in the empire, acquire landed property, and engage in all trades and professions. They could send their children to the general schools and were not subject to legal restrictions with respect to marriage. In 1851, that constitution was abrogated, and the Jews found themselves again deprived of their elementary human rights; but with the best efforts of the clericals, the old order in Austria could not be quite restored. In December 1867, after the empire had sustained a series of severe reverses, a new constitution was promulgated which restored full rights to the Jews and completed their emancipation.

In almost the same words as were inscribed in the Austrian constitution of 1849, the Prussian constitution of 1850 proclaimed the divorcement of civil and political rights from religious affiliation, although in practice Prussian officials still managed to exclude Jews from government and university positions. Nevertheless, that provision represented a notable advance, and in Bavaria and other German states Jewish rights were also extended. It was not, however, until 1871 that full emancipation was enacted for the whole of Germany, which had in the meantime been transformed by Bismarck into a well-knit empire, after a series of wars in which Denmark, Austria, and France were successively humbled by Prussia.

In the Italian peninsula, emancipation survived the reaction of 1849 only in the kingdom of Piedmont. But out of that kingdom came the three men—Victor Emmanuel the king, Cavour the statesman, and Garibaldi the hero—who achieved a unified Italy. When, in September 1870, Victor Emmanuel took possession of Rome as King of Italy, and the temporal power of the pope came to an end, the wretched ghetto of that city was at long last abolished, and all Italian Jews were fully emancipated.

5

THE interval between the return of Pius IX to Rome and his final deposition as temporal ruler is marked by an outrage which made men throughout the world wonder if the Dark Ages had really come to an end. On June 23, 1858, by order of the holy office of the Inquisition in Rome, Edgar Mortara, a six-year-old Jewish child, was torn from his parents by a troop of papal soldiers and placed in a convent to be brought up as a Catholic. The Mortara family lived in Bologna which, at the time, was still under papal jurisdiction, and the reason given for the abduction was that four years earlier, when the child was seriously ill, his nurse, according to her own confession, had secretly baptized him. The sacrament having been administered, the child, so the pontiff maintained, no longer belonged to his parents but to the church. All efforts of the parents to recover their child remained futile.

News of the abduction spread throughout the world, and the Mortara case created a sensation. In every land Jews appealed to their governments for diplomatic aid. Napoleon III of France and Francis Joseph of Austria, both Catholic sovereigns, appealed personally to Pius IX; Protestant rulers also expressed their sympathy; decent humanity everywhere was outraged, but the pope remained unmoved. "I snap my fingers at the whole world," he is reported to have said. The rabbis of Germany sent him a petition, which remained unanswered, and Sir Moses Montefiore journeyed to Rome, where the pope refused to see him. Edgar Mortara was brought up as a Catholic and remained one. Pius IX, angered by the notoriety which the case received, vented his resentment upon the Jews under his jurisdiction; but the Mortara case, it is believed, contributed not a little to his reverses in 1870. "If you only knew how much it cost me!" he once declared to the youth whom he had torn from his parents and his faith.

6

THE same year that witnessed the triumph of medieval bigotry in the ruthless abduction of little Edgar Mortara, brought the Jews of England a triumph of another order. In 1858 they won a decisive victory after more than a century of struggle for their civil and political emancipation.

As early as 1753, Parliament had passed a law which empowered it to naturalize members of the Jewish faith. It was a century since, as a result of the exertions of Menasseh ben Israel, the country which had been closed to the Jews since 1290, was reopened to them. During that century they had made good progress. Not even the restoration of Charles II in 1660, which their enemies, including the Corporation of the City of London, attempted to exploit to injure and blackmail them, could seriously undermine their position. On two separate occasions, in fact, Charles assured them of his protection, and in 1685 the Crown Council of his successor, James II, informed them they could "quietly enjoy the free exercise of their religion." With the wealth they brought to England and their commercial connections, they had become an important asset to the country.

In 1701, the Sephardic community, numbering several hundred members, dedicated their famous Bevis Marks synagogue which still stands. Its rabbi was the learned and philosophical David Nieto, and its membership included men of wealth and influence like Sir Solomon de Medina, the first Jew in England to be knighted. In 1692 Ashkenazic Jews had begun to arrive from Germany and Poland, but lacking the wealth and culture of the Sephardim, they were not welcomed by them and established synagogues of their own. It took a century for the walls of snobbery to come down and for the Ashkenazim to share in the leadership of British Jewry.

7

THE law of 1753, which would have made England the first European country to extend equality to Jews, was repealed only a year after its passage. Two years previously, a similar law for the benefit of the Huguenots who had settled in England, had come to grief, and now a violent campaign was launched against the enfranchisement of the Jews. The popular slogan was "No Jews, no wooden shoes," the "wooden shoes," of course, representing the Huguenots. Early in the reign of George III, moreover, the cause of emancipation suffered an even more serious blow in the passage of a law requiring voters, army officers, members of parliament, and all government and university officials to take an oath containing the words "upon the true faith of a Christian."

In that formula, the prejudice against the Jews appeared to be immovably entrenched, and many of the wealthy and ambitious among them sought the solution in baptism, if not for themselves, then for their children. The example was set by Samson Gideon, the head of the community, who took his children out of the faith; and it was followed by many of the leading Sephardic families, whose descendants gradually mingled with the British aristocracy and were lost in it. The most famous secession occurred in 1817 when thirteen-year-old Benjamin Disraeli, who was to become one of England's most illustrious prime ministers, was sent to the baptismal font by his father Isaac. Somewhat earlier, occurred the alienation of David Ricardo who, in 1819, became an outstanding member of Parliament, but is better known as the founder of the science of economics.

In the meantime, however, popular prejudice against the Jews began to ebb. More of them were arriving from Germany and Poland and, as small traders, they came into closer contact with the common people than did the Sephardic magnates. Many pious Englishmen like Lewis May, who founded a missionary society in London, labored for the speedy conversion of the Jews; and although they made few converts, their preaching inspired more tolerance and respect for the people who gave the Christians their Bible and Redeemer. But curiously enough, what contributed more, perhaps, to the change of attitude was the prominence achieved by Jews in pugilism, first in the affections of sports-loving Britons. In 1789, Daniel Mendoza became the boxing champion of England, and he was followed by other Jewish champions of the highly admired sport. The Jewish boxers, moreover, elevated the sport into a fine art in which skill counted for more than brute strength, so that members of the aristocracy also became devoted to it and admired its teachers and champions.

By the beginning of the nineteenth century the leadership of the community had to a large degree passed into the hands of the

Ashkenazim: the Rothschilds, the Goldsmids, the Salomons. The barriers between the two groups were coming down. In 1812, Judith Cohen, daughter of an Ashkenazi, became the wife of Moses Montefiore and, by marrying Judith's sister, Nathan Meyer Rothschild, as Montefiore's brother-in-law, established close relations with the Sephardic leaders. The latter had, in 1760, established the Board of Deputies to promote and safeguard Jewish rights, and by 1830 that body, which was destined to exert influence in many lands, numbered Ashkenazim also among its members.

8

THE previous year had witnessed the emancipation of the Catholics in England, and now a bill was introduced in Commons on behalf of the Jews. It was supported by petitions signed by thousands of leading Englishmen and it had staunch advocates in both houses. Among its champions was the poet, historian and statesman, Thomas Babington Macaulay, who in 1830 delivered his maiden speech in Commons in support of the measure and a year later published his famous essay on the political disabilities of the Jews. But after passing in Commons the bill was rejected by the Tory House of Lords. Year after year, it was presented and met the same fate. In the meantime, however, other political offices were opened to the Jews, in each case not without a struggle. In 1835 David Salomons was elected sheriff of London county, and when he refused to take the prescribed oath, Parliament adopted a law changing the wording of the oath, but for that office only. Ten years later, when David Salomons was elected an alderman, the change was extended to municipal offices. By 1846, the forbidding oath barred the way to Parliament only. The following year, and again in 1850, Baron Lionel Rothschild was elected to that body, but the House of Lords again defeated every attempt to modify the oath and prevented him from being seated.

The following year the solemn decorum of the House of Commons was rudely disturbed, and the struggle against the disfranchising formula assumed the character of an exciting drama. David Salomons was again the hero of the piece and the forbidding formula the villain. Having been elected to Parliament, he refused to take the oath, and when ordered to leave, he refused to do that also. He addressed the Commons in defense of his conduct and made a deep impression. In view of the tumult that arose it was moved to adjourn, and Salomons insisted on registering his vote on the motion. He voted also on two other occasions, and later the courts fined him £500 for each vote.

The country was stirred by Salomons' boldness; he became even more popular, and in 1855 he was elected Lord Mayor of London. The struggle against the formula continued: it was still a tug of war between the House of Commons and the House of Lords. At length, in 1858, the Lords agreed to a compromise which permitted each house to modify the oath as it desired in order to admit Jewish members. The same year Lionel Rothschild was seated as the first Jewish member of Parliament. He had taken the oath with covered head as prescribed by orthodox usage, replacing the words "upon the true faith of a Christian" with "so help me God."

Two years later, the parliamentary oath was changed for all members and for both houses, and in 1885 Lionel's son Nathan Meyer was raised to the peerage and became the first Jewish member of the House of Lords. A few restrictions, particularly in the universities, still remained; they were not removed until 1890 when all British subjects, without regard to religion, were made eligible for every position in the British Empire, except that of monarch. And it should be added that in no country has emancipation been better honored, in spirit as well as in letter, than in Britain.

CHAPTER FIFTY-THREE

In Czarist Russia

VIEWED against the somber back-drop of eighteen centuries of scorn and proscription, the middle decades of the nineteenth century, the decades of emancipation, were like the dawn of a new day for the ghetto prisoners of western and central Europe. The ghetto walls had come down and the prisoners were stepping out to share in ever-growing measure in the life of the

THE EAST EUROPEAN CENTER

nations. The current of hope ran high and strong: words like "culture," "enlightenment," "progress," and "humanity" were uttered with conviction; and the long centuries of the past were like a black night which made the approaching day appear all the brighter. For such is the way of men: past woes they quickly forget, and they paint the future in the hues of their hopes and desires. But the new dawn, true or false, was for the Jews of western and central Europe only, with the largest aggregation still in eastern Europe, where the waves of revolution rolling out of France broke without effect, and repression and persecution continued to flourish.

By far the greater part of the million Jews that made up the Polish community found itself, after the final partition of Poland in 1795, under the scepter of Czarina Catherine II. It was an ironic trick of fate for Russia to be endowed with so many Jews. For centuries, that country had denied them the right of domicile within its borders, although in practice the policy was not always completely enforced: the general economic welfare, especially in Little Russia, depended too much upon the Jewish merchant. Those rulers who, like Peter the Great (1682-1725), might have followed a more liberal policy, were not disposed to antagonize the clergy, who harked back with dread to a period in the fifteenth and sixteenth centuries when nobles and even priests of the Orthodox church were powerfully attracted toward Judaism. The official policy was epitomized in the reply of Catherine's predecessor, Empress Elizabeth (1741-1762), daughter of Peter the Great, to a petition to permit Jews to settle in Russia for the wealth they would add to the country. "From the enemies of Christ," said the pious Elizabeth, "I desire neither gain nor profit."

Saddled now with hundreds of thousands of these "enemies of Christ" and with millions of hardly more welcome Polish Catholics, Empress Catherine II, who liked to mouth liberal phrases, promised religious liberty to all her new subjects "and certainly to the Jews also." But Catherine's religious liberty did not include the right to settle in "Holy Russia," or to trade on equal terms with Christians. Jewish merchants were taxed twice as much as others, and in 1791, even before the second partition of Poland, the first of a series of edicts was enacted which established the infamous "Pale of Settlement," restricting the Jews to certain provinces of the enlarged empire, most of them carved out of former Poland, and setting up a wall of police vigilance which barred all of them except a privileged few from the rest of it.

But even in the Pale the Jews were not permitted full freedom of domicile. As early as 1808, it became the policy of the government to exclude them from the villages and herd them into the congested cities, where they were forced into competition with Christian merchants and artisans and with each other. For a century thereafter, the periodic expulsions from the villages, to which the czars and their minions resorted, brought misery and ruin to numberless Jewish families and only added to the hardships of the peasants in whose interest the policy was professedly applied. Very early, also, the government promulgated laws which reduced the powers of the local *kahals:* they were saved from total extinction only because they were found useful as tax-collecting and recruiting agencies.

2

THERE were three czars in Russia during the first half of the nineteenth century. In 1796 Catherine was followed by her unbeloved son Paul I, whom, five years later his officers murdered. Then came Alexander I, whose reign, which lasted till 1825, covered the Napoleonic period. Alexander's ambition was to be known as "the first gentleman of Europe." He loved to pose as a liberal and utter pious sentiments which Metternich knew how to utilize to promote his reactionary system. The third was Alexander's brother Nicholas I (1825-1855), whose reign of three decades was a Thirty Years' War against his Jewish subjects.

Under Paul I, the Jews became the objects of official solicitude, which they had good reason to suspect and fear. A number of investigations into their condition were conducted by Derzhavin, a statesman and pious poet, whose general attitude is expressed in the following sentence which occurs in his report: "Inasmuch as Providence, to attain its unknown ends, leaves this people, despite its dangerous characteristics, on the face of the earth, and refrains from destroying it, the government under which it takes refuge must also suffer it to live." The Polish nobles, asked by Derzhavin to state their views, shifted the responsibility for the misery of their serfs from themselves, where it belonged, to the Jewish innkeepers.

The accession of the "liberal" Alexander I aroused great hopes, and in 1804 he approved a far-reaching statute which aimed at nothing less than a metamorphosis of his Jewish subjects. It set out to change overnight, as it were, their occupations, language, habits, and even their garb. The statute, which became known as the "Jewish Constitution," desired above all to make farmers of them, and to this end, Astrakhan and the Caucasus were added to the eleven provinces which constituted the Pale of Settlement. Public schools and universities were opened to them, they were permitted to establish secular schools of their own, and were required to use Russian, Polish, or German in the conduct of their business or in communicating with the authorities. But the law further curtailed the powers of the *kahals* and, worst blow of all, it provided that by January 1808, the villages of the Pale must be cleared of all Jewish inhabitants. Czar Alexander was highly pleased with the statute: the Jews, he felt, owed him a debt of gratitude which he hoped they would repay by producing at least one Russian Mendelssohn.

As the day set for the expulsion from the villages approached, the alarm among the Jews increased. The government gave the victims a short reprieve: it feared they would welcome the armies of Napoleon who were already marching through the Polish provinces of Prussia. But in the Treaty of Tilsit of July 1808 Napoleon and Alexander came to terms, and shortly afterwards the expulsions began. They were an impressive demonstration of the brutality and stupidity which even a well-meaning Czarist government could display. The victims, it is reported, "were driven like cattle into the towns and cities and left there in public squares in the open air." There being too many of them to maintain themselves in the cities, they would, it was expected, turn to farming. But there was no land for them, not even means of transportation. Several small agricultural settlements had, it is true, been established in the south, but the government would provide no funds for additional ones. From every standpoint, including that of improving the lot of the peasants, the expulsions were a dismal failure and were so branded by an official committee which put a stop to them. "It is not true," the committee reported, "that the village Jew enriches himself at the expense of the peasants."

But a more compelling reason arose for ending the expulsions. The Treaty of Tilsit proved to be a short and uneasy truce, and in 1812 Napoleon's "Grand Army" was on the march, sweeping across Lithuania and White Russia, both regions thickly inhabited by Jews. But if Napoleon expected them to flock to his standard as he did when he invaded Palestine thirteen years earlier, he was again mistaken. The prospect of emancipation, which the triumph of his arms held out, failed to attract them. For with all their differences, Chassidim and Misnagdim were agreed that emancipation, which would open the door of European secularism to their children, would undermine the Jewish faith. Instead, Jews fought in the Russian armies and served them as purveyors and intelligence agents. In government circles a more favorable attitude came into evidence, and representatives of the *kahals* were able to secure certain concessions, including the suspension of some of the drastic measures prescribed in the "Jewish Constitution" of 1804. But the better day which seemed to be dawning for the Jews of Russia was blotted out by the black reaction that followed the Congress of Vienna. That Congress, moreover, ceded to Russia the greater part of the former duchy of Warsaw, delivering new masses of Jews to the tender mercies of the czars.

3

IN THE last decade of his reign, Alexander's liberalism was overshadowed by a religious mysticism out of which grew the Holy Alliance of Russia, Prussia, and Austria. The monarchs of those three lands bound themselves to be guided by "Christian principles" and to govern their subjects in a spirit of love, even as a father governs his children. In practice, however, the Holy Alliance became a powerful instrument of oppression. The same mystic trend led the czar to conceive an ardent desire to bring about the conversion of his Jewish subjects. He became the patron of a "Society of Israelite Christians" which was founded in 1817, and the following year, at the conference of the European powers which was held in Aachen, he laid before the diplomats a plan for the emancipation and conversion of the Jews which had been prepared for him by the English missionary Lewis Way. The conference did not reject Way's plan. It even adopted a resolution recognizing "the justice of its general tendency" and recommending the problem as "one which must claim the attention equally of the statesman and humanitarian." The diplomats knew how to honor the czar's mood with well-sounding but meaningless phrases.

In the meantime, strangely enough, the czar was compelled to take note of the fact that many of his subjects were moving in the opposite direction and adopting some of the rites of Judaism. They were the *Subbotniki*, "Sabbatarians," who practised circumcision and observed as their sabbath the seventh day of the week instead of the first. The sect had long been in existence, and in 1812 was even recognized by the government. Toward the end of his reign, however, Alexander made a determined attempt to suppress it. Thousands of *Subbotniki* were exiled to Siberia and the Caucasus. Jews were forbidden to employ Christian domestics lest they should become "Judaisers," and those living in districts where the sect flourished were banished. The old policy of herding them into the towns was also revived; in 1824 thousands were brutally expelled from the villages of the provinces of Moghilev and Vitebsk. A government report on the effects of this expulsion, issued ten years later, contained the following statement: "While it has ruined the Jews, it does not in the least seem to have improved the condition of the villagers."

4

WITH all these barbarities, Alexander's reign left a good memory, for the reign that followed was a veritable nightmare for the Jews of Russia. Nicholas began by suppressing a military revolt, and for thirty years held Russia in a vise of steel. What he meant for his Jewish subjects is indicated by the fact that, of the 600 laws bearing on Jews enacted in Russia between 1640 and 1881, more than half were decreed during his reign.

In foreign policy the "iron czar," as Nicholas I was called, was an ardent collaborator of Count Metternich, and his domestic policy was controlled by the ultimate aim of Russianizing all his subjects and gathering them under the wings of the Greek Orthodox Church. All changes were to be imposed by the autocrat and accepted without question, and it goes without saying that the more "different" any group of his subjects might be, the harder would this policy bear down upon them.

The most "different" were undoubtedly the Jews. Not only was their religion different, but also their language and even their garb, of which the long coat or caftan was the principal feature. The economic pattern of their life was different, lacking as it did a basis in agriculture and largely restricted to trade and handicrafts in the cities, and innkeeping in the villages. With a way of life rooted in a remote past and minutely regulated by the sacred code of the *Shulchan Aruch*, innovation would be tantamount to sacrilege and compliance to apostasy. In other lands of the Diaspora the "peculiar" character of this people was usually taken for granted: whether tolerated or resented it was regarded as immutable. Now, however, a powerful government proposed to change it: Nicholas I of Russia set himself the same goal which two thousand years earlier had been essayed by Antiochus IV of Syria.

5

THE first and most direct measure for the attainment or the goal was a decree issued in 1827 imposing a drastic system of military service upon the Jews. It was the infamous "cantonist" system, by which Jewish boys under eighteen, many of them not yet in their teens, were drafted into the army and exiled for twenty-five years or more from their homes, to which most of them never returned. The system was really a variant of the simpler method discovered by the Pharaoh of the Exodus, who ordered that "every son that is born ye shall cast into the river."

Not until a century later, when the Germans displayed their skill in the arts of torture and mass murder, was there a more fiendish contrivance inflicted upon the Jewish people. Legally a cantonist was the son of a soldier, the property of the state, who was trained from boyhood for the army; but any Jewish boy was liable to conscription as a cantonist. Upon each community a definite quota of conscripts was imposed, for which the local *kahal* was held strictly accountable and, in case of default, the officers of the *kahal* were themselves often conscripted.

But the real purpose of the system, in spite of the flowery

phrases with which the decree attempted to cover it, was plain enough. The youths and small children, torn from their homes, were to be compelled to renounce their faith, and the means to be employed to that end could be easily imagined. Throughout the Pale, the helpless communities were thrown into panic. Mothers hid their little sons wherever they could, and youths fled into the forests where they were hunted like animals. A rumor shortly arose that early marriages were about to be prohibited by government decree, for this custom, which was prevalent among the Jews, made many youths heads of families and conscription more difficult. Thereupon, fathers and mothers made frantic haste to marry off their children. The *behala*, or panic, continued to grow.

Despite the terrible pressure to which they were subjected, the *kahals* were unable to deliver their quota of conscripts and, as in every social upheaval, a class of debased creatures came forward to feed on the suffering of their fellows. They were the professional *chappers*, or "captors," who went about kidnapping youths and little boys in order to fill the quotas. Nor did the *chappers* confine themselves to boys of twelve and over, as the law required. They tore little ones as young as eight from the arms of their parents, and delivered them to be sent away as cantonists.

The victims were dispatched to distant provinces of the empire, far from the Pale of Settlement; but large numbers, probably more than half of them, never reached their destination. They succumbed to disease, to the hardships of the journey, to the brutality of their conductors. Those who reached the camps were put in charge of trainers, whose principal function was to make them consent to baptism. It was no easy task, so they starved and flogged the little conscripts, kept them endlessly awake, let them suffer thirst after feeding them with salted fish, compelled them to eat pork, and practiced other tortures upon them. Communication with their parents was banned, and the baptized and unbaptized were kept strictly apart. Naturally, very few of those who held out against baptism survived.

6

THE war against the Jews on the economic front was in no way relaxed. Early in the reign of the "iron czar," thousands of them were expelled from the villages in the provinces of Grodno and Kiev, from the city of Kiev proper, and from the fortified cities on the Black Sea. The "Statute Concerning the Jews," enacted in 1835, in which the existing laws were assembled and new ones added, narrowed the Pale of Settlement, limited the right of Jewish merchants to sojourn in cities outside the Pale, and restricted still further their right to employ Christian domestics. Hebrew books were subjected to censorship, and later in his reign Nicholas even prohibited his Jewish subjects from letting their earlocks grow or wearing the caftan. The autonomy of the *kahals* was abolished, although the officials were allowed to remain in order to collect taxes and furnish conscripts.

The climax of humiliation and injury came in 1852 when the Jews of the empire were divided into "harmful" and "harmless," the former to become the objects of new persecutions. They were saved in a measure by the outbreak of the Crimean War. In that war, thousands of Jewish soldiers died for a ruler who was their enemy in a much truer sense than the French and British soldiers whose cannon they faced.

Some of the laws, like those aiming to abolish the cherished traditional garb or limiting sojourn in cities outside the Pale, were easier to enact than to enforce. They only furnished a corrupt bureaucracy with additional opportunities for blackmail, and the total effect of the expulsions, restrictions, and extortions was to drive the Jewish masses in the towns and cities of the Pale from a condition of poverty to one of destitution.

7

IN THE former grand duchy of Warsaw, the lot of the Jews was, prior to 1831, better on the whole than that of their brothers in Russia. The duchy had been transformed by Alexander I into the Kingdom of Poland, with himself as king but with a large measure of autonomous rule.

Many of the Jews in the kingdom looked forward to speedy emancipation and, in emulation of their brothers in western Europe, not a few of them sought to "deserve" the boon by shedding their Jewish "peculiarities." They called themselves "Poles of the Mosaic Persuasion" or "Old Testament Believers." David Friedlaender of Berlin, who was looked upon as wearing the mantle of Moses Mendelssohn, was even officially asked to submit his views on emancipation: he remained true to his zeal for Reform by recommending that the Jews surrender their traditional way of life before being granted civil equality. The recommendation was entirely to the government's taste, and instead of granting emancipation, the restrictions to which the Jews were subjected were tightened. Nor could the "Old Testament Believers," with all their servility, gain the exceptional status for themselves which they sought.

When in 1831 the Poles took up arms for their independence, the aristocratic leaders of the revolt rejected a plan to organize a Jewish regiment, for which a call had been issued by Joseph Berkovich, son of Berek Yoselovitch, the man who raised the Jewish regiment which fought for Poland in 1794. Nor were they admitted into the regular army; and in the militia, which many of them joined, they had to operate as separate units.

With the suppression of the revolt, the kingdom, though not yet formally abolished, became virtually a Russian province, and the policy of oppression and Russianization was gradually extended over it. In 1843, the twenty-five year term of military service was imposed upon the Polish Jews, though they were spared the atrocious cantonist system, and two years later the tax on the traditional garb was also levied upon them.

8

IN THE meantime, the blood libel had made its way into "Holy Russia," where it found congenial soil. The cantonist system had, in addition to the "captors," produced a crop of depraved renegades and informers who joined forces with local demagogues to fasten the libel on individuals and entire communities. A hideous case which dragged on from 1823 to 1835 was fabricated in the town of Velizh, province of Vitebsk. On the instigation of the governor-general of White Russia, and with the aid of "testimony" furnished by prostitutes and apostates, a fantastic web of falsehoods was prepared, in which the leading families of the community were enmeshed. In 1826 Nicholas ordered the synagogues of the town closed and all religious services suspended. It was only after the case was reviewed by the Council of State, the highest court of the empire, that the prisoners who had survived the ordeals to which they were subjected were released, and the synagogues, which had been closed for nine years, reopened. In 1853, the city of Saratov in central Russia was the scene of another blood accusation, bringing torture and penal servitude to a number of innocents, of whom the last survivor was only pardoned in 1867 in response to an appeal made by Adolphe Crémieux to Nicholas' successor.

9

SERGIUS UVAROV, the czar's Minister of Public Instruction, satisfied himself that the cantonist system and the other coercive measures of the government were not sufficient to bring about the "radical transformation" of the Jewish people which he and his master desired. The root of the evil, he found, was the Jewish educational system, with its emphasis on the Talmud, which preserved their separateness. Uvarov had heard of the "enlightenment" and the reform which flourished in the West, of the secular schools for Jewish children in Prussia and Austria. He became convinced that the transformation policy would succeed only if the *cheder* and *yeshivah* were abolished and replaced by a system of government schools, where the children would be alienated from the influence of the Talmud and from all that made the Jews a separate people. With one hand the autocrat was to swing the knout of persecution, and with the other hold out the gift of "enlightenment." In 1840, therefore, a decree was issued ordering the establishment of a system of crown elementary and secondary schools for the Jews of Russia.

For the success of his "benevolent" project, Uvarov depended to a large extent on the handful of "enlightened" Jewish intellectuals who were already to be found in Russia; but for his principal adjutant he chose Max Lilienthal, a native of Bavaria and a graduate of a German university. Lilienthal, still in his twenties, had already proved his ability as head of a modern Jewish school in Riga. In 1841, and again the following year, Lilienthal, at Uvarov's behest, visited the leading communities of the Pale in an effort to persuade them that the government meant well by them. He was eminently unsuccessful. He himself had been beguiled into accepting Uvarov's professions of good faith, but the Jewish masses and their leaders knew what to think of favors that were being offered to them by the same hand that was snatching away their children. "You are a stranger," the leaders of the Vilna community told Lilienthal in 1842. "Do you know what you are doing? The government intends to have only one religion in the empire." In Minsk it was pointed out to him that without equal rights, general culture would only add to the woes of the Jewish youth. They would balk at the inferior positions which alone were open to them and finding no solace in their religion, many of them would seek a solution in baptism.

That such was the real aim of the government eventually became clear to Lilienthal also. In 1845 he turned his back on the Russian officials and their favors, and migrated to America. In the meantime, however, the system of crown schools had been set up, as well as two seminaries to train "modern" rabbis and teachers. The cost of maintaining the schools was passed on to the Jews in the form of special taxes on kosher meat and sabbath candles. The traditional schools and academies, though not immediately abolished, were marked for extinction, and inducements were offered to parents to send their children to the new schools, one form of bait being a reduction in the length of military service for their graduates.

The great majority of parents, however, saw in the crown schools a Trojan horse, loaded with enemies who were bent on destroying the only thing that gave their martyred life meaning and consolation—their faith. Against the passive resistance of the masses the schools were helpless, and before the reign of the "iron czar's" successor ended they were all abolished.

10

IN GERMANY, France, and England, Jewish leaders had, like Lilienthal, begun by assuming that Uvarov's educational projects were conceived in good faith. Some even hailed them as marking the advent of a new era for the Jews in Russia, and the famous artist Moritz Oppenheim was commissioned to paint a picture, symbolizing the dawn of the new day, for presentation to the czar. The picture was never finished. The new wave of persecutions, which included expulsions not only from the villages but also from the towns and cities of the western frontier zone, abrogation of the powers of the *kahals*, and imposition of new taxes on a people already pauperized, spoke louder than pious phrases. But might not the martyred Jews of Russia be helped by the intercession of their influential coreligionists of the West? In London the attempt was considered worth making, and in 1846, Sir Moses Montefiore, whom the Damascus Affair had already made famous, traveled to Russia with a personal letter from Queen Victoria to Nicholas.

The czar received Sir Moses in audience, and his journey through the cities of the Pale was a triumphal progress, with official receptions by the local authorities and enthusiastic demonstrations by the Jews, who were thrilled by the visit of the world-famous philanthropist. When it was all over, Sir Moses submitted a number of proposals for the relief of his persecuted people, but the czar and his ministers left things as they were. The same year Isaac Altaras, a wealthy merchant from Marseille, sought permission for large numbers of Jews to leave Russia and settle in Algiers, where the French government was prepared to welcome them, but this effort also bore no results. From the "decadent" West, Holy Russia listened to advice with official courtesy, but with secret resentment and scorn.

CHAPTER FIFTY-FOUR

Russianization and "Enlightenment"

THE reign of Nicholas I was no exception to the rule that aggression and war go hand in hand with tyranny. His decisive help in crushing the Hungarian revolt of 1849 had already earned him the designation of "gendarme of Europe," and to this distinction he was anxious to add the title of "protector of the Christians in the Ottoman Empire." The occasion for asserting his protective urge was a series of quarrels between Greek Orthodox and Roman Catholic monks over holy places in Palestine.

But neither France nor England, not to speak of Turkey, were convinced that the czar's intentions were purely benevolent, and in the Crimean War (1854-56) which followed, Russia was humbled and the corruption of the czar's autocracy exposed.

To secure more Jewish conscripts for that war, a new fiendish contrivance was devised. It extended immunity from conscription in return for seizing Jews without passports, of whom there were many, and dragging them to the recruiting stations. The abuses to which the regulation lent itself, and the temptations it roused, had the hideous effect of making Jews prey upon each other.

The death of Nicholas I, which occurred while the war was still in progress, made his son Alexander II (1856-1881) the "Autocrat of all the Russias." The youthful Alexander, however, seemed to be made of more humane stuff than his "iron" father; besides, the humiliations the war inflicted on Russia had a chastening effect on the government. The first ten years of the new reign, therefore, were marked by a policy of liberal reform from which the Jews also benefited. The emancipation of the Russian peasants from the medieval serfdom in which they were still held, the introduction of zemstvos or provincial assemblies, with power to share in local government, and a radical revision of the worm-eaten and chaotic judicial system of the country, were the three principal reforms during that period.

For the Jews, the first year of the new reign saw the abolition of the atrocious cantonist system, together with most of the other special conscription regulations from which they suffered, including the one which permitted the seizure and summary conscription of those without passports; but children who had already been forced into baptism were not permitted to return to their parents' faith. The classification of the Jews into "harmless" and "harmful" was suspended, and the Pale of Settlement was gradually extended.

Members of certain occupational categories were even permitted to settle in cities outside the Pale. The privilege was first granted to leading merchants and their families, and extended in time to university graduates, artisans, distillers, apothecaries, and dentists. In 1870 the privilege was further extended to include those who had performed military service. However, complete equality was ruled out; in granting the concessions, the controlling motive was not so much to benefit the Jews as to meet the demand in the interior of Russia for capital and men of enterprise, as well as for mechanics and members of certain professions.

2

GRATEFUL as the Jews were, these measures brought relief to only a tiny fraction of the masses who were still permitted no escape from the congestion and poverty of the Pale. Their numbers moreover, largely as a result of early marriages, continued to grow, and by 1860 probably four million of them were living under the scepter of Alexander II in the Russian provinces and in Poland. The futility of attempting, by force or guile, to wean them away from their faith was now apparent to the czar and his ministers. Nevertheless the government clung to the crown schools of the previous reign, not so much as a means of conversion as of cultural assimilation, and the attempts to suppress the *cheder* were continued. In time, however, the ministers realized that they were engaged in a losing fight, and by 1873 the crown schools were all closed.

Nor did the Jewish masses receive with any more eagerness the "enlightenment" which some of their own people urged upon them. For the government policy of Russianization found zealous supporters among those who, by wealth or education, had won the right of residence outside the Pale and were striving to adapt the teachings of Mendelssohn to their people in Russia. Among them were some who scorned and ridiculed Talmudic as well as Chassidic Judaism, urging a complete break with the Jewish way of life in return for the small favors they already received and the bigger ones they expected. In St. Petersburg, as Leningrad was then called, a number of them organized in 1863 a "Society for the Diffusion of Enlightenment among the Jews of Russia," which soon had branches in Riga, Kiev, Odessa, and other cities. Among its founders were the banker and philanthropist Joseph Ginsburg and his son Baron Horace Ginsburg, the "Rothschilds of Russia," who gave liberally to promote its program of making Russian the language of the Jewish masses, helping them to become farmers and artisans, and modernizing the education of the Jewish young. The Society included the promotion of Hebrew literature among its aims but its basic purpose, as explained by Leon Rosenthal, another one of its founders, was to eradicate certain "peculiarities" of the Jewish masses, in particular their "separateness and fanaticism" which, he declared, were responsible for the disabilities from which they suffered.

The Society was only one of many manifestations of the trend toward secular culture and away from those "peculiarities," a trend which gained ground especially during the first, or liberal, period of the reign of Alexander II. In increasing numbers, the youth flocked to the high schools and universities where they quickly absorbed the literary and scientific culture of Europe and even more quickly renounced the traditional learning and mode of life which had kept their people alive through the ages. The government did not yet set limits on the admission of Jews to the higher institutions of learning: it counted, and not in vain, on their gratitude to further its policy of Russianization. But if the government was pleased with their enthusiasm for Russian culture, it found cause for alarm in their equal enthusiasm for the social and political doctrines which were seeping into Russia out of the West. In their youthful and heady fervor, they saw the Messiah of socialism and universal brotherhood coming up on the horizon, and they treated the Messiah of their fathers with scorn and ridicule.

And among them were not a few who proceeded to hasten the advent of the new Messiah or the Revolution. They joined the movement of the radical Russian youth which, taking for its watchword "To the people!" went to live among the peasants in order to prepare them for the great day; nor were they absent from the bolder revolutionary circles and ventures which attracted the watchful attention of the police. Their world outlook was universal, and with regard to their own people they were fully persuaded that the over-all salvation of Russia would not pass them by. In later decades, some of them even advanced the slogan that "the wheels of the revolution must be lubricated with Jewish blood."

3

THE same forces which lured the generation in western Europe, now operated on many of the young in Russia: the gravitational pull which a dominant majority exerts upon a suppressed minority; the fascination of the new learning and the hope it held out to the disfranchised; the influence of catchwords like "enlightenment and progress" versus "obscurantism and superstition"; the tendency to accept uncritically whatever enjoys the approval of the privileged. In Russia, however, the multitudes stood like a wall against the innovations, clinging to their "peculiarities" as their most precious possessions, and in their distrust of the innovators, rejecting their counsel out of hand, without regard to the merits of whatever they proposed. The purveyors of "enlightenment" forfeited the confidence of the masses by flouting their religious sentiments, nor did they scruple at times to invoke the aid of the government in their war against the "obscurantists," especially against the Chassidic rabbis and their "courts." The rift was even more conspicuous in Poland. In Warsaw the wealthy and educated few curried favor with the Poles not only by asserting their Polish patriotism on every appropriate and inappropriate occasion, but by rejecting their Jewish nationality. They preached Polonization to the Chassidic masses who, of course, turned a deaf ear to all their advice and admonitions.

4

AMONG the different brands of "enlightenment" with which the millions of Jews in the Pale were wooed or menaced, from the Russianization and Utopianism of the revolutionaries, to the Polonization of the "Old Testament Believers," the most effective was the one which adopted the Hebrew language as its vehicle of expression and the rebirth of Hebrew literature as its principal goal. The movement is known as *haskalah*, the Hebrew for "enlightenment," and its practitioners as *maskilim*. The *maskilim* were anxious to modernize Jewish life without, however, entirely breaking with the past. They protested against soulless and excessive ceremonialism, exposed the misdeeds of those who controlled the *kahals*, and sought to open the minds of the young to the beauties of nature and the wonders of European culture. But it cannot be said that they were always careful of the religious sensibilities of their people, or that they fully understood the powers of self-regeneration that lay inherent in the ancient faith. The *maskilim* failed to win the confidence of the masses, for very much like the *measfim* of Mendelssohn's time, they exerted an influence which by and large tended toward assimilation; and if the movement as a whole was saved from following that road to the end, it was due not so much to a lack of direction and momentum as to the shock of the bloody events that occurred on the accession of Alexander III. It was the pogrom wave of 1881 which diverted the path of *haskalah* from assimilation to Jewish national regeneration.

Already in the reign of Nicholas I the herald of *haskalah* had made his appearance in the person of Isaac Baer Levinsohn (1788-1860). Like Max Lilienthal, Levinsohn was beguiled into accepting the crown schools in good faith, and as early as 1828, he published a Hebrew work in which he urged his people to add secular studies to their educational program. He wrote a vigorous refutation of the blood libel and a defense of the Talmud, but his relations with government functionaries, whose financial aid he often solicited, were not dignified. Levinsohn has sometimes been called the Mendelssohn of Russia and credited with being the founder of the "Science of Judaism" in that land. But he lacked the intellectual force and literary grace of the Berlin sage, nor could he compare in erudition with Leopold Zunz.

Vilna in the north and Odessa in the south became the leading centers of *haskalah*—Vilna, the "Jerusalem of Lithuania" and the intellectual power-house of east European Jewry, Odessa, the cosmopolitan seaport and the most civilized metropolis in Russia. In Vilna, the two leading pioneers of the Hebrew literary revival, Mordecai Aaron Ginsburg and Abraham Dov Lebensohn, flourished in the first stage of the movement, which coincided with the reign of Nicholas I. Both of them, the first in prose, the second in poetry, labored to bend the sacred language to secular uses, an effort which the pious masses and their leaders regarded with profound suspicion. They were a small and friendless circle, these early *maskilim*, disposed in their isolation to credit the czar and his officials with good intentions, and their tragedy became deeper when events demonstrated that the instincts of the masses were surer than their own wishful thinking.

5

BUT the tender shoot of the new Hebrew literature, and the appeal for modernism which it bore, continued to grow in spite of the uncongenial soil in which it was planted. It bore blossoms of rare charm in the lyric poetry of Micah Joseph Lebensohn, son of the poet Abraham Dov. Micah Joseph's life was cut short by tuberculosis in 1852, when he was only twenty-four, but in the few years of his creative life he awakened the lyre of Yehudah Halevi and Moses Chayim Luzzatto, adding a new and poignant strain which flowed from the sorrows and tensions in his own soul and in the life of his people. The man who spanned the first and second periods of *haskalah* was Abraham Mapu (1808-1867), whose novel *Ahabath Zion* (Love of Zion) had an extraordinary influence on the youth of his generation. Written in the pure style of the Bible, it painted a glowing picture of the life of Judah in the days of Isaiah, opening a world of wonder and beauty to the youth of the Yeshivoth who, of course, had to read it clandestinely. What a contrast it held up between the free and heroic past and the dismal present!

In the second period of *haskalah*, the leading poet was Judah Leib Gordon (1830-1892), who trained his muse to the arduous task of "enlightenment" and the correction of abuses which he found in the inner life of the communities. *Awake, My People*, the title of one of his first songs, became the battle-cry of the movement, and his epigram "Be a man in the street and a Jew at home," epitomized the policy of Russianization which he advocated. Gordon fought savagely against the Orthodox, who never forgot that he began his career as a teacher in a crown school. For seven years, until he was banished from St. Petersburg on the suspicion of being a revolutionary, he was secretary of the "Society for the Diffusion of Enlightenment." In the last decade of his life, however, his general outlook underwent a change. A great deal had occurred to disillusion him and make him a penitent. He abandoned his crusade for "enlightenment," championed the movement for the colonization of Palestine, and from having been the castigator of his people, he now became their defender.

But of all the standard-bearers of *haskalah*, the most influential was Shalom Jacob Abramovitch (1836-1917), better known by his pen name Mendele Mocher Seforim (Mendele the Bookseller), who spent the last thirty-six years of his long life in Odessa. Mendele, or "the grandfather," as he is endearingly called by his numerous disciples, blazed new trails both as *maskil* and writer. Not content to be read only by the educated minority who understood Hebrew, he chose as his principal medium the Yiddish of the masses, although he began and ended his literary career in the sacred tongue and himself translated into Hebrew most of his Yiddish writings. He is thus the acknowledged creator of a new Jewish literature, the Yiddish which has, since his day, won for itself an honored place among the literatures of the world. But by reason of his genius, and the flexibility which the ancient tongue acquired in his hands, he is looked upon by many as the founder of modern Hebrew literature also.

As advocate of "enlightenment," Mendele's instinctive love for his people saved him from the assimilationist vagaries and supercilious attitudes of his predecessors and contemporaries. Not that he spared the faults and follies which he had ample opportunity to observe in the teeming towns of the Pale. In fact, though his writings embrace numerous genres, his best remembered works, like *Fishke the Cripple*, *The Old Mare*, and *The Puny Little Men*, are satirical novels, dealing with vagrant beggars and paupers and the "respectable" community leaders who prey on them. Mendele ridicules and exposes, but there is no mistaking the tenderness in which his irony is steeped, nor the artistry of the literary master.

6

IN THE early sixties, the reign of Alexander II which began so auspiciously with the emancipation of the serfs and other reforms, entered upon a new and reactionary phase from which, until his assassination in 1881, the czar rarely departed. His youthful subjects were not satisfied with those reforms; the university students, who were aware of the political changes in western Europe, demanded a democratic constitution, and some of them even went so far as to dream of a socialist republic. Secret revolutionary societies arose whose members, as if to flaunt their recklessness, called themselves Nihilists; and to counter the merciless policy of suppression to which they were subjected, they adopted terror, or assassination, as their principal political weapon.

It was the Polish revolt of 1861-63 which, more than anything else, produced the somber change that came over the czar and his officials. In the course of that uprising, both sides, the Polish rebels and the czar's officials, sought the support of the Jews. Jewish lives were lost in the clash between the populace and the Cossacks in Warsaw in February 1861, and the Orthodox rabbi, Berush Meisels, as well as the young preacher Marcus Jastrow, joined with the Polish ecclesiastics at the funeral of the victims. For a moment it appeared as if the fond dream of the "Old Testament Believers" was to come true: Poles called themselves and the Jews "children of the same mother," demanded Jewish emancipation, and the concessions the Russian government offered the Poles actually included the removal of many of the disabilities against the Jews. The rebels, of course, wanted much more than the czar offered. They kept up the revolt, but with some exceptions, the Jewish masses, especially in Lithuania, held aloof, displaying an instinctive and healthy distrust of the new-found love of their Polish compatriots. The revolt, which was quickly crushed, was followed by brutal reprisals. The deep-rooted hostility of the Poles for the Jews came to life again and, in the hands of the publicists and politicians, it took the form of a full-fledged economic and political program of discrimination and repression.

7

AS FOR the czar and his ministers, they seemed to be never free from anxiety over Jewish "separatism" and "exploitation." The policy of Russianization, except for the few intellectuals who made a big noise about it, was a failure: the masses continued to send their children to their own schools, to speak their own language, to wear their earlocks and caftans, to live in accordance with the *Shulchan Aruch*. And as if to confirm the anxiety and resentment of the Russian statesmen, a new Pfefferkorn appeared on the scene, an apostate and informer named Jacob Brafman who claimed to have proof that the *kahal* organizations, which had by now been reduced to a mere shadow of what they had once been, continued to wield their former powers in secret, nullifying all the efforts of the government to bring about a fusion of the Jews with the rest of the population. Brafman went further. In a series of articles which appeared in the official organ of the province of Vilna and were later reprinted by the government under the title of the *Book of the Kahal*, the renegade charged that the Jews of the world had a secret international *kahal*, of which the Russian was a part, with the French *Alliance Israélite Universelle*, organized in 1860 for the protection of Jewish rights, also a member. The czar's officials found in Brafman's book everything they desired and, as is always the case, no refutations of the calumny made any impression upon those who were eager to believe it.

The remedy proposed by the renegade—the immediate abolition of the educational, social, and charitable institutions of the Jewish communities—was found to be too drastic, but about 1870, new restrictions were decreed against the Jews to "break down their separatism." Their right to participate in municipal government was curtailed, and they were singled out for special conscription regulations. For the population at large, those who were the only sons of families, for example, were exempted from military service, but if they were Jews they were subject to conscription. It was obvious that the new decrees were punitive in character and sprang not, as professed, from a desire for amelioration, but from prejudice and malice.

The charge of "exploitation" was naturally seized upon by all those who were irked by Jewish competition. Among them were the Greek food merchants in Odessa, who in March 1871, with the connivance of the authorities, went over to direct action. For three days, they and their Russian coreligionists conducted an Easter pogrom against the Jews of the most civilized city in Russia. For three days Jewish homes and shops were looted and wrecked. Jews were beaten and synagogues defiled, and it was only when the rioting threatened to get out of hand and become a massacre that the authorities acted, and the outbreak was easily suppressed. The Odessa pogrom gave a rude shock to the "Russianized" Jewish intellectuals: for a time the local branch of the "Society for the Diffusion of Enlightenment" kept its doors closed.

The general trend toward reaction, and the warm welcome which the czar's officials extended to the "revelations" of Jacob

Brafman, encouraged other blackguards to go into the profitable business of defaming the Jews. Hippolyte Lutostanski, a defrocked Catholic priest who became a Greek Orthodox monk, tried without success to blackmail the Jews of Moscow by threatening to publish a lurid pamphlet he had written on the blood accusation. In 1876 the pamphlet appeared; it won favor in official circles and was distributed among the secret police. Two years later, a charge of ritual murder was lodged against the handful of Jews who were living in the province of Kutais in the Caucasus, and although the accused were all acquitted, the poison in the atmosphere became thicker. The alliance between official authority and the criminal dregs of society was preparing czarist Russia for a wider and bloodier outbreak of violence against the Jews.

CHAPTER FIFTY-FIVE

Pogroms and Self-Help

NEITHER the policy of brutal suppression which the police of Alexander II pursued against the Nihilists, nor the patriotic fervor which swept the country in 1877 during the war against Turkey, could stem the growth of the underground revolutionary movement. Finally the czar determined to try a different course: he would make away with the discontent by removing the causes on which it fed. On March 13, 1881, he signed a decree ordering substantial reforms in the government, but the same day, as he was driving near his winter palace in St. Petersburg, the Nihilists assassinated him.

The following day his son succeeded him as Alexander III, and the first act of the new "Czar of all the Russias" was to suppress his father's decree of the day before. Soon enough it became clear that, in its basic objectives, the new reign meant a reversion to the reactionary regime of Nicholas I. The teacher and mentor of the new autocrat was the gloomy fanatic Constantine Pobyedonostzev, official head of the Holy Synod of the Greek Catholic Church, whose three-point program, which Alexander III approved, called for absolute autocracy, supremacy of the official religion, and compulsory Russianization. The ultimate aim of the policy was a Russia of one nationality, one language, and one religion.

The peril of the Jews under a regime dominated by such an aim may be easily divined, but their plight was further aggravated by the menace which the autocracy faced in the revolutionary movement. The reactionary press promptly and falsely accused them of taking a leading part in the movement and of being chiefly responsible for the death of Alexander II. Not that Jews were absent from the circles of the Nihilists. It would have been strange indeed if the children of the most oppressed nationality in Russia in whose veins ran the blood of the Hebrew prophets, had not been stirred by the vision of universal freedom and brotherhood which inspired the revolutionaries. But the young Jewish intellectuals who managed to separate themselves from the masses of their people in the Pale and join the underground movement were of small account in number and influence. For the czar and his mentor, however, they were an important asset. They and their people could be used as a lightning rod to ward off the wrath of the Russian people from the heads of their real oppressors, as an outlet for those passions which might otherwise turn into revolutionary channels. The scapegoat was right there, ready to hand.

The procurator of the Holy Synod, moreover, had no illusions about his ability to fit the Jews into his three-point program for Russia. For them his solution had the merit of great simplicity; he expressed it on one occasion in a simple arithmetic formula: one-third of the Jews would be forced to emigrate, another third would accept baptism, and the remaining third would be starved to death. In the last third he might have included those who would perish by the more direct method of the pogrom.

2

ALMOST immediately, in fact, the pogrom was adopted by the new regime as a definite instrument of policy for the suppression of the revolutionary movement and the "solution" of the Jewish question. Only six weeks after the beginning of the new reign came the first of a series of outbreaks which startled the civilized world and reduced the Jews of Russia to terror and despair. But even those weeks, it is now certain, were not wasted: they were spent in preparation, for there can be no doubt that the pogroms were organized and directed by a central agency. They could not otherwise have occurred at practically the same time, nor carried through with the same pattern. For two days, in accordance with this "technique," the military and the police permitted the work of destruction to go on unchecked, and on the third day they suppressed it.

The pogrom wave of 1881 was initiated by an outbreak in the city of Elizabethgrad in south Russia where for two days, on April 27 and 28, the mob was given a free hand to wreck and loot Jewish homes and shops. The riffraff of the city, as well as peasants who came in from adjacent villages, were given reason to believe that their work had the approval of the authorities. Soon afterwards, there were outbreaks in a large number of neighboring villages and towns; and early the following month, on May 8 and 9, the rabble attacked the Jewish quarter of Kiev, metropolis of the Ukraine, demolished a thousand houses, wrecked the synagogue, killed and maimed and raped, with no real interference on the part of the civil and military authorities. On the third day the bloody orgy was suppressed.

From Kiev, the contagion spread to the provinces of Volhynia and Podolia, and there were pogroms in scores of places. In some of the villages the simple peasants were afraid *not* to destroy the homes of their Jewish neighbors, lest they should be punished for disobeying the czar's "orders." In Berdichev the police commissioner, for a handsome consideration, of course, permitted the Jews to defend themselves, and the outbreak was nipped in the bud. Odessa, where the authorities were afraid to give the teeming rabble of the dock district a free hand, also diverged from the official pattern. The rioters were attacked and generally driven off by the soldiers and police, and in a number of instances by a Jewish self-defense. In July 1881, a second wave of pogroms began in Pereiaslav east of the Dnieper, and by the last month of that fateful year it had rolled west as far as the capital of Poland, where the Jews were attacked and pillaged in accordance with the standard "technique." Finally, on April 10, 1882, the bloodiest and most destructive outbreak of all occurred in Balta, province of Podolia, where the mayor, the police commissioner, the commander of the garrison, and the other local authorities openly worked hand in hand with the mob.

3

IT IS doubtful if this carnival of violence, in which the riffraff of south Russia was permitted to indulge for over a year, proved the existence of a deep-rooted animosity against the Jews on the part of the Russian people. There was no lack of evidence against such a conclusion. The normal relations between the two peoples were not unfriendly, and there were Russians, among them a good number of priests, who stood up to the rioters at the risk of their lives. The rabble, it must be recalled, was persuaded that the czar desired the Jews to be punished, and no sizable human aggregation would fail to furnish enough miscreants for a criminal enterprise if they were assured of official protection.

Nevertheless, the government of Alexander III had the effrontery to seek exoneration for its deliberate failure to suppress the mob by declaring that the pogroms were due to "the harmful consequences of the economic activity of the Jews for the Christian population." This statement came from Count Nicholas Ignatiev, the czar's Minister of the Interior; and at some of the trials which followed, the public prosecutor, instead of accusing the criminals at the dock, took his cue from the minister and denounced the victims. It was the public opinion of the world that forced the czar's government to make these hypocritical and clumsy attempts at self-exculpation. In London, a meeting of protest had been held at the Mansion House with the Lord Mayor as chairman; in Paris there was a similar demonstration under the chairmanship of Victor Hugo; and in the United States there were impressive gatherings in New York and Philadelphia. The American minister to Russia was even notified by Secretary of State Frederick T. Frelinghuysen that the government of the United States hoped "that the Imperial Government will find means to cause the persecution of these unfortunate beings to cease," and a resolution in much stronger terms was adopted by the House of Representatives.

If, however, the czar's government was perturbed by these protests, it showed soon enough that it had no intention of relieving the plight of the Russian Jews. True, its pogrom policy was, after the outbreak in Balta, abandoned, and the few eruptions that followed in 1883 and 1884 were effectively suppressed; but on the same day—May 15, 1882—that the government published its resolve to proceed against "any attempt at violence on the person and property of the Jews," the czar sanctioned the so-called "Temporary Rules," or "May Laws," an emanation from the malevolent brain of Count Ignatiev. The "Temporary Rules," which became permanent, prohibited the Jews from settling or acquiring property in the villages of the Pale, thus increasing the congestion in the towns where, moreover, Jewish traders were dealt a staggering blow by being forbidden to keep their shops open on Sundays and Christian holidays. Very soon afterwards, the rascally Ignatiev was charged with fraud and dismissed from office; but his successor, Dmitri Tolstoi, was a reactionary of the same stamp and the May laws were ruthlessly enforced. The methods of the mob were too crude: the government took over the task and sought to accomplish the same result by the "civilized" method of the "cold pogrom."

4

IF THE pogroms and the May Laws were designed to implement the formula of the procurator of the Holy Synod for the solution of the Jewish problem, they were indeed accomplishing their object. Jews in great numbers began streaming toward the borders of Russia, looking frantically for an escape. "The western frontier," declared the suave Ignatiev, "is open for the Jews." The government of Spain, regretting the expulsion of 1492, declared its willingness to receive the fugitives who, however, were not attracted by the offer. The great majority looked longingly toward the fabled land across the Atlantic where so many of their people from other lands had already found refuge. They were helped on their journey by the *Alliance Israélite Universelle* and, on their arrival in America, by those who had preceded them. Most of their leaders in Russia, however, fearful of being charged with encouraging Jews to "desert the fatherland," refrained from taking steps to organize and regulate the swelling stream of immigrants. Had the leaders been more courageous and realistic, the fugitives would have been spared a great deal of the suffering they endured.

5

THROUGH the rest of his reign, the "cold pogroms" devised by the ministers of Alexander III continued, one of the vilest of them being the *numerus clausus*, the "closed number" or school quota, which was imposed in 1887. By this decree, the number of Jewish students in high schools and universities located in the cities of the Pale, where the Jewish population ranged from 30 to 80 per cent, was restricted to 10 per cent of the total number of students. Outside the Pale, the proportion was limited to 5 per cent, and in the two capitals—St. Petersburg and Moscow—to 3 per cent.

The *numerus clausus* drove large numbers of young men and women to the universities of western Europe. There, in spite of the privations they suffered, they were able to quench their thirst for knowledge; but when they returned to their native land, they found their chance for earning a livelihood balked by the wall of legal restrictions, of which the denial of the right to freedom of domicile and movement was the most disastrous. The right to live in cities outside the Pale, which had in the previous reign been extended to first-grade merchants, artisans, and university graduates, was now restricted, and police raids, followed by summary expulsions, were carried out almost daily in St. Petersburg, Kiev, and other forbidden cities. The May Laws continued in force, with police officials straining their ingenuity to devise all sorts of rigors in their enforcement, if for no other reason than to create additional opportunities for blackmailing the victims.

In 1889 an imperial decree deprived Jewish graduates of law schools of the right to practice their profession, and even the policy of promoting handicrafts among the Jews was now abandoned. In 1884 a Jewish school for handicrafts, which had existed in Zhitomir for twenty-three years, was ordered closed on the ground that the Jews formed the majority of artisans in that region and thereby hampered "the development of handicrafts among the original population."

Together with the disabilities which the government inflicted upon them, the Jews of the Pale, as a result of special conscription regulations, were made to contribute a larger proportion of recruits than the Christians. And to justify the harsh and humiliating discriminations, they were constantly charged with evading military service, while the doors leading to promotion in the army were shut tight against them.

6

AS THE reign of Alexander III wore on, the official mood, which of course took its cue from the ruler, became more and more reactionary, venting its savagery primarily upon the Jews. In 1890 Dournovo was Minister of the Interior, with von Plehve, who was destined to out-Haman all the previous Russian Hamans, as his assistant. Rumors arose—which soon reached England and America—that those two functionaries were preparing new blows against their pet victims. On December 10, 1890, an imposing meeting of protest was held in London, with the Lord Mayor presiding. It adopted a resolution deploring "the severe and exceptional edicts and disabilities against the Jews in Russia," and declaring that "religious liberty is a principle which should be recognized by every Christian community as among the natural human rights." In addition, the Lord Mayor, in the name of the citizens of London, forwarded a memorial to the czar, imploring him to "annul those special laws and disabilities that crush and cow your Hebrew subjects." In the United States, a resolution of protest was introduced in Congress, and Secretary of State James G. Blaine instructed the American Minister to Russia to exert his influence to avert the threatened measures against the Jews.

But the only effect of the London petition and the diplomatic exertions of the United States was to evoke an elaborate display of the hypocrisy and duplicity at which the czar's ministers were past masters. In the spring of 1891 the new blows fell, taking the form of large-scale and ruthless expulsions of Jewish residents from St. Petersburg, Kiev, Moscow, and other cities, the victims being the merchants, artisans, and intellectuals who had been permitted to settle outside the Pale by Alexander II. In Moscow especially, the expulsion of twenty thousand persons who had lived in the city for decades was carried out with revolting brutality.

The same year the czar and his ministers welcomed a proposal from Baron Maurice de Hirsch, the great captain of industry and even greater philanthropist, to transplant over a period of twenty-five years some 3,000,000 Russian Jews to Argentina and other regions in the Americas. The Baron had founded in London the Jewish Colonization Association, commonly known as the ICA, with a capital of fifty million francs. To negotiate with the czar's government, as well as to determine the fitness of the Russian Jews for agricultural colonization, Hirsch sent Arnold White, a member of the British Parliament, to Russia as his personal representative. The officials in St. Petersburg assured White that the Jews were hopeless "usurers and parasites," but contact with the Jewish masses convinced him that the ogre which the czar's statesmen conjured up "has no existence in fact." White advised Hirsch to proceed with his project. "If," he reported, "courage—moral courage—hope, patience, temperance are fine qualities, then the Jews are a fine people."

It was a noble and imposing project, but it failed. In the first ten years, instead of the contemplated million, only ten thousand Jews were settled in Argentina. The problem of the Jewish people in Russia, it was clear, was not to be solved by philanthropy.

7

IF THE problem was too vast for philanthropy, even the princely philanthropy of a Baron de Hirsch, was it possible to find some other solution for it? With the wounds of the pogroms still unhealed, and hosts of refugees in flight from Russia, an answer to this question was offered by Leon Pinsker, a Jewish physician in Odessa. Pinsker, who was born in 1821, had been one of the founders of the "Society for the Diffusion of Culture among the Jews of Russia," and over many years had labored zealously for the cause of Russianization and emancipation. Now he rejected those nostrums. In September 1882 he published a pamphlet with the significant title *Auto-Emancipation*, in which he advocated a heroic and radical solution: his scattered people, he declared, must become a nation again in a territory of their own.

Pinsker's pamphlet created a great stir not only for the boldness of his remedy, but for the fearlessness of his diagnosis. His was a physician's approach to the problem. Anti-Semitism, or Judeophobia, he found to be a "psychic aberration," hereditary and incurable, induced by the "ghostlike apparition of a people without . . . land or other bond of union, no longer alive and yet moving about among the living." All attempts at reasoning with it he dismissed as futile. "Prejudice, or instinctive ill-will, can be satisfied by no reasoning, however forceful and clear." He deprecated the idea that "humanity and enlightenment" will ever solve the problem, and called for "the creation of a Jewish nationality . . . living upon its own soil." Nor must that soil, he contended, necessarily be Palestine; but wherever it is, such a refuge "cannot come about without the support of the governments": it would have to be "politically assured." Eighteen months after the appearance of *Auto-Emancipation*, its author, having by closer contact looked deeper into the hearts of his people in Russia, wrote in their name: "Let us obtain dry bread by the sweat of our brow on the sacred soil of our ancestors!"

Leon Pinsker stands out as the Jewish intellectual of his day who expressed most boldly and clearly the conclusions to which many others had been driven by the wave of pogroms which ushered in the reign of Alexander III and the ministerial blows that followed. The first of these conclusions was that the policy of Russianization was bankrupt. Neither the mob nor the ministers distinguished between the "enlightened" and "unenlightened," between the assimilated and unassimilated. They, the Russianizers, whether they preached the gospel in Hebrew or in Russian, now beat their breasts in repentance and took the road back to their own people. Among the most prominent of these repentant apostles of "enlightenment" was Lev Levanda (1835-1887), who achieved popularity and influence with his novels and stories of Jewish life. He wrote in Russian, and until 1881 looked upon the acquisition of Russian culture as the only way out for his persecuted people. The events of that year laid all his idols in ruins, and before he died he took his stand with Pinsker in the movement for self-help.

This cycle of spiritual struggle and change, through which standard-bearers of *haskalah* like Judah Leib Gordon and Lev Levanda passed, is illustrated best by the career of Moses Leib Lillienblum (1843-1910). In his twenties, Lillienblum entered the lists against the *Shulchan Aruch*, pouring all his wrath and scorn upon the "obscurantists" who controlled the *kahals*. In his thirties, he lost his way completely in the frivolous and nihilistic atmosphere of Odessa. In his forties, after the savage waves of pogroms had swept away the fatuities of *haskalah* and the illusions of Russianization, Lillienblum saw no other way for his people but a return to Palestine.

Among the few intellectuals who never cherished the illusions of the Russianizers was Perez Smolenskin (1842–1885), a rare and exalted spirit who spent the last seventeen years of his life in Vienna, where he founded and edited the Hebrew periodical *Ha-shachar*, "The Dawn." He fought valiantly against assimilation and for national conservation. He considered the Hebrew language and, later, the colonization of Palestine the most important instruments of Jewish survival, and in 1882 he inspired the organization in Vienna of the first society of Jewish students dedicated to national revival. For its name, the society took the Hebrew word *Kadimah*, which means both "forward" and "eastward."

8

KADIMAH expressed a spirit and a goal which were not confined to the students in Vienna who chose the word as the name for their society. The hope of restoration to the land of their glorious past had sustained the exiled people in all their wanderings across the centuries. It was the recurring theme of all their prayers, the inspiration of their mystic lore. It had given rise to widespread messianic ferments, and impelled numerous saints and poets to defy hardships and perils in order to breathe the air of the holy land and be laid in its soil. Now, amid the rubble of the recent hopes which lay strewn around them, the ancient hope took on fresh strength and found new forms of expression.

Even before 1882, when Pinsker issued his stirring call for auto-emancipation, something which may well be called a movement had already been launched in Russia. It named itself *Chibath Tziyon*, "Love of Zion," and it gave rise to numerous societies of "Lovers of Zion" (*Chovevei Tziyon*) in Russia, Rumania, Galicia, and as far west as the United States. In November 1884, delegates from most of these societies, meeting in Kattowitz, Silesia, united into a federation, making Leon Pinsker their president and Moses Leib Lillienblum their secretary.

The principal task which the united societies assumed was to find support for those whom the new movement had already sent forth to Palestine. For while the great current of migration which the persecutions set into motion was flowing westward, chiefly toward America, a small stream was moving toward the ancient homeland. In 1882, its first pioneers, hailing from Rumania as well as Russia, had already planted three agricultural settlements. Among these pioneers were students belonging to the movement known as BILU, young men and women who renounced their careers in order to pave the way for the restoration of their people. The name they adopted is compounded of the initials of the Hebrew words meaning "House of Jacob, come and let us go!"* Those who went were armed with faith and enthusiasm only, and were thrown into a life of privation, toil, and danger. They were unprepared for the enormous difficulties involved in colonizing a soil which had stood waste, neglected, and disease-ridden for centuries. Many of them succumbed, but with the help of the "Lovers of Zion" societies in Russia and, even more, with the lavish generosity and unflagging personal devotion of Baron Edmond de Rothschild of Paris, the first settlements, and others which followed, emerged from their precarious condition and became self-supporting. They have been called the "Jewish Pilgrim Fathers," these BILU pioneers who served as the vanguard of an army of reclamation and restoration in the decades that followed.

CHAPTER FIFTY-SIX

America, City of Refuge

IN A STEADY stream the victims of czarist terror, especially after the pogroms of 1881, sought and found refuge in the great republic of the New World. There the Jewish community, during the century preceding this influx, had grown and prospered, for during that interval the original Sephardim had

* Isaiah II, 5.

been reinforced by Ashkenazim who came from the Germanies. The reactionary wave that followed the Congress of Vienna sent large numbers of German Jews to America, and with the extinction of the hopes which the revolutions of 1848 had kindled, still more of them flocked to the distant land of liberty and opportunity. At the outbreak of the Civil War a dozen years later, the community in the United States is believed to have already numbered approximately 150,000.

For nearly two decades before the Congress of Vienna, immigration was halted by the Napoleonic Wars in Europe. Nevertheless, the tiny community contributed a goodly number of officers and men to the War of 1812. In the annals of that war we come upon the names of Colonel Nathan Moses, Major Abraham Massias, who foiled British attempts to invade Georgia, Captain Mayer Moses, Captain David Warfield and Captain Mordecai Myers, the last distinguished for many heroic deeds. Judah Touro, son of a Newport rabbi, who was to become an outstanding merchant and philanthropist, served as a private and during the siege of New Orleans was wounded in a daring exploit. Another Jewish soldier in the War of 1812 was the grandfather of the famous American novelist, Bret Harte. Uriah P. Levy, who in the course of a stormy career fought successfully for the abolition of corporal punishment in the United States Navy and eventually attained the rank of commodore, was one of the naval heroes of the war; another was Captain John Ordroneaux, a Jewish privateer of French origin, small in stature but great in skill and daring.

These soldiers and sailors were nearly all Sephardim whose fathers, in the case of many of them, had served in the Revolution. In the Mexican War (1846-48), the Sephardim were still conspicuous, but Ashkenazim now began to play a part, with one company of militia recruited in Baltimore consisting mostly of Jewish immigrants from Germany.

2

THE most colorful figure in the decades after the War of 1812 was Mordecai Manuel Noah (1785-1851), journalist and dramatist, diplomat and politician, orator and jurist. Noah served as American consul in Tunis, where he carried out an important and difficult diplomatic assignment; he also served as High Sheriff of New York, as Surveyor of the Port of New York, and as Judge of the New York Court of Sessions. He edited many newspapers, fought a number of duels, and wrote successful plays. He climaxed his kaleidoscopic career with a spectacular attempt to restore his people to nationhood.

Noah, who seemed to thrive on opposition and trouble, made his mark in all his enterprises, but closest to his heart was the plight of his persecuted people in Europe, whose sorrows he had occasion to witness in the course of his travels. In 1825, with the help of friends, he purchased Grand Island in the Niagara River near Buffalo, and issued a manifesto to the Jews of the world to come and settle there. In memory of the place where his namesake of the Bible had found a resting-place, Noah called his island "Ararat, a City of Refuge for the Jews." In September of the same year he was the central figure of an imposing dedication ceremony in Buffalo which, however, marked the end as well as the beginning of the romantic undertaking.

But it must not be supposed that Noah was content to find in "Ararat" only an outlet for his dramatic flair. In the first place, he was persuaded that Grand Island, lying near the Great Lakes and the Erie Canal, might be developed into an important commercial center. Second, he looked upon this "city of refuge" as only a temporary asylum and a proving ground for the eventual restoration of a Jewish nation in Palestine. The Grand Island project died at birth, but his faith in Palestine survived. In 1844 he delivered a great oration in Philadelphia, published later under the title of *Discourse on the Restoration of the Jews,* which entitles the quixotic Mordecai Manuel Noah to a place as one of the precursors of the Zionist movement.

3

FOUR years later the whole country became a city of refuge for the proscribed and disinherited of the Old World, with many Jews among them, most of whom hailed from Germany. Unlike their Sephardic predecessors whom, before long, they surpassed in number, they brought with them neither wealth nor commercial connections. But they quickly fell in step with the pioneering surge of the striding young republic. Many of them pushed beyond the Alleghenies into the valleys of the great rivers. They made their way southwest into Louisiana and Texas. They joined the gold rush to California, and on the Day of Atonement of 1849 they worshipped together for the first time in a tent in San Francisco. Many who began as pack-peddlers among the Indians or in the sparse and scattered settlements of the Middle West and South, rose to be merchant princes and industrial magnates.

Nor did they lose time in organizing their congregational life. They built houses of worship and schools for the children, and set aside plots of ground to bury their dead. There was room in the great land of "the vanishing frontier" for all men who were ready to toil and venture, and in short order the descendants of those who had cut through the deserts in the footsteps of Moses cast off the yoke which the ghettos of Europe had laid upon them, and became pioneers of the wilderness and prairies of the New World. They were often a curiosity to their neighbors, many of whom had never before seen a descendant of the people of the Bible. Joseph Jonas was the first Jew to settle in Cincinnati, where he arrived in 1817, and of him it is told that among those who came to look at him was a Quaker woman, eager to examine "one of God's chosen people." She walked around him a few times, and finally told him with evident disappointment: "Thee art no different to other people."

By 1856, there were five synagogues in Cincinnati, and among the rabbis were Max Lilienthal, whom the officials of Nicholas I had once duped into supporting their crown schools, and Isaac M. Wise, the foremost champion of Reform Judaism in America. In Cleveland, Chicago, St. Louis, New Orleans, and other cities of the Middle West and South, there was a rapid development of congregational life. But there was division among them as well as integration; some groups, finding the main body too Orthodox or too Reform, broke away to set up their own houses of worship.

The majority of the new arrivals remained, of course, in the large centers of the East, where the original Sephardim, who in the main held fast to their Orthodox tradition, maintained an aristocratic aloofness from the newcomers. For a long time, the latter clung to their German speech; and they also brought with them the doctrines and ritual of the Hamburg Temple and of the Reform fraternities of Berlin and Frankfort. Not that Reform was a thing unknown among the Sephardim. As early as 1824, in fact, a small group seceded from the Sephardic congregation in Charleston, South Carolina, to institute services along Reform lines. And in 1834, at the dedication of a new synagogue of the Shearith Israel congregation in New York, a plea for Reform was made by none other than Mordecai Manuel Noah. Nor were the immigrants from Germany uniformly devoted to Reform, for the middle-of-the-road position represented by Zechariah Frankel of Breslau and Michael Sachs of Berlin was not absent among them, its principal exponent in America being Isaac Leeser (1806-1868), who in 1829 was chosen preacher of the Mikveh Israel congregation in Philadelphia.

4

LEESER laid the foundation of what is today designated as Conservative Judaism. He combined enthusiasm for the traditional sanctities with an unusual capacity for work and ability as an organizer. He produced textbooks and prayer books, and for twenty-five years published and edited *The Occident*, in its day the leading Jewish periodical in the English language. In his hands *The Occident* became a formidable weapon against the rising tide of Reform in the New World, and in the midst of all his other labors he found time to produce a translation of the Hebrew Scriptures, which for a long time served as the standard Jewish version in English. Leeser also knew how to communicate his zeal to others. He stimulated the creation of philanthropic and educational institutions, including the Jewish Hospital of Philadelphia and Maimonides College. It was under his inspiration that, in 1838, the first Sunday School for Jewish children in America was established by Rebecca Gratz, a member of his congregation who, however, enjoys greater fame from the fact that Sir Walter Scott is believed to have taken her as the model for Rebecca, daughter of Isaac of York, in his *Ivanhoe.*

Conservative Judaism had many other learned exponents and doughty champions: Sabato Morais, the successor of Leeser in Mikveh Israel, founder and first president of the Jewish Theological Seminary of America; Benjamin Szold, who led his congregation in Baltimore back to the traditional ritual from which it had departed; Marcus Jastrow, who after long years of courageous leadership in Warsaw and Germany was, in 1866, elected rabbi of Rodeph Sholem in Philadelphia, where he collaborated with Leeser; Alexander Kohut, who came from Hungary in 1885 and joined Morais in the Jewish Theological Seminary; and many others.

5

NEVERTHELESS, the most striking religious trend of the so-called German period in the story of American Jewry, beginning in the forties and lasting until the eighties, was in the direction of Reform. The movement, in fact, made more progress in America than in the land of its birth, and in Isaac Mayer Wise it found a peerless leader. Wise landed in New York in 1846 at the age of twenty-seven, and after a number of years as rabbi in Albany, he was called to Cincinnati, which he and Lilienthal made the Reform center of America. Before he died in 1900, he had brought into existence the three principal institutions of Reform: the Union of American Hebrew Congregations, the Hebrew Union College for the training of Reform rabbis, and the Central Conference of American Rabbis, where, at annual sessions, basic principles and issues are discussed and determined.

In the ideology of American Reform, one of the leading doctrines is the "Mission of Israel," which asserts that the Jewish people had been scattered among the nations not, as the Orthodox believe, in punishment for its sins, but in order to teach mankind the unity of God and serve as an example of righteous living. Naturally this doctrine has for its corollary the denial of a national destiny for Israel and the rejection of the expectation of national restoration. The changes in ritual were the same as those which the reformers had introduced in Germany. The prayers were considerably abridged, with most of them in English instead of Hebrew. The organ was introduced, as well as mixed choirs; men and women were seated together, the men with heads uncovered. Sunday services were instituted and the second days of the festivals abolished. There were, of course, varying degrees of Reform, just as there were gradations in the concessions which Conservative congregations were prepared to make to "the environment." On the whole, the Reform leaders of the East, men like David Einhorn of Baltimore, Samuel Hirsch of Philadelphia, and Samuel Adler, rabbi of Temple Emanu-El, the first Reform congregation in New York, were inclined to go further than their colleagues in the Middle West.

In the New World, however, religious division was not accompanied by the bitterness and conflict which disturbed the Jewish communities in Germany. There were, of course, occasional blasts and counterblasts between the different groupings, but there was something in the general atmosphere of America that took the wind out of the sails of religious controversy. The right of men to differ in the matter of religion was taken for granted, and there was no tradition of a coercive authority in the realm of religion such as existed in Europe. Nor did the great influx of Orthodox Jews from eastern Europe affect the general serenity of the religious atmosphere. If, in later decades, the air resounded with denunciation of Reform, it came less from the orthodox than from the advocates of Zionism which Reform began by denouncing and rejecting.

6

LIKE the people of America as a whole, the Jews were divided by the overshadowing slavery issue and the Civil War to which it gave rise. But most of them by far, true to their immemorial aversion to human bondage, and fresh from the libertarian struggles in Europe, stood with the abolitionists, and in 1860 flocked to join the newly-formed anti-slavery Republican party. They were among those who, with pen and tongue, and not seldom at the risk of their lives, denounced the spreading evil, and the fiery John Brown numbered three of them in his small band of desperate zealots. Again, as in the War for Independence, the cause of freedom found wings in biblical ideals. The passions and the imagery of the Bible abound in Julia Ward Howe's stirring *Battle Hymn of the Republic* and *The Reveille* of Bret Harte, both of which captured the imagination of those who fought to save the Union and put an end to slavery. The wealthy and aristocratic Sephardim of the South, however, even as their Christian neighbors, looked upon slavery as a natural institution, and upheld the right of secession, although there were not a few among them who, like the renowned merchant and philanthropist Judah Touro, liberated the slaves they owned.

There is considerable divergence in the estimates of the number of Jews who fought on both sides in the Civil War. There is general agreement, however, that their proportion in the armed forces exceeded their ratio to the general population. The number of officers among them, on the general staff as well as in the field, was strikingly high, especially in the South where the Jews who took up arms generally belonged to the wealthy. But most of the Jews under arms were, of course, in the armies of the North. The names of nearly 700 Jewish officers have been found in the records, among them 8 generals, 21 colonels, 9 lieutenant colonels, 40 majors, and 205 captains. The northern general officers were Major General Frederick Knefler, General Leopold Blumenberg and Brigadier General Philip J. Joachimsen. Seven Jewish soldiers who fought for the Union were awarded the Congressional Medal of Honor, the highest decoration for valor. Max Frauenthal, who fought for the Confederacy and whose name was corrupted to "Fronthall," became a legend—a man who displayed unusual bravery was described as "a regular Fronthall."

There were Jews who rose to distinction in civil and political affairs also. Among them were Moritz Pinner of Missouri, an ardent abolitionist, and Lewis N. Dembitz of Kentucky, lawyer, author, and a leader in the affairs of Conservative Judaism. Both of them were members of the Republican Convention of 1860 which nominated Lincoln for the Presidency. Sigismund Kaufman of New York, also an active abolitionist, was a member of the Electoral College.

But the most important post during this period was held by Judah P. Benjamin, Secretary of State in the cabinet of Jefferson

Davis, who has been called "the brains of the Confederacy." Benjamin's sense of affiliation with his faith and people was, throughout his career in America and later in England, practically dormant, although from time to time it was awakened by his political enemies when they reminded him of his origin. All accounts agree that he was a man of amazing intellectual power and resourcefulness; nevertheless he failed to appreciate the moral advantage which the North possessed in the struggle against slavery, a fault of vision serious enough in any statesman but doubly reprehensible in a Jew. Benjamin was surprised when British workmen, their factories deprived of cotton by the northern blockade, proved willing to suffer hardships for the triumph of freedom. When the cause for which he labored was lost, Benjamin escaped to England where, as a top-ranking barrister, he quickly repaired his fortunes and rose to fresh fame and honors.

7

AS TIME went on the Jewish community in America, growing in numbers and influence, came naturally to be looked upon by less fortunate Jewries in other lands as a "big brother." The role was just as naturally accepted, and it was performed with credit on practically all occasions, including those when it became necessary to obtain government intercession for victims of persecution and wrong. Nor was that role a wholly altruistic one. For there were times when calumnies which brought suffering on their people in other lands involved their own good name which had to be protected.

The Damascus Affair of 1840 was such an occasion, and we have seen how it roused the Jews of America as well as those of England and France. It was also the first occasion on which the government of the United States interceded with a foreign government against anti-Jewish oppression, and the action came even before the meetings of protest were held in New York and Philadelphia.

A decade later, the Jews of the United States became involved in a long series of efforts for the protection of their own rights as American citizens. These rights were being denied them by the Swiss Confederation, where their coreligionists were still unemancipated. Under a treaty ratified by the Senate in 1855, American Jews wishing to reside in Switzerland would be subject to the disabilities from which the Swiss Jews suffered. Five years earlier, that treaty, with a different version of the discriminatory provision, had been laid before the Senate and rejected. President Millard Fillmore condemned it as "hostile to the institutions of the United States and inconsistent with the Constitution and laws." Now, under President Franklin Pierce, the government of the United States had assented to acts of discrimination against its citizens on purely religious grounds. Clearly, the Jews of America could not remain silent.

In 1857 President James Buchanan promised a Jewish delegation that the wrong would be righted, and long and weary exchanges between the two governments ensued, leading to no results. The Swiss constitution itself would have had to be changed before American Jews could expect the same treatment in Switzerland as other Americans. But that was something the canton of Basel, in particular, would not hear of. Its contention was that in that case it would have to open its doors to the "usurious Israelitish population of the French province of Alsace." Thereupon the American ambassador to Switzerland, Theodore S. Fay, set out to learn the truth about the "Israelitish population" of Alsace, and in November 1858 he informed Secretary of State Lewis Cass that, as a result of the information he had gathered, "no Swiss authority will ever dare to advance that objection against us as an argument."

The matter dragged on. In the meantime, Swiss cantons were individually granting Jews civil rights, and President Lincoln made his stand plain by appointing a Jew as American consul to Zurich. Even Basel relented, though it was not until 1872 that it extended complete equality. The dispute was not liquidated until 1874 when the Swiss Confederation adopted a new constitution, placing the rights of aliens under federal instead of cantonal jurisdiction, and abolishing all distinctions based on religion. It was not a glorious victory. It took twenty-five years before Americans of Jewish faith could enjoy the same rights in a foreign land as Americans of other faiths, and it was through the work of time rather than the exertions of the American government that the wrong was erased.

CHAPTER FIFTY-SEVEN

The City Expands

THE giant Statue of Liberty, standing in the gateway to America and symbolizing the spirit which presided at her birth, has a bronze tablet inside its pedestal on which are engraved the lines of a sonnet concluding as follows:

Give me your tired, your poor,
Your huddled masses yearning to breathe free,
The wretched refuse of your teeming shore.
Send these, the homeless, tempest-tost to me.
I lift my lamp beside the golden door!

This summons, addressed to the lands of the Old World, was penned by Emma Lazarus, a gifted poetess who died in her prime in 1887. She had forsaken her ivory tower of classic poetry to sing of the glory and woes and hopes of her people, and joined the many others who gave help and welcome to the fugitives on their arrival in America.

Public opinion in America had been outraged by the brutal pogroms. The meetings of protest and sympathy held in New York and Philadelphia in February 1882, were imposing demonstrations in which all creeds participated, and Sephardim and Ashkenazim united to provide temporary shelter and other aid to the refugees, a large sum for the purpose having been raised by the Hebrew Immigrant Aid Society. Among those who took a leading part in this labor of duty and love was Michael Heilprin, himself a Russian Jew who had come to America in 1856. Thus, in an atmosphere of sympathy and helpfulness, was ushered in the third stage in the history of the Jewish people in America, the so-called "Russian" period.

It was a period marked by the greatest, in point of numbers, of all the migrations in the four millennia of the wandering nation—in the story that began with Abraham's arrival in Canaan and included the Exodus from Egypt, the evictions from the motherland, the expulsions from Spain and other lands. From its start in 1881 until the outbreak of the First World War in 1914, a period of one generation, the tide carried to the United States some two million of these refugees from the lands ruled by the czars. There was a large contingent from Rumania, where the government kept its quarter-million Jews in a state of vassalage as aliens, and another large contingent from the impoverished Jewish masses of Galicia, a province of the Austro-Hungarian Empire. This huge migration, however, must be set against the background of the still greater influx of many other nationalities and creeds from the congested and impoverished lands of the Old World, of people "yearning to breathe free" in the land of freedom and opportunity. For, in the same period, the total number of immigrants who were admitted into the United States was over twenty-two million.

2

ONLY a small proportion of the Jewish immigrants—no more, perhaps, than one in twenty—had to be assisted by the social agencies. The country was in an era of expansion, labor was in demand, and the problem of earning a livelihood, the first problem that faced the immigrants on their arrival, was speedily solved. Most of them settled in the large cities of the East, particularly in New York, where they went into the needle trades as wage earners, many of them rising rapidly to become contractors and manufacturers. They congregated in special quarters, "ghettos," as these sections came to be called, showing the same proclivity in this respect as immigrants of other stock, all of whom sought aid, understanding, and human warmth among their own. Nor did the garment industries alone attract them. They became shoemakers, carpenters, plumbers, cigarmakers, printers, and jewelers: there was hardly a handicraft, in fact, into which they did not penetrate. And many who began as peddlers and small shopkeepers came to be numbered among the leading merchants of their communities.

The ancestral urge to return to the soil, reinforced by the romanticized doctrines and appeals of the *maskilim* and other idealists, asserted itself very early among the new arrivals. It was indeed the cardinal motive with the members of the society *Am Olam*, "Eternal People," who arrived as early as July 1881; and it permeated the hopes and dreams of the multitudes who followed them. The songs of a people, divorced for many centuries from the soil, exalted the farmer's lot, and tailors in the sweatshops hummed, as they stitched, the popular ditty:

Of plow and soil
God speeds the toil.

As early as 1882, groups of these idealistic newcomers, equipped with little else but enthusiasm, made brave but ill-starred attempts to plant agricultural settlements in Louisiana, Kansas, Colorado, the Dakotas, Oregon, Virginia, and other states. They were more successful in New Jersey, especially in Carmel and in Woodbine, where in 1895 the Baron de Hirsch Agricultural and Industrial School was established. Since the general trend for the country at large was away from the farms and toward the cities, it was too much to expect that a people which had for centuries been forced to dwell in cities would move in the opposite direction. Nevertheless, the Jewish farming population of America slowly increased and in 1945, by the records of the Jewish Agricultural Society, it numbered 100,000.

A striking feature of the shifting economic landscape of the new immigrants was the fact that the sons rarely followed the occupations of the fathers. A better life for their children was the goal of all parents; few sacrifices were considered too great to attain it. And this ambition, joining hands with the traditional respect for learning, sent the boys and girls flocking to the high schools, colleges, and professional schools. In time, this eager quest gave birth to new problems. It threw the economic structure of American Jewry out of balance, with too many in the professions and commerce competing in the main against each other, and made it particularly vulnerable in times of economic crisis or recession. In native quarters, moreover, resentment arose against recent arrivals who were reaching out successfully for the higher economic and social levels. They, the less recent arrivals, felt that those positions belonged to them. The result has been the imposition of unofficial quotas against Jewish students, especially in medical and engineering schools.

3

THE tide of refugees, fleeing from the pogroms and persecutions of Alexander III and his successor, continued to mount. From 1887 the annual number of new arrivals ranged from 30,000 to 35,000, rising sharply in years like 1891 when czarist brutality rose to new levels. In the pogrom years of 1905, 1906, and 1907, the annual influx rose to well over 100,000. To the superficial observer, the congested "ghettos" of New York, Philadelphia, Chicago, and other large cities, continued to harbor the same mass of "crude and clannish" aggregations; in reality there was a continuous exodus from the "ghettos" of those who had acquired the language and ways of the new land, who had passed through the relentless wringer of Americanization. But as long as new arrivals came and took their places, the optical illusion persisted. Indeed, only the observer who was equipped with the insight that comes from sympathy and detachment was able to apprehend the true character of the period—the epic swell of its swarming masses, the visions, old and new, that inspired them, the pitfalls they encountered, their tragedies and triumphs.

America set them on the path of freedom and new life, but it was not a path strewn with roses. Life in the tenements was harsh and unlovely, representing as it did a transition stage in many respects not unlike that of the mining towns of the West. The sudden shift from one physical and cultural environment to another engendered a host of problems, not the least of them being the intensity of the conflict, to which, for that matter, there is never and nowhere a pause, between the old generation and the new. The normal causes of dissension were reinforced by the enormous difference in tempo in the Americanization of the two generations. For the old, the process was naturally slow and laborious; for the young it was pleasant and swift, speeded as it was by a highly efficient system of free secular education. Nor could the rifts that ensued be healed by an inadequate system, if system it could be called, of Jewish education. In these tensions, and in the temptations of a quasi-frontier life, the ancient virtues were sometimes undermined, Jewish names began to appear in the roster of crime, and anti-Semites as well as the sworn enemies of the immigrant were quick to seize upon these lapses, exaggerating them and exploiting them for their purposes.

With all the opportunities which the new land afforded, the task of earning a livelihood demanded grinding toil and self-denial. In the needle industries, which absorbed most of the newcomers, the "sweating system" arose, with numerous little shops in unsanitary quarters where men and women toiled long hours and were miserably underpaid. The system is now practically a thing of the past: its destruction was the work of the Jewish labor movement.

That movement, crystallized today in a group of powerful organizations, including the Amalgamated Clothing Workers of America, the International Ladies Garment Workers' Union, and others, had its beginnings in small, pathetic efforts in the eighties and early nineties, efforts which were bedeviled by two basic impediments. The first was a lack of conviction and stability on the part of the workers which led them to rally to the union when strikes were declared and to abandon it after they were won or lost. The second arose from the attitude of the leaders, practically all of whom brought to their task the revolutionary social philosophies which they had imbibed in the Old World, and for which many of them had suffered in Russia. To these early leaders of the Jewish labor movement, a trade union was not primarily an instrument for achieving higher wages, shorter hours, and better working conditions for its members through collective bargaining or, if necessary, by striking; it was primarily an instrument for revolutionary education and action. And their futility, not to speak of the din they created, was aggravated by the fact that they were at odds among themselves with regard to objectives and methods.

The early leaders, with a few exceptions like Abraham Cahan, editor of the Yiddish daily *Forward*, and Joseph Barondess, leader of the first successful strike of the cloakmakers in 1890, never became fully aware of the new world to which they had been transplanted; but their followers did. In the new climate of opportunity and success, the millenarian doctrines which many of the immigrants brought in their baggage, and which anti-Semites seized upon and denounced for their purposes, withered and died; and if the din of clashing social theories and rival revolutionary slogans continued to resound on the East Side of New York, it was again because the steady stream of immigration brought contingents of newcomers who began where their predecessors had left off. Nearly all the Jewish unions, notwithstanding the fact that the Socialist party exercised a sort of tutelage over them, became affiliated with the conservative American Federation of Labor whose leader, it may be noted, was a Jewish cigarmaker named Samuel Gompers. In 1863, at the age of thirteen, Gompers migrated to America from England, became president of the organization in 1882 and, except for one term, was re-elected to that office year after year until his death in 1924.

The tutelage which the Socialists, through press and party, were able to exercise over the Jewish labor movement sprang chiefly from the zeal they alone displayed for the welfare of the immigrant workers. The latter were grateful; and when they acquired citizenship they often voted as the Socialist union leaders and journalists advised them. Nevertheless, socialism failed to hold them: much sooner than later they began to cast their vote for one or the other of the two parties which still dominate the American political scene.

4

AN AVIDITY for the things of the mind and spirit asserted itself promptly among the new immigrants. It found its primary nutriment, of course, in the synagogues, which increased and multiplied; but it led also to a rapid development of a Yiddish press, stage, and literature. Even before the large influx from Russia, as far back as 1870, the first newspaper in Yiddish had begun a brief existence. Four years later, Kasriel H. Sarasohn established the weekly *Jewish Gazette*, and in 1886 he launched the conservative *Jewish Daily News*. In 1897 came the Socialist *Forward;* four years later the Orthodox *Morning Journal;* and in 1914 *The Day*. Still more daily newspapers were launched in New

York, as well as in Chicago, Cleveland, Philadelphia, and other large centers.

The opinion which is sometimes heard, that the Yiddish press retarded the Americanization of the immigrants, is a profound error. The contrary, indeed, is the truth: it initiated its readers into the history and institutions of their adopted land in the only language they understood. In addition, these journals provided a medium for talented essayists, poets, and novelists whose labors brought an efflorescence of Yiddish literature in America. Abraham Goldfaden, the creator of the Yiddish theatre, and the incomparable humorist Sholom Aleichem ended their careers in America; and among the others who belong to both the Old World and the New are the essayist Reuben Brainin, the poet Morris Winchevsky, the novelist Sholem Asch, and the dramatist David Pinski. The outstanding poets of the earlier period were Morris Rosenfeld, the "proletarian" poet who sang of the sorrows and aspirations of the humble and exploited; and the more profound and versatile Solomon Bloomgarden, better known by his pen name Yehoash and famous also for his translation of the Hebrew Scriptures into Yiddish. The later period has seen the rise of a large number of gifted poets and novelists, whose work would shed luster on any literature, some of whom write in Hebrew as well as Yiddish.

The Yiddish theatre at its best attained a degree of excellence not surpassed by any other stage. Its first actors—Jacob Adler, Sigmund Mogulesco, Kennie Lipzin, Rudolph Schildkraut, and others—had their schooling in the Old World; and a number of those who, like Paul Muni, Bertha Kalisch, and Jacob Ben-ami, rose to fame on the American stage and in Hollywood, began their careers playing in Yiddish to "ghetto" audiences. Among the dramatists of the earlier period, the most prolific as well as the most serious, whose plays betray the influence of Ibsen and other Europeans, was Jacob Gordin, while the outstanding dramatists of the current period are Peretz Hirschbein, at his best in the folk drama, Ossip Dymov, and H. Leivick, distinguished also as a poet.

5

LIFE in the teeming "ghettos" of New York and other large cities had that hectic quality which adheres to all novel and transitional stages. Within the general aggregation smaller ones appeared, made up of newcomers hailing from the same region or town of the Old World, and clinging to each other for aid and comfort. Organizations sprang up and multiplied profusely: societies for mutual aid, for the propagation of social panaceas, for education, and charity. The life-span of most of them was short, but they served as a proving ground for the larger and more stable communal life that followed. For mutual help, nation-wide fraternal federations came early into existence. The largest of them, the Independent Order Brith Abraham, was launched in 1887. Philanthropy, for which the Jewish community as a whole stands in highest repute, and in which the lead was taken by the older and wealthier immigrants from Germany, grew and developed into huge and integrated networks of institutions throughout the land. And even the promotion of the religious education of the young has become the object of collective effort.

But the basic institution around which the immigrants gathered was, of course, the synagogue. Radicals and "intellectuals" might keep ever so disdainfully aloof; the masses of the new arrivals lost no time in setting up the worship they brought with them on their journey, and which had gone with their fathers on numberless journeys in the past. Thousands of synagogues over the country, most of them in poor and ill-furnished quarters, sprang into existence. In nearly every case the membership consisted at first of *landsleit*, men who hailed from the same Old World community —a bond of peculiar strength in a new and strange environment made doubly strong by the force of nostalgia. Their faith, of course, was Orthodox and in time, as the members grew in numbers and economic strength, the worship was moved into handsome synagogue structures, around which, as in all lands and generations, other communal activities—educational, social, and charitable—clustered.

Thus, with the influx from Russia which began in the eighties, Orthodox Judaism in America acquired fresh strength and, in point of numbers if not in influence, took the lead over the Reform and Conservative groups. Its failure to achieve greater influence stems from a number of causes, chief of which, until at least the most recent times, has been the refusal of the separate synagogues to acknowledge a central authority. The first attempt to establish such an authority was made in 1888 when Rabbi Jacob Joseph of Vilna accepted the invitation of a group of some fifteen Orthodox congregations in New York to become their chief rabbi. The attempt failed, chiefly as a result of the unwillingness of other rabbis to recognize his leadership. Similar efforts made later in Chicago and in Boston were equally unsuccessful, although certain outstanding rabbinical leaders like Moses Margolies in New York and Bernard Levinthal in Philadelphia, were, by tacit consent, accorded special recognition. In the first decade of the new century, however, Orthodoxy in the New World began slowly to emerge from its disorganized state. In 1902 the Union of Orthodox Rabbis of the United States and Canada was brought into existence, and somewhat later came a union of the Orthodox congregations. The Rabbi Isaac Elchanan Theological Seminary and Yeshiva University has, since 1896, been transformed from an Old World Talmudic Academy to the rank of a higher institution of learning, combining the humanities and modern science with the ancient lore and faith.

6

STRANGELY enough, the persecution mania of czarist Russia came to plague the Jews of free America. Since 1832 a commercial treaty had been in force between the United States and Russia, under which the czar's government claimed and exercised the right of discriminating between American citizens of Jewish faith and those of other faiths. It went even further. Denying the right of the czar's subjects to become citizens of another country, it claimed jurisdiction over Russian Jews who had become naturalized in the United States and were visiting their native land. Until the large influx from Russia began, the issue was more or less academic, but as early as 1879 a resolution was passed by the House of Representatives calling for amendment of the treaty in order "that the rights of the citizens of the United States should not be impaired at home or abroad because of religious belief."

For more than thirty years thereafter the discriminatory treatment of American-Jewish citizens by Russia under the Treaty of 1832 was a constantly growing irritation—with Russian consulates in the United States refusing visas to American Jews desiring to visit Russia, with earnest but futile representations by the American State Department to the wily and hypocritical ministers of the czar, and with sporadic resolutions in Congress, some of which were buried in committee. One such resolution was introduced in 1894 by the Jewish congressman Isidor Raynor of Maryland, who later represented his state in the Senate. In 1902 Henry M. Goldfogle of New York, also a Jewish congressman and chosen by a Jewish constituency, submitted a resolution which the House duly passed without, however, affecting the situation. In 1905 President Theodore Roosevelt made a personal but fruitless appeal to the czar through Count Serge de Witte, then in America to represent his sovereign in the negotiations that ended the Russo-Japanese War.

Shortly afterwards, the struggle against the Treaty of 1832 was taken up by the American Jewish Committee, a body formed in 1906 which included the most distinguished Jews of America. The Committee aimed and claimed to be representative without, however, exposing itself to the hazards of democratic elections. Since it was frankly an assembly of Jewish notables, self-selected and self-perpetuating, the Committee did not escape criticism and challenge, but because of the character and prestige of its leadership, it established before long an impressive record of achievement in the defense of Jewish rights and the promotion of Jewish interests. Chiefly instrumental in its creation was Mayer Sulzberger of Philadelphia, eminent jurist and profound Jewish scholar who became its first president; and among his associates were the brilliant lawyer Louis Marshall who succeeded him to the leadership in 1912; the versatile Cyrus Adler who became the Committee's president on the death of Marshall in 1929; Jacob H. Schiff, outstanding banker and princely philanthropist; and Oscar S. Straus, statesman and scholar, who served his country as Ambassador to Turkey and as Secretary of Commerce and Labor in the cabinet of Theodore Roosevelt. One of the first tasks of the Committee, in which it rendered effective service, was to combat the mounting agitation for the restriction of immigration, an agitation aimed principally against the Jews of eastern Europe, for whom America was the only haven of escape from their tormentors.

In February 1911, President William Howard Taft received a

delegation consisting of representatives of the American Jewish Committee, the Order B'nai B'rith, and the Union of American Hebrew Congregations, to discuss the long-standing "Russian passport question," as the issues arising from the Treaty of 1832 came to be called. The President's attitude proved gravely disappointing: he appeared to be deeply concerned over the possible risks which any drastic action might impose on American investments in Russia. Thereupon the "undemocratic" leaders decided to resort to the thoroughly democratic method of rousing the public opinion of the country against the injustice. Numerous mass meetings were held, the support of the press was enlisted, state legislatures adopted resolutions, and again resolutions were introduced into the houses of Congress. It became an American and not merely a Jewish issue, the most impressive meetings being staged by a non-sectarian body of which the chairman was Andrew White, a former United States ambassador to Russia.

The democratic process was completely vindicated. In December 1911 President Taft who, it is thought, was not averse to having this wide public pressure for a step he really favored, formally denounced the Treaty of 1832, and a year later, in accordance with its provisions, the abrogation of the treaty was an accomplished fact.

CHAPTER FIFTY-EIGHT

Anti-Semitism and the Dreyfus Affair

America and Czarist Russia—what a contrast these two broad lands presented in the fortunes of the Jewish people, with freedom and security in the one, and oppression and terror in the other! But what were the fortunes of the Jews in the other lands of Europe, in those where emancipation had at long last been attained: in Austria-Hungary where the Ausgleich of 1867 had terminated all legal disabilities; in Germany, where the "blood and iron" unification of 1871 brought similar constitutional guarantees; in Italy where, in the same year, the triumphant *Risorgimento* ended the temporal power of the papacy and swept away the foul Roman ghetto; in England where in 1858 Jews could sit in Parliament without forswearing their souls; and in France, "the cradle of liberty," where the Great Revolution emancipated them as early as 1791. Did the great prize for which they strove so hard bring them the dignity and security they hoped for? Did it solve the Jewish question in Europe?

There were many Jews who thought it did, and they lost no time in taking advantage of the opportunities their new-won freedom held out to them. In industry and commerce, in the legal, medical and other professions, in science, literature, and art, in journalism and even in politics, they quickly moved forward into the front ranks. The much decried "peculiarities" which centuries of ghetto life had stamped upon them seemed to fall away overnight. The European Jew became a thorough European, his beard trimmed or shaved, his clothes cut to fashion, the language of the land perfect on his tongue and pen. And if occasionally he appeared to be a little unpoised and ill at ease, by turns too shy and too bold, would not his good neighbors understand and overlook these small vestiges of oppression and segregation?

His good neighbors, alas, understood and overlooked nothing. They saw in him the same phantoms and terrors that haunted them in the Middle Ages, and they added new ones. Anti-Semitism was the new monster that rose up to plague the Jew in the modern world. The monster was not really new, but he came decked out in new trappings, and neither emancipation nor assimilation could slay him. The Jewish question in Europe was not solved; the Jews were not to be left in peace.

2

MODERN anti-Semitism was made in Germany, whence it spread rapidly throughout Europe and invaded other continents. The soil of Germany after the Franco-Prussian War was peculiarly suited for the rank growth. The swift triumphs achieved by the Prussian army and the "blood and iron" statesmanship of Otto von Bismarck intensified the morbid race consciousness of the Germans, the solemn conviction that they were the world's master race. The Jew, they were taught to believe, was an inferior alien among them, congenitally incapable of absorbing the "authentic German spirit," and therefore a stumbling block in the path of their destiny. This solemn twaddle was taught in the schools and universities; it was disseminated in numerous books, pamphlets, and periodicals; it was preached from the pulpits; it impregnated the intellectual atmosphere of Germany like a miasma.

By pulpit spellbinders like the court preacher Adolf Stoecker, anti-Semitism was exalted for the greater glory of Christianity: he it was who in 1879 inspired the organization of the League of Anti-Semites, and in 1882 presided over the first International Anti-Semitic Congress which was held in Dresden. On the other hand, with philosophers like Eugen Duehring, a progenitor of the Nazi ideology, anti-Semitism went hand in hand with hatred of Christianity as a product of the Jewish spirit; and the ponderous historian Heinrich von Treitschke, who even figured as a liberal, proclaimed and popularized the slogan: "the Jews are our misfortune." But the writer who did most to poison the intellectual atmosphere of Germany was, curiously enough, an Englishman. He was Houston Stewart Chamberlain, whose *Foundations of the Nineteenth Century*, first published in 1899, became the bible of German "scientific" anti-Semitism and the Pan-Germanic movement. Chamberlain married a daughter of the German composer Richard Wagner, himself a venomous anti-Semite, and at the outbreak of the First World War in 1914 turned traitor to the land of his birth.

Chamberlain gathered the threads of anti-Semitic doctrine already spun by his predecessors and elaborated them into a fantastic web. History, according to Chamberlain, reveals only one gifted race: the Germans, who created all things great and good. The Jews, on the other hand, represent a direct antithesis, and their continued existence is an historic crime. For the great men who throng the pages of Jewish history, Chamberlain found a singular explanation. Those men, like David, and Solomon, and the Hebrew prophets, were of Germanic descent! One of the nations in Canaan whom the Jews conquered, the Amorites, was conveniently discovered to be a Germanic tribe, and it was they who sired all the great of ancient Israel. As for Jesus of Nazareth and the apostles, the explanation was even more simple and startling: Palestine was garrisoned at that time by Roman soldiers among whom there were already many Teutons. Nor did the explanation, so blasphemous to the Christian consciousness, disturb the teacher and his numerous "Christian" disciples. Such was the "science" that gained the widest currency among the German intellectuals, with Emperor Wilhelm II himself one of its ardent admirers. Franz Oppenheimer, the brilliant Jewish socialist, found a word for Chamberlain: he called him "the court-fool of absolutism."

3

BUT the Germans are not a nation of intellectuals only. For the majority of them—the peasants and artisans, the shopkeepers and civil employees—a simpler brand of anti-Semitism was available. The stock market crash of 1873 and the economic depression which followed were, of course, the result of a Jewish conspiracy, in which the *Alliance Israélite Universelle*, the head and front of the "Jewish International," played the leading part. The German Catholics charged the Jews with responsibility for the bitter Kulturkampf which, from 1872 to 1879, Bismarck waged against their church. To make any cause or policy odious, the surest way was to identify the Jews with it, and anti-clericalism, the policy of Bismarck and the National Liberal Party, was no exception. The embittered and frustrated Pius IX, who still sat on the papal throne, himself led the anti-Semitic campaign.

By 1880, however, Bismarck himself made common cause with the anti-Semites. He found the alliance useful first in his struggle with the fast-growing Social Democratic party. That party came into existence in 1875 when the followers of Karl Marx united with those of the brilliant orator and labor leader, Ferdinand Lassalle, both of Jewish origin. What then could be more natural than to brand socialism and all its works as another Jewish conspiracy? In 1879, moreover, Bismarck embarked on a policy of reaction and broke with the National Liberal party, finding support from the anti-Semites to whom liberalism was also a Semitic fabrication. Were not the two Jews, Eduard Lasker and Ludwig Bamberger, who had given him invaluable aid in the creation of the Reich, the most relentless opponents of his new course? The advantages of enlisting anti-Semitism for the promotion of any political program were much too tempting.

Not that Bismarck and his Junkers were prepared to countenance the so-to-speak "uncivilized" forms of anti-Semitism. Germany must not sink to the level of Russia. Germany was a "cultured" nation and could not tolerate civil disturbances. Besides, violence had a way of spreading into unexpected quarters. The government policy, therefore, was to encourage anti-Semitism without permitting it to get out of hand. Unfortunately, however, this attempt to feed the tiger and keep the lamb whole proved a failure: the beast was much too ravenous. Not only were Jews in practice despoiled of their civil rights, but they were assaulted in the streets of Berlin and other cities. In Neustettin a synagogue was burned and in 1891 a charge of ritual murder was trumped up in Xanten, near the lower Rhine. At the trial, the prosecuting attorney himself called for the acquittal of the accused, but public passion had been whipped up to so dangerous a pitch that the city became unsafe for its Jewish inhabitants. In 1900 a similar accusation was attempted in the West Prussian town of Konitz; it failed to stand up, but the town had to be placed under martial law.

Indeed, the alarming fact soon became apparent—alarming not only to the Jews, but to decent Christians and even to some "scientific" anti-Semites—that the agitation had become the stamping ground of distinctly criminal types: blackmailers, forgers, incendiaries, perjurers, and even psychopaths. Stoecker himself was found guilty of political intrigue involving moral turpitude. Herman Ahlwardt, his successor as German anti-Semite Number One, a member of the Reichstag from 1893 to 1898, was imprisoned for libel and extortion, and the rabble-rouser Count Pueckler, his collaborator, wound up in an insane asylum. Dr. August Roehling, author of a scurrilous work entitled *The Talmud Jew,* was exposed as a forger and perjurer, and other anti-Semitic leaders, both in and out of the Reichstag, were convicted of embezzlement, falsification, and perjury! The movement attracted so many shady characters and public morality became so debased by it that in 1891, the year of the Xanten affair, hundreds of prominent Germans organized a Society to Combat Anti-Semitism, and a "respectable" anti-Semite like Wilhelm Marr, one of the "philosophers" of the movement, turned with "loathing amounting to nausea" from the noisome brood he had helped to engender.

4

NOT less unsavory was the anti-Semitic movement in the Austrian dominions, where the plight of the victims was aggravated by the chronic strife between the nationalities in the crazy-quilt empire of Francis Joseph. In the endless conflicts between Czechs and Germans in Bohemia, Poles and Ruthenians in Galicia, and Magyars, Slovaks, and Rumanians in Hungary, the Jews found themselves between the upper and nether millstones. When, as they usually felt compelled to do, they took sides in the electoral feuds, they incurred the bitter hostility of the party they opposed without necessarily earning the gratitude of the one they espoused. The least grateful were the Germans, particularly the Pan-Germans, who took their cue from the Treitschkes and Stoeckers in Berlin. In German Austria, where Roehling's screed against the Talmud found a wide circulation, the Berlin brand of anti-Semitism became, in the early eighties, the program of a political party. It was led by the Pan-German Georg von Schoenerer whose criminal violence brought him, in 1888, a term in prison. But the most unscrupulous anti-Semitic demagogue was the Viennese lawyer Dr. Karl Lueger, founder of the Christian Socialist party. In 1897, with the support of the Clericals and Pan-Germans, he became mayor of Vienna. Lueger, who numbered among his followers a large assortment of criminal types, became the inspiration and model of anti-Semitic demagogues who, a generation later, improved on his methods and applied them to Germany and the whole world.

German Austria, and particularly Vienna, became worm-eaten with anti-Semitism. Jews were forced out of municipal posts and denied other economic opportunities. The virus was particularly active in the secondary schools and universities, but the noble Teuton students had no stomach for meeting the victims of their malice on "the field of honor," where students normally settled their quarrels. When Jewish students began to exhibit a disturbing skill with foil and pistol, a congress of German students which met in

Waidhofen in 1897, solemnly resolved that the Jews were not entitled to "honorable satisfaction." However, in the Austrian army and navy—which of course were under direct imperial control—the monster was held in check, and Jews even rose to the rank of general and admiral. The emperor himself detested anti-Semitism and its practitioners: it was only after the voters of Vienna had given Lueger a majority three times in succession that Francis Joseph felt constrained to confirm his election.

5

IN HUNGARY, where the Magyars needed the Jews to retain their hegemony over the other nationalities, anti-Semitism, though not absent, was held in leash. But in 1882 it broke out in all its ugliness in the form of a fantastic blood libel in Tisza-Eslar, a village on the River Theiss. The anti-Semites knew how to exploit the lie to inflame the populace. There were serious riots in Pressburg and other places, and for two years the hideous affair dragged on with the usual apparatus of perjury, torture, intimidation, and terror before the accused, on the recommendation of the state's attorney himself, were acquitted. In Bohemia and Moravia, where Czechs and Germans were in a state of chronic hostility, the Czechs were bitter against the Jews for supporting their opponents, while the Germans were anti-Semitic as a matter of patriotic duty. There too the tension reached its climax in a blood libel which led to riots against the Jews. In 1899, in the town of Polna, a cobbler named Leopold Hilsner was condemned to death on a murder charge in which the medieval legend played a part. The trial was denounced by Thomas Masaryk, later the first president of the Czechoslovak republic, but all efforts to obtain a new trial were in vain. The sentence, however, was commuted to life imprisonment, and in 1916 Hilsner was pardoned.

6

IN GALICIA, the Polish province of the Austrian empire, there were nearly a million Jews who found themselves caught between the Poles and Ruthenians in their unceasing struggle for supremacy. Normally, the Jews supported the Poles, without, however, appeasing either the Polish *shlakhta* and clergy, who were still in political control, or the rising Polish middle class in the cities, bent on suppressing its Jewish competitors. The weapon the Poles found most effective was the economic boycott. The destitution among the Jews mounted to a degree which neither the tens of thousands who migrated to America and other lands, nor the efforts of Baron de Hirsch to divert them to new sources of livelihood, could mitigate. In 1898 the suffrage was extended, the Poles split into a number of parties, and when the Jews cast their votes for the Social Democrats as being the least anti-Semitic, the other parties unleashed a wave of pogroms against them which claimed thousands of victims. The disorders were suppressed only after the inflamed peasants began to attack the estates of the nobility also.

In eastern Galicia, the policy of supporting the Poles, into which the Jews found themselves dragooned, brought them the hostility of the Ruthenians, who were in the majority. In 1907, led by the Zionists, the Jews concluded a pact with the Ruthenians which allayed their resentment, but it naturally called down upon them the wrath of the Poles. Anti-Semitism became a major plank in the program of the Polish National Democrats whose party embraced Russian Poland also. The Endeks, as its members were called, intensified the economic boycott and had no hestitation about resorting to violence.

7

THUS from Germany eastward, into all the lands where emancipation had brought the promise of a new era to the Jewish people, came this new version of the ancient enmity to harass and torment them. But in all those lands the centuries had piled up heaps of inflammable material which the baleful sparks from Germany could easily ignite. Would the evil flames spread westward also? Would they find fuel in glorious France, the cradle of liberty and the native home of European civilization? The answer came in 1894 when an anti-Semitic conspiracy convicted an innocent Jewish army officer, Alfred Dreyfus, of high treason, and the Third French Republic was brought to the brink of civil war and downfall.

Never, in point of fact, did "scientific" anti-Semitism capture the imagination and passions of Frenchmen as it did of Germans.

Strangely enough, however, it made its appearance in France even before it did in Germany. In 1855, more than a generation before the renegade Englishman, Houston Stewart Chamberlain, popularized it in Germany, the French diplomat and writer Count Joseph Arthur Gobineau published his *Essay on the Inequalities of Human Races*. In this four-volume work the count propounded the major doctrines of "scientific" anti-Semitism, including the congenital superiority of the Germanic race and the intellectual and spiritual sterility of the Semites, especially the Jews. Nor did he fail to give credit to the intervention of Teutons for the birth of such Jews as David and Solomon, the Hebrew prophets, Jesus of Nazareth, and Paul of Tarsus. Gobineau's influence, however, was restricted, and it was probably greater in Germany than in France.

The flaming apostle of anti-Semitism who achieved popularity in France, was Edouard Drumont, whose *La France juive* (Judaized France) appeared in 1886. The atmosphere at the time was charged with partisan hatreds, and the reactionary anti-republican forces found it profitable to make the Jews responsible for the rise of the Third Republic in 1871, and for all the other ills, political and economic, with which France was afflicted. Drumont's chef-d'oeuvre became one of the best sellers of the century, diligently promoted by the clericals and royalists who were eager to see the downfall of the republic. In 1892, Drumont began publishing the anti-Semitic newspaper *La libre Parole*, which specialized in making aspersions on the patriotism of Jewish officers, of whom there were about five hundred in the French army, and the stage was set for the momentous Dreyfus Affair.

8

ALFRED DREYFUS, a captain of artillery attached to the general staff, was born in Alsace in 1859, and when, after the Franco-Prussian War, France was compelled to cede that province to Germany, Alfred's family chose to remain French and settled in Paris. There was nothing in the captain's personal circumstances to drive him to criminal conduct. He was happily married, he was wealthy, he was an able officer, and he seemed assured of a brilliant career in the army. In 1894 that career was abruptly terminated by a charge of high treason. A document, which became famous as the *bordereau* (memorandum), had come to light revealing that French military secrets had been communicated to agents of the German government. The handwriting of the *bordereau* was declared to be that of Captain Dreyfus, who was duly court-martialed and sentenced to life imprisonment after being publicly degraded.

On January 5, 1895, in the presence of his fellow officers and a crowd gathered in and around the *Champ de Mars*, the degradation of Captain Dreyfus was solemnly carried out. His insignia were ripped off, and his sword broken. "Death to the traitor! Death to the Jews!" the mobs shouted. "You are degrading an innocent man!" Dreyfus cried. He was then transported to the pestilential little Devil's Island off the coast of French Guiana where, his enemies were sure, he would spend the rest of his life.

But the Dreyfus family refused to let the matter rest, and they were ably assisted by the writer Bernard Lazare, champion of his people and implacable enemy of injustice. A year after the conviction, Colonel Picquart, the new head of the Intelligence Service, discovered to his amazement and dismay that the *bordereau* was not in the handwriting of Dreyfus but of a Major Esterhazy, an officer who was well-known as a dissolute scamp. But the Minister of War and the generals were adamant against reopening the case, and the reactionary press, of course, supported them. "What difference does it make to you whether this Jew remains on Devil's Island or not?" Picquart was asked by his superior; and when Picquart insisted, he was removed and his place taken by Colonel Henry, who could be relied upon to shield the real traitor. In the hope of silencing the Dreyfus family and others who made a fuss about justice, the generals staged a secret court-martial for Esterhazy which, of course, acquitted him.

But now a new champion entered the arena whose leonine voice could not be stilled. He was the outstanding French novelist Emile Zola, who on January 13, 1898, published his shattering *J'accuse!* In this open letter to Felix Faure, President of the French Republic, Zola charged the generals with the crime of "high treason against humanity." But Zola was himself arrested and convicted of libel. All France was now in a state of feverish excitement, the great majority joining in the hue and cry against Dreyfus. There were rumors of an imminent *coup d'état* to overthrow the republic, the judges feared to impose any but the severest sentence, and Zola fled to England. Anti-Semitic riots flared up in many cities of France, in Paris, Marseille, Bordeaux, Lyon, and others. The agitation spread to the French colony of Algeria, where it led to bloody pogroms.

But the demand for a new trial for Dreyfus could not be stifled: it persisted not only in France but throughout the world. New champions arose who took up his cause: Jean Jaurès, leader of the Socialists who were perturbed by the triumph of the reactionary coalition of clericals and royalists; Georges Clemenceau, the intrepid Radical statesman whose newspaper, *L'aurore*, was the first to publish Zola's *J'accuse;* Anatole France, the foremost man of letters in France, who was partly of Jewish descent; Aristide Briand, the statesman who was later the author of the law for the separation of church and state; Scheurer-Kestner, the vice-president of the French Senate, and others. But now events took a startling turn which made a new trial inevitable. On August 31, 1898, Colonel Henry, caught in the meshes of the forgeries he committed to shield Esterhazy, cut his throat with a razor, and the man he shielded fled to England. Now the reactionaries redoubled their agitation; Déroulède, one of their leaders, made an attempt to overthrow the Republic, and popular passion continued to rise. In February 1899, France voted for a new president with the Dreyfus Affair the burning issue, and the excitement reached its climax. But the successful candidate was Émile Loubet, who stood for a new trial for Dreyfus: the heart and intelligence of France were still sound.

From August 7 to September 9, 1899, Dreyfus faced an open court-martial at Rennes, and was again found guilty "with extenuating circumstances"! The verdict, it was clear, was another attempt to feed the tiger of reaction and keep the lamb of justice whole. The trial, as the London *Times* expressed it, was "foul with forgeries, lies, contradictions, and puerilities." Ten days after the trial, Dreyfus, sentenced to ten years' imprisonment, was pardoned by President Loubet.

The Rennes trial was followed by another desperate attempt by the reactionaries against the republic. The plot was discovered and its leader, Jules Guerin, secretary of the anti-Semitic League, together with a group of followers, entrenched himself in his headquarters and defied the government. It took more than a month and 5000 troops to rout them out! Now the government struck at the root of the evil—the preponderant influence which the religious bodies of the Catholic church, like the Jesuits, the Dominicans, and others, exercised on the royalists and the army. In 1901 the Associations Act was passed which broke the power of these orders over the education of the young. In 1905 the anti-clerical bloc in the Chamber of Deputies, which the Dreyfus Affair had welded together, went further. The Separation Law of that year abolished the connection of church and state which, under the Concordat between Napoleon I and the papacy, had existed in France for over a century.

The final act of the Dreyfus drama took place on July 12, 1906, when the *Cour de Cassation*, the Supreme Court of France, overthrew the verdict of the court-martial of Rennes and unanimously found Dreyfus innocent. The captain was promoted to the rank of major and awarded the ribbon of the Legion of Honor. Colonel Picquart was made a brigadier general and three months later entered the first cabinet of Clemenceau as Minister of War. The remains of Emile Zola, who did not live to see the triumph for which he had fought so valiantly, were laid to rest in the Pantheon. French anti-Semitism received a blow from which it never quite recovered.

9

THE anti-Semitism which sprang from the "blood and soil" of Germany, with its pompous parade of "science," its metaphysical and mystical twaddle, its hierarchy ranging from Fichte and Hegel down to the village schoolmasters, found no response from the realistic and hardheaded people across the North Sea. England, in fact, had permitted its native Jews to rise to a height which can only be compared with that attained during the golden era by their coreligionists in Spain. Wherever Jews were oppressed they sought and obtained help from the influential community in England, where men of all religious and political faiths often united to denounce bigotry and persecution.

Nevertheless, England did not remain immune to the more popular brand of the anti-Semitic virus. In their flight from eastern Europe, too many of the fugitives, it seemed, settled in England, and agitation to restrict the admission of aliens arose and became particularly clamorous in 1902 when, after the Boer War, unemployment became a serious problem. The "aliens"—and it was an open secret that the word stood for immigrant Jews—were accused of depriving Englishmen of their jobs. Naturally, the agitation was embellished with charges of a more distinctly anti-Semitic character. The "aliens" were accused, for example, of engaging in unproductive occupations. But the great majority—about 85 per cent of them—were artisans: tailors, shoemakers, cigarmakers, cabinetmakers, and others. Only about 7 per cent were traders. There were a number of parliamentary commissions whose investigations failed to substantiate any of the serious charges; and in 1905 one of these commissions, which specialized in the statistical aspects of the problem, exposed the exaggerations of the alarmists by revealing the fact that of the 300,000 Jewish immigrants who had been admitted since 1891, only 105,000 were still in England, the others having moved on westward to the Americas. But the clamor persisted, and Parliament finally passed the Aliens Bill which went into effect in 1906, with restrictions that reduced the number of Jews admitted that year to a third of the number admitted the year before.

The Aliens Bill did not have easy sailing in Parliament or in the country at large. Englishmen who cherished their reputation for fair play were disturbed by the false and bigoted claims which were advanced on behalf of the measure, let alone the comfort it provided for the persecutors in Russia and Rumania. Nor did the deeper social and moral implications of anti-Semitism escape them. "The amount of anti-Semitism in a country has generally been proportionate to the amount of bigotry, mental depravity, and moral callousness it contained," was the verdict of G. F. Abbott, author of a volume entitled *Israel in Europe*.

As for the Jews, the specious assurance that the bill was not aimed at them in particular failed to reassure them. It so happened that in 1904, in the midst of the agitation, a small group of Jews who had settled in the town of Limerick in Ireland became the target of a vicious propaganda launched against them by a monk of the Redemptorist Order named Father Creagh, to which the townsfolk and the peasants round about responded only too readily. Even in Britain a feeling of uneasiness descended on the Jews. England, said the novelist Israel Zangwill, "was catching the epidemic which rages everywhere against the Jew."

CHAPTER FIFTY-NINE

Theodor Herzl

THERE was at least one witness of that gruesome spectacle on January 5, 1895, when Captain Alfred Dreyfus was publicly degraded, who realized its full significance and on whom it made a shattering impression. He was an Austrian journalist named Theodor Herzl, living in Paris as correspondent of the influential Vienna newspaper *Neue Freie Presse*. He was thirty-five, tall, strikingly handsome, of grave and noble bearing, with the full black beard and regal port of an Assyrian monarch—endowments which played their part in perhaps the most singular career of modern times, bold, brilliant, and creative.

Theodor Herzl was already launched on a career of another sort when the glowing coal was pressed to his lips. He was making his mark in journalism and literature, nor did his racial origin impede or oppress him very seriously. True, both in Budapest where he was born and in Vienna where his family went to live when he was eighteen, this origin had, on a number of occasions, been unpleasantly brought home to him by teachers and schoolmates; and when, after getting his doctorate in jurisprudence in the University of Vienna, he began practicing law in Salzburg, he soon realized that the same origin made the prospects of a successful career in that profession rather dubious. But he possessed a native dignity and pride that enabled him to meet aspersions with healthy disdain and, as for a career, he preferred literature to law in any case. He wrote plays, essays, and critical studies. Some of his plays had already met with success on the stage, and he was well established as a journalist, being particularly adept with the short, sparkling, little essay called the *feuilleton*. Apparently, Herzl was one of the young Jews whom emancipation seemed to have really emancipated. He was at home in the intellectual and artistic life of Europe; the threads that connected him to his people and its past were so tenuous that he could relish the glitter and superficiality of that life without distaste or misgivings. By every indication, Theodor Herzl was marked for a serene and "successful" life.

But the Power which guides the destiny of men and nations ruled otherwise. Theodor Herzl came away from that lamentable scene on the *Champ de Mars* a changed man. What hideous thing was this which had come over France? he asked himself—the France he so loved and admired, the land of the Great Revolution, the cradle of liberty and human brotherhood. It was not just Dreyfus for whose blood he heard the mob clamor; it was for the blood of all his people! Herzl was shaken to his soul's depths, and out of these depths there rose to the surface a store of vision and prophetic passion, the existence of which neither he nor his friends seem to have suspected.

The way for his imperiled people seemed to him perfectly clear. That way was a return to nationhood—indeed, to statehood. But Herzl felt neither inclined nor competent to become the leader of a great historic enterprise: there were others he thought more qualified by wealth and station. There were the English Rothschilds, for example; and there was Baron Maurice de Hirsch, a man not only of great wealth, but beyond question of great heart also.

Early in June 1895, Herzl was received by Baron de Hirsch in Paris and spent an hour with him. The Baron was intrigued and disturbed by this enthusiast with the magnetic eyes and regal bearing. A Jewish state? An international political movement? Another Messianic agitation? It was fantastic, dangerous! Who was this young journalist come to tell the great philanthropist that the Jewish tragedy was too immense and, yes, too sacred to be solved by charity?

Disappointed but not discouraged, Theodor Herzl, first a writer, sat down and wrote. And there was born a one-hundred-page pamphlet to which he gave the provocative title *A Jewish State.* It appeared the following year and it led some of Herzl's friends to fear for his sanity. The little book had the precision of an architect's blueprint, but through it all ran a fervor and pathos that were profoundly moving. "We are a people—one people," was its basic idea and point of departure. From it proceeded the propositions, first, that the Jewish problem could only be solved through the collective effort of the Jews themselves, operating as a political entity; and second, that the goal of this effort must be the establishment of a Jewish state. Nor would the nations withhold their approval from the undertaking, for such a state, by absorbing a host of formidable competitors, would benefit them also. For his own people, whose infiltration into European society since the emancipation had spawned the new anti-Semitism, there was no other way; this monster, under certain conditions of tension and conflict which might well arise, would, in its blind fury, attempt the total destruction of its victim.

Like the prophet Ezekiel who, while an exile in Babylonia, drew a complete plan for a new Temple, Herzl proceeded to describe the process of creating the new state. A "Society of Jews" was to be the recognized political agency of the Jewish people, and a "Jewish Company" its financial and executive arm. Territorial rights were to be secured by a charter with the approval of the European governments. Colonization was to proceed by organized groups and to be carefully controlled. To win economic and spiritual freedom, the Jewish masses would flock to the new land; and the intellectuals and many of the wealthy would also come. "A generation of wonderful Jews will spring from the earth. The Maccabees will rise again! Let the opening words be repeated: the Jews who will it shall have a state of their own."

"As I wrote, I seemed to hear the rushing of eagles' wings above my head," Herzl set down in his diary.

2

BUT the idea of restoring the Jewish people to nationhood, which came to Herzl like a revelation, was, as we have already seen, not a new thing. It was born with the destruction of their state at the hands of the Romans; it was enshrined in their prayers; it became linked with the advent of the Messiah. The constant theme of the singers of the Exile was the land of Israel's former greatness, and around it the cabalists wove the glowing web of their mystic fancies. How they loved that land, how they yearned to breathe its air, "which makes men wise," to kiss its bare stones, and weep upon its ruins!

O who will give me wings that I may fly away,
My broken heart upon thy ruined stones to lay!

Thus sang Yehudah Halevi, the greatest poet of the Exile, who himself made the pilgrimage. And all through the centuries, singly and in bands, the exiles continued to brave the perils of the journey in order to satisfy their longing. They came as pilgrims, they came as settlers, and many came in their old age to be buried in the sacred soil.

But even the notion of a restoration through systematic colonization and political action was not a new thing when Herzl received his great illumination. As early as 1825, the same light had dawned on the quixotic Mordecai Manuel Noah in America, and in the early eighties it had come to Perez Smolenskin, Moses Leib Lillienblum, Leon Pinsker, and a host of others in eastern Europe where a serious attempt was already under way by the BILU groups and the *Chovevei Tziyon* societies to translate the idea into agricultural settlements in Palestine.

Of Pinsker's *Auto-Emancipation* and the ferment it had stirred in eastern Europe, Herzl had no knowledge. Nor was he aware that in the six decades between Noah and Pinsker there had been still others, Christians as well as Jews, who spoke out and who labored for the national redemption of the Jewish people. In 1842, with the eastern question in the forefront of international affairs, Charles Henry Churchill, of the same clan which in 1940 was to give Britain its greatest war leader, wrote to Moses Montefiore: "I cannot conceal from you my most anxious desire to see your countrymen endeavor once more to resume their existence as a people." Ten years later an English theologian named Hollingsworth wrote an eloquent plea for the establishment under British protection of a Jewish state in Palestine where "the Jew can feel the deathless energies of his race and the high destinies of his future." An equally ardent but more influential champion was the eminent philanthropist and social reformer Anthony Ashley Cooper, Earl of Shaftesbury. In 1876, speaking of the "crowning bond of union" between the Jewish people and Palestine, he declared: "This is not an artificial experiment: it is nature, it is history!" The same year George Eliot's great novel *Daniel Deronda* appeared, perhaps the most powerful plea that has ever been made for "the revival of the organic center" of the Jewish people.

Some of the Christian supporters of the national revival of the Jewish people were animated by theologic considerations: it must come to pass in fulfillment of prophecy, and be followed by the conversion of the Jews. The most active of these advocates was Laurence Oliphant, traveler, author, and mystic, who in 1879 vainly sought permission from the Sultan of Turkey to establish a large Jewish settlement in Palestine. He was encouraged by Prime Minister Benjamin Disraeli as well as by the Foreign Minister, Lord Salisbury. In fact, many years earlier, when Disraeli was only an aspiring young novelist, his enthusiasm for the redemption of the people from whom he sprang and whom he never hesitated to champion, found expression in his romances of the East. Nor should any roster of the early Christian champions of Jewish restoration, however incomplete, omit the name of Jean Henri Dunant, the great Swiss humanitarian, founder of the Red Cross, who from 1863 to 1876 labored to arouse an interest among the Jews of western Europe for the colonization of Palestine. And in 1891, only five years before Herzl published his *Jewish State*, the Reverend William E. Blackstone of Chicago circulated a petition addressed to President Benjamin Harrison and Secretary of State James G. Blaine, praying them "to secure the holding at an early date of an international conference to consider the condition of the Israelites and their claim to Palestine as their ancient home." The petition bore the signatures of scores of leaders in the spiritual, intellectual, political, and economic life of America. From America, also, there had even proceeded by 1870 three separate attempts by Christians to plant agricultural settlements in Palestine; of these at least two, one established in 1852 by Warder Cresson of Philadelphia, the other a year later by Mrs. Clorinda S. Minor, also of that city, were linked with the larger purpose of speeding the restoration of Israel.

3

BUT of these Christian champions Herzl had no more knowledge than he had of the *Chibath Tziyon* movement in eastern Europe. Nor had he any knowledge of the Jewish advocates of national revival who had preceded him with vain attempts to pierce the indifference of their people in western Europe. Among them were the historian Joseph Salvador in France, the scholar and poet Samuel David Luzzatto in Italy, and the rabbi and philosopher Isaac Ruelf in Prussia. The Orthodox rabbi, Zevi Hirsch Kalischer, also in Prussia, not only wrote and preached but even took a hand in a colonizing experiment in Palestine. The profoundest of these western exponents of Jewish national rebirth was Moses Hess (1812-1875), Socialist leader and collaborator of Karl Marx and Ferdinand Lassalle, whose *Rome and Jerusalem*, published in 1862, Herzl did not read until 1901. "I was delighted and uplifted by him," Herzl records in his diary. "What a lofty and noble spirit! All I have aimed at is already to be found in him . . . Since Spinoza the Jewish people has produced no greater spirit than this dimmed-out and forgotten Moses Hess!"

4

IT MAY have been an advantage rather than a handicap to Herzl, this ignorance on his part of what others had said and tried to do for the goal he urged: it enabled him to proclaim that goal with a simplicity and directness his *Jewish State* might otherwise have lacked. In the last analysis, however, Herzl's importance lay not in what he wrote, but in what he was. In every way—physically, intellectually, and morally—Herzl was superbly gifted, and he proved to be a great leader and practical man of affairs as well as a prophet. He has been hailed as the first creative statesman of the Jewish people since the Dispersion. Reluctant as he was to take the lead, Herzl had "put his hand to the plow," and he could not look backward. In the eight years that followed, until his untimely death in July 1904, he spent himself in the service of Zionism, as the movement he launched came to be called.

The simple plan of action set forth in the *Jewish State* was, in essence, actually followed. The "Society of Jews," which was to enlist public sentiment, negotiate with governments, and represent the Jewish people politically, became the World Zionist Organization. The "Jewish Company," which was to finance and administer the work of colonization, became the Jewish Colonial Trust, to which in time were added the Jewish National Fund and the Palestine Foundation Fund. The "Company," in Herzl's plan, was not to begin operations before the "Society" had obtained from the Sultan of Turkey or some other sovereign a public grant or charter over a definite territory. A tract in Argentina, Herzl was at first inclined to think, might also serve the purpose; it was only after he came to know the Jewish masses of eastern Europe that he realized the land must be Palestine and no other.

Contact with reality compelled still other modifications in his basic plan. The "Company," Herzl proposed, should be launched with a capital of $250,000,000. Why not? The rich as well as the poor, the influential as well as the lowly, would flock to the cause and insure its speedy realization. But his efforts to enlist the rich and the exalted brought little response. Other philanthropists besides Baron de Hirsch, who were spending large sums to relieve Jewish distress, turned a deaf ear to the proposals of the "dangerous visionary." Of the many Jews whose words carried weight in Europe, only Max Nordau, the brilliant French critic and social philosopher, and Israel Zangwill, the English novelist, placed themselves unreservedly at his side. The important Jewish organizations of western Europe—the French *Alliance Israélite Universelle*, its Austrian counterpart, the *Israelitische Allianz*, the Jewish Colonization Association in London—came out in opposition. Even the *Chovevei Tziyon* in Russia began by holding aloof. The Maccabeans, a society of Jewish intellectuals in London, listened to Herzl politely but coldly, and there were Orthodox rabbis who proclaimed that not in Herzl's way, but through God's anointed Messiah, would the great deliverance come about. The most bitter opponents of all were the Reform rabbis. The Jews, they asserted, were not a nation and must not seek to become one. Their mission was to be scattered among the nations of the earth to serve the cause of truth, justice, and universal peace. Zionism would only strengthen anti-Semitism. Besides, was it patriotic for Jews to talk of setting up a state of their own? What of the states which had emancipated them and to which they owed allegiance? Thus spoke the Reform rabbis of Germany and America.

So Herzl found himself left with the poor and the lowly. They were, for the most part, the suffering masses of eastern Europe, those who knew they were a people and should be a nation, who saw in Zionism a movement which ran true to their character and destiny.

5

IT WAS a staggering flood of opposition that Herzl encountered, but he was not dismayed. Very soon he saw enough to convince him that, notwithstanding the upraised brows and frigid smiles that greeted him in the salons of the mighty, he had touched the vital nerve of his people. He saw it in the response of the Jewish students of Austria and Germany: they sent him an address with thousands of signatures, and the *Kadimah* society in the University of Vienna, led by Nathan Birnbaum, was particularly enthusiastic. He saw it among the Jews of Sofia when, in the spring of 1896, he passed through that city on his way from Constantinople; and he saw it among the Jews in the East End of London. From Russia, Galicia, Rumania, Hungary, and Bulgaria he received expressions of adherence and demands for action. So Herzl went forward from words to deeds and his deeds were marked by the same largeness of vision that illumined his first conception.

He began by calling a representative Jewish congress which became the basic instrument of the movement. "The direction of Jewish affairs," said he in the call to the congress which went out in the name of a commission created for the purpose, "must not be left to the will of individuals, no matter how well-intentioned they may be. A forum must be created before which each one may be called to account for what he does or fails to do in Jewry." The time set for the first congress was August 1897; the place,

Munich. At once there arose a storm of objections. There was alarm in the western countries, where Jews still trembled for their new-won emancipation. They were afraid of an open discussion of Jewish affairs in a democratic body; they wanted no such symbol of Jewish unity, publicly displayed and with political implications. The leaders in the Jewish community in Munich protested against the holding of the congress in their city, and a group of German rabbis, the *Protest Rabbiner*, as Herzl designated them, published a denunciation of the proposed assembly as an aspersion upon their loyalty to the fatherland.

But the congress was duly held, not in Munich, but in the Swiss city of Basel. It brought together 197 delegates from almost every land of the earth, chosen by the vote of all those who, having paid the *shekel*, had demonstrated their adherence to the Zionist goal. For the first time in eighteen centuries, the Jewish people, or at least a considerable part of it, assembled to take its destiny into its own hands. "Zionism," said Herzl, "is the Jewish people on the march." The aim of the movement was defined by this First Zionist Congress in a statement, since then known as the Basel Platform, as the creation of "a publicly-assured, legally-secured home for the Jewish people in Palestine."

Now the movement was definitely launched, and the Congress became its instrument of organization and political action, the brain and arm of the "Society of Jews" called the World Zionist Organization. One by one, it brought to life all those institutions, like the Jewish Colonial Trust and the Jewish National Fund, which corresponded to the "Jewish Company." As emissary of the Congress, Herzl was soon to appear before the Sultan of Turkey and other monarchs in his tireless efforts to obtain the charter which would make possible the large-scale colonization of Palestine.

But the Zionist Congress was not only the head and arm of the movement; it was also its voice. From the platforms of the Congress and in the hearing of the world, that voice rang out boldly, denouncing the oppressors of the Jewish people, demanding its rights and proclaiming its hopes. Usually it was Max Nordau, he of the great heart and withering word who, with magnificent eloquence, reviewed the situation of his people at the opening session of each

Congress. And when Nordau spoke the world listened. And dominating the proceedings with the magic of his personality was Theodor Herzl, who stood before the delegates like some fabled monarch of the past, a living demonstration of the forces still latent in his persecuted people. In truth, after centuries of martyrdom, an heroic chapter was begun in the story of this people. Poets lifted up their voices and sang. One of them, Naphtali Herz Imber, wrote *Hatikvah*, "The Hope," which became the anthem of the movement. Another, Chaim Nachman Bialik, then in his twenty-fourth year and destined to become the foremost Hebrew poet of modern times, voiced the sorrow and longing of his people in a poem addressed to the delegates and concluding with the lines:

Your memory like a quenchless sun will light
The heavy darkness of your people's night.

6

IN ALL parts of the world, men and women flocked to join the movement, and in the lands of oppression the masses were stirred in a manner reminiscent of the messianic ferments of past centuries. But the differences were even more striking than the resemblances. Herzl may have had the magnetic attraction of a messiah, and undoubtedly the mainspring of the new surge lay deep in the same immemorial longings and expectations; but the movement he launched operated not with mystic charms and incantations but with political and financial realities. At the Third Congress, Herzl reported the founding of the Jewish Colonial Trust with headquarters in London, but with a capital of only £250,000. The Fifth Congress, held at Basel in 1901, saw the establishment of the Jewish National Fund for the purchase of land in Palestine, the land to be leased to colonists, but to remain a possession of the people forever. The Fourth Congress had been held in London and made a profound impression in the press and government circles. British statesmen began to take the movement seriously.

In the meantime, Herzl labored incessantly to win the support of other governments also, particularly that of Turkey. In the fall of 1898 he had two audiences with Kaiser Wilhelm II of Germany, the first in Constantinople, the second outside Jerusalem. The Kaiser was visiting the Near East and was known to have great influence with the Sultan Abdul-Hamid. In May 1902 he was received in audience by Abdul-Hamid himself. The sultan was vague about a charter for Palestine, and Herzl lacked the large sums which might have made him more specific: the Jewish bankers were indifferent or cautious and the masses desperately poor. In the summer of 1903, he visited the Russian capital on the invitation of Minister of the Interior von Plehve, and the same year he had audiences with Victor Emmanuel II of Italy and the pope. He stood before the crowned heads of Europe like a monarch, this king of dreams and hopes which had survived so many crowns and dynasties. And amid all his labors, Herzl found time to write his *Altneuland* (Old-new-land), a novel in which he anticipates the reality for which he strove. In this Utopia, he sees Palestine covered with modern cities and villages and a new society of proud men and women devoted to social justice and the universal welfare of humanity.

7

BUT all this time the distress of his people in eastern Europe kept mounting and, while the flood of refugees grew in volume, the opportunities for asylum were shrinking—a fact which Herzl saw plainly enough when, in July 1902, he testified as an expert on Jewish conditions before the British Aliens Commission. In April 1903, the frightful pogrom took place in Kishinev, and when in the summer of that year Herzl traveled through Russia, he was appalled by the misery of his people. In Vilna, the streets were dense with the throngs who came out to greet him, and in the community house, when the rabbi gave him the priestly benediction, the people burst into loud weeping. In the small hours of the following morning, an immense crowd gathered at the railroad station to bid him farewell, and the czar's police, always suspicious and fearful, dispersed the people with swinging knouts. Herzl was terribly shaken: he had entered the Inferno and seen with his own eyes.

But he did not abandon hope.

8

ON AUGUST 23, 1903, the Sixth Zionist Congress assembled in Basel, and in his opening address Herzl announced the receipt of an offer from the British government of a large tract in Uganda, in Africa, for colonization by Jews with guarantees of self-government. That, in fact, was the second British offer; the first, made earlier that year, proposed the region south of Palestine called El-Arish, but it had been found unsuitable because it lacked water. "Of course," Herzl said to the delegates, "Africa is not Zion and can never become Zion"; and Nordau called it a *Nachtasyl*, a "shelter for the night," a temporary haven for those fleeing from the knout and the pogroms. The ultimate aim of the Jewish people Herzl declared to be no other land than Palestine, and he ended his closing address with the immemorial oath: "If I forget thee, O Jerusalem, let my right hand forget its cunning."

But most of the delegates, and especially those who represented the Zionists of Russia, were profoundly disturbed. They, who suffered most, clung to Palestine with the greatest tenacity and looked upon the *Nachtasyl* with the deepest suspicion. The Congress was torn with strife and bitter recrimination. Nevertheless, the proposal to send a commission to investigate the territory offered by Britain received a majority of those who voted, but it was clear that the movement faced an irreparable schism. In October of the same year, the leaders of the movement in Russia met in a secret conference in the city of Charkov and sent a deputation to present a set of ultimatums to Herzl. With infinite patience Herzl answered his opponents and repeated his assurances: the deputation, having come as accusers, went away as the accused. In April 1904, there was a meeting of the Greater Actions Committee, the body that exercised authority in the interval between congresses, and the leader received a vote of confidence. The breach seemed to be healed.

Herzl continued his endless labors, but for a long time now his heart had been unable to keep pace with his will. He went to the little mountain town of Edlach near Vienna in the hope of finding rest and cure. Early in July, he was forced to bed, and on the afternoon of July 3, 1904, after keeping death at bay by sheer power of will until he could see his mother and children again, Theodor Herzl, at the age of forty-four, breathed his last.

9

ON FEBRUARY 8, 1898, when the movement he launched was only six months old, Theodor Herzl, addressing an audience in Berlin, had said: "I believe I may say to you that we have given something to the Jewish people: to the young a vision; to the old a dream; to all men something beautiful." He was paraphrasing the ancient Hebrew prophet Joel,* this modern Hebrew prophet of the winged word and shining deed.

CHAPTER SIXTY

The Last of the Czars

IN AUGUST 1897, when the First Zionist Congress assembled, Nicholas II had been czar of Russia for nearly three years. He was to hold the imperial throne for twenty more and to part with it, together with his life, in the revolutionary storm which burst over him in 1917. The fates were in a particularly ironic mood when they decreed that this dull mediocrity, devoid of courage or imagination and clinging with superstitious tenacity to the trappings of a dead past, should find himself called upon to rule the waves of war and revolution. And it was he in whose palsied hands lay the weal or woe of the largest Jewish aggregation in the world—nearly six million of them, four in Russia proper and two in the former provinces of Poland.

Very soon after his accession, and in a manner that left no room for illusions, the new czar took occasion to crush the timid hopes which had a way of sprouting up with every new reign. "Let

* And it shall come to pass afterward,
That I will pour out My spirit upon all flesh;
And your sons and daughters shall prophesy,
Your old men shall dream dreams,
Your young men shall see visions.—*Joel* 3; 1.

everybody know," he declared in January 1895, "that I shall guard the principle of autocracy as firmly and uncompromisingly as it was guarded by my late and unforgettable father." And as an earnest of this resolve, he retained his father's reactionary ministers, including that reincarnation of Torquemada and Philip II of Spain, the gloomy fanatic Pobyedonostzev.

It was clear to the Jews that the removal of the long-standing restrictions, like the suffocating Pale of Settlement, was an empty dream, and it was not long before new persecutions came to plague them. An imperial decree issued in January 1899 imposed fresh curbs on the first-guild merchants in Moscow who, after the brutal expulsions of the Jewish artisans in 1891, had still managed to maintain themselves in the "holy" metropolis. The walls of the Pale were even more heavily guarded, health resorts were brutally barred to Jewish patients, and the process of expelling Jewish innkeepers from the villages was accelerated by a variety of administrative decrees. In Kiev, the *oblavas*, or police raids, in which Jews were rounded up and driven from the city, became notorious for their frequency and brutal efficiency.

This rigid enforcement of the old curbs and the imposition of new ones had a catastrophic effect on the already precarious economic plight of Russian Jewry. Early in the new reign, the liquor trade was made a government monopoly. The Jews in the villages and towns who found themselves driven to pursue the dangerous traffic would have gladly changed it for another occupation, but the monopoly deprived thousands of them of this source of livelihood without permitting them access to others. The new paupers flocked to the cities, where the destitution of the Jewish proletarians became more appalling. Agriculture was closed to them by the "temporary rules" of 1882, which were still in force; even attempts to promote handicrafts among them were officially discouraged, and entry into the liberal professions was heavily restricted. In the legal profession it was made practically impossible, and the *numerus clausus* in all types of educational institutions was pulled tighter and more rigorously enforced. Apparently the government followed the deliberate aim of decimating the population of the Pale by the method of starvation.

Nor was the policy of adding terror to economic strangulation neglected. As early as February 1897, the thriving town of Shpola in the province of Kiev was the scene of a well-prepared orgy of destruction and plunder, in the course of which Jewish homes, shops, and warehouses were completely wrecked. Two years later a similar outbreak took place in Nikolaev. When, however, in August 1902, thousands of Poles in the Catholic shrine city of Czestochowa massed to attack the Jews, the authorities found no difficulty in dispersing them: apparently, the czar's officials were not prepared to let the Poles share the privilege with the Russians.

The ignorant town rabble and peasantry of both nationalities interpreted the official persecutions and humiliations of their Jewish neighbors in only one way: that it was lawful and pleasing to the czar to attack them. One Russian peasant, arrested for his part in the Shpola pogrom, is reported to have voiced the following grievance: "They told us," he protested, "that we had permission to beat the Jews, and now it appears it is all a lie!" The real culprits, of course, were the czar, his ministers, and the anti-Semitic agitators led by the semi-official newspaper *Novoye Vremia* (New Times). It was an agitation which the leading Russian men of letters, including such outstanding figures as Vladimir Solovyov, Leo Tolstoy, Maxim Gorky, and Vladimir Korolenko, could, with all their efforts, do little to stem.

2

UNTIL the spring of 1903, the world at large knew little and cared less about the sufferings of the Jews under Nicholas II. The governments were not, of course, uninformed, but the official attitude had to be diplomatically "correct." Thirteen years earlier, on the eve of the brutal expulsions of 1891, that attitude had been stated in super-correct phrases in Parliament by spokesmen of Her Britannic Majesty's Government. Replying to interpellations with regard to the impending persecutions, knowledge of which had seeped into western Europe, those spokesmen declared that "these proceedings, which, if rightly reported to us, are deeply to be regretted, concern the internal affairs of the Russian Empire, and do not admit of any interference on the part of Her Majesty's Government." Some fifty years later, it may be noted, the same "correct" attitude was observed when even more "deeply regrettable proceedings" against the Jews occurred, which concerned the internal affairs of the German Reich and served as one of the preludes to the Second World War.

To the man on the street in the cities of the liberal West, Nicholas II even figured as an idealist and humanitarian! Was it not he at whose call the International Hague Conference had been called in May 1899 for the purpose of promoting peace and disarmament? Only the thoughtful minority found it incongruous that a call for international peace should be issued by an autocrat who was ruthlessly stifling every free impulse of his own people; and a touch of lighter irony was provided by the fact that in the same call the czar leaned heavily on the ideas of one Ivan Bloch, a distinguished political economist and writer who was of Jewish origin.

In April 1903, however, the civilized world received a rude shock. On Easter Sunday and the day following, a pogrom of unprecedented frightfulness was enacted in Kishinev, the capital of the province of Bessarabia, where for centuries the large Jewish community had been living at peace with its Christian neighbors. There could be no doubt that the bloody carnival had been carefully planned and organized by the authorities, its inspiration having been traced to the Ministry of the Interior headed by the notorious Vyatcheslav von Plehve. The outbreak was preceded by a period of intensive incitation, from which a charge of ritual murder was not omitted, and the only action taken by the police throughout the bloody proceedings was to step in and disarm a group of Jews who were trying to defend themselves. The drunken mobsters were not interfered with; they plundered to their hearts' content and then went over to murder, rape, and other bestialities too hideous to record. On the morning of the second day, the governor of the province informed a Jewish deputation that, *having received no instructions from the capital*, he could do nothing to stop the carnage. Toward evening, a telegram arrived from the Minister of the Interior and the pogrom was promptly brought to an end. Forty-five Jews had been slain, hundreds wounded, and fifteen hundred houses and shops had been plundered and wrecked.

As knowledge of the full extent of the official crime filtered out of Russia, the civilized world, not yet inured to large-scale horrors, was profoundly shocked. Pulpits and platforms resounded with protests, and in England, France, Germany, and America, as well as in Russia itself, relief measures were launched for the wounded and plundered. The reaction was strongest in the United States, where scores of public meetings were held throughout the land, the one in New York under the chairmanship of Seth Low, the mayor of the city, with ex-President Grover Cleveland as principal speaker. In Russia the Jews were filled with shame as well as wrath. Too many of the victims had failed to exact a price for their lives. In his *City of Slaughter*, the poet Bialik expressed these feelings with shattering effect; and in cities and towns throughout the Pale, young men and women, Socialists and Zionists alike, came secretly together, organized for self-defense, and swore that never again would their people be slaughtered like sheep.

Von Plehve became aware of this movement for self-defense and issued orders to his minions to suppress it without mercy. Later that year, however, in September 1903, the Jewish self-defense proved its mettle in a bloody affray which broke out in the White Russian city of Homel. The rabble was easily dispersed and returned only after it was shielded by a cordon of troops, who fired on the defenders. But in spite of the protective screen, the fury of the inflamed mob was held in check, and the casualties on both sides were almost equal.

3

IT WAS apparent to all observers, including the great moralist and writer Leo Tolstoy, that the czar's government, in fomenting and preparing the anti-Jewish outbreaks, was pursuing a policy which it believed would result in neutralizing the revolutionary ferment which was rising throughout the land. In his moving protest against the Kishinev horror, a protest which von Plehve's censors suppressed, Tolstoy declared that the attitude of the government was proof that it "stops at no cruelty whenever it finds it necessary to check movements that are deemed dangerous by it." The policy was embodied in the simple formula: "Drown the revolution in Jewish blood!" No doubt there were Jews in the revolutionary movement, and it would have been strange if the people who suffered most from czarist oppression had not been among the most eager to overthrow it. Most of the Jewish radicals belonged to the Socialist *Bund*, as the "General Jewish Workers' Union of Lithuania, Poland, and Russia," organized in 1897, was briefly designated. But the efforts of the *Bund* were directed more against the Jewish employers of Jewish labor in the Pale than against the czarist regime. The Bund opposed Zionism, espoused Yiddish as against Hebrew, advocated national-cultural rights in Russia, and as far as the general revolutionary movement was concerned, took its stand with the Social Democrats, who discountenanced terrorism as a weapon against the autocracy. In the ranks of the Social Revolutionary party, who did advocate terrorism, the number of Jews was insignificant.

If von Plehve needed evidence that the revolutionary movement was not the inspiration of Jewish malcontents, but an authentic Russian product, he had it on July 28, 1904—although he was left in no condition to draw the necessary deductions. On that day, in St. Petersburg, he was assassinated. A bomb was thrown at him by a Social Revolutionary terrorist, a "genuine" Russian by the name of Sasanov. Seven months later, Grand Duke Sergius, governor-general of Moscow, the man who carried out the expulsions of 1891 and who vied with von Plehve as the best-hated minion of the autocracy, met the same fate at the hands of another "genuine" Russian, the Social Revolutionary Kalayev.

4

EARLIER that year, on February 8, 1904, began the disastrous war with Japan, in which some 30,000 Jewish soldiers, a number greater than the ratio of Jews to the general population called for, fought for a government that treated them as enemies. The pogrom policy was for the moment abandoned in the hope that the patriotic fervor which the war was expected to unleash would be a more effective counterrevolutionary specific. But either the new policy was not effectively enforced, or the government had raised a Frankenstein which it was no longer able to control. Toward the end of the year, there were outbreaks in a number of places in South Russia, of which the bloodiest occurred on Yom Kippur Day in Kherson; and in different parts of the land, "mobilization pogroms" were carried out, in the course of which disgruntled Russian reservists, on the way to the front, gave vent to their mingled feelings of resentment and patriotism by looting and wrecking Jewish homes and shops.

As the czar's forces on land and sea in the Far East suffered one humiliating defeat after another, the revolutionary temper in Russia continued to rise. The autocratic regime blew hot and cold. Von Plehve's successor toyed with a policy of concession and pacification, but on January 22, 1905, a day which has come to be known as "bloody Sunday," a procession of workers in the capital, bearing a petition to the czar, was met with a hail of bullets. The revolutionists responded with a wave of demonstrations, strikes, and acts of terror throughout the land. Dozens of Jewish communities submitted petitions, asking—and sometimes demanding—immediate emancipation; and in April 1905, a League for the Attainment of Equal Rights for the Jewish People in Russia was formed in Vilna. The general unrest continued to mount and the czar's government became jittery. It proposed some vague, but obviously double-faced concessions "relating to the perfection of the well-being of the state," which the revolutionists rejected, demanding a Constitution and a democratically elected Parliament.

5.

BUT the autocracy was not yet at the end of its resources, and for its main expedient it reverted to the old policy of "drowning the revolution in Jewish blood." Now the policy was implemented on a larger and more elaborate scale, and the dregs of Russian society were organized into the infamous Black Hundreds to carry it into effect. The underworld was brought to the surface and paraded as the "genuine Russians," faithful to their "little father," hating the revolution and all its works, and determined to destroy its instigators who were, first and last, the Jews. In the spring and summer of 1905, the Black Hundreds began rehearsing for their task. In the spring, peasants made sporadic attacks on Jews in a number of widely separated localities, but were generally beaten back by the self-defense. The most serious affray occurred in the city of Zhitomir, capital of Volhynia, where in spite of the assistance the rabble had from the police and military, the gallant defenders rendered a good account of themselves. In the summer the propaganda machine of the Black Hundreds reached new heights, charging the Jews with responsibility for the Russian defeats in the Far East, whereupon soldiers and Cossacks attacked the Jews in a number of localities, including the industrial cities of Lodz and Bialystok.

6

IN THE meantime, the revolution was taking its thunderous course. The bogus parliament which the government thought would allay the storm was indignantly rejected and, with the country in the throes of demonstrations, strikes by students and workers, and a general strike in preparation, the czar proclaimed civil, religious, and political liberty for the Russian people, with provision for a representative parliament, or Duma, vested with legislative power.

Great was the rejoicing in Russia among all lovers of liberty and especially among the Jews. Great but short-lived, for it lasted exactly one day. Beginning October 31, 1905, the day after the imperial manifesto, and lasting for a week, Jews in hundreds of cities and towns throughout the land were attacked by the Black Hundreds. Everywhere the underworld "patriots" were shielded by police and soldiery, against whom the self-defense was almost powerless. Hundreds were killed—in Odessa alone there were three hundred dead—thousands were maimed, and scores of thousands made destitute. In a number of places non-Jewish revolutionists were also attacked, for the widespread disturbance was intended to have the appearance of a spontaneous patriotic uprising. But there was nothing spontaneous about it. The "uprising" had been conceived, organized, and financed by agencies of the central government with the knowledge of the czar himself, and the Jews, regardless of political affiliation, were marked as the principal victims.

The "uprising" threw the revolution into chaos: before long the Black Hundreds, now parading as the "League of the Russian People," were to become the second government of Russia. But neither the open threats of the Russian pogromists, nor the snarlings of the anti-Semites in the Polish provinces, intimidated the Jews from voting for their own candidates to the First Duma. That body, which began its turbulent career of less than three months on May 10, 1906, contained twelve Jewish deputies, among them the brilliant Zionist orator Shmaryah Levin and the eminent lawyer Maxim Vinaver.

On June 14, while this Duma, dominated by the liberal Constitutional Democrats, was struggling with the reactionary government, a second pogrom, more sanguinary than the first, occurred in the large industrial city of Bialystok. The technique of pogrom-making had undergone improvement: the outbreak, in which the police and garrison took the leading part, was set off by a shot fired on a religious procession by an *agent provocateur*. The Duma appointed a special commission which, after investigating the pogrom on the spot, fastened the guilt on the military and civil authorities, branded the official reports as "contrary to the truth," and found that "there was no race hatred, either religious or economic, between the Christian and Jewish populations of the town." The Duma demanded the immediate resignation of the Government, but two days later, on July 22, an imperial order put an end to that body. The opposition, defying the government, issued the famous Viborg Manifesto, with all the Jewish deputies among the signers, but the counterrevolution triumphed, its principal weapon being always the pogrom. In September 1906 the place chosen by the Black Hundreds for the use of this weapon was the city of Siedlitz, where again the fuse was set off by an *agent provocateur*. In the trials that followed these orgies of looting and murder, punishment was reserved for the Jewish defenders, while the guilty generally obtained acquittal or pardon.

7

"HOW do you bear it?" was the question Theodor Herzl repeatedly asked when, in August 1903, he traveled in Russia and for the first time came into contact with Jewish misery in the towns and cities of the Pale. How did these huddled masses—the tailors, shoemakers, and weavers, the shopkeepers and petty traders—bear up under the knout of persecution and terror? Multitudes, of course, sought escape by emigration: in 1905 and 1906 nearly 230,000 of them left for America. But the millions who remained bore up remarkably well. It would be a distortion to picture the life of those millions as an endless round of gloom and sorrow. The ancient spiritual font remained unexhausted, and the years of pogroms and revolution even brought a new surge of spiritual and intellectual energy.

Into the life of these millions two new currents had been injected—socialism and Zionism—and, curiously enough, both were able to find sanction in the ancient heritage, particularly in the teachings of the prophets. In the main, however, the two were rivals, although in at least one party, the Poale Zion (Workers of Zion), they converged and flowed together. On the "Jewish street," as the social and intellectual milieu was designated, the turbulent times, reinforced by an ingrained penchant for dialectics, spawned numerous other parties which, in spite of the futilities they at times indulged in, bore testimony to mental vigor and high morale.

There were, of course, a goodly number of the young who turned their backs on the "Jewish street," who threw in their lot with the Russian youth struggling to break the czarist yoke, and who, if they thought of their people at all, consoled themselves with the belief that the liberation of Russia would "automatically" solve the Jewish problem. But the great majority held fast to their own, and even with the radicals among them, there was a marked concentration around Jewish cultural values, a will to preserve their people's distinctive character, different as the roads might be by which they sought to attain that goal. The Zionists, without renouncing interest in the Diaspora, looked forward to the restoration of Jewish nationhood in Palestine. Proletarian parties like the *Bund*, as well as the bourgeois groups who rallied around the League for the Attainment of Equal Rights, thought it possible for their people to preserve themselves permanently as a distinct nationality among the Russians and Poles: their program called for cultural autonomy to be guaranteed by certain group rights which, after the First World War, came to be called minority rights.

The din of contending political and cultural programs resounded loud in the "Jewish street." The Zionists were devoted to the Hebrew language and literature, their opponents to the Yiddish, but the sharp contest between them stimulated the efflorescence of both. Some of the foremost men of letters, including the novelist Mendele Mocher Seforim, the incomparable humorist Sholem

Rabinowitz (1859-1916), who wrote under the pen name of "Sholom Aleichem," and the poet and folklorist Isaac Leib Perez (1851-1915), wrote in both languages. Hebrew was the vehicle of Bialik and other distinguished poets, among them Zalman Shneour, Saul Tchernikovsky and Jacob Cohen, and of essayists and publicists like Achad Ha'am and Joseph Klausner. The poet Simon Frug (1860-1916) wrote in Russian as well as Yiddish; the latter was also the language of many other gifted novelists, dramatists, and poets. In Warsaw and Vilna, Hebrew and Yiddish dailies were published whose readers ran into the hundreds of thousands. Simon Dubnow (1860-1943) was first among the historians; he took a leading part in the struggle for cultural autonomy and minority rights.

8

FOR the vast majority of those millions, however, the parties and programs were like the waves of a sea swept by storm. Underneath were the calm spiritual depths out of which they, like their ancestors before them, continued to draw strength and solace. Life was hard and insecure, there was no freedom from want or freedom from fear, but the ancient faith, with its Sabbaths and festivals, its sanctified learning and institutions, its cherished rites and customs, was like the tree which Moses cast into the bitter waters of Marah, making them sweet.

Zionism came as an additional source of moral strength to the Orthodox masses, for though some of their leaders, especially among the Chassidim, rejected the movement, others like Samuel Mohliver (1824-1898) of Bialystok, Isaac Jacob Reines (1839-1915) of Lida, and Meyer Berlin, son of Naphtali Judah Berlin, the illustrious head of the great Yeshivah of Volozhin, joined the new cause and attained distinction in its leadership. The line of great spiritual leaders, men like the inspired moralist Israel Salanter and the monumental scholar Isaac Elchanan of the previous generation, was not broken. In the Lithuanian town of Radun, for example, lived the saintly Israel Meir Cahan (1833-1933), better known as the *Chofetz Chaim*, whose great influence was enhanced by the Yeshivah which he founded and directed.

Throughout the Pale, Talmudic academies continued to flourish.

First in renown was the Yeshivah of Volozhin, founded in 1803; in a checkered existence of more than a century, it produced nearly all of the most illustrious rabbis of Russia and Poland. In Lubavitch and other places, Sholem Baer Schneerson, leader of the *Chabad* school of Chassidism, established Yeshivoth where the Talmud and the legacy of the *Baal-Shem-Tov* went together. And other academies, whose teachers attracted students from near and far, many of whom ate the bitter bread of charity and spent all their waking hours in the study of Torah, were located in Telz, Grodno, Slobodka, Mir, Lida and many other places. In calm and storm, the cultural level of the Jewish masses of eastern Europe was high, incomparably higher than that of their neighbors to whose tender mercies they were so mercilessly exposed.

9

THE Russian Revolution of 1905, which gave rise to such glowing hopes of freedom, especially among the six million prisoners of the Pale, was smothered in a welter of pogroms, executions, banishments, and other acts of government terror. The Second Duma, which met early in 1907 and in which, as the result of juggling with the electoral law, the Black Hundreds were well represented, was still not to the czar's taste, and early in the summer of the same year it suffered the fate of its predecessor. New changes in the electoral law finally brought the government the Duma it wanted—the Third or Black Duma which, completely dominated by reactionaries and anti-Semites, convened in the fall. It was an assembly of the ungodly which took delight not only in contriving new injuries upon its principal victim, but in publicly making merry at his expense. There were new expulsions from cities outside the Pale and from villages inside of it. The *numerus clausus* in the schools and gymnasia was enforced with new refinements of cruelty. The Black Duma lived long and happily: its successor was not chosen until the spring of 1912.

In the Polish provinces, especially in Warsaw, the election contest of 1912 produced a new high in the anti-Semitism of the Poles which, to a great extent, was nourished by a morbid chauvinism. The Poles had become accustomed to vent their just grievances against the czar upon a people that suffered much more than they did at the hands of the same despot. For several years before the election campaign, the Polish economic boycott against the Jews had been in full swing, and during the campaign the Polish chauvinists in Warsaw demanded, under threat of drastic reprisals, nothing less than that the Jews should vote for their anti-Semitic candidate! When the Jews of Warsaw, who could have elected their own deputy, helped instead to elect a Polish Socialist, the boycott against them was prosecuted with even greater bitterness. The atmosphere of Poland, whose cities and fields were shortly to become an immense battlefield, became charged with poisons which added immeasurably to the havoc wrought by the enemy upon the Jewish communities.

And while Warsaw in the west was the scene of this anti-Semitic rampage, the holy city of Kiev in the east offered the world the spectacle of a blood libel unsurpassed by anything the Middle Ages had produced. This was the fantastic Beilis Case, which dragged on from 1911 to 1913, furnishing the czar and his henchmen with an enormous supply of anti-Semitic fuel. The murdered body of a Russian lad had been found not far from a brick kiln, and Mendel Beilis, employed as a watchman in the brickyard, was arrested on the charge of ritual murder. The hand of the Black Hundreds was visible from the very start of the case and when, in September 1911, the czar's prime minister Peter Stolypin was assassinated by a terrorist whose grandfather was a baptized Jew, the government itself entered the arena. An elaborate structure of distortion and perjury was built up to convict the entire Jewish people of the crime charged against Beilis. The judges were carefully chosen, the jury was made up of credulous peasants and townsmen. But Beilis was acquitted, although the ignorant jurors were inveigled into declaring that a ritual murder had been committed!

The case had roused the decent humanity of the entire world, including that of Russia. Twenty-five members of the St. Petersburg bar, having protested against the manner in which the Minister of Justice was handling the case, were convicted of agitating against the government. But only a month after this fresh assault on justice, the autocratic regime entered upon its final test: the nations were in the throes of the First World War.

CHAPTER SIXTY-ONE

Survey, 1914: The East

SOUTHWEST of Russia lies Rumania, northernmost country of the Balkan Peninsula, in ancient times called Dacia, where long before its conquest by the Romans in 107 C.E., Jewish settlements were already established. Politically Rumania began as two separate principalities, Moldavia in the north and Wallachia in the south, both of which, early in the sixteenth century, were subjugated by the Turks. But the provinces continued to be ruled by Christian princes; they paid tribute to the conquerors but were otherwise allowed a free hand.

Notwithstanding the harsh treatment the Jews suffered at the hands of most of these princes, their numbers continued to grow. A few Sephardim from Turkey had come in with the conquerors; in times of persecution, particularly during the Black Decade of 1648 to 1658, many fugitives streamed in from Poland; during the cruel reign of Nicholas I, Jews from Russia fled to Moldavia. It was not a safe asylum that they found in the Rumanian principalities. In the sporadic wars between Russia and Turkey, especially during the war of 1769-1774, Cossacks and Turkish irregulars fought back and forth across the provinces, and were at one only in plundering and massacring the Jews. In 1710 the blood accusation made its appearance for the first time in Moldavia and claimed many victims. It reappeared in 1714 in the city of Roman, where at the last moment the Jews were saved by the discovery of the real criminals. The Greek Orthodox clergy became the spearhead of the animosity against them, and again and again the blood accusation came to plague them. The climax occurred in 1797 in the city of Galatz, where the mob wiped out practically the entire community.

Early in the nineteenth century the legal precedents were established under which the Jews of Rumania, whether native or foreign-born, were given the status of aliens. A special poll tax was levied upon them and a commission set up to expel those not engaged in certain specified occupations, or not in possession of a certain minimum capital, all of whom were classified as "vagabonds." Now and then a prince came to power who abolished the persecutions and even accorded the Jews special privileges; but under the influence of the clergy the hostility of the populace continued dormant, if not active. In Bucharest, Galatz, and other cities, there were a few rich Jews engaged in international commerce and banking, but the great majority lived in the villages and small towns as petty traders and artisans. Chassidism made rapid progress among them, as it did in the neighboring Polish provinces.

2

IT WAS a great event in the history of Rumania when in 1859 Alexander Cuza became the ruler of both principalities which, though still subject to Turkey, were now united. The unification inspired the Jews of Rumania with hopes of emancipation, and their coreligionists of western Europe, with Adolphe Crémieux in the lead, endeavored to help them. But all their hopes were doomed to frustration. Cuza's constitution deprived them of the suffrage, and in 1866, that of his successor Carol, a scion of the Hohenzollerns, provided that "only such aliens as are of Christian faith may obtain citizenship." That was the infamous Article 7, and it was substituted for another which had declared that "religion is no obstacle to citizenship." The substitution was made after a series of street riots against the Jews which were staged in Bucharest while the National Assembly was framing the constitution, and in the course of which the principal synagogue of the capital was destroyed.

Under the policy of keeping the Jews in the legal status of aliens, their position became tragically grotesque. They were compelled to fulfill all duties, including service in the army, but when it came to rights, they could be treated like pariahs or vagrants. They were denied all political rights, and even their civil rights, including those of residence and occupation, could be curtailed or abolished at will. The Jews of Rumania, moreover, were not only aliens but stateless: they were not citizens of the land in which they lived and in which their ancestors had lived for centuries, nor were they citizens of any other land. This singular situation exposed them to all manner of outrages of which the most infamous, which stirred the indignation of the civilized world, occurred in July 1867.

The Minister of the Interior was John Bratianu, a hard-bitten anti-Semite of the modern variety representing the Liberals, a party well known for belying its label. It comprised the merchants, bankers, lawyers, and others of the rising middle class, who were opposed to the boyars, the big landed proprietors, on the one hand, and to the peasants on the other. The deepest animosity of these "liberals," however, was reserved for their immediate competitors, the Jews, against whom the minister launched a veritable reign of terror. He resurrected the old laws against them, and under a new decree against "vagabond foreigners" many Jews were arrested and expelled. In July 1867, a number of these victims were taken across the Danube to be dumped on the other side which belonged to Turkey, and when the Turkish officials refused to receive them, some of them were forced at bayonet point into the river, where they perished. There was an outcry in France and Great Britain, and Bratianu had to step out of the cabinet. The Conservatives came into power, but the expulsions continued, and Jews were attacked by mobs whom the government was not disposed to punish.

The plight of the Jews in Rumania stirred sympathy and indignation in America also, and in 1870 President Ulysses S. Grant appointed as consul-general for Bucharest the Grand Master of the Order B'nai B'rith, Benjamin F. Peixotto, with the understanding that he would endeavor to protect his coreligionists. With all his exertions, however, Peixotto could accomplish very little. In 1872, leading Jews from England, France, Germany, and the United States assembled in Brussels at the call of the *Alliance Israélite* and the Anglo-Jewish Association, but their efforts to bring pressure on Rumania to relax its persecutions brought no results, and shortly afterwards the smooth and venomous Bratianu returned to power as prime minister.

3

AN OPPORTUNITY, which appeared providential, for putting an end to the martyrdom of the Rumanian Jews arose in 1878. The year before, Turkey had been thoroughly beaten in a war with Russia, and Rumania, which had taken up arms on the side of Russia, demanded complete independence. The European statesmen considered it most urgent to settle the entire Eastern question, and in June 1878 they came together in the Congress of Berlin to accomplish nothing less. Prince Bismarck presided, Benjamin Disraeli, already Lord Beaconsfield, represented the British Empire, and both supported a proposal that the independence of Rumania should be recognized, but only on condition that it grant equal political and civil rights to all inhabitants regardless of religious beliefs. The principle was embodied in Article 44 of the Treaty of Berlin, which Rumania accepted.

That Article became famous because of the success Rumania achieved in making a complete mockery of it. It was violated with a maximum of chicanery and cynicism, and the European powers, who began by insisting on its observance, ended by sacrificing the Jews to their political and economic interests in Rumania. For two years the powers withheld their recognition of Rumania's independence, and her demagogues, again headed by the notorious Bratianu, utilized the time to play the double game of making hypocritical gestures toward complying with the Article, and of inciting mob outbreaks against the Jews to lend plausibility to the claim that it was unenforceable. The Rumanian constitution was, of course, amended to comply with the treaty, and 883 Jews who had fought in the war against Turkey were naturalized. But the government clung to the convenient doctrine that the Jews were aliens, and under the amendment, applications for naturalization must "in every individual case be decided by the Parliament." The latter played its part well. From 1880 to 1900 it approved only 85 applications.

As aliens, the 250,000 Rumanian Jews were completely at the mercy of a vicious and deep-seated anti-Semitism. The large landowners, as in the agrarian disturbances of 1907, found them an invaluable outlet for the wretchedness of their peasants, while the professional and commercial classes, in mortal dread of Jewish competitors, were never loath to rouse the students and town rabble against them. They were legislated out of the villages and small towns, deprived of numerous sources of livelihood, and barred from the schools and universities. Until 1908, the shameful oath *more Judaico* was exacted from them in court proceedings, and prominent Jews who incurred the government's displeasure, like the rabbi and scholar Moses Gaster, later the head of the Sephardic community in London, were summarily exiled. They were without any rights, but the duties of citizenship, including military service, continued to be required of them.

In 1902, John Hay, Secretary of State in the cabinet of Theodore Roosevelt, denounced Rumania in a note addressed to the signatory powers of the Treaty of Berlin, calling Rumania's treatment of the Jews an "international wrong." But the protest had no practical effect. Nor was the attempt made in 1913, at the end of the Second Balkan War, by American and British Jewish leaders to relieve the lot of their Rumanian coreligionists any more successful. Even the promise to naturalize the Jews who fought for Rumania in that war was broken. Emigration alone could bring them relief, and thousands of them flocked to America, England, and Palestine.

Such was the plight of the Jewish masses in Rumania when in August 1916 that country, bursting with rapacious ambition, leaped into the flames of the First World War.

4

IN BULGARIA, legend traces the presence of Jews as far back as biblical times, but it can be safely assumed that in the eighth century hard-pressed Khazars found refuge in that land, where they mingled with their coreligionists. About the middle of the fourteenth century a queen named Theodora, whose real name was Sara, sat on the Bulgarian throne, and the favor she showed her people is reported to have stirred up resentment against them. By 1450, the Turks were masters of the Balkan Peninsula and Jews, persecuted in France and Bavaria, fled to Bulgaria, establishing Ashkenazic communities. These, however, were overshadowed and gradually absorbed by the large influx of Sephardim who arrived not long afterwards as exiles from Spain and Portugal. In 1666 these communities fell an easy prey to the messianic frenzy set off by Sabbatai Zevi.

In 1878 the Congress of Berlin made Bulgaria an autonomous principality, still under Turkish suzerainty. It became an independent kingdom in 1908, but the equal rights which its constitution promised were largely nullified by the inroads of anti-Semitism, which became especially malignant after 1890. There were some 40,000 Jews in Bulgaria, about half of them in Sofia, the capital, when the ruler, King Ferdinand, eager to avenge himself on Serbia for the humiliations he had suffered after the Balkan War of 1913 and hoping to dominate the Peninsula, took his country into the First World War. In October 1915 he threw in his lot with the Central Powers against the Allies.

5

IN SERBIA which, after the war, was united with Croatia and Slovenia to form the Kingdom of Yugoslavia, there were sizable Jewish communities in Belgrade, Monastir, Sarajevo, and other cities. Their members were recruited largely from the Spanish and Portuguese exiles of the early sixteenth century. By grace of the Congress of Berlin, Serbia, like Rumania, had become an independent kingdom in 1878, but unlike Rumania, Serbia honored the undertaking it assumed to establish full equality for the Jews within its borders. Both in Serbia and Bulgaria, Zionism was embraced with enthusiasm, giving Jewish life in those countries a new surge. At the outbreak of the War of 1914, kindled by that fatal shot in Sarajevo on June 28, the Jews in Serbia and the other provinces of present-day Yugoslavia numbered some 50,000.

6

THE story of the Jews in Greece, particularly after the country won its independence from Turkey in the third decade of the nineteenth century, is not a happy one. The most somber incident occurred in 1891 on the Island of Corfu where, as the result of a blood libel, the Jewish quarter was besieged and reduced to starvation, and 1,500 of its inhabitants fled to Italy, Turkey, and Egypt.

After 1912 when, as a result of the First Balkan War, Greece acquired Salonika, that flourishing seaport, for centuries the home of a vigorous Jewish community, became the scene of violence and persecution. Those were the methods by which the government hoped to Hellenize the city, where the Jews formed the majority of the population and the Jewish Sabbath was a general day of rest. In the First World War, Greece delayed throwing in its lot with the Allies until June 1917, but in September of the following year Salonika became the starting point of the victorious campaign which forced Bulgaria to surrender. The Jewish population of Greece was approximately 100,000, most of them in Salonika, and they were well represented in the Greek contingents that fought with the Allies.

7

WHEN Turkey, in October 1914, joined the Central Powers, it harbored some 75,000 Jews, besides those in Palestine. The largest communities were in Constantinople and Adrianople; most of their members were Sephardim. That golden period in the sixteenth century when Joseph Nassi was Duke of Naxos, and Safed was the city of the great codifier Joseph Karo, was now only a memory. The communities languished in poverty and cultural depression, a condition from which the *Alliance Israélite* did much to lift them through a network of elementary and trade schools. Legally the Jews in Turkey were fully emancipated, and the Young Turks, when they dethroned Abdul-Hamid in 1908, confirmed their equal status. In practice, however, their rights were not always respected.

8

A GLANCE at a few clusters of this world people that stood away from its main currents, light up its varied destiny and strange powers of survival.

In very early times Jews from Babylonia spread abroad into Persia, or Iran, where there are now approximately 60,000 of them, their largest community in Teheran. For some five centuries after the Abassid caliphate (750-1040), their story is shrouded in obscurity. In 1155, and for years afterwards, they were agitated by a formidable messianic movement led by David or Menachem Alroy, a movement which young Benjamin Disraeli made the theme of one of his romances. From the sixteenth century they were sorely afflicted by persecutions instigated by the Shiite Moslem clergy—persecutions which were not abolished until a revolution in 1920 placed the crown on the head of a new shah.

Farther east and, it is believed, in even earlier times, the tides of Jewish history deposited communities as far as India and China. In Bombay, there are some 15,000 "brown" Jews who call themselves "Beni-Israel," and proudly preserve the memory of their origin as well as many of the ancient rites, including circumcision and the Sabbath. They are keen and industrious, they make good soldiers, and the British found them excellent officer material. In Calcutta also, there are small communities, but these trace their origin to much later immigrants from Iraq and Arabia. Among them the Sassoons, the "Rothschilds of the East," are renowned alike for their wealth and benefactions.

In China, Jews from Europe have in recent times established themselves in Shanghai and a few other cities, and developed an active community life; but remains of very ancient Jewish life, now almost vanished, have been discovered in China, the oldest in Kai-fong-fu, some 500 miles south of Peiping.

But of these isolated lagoons, the most interesting is the group of approximately 50,000 black Jews in Ethiopia or Abyssinia known as Falashas, the word in Abyssinian meaning "immigrants." Their origin is in dispute, but at one time they ruled the country. The first Jewish king, according to legend, was a son of King Solomon and the Queen of Sheba, whom she bore on her return from her celebrated visit to David's son in Jerusalem. The Falashas have retained a large part of their faith, including the Sabbath and the biblical festivals. In 1911, due largely to the efforts of the Orientalist Jacques Faitlovitch, who made three extended journeys among them, pro-Falasha committees were formed in Italy and other countries and a teacher's seminary for youthful Falashas was established in Eritrea.

Across the Red Sea from Abyssinia and Eritrea lies Teman or Yemen, the "Happy Arabia" of the ancient Romans, where legend places Jews as early as the reign of Solomon. Maimonides, it will be recalled, addressed a famous letter, the *Iggeret Teman*, to his brethren of that land, urging them to remain steadfast to their faith in spite of persecutions. They did so, and even developed a significant scholarly and literary activity in Hebrew. They also won high standing as skilled artisans, but their lot has been a checkered one. In 1910 their number was estimated at some 15,000 and their condition was deplorable, their status under the Imam, or ruler, being that of pariahs and virtual slaves. The same year many of them managed to escape to Palestine, where they found a new and happier life.

A vivid demonstration of the power of the ancient faith appeared several years after the First World War, when Samuel Schwartz, an Austrian mining engineer, discovered sizable groups of Marranos in Portugal who, four centuries after their ancestors had been forcibly converted, still adhered to the Jewish Sabbath and observed the Passover festival and the Day of Atonement. On the initiative of the *Alliance*, an international committee was set up to assist these "underground" Jews to return openly and fully to their faith. They are believed to number some 10,000 families, and under the gallant leadership of one of their own, Anton Carlos de Barros Bastos, they have developed a communal life in Oporto, Braganza, and other cities of northern Portugal.

9

CULTURALLY, the Arabic-speaking coast lands of North Africa, the Berber states of Morocco, Algeria, and Tripolitania, also belong to the East. In Fez, Tangier, Kairwan, Tunis, Tripoli, and many other towns and villages of those lands, there are Jewish communities harking back to medieval and ancient times. In the fifteenth and sixteenth centuries they were augmented by Marranos and fugitives from Spain and Portugal; in more recent times by refugees from other lands. From time to time they knew persecution and even pogroms, but French annexation brought them relief, and the schools established by the French *Alliance* further improved their condition. Their total number in 1914 was approximately 250,000.

In Egypt too, the land that played so important a role in the dawn of Israel, there were substantial Jewish communities in Alexandria and Cairo, with some of their members prominent in the industry, commerce, and finance of the country.

10

FROM Cairo it is an overnight journey by train to Palestine, the ancient motherland, whose fortunes were now linked with the world-wide movement launched by Theodor Herzl in 1897.

In spite of obstacles and setbacks, the movement continued to gather strength. At the Seventh Congress in 1905, the threatening schism over the Uganda offer, now that Herzl's strong hand was absent, actually occurred. The report of the survey commission was unfavorable, and when a resolution was adopted to exclude from consideration all territories except Palestine and countries adjacent to it, Israel Zangwill, followed by a group of dissidents, bolted the Congress and formed the Jewish Territorial Organization. Until 1918, when Zangwill disbanded it, this body looked in vain for a region other than Palestine "for Jews who cannot or will not remain in the lands in which they at present live."

But the movement as a whole sustained the death of the leader and the defection of the Territorialists in a manner that bore testimony to its inherent vitality. True, the imposing sums which would have procured the longed-for charter were not forthcoming, nor did the Colonial Trust obtain the capital it called for; but before long the Anglo-Palestine Bank, a subsidiary of the Trust, began operations in Palestine, and in 1908 the organization opened its Palestine Office in Jaffa. The Office was placed under the direction of Arthur Ruppin, a scholar and colonization expert who identified himself wholly with the aims and spirit of the movement, and served it until his death in 1943. The *Keren Kayemeth*, or "Permanent Fund," as the Jewish National Fund was designated in Hebrew, captured the imagination of the masses and its income steadily increased.

The establishment of the Palestine Office for the promotion of urban and rural colonization marked the end of an intense struggle within the movement, which began with the liquidation of the Uganda controversy. It divided those who believed that all efforts at colonization must await the attainment of the charter, and those who were opposed to delay in expanding Jewish holdings in Palestine in every sphere, cultural as well as economic. The first, led by Max Nordau, were the political Zionists par excellence, those who clung to what they considered the legacy of Theodor Herzl. The second, whose leader was Menahem Mendel Ussischkin (1863-1943), an engineer from Russia and the dominant figure in the group that hailed from the *Chovevei Tziyon*, saw immediate work in Palestine not only as good in itself, but also as an important political asset, capable at the right moment of tipping the scales in favor of the Basel Platform.

The decision to establish the Palestine Office meant, of course, a victory for the second policy. The decision came while the organization was still headed by David Wolffsohn (1856-1914), Herzl's friend and successor, who tried to steer a middle course between the two standpoints, and the policy became fixed in 1911 when Wolffsohn was succeeded by the eminent scientist Otto Warburg.

II

AS EARLY as 1901, the Congress no longer presented the ideological uniformity with which the movement had begun. The Basel Platform was the broad common ground on which all its adherents stood, but room was found on it for a variety of outlooks whose followers drew together to form separate parties. Like other European legislative bodies, the Congress came to have a Right, a Left, and a Center. The Right consisted of the Mizrachi (literally, "Easterners") who took for their watchword "the land of Israel for the people of Israel, in conformity with the Torah of Israel." The Mizrachi, who became a separate federation within the movement, were led by Rabbi Isaac Jacob Reines (1839-1915) of Lida, and stood for the recognition of traditional Judaism in the affairs and institutions of the movement. The Left, which also became a separate world-wide federation within the movement, was the party of Poale Zion, who called for the application of collectivist principles in the upbuilding of Palestine which, they hoped, would eventually develop into a cooperative socialist commonwealth. The Center consisted of the so-called General Zionists, who were unwilling to predetermine the social constitution of the national home for which they labored, desiring only that the Basel Platform should be realized as speedily as possible.

Running through the whole movement like a separate current and exerting considerable influence, though not formally organized, was the brand known as Cultural Zionism. It laid its emphasis on a "spiritual center" in Palestine rather than a state, a center which would function as a power-house to quicken and preserve Jewish communities throughout the world. Its outstanding champion and exponent was Asher Ginsburg (1856–1927), better known by his pen name Achad Ha'am (One of the People), a dominating figure in the revival of Hebrew literature. He was the leading essayist and prose writer, as Bialik was the leading poet, a stylist who fashioned the Hebrew language into an instrument of cameo precision and elegance.

12

IN THE meantime the Second Aliyah, or migration wave into Palestine, had begun, the first having been that of the BILU students and others which began in 1882. The new arrivals were better prepared, physically and psychologically, than their predecessors. Most of them came from Russia after the abortive revolution of 1905, and they brought an amazing baggage of ideas and idealisms for their own and their people's regeneration. Palestine, they were resolved, was to be Socialist as well as Jewish, and by a remarkable alchemy they fused their passion for social justice with their conception of the realities of the national restoration problem: the Socialist way, in other words, was not a luxury for them, but a stern necessity. They were the pioneers who set up at least three standards that have exercised a controlling influence on the colonization program as a whole. The first was the principle of self-labor, which demanded that the Jewish colonist live by the work of his own hands, and not by employing hired labor. The second was the principle of cooperation, which found its fullest expression in the collectivist type of farm settlement known as the *kvutzah;* the first of its kind, Dagania, was planted in the upper Jordan valley in 1909. The third standard was the principle of self-defense for the protection of Jewish life and property and the vindication of Jewish honor.

In 1907 that principle found its embodiment in Hashomer (The Watchman), an organization of mounted guards who took over the dangerous task of protecting Jewish settlements against brigands who prowled in the night; and in the same year, this first contingent of armed Jews to make its appearance in Palestine in modern times received its baptism of fire. Hashomer aimed to resurrect the ancient Zealot spirit, and its members, rigidly selected, became feared and famous for their hard riding and straight shooting. Hashomer furnished the vanguard for every post of danger, and by 1914 nearly all the colonies had placed themselves under its protection. Among its founders were the modest but iron-willed Israel Giladi, in whose memory stands the village of Kfar Giladi in Upper Galilee, and Isaac Ben Zevi and David Ben Gurion, both of whom have played an important and prominent part in the growth of the Yishuv, or settlement, as the Jewish community in Palestine is briefly designated.

13

THERE was another standard, the revival of the Hebrew language, to which the entire Yishuv became passionately attached. It was set up by no party or group; the chief credit was due, rather, to a single individual, Eliezer Ben Yehudah (1858-1922), whose scholarship, toil, and tenacity produced the astounding result of restoring the tongue of the ancient farmers, priests, and prophets of Israel to the lips of their modern descendants.

Shortly before the outbreak of the First World War, this revival was considerably advanced as the result of a language conflict in connection with a Technical Institute which was about to be opened in Haifa. On the board of this Institute, which had received the support of the *Hilfsverein der deutschen Juden*, a body organized in Berlin in 1901 with aims similar to those of the French

Alliance, were some who insisted that its language of instruction should be German. A bitter controversy ensued which found echoes throughout the world. The Zionist members of the board resigned, teachers and pupils of other *Hilfsverein* schools in Palestine went out on strike, and new schools came promptly into existence. They became the foundation for a Hebrew educational network ranging from kindergarten through elementary and secondary schools, and including teachers' seminaries and the Bezalel School of Arts and Crafts in Jerusalem; the whole crowned later by a university which is one of the glories of the Yishuv.

14

BY 1914 there were some 50 Jewish agricultural settlements in Palestine with a population of 15,000 and covering an area of somewhat more than 100,000 acres. In size, they ranged from mere outposts like Metullah, far up in Galilee, to compact little towns like Petach Tikvah (Gate of Hope) in Judea. In social organization, they included collectivist *kvutzoth*, cooperative villages of small separate homesteads known as *moshavim*, and individualist settlements of the original type. But there was also progress in urban colonization and in other fields. The city of Tel Aviv, which had its beginnings in 1909 on the sand dunes north of Jaffa, had already grown into a large and thriving suburb. Several years later, the first steps toward solving the health problem of the country were taken by the American philanthropist Nathan Straus and by Hadassah, the Women's Zionist Organization of America, which owed its origin and program to the inspiration of Henrietta Szold. In 1913, Hadassah initiated its present large network of health institutions with a system of district nursing and anti-trachoma education.

From 1896 when Herzl's *Judenstaat* appeared, to 1914 when the lights of Europe went out, the Jewish population of Palestine had risen from less than 45,000 to over 100,000. It had grown by the much decried process of "infiltration," the method which Max Nordau and his followers condemned as being woefully inadequate for the solution of the Jewish problem. That problem had certainly not been solved, but a light had been kindled in the East, and it shone with promise, if not with fulfillment.

CHAPTER SIXTY-TWO

Survey, 1914: The West

EXCEPT in Palestine, where the small Yishuv already presented an intriguing combination of East and West—an "ingathering of the exile," as it was often called—the lot of the larger or smaller Jewish communities in the lands of the East was repression or stagnation or both. But westward from czarist Russia, across Europe and on into the New World, the picture brightens. Not that there was a lack of hostility, of dark glances and ominous rumblings; and there were disturbing inner problems to which the new horizons opened by emancipation gave birth. But at least the formal guarantees of emancipation were secure—or so they appeared—and the inner problems were a challenge to the vitality of a people already tested and tempered by four millennia of history. Survival or dissolution depended on the path they chose, and the choice lay largely in their own hands.

2

AS WE leave czarist Russia and "liberal" Rumania, we come upon the congeries of lands and races that made up the Austro-Hungarian Empire. Galicia, the Polish province of that empire, contained in 1910 nearly 900,000 Jews. Their economic situation was deplorable, nor could it be relieved by philanthropy or the sizable emigration which flowed to America during the decade between 1900 and 1910. Politically, the Jewish minority, with its hosts of Chassidim indifferent to politics, with its party divisions, and its uneasy position between the mutually hostile Poles and Ruthenians, was ineffective. The "Jewish Club" in the imperial *Reichsrath*, formed in 1907 and consisting of four deputies led by Benno Straucher, lasted only four years. The other ten Jewish deputies in the parliament of the empire refused to join it, preferring to identify themselves with German or Polish blocs. It was a division that played into the hands of the rabid Polish National Democrats, enabling them to intensify their policy of economic extrusion and cultural suppression.

Somewhat more than 10 per cent of the Jews of Galicia lived on the soil, but among the remainder an abnormally high proportion was engaged in petty trade and petty industry. The number of artisans among them was especially small, a condition that sprang in large measure from official restrictions and chicanery. Nearly all the large Jewish philanthropic bodies in Europe labored to improve their economic lot, and shortly before the First World War an organized attempt was launched at self-help.

In its inner life, Galician Jewry, throughout the nineteenth century and into the twentieth, was an ideological battleground. Chassidim and Misnagdim fought for control of the communities, and both fought the *maskilim* or "enlighteners." Zionism won numerous adherents, nor were the "Poles of the Mosaic persuasion" absent from the arena, and the different groups brought their conflicts to the polls, which sometimes became scenes of violence.

3

IN HUNGARY the emancipation won in 1867 had been seriously threatened by a rising tide of anti-Semitism of which, as we saw, the Tisza-Eslar blood libel of 1882 was the climax. By 1895, however, the tide had receded, the position of the Jews was legally secured and, particularly in the cultural and professional spheres, they rose to a height probably unsurpassed in any other country in the world. In Budapest, the capital, where they made up a quarter of the population, more than half the physicians and nearly half the lawyers and journalists were Jews, and they were prominent in the government service and in the municipal administrations. One reason for their rapid rise was the fact that in the struggle of the dominant Magyars against the other nationalities in Hungary, the Jews, for better or worse, supported the Magyars. The outbreak of war in 1914 found them eager to shed their blood for the Magyar fatherland. They numbered nearly a million, and in their internal affairs there had been since 1871 a sharp division between the Orthodox and their opponents, with separate communal organizations, including educational and charitable institutions for each.

In Austria proper there were approximately 175,000 Jews, nearly all of them in Vienna. They were the cultural leaven of the land, with men of letters like Arthur Schnitzler, Richard Beer-Hoffman, Felix Salten and the brothers Stefan and Arnold Zweig; with composers like Gustav Mahler and Arthur Schoenberg; with scientists like Sigmund Freud. Nor were they absent in the financial, industrial, and political life of Vienna, although since the advent of the anti-Semitic Christian Socialist party and the triumph of its leader Karl Lueger in 1897, they were compelled to devote much of their strength to the struggle against anti-Semitism. The leading champion in the struggle was Joseph Samuel Bloch (1850-1923), rabbi, scholar, and three times elected to the *Reichsrath*, whose victory in a lawsuit against the anti-Semite August Roehling attracted world-wide attention.

The internal affairs of Vienna Jewry were regulated by an all-inclusive community organization, the *Israelitische Kultusgemeinde*, established in 1890 with power to levy taxes for communal purposes. Three years later a rabbinical seminary was opened and a network of communal institutions came into existence. In 1914, the chief rabbi was Moritz Guedemann (1835-1918), who won distinction as an educator and historian. Toward Herzl and Zionism, Guedemann blew hot and cold, but the movement found numerous adherents and was chiefly responsible for the rapid development of athletic societies among the Jewish youth, for which Vienna became famous.

In those provinces which, after the First World War, were united to constitute the republic of Czechoslovakia, there were in 1910 approximately 360,000 Jews, of whom 140,000 lived in Slovakia, then part of Hungary. Bruenn in Moravia, Prague in Bohemia, and Pressburg in Slovakia contained the most important communities. In Bohemia, there was continuous conflict between Czechs and Germans, and for the most part the Jewish orientation before the war was toward the Germans. Prague was a city teeming with Jewish tradition, and like Vienna, it contributed many Jewish artists and literary figures who enriched the intellectual life of Europe, men like Franz Kafka, Max Brod, Franz Werfel and others.

4

IN GERMANY the turn of the century brought a change in the mood and methodology of anti-Semitism. Germany, aspiring to lead the world in the arts of civilization, could not afford to be bracketed with czarist Russia. German anti-Semitism eschewed the tactics of Stoecker and Ahlwardt and became "refined." But there was no shrinking of its dimensions, no abatement of its neurotic obsessions, no relaxation of its purpose. Its victims were still subjected to a variety of discriminations. They had small prospect of attaining officer's rank in the army, of sitting as judges in the courts, of holding positions in the schools and universities. Immigrant Jews from the East, the so-called *Ostjuden,* became the targets of a special hue and cry in which some of the highly Teutonized native Jews did not scruple to join.

Nevertheless, at the outbreak of war in 1914, the Jews of Germany were not wanting in a sense of security. There were only some 500,000 of them, or less than 1 per cent, in a population of over 60,000,000; the largest communities were in Berlin, Frankfort on the Main, Breslau, Hamburg, Cologne, Leipzig, and Munich. The economy of the country was on the upsurge, and they played an important role in its progress. Their occupational distribution which, of course, had been determined by their history, was neither balanced nor wholesome. There were too few farmers and artisans among them and too many in commerce, industry, and the professions. But they held leading positions in commerce, industry, and finance, and added substantially to the power and glory of the fatherland.

They did this, moreover, not only by their economic activity, but even more by their contributions to German literature, science, and art. The number of Jews in Germany who achieved distinction in those fields would fill a sizable "Who's Who," and names like Jakob Wassermann, Lion Feuchtwanger, Joseph Popper-Lynkeus, Maximilian Harden, and Ludwig Fulda in literature; Hermann Cohen, Georg Simmel, and Ernst Cassirer in philosophy;

Hermann Minkowski and Albert Einstein in pure science; August von Wassermann, Paul Ehrlich, and Otto Meyerhof in medicine; Otto Wallach and Fritz Haber in chemistry; Max Liebermann in painting; Erich Mendelsohn in architecture; Benno Elkan in sculpture, and Max Reinhardt in the theater, belong more to a history of Germany or of European culture than of the Jewish people.

In the internal affairs of German Jewry, the strife between Orthodoxy on the one hand and the different grades of Reform on the other, continued to dominate the scene until the advent of Zionism at the turn of the century brought about a new alignment. Both camps greeted the newcomer with hostility. The Orthodox saw in the Zionist cultural program an attempt to secularize Jewish life, while the Reformed, as well as those who were indifferent to religion, saw in the movement a reflection on their German patriotism and a peril to their civil status. The new movement was undoubtedly calculated to stem, or at least retard, the process of total assimilation which was moving forward, not so much now by the road of baptism as by that of intermarriage.

The center of German Orthodoxy was Frankfort on the Main, where the legacy of Samson Raphael Hirsch was zealously guarded. Under the direction of Jacob Rosenheim, that city became the headquarters of Agudas Israel, the world organization of Orthodox Jewry founded in 1912. Berlin, which had a Jewish population of over 100,000, was the center and hub of many Jewish activities and agencies, including the Union of German Jews organized in 1904 for the protection of Jewish rights, the *Hilfsverein der deutschen Juden*, and the World Zionist Organization, which had its central office in the German capital. A disturbing symptom of the period was the rivalry between the German *Hilfsverein* and the French *Alliance*, both of which, in the schools they founded and conducted in North Africa and the Levant, appeared to be as much interested in extending the cultural influence of Germany and France respectively as in improving the lot of their coreligionists.

This rivalry, as well as the dissensions among the Jews of Germany and other lands, should have served as an effective refutation of one of the favorite myths of the anti-Semites, the bogy of an international Jewish conspiracy. It failed to do so: the legend continued to gestate, and when the war was over it flourished again and bore new and bitter fruit.

5

BY 1914, the passions which the Dreyfus Affair had stirred up in the French Republic were only a bad memory. French anti-Semitism, to be sure, was not dead: its embers were still nursed by the beaten and disaffected clericals, and a lively, though not very formidable, flame was kept burning by the monarchists, the *Camelots du Roi,* "the king's newsboys," as they called themselves, who rallied around Léon Daudet and his vituperative *Action Française.* But the French Jews were not much disturbed by it. They entered into the life of the Republic, making notable contributions to every phase of it, including the political, with Léon Blum, leader of the Socialists; Louis Klotz, Minister of Finance, and Maurice Bokanowski, son of an immigrant from Russia, who in 1926 was to become Minister of Commerce and Industry. They are estimated to have numbered no more than 130,000, with about 100,000 in Paris, but they had an honored place among French writers, scientists, musicians, journalists, dramatists, and actors. Sarah Bernhardt, hailed as the greatest actress of the period, was holding audiences all over the world in her spell, and Henri Bergson, who in 1928 was to receive the Nobel prize for literature, was already winning his place as the most important thinker of his generation. In 1912 there were 8 Jewish generals in the French army, in addition to 14 colonels and hundreds of other officers.

The separation of church and state in 1905 had required a reorganization of the Jewish consistory on a voluntary and self-supporting basis: Zadoc Kahn, distinguished preacher and scholar, who died the same year, was the last official Grand Rabbi of France. In Jewish learning, French Jewry could point to an impressive number of eminent scholars, including the brothers Salomon and Théodore Reinach, Arsène and James Darmesteter, Joseph Halévy, Moise Schwab, and others. Beginning in 1903, the pogroms in Russia sent a small stream of refugees into France who before very long introduced fresh vigor into the life of the community.

6

ITALY was one of the few lands where anti-Semitism found no welcome, and Jews rose to the highest positions in all spheres of Italian life. In 1902 General Giuseppe Ottolenghi was Minister of War; in 1907 Ernesto Nathan was Mayor of Rome; in 1910 Luigi Luzzatti was Prime Minister. They contributed high-ranking officers to the army and navy and numerous professors to the universities. In 1899 a seminary was established in Florence which provided most of the rabbis for the communities of Italy, but notwithstanding the splendid synagogues that were erected in Florence, Rome, Milan, and other cities, it cannot be affirmed that for creative Jewish learning this Italy could compare with that of the Middle Ages or of Samuel David Luzzatto.

In May 1915, Italy joined the Allies against the Central Powers, and no one greeted the prospect of Italian aggrandizement with more enthusiasm than the 40,000 Italian Jews.

7

IN THE smaller lands of western Europe: Belgium, the Netherlands, Switzerland, Denmark, Norway, and Sweden, there were in 1914 Jewish communities of varying size, subject in the main to the same centrifugal and centripetal forces as in the larger countries. In Switzerland, where they numbered approximately 20,000, with the principal communities in Zurich, Basel, and Geneva, they were an important factor in the textile and lace industries. The law prohibiting the ritual method of slaughter, adopted under anti-Semitic pressure in 1894, was still in force.

In Belgium, where equality came after the revolution of 1830, there were some 60,000 of them, with the largest concentration in Antwerp, where they dominated the diamond industry. Belgium was on the whole successful in immunizing herself against the anti-Semitic virus; and this may also be said of The Netherlands, where the largest Jewish communities were to be found in Amsterdam, Rotterdam, and The Hague. They were the chief factor in the diamond industry and played an important part in merchandising; but while there were wealthy men among them, the majority, as in all countries except Germany, were proletarians. Their contributions to Dutch political and cultural life were considerable. Tobias Asser, who received the Nobel peace award in 1911, was the foremost authority on international law; Jacques Oppenheim, another jurist, was a leading authority on constitutional law. Jozef Israels, who died in 1911, was pre-eminent among the painters, and Herman Heyermans and Michel van Campen stood out in an impressive list of Jewish men of letters. In the religious life of the community, Orthodoxy was in the ascendant, and Zionism made a strong appeal to the youth.

In Norway, there was a tiny community in Oslo. In Sweden, where the last barriers against the equality of the Jews were removed in 1870, they numbered in 1914 only a little over 6,000, but they played no insignificant role in the cultural life of the country, with Ernst Josephson one of the foremost painters, and Oscar Levertin a distinguished poet.

In Denmark, where nearly all the 5,000 Jews lived in Copenhagen, their contribution to the culture of the country was little short of amazing. The most famous man of letters was the critic Georg Morris Cohen Brandes, but he was only one of a galaxy of poets, scientists, artists, composers, and virtuosos. Nor were they absent from the political and industrial life of that great little land.

8

IN 1880, the number of Jews in Great Britain stood at 60,000, but by 1914 it had risen to 250,000, with the largest communities in London, Manchester, Leeds, and Glasgow. In spite of occasional anti-Semitic undertones, like those which accompanied the agitation for the Aliens Act at the turn of the century, the Jews of Britain were spared the sustained hostility with which their fellows on the continent had to contend. No insurmountable barriers were raised against them in the economic, political, and cultural life of England, not even in the social sphere. They had long before established themselves in commerce, industry and finance; they now made their mark also in literature and the press, and rose even higher in public service.

As early as 1871, Sir George Jessel, acknowledged as one of England's foremost jurists, had been named solicitor-general, and ten years later he became president of the court of appeal. By 1914, his career was surpassed by Rufus Isaacs, later Lord Reading, who rose to be Lord Chief Justice of England. Edwin S. Montagu, son of Lord Swaythling, was Undersecretary of State for India; Lord Pilbright, originally Baron Henry de Worms, was Colonial Undersecretary; and Sir Alfred Mond, later Lord Melchett, one of England's foremost industrialists and Zionist leaders, had already been elected to Parliament. Sir Herbert Samuel was a member of the Asquith cabinet; Sir Matthew Nathan, who was entrusted in 1916 with the defense of London, had already distinguished himself as soldier and colonial administrator. Numerous other Jews of Britain had started on careers of public service which reached their climax during and after the war.

Those men were descendants of the earlier Sephardic and Ashkenazic immigrants, but the more recent arrivals also registered progress. They began by herding together in special quarters in London and other cities, and London's Whitechapel took on the appearance of a ghetto. They entered in large numbers as workers and entrepreneurs in the clothing and furniture industries, as well as in the fruit and tobacco trades. Champions of a large assortment of social panaceas, including philosophical anarchism and socialism, made Whitechapel their stamping ground, but what little influence they won was superficial and transitory. The process of Anglicization went steadily forward: the children found their models in those coreligionists of theirs who had risen to such heights in British society.

The religious organization of British Jewry had, in the course of the nineteenth century, made important progress. The Sephardic community was headed by a rabbi with the title of Chacham, while the leader of the Ashkenazic congregations was officially recognized as the chief rabbi of the empire. The best known Chacham was Moses Gaster, versatile and brilliant scholar and writer, and an ardent collaborator of Theodor Herzl. Among the outstanding Ashkenazic leaders were Nathan Marcus Adler and his son Hermann (1839-1911), and Joseph H. Hertz, who assumed the post of chief rabbi in 1913. Both communities were thoroughly Anglicized, but Orthodox. Reform failed to make large gains in

England, although it had able leaders in Claude Goldsmid Montefiore, grandnephew of Sir Moses Montefiore and a scholar of wide attainments; and in Lily Montagu, daughter of the banker Samuel Montagu, the first Lord Swaythling, himself rigidly Orthodox. The most important advance achieved by Reform in England was the opening of the Liberal Synagogue in London in 1911.

A seminary for the training of rabbis, cantors, and religious teachers, known as Jews' College, had been established in 1852. Notable contributions to Jewish scholarship were made under the influence of its rectors and by men like the genial and brilliant Solomon Schechter before his departure for New York in 1902; Israel Abrahams (1858–1925), whose works achieved wide and merited popularity; Joseph Jacobs, Lucien Wolf, the brothers Leon and Cecil Roth, and others. The most influential Jewish publication in the country, and perhaps in the world, was the London weekly, *The Jewish Chronicle*, which was founded in 1841.

This publication and its editor, Leopold Greenberg, placed themselves at the service of Theodor Herzl and his bold adventure. Despite the aloofness of many British Jews in high station and the downright hostility of men like Claude Montefiore and Sir Edwin Montagu, Zionism in England continued to make gains. In large measure its advance was due to the interest the movement evoked in British government circles, an interest which found early expression in the El-Arish and Uganda offers, and was to reach its climax in the Balfour Declaration of 1917.

9

BRITISH dominions across the seas have also harbored numerous Jewish communities. In Canada, a Sephardic congregation was established in Montreal as early as 1768. Emancipation came in 1832, and immigrants began arriving from Germany and Poland who moved westward with the railroad. In 1901 the current grew in volume, and in two decades the Jewish population of Canada leaped from 16,000 to 126,000, most of them located in Montreal and Winnipeg. But there are also hundreds of Jewish farmers in Canada, many in settlements founded with the help of the Jewish Colonization Association. The great majority of the Canadian Jews are Orthodox and support the Zionist movement; in general, their communal institutions are patterned after those of their coreligionists in the United States.

After Canada, the British dominion having the largest Jewish settlement is the Union of South Africa. It numbers approximately 90,000, most of them hailing from eastern Europe, particularly from Lithuania. The great majority arrived after 1890, but Jews played an important part in the pioneer days of South Africa: they developed some of its leading industries, including wool and hides, shipping, fisheries, diamonds, and sugar. They have been prominent in the political life of the country, and have developed religious, educational, and philanthropic institutions of a high order, particularly in Johannesburg and Cape Town, where the largest communities are located. Their internal affairs are controlled by their own Board of Deputies, and they have displayed a marked devotion to the Zionist cause.

Jews made important contributions to the economic growth of Australia also, the brothers Jacob and Joseph Montefiore figuring prominently in sheep raising and commerce. The dominion has a Jewish population of some 25,000, the principal communities in Sydney, Melbourne, and Perth.

In New Zealand the handful of Jews, some 2,500 in number, have played a conspicuous role in the political life of the dominion. Sir Julius Vogel was one of New Zealand's leading statesmen: he was prime minister in 1873 and held other important posts. The largest community is located in Wellington, the capital.

10

THE turn of the century saw the dramatic rise of the United States to the status of a world power, largely as a result of the swift and decisive war against Spain which began in April 1898 and was over in August of the same year. In that war, the Jews maintained the high record of service they established with the Revolution. Of the thousands who volunteered in the army and navy, the majority were recent immigrants, many of whom had had training in the armies of Russia and Rumania. Jewish sailors went down with the battleship Maine, and Jewish cavalrymen fought in Cuba in Theodore Roosevelt's famous regiment of Rough Riders. Lieutenant Commander, later Rear Admiral, Adolph Marix, gained distinction in the investigation of the sinking of the *Maine*, as well as for "eminent and conspicuous conduct in battle." Lieutenant Joseph Strauss rose to the rank of Rear Admiral during the First World War, and in 1921 was Commander of the Asiatic Fleet. In 1917, when the entry of America on the side of the Allies made the outcome of the war a foregone conclusion, the Jews of the United States were estimated to number about 3,400,000 in a total population of 103,640,000.

One of their principal concerns in the first two decades of the twentieth century was the rising tide of opposition to the liberal immigration policy which had permitted those seeking refuge from persecution to find it in America. It was an opposition with growing anti-Semitic undertones. The immigration law of 1907 imposed a number of restrictions which did not, however, materially affect the total number admitted. A literacy test was being strongly advocated but was not enacted until ten years later and over the veto of President Woodrow Wilson.

II

THE same decades saw impressive achievements in the cultural sphere. By 1906, the twelve volumes of the *Jewish Encyclopedia*, one of the boldest ventures in Jewish scholarship, had come off the press, and a new translation of the Hebrew Scriptures, published by the Jewish Publication Society of America in 1917, and recognized as the authentic Jewish version in English, was already under way. The Society, founded as early as 1888, as well as a number of commercial publishing houses, were producing books, in Yiddish as well as English, of substantial if not uniform merit.

Since 1902, the Jewish Theological Seminary in New York had been rising in importance under the presidency of Solomon Schechter who, unlike most devotees of the "Science of Judaism," attached as much importance to the mystical as to the rational, and questioned the findings of the "higher critics" of the Bible. He inspired the organization in 1913 of the United Synagogue of America, a body which, aiming "to assert and establish loyalty to the Torah," and "to preserve in the service the reference to Israel's past and the hopes for Israel's restoration," represented a clear challenge to Reform.

Zionism struck roots promptly in the American community. It was acclaimed by most of those who hailed from eastern Europe, among whom were not a few *Chovevei Tziyon*, and as early as July 1898, the separate Zionist societies which had come into existence united in the Federation of American Zionists. The first president was the orientalist Richard J. H. Gottheil; in 1904 he was succeeded by the eminent physician Harry Friedenwald of Baltimore. The movement, of course, did not go unchallenged: its chief opponents were Reform rabbis who accused it of misunderstanding "Israel's mission," and cosmopolitan radicals, to whom every manifestation of nationalism was "reactionary." But, though slowly, it gathered strength, and by the outbreak of the war in 1914 was of sufficient stature, both in leadership and following, to meet the crises as well as the opportunities with which the world movement was confronted by the conflict. One of the most valuable assets it acquired was the adherence of a Boston lawyer named Louis Dembitz Brandeis, who brought to the movement a remarkable gift for practical idealism, clarity of vision, moral force, and skill in the handling of large affairs, a rare combination of qualities which made him also one of the greatest Americans of his generation. In his espousal of Zionism, Brandeis was considerably influenced by Jacob de Haas, a collaborator of Theodor Herzl, who became a leader of the movement in America. Even more prominent among the leaders was Stephen Samuel Wise, of untiring energy and sweeping oratorical power, and Louis Lipsky, who began as a journalist and then devoted an unusual gift for trenchant expression as speaker and writer to the continuous service of the movement.

With all their cultural progress, however, the Jews of America were unable to achieve unity of organization and action. The three main divisions, to which the terms Right, Left, and Center might, though not without reservations, be applied, persisted; the Right being represented by the notables of the American Jewish Committee, the Left by the socialistic labor leaders, the Center by the Zionist groups and the American Jewish Congress. The latter, led by Stephen S. Wise, Bernard G. Richards, and the heads of the fraternal orders whose membership consisted of the more recent arrivals, insisted that Jewish life in America must be "democratized," and found itself in almost continuous conflict with the Right and Left, who sometimes joined forces to combat the Center.

An attempt in 1909 led by Judah L. Magnes, who both as rabbi and communal leader was something of a stormy petrel in Jewish life, to create a *Kehillah*, or over-all communal organization for the vast aggregation in the City of New York, proved a failure. The centrifugal forces, springing from differences in countries of origin, length of residence in the New World, cultural background, economic station, and religious outlook, proved insurmountable. At one extreme stood the leaders, though not the rank and file, of the labor movement, whose outlook was militantly radical and antireligious. At the other were many of those who had achieved wealth and material ease and were eager to lose their Jewish identity in Ethical Culture, Christian Science, or in general aloofness. Between the two stood the great amorphous majority, recognizing a common kinship of origin and religion, but too far apart in their understanding of its implications to unite on a permanent communal program. Occasionally differences were submerged and there was common action, but they were occasions of sorrow or alarm, like a pogrom wave in Russia, or a cataclysm like the one that shook the world in the summer of 1914.

Part Six 1914 TO 1948

The World Wars

Disaster and Daybreak

CHAPTER SIXTY-THREE

The First World War

BY THE middle of that summer of disaster in 1914, the great European powers—Germany and the Austro-Hungarian Empire on one side; Russia, France and Great Britain on the other—were locked in the most colossal conflict that had, until then, scourged the human race. For more than four years, until November 11, 1918, the carnage continued, the vortex having in the meantime drawn in the other great powers of the earth—Japan, Turkey, Italy, and finally the United States—and nearly all the smaller ones.

Rivers of ink have been spilled in the controversy over the degree of guilt of the different belligerents, and perhaps there is not one among them, if sins of omission are considered as well as sins of commission, whose hands are spotless. Nearly all of them had their scores to settle and their greeds to satisfy, and against the lure of national ambition the ethical imperatives of Christianity, to which they were paying lip service, went up like a straw fire. Nevertheless, a single fact stands out which fastens the immediate responsibility where it belongs: Austria would not have sent its ultimatum to Serbia on July 23, nor declared war on that little land five days later, without the assurance that Germany would support it in every eventuality. For Germany it was *der Tag*, "the day" the Treitschkes and Bernhardis, who glorified war and nursed the prospect of German world domination, had foretold and awaited.

2

FOR over three years—from August 1914 to the fall of 1917—the borderlands between Russia and the Central Powers, stretching from the Baltic to the Black Sea, made up the eastern front across which the embattled armies advanced and retreated.

From East Prussia, which they invaded early in August 1914, the Russians were hurled back the same month in the Battle of Tannenberg. In Galicia they were more successful: early in September they captured Lemberg and by March 1915 had driven on into the Carpathians. But the same spring the Germans drove them out of Galicia, and by the fall they were masters also of Russian Poland and Lithuania, having seized both Warsaw and Vilna. In that campaign the Russian losses in killed, wounded, and prisoners amounted to two and a half million men: the regime of Nicholas II was crippled and demoralized; its incompetence and corruption stood plainly revealed.

The following year, while the Germans were pouring out their strength in the west before Verdun and on the Somme, the Russians had a brief illusion of recovery when they reconquered a part of eastern Galicia. The illusion was strong enough to tempt Rumania to join the Allies: in August 1916 it took the plunge, but before the end of the year its capital had fallen and nearly the whole of the country was overrun.

Early the following year—1917—the flames of revolution which in 1905 the czar, with the aid of the Black Hundreds, had managed to smother, erupted with irresistible fury, and on March 15, 1917, Nicholas II was compelled to abdicate. In July the provisional government under Alexander Kerensky attempted another offensive against the enemy. It was a forlorn hope. The Russian armies were completely demoralized, the Germans captured Riga, the Austrians recovered their losses of the previous year in Galicia. The eastern front was no more. The borderlands between Russia and the Central Powers—Estonia and Lithuania, Poland, Galicia, the Ukraine, and Rumania—appeared to be firmly in German and Austrian hands.

3

IN THE cities and towns of these borderlands lived the great majority—some 75 per cent—of the Jews of the world, and it was they who suffered most at the hands of the warring hosts. They suffered not only from the inescapable miseries to which all the inhabitants were exposed—from the destruction of homes, factories, and crops, from famine and pestilence—but they were the victims of special afflictions and indignities.

They suffered at the hands of their "friends" as well as their foes. The Russian High Command took for granted that a people whom the regime had so abused could not remain loyal to it, especially since the war brought them no relief from persecution and disabilities; and when the generals met with defeat and disgrace, what more natural than to shift the guilt to the eternal scapegoat? So they charged the Jews with having commerce with the enemy, and to dramatize their attempt at self-vindication, they ordered the evacuation of entire communities into the interior of Russia. Men, women, and children were packed into box-cars in which many of them perished, or were driven off on foot and marched for hundreds of weary miles away from the war zones. Some of them were evacuated as far as Siberia. In addition, community leaders were seized as hostages and a number of Jews were executed as spies. The policy found support in the allegations of Polish anti-Semites, who took advantage of the situation to settle old scores with Jewish competitors.

The facts, however, bore out neither the slurs of Russian generals nor the slanders of Polish anti-Semites. Between six and seven hundred thousand Jews are estimated to have fought in the armies of Russia during the war. They were barred from promotion to officer's rank, but large numbers of them received awards for bravery, and scores of thousands shed their blood for a government that continued to treat them and their people as outcasts.

4

WHEN the Cossacks broke across the borders into Bukovina and Galicia, thousands of Jews, subjects of Austria-Hungary, fled westward of their own accord. Nearly half the Jews of Galicia became fugitives. They were not welcomed in cities like Vienna, the capital of their own country, where not even war could sterilize the virus of anti-Semitism, nor did their sufferings end in the camps which were hastily improvised for them. There were, however, high-ranking Jewish officers, including generals, in the armed forces of the Austrian Empire, where the total number of Jews in service is estimated to have exceeded 300,000. Many of them, particularly in the Hungarian contingents, were decorated for valor.

In none of the belligerent lands did the Jews flock to the colors with more alacrity than in Germany; more than 100,000 of them, or nearly 20 per cent of the total Jewish population, served in the armed forces, and the number of those who gave their lives is reliably estimated to have exceeded 28,000. Both these figures represent a larger proportion than the corresponding figures for the country as a whole; nevertheless, it was in Germany where the most elaborate and studied insult was inflicted upon the Jews during the war. On November 1, 1916, a special census was taken of Jewish soldiers at the front, on garrison duty, and in other categories. The count had been demanded by anti-Semites in the *Reichstag* and elsewhere, and although the results gave them no comfort, the agitation served their purpose of humiliating the Jews and fomenting hostility against them among soldiers and civilians alike. During the census, many Jewish soldiers were temporarily removed from the front in order to reduce the number in that category which the investigation would disclose.

The actual figures, not only in Germany but in all the belligerent countries, belied the defamations of the anti-Semites. The Jews constituted 1 per cent of the total population of all those countries; to the armed forces, however, they contributed 1,500,000 men, or more than 2 per cent of the total; and the 170,000 fatal casualties they sustained also represented 2 per cent of those who were killed in action. The armies of the Allied Powers, except the Russian, included thousands of Jewish commissioned officers. There were Jewish generals in the French and Belgian armies, and one of the most distinguished soldiers of the war was Lieutenant General Sir John Monash, commander of the Australians who fought in France.

5

WHATEVER sympathy existed among the Jews of America for the Central Powers—a sympathy kept alive by the hope of seeing the defeat of czarist Russia—was swept away by the downfall of Nicholas II and the legal emancipation of Russian Jewry that followed. And when on April 6, 1917, the United States declared war on Germany, the Jews of the United States flocked to the defense of their country with an eagerness exceeded by no other group of the population. "No class of people," wrote General John

J. Pershing, the commander in chief of the American Expeditionary Force, "served with more patriotism or with higher motives than the young Jews who volunteered or were drafted, and who went overseas with our other young Americans."

The statistics are just as eloquent. With the Jewish community only 3.27 per cent of the total population, it contributed 5.73 per cent of the Americans in uniform. There were 170,000 of them in the army, 24,000 in the navy, 12,000 in the marine corps, and a sufficient number in the other services to raise the total to nearly 250,000. Some 20 per cent were volunteers, and in the American Expeditionary Force, 75 per cent of them were in the combatant branches, while the proportion of the entire force in those branches was only 60 per cent. The Jewish commissioned officers numbered more than 9,000.

The "East Side Boys," as the Jewish soldiers who fought for America in the First World War were called, made keen and resourceful soldiers, and contributed their full quota to the roster of the heroes of the epic conflict. The Seventy-seventh Division, which penetrated farther into the German lines than any other unit, was 40 per cent Jewish. To that division belonged the famous "Lost Battalion" which was saved by Abraham Krotoshinsky, still a "greenhorn" in America. He succeeded in passing through the enemy lines in the Argonne Forest after 36 other men had been killed or captured in the attempt.

6

BUT the call to arms was not the only one which the American Jewish community heard and heeded. Another was the cry of distress from their brothers in the war zones of Europe. Organized efforts for the relief of the victims of invasions and deportations were initiated in European lands also—in Germany, Austria, Russia, and neutral countries—but the chief burden of giving and dispensing fell upon the Jews of America.

Three fund-raising agencies, each appealing to a different segment of the community, came promptly into existence, but a recognition of the urgency for speed and efficiency in the administration of relief overcame internal differences and by the end of 1914, the Joint Distribution Committee was set up. It gradually took over, also, the task of raising the funds. The committee was headed by the noted banker and philanthropist, Felix M. Warburg of New York, and first among its benefactors was Julius Rosenwald of Chicago.

As the war dragged on and the distress grew, the annual appeals brought more and more millions into the coffers of the "Joint," and in spite of the obstacles which multiplied after the entry of America into the war, a large network of relief activities was established in Europe. These involved constructive as well as immediate, or palliative, relief; nor did they exclude the religious and cultural needs of the war-ravaged communities of Europe. Help for the victims flowed also from the *landsmanschaft* societies and from individuals who sent aid to stricken relatives.

7

CALLS for help came not only from Europe but also from Palestine. For a time it appeared as if the war would scatter and obliterate the budding community in the motherland around which clustered so many old and new hopes, and which had a special place in the affections of all Jews, Zionist and non-Zionist alike. Not only did the war stem the flow of charity funds, known as the *Chalukah*, which sustained the pious old who had come to live their last days in the Holy Land, but it shut off the markets for the principal export commodities of the country, wine and oranges. It was imperative to feed the hungry and check epidemic disease. Most of the help came, of course, from America. It came in the form of funds, food, medical supplies, and medical personnel, the latter consisting of the American Zionist Medical Unit which was organized and dispatched by the Hadassah Women's Zionist Organization.

But the tribulations of the Yishuv were not only economic, but also political. Jemal Pasha, the Turkish military governor of Palestine, chose to look upon Zionist activity as treason, and upon the large numbers of the Yishuv who were subjects of the czar, with whom Turkey was at war, as spies and subversionists. His methods were ruthless: they included imprisonment, forced evacuation, torture, and execution. Thousands of Russian subjects were banished, most of them finding refuge in neighboring Egypt.

8

IT SOON became apparent, moreover, that the war would produce far-reaching political changes; to suppressed nationalities like the Poles and the Czechs, it opened vistas of freedom and self-determination, and Zionists all over the world felt that the opportunity which Herzl had sought in vain might now be at hand. The war had disrupted the apparatus of the World Zionist Organization, and in America a Provisional Executive Committee for General Zionist Affairs, headed by Louis D. Brandeis, was created not only to provide the Yishuv with material help but also to promote the political interests of the movement. Those interests, it became obvious, were more likely to be served by a victory of the Allies, involving as it would the defeat of Turkey; and the conviction grew that a direct military contribution to such a victory would add strength to Zionist political claims.

The conviction found expression in a determined effort which, before the war ended, brought the first Jewish military units in modern times to fight in and for the ancient motherland. The first attempt, launched early in 1915 among the exiles from Palestine who had found refuge in Egypt, led to the formation of the Zion Mule Corps, a body of 650 men who served in the ill-fated Gallipoli campaign, conveying food and ammunition, frequently under fire, to the soldiers in the trenches. Disbanded in the summer of 1916 after the abandonment of the Gallipoli enterprise, the Corps became the nucleus of the battalions, consisting of volunteers recruited in England, the United States, Canada, and the Yishuv, which are remembered as the Jewish Legion, and in Palestine were known as the "Judaeans."

Numerous obstacles, including those raised by government circles and anti-Zionist British Jews, had to be overcome before the first battalion, officially known as the 38th Royal Fusiliers, became a reality; and the effort called for unceasing exertion by a group of dynamic personalities, including Vladimir Jabotinsky, brilliant journalist and orator; Joseph Trumpeldor, Palestinian pioneer and hero of the Russo-Japanese War; Pinchas Ruttenberg, engineer and a leader of the Russian Revolution of 1905; and the labor leaders of the Yishuv. It was not until June 1917 that the British

Official Gazette announced the authorization of the Jewish units, but the first battalion, commanded by Colonel John Henry Patterson, arrived in time to take part in the campaign that drove the Turks out of Palestine. On September 22, 1918, it stormed the ford at Um-esh-Shert, opening the way for the Australian and New Zealand cavalry to break into Transjordania. It was near the spot on the Jordan River where, thirty-three centuries earlier, Joshua had led the children of Israel across into the Promised Land.

In the spring of the same year the second battalion, consisting of American and Canadian volunteers, had arrived in Palestine, commanded by Colonel Eliezer Margolin, a tried and gallant soldier and a proud son of his people. He led his men in the capture of the bridge across to Es-Salt, after three attacks by other units had been thrown back. A third battalion, commanded by Colonel Frederick Samuel and consisting largely of Palestinian Jews, took part in the final phase of the campaign, and on Armistice Day, American volunteers in sufficient number to make up three more battalions were in training in Canada and England. The exploits of the Jewish battalions were cited by the commanders in the field, but at staff headquarters in Egypt the attitude was not friendly: in this, as in larger matters of policy with respect to Palestine, the government in London failed to secure the understanding and cooperation of its subordinates.

9

EVEN before the first Jewish battalion arrived in the Near East, the basic policy of the British War Cabinet with respect to Palestine had been formulated and published. Under date of November 2, 1917, Lord Rothschild, as president of the English Zionist Federation, received a communication from Arthur James Balfour, the Secretary of State for Foreign Affairs, which had been approved by the Cabinet. It declared that:

> His Majesty's Government view with favor the establishment in Palestine of a national home for the Jewish people, and will use their best endeavors to facilitate the achievement of this object, it being clearly understood that nothing shall

> be done which may prejudice the civil and religious rights of existing non-Jewish communities in Palestine or the rights and political status enjoyed by Jews in any other country.

The Balfour Declaration, as this pronouncement came to be known, was hailed with solemn joy in the Jewish communities throughout the world. It seemed to augur the realization of the dream of Theodor Herzl and the hope nursed by his people through nearly two millennia of exile and persecution. History was found to repeat itself: the declaration was compared to the proclamation issued in 538 B.C.E. by Cyrus the Persian, which permitted the exiles of Babylonia to return and establish the Second Jewish Commonwealth.

For Britain, the Balfour Declaration was an act of practical statesmanship, frankly designed to enlist the good will and support of an influential world community in its hour of peril; nor were its rulers unmindful of the value a grateful and dependable Jewish settlement on the road to the Far East might have for the future. But those considerations, weighty as they were, do not exhaust the motives that lay behind the action. The Declaration was also the consummation of a deep and long-standing British sentiment, one which had its foundation in a widespread knowledge of biblical prophecy and a reverence for it. That sentiment, moreover, had found many previous expressions: in the brave words and deeds of British precursors of Zionism through the second half of the nineteenth century, and in the El-Arish and Uganda offers made by the British government to the Zionist Organization.

The Declaration was not an engagement into which Britain entered lightly. Many months of negotiation between the government and Zionist leaders, chief among them Chaim Weizmann and Nahum Sokolow in Europe and Louis D. Brandeis in America, preceded the adoption and publication of the final formula, not to speak of the influential anti-Zionist Jews who had to be appeased. Weizmann, who already held a prominent place in Zionist affairs, was teaching chemistry in the University of Manchester, and having rendered signal service to the British war effort through his scientific attainments, he came into personal contact with government leaders, among them David Lloyd George, the head of the War Cabinet, and Balfour. Both were already in sympathy with Zionist aims, and he succeeded in convincing them of the practical and moral advantages Britain would gain by supporting those aims officially and publicly. The brilliant and versatile Sokolow accomplished the task of winning the assent of the French and Italian governments, and he even succeeded in allaying the misgivings of the pope, Benedict XIV.

The United States was neither at war with Turkey nor technically one of the Allies, but its commanding power and influence made its support indispensable, and President Woodrow Wilson, convinced of the justice of the Zionist cause, required little persuasion from Brandeis and his associates, among them Stephen S. Wise and Julian W. Mack, to extend it generously and eagerly. Wilson, in fact, approved the text of the Balfour Declaration before its promulgation.

10

BUT in spite of the long time and distinguished statesmanship that were devoted to its formulation, the Declaration emerged not without omissions and ambiguities which were destined to bear bitter fruit. The term "national home" found itself subjected to a variety of interpretations. True, both David Lloyd George, President Wilson, Lord Robert Cecil, Winston Churchill, Jan Smuts, and other British and American leaders, made it clear that they understood it to imply an eventual Jewish Commonwealth. Lloyd George, in his book *The Truth about the Peace Treaties*, says:

> There has been a good deal of discussion as to the meaning of the words "Jewish National Home" and whether it involved the setting up of a Jewish National State in Palestine . . . It was contemplated that when the time arrived for according representative institutions to Palestine, if the Jews had meanwhile responded to the opportunity afforded them by the idea of a National Home and had become a definite majority of the inhabitants, then Palestine would thus become a Jewish Commonwealth. The notion that Jewish immigration would

> have to be artificially restricted in order to ensure that the Jews should be a permanent minority never entered into the heads of anyone engaged in framing the policy. That would have been regarded as unjust and as a fraud on the people to whom we were appealing.

And on February 8, 1920, Winston Churchill stated his understanding of the term as follows:

> If, as may well happen, there should be created in our own lifetime by the banks of the Jordan a Jewish State under the protection of the British Crown which might comprise three or four millions of Jews, an event will have occurred in the history of the world which would from every point of view be beneficial, and would be especially in harmony with the truest interests of the British Empire.

Less than twenty-five years later, however, with the Jews in Palestine still a minority, the vagueness of the term enabled Britons who were anxious to evade the pledge to claim that it had already been fulfilled; and they were able to bolster their claim by the fact that the Declaration spoke not of Palestine as the Jewish national home, but of a national home *in* Palestine, that preposition being ruefully reminiscent of another by which the Vienna Congress of 1815 stripped the Jews of the rights they had won in Germany. But perhaps the most serious deficiency of the Declaration was its apparent assumption that the boundaries of Palestine required no definition, an assumption which only five years later made it possible for a British White Paper to exclude Transjordania, the large and fertile region east of the Jordan, from its borders.

Nor was it realized at the time that certain commitments made two years earlier to Husein, Grand Sherif of Mecca and, after the war, King of Hejaz, would, because of their vagueness, afford Arab nationalists an opportunity to claim that Palestine was included in the regions where, as a reward for an Arab revolt against Turkey, Great Britain was "to recognize and support the independence of the Arabs." Those commitments were made by Sir Henry McMahon, the British High Commissioner in Egypt, and the Arabs have persistently repeated the claim in spite of a public denial by Sir Henry himself. In a letter to the *London Times* of July 23, 1937, Sir Henry wrote:

> I feel it my duty to state, and I do so definitely and emphatically, that it was not intended by me . . . to include Palestine in the area in which Arab independence was promised. I also had every reason to believe that the fact that Palestine was not included in my pledge was well understood by King Husein.

II

BUT the flaws and blemishes were either unrecognized or ignored. The enthusiasm which greeted the Balfour Declaration saw only its bright promise, which acquired added reality by the simultaneous progress of British arms from Egypt toward Jerusalem. On December 11, 1917, the Holy City was entered by General Allenby, who marched in bareheaded and on foot, like a pilgrim rather than a conqueror. Early the following year, a Zionist Commission, authorized by the British government and headed by Weizmann, arrived in Palestine to advise the military authorities in matters affecting "the establishment of the Jewish National Home," and to act as a link between them and the Yishuv. In July of the same year, the foundation stone of the Hebrew University was laid on Mount Scopus even while to the north the cannon were still rumbling.

Those events were important enough in themselves, but their symbolic significance was even more stirring. The Zionist Commission discovered soon enough that the military authorities were uninformed and obstructive, but the Jewish masses throughout the world went through a honeymoon of redemption. It had been even so with the exiles from Babylonia when they first saw the hills of Jerusalem. "When the Lord brought back those that returned to Zion," sang the Psalmist, "we were like unto them that dream. Then was our mouth filled with laughter, and our tongues with singing." That was in 538 B.C.E., but it took many decades of toil and struggle before the Second Commonwealth, under the leadership of Ezra and Nehemiah, was firmly established. The road to the Third Commonwealth was to prove equally steep and stony.

CHAPTER SIXTY-FOUR

New Europe and New Russia

IN THE meantime, that first attempt of the "master race" to establish its hegemony over the nations was running to its doom: *der Tag* was sinking into twilight and night. Not even the Bolshevik revolution of November 1917, nor the humiliating treaties which Russia and Rumania were forced to accept, lifting the burden of the eastern front from the German High Command, could save the "supermen" from defeat and disgrace.

A new combatant, the giant of the New World, had entered the lists. The ruthless campaign of the German submarines, by which England was to be starved and brought to her knees, was checked; a bridge of ships was built across the Atlantic; and by the summer of 1918, a million American soldiers had been landed in France. In March of that year, the Germans had begun their supreme effort in the west, but in July, with the Allied command unified under Marshal Foch and the Americans fighting in force, the Germans were decisively defeated in the Second Battle of the Marne and by November had lost nearly all their conquests in France and Belgium. In September, Bulgaria, after suffering a succession of defeats by the Allied army based on Salonika, had surrendered unconditionally, and the following month Turkey and Austria-Hungary did likewise. The Turks had been driven not only from Arabia, Palestine, and Syria, but another expedition had sent them reeling up the Tigris River from Bagdad to Mosul. As for Austria-Hungary, its subject nationalities, spurred by the imminent debacle of Germany, had risen in revolt, and the patchwork empire fell in like a house of cards.

Finally, on November 11, 1918, came the surrender of Germany itself. The first bid of the "master race" for world dominion, which had brought mankind incalculable woe, with over eight and a half million killed and twenty-two million wounded, had ended in defeat—but not, as later events were to reveal, in remorse or resignation.

2

OVER the face of eastern and central Europe, in the lands where for nearly four centuries the largest and most vital Jewish communities had toiled and struggled, the First World War brought sweeping changes. Military collapse and social revolution put an end to czarist Russia; the uneasy empire of the Hapsburgs broke up and vanished; and under the aegis of national "self-determination," states long dead came to life and new ones were born.

The three segments into which Poland had been broken by the partitions at the end of the eighteenth century were united to form a new state, with a corridor giving access to the sea at Danzig. North of Poland along the Baltic, the regions which Russia had been forced to yield became the republics of Lithuania, Latvia, Estonia, and Finland. To the south, the dissolution of the Austro-Hungarian Empire gave birth to Czechoslovakia, and brought considerable enlargement to Rumania, which was further augmented by the annexation of Bessarabia. Farther south in the Balkan Peninsula, Serbia, where the world conflagration started, was expanded into Yugoslavia, and Greece was rewarded by the cession of Thrace with its great port of Salonika, rich with memories of Jewish traders, scholars, and mystics. Austria became an impoverished little state, and Hungary, shorn of Transylvania and Slovakia, was left seething with Irredentist passions. Germany, defeated and humiliated, was compelled to disgorge the spoils of this and previous wars. Its emperor was a fugitive in Holland, its industrial regions in the west were occupied, and it embarked on a venture in democratic government for which neither the petrified Junkers, the arrogant and servile functionaries, the stodgy masses, nor the turgid intellectuals were prepared.

Thus it came about that nearly nine of the fourteen million Jews of the world found themselves subject to new political regimes and, in the case of the two and a half million who remained within the borders of Soviet Russia, to drastically new social and economic conditions as well.

3

NEVERTHELESS, except for the Soviet Union, which went her separate way and remained largely a sealed book, it can be said that the Jews in the other war-changed or war-created lands looked to the future with a measure of sober hopefulness. Those lands were, after all, the handiwork of the Versailles Peace Conference. That conference, which began in December 1918 and lasted till the following June, was of course dominated by the victorious democracies of the West; but, at least in matters not affected by their interests, they might be expected to honor the claims of justice.

One of those matters was the problem of the minorities. In every state of eastern and central Europe, the boundaries of which were drawn or redrawn by the Conference on the principle of national self-determination, there still remained minorities who, in race, language or religion, differed from the dominant majority. There remained, for instance, Germans and Ruthenians in Poland, Magyars in Rumania, Germans in Czechoslovakia. And in all of them there were Jews, the ubiquitous minority of the ages who, in their status as a minority, were distinguished by the uniqueness which characterizes their entire career. Their differences, to begin with, were more conspicuous than those of the other minorities; unlike the others, they were not concentrated geographically but lived in communities scattered throughout the lands; and, most important, there was no political entity controlled by their own kith and kin which, as in the case of the other minorities, might, as the need arose, come forward and champion their grievances. Would the new states grant their minorities the right to be different, the right to their own way of life, their religious and social institutions, their language and culture? The Peace Conference was led to the conclusion that they should, and not only in the interest of justice, but because the policy of suppressing the minorities had proved to be a fertile source of conflict and a menace to the general peace.

The racial, religious, and linguistic minorities of the states in question won the formal recognition of their rights, both as individuals and as groups, and the victory was due chiefly to the labors of the deputations whom the Jewries of those and other lands sent to the conference. They formed themselves into a Committee of Jewish Delegations at the Peace Conference, the leadership of which fell to Julian W. Mack and Louis Marshall, the heads of the American delegation in which both the American Jewish Committee and the more democratic American Jewish Congress were represented. The struggle of the Committee of Jewish Delegations for minority rights did not go unchallenged: it was opposed by the representatives of French Jewry and, to a large extent, by those of British Jewry, who felt uneasy about a demand which, if granted, might expose the Jewish communities to the charge of forming "a state within a state." But the Peace Conference not only made minority rights part of the treaties which the states concerned, willingly or unwillingly, had to accept; they enacted further that those provisions "shall be recognized as fundamental laws . . . and shall be placed under the guarantee of the League of Nations." In the case of Rumania, additional safeguards were added to prevent that country from resorting to its time-honored dodge of placing its Jews in the category of aliens.

However, neither in reborn Poland nor in aggrandized Rumania, the lands with nearly four and a half of the six million Jews for whom minority rights were enacted, did the two decades between the First and Second World War vindicate the enthusiasm with which the acquisition of those rights was greeted. In practice, minority rights, as well as other and more elementary human rights, were honored more in the breach than in the observance. Laws and treaties proved powerless against the ingrained animosity of the dominant majorities, enflamed by the fierce chauvinism that seized upon them in their new-found national grandeur. The position of the minorities was further undermined by the failure of the dream of which Woodrow Wilson was the inspired apostle. The "guarantee of the League of Nations" lost its meaning when the defection of the giant of the West reduced the League to a mere shadow of what it was intended to be.

Minority rights were not, of course, the only victim of the rejection of the League by the Senate of the United States. Other arrangements, like the mandates system, lost their vitality, and many students of international affairs have attributed the final breakdown of world peace two decades later to the same cause.

4

To the Soviet Union, the arrangements of Versailles did not, of course, apply. There, of the six million Jews who had lain under the heel of the czars, some two and a half million still remained in the caldron of revolution and civil strife which the country became immediately after the Bolshevist seizure of power. Nearly two million of them were concentrated in White Russia and the Ukraine, and the savage hordes which until 1922 swept back and forth across those lands repeated the crimes which their forebears committed under Chmelnitzki in 1648. If the counterrevolutionary chieftains—Petlura, Wrangel, Denikin, Grigoriev, and the others—had no other rewards for their motley followers, they could always give them a free hand to plunder and murder the helpless Jews, whom they, like the czar, thought it good policy to hold accountable for the revolution. To the ignorant and the prejudiced the policy appeared to be justified by the fact that there were Jews among the Bolshevist leaders, including Leon Trotsky, the creator of the Red Army, Grigoryi Zinoviev, and Leon Kamenev. The fact that Jews were also among the leading foes of the Bolshevists, and that it was a woman named Dora Kaplan who attempted to assassinate Lenin, meant nothing to the propagators of the lie that the Communist Revolution was the handiwork of the Jews.

The great majority of the Jewish workers, in fact, belonged to anti-Bolshevist parties, not to speak of the merchants, small traders, and independent artisans who made up an abnormally large proportion of the Jewish population. It was so large indeed that under the Soviet legal system, which deprived middlemen of political and civil rights, 35 per cent of the Jewish population found themselves among the *lishentzi* (rightless), while for the entire population, the ratio was only 5 per cent. In Ukrainia itself, the political alignment of the Jewish population was a matter of public record: in 1918, 63 per cent of the delegates to a democratically elected Jewish National Assembly represented bourgeois parties, and the remainder belonged to parties like the *Bund*, which were Socialist but anti-Bolshevist.

Like the old medieval libels, the new lie furnished a welcome sanction for the release of all the degenerate passions that lurk in the human animal. In Ukrainia, the civil war brought chaos and terror; the restraints which normally control human conduct disappeared; and, as always in a period of social upheaval, the first and most tragic victims were the Jews. For the two years beginning January 1919, the Ukraine was the scene of more than a thousand pogroms, with the dead alone, according to some estimates, running into the hundreds of thousands. In numerous places the Jews prepared themselves for defense; they could do little against the well-armed soldiers of Petlura and Denikin, but they gave a good account of themselves against the roving bands of brigands who infested the land.

The arch-culprit was the Cossack hetman Petlura. In 1926 he was shot to death in Paris by Shalom Schwartzbard, whose father had been slain in one of the hetman's pogroms; and a French jury, after hearing all the evidence, found the avenger not guilty.

5

BY 1922, the new Russia had put down the counterrevolutions and checkmated the armed interventions of the Allies whom it had abandoned when it accepted the shameful Treaty of Brest-Litovsk, imposed by Germany in March 1918. Now the country was ready to proceed apace with the most sweeping social transformation a nation had ever attempted, and the Jews who remained within its borders found themselves under a juggernaut that bore down upon them with devastating effect. Not that the new regime inherited the anti-Semitic virus of its predecessor. On the contrary, one of its first acts was to outlaw anti-Semitism as an instrument of reaction and counterrevolution, and to make its practice a grave crime—a policy which the Soviet Union was the first state ever to apply. The woes which the new order brought upon the Jews of Russia had a different origin: they sprang first from the fact that nearly 900,000 of them had derived their subsistence from occupations now proscribed, and second, from the implacable anti-religious policy of the new regime, which played havoc with the basic principle of their individual and collective life.

The economic test, which the classless society to which Russia was struggling to give birth now applied, rejected those who failed to meet it with even more rigor than the religious test of the Middle Ages. Deprived of the right to vote for the local soviets, the rejectees were excluded from the factories as well as government posts; their children were not admitted to the trade schools; their taxes were higher; their ration allotments lower; and they were subject to still other discriminations. The desperate plight of the declassed Jews was to some extent relieved by the help of relatives in America and by the more systematic aid of the Joint Distribution Committee, but in 1926, nearly half the Jews in Russia were estimated to require the aid of charity.

In 1924, the government itself launched a program of reconstruction for the declassed by allotting land in the Ukraine, where Jewish colonies had been established for generations, as well as in northern Crimea, White Russia, and in other regions of the Soviet Union, for Jewish agricultural settlements. To provide equipment and additional aid to the colonists, the Joint Distribution Committee, with the help of the ICA, the ORT, and other relief agencies, established the Agro-Joint; and although the ambitions of the Comzet, as the government commission in charge of the project was called, were not realized, some 3,000 families are believed to have been colonized every year since 1924, so that by the outbreak of the Second World War the population of the new settlements probably exceeded 200,000. In the Crimea there were 89 collective Jewish settlements, with a population of about 40,000.

One of the ambitions of the Comzet was to create an autonomous Jewish region in southern Russia, and when that hope proved illusory, the Comzet transferred it in 1928 to Biro-Bidjan, an extensive region on the Amur River in eastern Siberia. Although the cultural autonomy of the district was duly proclaimed, and Yiddish was made an official language, the great distance as well as the harsh climate failed to attract the requisite numbers, and of those who came to settle there, a considerable portion found it impossible to remain. Besides, the industrialization of Russia under the Five Year Plans enabled large numbers of Jews to find employment in industry, so that the impulse to colonization lost a good deal of its original force. Gradually, the number of the declassed diminished. The young managed to find their place in the new economic structure, but the tragic plight of their elders continued.

6

RUSSIAN Jewry under the czars, despite the calamitous discriminations imposed by the regime, had nevertheless played a leading part in the culture and aspirations of the world-wide community. The more recent spiritual and political currents, which quickened Jewish life throughout the world, expressing themselves in the Zionist movement and in the new Hebrew and Yiddish literatures, had found their chief support in Russia. In the Soviet Union, however, where the Jews were on a legal footing of equality with all the other inhabitants, the Jewish community became a shadow of its former self. Russia itself lived in practical isolation from the rest of the world, and the Jews of Russia lost contact with their kin in other lands. Their inner life, moreover, was subjected to a series of assaults which all but destroyed it.

In line with Communist policy, which looked upon all religions as instruments of class oppression, a ruthless campaign was launched against Judaism. Hundreds of synagogues were transformed into workers' clubhouses; the practice of circumcision was heavily penalized; and the religious education of the young practically barred. The Zionist movement was outlawed as "a tool of British imperialism and counterrevolution," and the Hebrew language and literature came under the same ban. Zionist leaders were arrested, exiled, and imprisoned. Yiddish, on the other hand, as "the language of the proletarian masses," was free and unfettered. Recognized as the language of a national minority, it was encouraged and subsidized, although, to serve the party line, its literature, like its orthography, was grotesquely distorted.

The campaign against Judaism, Zionism, and Hebrew was entrusted to a group of renegades and doctrinaire fanatics who conducted it with more than ordinary zeal and malice. They made up the so-called Jewish Section, or *Yevsektzia,* who used their power to vent their spleen against the immemorial sanctities which had become hateful to them. In 1930, the Section was abolished, but what has remained of the ancient spiritual bulwarks of Russian Jewry is a question which is still unanswered. What is clear, however, is that the substitute in the form of a Yiddish proletarian culture, which was to safeguard the Jewish nationality, has failed of its purpose. The process of assimilation is unchecked, for nowhere can the hope of Jewish survival rest upon a secular culture alone.

CHAPTER SIXTY-FIVE

Disaster Made in Germany

FOR mankind in general and the Jewish people in particular the two decades between the world wars—the "long truce," as the period has been called—ended with a disaster of unprecedented magnitude. It was a disaster made in Germany, brewed in a caldron in which, by a fatal juncture of conditions and events, all the necessary toxic ingredients were assembled.

The chief ingredient was a nation exhausted, humiliated, and demoralized—a neurotic, adolescent nation which, though defeated and broken, clung desperately to its morbid chauvinism, seeking the cause of its ruin in everything except its true source: itself. The second ingredient was a group of "victorious" nations around Germany, not far behind it in demoralization, bedeviled by economic distress and internal division, their noblest traditions submerged by the fatigue and cynicism that follow in the wake of war. Into the moral vacuum that existed in Europe, there now entered something which had all the appearance of a nightmare: a monster that shrieked and bellowed for a return to the jungle, gloried in the chaos and bloodlust of the jungle, and trampled upon all the ethical norms which the human race had achieved at such terrible cost. The thing called National Socialism, or Nazism, appeared in Germany and began its work of pollution, spilling over into other lands and absorbing all things vile, including its pale precursor, the fascism of Italy.

Finally, that brew of disaster found its active reagent in a group of leaders, all stamped with the seal of physical, mental, or moral degeneration. With cynical frankness, they made no secret of their intention to subdue the world to their purpose; and with fraud, duplicity, and terror they openly set about to corrupt and subvert men and nations. By the Fuehrer, or supreme leader of the group, its aim was expressed in simple words. "I want to see again in the eyes of youth," he said, "the gleam of the beast of prey. A youth will grow up before which the world will shrink." Never in human history had sheer evil stood forth so stark and naked, and, as was shortly to appear, so well-geared to accomplish its aim.

In this arch of evil, which from 1933 until the end of the Second World War threw its shadow over the earth, the keystone was anti-Semitism. Here was a passion and a program which answered to all the depraved instincts of the Nazi leaders and rabble, to all their sadistic lusts and greeds, and served to vindicate all their failures and frustrations. It was, moreover, peculiarly fitted to appeal to their counterparts in other lands, and whatever else the Nazi baggage contained that was vile and sinister became acceptable to anti-Semites the world over.

For the Nazis and their disciples the Jewish people became Enemy Number One. Indeed, it was a sound intuition which led these men, who called for the restoration of the ruthless Teutonic gods and demons, to single out for their most implacable hatred the people who were chiefly responsible for the recognition of the God of justice and loving kindness. Thus it came to pass, a century and a half after the French Revolution and nearly two generations after the Jews of Germany had been admitted to civil equality, that they, as well as their kin in nearly all the rest of Europe, some eight millions of them, suffered a catastrophe which dwarfs all previous disasters in their four millennia of history.

2

IMMEDIATELY after the First World War, Germany, defeated but unchastened, became a "democratic" republic, but it was like a man trying to lift himself by his boot straps. The economic problems, such as the reparations which the conquerors imposed, the catastrophic inflation of 1923, and the depression that smote the entire world in 1929, would have staggered an old and stable democracy; in Germany they doomed an experiment which would probably have failed in any case. For the basic vice was psychologic rather than economic. Not only did the Germans lack experience in self-government, but they were afflicted with an inveterate aversion for it, with what amounted to an organic need for control and authority. This deficiency, which their philosophers of course exalted into a sublime virtue, was aggravated by the frustrations of defeat, and by the association which inevitably arose in their minds between the republic and their misfortunes.

After a feverish career of fourteen years, marked by assassinations, bloody clashes between private armies, and revolutionary attempts by the Right and the Left, the Weimar Republic, so-called because in 1919 its constitution was drafted and signed in that city, came to an end, and in 1933 it was replaced by a dictatorship headed by one Adolf Hitler.

But even before the exaltation of this modern Genghis Khan—a designation which insults the memory of the twelfth century super-killer—his followers, actual and potential, open and hidden, had already found in anti-Semitism a consolation and a program. Those followers included the army officers, the industrialists, the Junker land barons, the intellectuals, the middle classes, all who had grown up on a diet of German superiority and invincibility. They had to have an explanation for their defeat and it had to be one that would cater to their arrogance. They found it in the fable of a "stab in the back" administered to the army by the Jews. The terms the conquerors imposed on Germany at Versailles—terms which it became fashionable to condemn as too severe but which were mild compared to those which Germany imposed on Russia at Brest Litovsk—were ascribed to Jewish influence. Every liberal and radical manifestation which all of those groups feared and hated, including the Weimar Republic itself, was, of course, denounced as a Jewish concoction. And, as in the case of the Russian Revolution, ample evidence was found to convince inflamed minds. Was not Rosa Luxemburg a leader of the Socialist uprising in January 1919? And the man who in November 1918 led the Communist revolution in Bavaria was Kurt Eisner whose enemies, before and after his assassination, made his Jewish origin their principal target, regardless of the fact that his assassin was also a non-Aryan. As for the Weimar Republic, the evidence was equally "convincing." The creator of the Weimar Constitution was the eminent political scientist Hugo Preuss, and one of its strongest champions was Hugo

Haase who in November 1919 was also struck down by the bullet of an assassin.

But the dominating figure in the early years of the republic, the man whom the world regarded as most likely to restore Germany to a dignified place in the community of civilized nations, and who, for that reason, drew upon himself the fiercest hatred of the "supermen," was Walter Rathenau. During the war, Rathenau had served his country as organizer of its industrial resources, a key post similar to the one held by Bernard Baruch in America. As Minister of Reconstruction and, later, as Foreign Minister under the Weimar Republic, Rathenau stood for the faithful performance by Germany of its treaty obligations, and he went a long way toward establishing genuine cooperation with France and Russia. He was, besides, a man of exalted spirit, a thinker and writer, and a proud Jew. Those crimes the "supermen" could not forgive, and on June 24, 1922, after a campaign of the vilest defamation, he too was assassinated. The civilized world was shocked, and the Republic gave Rathenau a state funeral; but the foul deed, for which the entire reactionary cabal was responsible, had removed a chief obstacle to the overthrow of the republic and the rise of the gutter to supreme power.

3

HOW it came about that a people of 65,000,000 surrendered voluntarily and unconditionally to that reckless and depraved group headed by Hitler, will probably always remain a mystery. Every enumeration of causes, including spiritual frustration, economic distress, and the fears and ambitions of groups and classes, fail somehow to add up to the fantastic and hideous total. It is not as if the German people were led blindfolded into a trap; by 1933 the exploits of the Nazi gangsters over more than a decade had made the character of the movement clear, and any remaining doubts had been removed by the leader himself in his writings, particularly in *Mein Kampf*, which he wrote after his ill-starred beer-hall *putsch* in Munich in November 1923. In this bible of nazism, which the Germans read with avidity and which ended by supplanting the Bible of their nominal faith, the nature of the enterprise, as well as its insane objectives, stand revealed. Throughout the world, moreover, the progress of nazism was observed without that sense of dismay to which it should have given rise. All through Christendom, and in Germany in particular, that triumph represents the most startling collapse of the ethics of Christianity which the ages have witnessed.

In this collapse the principal demoralizing factor was anti-Semitism and the diabolic cunning with which the Nazi hierarchy made use of it. From the frenzies of Adolf Hitler, the jeering of Josef Goebbels, the obscenities of Julius Streicher, and the distortions of the "philosopher" of nazism, Alfred Rosenberg, it is difficult to appraise to what extent anti-Semitism was a genuine passion with this hierarchy, and to what extent it was cold calculation. But to their followers, in Germany and elsewhere, it was the answer to all their prayers, the panacea for all their ills. And as for those in and out of Germany, including statesmen and others in high places, who were too wise to be taken in by the tricks of propaganda, the wild hue and cry against the Jews appeared at best as only an outlet for popular unrest, and at worst as a sword that hung over the heads of the Jews alone. The Nazi program, which secretly envisaged the enslavement or destruction of many nations, never made a secret of its purpose to annihilate the Jews. But there were those in all lands who refused to believe that so monstrous a deed was really intended, and there were others who refused to be disturbed by the prospect. A strange and fatal disease had smitten the nations, its symptoms a softening of the brain, or a hardening of the heart, or both.

4

QUICKLY the Nazis, summoned to power in January 1933 by Field Marshal Paul von Hindenburg, the senile president of the German Republic, replaced it with a dictatorship, and they lost no time in launching a campaign of terror against the Jews. It rose steadily until, by the outbreak of the Second World War less than seven years later, the German Jewish community was virtually obliterated. That community had been small in numbers—its 550,000 members representing less than 1 per cent of the country's population—but great in achievement. Among the 38 German Nobel prize winners, 11, or nearly 30 per cent, had been Jews, and not only the science, but the literature, the music, the art, and the drama of Germany had been enormously enriched by them. There had been tensions and defections in the inner life of the community, the urge toward self-effacement and total assimilation gaining steadily in force; but other tendencies had also asserted themselves, tendencies represented by men like Leo Baeck, the courageous communal leader, rabbi, and scholar; Martin Buber, the religious philosopher who revealed anew the spiritual treasures of Chassidism; and his collaborator Franz Rosenzweig, a spirit of heroic mold, for the last seven years of his life totally paralyzed, but producing works of rare depth and beauty. Nor had Zionism failed to attract large numbers of the youth, and in every city and town the ancient faith had been still zealously guarded and continued to dominate the communal life. And now a seven-year storm of hate swept over this community and destroyed it.

In those years of mounting savagery, certain events stand out. On May 10, 1933, books by Jewish authors—Mendelssohn, Heine, Auerbach, Wassermann, Feuchtwanger, Zweig and numerous others, as well as the Bible, were publicly burned, and the youth of the new Germany, party members, storm troopers, students, and teachers, danced and shouted around the bonfires. On September 15, 1935, at one of those monolithic rallies of the party robots in their shrine city of Nuremberg, the sweeping Nuremberg Laws were enacted which deprived all Jews of their citizenship, thus nullifying emancipation with a single stroke. But their civil status before the emancipation was incomparably higher than that which the Nuremberg Laws permitted them. For not only did the Nuremberg Laws restore the ghetto, but Jews were subjected to forced labor, deprived of their property and professions, and placed under the direct jurisdiction of the *Sicherheitsdienst* (SD), a department of the *Schutzstaffeln* (SS) later combined with the dread Gestapo, the *Geheime Staatspolizei*, or Secret State Police.

Less than a year later, a Race Bureau was established, which had no difficulty in persuading the scientists of Germany to prostitute their brains and pens in order to falsify history and sociology and diffuse their venomous lies through Germany and the entire world. Nor were the scientists alone in their infamy: the liberal professions and the arts were equally zealous. They expelled their Jewish members, and in the schools teachers inflicted torture on little children, holding them up to the ridicule and hatred of their classmates. In other lands, the sensitive few heard of those doings and were deeply disturbed. How, they asked, was it possible for a whole nation to sink so low? But the majority, including the governments, dismissed them as matters of internal policy with which other nations could not interfere.

5

FINALLY came November 10, 1938, when an orgy of violence, carefully prepared and thoroughly executed, swept through the *Reich*, which startled even the callous. Nazi Germany was already on the loose. In March of the same year, Austria had been overrun and annexed with all the techniques of fraud, subversion, and terror. In September had come the ignominious pact of Munich and the betrayal by England and France of Czechoslovakia, and, on the first of October, the dismemberment of this last refuge of democracy and decency in central Europe had begun. Then, on November 7, good Germans were enraged, and the Nazi hierarchs were no doubt delighted, to learn that in Paris a seventeen-year-old Jewish boy named Herschel Greenspan, driven frantic by news of the sufferings endured by his parents and thousands of other Polish Jews in the *Reich* who had been suddenly and brutally dumped across the Polish border, had shot and mortally wounded a minor official of the German embassy.

The official died on November 9, and before the dawn of the following day, the *Reich* "avenged itself" with an organized pogrom of unparalleled extent and ferocity. In hundreds of cities and towns throughout the land Jewish shops and homes were systematically looted and wrecked, five hundred synagogues were destroyed by fire, thousands of men, women, and children were beaten and maimed, scores, perhaps hundreds, were murdered, and thirty thousand of the more well-to-do were thrown into concentration camps and their property confiscated. This time there was a genuine feeling of uneasiness in the western democracies: apparently civilization was confronted with something new. But the huge pogrom was still a matter of German "internal policy" and not subject to the intervention of other governments. Besides, the beast would probably gorge itself on the Jews and become sated and tame, and the peace of Europe would not be broken. Franklin D. Roosevelt, the President of the United States, recalled his ambassador from Berlin: he alone of the leading statesmen of the world seemed to realize the enormity of the new thing the world was facing.

6

THE beast was not sated. In March of the following year, he devoured Bohemia and Moravia; in May, Germany and Italy concluded a formal military alliance; in August came a mutual non-aggression pact between Germany and Russia, giving the Nazis a free hand in eastern Europe; and on September 1, the mechanized Nazi hordes were streaming across the Polish borders. The "internal" war against the Jews had become the Second World War.

What in the meantime had been the fate of the German Jews whom the Gestapo torturers, the concentration camps, and the suicide waves had spared? By 1938 approximately 150,000 of them, the younger and more fortunate, had managed to escape by emigration, of whom some 35,000 found a haven in Palestine. November 10 was followed by intensified persecutions: a fine of a billion marks was imposed upon the victims; Jewish children who still attended the public schools were expelled; Jewish community life was hamstrung by decrees as well as by the arrest and incarceration of leaders and functionaries; and numerous other devices, damaging or only humiliating, were invented. Some refugees managed to find asylum in other lands on the continent, in England, and across the ocean in the United States, Canada, and Latin America. By the outbreak of the new war, those who remained in Germany were nearly all in concentration camps, in hiding, or were too old and feeble to merit the attention of the Gestapo.

In July 1938, on the invitation of the President of the United States, delegates from thirty-two countries met at Evian in France to devise measures, within the limitations imposed by their immigration laws, for speeding the rescue of the victims of the Nazi terror. There were noble speeches, but very little action. Many thousands of unfortunates found themselves caught between those immigration laws and the Nazis, and perished. It was a strange phenomenon. A new horror was on the rampage, and even the few among the nations who had eyes to see, stood paralyzed by their self-imposed limitations.

7

WAS nazism an offspring of Italian fascism? They had a great deal in common: a contempt for democracy, a delirious nationalism, terrorism as a state policy, an incurable compulsion toward aggression, the glorification of war. But unlike nazism, Italian fascism clashed with the temperament of the people it ruled, and it was only in 1938, under pressure from Berlin, that it adopted the credo of anti-Semitism. Fascism took possession of the Italian government in 1922, more than a decade before the triumph of the Nazis in Germany. The heroics of that "march on Rome" by Benito Mussolini and his Blackshirts, which made *il duce* dictator of Italy, have been exposed as a fraud, and to the movement as a whole there clung a suggestion of *opera bouffe* which the grandiose postures of the dictator did nothing to dispel.

But the original brand did not adopt the doctrines of racism. Until 1938, the 50,000 Jews in Italy, scattered in a population of 40,000,000, were on a par with their fellow citizens of other faiths, and even under fascism they continued to figure in the political, cultural, and military affairs of the kingdom. Jewish refugees from Germany found asylum in Italy; the universities kept their doors open to Jewish students from other lands; laws were enacted to protect the religious integrity of Jewish children in the public schools; and there were Jewish officials in the fascist government, some of them in high places, like Guido Jung who was Minister of Finance and Ludovico Mortara who was Chief Justice.

8

BUT apparently fascism and anti-Semitism cannot be separated, and it could not be otherwise even in Italy. The change began in 1935 with Mussolini's onslaught on Ethiopia, and it ripened in 1938 when, to all intents and purposes, Italy became a vassal of Germany. England's antagonism to his imperial progress, together with his desire to pose as the protector of Islam, led *il duce* to adopt a hostile attitude toward Zionism and to the people it represented. When, however, Italy entered into a military alliance with Germany, it seemed a foregone conclusion that the Nazi brand of anti-Semitism would be adopted by the junior partner. In the summer of 1938 the blow fell. It was preceded by a vicious newspaper barrage as in Germany, nor did it fail to enlist its retinue of "scientific" camp-followers—anthropologists, sociologists, and historians—to establish the superiority of the Italian "race" and the dangers that threatened it from the Jews! Laws were now decreed ordering the expulsion of all refugees and other Jews who had come in after January 1, 1919, and the schools and universities were "purged" of Jewish teachers and students. Nor would the policy stop there: its German sponsorship made that perfectly plain.

Thousands of Jews, in an environment where the ancient faith lay lightly on many of them, thought to save themselves by baptism. They relied on the help of the Vatican, for did not Pius XI, denouncing the new policy, declare that "spiritually we are all Semites"? But more effective help flowed from the Italian people, who were amazed and repelled by the new departure, seeing in it another act of subservience to the German master whom they hated. They continued to esteem and, whenever possible, to protect their Jewish friends and neighbors.

CHAPTER SIXTY-SIX

The "Long Truce" in Eastern Europe

RESURRECTED Poland required no pressure from Berlin to make anti-Semitism a national policy. The triumphant march of Nazism only added fuel to a long-standing passion which the heady nationalism that now swept over Poland had already inflamed. The new Polish chauvinism revealed its temper even before the sessions at Versailles were concluded. Disdaining to let the conference determine its boundaries, the new Poland took the matter into its own hands, attacked its neighbors north, east, and south, and in every case its ebullience ran over into "excesses," as the assaults were politely called, against the Jews.

Only ten days after the armistice, the Poles captured the Ukrainian city of Lemberg where they staged a pogrom with all the accompaniments of looting, arson, and murder. Not long afterwards, they seized the White Russian city of Pinsk where, without trial, they shot fifty of the leading men of the Jewish community and committed other outrages. Early in the spring of 1919, the Poles set out to "rectify" their northern boundary at the expense of Lithuania: they seized the cities of Lida and Vilna, where the soldiery disported themselves against the Jews in the same manner. Nor were the cities of the interior neglected: there were "excesses" in scores of places, in which all classes of the population took part. Beating Jews on the street, cutting off their beards, and throwing them from moving trains became favorite Polish pastimes. The American and British governments sent commissions of investigation to Poland, the American headed by Henry Morgenthau, former ambassador to Turkey, the British by Sir Stuart Samuel. The Polish ministers regretted and deplored and gave assurances, but nothing effective was done to curb the violence.

This mood of arrogant expansionism in which Poland began its new career could be sustained neither by its geography, nor social structure, nor economic resources. With no natural and defensible boundaries, Poland nevertheless chose to badger and attack its neighbors, instead of courting their good will. Instead of depending, like other minor powers, upon a strong League of Nations, Poland chose to swagger as a great power, and contributed to the humiliation of the League by flouting the obligations which it had assumed toward its minorities and which the League had guaranteed. With its peasantry pauperized by the land-owning *pans*, with the textile and leather industries, which the Jews had built up, all but ruined by the closure of the Russian market, with its mineral resources lying fallow, this beggar on horseback nevertheless chose to maintain a huge military establishment by which its gentry—the "colonels," as they have been designated—hoped to hold and augment their country's power.

The ideal Poland, as envisioned by its new chauvinists, was very much like the Russia for which Nicholas I had striven in his day:

it was to be a Poland of one nationality, one language, and one religion. This aim, however, did not deter the "colonels" from pursuing a policy of aggression which brought additional millions of different nationality and religion within Poland's boundaries. The biggest adventure of the sort occurred in the spring of 1920, when Soviet Russia, paralyzed by civil war, was invaded by the Poles under the leadership of the glamorous Jozef Pilsudski. The invasion ravaged the border regions, and again the principal sufferers were the Jews. In the summer, Russia found the strength to drive the Poles back, and Warsaw was only saved when the French came to its rescue. Nevertheless, Poland achieved an eastern boundary far beyond the so-called Curzon Line, and hosts of Ukrainians, White Russians, and Jews were added to its unhappy minorities.

2

ALL the minorities in Poland were oppressed, but the most vicious and sustained assaults were directed against the minority which lacked what the others had: the protection of a land and government of their own kith and kin. As the uneasy truce between the two world wars continued and, in the late thirties, reached the breaking point, the fury of the Poles went crescendo. The security of the sprawling Polish domains, hemmed in between Germany and Russia, both of whom nursed Irredentist resentments against the upstart, became more precarious; the economic plight of the impoverished land, weighed down by its top-heavy military establishment, became catastrophic; and the "colonels," aided and abetted by the clergy, found it convenient and easy to direct the mounting anxiety and distress against the eternal scapegoat.

The primary aim of the government was to dislodge the Jews from the middle-class positions they had occupied for centuries, and transfer them to the growing number of Poles who were flocking from the impoverished farms to the cities and towns. To attain that goal the weapon employed by the National Democrats, or Endeks, and other anti-Semitic parties, was the economic boycott, seasoned with terror, while the role of the government was to enact legislation designed to deprive the Jews of their livelihoods. Thousands of small enterprises—clothing factories, shoe factories, food and dry goods shops, and others—were boycotted or taxed out of existence. Large-scale enterprises, like the salt, liquor, and tobacco industries, sources of livelihood for thousands of Jewish families, were transformed into state monopolies, which, like the public utilities and the civil services, denied employment to Jews. Suddenly the government discovered that the ritual method of slaughtering cattle was inhumane, and the law which was passed prohibiting it drove more thousands to destitution.

The Polish Jews were reduced to an appalling state of poverty. The revolving Loan Funds, or *kassas*, to enable artisans to purchase tools and raw materials which, with the help of the Joint Distribution Committee, were established in hundreds of towns and cities, did something to mitigate their plight; but the number of families who at one time or another were compelled to resort to charity was staggering. Polish leaders brazenly declared that the Jews, whose forebears had lived in the land for nearly a thousand years, were a "superfluous" element of the population.

The ruin of the Jews, however, did not, as these leaders had promised, bring prosperity to the Poles. On the contrary, Poland's economic fortunes sank lower and lower, with a disastrous inflation which paved the way for the bloody coup in May 1926 by which Pilsudski established a military dictatorship over the country.

3

AS IN previous periods of its long career, so in the two dismal decades between the world wars the great Jewish community of Poland defied the "economic interpretation of history." That ancient source of consolation, their faith, with the hallowed institutions that were part and parcel of it, maintained its vigor. In Yeshivoth, synagogues, and homes, Talmudic learning continued to flourish, and Chassidic communities gathered around their revered leaders and cultivated their intense religious life from which gloom was banished as sin. To this enduring font, a new spring of hope and pride was added, especially for the young: the growing Yishuv in Palestine with its promise of national and personal redemption. For many of them between 1920 and 1939, it was more than a promise: during those years, 125,000 Polish Jews escaped into Palestine, and under the banner of organizations like

Hechalutz (The Pioneer), Poland became the principal source and training ground for the young men and women who drained the marshes, cleared the rocks, built the roads, and restored the waste places of the ancient motherland.

All groupings of Polish Jewry—and there were many—cultivated the things of the mind and spirit, applying themselves especially to the education of the young. To the traditional *cheder*, where most of the boys were still taught, were added the schools of *Tarbut* (Culture), supported chiefly by the Zionists, with emphasis on Hebrew, and Yiddish schools which were identified with the Socialist *Bund*. Both Zionists and Bundists found themselves challenged by the ultra-Orthodox Agudas Israel, which sponsored the Beth Jacob schools for girls, an educational enterprise that had its inspiration in the zeal of Sarah Shenirer, one of the remarkable women of the generation. There was a flourishing press in Yiddish, Polish, and Hebrew: in 1930 it included 130 newspapers and other periodicals, with a circulation of well over half a million. There was also a large and steady flow of books, both secular and religious, the combined annual editions running into the millions; and the theater stood on a high artistic level and was greatly prized.

The different groups and parties were eager to play their part in politics also. The "Poles of the Mosaic Persuasion," who, of course, refused to identify themselves with the Jewish minority, had lost their influence; the Zionists were now the dominant force, as was demonstrated in the general election of 1922 when 34 Jewish deputies and 12 senators who formed a bloc or "club" of their own, were returned to the parliament. The club was headed by Isaac Gruenbaum, Zionist leader and intrepid champion of minority rights. These rights, however, remained practically a dead letter, although the decree of 1927, issued by the more friendly Pilsudski government to regulate the inner organization of Polish Jewry, represented a more liberal tendency.

4

THE triumph of Nazism in Germany in 1933 inspired the Polish anti-Semites across the border with fresh boldness and a new vision. With fatuous blindness they ignored the handwriting on the wall announcing the doom of their own country, and rejoiced instead at the sanction they obtained from a nation which, unlike their own, ranked among the leaders of world culture. They dreamed of the elimination of the three and a half million Jews of Poland, and they saw it accomplished not by the slow method of legislation, but by the swifter courses advocated by the Nazis. The Polish disciples of Nazism grew more violent; riots and pogroms became almost daily occurrences. Poles discovered that they too were "Aryans," and proceeded to expel "non-Aryans" from professional and trade organizations.

The most violent manifestations developed in the universities. The faculties had already been "Aryanized," and now the students, encouraged by their teachers, launched a campaign of violence designed to drive the Jewish students from the classrooms. The Jewish students struck back at their attackers, and the universities resounded with riots and brawls which often compelled the authorities to close them. The "Aryans" came forward with a new device, which also hailed from Germany: they demanded that in every classroom the Jewish students should be segregated: the humiliation, they hoped, would be more effective than brass knuckles and less risky. In 1937 the government acceded to the demand, and ghetto-benches were legalized throughout Poland. The Jewish students refused to occupy them. They were supported by a few professors; the more radical trade unions also protested; and there were repercussions in academic circles in other countries, including America. The same year, the Camp for National Unity was organized as a single party on the Nazi model, with an elaborate anti-Jewish program. The anti-Semitic clamor in Poland became louder: it was only in September 1939 that it was stilled by the roar of Nazi cannon and the shrieking of Nazi bombs.

5

THE seizure of Vilna by the Poles dealt a staggering blow to the Republic of Lithuania, another offspring of the First World War, and to the 150,000 Jews who were left within its borders. Lithuania had begun by honoring the treaty provisions with respect to minority rights. It recognized a Jewish National Council with power to levy taxes for community needs; Jewish schools were subsidized by the state; and there was even a minister for

Jewish affairs in the cabinet. But year after year, as the chauvinism of the Lithuanians, embittered by Polish aggression, became more intense and economic distress deepened, these rights were whittled away or altogether abolished. Instead, the usual methods for purging the Jews from their middle-class positions, like their exclusion from government services, the nationalization of certain industries, the promotion of cooperatives, the enactment of Sunday closing laws, and the imposition of heavy taxes, were vigorously pursued until the majority of the Jewish population was reduced to pauperism.

In 1938, the Nazis, flushed with their triumph in Austria and Czechoslovakia, seized the Lithuanian port of Memel together with a large strip of adjacent territory, most of the Jews escaping with their bare lives. In spite of their destitute state, however, which only relief from abroad made supportable, the Jews of Lithuania remained true to their high tradition of scholarship and learning: they continued, at immense sacrifices, to maintain their schools and academies.

6

OVER half a million Jews were added to the subjects of King Ferdinand of Rumania as a result of the First World War, bringing the total to nearly 900,000, and all of them, during the interval between the two wars, learned what it meant to be at the mercy of cynical and corrupt politicians with experience and skill in violating treaty obligations. The ministers outdid themselves in chicanery to nullify not only the cultural rights which the peace treaty conferred upon the minorities, who made up nearly 30 per cent of Rumania's 18,000,000 inhabitants, but also the more basic rights of equal citizenship. A law of 1924 required applicants for citizenship to produce documents proving ten years' residence prior to 1918; the papers were in numerous cases unobtainable, and well over 100,000 Jews were left in the tragic category of people without a country.

The economic pattern of Rumania was very much like that of Poland, with a small class of boyars, or landowning gentry, exploiting millions of impoverished peasants whose sons and daughters were eager for the middle-class positions in the cities and towns.

Since those positions were in large measure held by the Jews, the gentry saw in anti-Semitism a convenient lightning rod for deflecting the bolts from their own heads. The youth of the land, especially the student youth, found in it a focus not only for their personal grievances and ambitions, but for their inflamed chauvinism as well. Under the inspiration of the venomous and veteran anti-Semite, Alexander Cuza, the few and overcrowded universities became the scenes of violent manifestations. There were numerous bloody brawls, and frequently the universities had to be closed. There were also two deliberate murders, one in 1921 by Cornelius Codreanu, leader of the Fascist Iron Guard, who in open court shot to death a police officer who had had the courage to arrest a number of student rioters; the other, three years later by a student "patriot" who, also in open court, killed a Jewish student who had dared protest against his exclusion. Both murderers were acquitted and the acquittals were hailed with frenzied demonstrations which boiled over into attacks on Jews. In 1926, the students held a Congress in Jassy, the following year in Oradea Mare; on both occasions they gave vent to their exuberance by attacking Jews and wrecking, burning, and looting their possessions.

The government made no serious efforts to discourage these outbursts; in 1926 Judah Loeb Zirelsohn, Chief Rabbi of Kishinev and a member of the Rumanian Senate, resigned from that body when a speech he delivered in protest against the official tolerance of pogroms was excluded from the record.

7

RUMANIAN anti-Semitism, fanned by the green-shirted demagogues of the Iron Guard, openly encouraged by leading prelates like Miron Christea, the Grand Patriarch of the Greek Orthodox Church, and abetted by government and big business, continued to mount. It was a perfect outlet for all woes and frustrations, a simple and safe expedient for achieving the status of a "hero," a tempting target for every sadistic urge. Not even Julius Maniu, leader of the National Peasant party, who realized that anti-Semitism was a device for diverting attention from the real authors of his country's woes, and who in 1928 became head of the government, could stem the turbulent flood. In 1930, the agitation gained fresh fuel when King Carol returned to Bucharest from his self-imposed exile to the delights of Paris, and assumed possession of the throne, bringing with him his mistress Magda Lupescu, the daughter of a Jewish apothecary. Was it not the final proof that the country was completely in the hands of the Jews?

But the most powerful stimulus to the ambitions of the anti-Semites came, of course, in 1933 when the Nazis took possession of Germany. Now the Cuzas, the Codreanus, and the Christeas knew where to turn for inspiration and direction. They began by attempting to bring an end to Rumania's alliance with France and to hitch their country to the chariot of Nazi Germany. They proceeded to purge Jews from the arts, the professions, and even from commerce and the trades. In December 1937, an inconclusive election brought the Fascist Octavian Goga into the post of prime minister for a period of seven weeks. His wild measures brought the country to the brink of ruin, but a law was framed and adopted under his successor, Christea, by which Rumania, in violation of its treaty obligations, deprived over 300,000 Jews of their citizenship and with it of the right to earn a livelihood.

But Codreanu and his Iron Guard, still unsatisfied, prepared to seize the government; whereupon a typically Balkan political maneuver followed: Codreanu and his principal aides were first jailed, then liquidated. Nazi agents, in the meantime, were busy in Rumania, corrupting and intimidating, always fanning the fires of anti-Semitism, their principal device for confusing and subverting men and nations. As the Nazi monster, coiling eastward across Czechoslovakia, revealed his true visage, Rumania recovered somewhat from its blind obsession. It was too late: in helpless dismay it waited for its doom.

8

IN NO country of Europe was the status of a large and noble Jewish community altered so promptly and tragically by the aftermath of the First World War as in Hungary. Here was a land of which, twenty-five years earlier, Baron de Hirsch had ventured to prophesy that it would never know the bane of anti-Semitism, a land to which the Jews were proudly and passionately attached, where they played a heroic part in war and a creative role in peace and where, besides, they were free and unafraid to lead their own inner life. Only a year after the armistice, all of that was changed; and by the end of the interval that separates the two wars, more than half of the 700,000 members of the community had been legislated out of their livelihoods and all of them reduced by law to the status of outcasts. Two major causes operated to produce the tragedy. The first was the abortive social revolution in the spring and summer of 1919 and the rampage which the reaction unloosed against the Jews; the second was the triumph of nazism in Germany in 1933 and the ferocious anti-Semitic passions it aroused in Hungary, as it did everywhere else.

The Treaty of Trianon, which the victorious Allies imposed on Hungary, reduced that country to less than a third of its former size. It dealt the proud Magyars a demoralizing blow, and the moment seemed auspicious for an attempt to change the economic order after the manner of the Bolshevist Revolution in Russia. The attempt, led by Bela Kun, the son of a Jewish peddler, was smothered in a welter of blood and chaos. The Allies tightened the blockade around the destitute country. The Rumanians seized and looted Budapest in an orgy of terrorism. They were followed by a government of the feudal barons, headed by Admiral Horthy, who proceeded to erase every vestige of the revolution, particularly the agrarian reforms.

Naturally the full fury of the White Terror fell upon the Jews. It would no doubt have fallen upon them in any case, notwithstanding that, as members of the middle class, they were the first victims of Bela Kun and his Bolshevism; but the fact that the revolutionary leader was a Jew inflamed the lust of the Awakening Magyars, the Hungarian counterpart of the Rumanian Iron Guard. The terror raged practically unchecked by the authorities. Communities were devastated, thousands of Jews were murdered, other thousands were blackmailed and plundered. Not even the baptized found safety from the greed which paraded as patriotism, and which the barons found an effective outlet for the discontent of the wretched peasants who coveted their land. Nor did the Awakening Magyars neglect to "provide" for their middle classes also. The entire apparatus of boycott against Jewish trade was imported from Poland, and the terror was extended to the universities where, in 1922, a *numerus clausus* was instituted by law. After a struggle of more than five years, waged by Jewish bodies outside Hungary through the League of Nations, the law was "changed": Jews were not explicitly named, but the effect of the new provisions was exactly the same.

After a reign of terror which lasted nearly two years, a better day dawned for Hungary and its Jewish community under the government headed by Stephen Bethlen. In the elections of 1922, the anti-Semites were defeated and the country seemed disposed to return to its pre-war tradition of decency when the march of nazism in Germany, combined with the world-wide economic depression, restored the anti-Semitic specter in a form even more menacing. Two methods of "solving" the Jewish problem in Hungary began a struggle for mastery. The first, advocated by groups of stalwarts like the Awakening Magyars and by politicians like Julius Gombos, who were prepared to deliver their country, lock, stock and barrel, to Germany, was the gangster method of the Nazis as legalized in the Nuremberg Laws. The second was the "civilized" method of the government, by which as many Jews as possible were to be deprived of their livelihood as quickly as possible. Under the premiership of Bela Imredy, the second prevailed. In May 1939, a law was passed with stringent quotas for Jews in industry, commerce, finance, and the arts and professions, and more than half of them were brought face to face with the immediate prospect of destitution and, eventually, with extinction.

A note of grim comedy was added to the situation when Imredy was compelled to resign because the Hungarian Nazis, in their rage against the "civilized" method of the government, searched and found that the prime minister was himself descended from a Jewish great-grandmother. A more somber note was injected when his successor, Count Paul Telecki, who had engineered the law through the parliament, committed suicide when he saw his country fall into the grip of Germany. But there was small consolation in those events for the proud Jews of Hungary, who had given so much to the civilization and defense of their country. Some seventy years had passed since their emancipation in 1867, and the hopes which that event aroused now lay in ruins around them.

9

THE Treaty of Saint-Germain, with which the victors of the First World War snuffed out the once proud and mighty Austrian Empire, left Austria proper an impoverished little republic, with a population of somewhat more than six million, of whom a disproportionate number, amounting to more than two million, lived in Vienna. That gay and elegant metropolis was now a queen of rags and tatters, but still a queen. In it too there lived nearly 90 per cent of the 200,000 Jews in the country, and they fell victim to all the economic ills with which the stripped and exhausted state was afflicted and, in addition, to the relentless hostility nourished by the church, the Pan-Germanic movement, and the reactionaries. As the star of the Nazis mounted, this hostility of course received new stimulation from the more virulent brand that flourished in Germany.

The old animosity found numerous ways to express itself. In 1919, it pounced upon the hundreds of thousands of refugees from Galicia and other provinces, and succeeded in expelling the great majority of them. From Poland and Rumania, it imported the boycott and the "crusade" against Jewish students in the universities. It had its armies and shirted rowdies who paraded and shouted and rioted.

In Vienna the Jewish youth, particularly in the university, exacted a price from the anti-Semites for their exuberance. In Vienna, the Jews were not unbefriended, for while the federal government of the Republic was clerical, the municipal administration of Vienna was Socialist. Under its bold and liberal government, in which a number of Jews, including Otto Bauer, Julius Deutsch, and Hugo Breitner, played a distinguished part, the metropolis, after 1923, began to make remarkable progress, particularly in public health and housing for workers. The workers of Vienna were not slow to see the enemy of their best interests in anti-Semitism; every project for their welfare was denounced by the reactionaries as "Jewish" and "Bolshevist."

The ten years that followed were marked by a struggle between the clerical Federal Diet and the Socialist municipality of Vienna. The depression which began in 1929, highlighted in 1931 by the failure of the *Credit Anstalt*, had a crippling effect on the municipal government; and early in 1934, the struggle ended disastrously for Vienna when Engelbert Dolfuss, the clerical chancellor of the Republic, turned the guns of his *Heimwehr* on the workers' apartments, killing hundreds of the occupants, men, women, and children, and afterwards liquidating the Socialist leaders.

But the victory did not put an end to the internecine strife. Now it became a tug of war between the clerical Fascists led by Dolfuss, who stood for the independence of Austria, and the Pan-German Nazis who yearned for Austria's absorption into the Third Reich. Both, of course, were wedded to anti-Semitism, but the Dolfuss brand was less virulent, and the Jews were reduced to hoping and praying that the chancellor would prevail. They hoped and prayed in vain. On July 25, 1934, Dolfuss was assassinated by the Nazis, and his successor Kurt Schuschnigg, after resisting the tightening ring of provocation, threats, and terror for nearly four years, yielded to an ultimatum from the German *fuehrer*. He resigned his office to a Nazi who, on March 13, 1938, proclaimed the union of Austria and Germany.

The invasion and seizure of the helpless little state, which had occurred the day before, unleashed a flood of Nazi savagery against the Jews that was so far without parallel. The Nuremberg Laws and all the techniques of Gestapo sadism, which in Germany had taken five years to perfect, were applied overnight in Austria. The criminal dregs of society were invited to give free play to their lusts, and they were joined by large numbers of the average and "respectable," in whom the same appetites are normally held in leash. Unspeakable humiliations were inflicted on rabbis and other leaders of the community; men who stood in the vanguard of European culture were hounded, beaten, and exiled; many thousands were herded into old and new concentration camps; Jewish establishments and homes became the prey of official and unofficial looters; and the number of suicides is estimated to have reached two thousand.

It was twilight and night for the Jewish community in Austria. It was the doom of Austria also, and especially of Vienna—the Vienna of civilized and decent human beings, of sparkling music and books and drama, of elegant art and solid science, the Vienna that owed so much to Jewish writers, musicians, artists, and scientists. In place of all that now lowered like a vulture the vast, formless, and obscene shadow of Nazism.

10

PERHAPS the only European creation of the Peace Conference that answered to President Wilson's plea "to make the world safe for democracy," was the Republic of Czechoslovakia. Here was a new state wedged into central Europe, surrounded by neighbors who eyed it with no good will and saddled with disgruntled minorities, which, nevertheless, stood as a bulwark and beacon of democracy and decency. Prague, its capital, became a center of European culture, more vigorous if less mellow than Vienna, and without the economic and racial tensions that disturbed the Austrian metropolis.

The new republic was exceptionally fortunate in its statesmen. Thomas Masaryk, who was chosen to be its first president in 1918 at an assembly in the United States, when Czechoslovakia was only a dream, was a distinguished scholar and an experienced political leader. He was, above all, an ardent champion of justice: in 1899 Leopold Hilsner, accused of ritual murder, had found in him a fearless and powerful defender. And Eduard Benes, Masaryk's pupil and foreign minister who in 1936 succeeded him to the presidency, displayed the same qualities as his master. The Czechoslovak republic accepted the principle of minority rights willingly, and applied it with sincere good will, the only state in Europe to do so. The 350,000 Jews who lived within its borders were equal citizens, their rights as a religious and cultural group respected, and they were free from the bane of official and unofficial anti-Semitism.

But after 1933 the shadow of Nazi Germany began to darken its eastern neighbor. The technique of subversion and disintegration was simple enough: its principal weapon was the lie, shouted from Berlin and echoed by Konrad Henlein's Nazi party across the border, that the German minority in the Sudetenland was being oppressed and tortured by the Czechs. At the other end of the Republic, the same technique was adopted by the Slovak separationists, led by the priest Andreas Hlinka. Both Germans and Slovaks, it goes without saying, added anti-Semitism to their arsenal, the Hlinka Guards in Slovakia vying with the Iron Guard of Rumania in the criminal depravity of its followers and in terror against the Jews.

In its mortal peril, the Czechoslovak republic relied on its creators and guarantors, primarily on England and France. It was a vain trust. In September 1938, the abject surrender in Munich of Neville Chamberlain and Edouard Daladier, the prime ministers of Britain and France respectively, gave the signal not only to Germany but to Poland and Hungary also to violate their neighbor's frontiers and seize its territory. For another half-year, the mangled republic preserved a nominal independence; then, in March 1939, the Nazi mechanized hordes overran the provinces of Bohemia and Moravia. Slovakia, now a puppet of Hitler, declared its independence, and the last flickering light of freedom in central Europe was extinguished.

Now the Jews of Prague and the rest of the murdered republic, all except the small number who managed to escape, became the victims of the bestiality that had overwhelmed the Jews of Austria a year earlier; and among them were many who had fled to Czechoslovakia from Austria and Germany. The Nuremberg Laws were promptly introduced, and the Gestapo machinery of plunder, torture, and concentration camps, which practice had made perfect, was brought to bear against helpless men, women, and children. The Hlinka Guards in Slovakia deserve a special citation for infamy and depravity.

In one respect, however, the Nazis failed: their confidence that the Czechs would be pleased by the spectacle of the spoliation and torture of their Jewish neighbors, an expectation which figured in the blueprint of all their aggressions, proved false. The Czechs refused to be placated: for their conquerors they nursed in their hearts nothing but contempt and hatred, a hatred wary and patient, but implacable.

CHAPTER SIXTY-SEVEN

The "Long Truce" in the West

BY THE end of the two decades between the wars, the countries of central and eastern Europe, with the exception of the Soviet Union, had been forced into the orbit of Nazi Germany. It was done by violence, by fraud, by economic pressure, by fifth columns, by intimidation, by invasion. In most of those countries the democratic tradition was neither old enough nor strong enough to withstand the aggressor's ideology; and it is significant that even in attempting to resist him some of them were driven to adopt his political system. Thus, in 1934 King Boris of Bulgaria established a dictatorship; the same year the assassination of Alexander of Yugoslavia hardened the dictatorship which he had set up five years earlier; and in 1936 Greece found her dictator in General Metaxas. In all three, the Jewish communities—50,000 in Bulgaria, 70,000 in Yugoslavia, 100,000 in Greece—watched this rise of totalitarianism with deep foreboding, accompanied as it was, especially in Greece and Bulgaria, by anti-Semitic rumblings. In the west, however, the Nazi octopus met with a resistance that lay deeper and in the end, after the most titanic struggle in history, destroyed him. The west included Germany's immediate neighbors; it included Great Britain; it included finally the United States and the entire Western Hemisphere.

2

FRANCE, living in the shadow of the monster and exposed to all his corrosive arts, nevertheless remained true to its liberal and democratic tradition. For the Jewish community, which by 1939 after an influx of one hundred thousand refugees from Germany and Poland, numbered a quarter of a million souls, France stood firm as a symbol of equality and decency, and the Jews maintained their high place in the life of the nation. They raised it.

in fact, when on June 4, 1936, Leon Blum, leader of the *Front Populaire*, and embodying in himself an integration of French and Jewish loyalty, became the head of the first French Socialist government.

Not that France was immune to anti-Semitism. Leon Daudet and his *Camelots du Roi* still fanned the smoking embers of the Dreyfus Affair. There were French admirers of nazism, like François Coty, a manufacturer of cosmetics, who specialized in disseminating that malodorous forgery, the Protocols of the Elders of Zion. There were Fascist writers like Charles Maurras. There were the *Cagoulards*, a secret society which borrowed the trappings of the American Ku Klux Klan, receiving its inspiration and maintenance from Germany. There was even an anti-Semitic flurry against Blum in the Chamber of Deputies when he first appeared as premier. But the nation as a whole, and the governments which succeeded each other all too often, had no illusions about the aims of the movement or the source from which it was fed. In 1939, the government even adopted curbs against anti-Semitism, making race defamation a criminal offense.

But the Third Republic, particularly after the world depression which began in 1929, floundered in a sea of troubles that threatened to overwhelm it. The antagonism of parties and classes grew more bitter, bringing armed clashes in the principal cities at a time when the position of France as the leading continental power was being undermined by the growing strength of Nazi Germany and the mounting bluster of Fascist Italy. Both of them, moreover, with cynical frankness, aided and abetted the rise of a Nazi-Fascist Spain on its southern border. Turn where it would, France found no aid or comfort. The League of Nations had been reduced to impotence; the policy of collective security, of which the Soviet Foreign Minister, Maxim Litvinov, was the leading advocate, foundered on the rock of suspicion against Communist Russia; while Britain, upon whom France was compelled to lean more and more heavily, embarked upon the policy dear to the heart of the reactionary Cliveden Set, the policy of appeasing the Nazis and Fascists of which the surrender at Munich was the high water mark and symbol.

In the main, Frenchmen thought they were safe behind their

Maginot Line; but the Jews of France, those whose past was rooted in the country and, even more so, the recent refugees, watched with growing dismay the Fascist encirclement of the land they loved and the progressive decay of its domestic peace. Their alarm was shared by men throughout the world for whom France was still the bright symbol of democracy and European culture. This France, the France of decent and civilized men, the France that the corruptionists of Berlin called decadent, appeared to be ripe for the black reaper.

3

THE machinery of corruption and disintegration set up by the Nazi regime was, of course, directed against the smaller countries of western Europe also. In Belgium it produced Leon Degrelle and his Rexists, who entered the political arena in 1936. In Holland the *fuehrer* was Alfred von Mussert, who by 1935 had built up a not inconsiderable following. In Switzerland it was Wilhelm Gustloff, whose career of subversion and terror was ended abruptly early in 1936 by the revolver of a Jewish student named David Frankfurter. There were Nazi cells in Denmark and Sweden, while in Norway, Vidkun Quisling achieved the distinction of giving all languages a new word connoting treason, stratagem, and spoils. It goes without saying that the principal weapon employed everywhere was anti-Semitism, the bait with which the demagogues won their following.

But in all those countries the democratic tradition was old and strong, and the pollution that flowed from Berlin and Nuremberg was only a froth on the surface of their national life. The Jews, however, were deeply disturbed by it. In 1934, the leaders of the Swiss community won a libel suit against a Nazi editor who was promoting the Protocols of the Elders of Zion; the plaintiffs had no great difficulty in proving the screed a forgery. In Holland, racial defamation was made a criminal offense, and in all those lands governments and public opinion, moved by a sense of justice as well as by the realization that anti-Semitism was clearing the roads for German invasion, held the agitation in check. But with all this sympathy and good will, the Jews lived with a feeling of insecurity, mounting at times to a sense of impending disaster which the hardships and tensions produced by the world depression did nothing to allay.

4

BRITAIN too held fast to its democratic heritage; even its appeasers justified the succulent repasts which Prime Minister Neville Chamberlain was allowing the ravenous monster on the ground that the country was woefully unprepared for war, psychologically as well as militarily. Thousands of fugitives from the furnace of Nazi terror were admitted into England. The persecutions, and especially the huge pogrom of November 10, 1938, evoked a storm of protest from the leaders of British public opinion, and former prime minister Stanley Baldwin headed a campaign which raised a considerable fund for the relief of the victims. The British government, as well as the French, explored though without success the possibilities of settling large numbers of Jewish refugees in some of their colonial possessions. Nevertheless a curious lack of understanding of the character of nazism persisted in large and influential British circles. There were high-placed Britons, like Nevile Henderson, the ambassador to Germany himself, who stood before the sinister apparition with helpless incredulity.

But the Jews, in England as everywhere else, understood it only too well: for, in the words of the Psalmist they could say: "the plowers plowed upon my back, they made long their furrows." Small wonder, therefore, that manifestations of anti-Semitism in England disturbed them profoundly. In the first decade of the "long truce," those manifestations bore a surface respectability: they cropped up in the ultraconservative press like the London *Morning Post*, where the Bolshevist bogey was furnished with Jewish features, and they appeared in the polished writings of Gilbert Chesterton and Hilaire Belloc. It was, however, another matter when in the early thirties a *fuehrer* arose in England. He was the wealthy and socially prominent Sir Oswald Mosley, who became the head of a Union of British Fascists, drawing their inspiration, as well as their trappings and methods, from Rome and Berlin. When, as was inevitable, anti-Semitism became their staple and rowdyism their pastime, the Jewish youth of London reacted vigorously. Late in 1936 they broke up a mass demonstration of the Union, and shortly afterwards its semi-military formations, modeled on the Nazi storm troopers, were outlawed.

In Britain, the Jewish community numbered about 300,000, and in the British dominions there was an equal number, of whom 175,000 were in Canada and 95,000 in South Africa. But, as the mandatory for Palestine, Britain stood in a special relationship to the entire Jewish people. It was natural, therefore, that Jewish communities the world over should be keenly interested in social and political currents in England. They rejoiced when the British social fabric proved itself capable of repelling the incursions of the Nazi ideology. They were not so happy with the appeasement policy of the British statesmen who seemed to hope they could feed the Nazi-Fascist tiger and keep the lamb of democracy whole. They were embittered and amazed by the British course in Palestine, a course of vacillation and concession to violence, of retreat from solemn pledges and legal obligations, the course which had its climax in the White Paper of May 1939, issued by the same cabinet which had approved the Munich surrender eight months earlier. It was a curiously paradoxical attitude which the Jews of the world held toward England: an attitude of admiration and gratitude, but one also of bitter resentment and distrust.

5

THOUSANDS of fugitives from Nazi terror found asylum in Canada and in the countries of Central and South America. In Canada, fascism exerted a strong lure on the French Catholics in the province of Quebec, where there were marked anti-Semitic manifestations. With the exception of Argentina, the republics of Central and South America, held by the gravitational force of the economic power and the good neighbor diplomacy of the United States, hewed in the main to the democratic line, although the Falange, inspired and nourished by Fascist Spain, continued its subversive efforts in all of them. Argentina fell into the hands of a Fascist military dictatorship, and that country, harboring the largest Jewish community on the continent, became the base of Nazi intrigue in the Western Hemisphere.

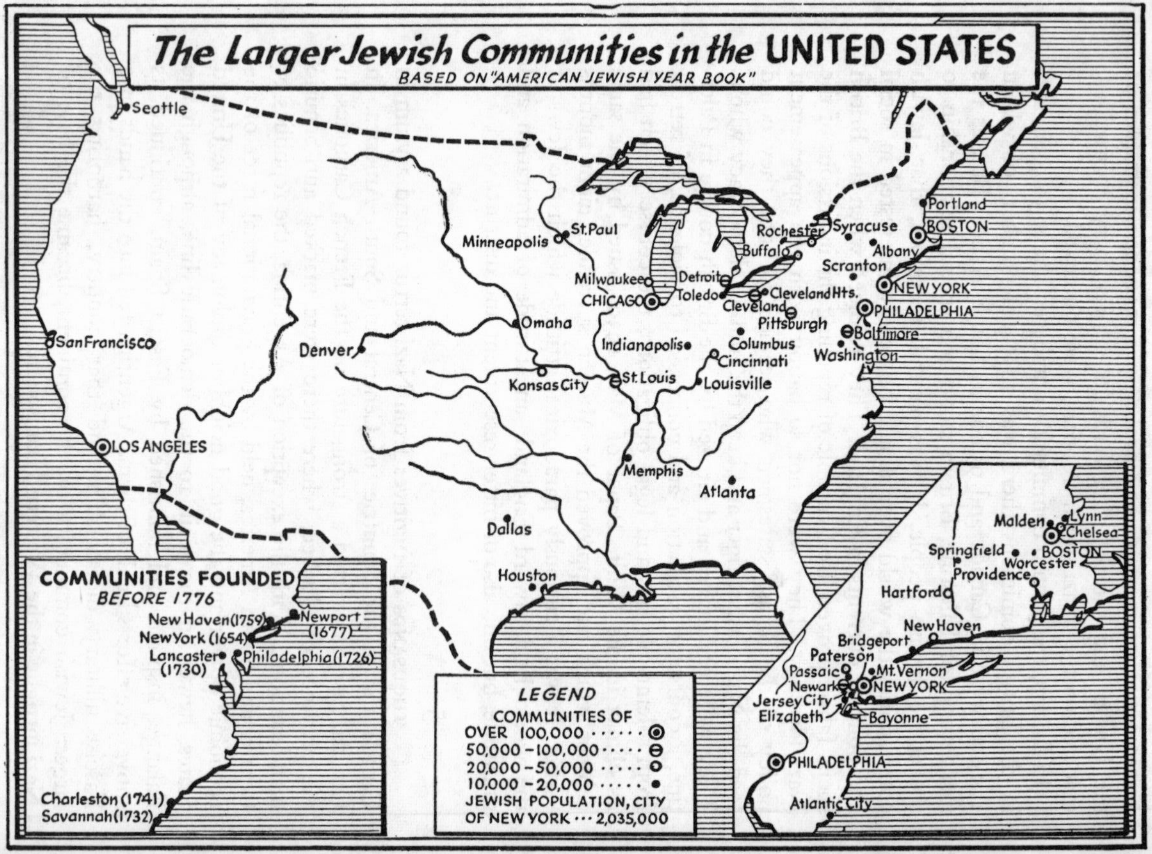

The Larger Jewish Communities in the UNITED STATES
BASED ON "AMERICAN JEWISH YEAR BOOK"
Seattle
San Francisco
LOS ANGELES
Denver
Minneapolis
St. Paul
Omaha
Kansas City
Dallas
Houston
Milwaukee
CHICAGO
Indianapolis
St. Louis
Memphis
Louisville
Cincinnati
Columbus
Atlanta
Detroit
Toledo
Cleveland
Cleveland Hts.
Pittsburgh
Buffalo
Rochester
Syracuse
Albany
Scranton
Portland
BOSTON
NEW YORK
PHILADELPHIA
Baltimore
Washington
COMMUNITIES FOUNDED
BEFORE 1776
New Haven (1759)
Newport (1677)
New York (1654)
Lancaster (1730)
Philadelphia (1726)
Charleston (1741)
Savannah (1732)
LEGEND
COMMUNITIES OF
OVER 100,000
50,000 – 100,000
20,000 – 50,000
10,000 – 20,000
JEWISH POPULATION, CITY OF NEW YORK ... 2,035,000
Malden
Lynn
Chelsea
BOSTON
Springfield
Worcester
Providence
Hartford
New Haven
Bridgeport
Paterson
Passaic
Mt. Vernon
Newark
NEW YORK
Jersey City
Elizabeth
Bayonne
PHILADELPHIA
Atlantic City

In the annals of the Jewish people Argentina figures as the one land other than Palestine where the most determined effort was made to bring them back to their earliest calling, the cultivation of the soil. In 1930, the results of that effort, promoted by the lavish philanthropy of Baron de Hirsch, were approximately 40,000 Jews still living in agricultural settlements. In Buenos Aires and other urban centers there was a vigorous Jewish communal life, expressing itself in religious, charitable, and cultural institutions, with newspapers, daily and weekly, in Yiddish and Spanish.

There were sizable communities also in Brazil and Uruguay. In the latter, where some of the Jews are farmers and professional soldiers, the largest group is in Montevideo. In Brazil, where their story goes back to the discovery of the land, and whence sailed the first group to settle in what became the United States, they numbered in 1930 about 30,000, half of them in Rio de Janeiro. To all those lands, the refugees, many of whom were equipped with capital and industrial skill, have brought economic benefit, and to the existing Jewish communities they have added fresh vitality.

6

FOR the Jewish community of the United States, the "long truce" was a period of impressive growth. In numbers it rose from three and a half million to nearly five. It extended its role in every sphere of the nation's life, and in growing measure it drew on its resources for the alleviation of Jewish distress abroad, the defense of Jewish rights everywhere, and the upbuilding of the national home in Palestine. In the religious and cultural sphere also, the two decades witnessed an intensification of effort on the part of every group, especially the Orthodox, although the centrifugal forces, reflected in the general tendency toward secularization and in the urge to total assimilation, took a heavy toll, especially in the smaller communities of the land.

There was a quickening also of the sense of cohesion, or at least of the desire for it, with no leveling, however, of the ideological barriers separating the various groups, and with only occasional union for common action. In general American Jewry was far from constituting that compact and purposeful organism which the sworn anti-Semites professed to see in it. It did not think alike, or vote alike, or act together. Often enough, its inner tensions presented a spectacle that was far from edifying, and only common danger at home or distress abroad proved capable of uniting them for limited objectives. American Jewry, however, was now the largest aggregation under a single political jurisdiction in the world, and its numbers, wealth, and influence, if not its spiritual eminence and cohesion, gave it that hegemony over the world community which before the First World War had been held by the Jewry of Russia.

In the early twenties, moreover, the Jews of America were faced with the realization that the period of large-scale immigration, which brought them a constant stream of replenishment from the Old World, was over, and that they now had to look to their own spiritual fences. The period came to a definite halt with the Johnson Immigration Act of 1924, which rested on a *numerus clausus* or quota system. It provided that the annual quota to be admitted from any country was not to exceed 2 per cent of the number of foreign-born hailing from that country who resided in the United States in 1890. The aim of the formula was to discriminate between nationalities, to reduce drastically the number of immigrants from eastern and southern Europe, in particular Jews and Italians, and to encourage immigration from northern and western Europe. The act accomplished its purpose. It reduced the admission of Jews to a tenth of its pre-war volume, deflecting large numbers to Canada, South America, and Palestine, but dooming much larger numbers to the blind alleys in Europe in which they were suffocating.

The passage of the Johnson Bill was preceded by years of racist propaganda. The "chosen" stock in those days was not the "Aryan" but the "Nordic," and rivers of ink and gales of breath were spent in extolling the noble Nordic and bemoaning his imminent submergence by the "inferior hordes" from eastern Europe. The Nordics were found to possess every virtue, the others every vice, including the gravest of all, a penchant for social radicalism. Little did those eulogists and lamenters dream that in less than two decades their sons would again be streaming across the Atlantic to fight and die on a hundred battlefields against a "Nordic" nation which took those encomiums too seriously.

7

THE prejudices that culminated in the Johnson Act were more or less veiled: the law embraced others besides Jews, and many of its advocates denied being swayed by racial bias, maintaining their stand solely on the ground of economic necessity. However, the years under review witnessed a series of manifestations that were much more outspoken. During the first decade the stage was held by a resurrected Ku Klux Klan and by no less a personage than Henry Ford, the leading and most admired industrial magnate of America.

Over the postwar atmosphere of the land hung a miasma of fear of an imminent Bolshevist revolution, heightened by the deflation and labor unrest of the early twenties. It was an ideal atmosphere for bigots, demagogues, and adventurers, and the Ku Klux Klan, which had flourished in the South after the Civil War, rose from its grave garbed in its ancient cerements. It burned fiery crosses and rode again in the night; but this time it rode not only against Catholics and Negroes, but also against Jews. It gathered millions of members under its banner of hate, and it sputtered out again largely as the result of a rise in the economic barometer of the country and, to no small extent, because of the exposure of the frauds and crimes of not a few of its leaders.

The anti-Semitic career of Henry Ford was even more sinister and grotesque. Duped by an unscrupulous coterie of subordinates, the motor magnate lent his name and his wealth to a vast network of vicious propaganda, spearheaded by his *Dearborn Independent* and whipped up by a world-wide distribution of the Protocols. Then, in 1927, after blowing hard for six or seven years, the storm was suddenly stilled. Henry Ford saw the light. It flashed on him in the course of a libel suit brought against him by a lawyer named Aaron Sapiro, and it led the penitent tycoon to address a humble letter of apology to Louis Marshall, the head of the American Jewish Committee, in which he asked the forgiveness of the Jews "as fellow men and brothers," assuring them that "henceforth they may look to me for friendship and good will." It was a notable victory, although the ground swell of the hate waves launched by the motor magnate continued, and shadows of doubt were thrown over his change of heart by persistent rumors of his sympathy with Fascist movements. Particularly disturbing was his association with Charles Lindbergh who, until the attack on Pearl Harbor, was the darling of the American Fascists and the apparent answer to their prayer for a "man on horseback."

8

THE economic disaster that smote the country in the fall of 1929 and continued its ravages through the early thirties, would alone have sufficed to bring an upsurge of anti-Semitism; but now, in line with its world strategy, nazism crossed the Atlantic and became the instigator and model of a swarm of Fascist movements and organizations—the Silver Shirts, the Christian Front, the Knights of the Camelia, and numerous others. Whatever differences existed among their *fuehrers* and followers, anti-Semitism was the thing they all had in common. The boldest of them was the German-American Bund, the transmission belt between Nazi agents from Germany and native Fascists, whose members, until their leader Fritz Kuhn was convicted of embezzlement and sent to prison, dreamed of a Nazified America, and prepared for "the day" by drilling in storm troop uniforms and training their boys and girls in a network of camps in imitation of the Hitler Youth in the fatherland.

But the prophet who commanded the admiration and affection of all these sowers of hate and discord was the priest, Charles Coughlin. Here was a voice of sanctimonious venom that out-Goebbeled Goebbels. From his "shrine" in Detroit, he disseminated his slanderous *Social Justice*, and addressed his unctuous defamations to a radio audience that ran into the millions. His basic line was made in Germany. It consisted, on the one hand, of identifying Jews with communism and communism with Jews, and, on the other, of charging all the economic ills of the world to the "international bankers," a term which became a synonym for Jews. Both communism and capitalism were part of an Elders of Zion plot to subvert and destroy the nations. The contradiction involved in the two credos gave the priest and his disciples no qualms. In the heat of passion, and with the aid of a little pious casuistry, it melted like snow in a summer sun.

Naturally, this fungus growth, fertilized as it was by the pollution that flowed from Berlin, Nuremberg, and Munich, alarmed the Jews of America, and they took measures to defend themselves. They were in the lead of the boycott that was launched against German goods and services, although they were not of one mind as to its wisdom, some of the leaders being fearful that it would only add to the afflictions of their people in Germany. Bodies like the American Jewish Committee, the American Jewish Congress, the Anti-Defamation League of the Order B'nai Brith, the Non-Sectarian Anti-Nazi League headed by the distinguished attorney, Samuel Untermyer, worked hard to sterilize the poisons disseminated by the Fascist groups, and the Jews took a prominent part in projects like the National Conference of Christians and Jews for the promotion of understanding and good will among the different faiths. But the surest bulwark of defense for the Jews of America lay in the traditions of the American people. With all their clamor, the Fascist eruptions represented only the "lunatic fringe" of America. The great body of the American people, their government, their press and pulpit, their leaders of thought and action, by and large despised the bigots and demagogues, and to their contempt was added a feeling of anxiety as they saw Nazi Germany, the fountainhead of the agitation, with fifth columns planted in the bosom of every country, moving forward on its career of aggression and world menace.

9

NOR did the raucous clamor of the lunatic fringe succeed in curbing to any great extent the progress of American Jews in the life of the nation. They were now in nearly every branch of industry and commerce, particularly in large and small-scale merchandising, in the manufacture of wearing apparel, in building construction, and in motion picture production. They achieved eminence in science and the professions, with men like Albert A.

Michelson, J. Robert Oppenheimer, and Albert Einstein, now also an American, in physics; Simon Flexner, Joseph Goldberger, and a host of others in medicine; Edwin R. A. Seligman, Franz Boas, Mordecai Ezekiel, and Isadore Lubin in the social sciences. They made distinguished contributions to journalism, belles-lettres, and scholarship, with some of the writers—Ludwig Lewisohn, Maurice Samuel, Waldo Frank and others—devoting their talents largely to Jewish themes.

They won even greater prominence in the arts: in music with composers like Ernest Bloch and George Gershwin; virtuosos like Jascha Heifetz, Yehudi Menuhin, Mischa Elman and numerous others, and popular song writers like Irving Berlin and Jerome Kern; in painting and sculpture with artists like Jo Davidson, Jacob Epstein, and Jules Butensky; and in architecture and bridge-building. Finally, in the art of entertainment the names of Jewish comedians, playwrights, actors, and producers had become American household words.

Equally impressive has been their contribution to public service and statesmanship. They have sat as judges in the federal courts, including the Supreme Court, and in state, county, and municipal courts throughout the land. They have been elected in substantial numbers to the legislative branches of the state and federal governments, and as governors in Idaho, Utah, Oregon, New Mexico, Illinois, Florida, and New York. They have served in presidential cabinets, held important posts in executive and administrative agencies, and gone to foreign countries as envoys and ambassadors.

Their number is legion, but if a few names should be selected they might, in addition to those of Louis D. Brandeis, Benjamin N. Cardozo, and Felix Frankfurter, who have sat on the bench of the United States Supreme Court, be those of Bernard Baruch, who achieved a position of extraordinary influence as the "elder statesman" of America; Herbert H. Lehman, elected three times as governor of the State of New York and later named General Director of the United Nations Relief and Rehabilitation Administration (UNRRA); Henry Morgenthau, Jr., Secretary of the Treasury during the critical years of depression and war; and David E. Lilienthal, for thirteen years director of the Tennessee Valley Authority and, in 1947, first chairman of the United States Atomic Energy Commission. There was a bitter struggle before the appointment of Lilienthal to the Commission was ratified by the Senate, a battle strongly reminiscent of the one that raged in 1916 over the appointment of Brandeis to the Supreme Court.

There were men in the American Jewish community, some of them influential, who followed the achievements of their coreligionists with pride, no doubt, but not without anxiety. They would have preferred to see them advance less rapidly and less conspicuously, and they even attempted on occasion to apply the brakes to their progress. Their counterparts, for that matter, existed in other countries also: in France, for example, they attempted in 1936 to dissuade Leon Blum from accepting the post of premier. In the hectic atmosphere of a world that was constantly growing smaller, and surrounded by the savage propaganda manufactured or inspired by Germany, it was not unnatural that a haunting sense of insecurity should beget a desire for self-effacement.

10

THE six or seven boom years preceding the collapse of 1929 saw a marked expansion of the institutional life of American Jewry, with handsome centers springing up in large communities and small, with philanthropic agencies gaining in strength and coordinated control, and with increasing support for relief and reconstruction abroad and for the rebuilding of the national home. Although the sums raised for those purposes by voluntary contributions compared well with similar efforts on the part of other religious communities, they did not, in the opinion of many, represent what those who were appealed to could and should have given. Nor can it be said that, in general, a deepening of the content of Jewish life went hand in hand with the material expansion. Perhaps the most serious dereliction lay in the failure to make adequate provision for the religious education of the young, although a few brave efforts to face the problem were not wanting, the most notable being the Jewish Education Association of New York, inspired and led by Bernard Semel, and the work conducted for Jewish students on college campuses by the Menorah Association and the Hillel

Foundation of the Order B'nai B'rith. In the larger communities, notably in New York under the leadership of Samson Benderly, central educational agencies were established for the improvement of educational standards and techniques. The most recent development has been a marked growth of the so-called small Yeshivoth. These orthodox all-day elementary schools, where the religious and secular subjects are taught under the same roof, are expected to produce the future communal and religious leaders.

A new movement, which took the name of Reconstructionism, made its appearance in the realm of religion. Like the champions of Reform in Germany a century earlier, its proponents, led by Mordecai M. Kaplan, a teacher in the Jewish Theological Seminary of America, called for changes in doctrine and liturgy which, they asserted, the science and social progress of the times demanded. Unlike the earlier Reform advocates, however, the Reconstructionists held fast to Jewish national values and championed the revival of Jewish nationhood in Palestine. The Orthodox and many of the Conservatives denounced the proposed changes, particularly the denial of the selection of the Jewish people and of the revelation at Mount Sinai. Reconstructionism, they affirmed, was guilty of attenuating the concept of God and of divesting religious observances of their original and divine sanction. The movement, in their view was, to all intents and purposes, secular rather than religious in character.

At the other end of the religious gamut, Chassidism became a factor in the larger communities of the country. From the Old World came a number of Chassidic leaders, scions of illustrious "dynasties," who attracted groups of zealous adherents. Distinguished among them was Joseph Isaac Schneerson, the "Lubavitcher Rebbe," a direct descendant of Shneur Zalman of Liady (1748-1812), the founder of the intellectual or *Chabad* branch of the movement. In New York and other communities, the "Lubavitcher's" devotees established elementary and higher schools for the teaching of Torah in the spirit of Chassidism.

The Yiddish press, embracing dailies, weeklies, and at least one literary monthly, *Die Zukunft* (The Future), continued to prosper, and new Yiddish writers of talent made their appearance, although the market for their books failed to expand or even to hold its own. Books of Jewish content in English did, however, find a larger public, and periodicals in English multiplied. Books and periodicals made their appearance in still a third language, Hebrew. The weekly *Hadoar* (The Post) began publication in 1921, the monthly *Bitzaron* (Citadel) in 1939, and, with the arrival in America of Abraham Joseph Stiebel, the foremost patron of modern Hebrew literature, the quarterly *Hatekufah* (The Era) also began to appear in the New World. Hebrew literature in America derived its inspiration, first, from the Zionist movement and the astounding literary productivity of Palestine, and, second, from the Federation for Hebrew Culture (*Histadruth Ivrith*), organized by a group of enthusiasts in 1916.

II

IN THE Zionist movement, the early years of the third decade produced a schism when in 1921 Louis D. Brandeis and his adherents withdrew from the general organization and established instruments of their own for the economic development of Palestine. The break was ascribed to a clash between "east and west," between the temperament and methods of Weizmann and his followers, and those of Brandeis and his. In the course of the next decade, however, the breach was healed: the gulf was found to be not so deep after all. By 1930, Julian W. Mack and Robert Szold, leading members of the "Brandeis group," were back in the administration of the Zionist Organization of America.

Brandeis himself continued to be a dominating influence in the movement, as, indeed, he was in American life generally. His home in Washington was a shrine to which Zionists of all affiliations repaired for counsel and inspiration. Powerful impetus came also from the world leaders of Zionism who from time to time came to labor for the cause in the American community. Among them were Chaim Weizmann, the world head of the movement; Nahum Sokolow, its scholarly and persuasive "diplomat"; Menahem Ussischkin, the "iron" man of Zionism; the matchless orator Shmaryah Levin, and the Hebrew poet-laureate, Chaim Nachman Bialik.

In the meantime, Weizmann devoted his diplomatic skill to the task of drawing into the Jewish Agency the wealthy and influential non-Zionists of every land, particularly of America, the Agency being the body recognized in the Palestine Mandate as representing the entire Jewish people in matters affecting the National Home. Outstanding among American non-Zionists who were enlisted in the Agency were Louis Marshall, ardent champion of his people and a distinguished figure on the American as well as the Jewish scene; Felix M. Warburg, banker, philanthropist, and communal leader, head of the house of Kuhn, Loeb and Company; and the versatile Cyrus Adler, president of the Jewish Theological Seminary of America, of Dropsie College for Hebrew and Cognate Learning, and also of the American Jewish Committee. At the Sixteenth Zionist Congress, held in Zurich in 1929, the extension of the Jewish Agency was, formally at least, accomplished.

Nor did the movement fail to impress the public opinion of the country at large. In 1922, the terms of the Balfour Declaration were endorsed in a joint resolution adopted unanimously by both houses of Congress and signed by President Warren G. Harding. Two years later, the Mandate, which is based on the Declaration, was embodied in a Palestine Convention or treaty between Great Britain and the United States.

With the outbreak of the Second World War, the principal Zionist organizations in America—the Zionist Organization of America, the Hadassah Women's Zionist Organization, the Poale Zion, and the Mizrachi—joined hands in an Emergency Council to safeguard and promote Zionist interests. New men and women became prominent in the leadership of the various groupings, among them Abba Hillel Silver, Emanuel Neumann, Morris Rothenberg, Louis Levinthal, Israel Goldstein and Bernard A. Rosenblatt among the General Zionists; Hayim Greenberg in the labor wing of the movement; Rose Jacobs, Judith Epstein, Tamar de Sola Pool and Rose L. Halprin in Hadassah; and Gedaliah Bublick and Leon Gellman in the Mizrachi. In addition, an array of Christian leaders in every walk of American life, including men like Robert F. Wagner, the senior senator from the State of New York, and Henry A. Atkinson, director of the Church Peace Union, organized to give moral and political support to the cause.

CHAPTER SIXTY-EIGHT

Palestine Resurgent

But the most important development of Jewish life between the wars did not take place in eastern Europe, where the communities were like frail barks in the raging floods of anti-Semitism. Nor did it take place in western Europe, where the shadow of Nazi Germany was growing steadily longer; nor even in America, where the most absorbing concerns of the community were the raising of funds for relief abroad and philanthropy at home and the struggle against the rising menace of anti-Semitism. It took place in the little land called holy, where, some 4,000 years earlier, the career of the Jewish people began and where it reached the zenith of its ancient glory.

By a concatenation of forces, immemorial as well as immediate, the ancient motherland emerged from the shadows of the centuries and began to resume her central place in Jewish destiny. Poets and pietists found their faith confirmed, nor could even the casual observer fail to be inspired with a sense of direction and purpose in the long and bitter journey of the Jewish people. For the resurgence of Palestine had import not only for the Yishuv; it lifted all the scattered communities to new dignity, revealing as it did the creative strength of a people which, for nearly two millennia, had been living on the margin of the world's economy and toleration.

2

AS A WORK of economic reconstruction, few if any accomplishments during the period have been found to surpass it. From the end of the First World War to the outbreak of the Second, the population of the Yishuv had risen from some fifty thousand to nearly half a million, and the total in 1947 was estimated at seven hundred thousand. In 1943, the number established on the soil in

PALESTINE
RESURGENT
JEWISH SETTLEMENTS
(not all of them included)
ARAB-JEWISH CITIES
ARAB CITIES
RAILROADS
MEDITERRANEAN
SEA
LEBANON
SYRIA
GOLAN
BASHAN
HAURAN
GILEAD
TRANS-JORDAN
GALILEE
SAMARIA
JUDEA
NEGEB
EGYPT
Metullah
Kfar Giladi
Tel Hai
Kfar Szold
Kfar Blum
Lake Huleh
Hanita
Birya
Safed
Acre
Kfar Masaryk
Emek Zebulun
HAIFA
Mt. Carmel
Kfar Chassidim
Sea of Galilee
Tiberias
Dagania
Nazareth
Emek Hayarden
Gesher
HYDRO-ELECTRIC WORKS
Valley of Jezreel (The Emek)
Affuleh
Ein Hashofet
Zichron Yaakov
Binyamina
Ein Harod
Beth Alpha
Beth-shean
OIL PIPE LINE
Hedera
Kfar Brandeis
Givat Hayim
Jenin
Tirath Zvi
Jordan
Nathanya
Emek Hepher
Tulkarm
Nablus
Shefayim
Rishpon
Herzliah
Ramath Gan
Petach Tikvah
TEL AVIV
Jaffa
Tel Litvinsky
Ben Shemen
Rishon-le-Zion
Lydda
Nes Ziona
Rehobot
Ramallah
Amman
Givat Brenner
Kiryath Anavim
POTASH WORKS
Mt. Scopus
JERUSALEM
Nitzanim
Beer Tuvia
Kfar Warburg
Bethlehem
Negbo
Dead Sea
Hebron
Gaza
Dorot
Ruhama
Gvuloth
Beersheba
Tel Zofim
SCALE OF MILES
0
10
20
30
Beersheba
Dead Sea
Beth Eshel
Tel Zofim
Emek Haraba
Akaba
25 MILES

some three hundred agricultural settlements amounted to 25 per cent of the total, a proportion that compares well with that of rural populations in other lands. Large stretches of swampland, for centuries the breeding ground of the malarial mosquito, the most important area of the sort being the storied Valley of Jezreel, had been drained and put to the plow. Other areas, parched and stony wastes, after being cleared and watered, had become forests, grain fields, and gardens. Along the coastal belt, sand dunes were irrigated and transformed into orange groves, and deep boring brought water to land in the Negeb and elsewhere, which had been arid and sterile for centuries. Scientific methods and modern machinery revolutionized the country's agriculture; among the innovations were soil conservation, intensive farming, crop rotation, the introduction of new breeds of cattle and poultry as well as new crops like bananas and tobacco.

In urban and industrial development the progress was equally marked. Around the ancient somnolent cities of Jerusalem and Haifa modern suburbs had sprung up; some of the older colonies like Petach Tikvah and Rehobot, had grown into compact little towns; and the queenly city of Tel Aviv (Hill of Spring) had risen up from the sand dunes on the coast and now had its own harbor installations. In 1943, nearly 70,000 workers in 2,000 factories and twice as many small workshops were employed in these urban centers, most of them working for the armies operating in the Middle East, producing some 200 military items. The power that drove the wheels came from the Jordan River which had been harnessed by the Palestine Electric Corporation, the creation of that soft-spoken revolutionary and dreamer, Pinchas Ruttenberg. In the Dead Sea, vast stores of potash and other chemicals had been discovered and were being extracted. Fishing villages were springing up along the coast of Lake Tiberias and the Mediterranean, and a modest shipping industry had come to birth. The fugitives from the terror in Poland and Germany had given industry a fresh spurt: refugees from Lodz, for example, developed the manufacture of textiles, those from the west established factories for making optical instruments and cutting diamonds. The country was buoyant with initiative and enterprise; its exhibits became a new Mecca for the neighboring lands; Palestine had become the industrial and commercial enzyme of the Middle East.

But any account of the Yishuv would be incomplete if it failed to stress the spirit of social idealism that brooded over it, especially in the agricultural settlements. That spirit asserted itself as early as 1901 in the statutes of the Jewish National Fund, stipulating that the land it purchases must forever remain the inalienable possession of the whole people. The same spirit animated the pioneers of the Second Aliyah in the first decade of the twentieth century, who in 1909 established the first *kvutzah*, or collectivist farm settlement, at Dagania, the model of many other *kvutzoth*, dedicated to the principle of "no exploiters and no exploited." The same spirit animates also the *moshavim* or small-holders villages, where the cooperative principle is applied in the purchase and use of farm machinery and in the marketing of the crops; in the large network of producers and consumers cooperatives in the cities; in the system of health services established by the Histadrut, the General Federation of Jewish Labor, and in other institutions.

The Histadrut is like no other labor organization in the world. With a membership in 1947 of 170,000, it regards itself not primarily as a vehicle for promoting the interests of its members, but as the vanguard of Jewish national redemption, charged with the task of preparing a home for the homeless of their people; a home, moreover, which is to rest on the principles of social justice as proclaimed by the lawgivers and prophets of Israel and elaborated by the experience and struggles of modern societies.

3

IN THE matter of public health and education, two criteria by which the level of any society may be gauged, the Yishuv has had to face problems no less formidable than in the economic sphere, and its progress has been no less impressive. A Health Council, *Vaad Habriuth*, coordinates the work of a number of health agencies, the most important being the *Kupat Cholim*, or Sick Fund of the Histadrut, and the Hadassah Medical Organization. The latter, maintained by the Hadassah Women's Zionist Organization of America, conducts hospitals, clinics, health and diagnostic centers, hygienic services for school children, as well as a nurses' training school. The *Kupat Cholim* provides similar services for its members. The zeal of the Yishuv for the health of its people has been rewarded by a sharp reduction in infant mortality and in the diseases that once ravaged the country, particularly malaria and trachoma, a reduction from which the Arabs have also benefited. The national home has produced a new physical type: the muscular Jew, robust, bold, and self-reliant.

The educational pyramid of the Yishuv has for its base the hundreds of elementary schools in towns and colonies with a school population of nearly 100,000. The system also includes secondary schools, trade schools, seminaries for teachers, agricultural schools, and the Haifa Technical Institute, an engineering college to which a Nautical School has been added. The apex of the pyramid is the Hebrew University on Mount Scopus opposite Jerusalem. On April 1, 1925, before a distinguished gathering representing leading institutions of learning throughout the world, the University was formally dedicated by Arthur James Balfour. Its faculties of the humanities and science, as well as its medical center, include illustrious savants, many of them refugees from Nazi terror, and the University has already made important contributions in a number of fields including medicine, agriculture, archaeology, and Arab lore. Vigorous action was begun in America in 1946 to provide the University with a medical school. And to the higher institutions of learning in the Yishuv should be added the Weizmann Institute at Rehobot, dedicated to scientific research, especially in chemistry.

The zest for education has created problems, not all of them financial, the most serious being the lack of unity in the school system, with secular Labor schools, religious Mizrachi schools, and middle-of-the-road "general" schools. Talmudic education is, of course, also well represented, some of the renowned Yeshivoth of eastern Europe having established themselves in the national home. Outstanding among the religious leaders of the Yishuv was the wise, profound, and saintly Abraham Isaac Kook (1865-1935), who was Chief Rabbi of the Ashkenazic community from 1919 until his death.

But apart from the formal school system, the cultural efflorescence of the Yishuv is probably the most luxuriant in the world.

It publishes more books, newspapers, and other periodicals, for its size, than any other community in the world. Nowhere else are the talented men and women—the poets, novelists, and essayists, the scholars and scientists, the artists, musicians, and dramatists—relatively so numerous and held in such high esteem. The Hebrew language, responsive to all demands, technical as well as belletristic, is of course their medium; and they have brought to their audiences not only original works but also, in glowing translations, those of the monarchs of world literature, ancient as well as modern.

Though resting on a common national purpose, the Yishuv, constituting as it does a miniature ingathering of the Diaspora, presents a highly diversified social landscape. East and West are mingled but not yet fused, the East represented by Jews from Yemen and other lands of the Orient, the West by Europeans and Americans. Religious conformity ranges all the way from rigid Orthodoxy, sometimes, as in the case of the Agudas Israel, militant in character, to a disregard of ritual forms. But in all cities and colonies the day of rest is the Seventh Day, and the holidays are universal festive occasions. Some of them, like Shabuoth, Purim, Hanukkah and the New Year of the Trees (on the fifteenth day of the month of Shebat), have acquired forms of observance springing from the new life in the homeland and unknown in the Diaspora.

Politically also, the Yishuv presents a wide diversity. Its internal affairs are governed by an elected assembly of 171 members who choose a small executive body, the *Vaad Leumi* (National Council). In both are represented parties of the Left, the Right, and the Center, who divide on questions of political orientation, as well as on economic and religious grounds. Those divisions, social, religious, and political, add to the problems of the Yishuv, but they do not annul its basic unity of purpose, its calm and relentless determination to recreate at long last the national home of the Jewish people.

4

THIS keen and vibrant human society, this miniature Commonwealth brought to life in two brief decades, would have been miracle enough had it been forced to contend with the obstacles of nature only—eroded and denuded hillsides, swampy and malarious valleys, sandy wastes, tropical heat, drought, and disease. But in addition, it has had to contend with even more serious obstacles: the hostility and malevolence of man.

That this daring enterprise, this sudden injection of a new dynamic into the stagnant Near East, would alarm those Arabs who preferred the stagnation and profited from it, was, of course, to have been expected. What effect, the Arab landlords wondered, would the example of the sturdy, progressive Jewish farmers have upon the Arab peasants who furnished their revenues? It was also to have been expected that the heady postwar nationalism which ran riot in Europe would spill over into the Near East and leave Arab politicos dissatisfied with the enormous gains in freedom and independence the First World War had brought them, and at such little cost; that they would not willingly consent to the restoration of Palestine, that "little notch" in their vast domains, as Balfour called it, to the Jews. All that was to be expected, in spite of the fact that the official spokesman of the Arabs at the Peace Conference, the Emir Feisal, son of King Husein of the Hejaz, wrote to Felix Frankfurter (then a member of the Zionist Delegation at the Conference) that he regarded the proposals of the Zionist Organization "as moderate and proper"; that the Arabs would do their best "to help them through"; that they "will wish the Jews a most hearty welcome home." What came as a shock, however, was the antagonism of British officials, first of the military government, which was not replaced until July 1920, and then of officials in London as well as Jerusalem.

It was, of course, folly to assume that the ordinary colonial administrator, high or low, brought up in the traditions of British imperialism, would have the necessary understanding and imagination to lend himself to the implementation of the Balfour Declaration and the Palestine Mandate. This undertaking to restore a people to nationhood on their ancestral soil was something unique in history, just as, for that matter, the entire career of the Jewish people is historically unique. It was an undertaking that cut across every habit and prejudice of the colonial administrator. He was now called upon to deal not with "natives," who were to be cajoled or intimidated, but with a highly sensitive and intelligent people who knew their rights and had the temerity to regard themselves as his equals. He was above all called upon to promote a policy that clashed with some basic imperialist axioms, a policy that envisaged the creation not only of an agricultural community as an outlet for British manufactures, but of a community for which industry was essential to its life and growth. It was a venture to which the time-honored axiom of "divide and rule" might prove fatal, for it was obvious that unless Jews and Arabs learned to live together in peace the project would fail. How was the run-of-the-mill colonial official, if left to his established habits, to adjust himself, mentally and emotionally, to this new and unique undertaking?

5

THE proposals which the Zionist Organization made to the Peace Conference in February 1919, and to which Feisal referred in his letter to Frankfurter, called for "the fullest freedom of religious worship for all creeds in Palestine," and pledged "no discrimination among the inhabitants with regard to citizenship and civil rights on the grounds of religion or race." But the Peace Conference failed to make a prompt decision, and the opposition had time to mobilize and act. In March 1920, the Jewish outposts of Tel Hai and Kfar Giladi in Upper Galilee were attacked by Arab insurgents, and five of the heroic defenders, including their leader, Captain Joseph Trumpeldor, were killed. "It is good to have a country to die for," were the last words of Trumpeldor, one of the many brave and lofty spirits which the national revival has produced. In April of the same year, there was a mob outbreak in Jerusalem in which Arabs and Jews lost their lives. Those events did spur the Allied Supreme Council to take action, and at its meeting at San Remo in Italy later the same month it made the Balfour Declaration part of the treaty with Turkey and assigned the Mandate for Palestine to Great Britain. But the Mandate had still to be ratified by the League of Nations, and sleepless vigilance and effort in the face of enemies in and out of Palestine were required before the Council of the League, in July 1922, gave the Mandate its official endorsement. Then, at long last, the Jewish

National Home became a formal part of the new international structure.

The Mandate is not entirely free of ambiguities, but that its primary purpose is to implement the Balfour Declaration is altogether clear. Indeed the Mandate is much more explicit than the Declaration. It recognizes "the historical connection of the Jewish people with Palestine" and "the grounds for reconstituting their National Home in that country." It makes the Mandatory Power "responsible for placing the country under such political, administrative, and economic conditions as will secure the establishment of the Jewish National Home." It recognizes a Jewish Agency "for the purpose of advising and cooperating with the Administration in matters affecting the Jewish National Home," and makes Hebrew one of the official languages of the country, the others being English and Arabic. It requires the Administration of Palestine to facilitate Jewish immigration and to encourage "close settlement of Jews on the land, including state lands and waste lands not required for public purposes." The Mandate, of course, stipulates that "the civil and religious rights of all the inhabitants of Palestine, irrespective of race and religion," be safeguarded, and finally it requires the Mandatory to submit an annual report to the Council of the League of Nations on what it is doing to fulfill its obligations.

6

FROM July 1920 to June 1925, the Palestine Administration was headed by Herbert Samuel, an experienced statesman whose appointment as High Commissioner was hailed as the beginning of a new era in the history of his people. They were years of substantial progress for the national home, although in the spring of 1921 Arab intransigents again resorted to violence which was effectively suppressed, in large part by the Jewish self-defense. Samuel omitted no opportunity to placate the Arabs, and one upon whom he lavished high office and great power proved to be the principal thorn in the side not only of the Jews, but also of the British. He was Amin El Huseini, who had been given a long prison sentence for his part in the riots of 1920. Samuel pardoned him and enabled him to become the mufti, or religious head of

Jerusalem, and president of the Supreme Moslem Council, a body in control of sizable religious funds which could be diverted for less holy purposes.

But until the summer of 1929, the country was at peace, and the work of reclamation went forward. An economic crisis which began late in 1925 was gradually overcome, while the new High Commissioner, Field Marshal Lord Plumer, a blunt soldier, hewed straight to the line laid down by the Mandate. Lord Plumer left his post in 1928 and government authority rested with a group of minor officials who proved unequal to a new and graver crisis with which the mufti and his adherents, after careful preparation, confronted them.

The immediate issue revolved around the Wailing Wall, the one relic of the ancient Temple at which Jews, from time immemorial, had come to pray, but which was legally under the jurisdiction of the Supreme Moslem Council. Now the Council declared that the Jews were exceeding their rights at the Wall. For months an intense religious incitement was carried on until, on August 23, 1929, violence broke out in the capital, whence it spread quickly through the rest of the country. It continued for a week and cost the lives of about 130 Jews and an equal number of Arabs. The officials had declined to suppress the agitation and failed to act promptly and decisively even after the outbreak. It was the Jewish self-defense that prevented a much heavier loss of life and destruction of property.

The outbreak of 1929 was followed by a series of contortionist efforts on the part of the government in London to satisfy the Arab die-hards and make a show of honoring the Mandate. The majority report of a commission of inquiry headed by Sir Walter Shaw appeared to justify the claim, which, however, proved to be groundless, that Arab peasants were being dispossessed by Jews; and another investigation, conducted by Sir John Hope Simpson, a colonization expert, professed to find no economic future for the country. Basing itself on these gloomy reports, a White Paper, prepared by Lord Passfield, the Colonial Secretary of the Labor government headed by Ramsay MacDonald, was issued in October 1930, presaging the early liquidation of the national home. There was a world-wide outcry, whereupon the prime minister sent

Weizmann a letter "interpreting" the Passfield Paper and assuring him that Britain intended to fulfill its obligations. But the net result of these maneuvers was to convince the Arab irreconcilables that the Mandate policy was not, as Lord Balfour once termed it, *une chose jugée*, and that Britain, under sufficient pressure, could be brought to abandon it. The policy was a nettle which neither the Colonial Office in London nor the Administration in Palestine was disposed to grasp.

7

IN SPITE of official handicaps, which the MacDonald letter failed to ward off, the outbreak of 1929 was followed by seven years of peaceful and unprecedented growth for the national home. Its population more than doubled; its urban centers, particularly Tel Aviv, Jerusalem, and Haifa, expanded; there was a large flow of public and private capital; and industry increased in size and variety. Existing colonies were enlarged; many new ones were established; and the citrus crop, the principal export commodity, grew by leaps and bounds. Toward this expansion, tens of thousands of refugees from Germany contributed in large measure. Palestine indeed had become one of the principal havens for those fleeing from Nazi terror.

It was not to be expected, however, that the Arab intransigents, headed by the mufti, would look upon this expansion of the Yishuv with equanimity, nor that they would fail to take advantage of the opportunities which the triumph of the Nazis in 1933 and the onslaught of Italy on Abyssinia in 1935 offered them. For their part, both nazism and fascism saw in Arab discontent a perfect instrument for undermining the British position in the highly strategic Middle East, while the British became more than ever disposed to yield to Arab pressure at the expense of the national home.

By the beginning of 1936, Italian aggression in Abyssinia, which England and France tried but failed to halt, emboldened both Egypt and Syria to demand full and immediate sovereignty, and the Palestine Arab leaders felt that their big moment had arrived. Arms and money were no problem now: Berlin and Rome took care of both. In April 1936 a new wave of violence and bloodshed began, and it did not end until the outbreak of the Second World

War in 1939. Jewish settlements throughout the country in cities and colonies were attacked. Crops were burned, trees uprooted, and the roads became unsafe. The number of victims rose into the hundreds, and included Britons besides Jews, as well as many Arabs who refused to join the mufti's henchmen or pay the tribute they demanded. It took the British officials a long time to realize that they were confronted with a full scale revolt, and by the time they did so, large military forces were required to suppress it. After long and vain endeavors to appease them, the Arab leaders were apprehended and deported, but the mufti managed to escape, and throughout the Second World War served as agent and propagandist for the Axis.

The Jewish Settlement Defense, which numbered some 25,000 men, was from the outset faced with a problem that was moral rather than military. The brigand bands, most of them recruited in neighboring countries, operated without scruple, burning crops and groves, shooting down farmers in the fields, blasting vehicles on the highways, killing women and children as well as men. Should the defenders adopt a policy of reprisals in kind? Their answer was No. They adopted instead the principle of restraint: the Hebrew word for it, *havlagah*, became famous. It was only toward the end of the period of nearly four years during which the terror continued, that some of the groups departed from the policy of non-retaliation. The outbreak brought 2,877 fatal casualties, of which 450 were Jewish, 140 British, and 2,287 Arab.

Units of the Jewish Settlement Defense, which worked in cooperation with the British forces, patrolled the highways, stood guard over colonies, fields, and groves, and escorted laborers to and from their work. The Mosul pipeline, with its outlet at the port of Haifa, and outlying settlements were guarded by special Jewish night squads who were trained in commando tactics by Charles Orde Wingate, a brilliant soldier, a man of lofty spirit, and an ardent champion of the Jewish national revival. Many Jewish settlements were attacked but not one fell or was abandoned, not even those that lay in the most isolated parts of the country. But not only were the existing settlements retained; some fifty new ones were added, many of them on sites deliberately chosen because they were exposed to maximum danger. Symbolic of the ordeal which the Yishuv successfully withstood is the fact that while 200,000 trees were uprooted, 1,000,000 new ones were planted.

A special technique was developed for setting up new outposts overnight. The groups arrived at the chosen spots in lorries, bringing all they needed, and, in a matter of hours, outposts sprang up as if by magic. Around them ran a wooden stockade, reinforced with stone and concrete and strung with barbed wire, and in the center stood a watchtower with a revolving searchlight commanding a broad area on every side. Soon afterwards, and usually at night, the new settlement might be attacked, but the assailants were always thrown back and rarely ventured to repeat the attempt.

8

WITH all its impact and all the support it had from the Axis powers, the Arab outbreak was unable to muster anything which the government, aided by the Yishuv, was unable to cope with. Palestine did not have to be sacrificed to the rising star of fascism. Nevertheless, the Jewish National Home, like Czechoslovakia, was sacrificed to the same futile policy of appeasement. Arab terrorism failed in Palestine, but it succeeded in London.

As early as November 1936 a Royal Commission, headed by Lord Peel, arrived in the country and spent three months investigating the causes of the outbreak. The Commission rejected most of the Arab grievances, stressing the economic and hygienic benefits which Jewish enterprise had brought the Arabs, and deprecating the extent to which "the policy of conciliation" had been pursued. It even recommended "the careful selection of British officers intended for service in Palestine and a course of special training." In the end, however, it found Arab and Jewish aspirations irreconcilable and recommended "a surgical operation": the partitioning of Palestine into a Jewish state and an Arab state, with certain places, among them Jerusalem, to remain under permanent British control.

In August 1937, the Zionist Congress, meeting in Zurich, rejected the findings of the Commission, insisted that the Mandate was workable, and that a peaceful solution in Palestine was possible. The government in London had declared itself in general agreement with the Commission's conclusions, but in November 1938, with the report of still another commission before it, it found the partition proposal impracticable.

In the meantime, international tension was mounting to the breaking point: Europe was moving relentlessly toward war. In September 1938 had come the Munich surrender; and in February 1939, at the bidding of the Chamberlain government, Arab and Jewish representatives met separately in London, the Arabs refusing to sit with the Jews. The fact that representatives of the neighboring Arab states had also been invited showed the direction in which the official wind was blowing.

In May 1939 came the Munich of the Jewish National Home. It took the form of another White Paper, announcing the complete stoppage, except with Arab consent, of Jewish immigration into Palestine at the end of a five-year period. It provided also for the independence of Palestine after ten years, with the Jews, of course, still a minority and destined to remain one. Land regulations, based on the White Paper and issued somewhat later, made it impossible for Jews to purchase land in 94 per cent of the country. A system of racial disabilities, not unlike the Nuremberg Laws, was imposed on them in their own national home!

The Permanent Mandates Commission of the League of Nations rejected the new British policy, and in England itself the incredible reversal, made in the vain hope of obtaining Arab support in the approaching war, did not go unchallenged. In Parliament strong voices rose up in denunciation of the White Paper, the strongest of them the voice of Winston Churchill, who called it "another Munich" and "a plain breach of a solemn obligation." For the Labor Opposition, Herbert Morrison called the White Paper "a cynical breach of pledges given to the Jews and the world, including America," and declared that "the Government must not expect that this is going to be automatically binding upon their successors." The Paper was adopted in Commons by an abnormally small majority, with scores of members abstaining from voting. England appeared to be ashamed of what England was doing.

Three months later, the world was again at war and the Jews in the Yishuv and throughout the world forgot their grievances against England and threw themselves into the struggle against the enemy of mankind. But the White Paper was not withdrawn or suspended. Applied with brutal rigor, it added greatly to the woes of the Jews of Europe and to the number of those who perished in the immeasurable holocaust that now descended upon them.

CHAPTER SIXTY-NINE

Holocaust in Europe

For nearly a thousand years, ever since the decline of the great community in Babylonia which created the Talmud, the Jewish center of gravity had lain in Europe. The period saw the rise and fall of the brilliant community in Spain, and the growth of large creative centers in eastern Europe. It saw the struggle for civil emancipation apparently won, and the attainment to power and dignity of sizable groups in England, France, Germany, and other European states. By the end of the period, an important concentration had arisen in the New World and the ancient motherland was being reclaimed; but in 1939, Europe was still the continent where lived more than 60 per cent of the sixteen million Jews of the world, and where Jewish life in all its multiformity found expression.

The Second World War swept like a scythe over the Jewish communities of the European continent. The final tally has not been made and probably never will be, but a summary appeared in the text of the formal indictment lodged in October 1945 against the major German war criminals, the top-ranking Nazis who were brought to the bar of justice in the famous Nuremberg trials by the United States, France, Great Britain, and the Soviet Union. The men on trial included twenty-four of the heads of the German government, its army and navy, industry and finance, and of the Nazi party and its affiliates. They did not include Adolf Hitler, Josef Goebbels, and Heinrich Himmler, head of the Gestapo, all three of whom had committed suicide. Before it was over, Robert Ley, head of the Labor Front, had also managed to do away with himself, and Hermann Goering, the deputy *fuehrer*, cheated the gallows by taking poison on the eve of his execution.

"Of the 9,600,000 Jews who lived in the parts of Europe under Nazi domination," said the indictment, "it is conservatively estimated that 5,700,000 have disappeared, most of them deliberately put to death . . . Only remnants of the Jewish population of Europe remain." Three out of every five, in other words, have perished. "The conspiracy . . . to exterminate the Jews was so methodically and thoroughly pursued," said Robert H. Jackson, the chief American prosecutor, in his charge at the opening of the trials, "that despite the German defeat and the Nazi prostration, the Nazi aim largely has succeeded . . . History does not record a crime ever perpetrated against so many victims, or one ever carried out with such calculated cruelty."

Count Three of the indictment mentions victims running into enormous totals and including also non-Jews; it states, for example, that "about 1,500,000 persons were exterminated in Maidanek, and about 4,000,000 persons were exterminated in Auschwitz (Oswiecim)," and it names other places where the victims ran into the hundreds of thousands. But, says Count Four, "millions of the persons . . . mentioned as having been murdered and ill-treated were Jews." In his opening charge, the American prosecutor asserted that "the most savage and numerous crimes planned and committed by the Nazis were those against the Jews."

To give substance to the general accusation, the indictment records a few instances. "Among other mass murders of Jews," it states, were the following:

> At Kislovodsk all Jews were made to give up their property; 2,000 were shot in an anti-tank ditch at Mineraliya Vody; 4,300 other Jews were shot in the same ditch; 60,000 Jews were shot on an island on the Dvina near Riga; 20,000 Jews were shot at Lutsk; 32,000 Jews were shot at Sarny; 60,000 Jews were shot at Kiev and Dniepropetrovsk; thousands of Jews were gassed weekly by means of gas-wagons which broke down from overwork.
>
> As the Germans retreated before the Soviet Army, they exterminated Jews rather than allow them to be liberated.

> Many concentration camps and ghettos were kept up in which Jews were incarcerated and tortured, starved, subjected to merciless atrocities and finally exterminated.

"The eastern Jew has suffered as no people ever suffered," said the American prosecutor. But his brother from the west suffered no less. "Millions of Jews from Germany and from occupied western countries," says the indictment, "were sent to the eastern countries for extermination."

2

THE extent of the crime may be capable of computation: its dimensions may be expressed in arithmetical terms. But, is it possible to measure the bestiality of the criminals or the agonies of the victims? Words are vain and impotent; nevertheless the official indictment is not altogether silent on that score, and the following precise and legalistic description is perhaps more eloquent than a jeremiad:

> The murders and ill treatment were carried out by diverse means, including shooting, hanging, gassing, starvation, gross overcrowding, systematic under-nutrition, systematic imposition of labor tasks beyond the strength of those ordered to carry them out, inadequate provision of surgical and medical services, kickings, beatings, brutality and torture of all kinds, including the use of hot irons and pulling out of finger nails and the performance of experiments by means of operations and otherwise on living human subjects.

Finally, no account of this, the most stupendous crime in history, should quail from citing the most bestial aspect of it, the mass murder of children. Again we quote the restrained language of the indictment:

> Along with adults the Nazi conspirators mercilessly destroyed even children. They killed them with their parents in groups and alone. They killed them in children's homes and hospitals, burying the living in the graves, throwing them into flames, stabbing them with bayonets, poisoning them, conducting experiments upon them, extracting their blood for the use

of the German Army, throwing them into prison and Gestapo torture chambers and concentration camps, where the children died from hunger, torture, and epidemic diseases.

The following paragraph is taken from the summary of the verdict, delivered September 30 and October 1, 1946, of the International Military Tribunal before which the trial of the ranking Nazis took place. The Einsatz Groups, mentioned in the last sentence, were special units "given the duty of exterminating the Jews in the east":

> The hair of the women victims was cut off before they were killed to be used in the production of mattresses. The clothes, money and valuables were sent to the appropriate agencies for disposition. The gold teeth and fillings were taken from the heads of the corpses and sent to the Reichsbank. After cremation the ashes were used for fertilizer, and in some instances attempts were made to utilize the fat from the bodies of the victims in the commercial manufacture of soap. Adolf Eichmann, who had been put in charge of the program to exterminate the Jews, has estimated that the policy pursued resulted in the killing of 6,000,000 Jews, of whom 4,000,000 were killed in the concentration camps and 2,000,000 were killed by the Einsatz Groups.

The intellectual and spiritual leaders—the rabbis and scholars, the poets and teachers—were as a matter of Nazi policy among the first to be liquidated. Their number was legion, among them Simon Dubnow, the dean of Jewish historians; Hillel Zeitlin, religious teacher, poet and mystic; Noah Prilutzky, folk-lorist, publicist, and communal leader; the historians, Emanuel Ringelblum and Ignatz Schipper; the scholar, Zalman Reisin; and Yitzchak Katzenelson, a poet who, before his final deportation to the murder-mill in Auschwitz, managed to give some expression to the agony of his people.

3

A LURID light on the passion that lashed the Germans to commit those deeds is thrown by their leader's *Political Testament*, prepared by him shortly before his suicide in April 1945. The document reveals the inner decay of the Nazi regime, the "nightmare of treason," as Hitler's fellow-suicide, Josef Goebbels, called it, highlighted by the treachery of Himmler and Goering. But, in the main, the *Testament* is a fantastic tirade against "international Jewry," reeking with maniac hate, yet shrewdly designed to perpetuate the fury and the Nazi creed which fed upon it.

Robert Ley, another Nazi in the top layer of the brown hierarchy and, of course, a ferocious anti-Semite, also gave the world a last testament, written just before he too ended his life. Like his master's, its principal theme was the Jews. But Ley proclaimed himself an abject penitent. Anti-Semitism, he declared, had been Germany's fatal mistake, the source of all its woes, and he implored the German people to renounce it. But his "repentance" is curiously unrelated to any moral consideration. Anti-Semitism was a mistaken policy: it failed to produce the expected results. And by all accounts, the same moral blackout envelops the German people as a whole, not only with respect to anti-Semitism and its crimes, but with respect to the unparalleled disaster which they brought upon all mankind.

4

REPORTS of the murder mills at Auschwitz, Birkenau, Treblinka, Maidanek, Sobibor, Dachau, Muthausen, Buchenwald, Belsen, and numerous other places, built and operated by the Germans with all their vaunted scientific thoroughness, were in circulation during the first year of the war, but it took the world a long time to take note of them and a still longer time to believe them. It was only on December 17, 1942, when the policy of mass murder had been in operation for at least two years, that Anthony Eden, British Foreign Secretary, informed the House of Commons that the Nazi plan to exterminate the Jews was in full swing. In America, as well as in Britain and its dominions, official and unofficial voices were raised in horror and action was demanded to rescue as many of the doomed as possible. In the United States, Congress and state legislatures adopted resolutions; there were petitions and memoranda, public demonstrations and days of prayer and fasting, and compassion.

Finally, in April 1943, delegates representing the governments of the United States and Britain met in Bermuda to consider measures of relief and rescue. Like the conference which took place five years earlier at Evian, it gave rise to many hopes, but, like its predecessor, it resulted only in lofty sentiments, vague assurances, and expressions of profound regrets. There were "technical" difficulties which the conferees found insurmountable: the British White Paper of 1939, which prevented the admission of the victims into Palestine; the immigration laws and lack of shipping, which prevented their admission into the United States. One Jewish body, more outspoken than the others, publicly branded the Bermuda Conference as "a cruel mockery."

In January 1944, President Roosevelt, yielding to continued pressure from Christian as well as Jewish sources, took more effective action. He set up a War Refugee Board, consisting of his Secretary of State, Secretary of War, and Secretary of the Treasury, "to forestall the plan of the Nazis to exterminate all the Jews and other persecuted minorities in Europe." In the summer the Board, with the help of a number of Jewish organizations, among them the Jewish Agency for Palestine and the Joint Distribution Committee, set up a rescue unit in Turkey which assisted in saving hundreds of Jewish lives. But there was a bitter tang in the accomplishments of the War Refugee Board; they indicated what might have been achieved by the democracies toward the rescue, not of hundreds, but of thousands if the effort had not been so little and so late.

5

OTHER efforts conducted by Jewish groups and individuals, some of them, like the *Vaad Hatzala* (Rescue Commission), set up in America, but stemming mainly from the Yishuv, had been in progress which accomplished more. In fact, whatever was achieved by the War Refugee Board in Turkey was largely the result of the superb courage and resourcefulness of the couriers from the Yishuv. Soldiers from the Yishuv, fighting in North Africa, the Balkans, and Italy, lost no opportunity to bring succor to their people, as did Jewish partisan groups in France, Yugoslavia, Poland, and Russia. Men and women from the Yishuv managed to reach ghettos and concentration camps, some by parachute, to rescue or to organize resistance.

The time is not yet for a full account of the epic deeds that were performed, of the heroes and heroines who survived and of those who perished. But not even this incomplete account can omit the name of Enzo Sereni, scion of a distinguished Italian-Jewish family, a bold and luminous spirit, who had become a humble pioneer in Palestine. Chosen leader of a group of Jewish parachutists, Sereni insisted on sharing the perils of his followers. He parachuted behind the German lines in Italy, fell into the hands of the Nazis, and was done to death in the hideous murder mill at Dachau. Nor can this account omit the name of Hannah Senesch, a member of the same Palestine group, young, ardent, and, like Sereni, remarkably gifted, who performed a similar feat and met a similar fate in a prison in Hungary. Five others of the same group—Zvi ben Yaakov, Abba Berditchev, Perez Goldstein, Raphael Reiss, and Habiba Reich-Martinovitch—are also known to have perished while on rescue missions in Europe. The four lines of Hannah's last poem became part of her legacy to the youth of Palestine and of the whole world:

Happy the match consumed igniting the flame;
Happy the flame ablaze in secret hearts;
Happy the hearts in honor beating their last:
Happy the match consumed that lighted the flame.

An outstanding rescue undertaking was the Youth Aliyah, inspired and led by Henrietta Szold, which up to the end of 1945 succeeded in saving over 17,000 Jewish children and bringing them to Palestine. The effort, begun in 1933 with the rescue of children from Germany, came to embrace other lands where the German murder machine was planted, and reached out also into the concentration camps.

Throughout Europe, particularly in France, Belgium, and the Netherlands, thousands of Jews, especially children, were kept from the bloody toils of the Gestapo by Christian neighbors and friends, many of whom, however, weaned the children away from their faith and insisted on retaining them. Switzerland became a city of refuge for thousands who escaped from France; and generous asylum was provided by Sweden to large numbers who fled across the channels from Denmark. Some 900 were received by the United States and lodged in a camp near Oswego, New York, under a plan to set up temporary havens for refugees in various lands—"free ports," some advocates called them. It was a brave plan, designed to save lives without offending the immigration laws, but it fell pitifully short of the hopes it awakened.

6

IN THE summer of 1943 came reports which the world found even more incredible than the first stories of the mass murders. The surviving Jews of Poland, penned in their walled ghettos and extermination centers, had thrown down the gauntlet to their executioners! The first rumors, which by the fall of that year had been fully substantiated, were of a revolt in the ghetto of Warsaw. They were followed by accounts of uprisings in the ghettos of Bialystok, Bendin, Vilna, Cracow, Tarnopol, Stryj, Czestochowa, and other cities. Finally, it was learned that outbreaks had occurred in extermination centers also, in Treblinka, Sobibor, Trawniki, Poniatowka, and others.

Jews were also playing an important part in the underground resistance of the occupied countries, particularly in Russia, France, Yugoslavia, and Czechoslovakia. There were Jewish officers among the Maquis, men like Captain Robert Gamzon, and Captain Yechiel Ashkenazi-Bader. Moreover, partisan bands consisting entirely of Jews were operating in Poland, France, Greece and Russia, cutting the enemy's communications, killing murderers, rescuing victims and protecting them in hiding places in the forests.

The spirit of the men and women who fought the enemy in the ghettos and forests of Poland is preserved in songs, some of which reached the ears of their brothers in other lands after the liberation. The following is a translation from the Yiddish of some of the lines of the *Partisan Song of the Vilna Ghetto:*

Never say: "Alas, this journey is my last."
Golden days are near though skies are overcast.
The hour for which we long is not too far:
Like a drum our tread will echo: "Here we are!"

This song was written down with blood and lead;
No song is this of birds from bondage fled.
'Mid crashing walls a people sang this song:
Revolvers clasped, they sang it bold and strong.

7

THE first steps in the uprising in Warsaw were taken in March 1942 on the initiative of Hechalutz, the Zionist pioneer organization. Fortified bunkers were prepared at various locations in the ghetto, other points were mined, and twenty-two combatant units were organized, eighteen consisting of Zionist groups and four affiliated with the Socialist *Bund*. Rifles, revolvers, hand grenades, and a few machine guns were obtained from friendly groups of the Polish underground, or purchased from Nazi soldiers and their Lithuanian, Ukrainian, and Latvian auxiliaries. Mordecai Anilevitch, leader of Hashomer Hatzair (The Young Watchman), one of the Hechalutz affiliates, was in general command. He was one of a number who left the comparative safety of the forests, where they operated as a guerrilla band, to provide leadership for the uprising.

They and many of their comrades in Warsaw and elsewhere, nearly all of whom perished in the struggle, have already become legendary figures: Abraham Diamant, "the Corporal"; Abraham Eiger, who, though mortally wounded, shouted defiance to the attacking Nazis from a balcony, predicting their doom; Lutek Rothblatt, commander of the Akiba unit; Isaac Zuckerman, one of the few survivors; and numerous others. The units commanded by Zechariah Artzstein and Joseph Farber were the last to continue the struggle inside the Warsaw ghetto. In the Bialystok ghetto the leader of the uprising was Mordecai Tenenbaum-Tamarov, and the hero of Czestochowa was Mark Fallman.

The names of many women should be included in the heroic roster: they were not behind the men in daring and endurance, and they were especially adept in the procurement of arms and as couriers between the ghettos and the partisan units in the forests. In Cracow ninety-three Orthodox girls, students of a Beth Jacob seminary, took their own lives so as not to fall into the hands of the foul enemy. Among the organizers and combatants in Warsaw and elsewhere were the indomitable and ubiquitous Tosha Altman; Tzivya Lubetkin, "the mother of the ghetto," who survived the holocaust; the heroic sisters Frumka and Chantcha Plotnitzky, and many others. Tzivya was one of forty surviving Jewish fighters who, after crawling for twenty hours, without food or water, through the sewers of Warsaw, emerged on the "Aryan" side, and on May 12, 1943, escaped in a commandeered truck to a forest outside the city.

Chaya Grossman was in the forefront of the uprising in Bialystok, and she too was of the few who survived. She attended the first postwar international Zionist conference, held in London in September 1945, and addressing the delegates, she said:

> Battle was the thing for which we strove. The moment of battle was the moment for which we hoped and waited . . . Our movement was great and strong, and it was glorious also in defeat. To live is no great matter. One must know *how* to live and—still more important—how to die. We knew that with our death all would not be lost, that our death would be transformed into an uplifting force, into a Torah for the education of our young . . . And one thing more I would say to you, although I find it hard to bring to my feeble lips: the heroes of our people are not exactly its famous leaders; they are the common men and women, the humble and the silent . . . For us the war is not over.

8

ACTIVE resistance in Warsaw began January 18, 1943. The inmates of the ghetto—thousands of them every day—had been evacuated to the gas chambers and crematoriums of Treblinka, the victims being assured they were being taken to the Ukraine for farm labor. The deportations had begun in the summer of 1942, and by the spring of the following year, only some 40,000 were left of the 450,000 whom the Germans had impounded in the small enclosure. But those who remained had learned the truth, and they had organized to exact a price for their lives.

On April 18, 1943, a pitched battle broke out between Jewish units and Nazi battalions equipped with artillery, tanks, bombing planes, machine guns, and flame throwers. After more than a week of furious fighting at close quarters, the Nazis, finding the cost too high, withdrew and bombarded the ghetto with ground batteries and bombed it from the air. They set fire to the ghetto and on April 28, launched a force of 6,000 heavily armed men against the survivors. But it was not until two months later that the last flickers of resistance were extinguished.

The following is one of the final paragraphs in a report of the uprising issued by the Jewish Fighting Organization of Warsaw and published by the World Jewish Congress in November 1944:

> With special equipment and bloodhounds the Germans proceeded to locate the Jewish underground bunkers. On May 8 they surrounded the main bunker of the Jewish Fighting Organization and cut off all five of the entrances leading to it. In view of the hopelessness of the situation, and in order not to be taken alive by the Germans, Aryeh Wilner called upon his comrades to take their own lives. Lutek Rothblatt first shot his own mother then himself. In that bunker most of the members of the Organization perished, including Mordecai Anilevitch, the commander in chief.

Strangely reminiscent of the last desperate resistance in Jerusalem against the legions of Titus nineteen centuries earlier, are these uprisings in the ghettos and extermination camps of Poland. In Jerusalem, after the Temple had been taken and burned, the Jews also fought in ruined buildings and streets and in the underground passages of the Upper City. There too a band of starved and ill-armed defenders defied the mightiest conquerors of the age, the Romans who, in the arts of torture and mass murder, however, were but tyros compared to the Germans of today.

9

THREE areas of this shrunken planet: Europe, America, and Palestine, may endure as centers of a creative Jewish life into the indefinite future, but the least likely to do so is Europe. Outside the Soviet Union, where all that is certain is that since the Communist Revolution, Jewish life has gone glimmering, only about 1,250,000 Jews are thought to have been left alive on the continent,

The Remnants of
EUROPEAN JEWRY
IN 1946
FINLAND
2,000
1,500
NORWAY
2,000
1,000
SWEDEN
6,500
20,000
DENMARK
7,000
5,000
SOVIET UNION
3,000,000
2,000,000
GREAT BRITAIN
300,000
350,000
150,000
30,000
Kovno
Vilna
Minsk
POLAND
3,325,000
120,000
Bialystok
Bergen-Belsen
NETH.
GERMANY
500,000
12,000
Warsaw
Treblinka
BELG.
60,000
30,000
Lodz
Lublin
Sobibor
Maidanek
Buchenwald
Theresienstadt
Kielce
Ratibor
Oswiecim
(Auschwitz)
Lwow
Tarnopol
CZECHO.
350,000
55,000
Nuremberg
Birkenau
Stryj
Dachau
FRANCE
250,000
180,000
AUSTRIA
180,000
5,000
SWITZ.
18,000
28,000
Evian
HUNGARY
450,000
200,000
RUMANIA
850,000
300,000
YUGOSLAVIA
75,000
10,000
ITALY
50,000
30,000
BULGARIA
50,000
45,000
GREECE
75,000
10,000
LEGEND
1933 → 100,000
1946 → 15,000
Displaced Persons not included

and their future has been a grave concern not only to themselves but to the governments of the world. The last months of the war in Europe unlocked to the gaze of the Allied armies sweeping across Poland, Germany, and Austria the Gargantuan horrors of the concentration camps and murder mills, and the civilian populations of the world were permitted to view a moderate sampling of those horrors in the cinemas. But in the various occupation zones of Germany and Austria hundreds of thousands of Jewish survivors were, in 1947, still subsisting in displaced persons camps. They could not be repatriated to countries like Poland, which had become vast graveyards haunted by the ghosts of their kin and all their past, and where, moreover, the old animosity, far from having dissolved in the crucible of common suffering, emerged stronger and more malignant than ever.

In Poland the fact that out of the pre-war community of more than three million Jews, only some thousands remained alive in the country, failed to slake the savage hostility with which the entire population seemed to be infected. Thousands of Jews who managed to survive in Poland or returned from other lands, including the Soviet Union, where about 250,000 of them found refuge during the war, fled for their lives from a wave of violence which the government, itself menaced by the same fury, confessed itself unable to stem. Nor, apparently, were the religious leaders of the Polish people, men like Cardinal Hlond, able or even willing to stem it. After the liberation, hundreds of Jews, some of them men and women who had fought in the Polish underground, were murdered in Poland, the most sanguinary incident being the pogrom in Kielce in July 1946, which took the lives of more than forty of them. Nor were conditions in Hungary and Rumania, with their larger Jewish communities, much better, although in those countries the more violent forms of hostility were not so prevalent.

Alas for the logic of those who reasoned that the Nazi doctrines would be buried in the ruins of vanquished Germany, and that the common struggle would erase old rancors and prejudices! Instead, fresh motives arose to sustain them: the Jewish possessions, for instance, which the Nazis had "Aryanized" and which the new owners were determined to hold, not to speak of the appalling misery that stalked the continent, making men bitter and callous and keen to find a pretext for denying to others a share of the little that was left.

10

BY ALL accounts, the majority of the Jewish survivors in Europe stood loins girded and staff in hand, eager to wander forth, and the land toward which their faces were turned was Palestine. With regard to the "displaced" Jews still languishing in the camps of Germany and Austria, the predominant urge toward Palestine was confirmed by many reports, official and unofficial. In August 1945, three months after Germany's surrender, Earl G. Harrison, a member of the Inter-Governmental Committee on Refugees, after a personal investigation at the behest of President Harry S. Truman, reported that the desire of the displaced Jews to leave Germany "is an urgent one . . . They want to be evacuated to Palestine now, just as other national groups are being repatriated to their homes." Very few Polish and Baltic Jews, he reported, wished to return to their countries, and for them and others who did not wish to return, "Palestine is definitely and pre-eminently the first choice." Nor was there any reason to believe that the great majority of the other remnants in central and eastern Europe, with the exception of the Soviet Union, saw their future linked with that continent.

The situation of those in the displaced persons camps in Germany, Austria, and Italy continued to deteriorate. They made brave efforts to organize their lives, though necessarily on a provisional basis, their principal sources of aid being the Joint Distribution Committee, the United Nations Relief and Rehabilitation Administration (UNRRA), and the American military authorities. The most buoyant groups consisted of those who were preparing themselves for life in Palestine. But the congestion and privations from which they still suffered, and, even more, the anguish of hopes so often betrayed or deferred, were not conducive to the building or preservation of morale. The heaviest blow sustained by them was the rejection by the British government of the unanimous recommendation of the Anglo-American Committee of Inquiry on Palestine, repeatedly urged by President Truman, to admit 100,000 of them without delay into Palestine. Moreover, the population of the camps, as a result of the flight of Jews from the postwar terror in Poland and other countries, had greatly increased. In January 1946, it was 80,000; by January 1947, it had risen to 256,000.

CHAPTER SEVENTY

Crimson Dawn

UNIQUE among all the aggregates of the sorely stricken Jewish people was the Yishuv in Palestine: outwardly unique in possessing all the basic economic and cultural assets of a national commonwealth; inwardly unique in its freedom from the peculiar social malaise with which minorities are afflicted. Numerically the Yishuv, in 1947, was still a minority, constituting less than 40 per cent of the population. But it led in enterprise and achievement and, even more important, its spirit was dominated by the sense of being "at home." This profound and almost mystical feeling of "at homeness," the fine distillation of four millennia of physical and spiritual association, is the very soul of the Yishuv. It explains the absence among its members of that sense of subordination and uneasiness which usually oppresses minorities, and it provides the key to their aspirations and reactions as a community.

The part which the Yishuv played in the war greatly enhanced its proud uniqueness and self-confidence. To all intents and purposes the Yishuv was one of the United Nations, its character as such underscored by the fact that in its devotion to the Allied cause it stood alone in an Arab world of aloofness or hostility, veiled and open. On the outbreak of war, a registration in the Yishuv for national service brought out 136,000 volunteers, 50,000 of them women. Its farm settlements, of which some forty new ones were established during the war years, increased their output, producing new crops to provide a substantial part of the food required by the armies based in Palestine. Its industrial facilities were expanded and geared to the manufacture of war materials, including cement, textiles, electrical appliances, leather and metal goods, chemicals and other items. Its considerable scientific resources were mobilized for war service in tropical medicine, surgery, meteorology, and the production of optical instruments and synthetic drugs and serums. Its efficient labor force built roads and camps, as well as fortifications like those near the Syrian border, erected at top speed by 10,000 Jewish workers toiling day and night.

But it was the Yishuv's military contribution which, more than anything else, emphasized its distinctiveness among the Jewish communities of the world. All of these communities gave their full share of fighting men to the armed forces of the United Nations, their total numbering a million men and women, but only those from the Yishuv were able to serve in units of their own with their own insignia and under their own flag. The right to do so did not come easily or quickly, and the reason was political rather than military: the British government was too careful of Arab sensibilities. Jewish volunteers were at first received in auxiliary or service units only. Gradually, however, the combatant ranks were opened to them, and the principle of "parity," under which an equal number of Jewish and Arab units were to be formed, had to be abandoned because Arabs were not eager to enlist.

By the winter of 1944 the number of Palestinian Jews in the British forces, among them 2,000 women in the Auxiliary Territorial Service, had grown to 33,000, and they had seen service in France, in Greece and Crete, in Cyprus and Malta, in North Africa from Egypt to Tunisia, in Abyssinia and Eritrea where their commandos gained special distinction. Their language was Hebrew and their non-commissioned officers, as well as many of their commissioned officers, were Jews. There were other Allied contingents in the British forces of the Middle East: Czech, Greek, Polish, and the British information service made the world aware of them. The Jewish contingent was as large or larger than the others, with a long and heroic record of service, but it took several years before the British ventured to call them Palestinian Jews rather than just Palestinians.

In Britain and America an unremitting agitation was conducted to authorize the formation of a large Jewish fighting force, but it met with even greater resistance than the similar demands that had been made during the First World War. Finally, however, in September 1944, the British government announced the formation of a Jewish Brigade "to take part in active operations," its flag to be the blue and white banner of Zion, and its shoulder insignia of the same distinctive design. The Brigade, commanded by Brigadier Ernest F. Benjamin, went into action against the Nazis in Italy in March 1945, took part in the Allied sweep into Austria and Germany and, before its demobilization, was garrisoned in Belgium and Holland. "The Jewish Brigade," said Prime Minister Churchill to the House of Commons on May 2, 1945, when he announced the surrender of all German troops in Italy, "fought in the front line with courage, and gave an excellent account of themselves."

There were indeed no keener soldiers than the fighting men from the Yishuv. Some of their individual and group exploits have been recognized and recorded, but many more will remain unknown. Only a few can be recorded in this chronicle. David Raziel, of rare courage and resourcefulness, lost his life in Iraq where he headed a group on a secret mission for the British during the pro-Axis revolt of that country in 1941. Twenty-three young men of the Yishuv, led by a British officer, all perished in a sabotage mission in Syria. The British and Free French invasion of Syria was vanguarded by a group of fifty scouts from Jewish outposts in Upper Galilee who, with supreme courage, prevented Vichy troops from blowing up two bridges that were vital to the advance of the invaders. That feat was equaled by other exploits in Syria, Greece, and especially Eritrea and Abyssinia, where Jewish commandos, operating in suicide squads, played an important part in the capture of Keren, Amba Alagi, and Gondar.

Jewish combat and auxiliary units played an important part also in the seesaw battles of the North African deserts, including the long siege of Tobruk, the initial deadlock at El Alamein, and the sweep of the Eighth Army westward which destroyed the redoubtable Nazi Afrika Korps and saved the Allied cause from disaster. In these operations Jewish commandos performed exploits unsurpassed by any others. From Tobruk to Tripoli the supply and transport companies, to which General Montgomery paid a glowing tribute, were mainly Jewish; and roads and railroads were repaired and superintended by Jewish units working under a constant hail of bombs. Their senior officer, who was killed in the line of duty, was Brigadier Frederick Kisch, Chief Engineer of the Eighth Army, a gallant soldier and veteran Zionist leader.

2

THROUGH all the war years, however, the Yishuv lay under an incubus even more galling than the sorrows, toils, and anxieties which the war imposed. It was the White Paper of May 1939. That instrument had no legal validity, having been rejected by the Mandates Commission of the League of Nations, but the government chose to adhere to it with a rigor which took no account of the catastrophe that befell the Jews of Europe. Thousands of fugitives fleeing from the most fiendish barbarism ever visited on human beings were denied admittance to the land where, they had once been assured, they could live "as of right and not on sufferance," their National Home. The result was that large numbers of them perished who might have been saved. An explanation of this cruel course has been offered that would sound cynical, were it not so plausible: Britain, fighting the Nazis, took the loyalty of the Jews for granted; it was the Arabs it had to appease, their leaders always hovering on the threshold of betrayal and sometimes, as in the pro-Axis revolt of Iraq in 1941, stepping over it.

A series of tragedies resulted, some of which even touched the heart of a world grown callous to human suffering. They will be remembered in association with the names of ships, the *Darien*, the *Salvador*, the *Pacific*, the *Milos*, the *Patria*, the *Atlantic*, the *Struma*, most of them small, unseaworthy craft, overcrowded with fugitives fleeing from torture and death. The *Salvador* foundered in the Sea of Marmara, 200 of her passengers going down with her. Some 1600 refugees who arrived on the *Atlantic* were interned upon landing, then exiled to the Island of Mauritius in the Indian Ocean. The *Patria*, crowded with 1900 refugees slated for deportation, blew up in the harbor of Haifa with a loss of more than 250 lives. Even more grim was the tragedy of the *Struma*. That small vessel, bearing 769 fugitives who were denied admittance to Palestine, was ordered away from Turkey, and in February 1942 she went down in the Black Sea. Only one of her passengers survived.

In the world at large, with nations going down and cities crumbling to rubble, those tragedies, which one touch of humanity or justice would have averted, produced only passing tremors. But the Yishuv was shocked and outraged. The victims were its own kith and kin, shut out without warrant in law or morals from their only place of refuge. The tension was further aggravated by ruthless military and police raids in search of arms. There was bloodshed followed by arrests, and heavy penalties were imposed in an attempt to disarm the Jews and leave them helpless in the face of Arab hostility and official chicanery.

Neither the end of the war, nor the victory of the Labor party, nor the pleas of the survivors of the concentration camps, nor the appeals of American public opinion led by President Truman himself, brought any relaxation to the rigor with which the White Paper was enforced. And, as if to make the intentions of the Mandatory Power still plainer, the former mufti of Jerusalem, organizer of the bloody attacks against the Yishuv in 1929 and 1936, was permitted to escape from France and establish himself in Egypt, where he assumed the direction of his followers as chairman of the Arab Higher Committee of Palestine. During the war, the mufti had been a close collaborator of the Fascists and Nazis and was directly involved in the policy of exterminating the Jews of Europe. The solemn official disavowals failed to convince the Yishuv or the world at large that his return had not come about with the connivance of the authorities. In addition, a number of his lieutenants, whose record of service to the Nazi cause was not less unsavory, were also permitted to return and begin where they had left off in 1939.

The course of the Labor government, its Foreign Office headed by a man who saw fit to season his declarations of policy with cynical anti-Semitic jibes, was particularly painful to the Yishuv, for the Labor Party had repeatedly repudiated the White Paper and demanded unhampered opportunities for the creation of a Jewish Commonwealth in Palestine. The Yishuv's reply to the policy of the Labor government, as announced on November 13, 1945, by Foreign Secretary Ernest Bevin, was firm and unequivocal. It rejected the White Paper and the concept of "illegal" Jewish immigration, and it would continue, it declared, to assist Jews to enter their national home and establish themselves in it. British troops and armament were poured into the country, ostensibly to preserve peace between Jews and Arabs. It was charged, however, that Britain's real object was to safeguard its imperial interests in the Middle East. Observers agreed that never before had there existed such peaceful and cooperative relations between the two communities of the country.

3

WITH the downfall of the Axis, three new factors came to the fore which bedeviled the Palestine situation. The first was the formation, under British tutelage, of the Arab League. The second was the anxiety that arose both in England and the United States over their vast oil interests in Arab countries, particularly in Saudi Arabia. The third was the growing rivalry between Britain and the United States on the one hand and the Soviet Union on the other, a rivalry which produced tension in many areas of the globe, including the Middle East.

The Arab League, contrived by the British as an instrument of imperial policy, is a loose association of the seven Arab states of the Near East—Egypt, Saudi Arabia, Iraq, Syria, Lebanon, Yemen, and Trans-Jordan, the first six of whom were, in 1947, members of the United Nations. The states of the Arab League appear to be held together only by their hostility to Zionism. Their differences, in fact, are more pronounced than their agreements, especially those between Saudi Arabia, ruled by King ibn-Saud, who in 1924 had ousted the Hashemite King Husein, and Iraq and Trans-Jordan, both still headed by Hashemite rulers. But the British hoped that their common antagonism to Zionism would be useful as a diversion from the mounting clamor in Arab countries, in Egypt especially, against continued British control. The anti-Jewish agitation which flowed from the League led, in November 1945, to violent demonstrations in Egypt, marked by indiscriminate looting, and to bloody pogroms in Tripolitania, outbreaks which, it was charged, were fomented for political objectives and were not suppressed by the British authorities as effectively as they could have been.

An even more important reason for the reluctance on the part of Britain—and America also—to offend Arab sensibilities was to be found in the huge oil interests which they control in the Middle East. In 1947, United States interests, through the Arabian-American Oil Company, owned all the oil rights in Saudi Arabia, including the Bahrein Islands, and a fourth of the rights in Iraq and Trans-Jordan, with total reserves estimated at nine to twelve billion barrels. Arabian oil, it was argued, was vital for the operations of the naval and air forces of both countries, and government officials and oil men professed to see the Arabs turning these resources over to Russia the moment Arab demands with respect to Palestine were rejected.

The fear of Russian aggression dominated the international scene, and the Soviet Union was represented as wooing the Arabs, the latter ready to yield to Communist blandishments unless Britain and America wooed them with greater ardor. It was a fallacious oversimplification of a complex situation, for the feudal Arab rulers desired anything but Communist domination, while many of those familiar with the other grave problems of the Arab states, both internal and external, discounted their apparently overshadowing interest in Palestine.

4

BUT even before the war ended, and in growing measure as the months that followed rolled up into years, a new factor came to the fore in Palestine, a force that stirred and amazed the entire world. It was the underground Jewish Resistance Movement, consisting of three military organizations: the Haganah (Defense), embracing most of the able-bodied men and women of the Yishuv; the Irgun Zvai Leumi (National Military Organization), faithful to the militant spirit of Vladimir Jabotinsky, the founder of Revisionism; and the Fighters for the Freedom of Israel, better known as the Stern Group, a smaller band of avowed terrorists. "There exists in this country a secret armed Jewish force," says a memorandum submitted March 25, 1946, by the commander in chief of the Haganah to the Anglo-American Committee of Inquiry.

The armed Jewish forces and the spirit which created them were, however, not new. They harked back to the Hashomer, the corps of mounted guards for the protection of Jewish settlements which came into being in the first decade of the century, when the country was still under Turkish rule. They harked still further back to the self-defense movement in the Russian Pale after the Kishinev pogrom in 1903. As the national militia of the Yishuv, the Haganah came into existence when the Jewish Legion was disbanded after the First World War, its spirit and purpose stamped upon it by men like the daring and high-minded Eliahu Golomb (1893-1945), one of its founders. And in 1921, 1929, and 1936, years when the Yishuv was the target of increasingly violent assaults usually met by the government with forces that were too little and too late, the Haganah went through ordeals of fire which left it stronger than before. Finally, to understand not only the antecedents of the Jewish resistance movement in Palestine, but also its spirit of grim determination, often expressing itself in desperate deeds, the latest and greatest catastrophe sustained by the Jewish people in its entire history must be kept in view. Six million martyrs in Europe called into action a new generation of heroes in Palestine.

> We will not permit the implementation of any solution that puts an end to the last hope of our people [says the memorandum]. To liquidate the Resistance Movement, it will be necessary to liquidate the entire Jewish community in the country and to uproot the eternal love of Zion among the Jews of the world . . . We are the militant Jewish people . . . We will confront the British government with a choice: Accept our vital demands or destroy us.

The memorandum goes on to examine the threats of an Arab-Moslem uprising in Palestine and other countries, and declares them to be groundless. "We ourselves can overcome any attack or trouble from that quarter [the Arabs in Palestine] without assistance from British or American forces." And the possibility of invasion from the Arab countries is practically ruled out by their internal problems and international tensions. Nor does the memorandum find the fear of a Soviet-Arab alliance any more real. "There is not a single Arab government," it states, "that draws its support from the masses of the people. Feudalism still thrives in Arab lands, and an abyss separates the enslaved and impoverished masses from the ruling groups. Any penetration of Soviet influence into Arab lands constitutes a danger to the dynasties and ruling classes."

5

IT BECAME increasingly evident that the strength, daring, and skill of the resistance movement would make the apparent aim of the British government—to stifle the Zionist enterprise—extremely difficult to carry out. With the conclusion of the war, acts of sabotage and reprisal, most of them the work of the Irgun and Stern Group, and involving loss of life, multiplied. Even before the war was over—in November 1944—Lord Moyne, who had been the colonial secretary when the *Patria* and *Struma* went down, was assassinated. There were attacks on military installations, including airfields; on police stations, railway lines, trains, and pipelines; and kidnapings of British officers who were held as hostages. On June 16, 1946, the Palmach, striking force of the Haganah, blew up the five bridges across the Jordan River, isolating Trans-Jordan which the British had transformed into a puppet kingdom. On July 22, 1946, came the most disastrous act of the Irgun—the blowing up, with a loss of nearly a hundred lives, of the British Army Headquarters and the Secretariat of the Palestine Government, both located in the King David Hotel in Jerusalem. Early in 1947 an officers' club in Jerusalem was blown up with sixteen dead and thirteen wounded, and on May 4, 1947, the Irgun blasted open the prison at Acre, liberating more than 200 prisoners.

The government retaliated with attacks on Jewish colonies and searches for arms, in the course of which property was ruthlessly destroyed and lives were lost. In November 1945, British troops fired on colonists at Givat Hayim, Shefayim, and Rishpon, killing 8 of them and wounding 75. The army made wholesale arrests, and imposed curfews and other restrictions which weighed heavily on the life of the Yishuv. Palestine, to all intents and purposes, became a land ruled by the army and police. On a single day, June 29, 1946, the army arrested over 2,700 men and women, including officers of the Jewish Agency and other leaders of the Yishuv, and occupied the Agency headquarters in Jerusalem. The *Vaad Leumi* (National Jewish Council) responded with a proclamation of non-cooperation with the government.

After the attack on the officers' club in Jerusalem, martial law was imposed on Tel Aviv and other Jewish areas. It affected almost half the population of the Yishuv and was not lifted until March 17, 1947, fifteen days later. The British claimed that the measure had proved successful: the guilty, they announced, had been discovered with the aid of informers. But the Jews knew that the claim was an idle boast. They were not prepared to turn informers for a government which, by destroying the last hope of the remnants in Europe, was, they maintained, itself responsible for the terror.

6

BUT the Haganah, the largest and strongest of the three underground forces, while refusing to adopt a course which would have plunged the Yishuv into civil war, deplored and denounced the acts of terror committed by the other two, as did also the Zionist Congress, the responsible leaders of the Yishuv, and the Jewish Agency. The Haganah concentrated on a policy of resistance which, it claimed, was constructive rather than destructive. This policy consisted first of organizing and conducting the "illegal" immigration into Palestine, and second, of extending and protecting Jewish colonization in the country.

The first involved the creation of a far-flung network of activities in Europe, in ships both in port and on the high seas, along the coast of Palestine, and in the settlements. It involved also operations of a military character, such as the destruction of radar stations and coast guard installations, and the mining of deportation ships by a squad of specially trained underwater swimmers who became famous as "the frog-men." Scores of ships, large and small, filled with refugees undeterred by peril or hardship, attempted to run the formidable blockade established by the British navy and air force. Some were successful: how many and how large the number of refugees they landed has of course remained secret. Dozens of others were intercepted, their passengers, usually after a violent encounter with naval boarding parties, taken to Haifa, and, beginning August 1946, transferred to detention camps in Cyprus.

The second part of the Haganah resistance program, the protection and extension of Jewish colonization, involved operations equally daring and spectacular. On March 5, 1946, for example, British troops occupied Birya, a tiny settlement and labor camp in Galilee, and removed and imprisoned its 24 settlers. Nine days later, 3,000 unarmed men and women of all ages and classes streamed to Birya to reclaim and rebuild it. There was tension and danger and more demolition, but in the end the British had to allow 20 occupants to remain. But even more dramatic was the role played by the Haganah in the establishment of new settlements, especially in the Negeb. On a single day, October 6, 1946, but after months of meticulous preparations, eleven new points were planted in that region. Immigration and colonization, the primary factors in the growth and safety of the Yishuv, became the two major concerns of the Haganah. Nor was the life of the Yishuv in every other sphere, industrial, commercial, and cultural, seriously impaired by the disturbed state of the country and the repressive measures of the government.

7

IT BECAME increasingly clear, however, that Britain's policy would not lead to the pacification of the country or to a solution of its political problem. Having repudiated the unanimous report and recommendations of the Anglo-American Committee of Inquiry, the government proposed a cantonization or federalization plan which still denied the Jews control of immigration and colonization. Even among the moderates the conviction grew that the Britain of Lord Balfour and Lloyd George was gone beyond recall; and the Twenty-second Zionist Congress, held in December 1946 in the Swiss city of Basel, rich with memories of Theodor Herzl and the early days of the movement, voted Chaim Weizmann out of power. For nearly thirty years he had been the world leader of Zionism and the persistent advocate and symbol of cooperation with England. The federalization plan was rejected by the Jewish Agency, and it was rejected also by the Arab leaders who remained unyielding in their demand for the immediate independence of Palestine and the total stoppage of Jewish immigration.

Finally, the government confessed its helplessness, and called upon the United Nations to undertake a solution of the problem "of the future government of Palestine." In May 1947, after a special session lasting three weeks and packed with tension and drama, the Assembly of the United Nations named a committee of inquiry of its own, with instructions to report back in time for the regular session of the Assembly in September of the same year. The high point of the special session was a declaration by Andrei Gromyko, the delegate from the Soviet Union, favoring either a bi-national state in Palestine or a Jewish state in part of the country. The declaration represented a complete reversal of what was believed to be the Russian position, and appeared to eliminate the fear which was so frequently voiced by British ministers, and which no doubt haunted also many of the officials of the State Department in Washington, that a pro-Jewish policy in Palestine would throw the Arabs into the arms of Communist Russia.

8

IN THE summer of 1947, while the United Nations Special Committee on Palestine was still conducting its inquiry, the world witnessed a remarkable dramatization of the tragedy and heroism of the homeless survivors seeking asylum in their promised homeland. The spectacle was provided by the Labor Government itself in an attempt to enforce a new policy under which the "illegals" were not to be taken to Cyprus, but returned to the country whence they had sailed.

On July 11 the *Exodus 1947*, a former American coastal vessel crowded with more than 4,500 men, women, and children bound for Palestine, slipped out of a southern French port. Seven days later, the ship was intercepted by a British squadron of five destroyers and a cruiser, and, although well outside the territorial waters of Palestine, was rammed and boarded. A battle ensued in which three of those on board, including William Bernstein, an American crew member, were killed, and seventeen wounded.

Three British prison ships then carried the "illegals" back to France, but they refused to disembark. Only in Palestine, they declared, would they land willingly, and the French government, while it offered them hospitality, would not permit the British to force them to accept it. For nearly a month the grim resolution of the refugees, huddled behind the barbed wire of the prison ships off the coast of France, stood pitted against the will of the British government. Early in September the British gave up the duel. The ships sailed to the British occupation zone in Germany where, after desperate resistance, the refugees were forced ashore and taken to detention camps. The heroic odyssey of the *Exodus 1947* produced a profound impression throughout the world.

9

IN THE meantime, the United Nations Special Committee on Palestine completed its labors and published its conclusions. It agreed unanimously that the British Mandate should be terminated at once, and the majority recommended that Palestine be partitioned into independent Jewish and Arab states, with Jerusalem and its environs internationalized and governed under the authority of the United Nations. The majority plan provided also that the economic unity of the country be recognized and safeguarded in respect to transit and communication facilities, currency, customs, and irrigation and reclamation projects.

On September 16, 1947 the United Nations General Assembly opened its sessions at Flushing Meadows, and on November 29 came the decision. With some changes, the Assembly, by a vote of 33 to 13, adopted the majority report, the most important change being the removal of the Arab city of Jaffa from the Jewish state. The large vote in favor of an independent Jewish state—7 more than the necessary two-thirds—was important enough, but even more significant was the presence among the 33 of the two leading world-powers, the United States and the Soviet Union.

The ten weeks before the final vote were tense with uncertainty and suspense. Palestine, one of the major problems of the postwar world, became the touchstone of the capacity of the United Nations for constructive action. For the first time the United States and Russia stood together on an important issue, and throughout the world men hailed their agreement as a good augury for the peace of the world as a whole. The speeches delivered by the Moslem delegates rang with defiance and menace. The Jewish spokesmen —Chaim Weizmann, Abba Hillel Silver, and Moshe Shertok— urged the adoption of the majority report as a measure of compensation, incomplete though it was, for the millennial hopes and sufferings of the Jewish people and their toil and sacrifice in Palestine.

In Jewish communities throughout the world the decision released a wave of joy and thanksgiving. Longstanding antagonisms seemed to dissolve and vanish. No event since the year 70 C.E., when the Romans destroyed the Jewish state, appeared so momentous. A new era had dawned in the history of the eternal people, the era of the Third Commonwealth.

But a sober realization of the problems and perils that would have to be met went hand in hand with the jubilation. The Jewish people, and the Yishuv in particular, had no illusions about it. And not a few, particularly in the Yishuv, even took the epochal decision with reserve, having known the fickleness of political promises and remembering the warning of the Psalmist: "Put not your trust in princes." Grim days were ahead for the Third Jewish Commonwealth in the immediate future, and the task of establishing its firm foundations would demand a heavy price. But the hand of the Lord was again upon His people and there could be no retreat.

10

THE supreme test of the Yishuv began promptly on the morrow of the United Nations decision. Thousands of well-armed and organized Arab mercenaries from the neighboring countries were allowed by the British to enter Palestine. Outlying Jewish settlements in Galilee and the Negeb were attacked, the area between Jaffa and Tel Aviv became a battleground, and in Jerusalem the Jewish quarter of the Old City found itself beleaguered. Destructive bombings and road attacks took a large toll, and the number of casualties on both sides continued to rise. The policy frankly pursued by the Mandatory Power was one of non-cooperation with the United Nations decision; its conduct gave aid and comfort to the Arab attackers and hampered the efforts of the Jews to defend themselves.

As the months passed and the tempo of battle mounted in Palestine, the hardest blow against the Yishuv was struck in the Security Council of the United Nations. With startling suddenness the government of the United States reversed its stand on partition. By the middle of April, with the termination of the mandate set for May 15, the General Assembly was again in special session at Lake Success to consider an American proposal to place Palestine under UN trusteeship. But while the Assembly, with its committees, subcommittees, and international rivalries, was pursuing its desultory course, the military arm of the Yishuv took the decision out of its hands by making partition a reality. In a series of brilliant actions, the Haganah, with the Irgun now operating under its command, dealt the Arab bands a crippling blow at the Battle of Mishmar Haemek, reopened the vital road to Jerusalem, seized the cities of Haifa, Tiberias, Safed, and Beisan, as well as numerous strategic Arab villages, and compelled Jaffa to surrender. The mandatory regime, in the meantime, was liquidating its authority and functions, and doing it in a manner apparently designed to leave the country in a state of chaos. The Yishuv, however, had in readiness for May 15 a Provisional Council of Government and an administrative apparatus of its own.

II

THE Yishuv had something else in readiness: the proclamation of its independence and statehood. On May 14, 1948, David Ben Gurion, premier of the Provisional Government, read the following declaration of sovereign statehood to the members of the National Council meeting in Tel Aviv:

> The land of Israel was the birthplace of the Jewish people. Here their spiritual, religious and national identity was formed. Here they achieved independence and created a culture of national and universal significance. Here they wrote and gave the Bible to the world.
>
> Exiled from Palestine, the Jewish people remained faithful to it in all the countries of their dispersion, never ceasing to pray and hope for their return and restoration of their national freedom.
>
> Impelled by this historic association, Jews strove throughout the centuries to go back to the land of their fathers and regain

statehood. In recent decades they returned in their masses. They reclaimed a wilderness, revived their language, built cities and villages, and established a vigorous and ever-growing community, with its own economic and cultural life. They sought peace, yet were ever prepared to defend themselves. They brought blessings of progress to all inhabitants of the country.

In the year 1897 the first Zionist Congress, inspired by Theodor Herzl's vision of a Jewish state, proclaimed the right of the Jewish people to a national revival in their own country.

This right was acknowledged by the Balfour Declaration of November 2, 1917, and reaffirmed by the mandate of the League of Nations, which gave explicit international recognition to the historic connection of the Jewish people with Palestine and their right to reconstitute their national home.

The Nazi holocaust which engulfed millions of Jews in Europe proved anew the urgency of the re-establishment of the Jewish state, which would solve the problem of Jewish homelessness by opening the gates to all Jews and lifting the Jewish people to equality in the family of nations.

Survivors of the European catastrophe as well as Jews from other lands, claiming their right to a life of dignity, freedom and labor, and undeterred by hazards, hardships and obstacles, have tried unceasingly to enter Palestine.

In the second world war, the Jewish people in Palestine made a full contribution in the struggle of freedom-loving nations against the Nazi evil. The sacrifices of their soldiers and efforts of their workers gained them title to rank with the peoples who founded the United Nations.

On November 29, 1947, the General Assembly of the United Nations adopted a resolution for re-establishment of an independent Jewish State in Palestine and called upon inhabitants of the country to take such steps as may be necessary on their part to put the plan into effect. This recognition by the United Nations of the right of the Jewish people to establish their independent state may not be revoked.

It is, moreover, the self-evident right of the Jewish people to be a nation, as all other nations, in its own sovereign state.

Accordingly we, the members of the National Council, representing the Jewish people in Palestine and the Zionist movement of the world, met together in solemn assembly by virtue of the natural and historic right of the Jewish people and the resolution of the General Assembly of the United Nations, hereby proclaim the establishment of the Jewish state in Palestine, to be called Israel.

We hereby declare that as from the termination of the mandate at midnight this night of the 14th to 15th of May, 1948, and until the setting up of duly elected bodies of the state in accordance with a constitution to be drawn up by a Constituent Assembly not later than the 1st day of October, 1948, the present National Council shall act as the Provisional State Council, and its executive organ, the National Administration, shall constitute the provisional government of the State of Israel.

The State of Israel will be open to Jewish immigration and to the ingathering of our exiles; will promote the development of the country for the benefit of all its inhabitants; will be based on precepts of liberty, justice and peace taught by the Hebrew prophets; will uphold the full social and political equality of all its citizens without distinction of race, creed or sex; will guarantee full freedom of conscience, worship, education and culture; will safeguard the sanctity and inviolability of shrines and holy places of all religions, and will dedicate itself to the principles of the Charter of the United Nations.

We appeal to the United Nations to assist the Jewish people in the building of its state and to admit Israel into the family of nations.

In the midst of wanton aggression we call upon the Arab inhabitants of the State of Israel to return to the ways of peace and play their part in the development of the state, with full and equal citizenship and due representation in all its bodies and institutions, provisional or permanent.

We offer peace and amity to all neighboring states and their peoples, and invite them to cooperate with the independent Jewish nation for the common good of all. The State of Israel is ready to contribute its full share to the peaceful progress and reconstruction of the Middle East.

Our call goes out to the Jewish people all over the world to rally to our side in the task of immigration and development, and to stand by us in the great struggle for the fulfillment of the dream of generations—the redemption of Israel.

Testifying to our faith in the Rock of Israel, we now affix our signatures to this Proclamation at a meeting of the Provisional State Council held on the ancestral soil in the city of Tel Aviv this Eve-of-Sabbath day, the fifth of the month of Iyyar, 5708 (Friday, May 14, 1948).

Now the nation was reborn on its ancient soil, the first country to extend recognition to Israel being the United States of America. Before it still loomed a hard struggle, perhaps the hardest, the battle against the Arab states on its borders. But the issue of that contest, the Yishuv felt, lay chiefly in the strength of its own right arm and in the might of its own spirit.

12

IN THE United States the great majority of the community, supported by the public opinion of the country as a whole, stood firmly behind the Yishuv. A cross section poll of American Jews, taken in November 1945 by the public opinion analyst, Elmo Roper, revealed that 80.1 per cent favored a Jewish state, 9.4 per cent were undecided, and only 10.5 per cent were opposed. In the presidential campaign of 1944, the platforms of both major parties contained planks in support of a Jewish Commonwealth in Palestine, and in December 1945 a joint resolution was adopted by both houses of Congress urging that Palestine "be opened for free entry of Jews into that country . . . that they may freely proceed with the upbuilding of Palestine as the Jewish national home."

Early in July 1947, the leading Zionist body in the United States, the Zionist Organization of America, held its jubilee convention. It was fifty years since Theodor Herzl stood before the first congress of the scattered people assembled in Basel to launch the movement for national restoration. For people and movement they were years of cataclysmic change and staggering disasters, but also of abiding hope and impressive achievement. The community in America had become the principal, perhaps the only, reservoir of strength in the Diaspora, and the Yishuv in Palestine had become a de facto Jewish commonwealth.

The movement in America had made enormous strides. The convention was informed that the membership of the organization had risen to over 225,000; together with the other Zionist bodies—the Hadassah Women's Zionist Organization, the Mizrachi, the Labor Wing of the movement and others—the number of organized Zionists in the country was well over half a million. As president of the organization, the convention elected Emanuel Neumann, for many years one of the foremost spokesmen of the movement and a leader in the affairs of the American and world organizations, as well as in the work of reclamation in Palestine.

13

IN ITS challenge to the Axis, American Jews rallied to their government with an eagerness not exceeded by any other group. On the home front as well as in the armed services, their contribution, in quality as well as quantity, is on the record. They served in the government and its war agencies, they were in the front ranks of the War Loan drives, they gave blood and money to the Red Cross, they cooperated eagerly in all civilian defense measures. A striking number of Jewish names are on the list of the scientists who contributed to the production of the atomic bomb, the weapon that gave Japan its *coup de grâce* and has since then confronted the world with a new and overshadowing problem.

In the armed forces, according to the statistics of the National Jewish Welfare Board, American Jews, men and women, numbered approximately 550,000, or slightly less than 12 per cent of the estimated population of the community. As in previous wars, that percentage was higher than the corresponding one for the country as a whole, the ratio of the armed forces to the general population having been estimated at about 10 per cent. Some 60 per cent of Jewish physicians under forty-five years of age were in uniform, and a high proportion of the rabbis served as chaplains. Over 25,000 Jewish soldiers and sailors were decorated for valor: they were among the winners of the Congressional Medal of Honor, the Distinguished Service Cross, and other awards. Nearly 8,000 were killed on the field of battle, among them the gallant Major General Maurice Rose, Commander of the Third Armored Division.

The two years following the war produced impressive evidence of the responsiveness of American Jews to the plight of the remnants of their people in Europe and to the need of strengthening and expanding the Yishuv. There was an unprecedented outpouring for relief in Europe and reclamation in Palestine. In 1946, a quota of $100,000,000 for those purposes was oversubscribed, and for 1947 the goal was fixed at $170,000,000. The funds, raised by the United Jewish Appeal, were allocated to the Joint Distribution Committee for its network of activities in Europe and North Africa; to the United Palestine Appeal for land purchase by the Jewish National Fund and for the immigration and colonization program of the Palestine Foundation Fund (Keren Hayesod); and to the United Service for New Americans for assistance to refugee immigrants in the United States.

14

THE Second World War has made the American Jewish community a dominant factor in the destiny of the Jewish people, just as the vital part played by America in the defeat of Germany and the supreme part it played in the defeat of Japan have made the United States the dominant force in the world. How will the community utilize its power and opportunity? How will it meet the obligations which power imposes?

The same questions are being anxiously asked about the role of America in the affairs of the world, but with respect to the Jewish community the factors which determine the answer are even more complex. In both cases the material strength is visible and fairly measurable, but the spiritual assets, like the degree of sensitiveness and understanding, of unity of purpose and will, are not easily appraised and, besides, they fluctuate with the shifting winds of circumstance. With the Jewish community, moreover, these imponderables are dependent on the variations in the general social climate. No minority, least of all the Jewish, is able to act without anxiously glancing over its shoulder at the mood of the majority.

For the war did not remove the uneasiness that oppressed American Jewry in the years that preceded it. A survey of anti-Semitism in the United States during 1946, made by the Anti-Defamation League of the B'nai B'rith, found that the situation was in some respects "comforting," the American people having become "increasingly aware of the dangers inherent in group prejudice." But the survey also found that the native Fascist miscellany, whom the war had driven underground, had re-emerged, the defeat of Nazi Germany having failed to destroy "domestic or world-wide Fascism"; and there was even a "growth of subtle forms of anti-Semitism, manifesting themselves in social, economic and educational discrimination." In addition, there was always the fear that the postwar years might bring new economic and social tensions demanding a scapegoat and, as usual, finding it in the Jew.

Thus the inner strength of American Jewry for meeting its obligation to insure the creative survival of the Jewish people cannot be easily assessed. Large numbers have drifted away from the ancient moorings, hoping for a quiet life in self-denial, seeking escape for themselves and their children in nostrums which the record of the past would show them to be vain. At the same time, however, there are many evidences of a will to self-realization, of an ingathering of inner resources.

As the record of the past shows with respect to other communities, the future of American Jewry would seem to rest with those who, without being the less American for it, will cultivate those spiritual possessions that are authentic to themselves. They are possessions which four millennia of history have sanctified and which, in the teeth of tragedy and suffering, have always brought an affirmation and renewal of life. They are the possessions which have given meaning to the long travail of the Jewish people across the centuries—meaning for themselves and for all mankind. For when all the philosophies of history have been written and the catalogues of "civilizations" compiled, the basic historic fact is still the struggle in the human heart and in human society between the holy and righteous God of Abraham, Moses, and Isaiah, and the idols of paganism. And they are essentially the same, those idol broods, whether they disport themselves elegantly on Mount Olympus or practice their savage lusts in the forests of Germany.

It was those spiritual possessions which, in the words of the well-known benediction, have "kept us alive, and preserved us, and enabled us to reach this season."

FOR ADDITIONAL READING

and

INDEX

For Additional Reading

GENERAL AND REFERENCE WORKS

The Holy Scriptures, A New Translation. Philadelphia, Jewish Publication Society, 1917.

Jewish Encyclopedia. 12 vols., New York, Funk & Wagnalls, 1906.

Encyclopedia of Jewish Knowledge. One vol., New York, Behrman House, 1934.

Universal Jewish Encyclopedia. 10 vols., New York, The Universal Jewish Encyclopedia, Inc., 1939–43.

SALO W. BARON, *A Social and Religious History of the Jews.* 3 vols. New York, Columbia University Press, 1937.

HEINRICH GRAETZ, *History of the Jews* [to 1870]. 6 vols., Philadelphia, Jewish Publication Society, 1895.

JOSEPH JACOBS, *Jewish Contributions to Civilization.* Philadelphia, Jewish Publication Society, 1919.

MARGOLIS AND MARX, *A History of the Jewish People.* Philadelphia, Jewish Publication Society, 1927.

CECIL ROTH, *A History of the Jews in England.* Oxford University Press, 1941.

CECIL ROTH, *The History of the Jews in Italy.* Philadelphia, Jewish Publication Society, 1941.

SOLOMON SCHECHTER, *Studies in Judaism.* 3 series, Philadelphia, Jewish Publication Society, 1908–1924.

PART ONE: THE FIRST COMMONWEALTH

Cambridge Ancient History. (Pertinent chapters in vols. 1, 2, and 3) Cambridge University Press, 1925.

STEPHEN L. CAIGER, *Bible and Spade.* London, Oxford University Press, 1938. (An excellent survey of archaeological discoveries bearing on the historicity of Biblical events. Brief and comprehensive.)

JOHN GARSTANG, *The Foundations of Bible History: Joshua, Judges.* New York, R. R. Smith, 1931.

ISRAEL GOLDBERG and SAMSON BENDERLY, *Outline of Jewish Knowledge.* Vol. 1: *Founding of the Nation.* Vol. 2: *The First Commonwealth.* New York, Bureau of Jewish Education, 1929–30.

CARLETON NOYES, *The Genius of Israel: A Reading of Hebrew Scriptures Prior to the Exile.* Boston, Houghton Mifflin Co., 1924.

MAX RADIN, *The Life of the People in Biblical Times.* Philadelphia, Jewish Publication Society, 1929.

GEORGE ADAM SMITH, *The Historical Geography of the Holy Land.* New York, R. Long and R. R. Smith, 1932.

A. S. YAHUDA, *The Accuracy of the Bible.* London, Heinemann, 1932.

PART TWO: THE SECOND COMMONWEALTH

The First Book of the Maccabees and *The Second Book of the Maccabees,* in the Apocrypha. London, Oxford University Press.

NORMAN BENTWICH, *Hellenism.* Philadelphia, Jewish Publication Society, 1919.

ISRAEL GOLDBERG and SAMSON BENDERLY, *Outline of Jewish Knowledge,* Vol. 3: *The Second Commonwealth.* New York, Bureau of Jewish Education, 1931.

R. TRAVERS HERFORD, *Judaism in the New Testament Period.* London, The Lindsey Press, 1925.

FLAVIUS JOSEPHUS, *The Jewish War.* Translated from the original Greek by William Whiston. (See footnote, p. 177 of this volume.)

MAX RADIN, *The Jews Among the Greeks and Romans.* Philadelphia, Jewish Publication Society, 1915.

T. H. ROBINSON and W. O. E. OESTERLY, *History of Israel.* Vol. 2. Oxford, Clarendon Press, 1932.

PART THREE: BABYLONIA AND SPAIN

The Mishnah, Translated by Herbert Danby. London, Clarendon Press, 1933.

The Talmudic Anthology, edited by Louis I. Newman and Samuel Spitz. New York, Behrman House, 1945.

ISRAEL ABRAHAMS, *Jewish Life in the Middle Ages.* Philadelphia, Jewish Publication Society, 1911.

ABRAHAM COHEN, *Everyman's Talmud*. London, J. M. Dent & Sons, Ltd., 1932.
SOLOMON IBN GABIROL, *Selected Religious Poems*. Translated by Israel Zangwill. Philadelphia, Jewish Publication Society, 1923.
JEHUDAH HALEVI, *Selected Poems*. Translated by Nina Salaman. Philadelphia, Jewish Publication Society, 1924.
HENRY CHARLES LEA, *A History of the Inquisition in Spain*. (Vol. 1). New York, Macmillan, 1906.
MAURICE LIBER, *Rashi*. Philadelphia, Jewish Publication Society, 1906.
M. MIELZINER, *Introduction to the Talmud*. New York, Bloch Publishing Co., 1925.
C. G. MONTEFIORE and H. LOEWE, *A Rabbinic Anthology*. New York, Macmillan, 1938.
GEORGE FOOT MOORE, *Judaism in the First Century of the Christian Era*. 3 vols., Cambridge, Harvard University Press, 1932.
ABRAHAM A. NEWMAN, *The Jews in Spain*. 2 vols., Philadelphia, Jewish Publication Society, 1942.
CECIL ROTH, *A History of the Marranos*. Philadelphia, Jewish Publication Society, 1932.
DAVID YELLIN and ISRAEL ABRAHAMS, *Maimonides*. Philadelphia, Jewish Publication Society, 1903.

PART FOUR: IN MEDIEVAL EUROPE

ISRAEL ABRAHAMS, *Jewish Life in the Middle Ages*. Philadelphia, Jewish Publication Society, 1911.
E. N. ADLER, *Jewish Travelers*. Philadelphia, Jewish Publication Society, 1905.
MARTIN BUBER, *Tales of the Hasidim: The Early Masters*. New York, Schocken Books, 1947.
S. M. DUBNOW, *History of the Jews in Russia and Poland*. Vol. 1. Philadelphia, Jewish Publication Society, 1916.
LOUIS GINZBERG, *Students, Scholars and Saints*. Philadelphia, Jewish Publication Society, 1928.
GLUCKEL OF HAMELIN, *Memoirs*. Translated by Marvin Lowenthal. New York, Behrman House, 1938.
RUFUS LEARSI, *The Wedding Song: A Book of Chassidic Ballads*. New York, Behrman House, 1938.
H. WALTER, *Moses Mendelssohn*. New York, Bloch Publishing Co., 1930.

PART FIVE: EMANCIPATION

Jewish Emancipation: A Selection of Documents. Edited by Raphael Mahler. New York, American Jewish Committee, 1941.

Publications of American Jewish Historical Society.

ALEX BEIN, *Theodor Herzl.* Philadelphia, Jewish Publication Society, 1940.

S. M. DUBNOW, *History of the Jews in Russia and Poland.* 3 vols., Philadelphia, Jewish Publication Society, 1916–20.

LEE M. FRIEDMAN, *Jewish Pioneers and Patriots.* Philadelphia, Jewish Publication Society, 1942.

PAUL GOODMAN, *Moses Montefiore.* Philadelphia, Jewish Publication Society, 1925.

THEODOR HERZL, *The Jewish State.* New York, Scopus Publishing Co., 1943.

THEODOR HERZL, *Excerpts from His Diaries.* New York, Scopus Publishing Co., 1941.

MOSES HESS, *Rome and Jerusalem.* Translated by Meyer Waxman. New York, Bloch Publishing Co., 1943.

LEON PINSKER, *Auto-Emancipation.* Translated by D. S. Blondheim. New York, Zionist Organization of America, 1944.

ERNST SIMMEL, *Anti-Semitism: A Social Disease.* New York, International Universities Press, 1946.

PETER WIERNICK, *History of the Jews in America.* New York, Jewish History Publishing Co., 1931.

PART SIX: THE WORLD WARS

The Black Book: The Nazi Crime against the Jewish People. New York, The Jewish Black Book Committee, 1946.

Palestine, a Study of Jewish, Arab and British Policies. Published for the Esco Foundation for Palestine, Inc. New Haven, Yale University Press, 1947.

ISRAEL COHEN, *The Zionist Movement.* New York, Zionist Organization of America, 1947.

ROBERT R. NATHAN, OSCAR GASS and DANIEL CREAMER, *Palestine: Problem and Promise, An Economic Study.* Washington, American Council on Foreign Affairs, 1946.

ABRAHAM REVUSKY, *Jews in Palestine.* New York, Vanguard Press, 1936.

ABRAM L. SACHAR, *Sufferance Is the Badge*. New York, Alfred A. Knopf, 1939.

B. W. SEGEL, *The Protocols of the Elders of Zion—The Greatest Lie in History*. New York, Bloch Publishing Co., 1934.

MARIE SYRKIN, *Blessed is the Match: The Story of Jewish Resistance.* New York, Alfred A. Knopf, 1947.

Index

B

D

F

I

N

O

Q

R

S